APPOINTING JUDGES IN AN AGE OF JUDICIAL POWER: CRITICAL PERSPECTIVES FROM AROUND THE WORLD

Edited by Kate Malleson and Peter Russell

The expansion in judicial power taking place throughout the world has led to a growing interest in the way judges are chosen. Reform of the judicial selection process is on the political agenda in many countries but the approach taken differs according to the type of system in place – whether a career judiciary, elected judiciary, or hybrid system.

One of the main purposes of this volume is to analyse common issues arising from increasing judicial power in the context of different political and legal systems, including those in North America, Africa, Europe, Australia, and Asia. It also seeks to assess the strengths and weaknesses of structural and procedural reforms being proposed or implemented. Among the issues addressed are the growing pressure to rethink the balance between judicial independence and accountability and the growing recognition of the importance of selecting judiciaries with a greater diversity in composition.

Featuring contributions by eminent scholars from around the globe, the volume is the first such analysis of judicial selection undertaken, and will be of interest to a wide international audience.

KATE MALLESON is a professor in the Department of Law at Queen Mary, University of London.

PETER H. RUSSELL is a university professor emeritus in the Department of Political Science at the University of Toronto.

Appointing Judges in an Age of Judicial Power: Critical Perspectives from around the World

Edited by
Kate Malleson and Peter H. Russell

UNIVERSITY OF TORONTO PRESS
Toronto Buffalo London

Toronto Buffalo London
Printed in Canada

ISBN-13: 978-0-8020-9053-9 (cloth)
ISBN-10: 0-8020-9053-2 (cloth)
ISBN-13: 978-8020-9381-3 (paper)
ISBN-10: 0-8020-9381-7 (paper)

Printed on acid-free paper

Library and Archives Canada Cataloguing in Publication

Appointing judges in an age of judicial power : critical perspectives from around the world / edited by Kate Malleson and Peter H. Russell.

Includes bibliographical references.
ISBN-13: 978-0-8020-9053-9 (bound)
ISBN-13: 978-8020-9381-3 (pbk.)
ISBN-10: 0-8020-9053-2 (bound)
ISBN-10: 0-8020-9381-7 (pbk.)

1. Judges – Selection and appointment. 2. Judicial power.
I. Malleson, Kate II. Russell, Peter H. III. Title.

K2146.A93 2006 347′.014 C2005-906214-2

University of Toronto Press acknowledges the financial assistance to its publishing program of the Canada Council for the Arts and the Ontario Arts Council.

University of Toronto Press acknowledges the financial support for its publishing activities of the Government of Canada through the Book Publishing Industry Development Program (BPIDP).

Contents

Foreword

No country can claim to be an enlightened democracy without the presence of certain attributes, including the rule of law and an independent judiciary. Moreover, no judiciary can expect to obtain the acceptance of and obedience to its judgments if certain badges of legitimacy are not present. One of the most important badges is that well-qualified candidates sit on the nation's bench. As a result, in an era when democratic constitutionalism has been breaking out around the world, in both old and new democracies, there has been an increased focus on how judges are selected or appointed. This attention has in turn caused much normative debate and discussion on how a country's judiciary should be appointed and, more particularly, on whether democratic theory points to a particular method as optimal or at least preferable.

This topic is especially important because a companion to the outbreak of democratic regimes has been the assignment of an increased role to the judiciary to be the arbiter of the human rights and fundamental freedoms that form an essential part of the newly enacted constitutional architecture. The impetus for this new constitutional design was greatly enhanced by the horrific abuses of human rights by fascism and Nazism leading to the Second World War, and totalitarianism after the war. However, virtually no country is immune from criticism with respect to its historical human rights record.

Given these realities the present collection could not be more timely. Who serves in the judiciary of a country is of utmost importance to the quality of democracy in that particular country. Kate Malleson and Peter Russell have made an invaluable contribution to the debate by bringing together authors from around the globe to provide commentary and analysis of judicial selection in old, new, and emerging democracies, as well as commentary on the appointment of judges to international courts.

It is most appropriate and commendable for the editors to have orchestrated this comparative treatment of the subject: valuable lessons can be learned from exploring experiences and approaches outside our national boundaries. Granted, comparative study has limitations; what works in one country may not be appropriate in another, for a number of reasons. But that does not negate the need for, and/or the benefits that can derive from, comparative examination and analysis.

As a lawyer and judge who has been actively involved in the judicial appointments process, I have benefited greatly from reading the papers in this book. The variety of the approaches taken in different jurisdictions along with the underlying analysis is most edifying and illuminating.

I thank and congratulate the editors and contributors to this volume for sharing their expertise and experience on a subject of great importance to the promotion of the rule of law and the administration of justice in the world.

THE HON. FRANK IACOBUCCI

Preface

The idea for this volume developed out of a series of annual meetings of the International Political Science Association's Research Committee on Comparative Judicial Studies. During the late nineties a recurring theme which seemed to play a more and more prominent role in the Research Committee's meetings was the growing importance of judicial selection and its relation to increasing judicial power. As academics with research interests in the Canadian and U.K. judiciaries this emerging focus came as no surprise, given the very obvious growth in judicial power in both our countries. More unexpected was the increasing evidence of how global this development appeared to be. We were also struck by how many common themes were thrown up in discussions of the relationship between judicial power and judicial appointments, despite the very different political and legal contexts of the different systems.

By 2003 it became clear to us that this subject was both sufficiently important and intellectually coherent to warrant a global review of current developments. The enthusiastic response to our tentative request for contributions from scholars around the world confirmed this view, and in January 2004 the Research Committee agreed to hold a further meeting at the London School of Economics dedicated to the subject of judicial appointments. Many of the chapters in this collection were presented as papers at that conference and the powerful discussions they generated convinced us that this was a worthwhile project. Fired up with enthusiasm after the meeting we commissioned nineteen chapters for the volume and received, by the required deadline, all nineteen of them. This rather unexpected success rate may have added to the workload (and costs) of our forgiving publishers, but that it was so relatively easy to persuade a large number of leading experts on judicial appointments from around the world to contribute such high quality chapters is a further indication of the global interest in the subject.

We are grateful for the enthusiastic and conscientious input of all the contributors and to our excellent research assistant, Heather Harrison Dinniss, who took on the task on producing a coherent manuscript from the flood of submissions under tight time pressure. We are also indebted to the University of Toronto Press for its support and efficiency in producing this volume.

As is inevitable with a book of this kind, changes have taken place in the judicial appointment processes of the individual countries between writing and publication. The contributions cover developments up to May 2004.

APPOINTING JUDGES IN AN AGE OF JUDICIAL POWER

Introduction

KATE MALLESON

Until relatively recently, the appointment of judges was a subject that rarely generated political debate. With the notable exception of the United States, the traditional view of the judiciary as a body of legal experts or civil servants rather than a branch of the state has meant that judicial appointments systems have not generally attracted significant public attention. However, in recent years the global expansion in judicial power has led to a growing interest in the way judges are chosen. In 1995 Tate and Vallinder identified the way in which this process of 'judicialization,' as it has come to be called, has taken different forms in different parts of the world.[1] In European civil law systems such as France, Spain, and Italy, its most obvious manifestation has been the increasing judicial activism of examining magistrates, most notably in investigating criminal charges against political leaders. In many common law systems, such as Australia, Canada, and England and Wales, the development of human rights adjudication (with or without a Bill of Rights) and the expansion of judicial review has been the primary source of judicialization. In areas of the world which have experienced rapid political change, such as South Africa and Central and Eastern Europe, the newly formed or reinvigorated constitutional courts are the location of increasing judicial authority. The political and constitutional contexts of the global expansion of judicial power therefore vary considerably, but a common feature of this trend is that it is accompanied by a growing public and political interest in who judges are and how they are chosen.

The increasing global interest in judicial selection across different political systems can be seen in both common law and civil law systems and includes the full range of appointments processes found within them – a career judiciary, an elected judiciary (direct and indirect), appointment by the executive, and hybrid systems. The jurisdictions considered in the chapters which follow have been chosen in order to encompass the spectrum of different systems from long-established liberal democracies at one end (such as the United States, Canada, and European jurisdictions), newer democracies in the middle (such as Israel and South Africa), through to those states which are emerging from autocratic regimes and moving towards the establishment of regimes based on the rule of law (such as China), the only common factor being that they are all found in countries which can be described as broadly democratic. Our project is, therefore, quite consciously intended to explore the way in which the expanding judicial role in these different contexts impacts on the judicial selection process and how this relationship relates to the process of developing, maintaining, and strengthening liberal democracies within a democratic system. Implicit in the scope of the volume is a commitment to the idea of an independent and strong judiciary as a defining feature of a healthy democracy. We have made this assumption explicit in the structure of the book by dividing it into two sections which distinguish between developments in new democracies or transitional states and those of established democracies. In between these two parts of the book is a chapter on appointing the judges of international courts.

This general categorization between new and established democracies allows us to identify the effect of the country's political environment on a number of common themes that arise from the increasing role of the judiciary. We cannot, of course, claim that the book discusses all the important jurisdictions. India and the judiciaries of South America are obvious examples of areas in which many significant changes have occurred in recent years. But we have sought to ensure that the scope of the jurisdictions covered is sufficiently wide that none of the major themes in judicial appointment around the world is neglected.

The first of these themes is the growing pressure to rethink the balance between judicial independence and accountability in judicial appointments processes. As Russell and O'Brien's recent volume on judicial independence has highlighted, the nature of this pressure for change differs according to the particular form of judicialization and the political system in which it occurs.[2] In countries where judicial activism has developed within established liberal democracies (Canada, Australia, Israel) the dilemma is how to increase judicial accountability by strengthening the link to the electoral process while avoiding the creation, strengthening, or revival of partisan political control. For systems in parts of the world such as Southeast Asia, China, and Russia, which are moving towards liberal democracy and away from strong state control, the challenge is to enhance the independence of the appointments process and to weaken the link with the executive while retaining the democratic legitimacy of their increasingly powerful judiciaries.

A comparative review reveals that these tensions express themselves in very different practical forms. In England and Wales, for example, two notable area of stress have been the appointments process for part-time judges and the overlapping constitutional functions of the lord chancellor. In Canada, debate over the continuing role of party politics in federal appointments has intensified, while in many civil law systems there is growing interest in the question of whether judicial independence is enhanced through a mixed system combining a career judiciary with selection from the legal profession (as in Holland), or whether the traditional career structure remains the best guard against inappropriate political involvement in the selection process. A striking feature of these debates and trends is the gap that often opens between theory and practice. Institutions or procedures that may on paper appear to lend themselves to manipulation of the selection system by politicians are often found in systems in which it is generally accepted that judicial independence is strong, and vice versa. This highlights the need for a rigorous comparative analysis of the relationship between formal judicial selection arrangements and the political culture which underpins them.

The analysis is further complicated by the need to strike a different balance between judicial independence and accountability in trial courts and the highest courts of review. Judges in top review courts are reaching decisions that often have far-reaching social and political implications, and greater emphasis must therefore be placed in the appointments process on their accountability. The case for such processes as public interviews or confirmation hearings for constitutional court judges, designed to provide the public with some knowledge about the values and attitudes of these powerful decision makers, is much more persuasive at the top court level. It is also arguable that the threat to judicial independence posed by such arrangements is reduced at this level. Judges in these courts have reached the top of the career ladder and are not looking for promotion, thus they are better able to withstand pressure from their selectors once on the bench. The dismay with which some U.S. presidents have greeted the judgments of their chosen Supreme Court appointees is testament to the ability of judges to defy the political aspirations of their appointers.

The rationale for judicial independence in the various types of courts also needs to be differentiated. The reason for ensuring that judges appointed at trial level are independent of their appointers is to ensure that judges can decide cases impartially as between the parties – without being affected by 'fear or favour,' as is commonly articulated in the judicial oath sworn by judges on taking office. In the top review courts, however, where judges are often called upon to decide between the competing ideologies, values, or policies which underlie the law, the notion of impartiality is more problematic. Is it realistic to require that the appointments system select judges who are impartial when judging between one set of values and another, in the same way as they must be impartial when judging between one party at trial and another?

The justification for the participation in some form of the elected branches of government in the appointments process of the highest ranks of the judiciary is, therefore, clear. Yet it is precisely at this level of court that the highest calibre of judges is needed, and great damage will be done to the legal system if the selection of candidates on the basis of partisan political affiliation rather than skills and ability undermines the quality of the bench. The challenge that all appointments processes for top review courts face is to ensure that the democratic legitimacy of the judiciary is maintained without introducing a form of politicization that reduces the quality of the judges appointed and transforms judges into politicians in wigs.

The search for the elusive balance between independence and accountability in judicial appointments processes has led to substantive reforms in many countries. Here too the direction which these reforms take may be quite different, and even diametrically opposite, depending on the particular contexts in which they arise. For example, direct elections, found predominantly in the United States, are generally falling from favour, while indirect elections are enjoying a renaissance through the growth of international courts. In these multistate tribunals the use of indirect elections, usually by the national legislature, holds out the promise of enhancing accountability by ensuring the participation of the different states in the selection process while limiting the danger of populist control of the courts.

In other instances variations in type of procedural reform arise within the same selection system. The most obvious example of this is found in judicial appointments commissions, which look likely to become the most popular selection system of the twenty-first century. Throughout common law and civil systems alike the use of commissions is increasingly being explored as a solution to the difficult problem of achieving a balance between independence and accountability in judicial selection. Canada, South Africa, Scotland, England and Wales, and many civil law systems in Europe now use some form of commission. Their great strength is their adaptability, which allows them to be shaped to meet the particular requirements of each system. As a result, the make-up, powers, and procedures of commissions differ significantly around the world. To date, very little comparative analysis of the forms, functions, and effectiveness of commissions has been undertaken. Important questions are thrown up by the move to commissions: Do they enhance the legitimacy of the selection process? Do they increase its transparency? Do they affect the composition of the judiciary, and if so how? Are they liable to be captured by certain interest groups? If so, can this be avoided? The analysis which runs through the book seeks to begin to address these questions.

The second central and recurring theme evident in the current debate on judicial selection is the growing recognition of the importance of selecting more diverse judiciaries. The lack of women and lawyers from minority ethnic backgrounds on the bench throughout different jurisdictions is one of the greatest challenges facing judiciaries today, and the failure of appointments systems to make significant progress in increasing diversity has been a key factor in many of the changes being introduced. In federal and provincial systems, regional representation is an equally important factor. Likewise, for international courts the inclusion of judges from the different regions or countries covered by their jurisdiction is the foundation upon which their legitimacy rests. The geographical balance of the courts' membership is often the most controversial aspect of the appointments processes to the international courts. For countries in which there are strong religious divisions, such as Israel, the religious backgrounds of the judges are equally critical. In many African jurisdictions the question of racial composition is inevitably at the fore. Nor are the categories of representation unchanging or universal. The South African Judicial Services Commission, for example, takes pride in its record of promoting disability equality in its appointments process, whereas in other systems the question of disability has barely found its way onto the diversity agenda. This last example provides evidence of the way a comparative review of judicial selection around the world reveals the changing shape of the debate and some possible directions it may take in the future. It also highlights the fact that it is in the newer democracies that some of the more innovative policies and practices in this area are found. While the mature democracies can generally claim a stronger record in relation to the protection of judicial independence, the weight of tradition and precedent found in those countries has often inhibited the development of reforms to judicial appointments processes that would expand the recruitment pool for judicial office and lead to a more diverse judiciary.

The increasing centrality of issues of composition in judicial selection raises a number of important empirical questions. Why do some judicial appointments systems seem to be making much faster progress in diversifying the composition of the bench than others? How can the recruitment pool be enlarged to increase the opportunity to select from a wider group of people? Two schools of thought can be clearly identified in many different systems. The 'trickle up' approach argues that greater diversity will happen naturally and automatically as societies and legal professions become more inclusive. Against this, critics claim that structural and cultural barriers remain strong and that only proactive change will bring about diversity. The book looks for evidence in the different countries to support these different positions. Which school of thought is dominant? What procedural, structural, or cultural reforms have been implemented to try to change the composition of judiciaries, and how successful have they been?

Underlying these empirical and practical issues are a number of particularly difficult theoretical questions: What is the rationale for seeking greater diversity in the judiciary? Should some forms of diversity take priority over others? Can the notion of a more representative judiciary be reconciled with the principle of judiciary impartiality? This comparative analysis seeks to shed light on how different countries have approached these questions in their particular legal and political contexts and which, if any, have identified coherent and rational answers.

Reviewing the impact of appointments processes on the composition of the judiciary also raises questions about the definition of merit. All selection processes in liberal democracies claim to be merit-based in the sense of choosing the best person for the job. Yet it is clear that there are many different definitions of merit, explicit or implicit. The priorities valued in an electoral system, executive appointment, or a career judiciary are bound to differ. Moreover the differences may be greater within these systems than among them. The book therefore seeks to identify some of the qualities considered necessary in a good judge and to scrutinize the basis for these different interpretations. For example, in some common law systems there is evidence of growing tension between the desirability of traditional legalistic technical skills and more communication, practical, and 'people' skills. On the other hand, in the emerging liberal democracies legal expertise and lack of corruptibility are valued more highly than ever in the struggle to build judiciaries with integrity and competence. Finally, there is evidence in some systems that a less individualistic approach to the definition of merit has emerged which links merit to the composition of the judiciary. In South Africa, for example, the selection criteria specifically allow for the background of candidates to be taken into account on the grounds that a more diverse judiciary enhances its 'collectively competence.'

The debate over the desirable qualities and characteristics required of a judge presupposes an assumption about what judges do. Yet a clear trend throughout judiciaries is the acceleration of change in the functions of judging. Greater specialization, more emphasis on active case management, and the emergence of more consumer-orientated adjudication processes in which judges are seen as service providers are evident in many different systems. At the same time, a sharper division in some systems between the work of trial courts and top review courts is apparent: the upper courts are increasingly required to assess policy implications and reach politically and socially sensitive decisions. The characteristics, background, knowledge, and skills required of judges appointed to trial courts and top review courts may, as a result, be very different. The idea that thirty years as an advocate is the best possible training for both types of court, traditionally entrenched in many common law systems, is now increasingly being questioned. How to meet the challenge of the changing judicial role in selection criteria and procedures is a pressing question in many systems. Should the higher courts include former politicians (as found in the French and German Constitutional Courts) or academics (as has become more common in Canada)? If the gap between the different ranks of judges is growing, is it best to have separate appointments processes for them (as in many European systems), or to employ essentially the same system (as in many common law systems)?

The book does not seek to provide definitive answers to all these questions, but instead attempts to construct a rigorous comparative framework within which to address them. Reviewing the ways in which different countries are facing the challenge of developing modern judicial selection systems fitted for the fast changing roles of their judiciaries provides valuable lessons for policy makers and academics. In common with all comparative study it reminds us that our own ways of doing things are not immutable or inevitable. For those of us who come from countries which have modelled themselves on the tradition-bound English legal system, this exploration can be a liberating intellectual process. But the rationale for this volume is not purely academic. Reform of the judicial selection process is now clearly on the political agenda in many different countries. Policy makers, judges, and lawyers are increasing familiar with, and interested in, the institutions and processes of different judicial systems. The emergence of a global debate on judicial selection means that a comparative analysis has a useful contribution to make in informing the shape and direction of change in this area.

NOTES

1 Tate and Vallinder, 'The Global Expansion of Judicial Power.'

2 Russell and O'Brien, eds., *Judicial Independence in the Age of Democracy.*

PART ONE

Appointing Judges in Established Democracies

1 The Scottish Judicial Appointments Board: New Wine in Old Bottles?

ALAN PATERSON

Introduction

Whatever else they may disagree about where judges are concerned, both the government and the commentators are of one mind with respect to current methods of judicial appointment in the United Kingdom – they are badly in need of rejuvenation.

This is a Damascan conversion for the executive but not for the critics, who have been pushing for reform in this area for over thirty years. Throughout this period they have campaigned for the replacement of an executive-dominated, covert, and non-transparent procedure with its perceived potential for political patronage, cronyism, and personal prejudice, advocating an independent appointments commission operating transparently and openly while drawing on a broader range of candidates in terms of gender, race, and social and educational background. Judicial appointment procedures have to be both independent of undue political influence and democratically accountable.[1] However, it was not until the 'New' Labour government was elected in 1997 that politicians began to talk openly of the possibility of introducing a judicial appointment commission. Having announced that a consultation would emerge later that year on the topic, Lord Irvine quietly withdrew the commitment a few months later. However, the coalition partners which formed the first administration of the new Scottish Parliament went further. After informal discussions the Scottish ministers set out their commitment to consulting on the system of judicial appointments in *A Programme for Government* in 1999. In the summer of 2000 a consultation paper entitled *Judicial Appointments: An Inclusive Approach* was launched. The responses were strongly in favour of an independent appointing body[2] and in March 2001 the justice minister,[3] in an address to Strathclyde University Law School, announced the establishment of a non-statutory Judicial Appointments Board. Despite the reservations of the bodies representing the judiciary in Scotland, the executive plumped for a board with an equal number of lay and legal members, and a lay chair.[4] Moreover, it was made clear that while merit selection was to be its watchword the board was also expected to seek to appoint a judiciary which is as representative as possible of the communities they serve. The board was finally established in June 2002 and in its first year appointed forty-four judges throughout Scotland.

Judicial Appointment: The Background

Judicial appointment in Scotland, as in other modern democracies, has struggled with the conundrum of the apparently insoluble tension between judicial independence and judicial accountability. It seems that every attempt to protect the judiciary from undue external influence makes that judiciary less accountable to the community it was appointed to serve. Striking the elusive balance between the two goals has become even more difficult with the decline in 'the moral authority' of the judiciary[5] in the last twenty years, the emergence of a more demanding consumer society which expects all aspects of government to demonstrate that they are serving society effectively, a more vocal media in relation to the judiciary, and the establishment of two Justice Committees in the Scottish Parliament.

To compound matters the key concepts in the discourse of judicial appointment – transparency, merit selection, independence, and accountability – have a spurious clarity that disintegrates on closer analysis, since each is culturally and contextually determined. Small wonder that liberal pragmatists and critical legal scholars find little common ground in this arena. However *transparency* is defined, the old system in Scotland was certainly not transparent. Appointment by constitutional custom was largely in the gift of one man – the chief government law officer.[6] The latter was not legally required to consult with anyone,[7] and had a relatively unfettered discretion to appoint whomsoever he wished within the minimal confines laid down in the Treaty of Union and subsequent legislation setting out the eligibility criteria for judicial appointment in Scotland.[8] This system had some merits. It could be swift, decisive, and bold, and it suited those who preferred to receive the 'tap on the shoulder' rather than the risk of rejection associated with open applications. It also promoted – at least in theory – political accountability.[9] On the other hand, it opened the door to actual or perceived cronyism, political or 'reward' appointments, gender bias, secret soundings, and even self-selection.[10] Secret soundings have, of course, been a major bone of contention in recent years in England and Wales, with the English Law Society withdrawing from the consultations process and the commissioner for judicial appointments attacking soundings in successive annual reports for their inherent bias against women and ethnic minorities.[11] The extent to which soundings were used in Scotland in the past is unclear (with the exception of the lord president), although in recent times it is probably the case that all the law lords have been consulted about the appointment of a new Scottish law lord, the two most senior judges have been consulted about High Court appointments, and sheriff principals have been consulted as to shrieval appointments to their sheriffdom as well as appointments of 'all-Scotland floating sheriffs' and part-time sheriffs.[12] The old appointment system could perhaps best be characterized as a partnership between the government and the judiciary. As will be discussed in greater detail below, the Judicial Appointments Board from an early stage turned its face against secret soundings and the use of personal knowledge, largely in the interests of fairness and transparency. However, even the lay members baulked at being so transparent as to hold public interviews of the candidates, as occurs in South Africa.

Merit selection is one of the shibboleths which dominates past and contemporary discussions of judicial appointment in Scotland and England. Throughout the constitutional debates of the last few years ministers have repeated like a mantra that any changes to judicial appointment mechanisms would retain the principle of merit selection. The Judicial Appointment Board might be charged with increasing the diversity of the Scottish judiciary, but only against the assurance that they would adhere to merit selection. While the latter reassures both the reformers and the conservatives, the concept has an apparent objectivity that masks its protean actuality. In Scotland the legal criteria for appointment as a judge are minimal in the extreme: five or ten years' standing as a Scots lawyer, none of which need be as a court lawyer or indeed as a practitioner at all. However, the actual criteria applied have been far more restrictive, with higher appointments effectively limited to practising advocates (barristers) of eighteen or more years calling and full-time shreival appointments restricted to practising advocates or solicitors of fifteen or more years calling. In practice, having held certain other offices, such as lord advocate,[13] dean of the faculty,[14] and advocate depute,[15] also improved the candidate's chances of preferment to higher judicial office.[16] As a result, a set of legal criteria which are sufficiently open to allow a wide pool from which to select on merit has effectively been reduced, as an unintended consequence of the cultural definition of merit, to one that favours white, male, middle-class, practising lawyers. A key issue for the board, therefore, is whether this cultural definition of merit can be altered.

Even when taken at their face value, the Siamese twins of *Independence* and *Accountability* – where more of one means less of the other, but both are needed – have the appearance of a Catch 22. In reality, however, each of these concepts is culturally determined. Typically, independence means freedom from undue political or other influence, whether over judicial decisions, judicial salaries, judicial promotions, or judicial removal. However, the definition of what amounts to 'undue' pressure depends in part on the political climate and culture of the jurisdiction in question, the tier of the judiciary under consideration and the leadership of the judiciary. It also matters whose standpoint is being adopted: the judiciary's, the media's, or the public's. Even where a consensus exists in one jurisdiction over what constitutes 'undue' influence, immunity from such an influence may not be enough to eliminate criticism if the case is of international significance. Thus the interaction between the judiciary and counsel in the Lockerbie bombing trial in the Netherlands, which was unexceptional in Scottish terms, was subject to a scathing attack from the academic appointed as the UN observer who perceived 'undue influence' in terms of the less adversarial system of civil law countries. In truth, judges cannot be insulated from all outside influence. They, like other members of the community, are, at least in part, creatures of their own particular environment, encompassing their education, training, relationships with other lawyers and fellow judges, membership in clubs, family life, hobbies and pastimes, and their exposure to the media. Even if they were not, they would be assumed to be so, as Lord Hoffmann discovered to his cost in the aftermath of the Pinochet appeal.[17] Conversely, as that and subsequent cases demonstrated, it is not enough for judges to take account of all influences of which they are personally aware – they are also expected to be aware of any influences which a 'fair-minded and informed observer' would regard as likely to affect them.[18]

If *judicial independence* has a centuries-old pedigree, *accountability* in judges is largely a product of late twentieth-century democratic liberalism.[19] As judicial power has grown in the last thirty years – through an expanded judicial review jurisdiction, the supremacy of European law, the implementation of the European Convention on Human Rights in the United Kingdom, and the power to rule on the compatibility of Scottish legislation with the Devolution settlement - so have concerns about a potential, consequential democratic deficit.[20] The logic has a deceptive simplicity. In a democracy, those who wield legitimate power in the name of the state are expected to be accountable for their acts. The traditional defence of the judiciary – that they are merely 'finding' the law rather than making it, and that the scope of their discretion is closely confined by statute – looks increasingly more difficult to sustain in an era in which some of the more forthright members of the senior judiciary have openly accepted that they change the law and that talk of law 'finding' belongs in the realm of 'fairy stories.'[21] To observers who accept this line of thinking, developing accountability mechanisms for the new judiciary is a significant constitutional problem, one which will only be exacerbated in England by the abolition of the lord chancellor and the 'setting free' of the judiciary as a distinct arm of government under the doctrine of the separation of powers. Given that many accountability mechanisms contain a potential threat to the independence of the decision makers it is perhaps not surprising that attention has turned to appointment mechanisms as a source of legitimacy and 'before the event' accountability.

In sum, the old Scottish system of appointing judges failed to deliver transparency and endorsed a definition of objective merit selection that contained hidden equal opportunity problems, while also failing to resolve the tension between independence and accountability satisfactorily. It is against these three challenges that the performance of the Judicial Appointments Board in Scotland will likely be assessed.

The Judicial Appointments Board

Issues

Once a government has made the decision to opt for a judicial appointments commission a number of subsidiary issues present themselves concerning its powers, scope, establishment, composition, and procedures. Each of these issues is discussed below.

POWERS

Here the choice is between a commission that actually makes the appointments and one that recommends them to the government, with the politicians having the final say.[22] The former approach shifts the balance of power in the appointing process from a judiciary/politician partnership to one where the balance of power lies with whichever grouping controls the make-up and operation of the commission. An appointing commission, therefore, is one in which 'politics' and stakeholder interests may come to play a role in its appointment, composition, and modus operandi. A recommending commission, on the other hand, leaves the politicians with a significant residual power in that they have the last word in the appointment process.[23] This power, however, is shared with those who control the composition and operation of the commission. Perhaps understandably, given the amount of power that they were being asked to forego, the Scottish executive opted for a recommending Judicial Appointments Board (as well as being a non-statutory pilot). The executive desired that the board should provide them with a ranked list of recommended candidates, but indicated that they would only reject a name or ranking from the board in very unusual circumstances, and even then only on cause shown and in writing. In practice the board has chosen to provide short, ranked lists to the executive except when a plurality of posts are to be filled, and the executive and the lord president accepted the names and rankings of the board without demur in each of the forty-four appointments made in the first year. For so long as the ministers maintain their self-denying ordinance,[24] the bulk of the power in the appointment process will effectively lie with the board.

SCOPE

One way for the executive to limit its loss of power to the board is to restrict the scope of the board to certain judicial appointments. Thus the Scottish Board currently plays no role in the appointment of the two most senior judges in Scotland, the lord president and the lord justice clerk. Equally, it has no say in the appointment of the two Scottish lords of appeal to the House of Lords. This, however, will change with the establishment of a Supreme Court in place of the House of Lords, when a special Supreme Court Appointments Commission is proposed, one of whose members will be drawn from the Judicial Appointments Board.[25] Perhaps less understandably, the board plays no role in the promotion of Court of Session judges to the Inner House (the Scottish equivalent of the English Court of Appeal), which lies entirely in the hands of the lord president. More surprisingly, the board has no say in the appointment of temporary judges, who have the status of Court of Session judges although appointed on a temporary, renewable contract. These individuals are predominantly drawn from the ranks of the existing shrieval bench, but in some cases the candidates are members of the bar. Such appointments are made by the first minister on the recommendation of the lord president. Currently, there are twenty temporary judges as compared with thirty-two permanent High Court judges, some of whom sit for many days a year. This has attracted criticism both because temporary judges appear to be a cheap way for the Treasury to avoid paying for more permanent ones, and because their appointment process is neither transparent nor demonstrably fair in equal opportunities terms.[26] Unfortunately, the ability of the lord president and the executive to exclude the board in the case of such senior appointments, if continued for a sustained period, may risk undermining public confidence in the board. Finally, the board is rarely involved in the appointment of sheriffs to the most coveted shrieval posts, such as those in Edinburgh or Glasgow, since these positions are typically filled by sheriffs from other parts of the country who apply for a transfer. Such appointments are by the first minister on the recommendation of the relevant sheriff principal. This has led to the somewhat curious position that the appointment process for sheriffs to less popular areas is handled by the board according to Nolan principles of transparency and fairness in equal opportunities terms, while the more favoured postings are filled by a process that has neither transparency nor demonstrable fairness in equal opportunities terms.

ESTABLISHMENT AND COMPOSITION

The extent to which a commission represents a significant shift of power away from the executive (and possibly also the judiciary) depends not merely on its scope or on whether it is a recommending or an appointing commission. It also depends on the way in which the commission is established, the nature of its composition, and the procedures it follows. In the case of the Scottish board the five lay members and the two lawyer members were appointed following open advertisement, Nolan-style civil service short listing, references, and interview.[27] The three judicial members, however, were nominated by their respective judicial bodies and only the sheriff was given an interview. The process scored highly on transparency, merit selection, accountability, and (to a slightly lesser extent) independence. Although the overall approach reduced the influence of the executive and the judiciary in the appointing process, the board remains open to influence from both these quarters. Nevertheless, the individual make-up of the board shows little sign of policiticization.

(None of those appointed has an affiliation with any political party, a link with either of the coalition partners in the Scottish government.) On the other hand, the three judicial members, while not representing their 'constituencies,' remain in touch with them and thus provide a diffuse but useful conduit for judicial interests and concerns to reach the board.

The debate over the composition of the board was unusual in that much of it occurred in public. As mentioned in the introduction, the executive set out its proposals in a consultation paper in the summer of 2000: *Judicial Appointments: An Inclusive Approach.* While all four of the Scottish judicial bodies who responded were strongly in favour of an independent appointing commission, it is fair to say that they also favoured a commission that would be numerically dominated by judges, as is the case in most jurisdictions with commissions.[28] In particular, the judicial groups saw little purpose in having many lay members on the commission. While in all likelihood these were genuinely held views and reflected what the judiciary considered to be in the best interests of the public, it is also clear that if the judiciary's views had prevailed they would have led to a major shift in power from the executive to the judiciary with respect to judicial appointments. To the credit of the justice minister, in the face of some vocal judicial reservations, he opted for a board with 50 per cent lay members, a lay chair, and only three judicial members. This is in marked contrast to the concordat thrashed out in private between the lord chief justice of England and Wales and the lord chancellor in early 2004 whereby, following another consultation exercise, it was agreed that the English Judicial Appointments Commission would have a minority of lay members, although it would have a lay chair. In part the Scottish justice minister was influenced by a desire to create a board with the appropriate skill set for the job. Lay members could bring experience of modern recruitment and selection processes from industry, as well as business experience, performance appraisal skills, and interviewing skills. They could also provide greater diversity and experience of the wider world than the judicial and legal members.

Moreover, to have established a board with a majority of judicial members would more likely than not have ensured that little would change from the status quo, as Baroness Hale has observed concerning the proposed English commission: 'Depending on the composition of the Commission, the [new] process might be even more under the control of the existing judiciary [than the old]. What Helena Kennedy[29] has called the "potential for cloning" could be just as strong.'[30] Similarly, the former permanent secretary to the lord chancellor, Sir Thomas Legg, has indicated that one reason why he has been a long-time opponent of a Judicial Appointments Commission was that the senior judiciary would inevitably have a heavy and often predominating influence on such a commission. As he noted, 'it is no reflection on our judges to say that this would be undesirable. No branch of government should be effectively self-perpetuating.'[31]

PROCEDURES

Essentially, the board advertises all positions within its remit as widely as possible, and requires candidates to fill in a detailed application form with three named referees. The board sifts the applications to produce a long list, and after taking up references sifts again to produce a short list for interview. The interviews consist of a prepared presentation followed by questions on the presentation and on judicial competencies. This modus operandi represents the last opportunity for the executive and the judiciary to reassert their former hegemony over judicial appointments. The executive, having accepted a 'long-stop' role with respect to recommendations from the board, as we have seen, has little scope for further influence on the board, other than to issue formal or informal guidance.[32] Although the executive asked the Judicial Studies Committee to provide a list of informal appointment criteria,[33] the board was not required to use them. In practice the board accepted the criteria with the exception of the suggestion that 'previous judicial experience is also desirable though not essential.'[34] The influence of the judiciary, on the other hand, remains an issue in the operation of the board. The exclusion of the board from shrieval transfers to popular posts and from the appointment of temporary judges could certainly be represented as successes for the interests of the Sheriffs' Association and the lord president respectively. Again, they alone were able to select which of their members should be nominated to the board. On the other hand, it was established from an early stage that the three judges were not on the board to represent their 'constituencies,' but as individuals with particular forms of judicial experience. Moreover the board, in sifting applications for long and short lists, grants no priority to the judicial members. Each board member reads every application and gives it a score on a scale of A, B, and C.[35] These scores are revealed at the start of the sifts in order to ensure that each board member's vote counts equally. Secondly, at an early stage in its life the board, largely at the instigation of lay members, decided that it would eschew judicial consultations or soundings (as opposed to nominated referees) on equal opportunities grounds, since women and ethnic minority lawyers are less involved in judicial networks than white, middle-aged, middle-class men. This took considerable courage as there is an instinctive and understandable desire by lawyers to seek the views of senior judicial figures over significant appointments.[36] Equally courageous and disconcerting to some of the legal members of the board was the decision to exclude the articulation of personal knowledge about a candidate from members of the board. Once again the majority perception was that equal opportunities concerns arose over the use of personal knowledge unless the member knew all the candidates equally well. Even where one or more member could claim to know all the short-listed candidates for, say, a senior judicial appointment, the reservations over the use of personal knowledge persisted. It was felt that to replace the preferences of one man (the lord advocate) with the preferences or concerns of one or two legal members of the board was hard to square with the shift to transparency, openness, and equal opportunities that the establishment of the board was supposed to entail. Indeed, in some respects to allow personal knowledge in would be worse than the old system, since applicants would expect to be judged on objective, open, transparent criteria only to have their progress hindered or assisted by 'unofficial knowledge' that would not be put to them or open to verification.[37]

Additionally, all interviewing panels consist of equal numbers of lay and legal members of the board and are chaired by one of the lay members. Finally, during the interviews the judicial members have no particular primacy in the questioning and when the scores and rankings for candidates are being agreed, the lay members are asked to give their views before the legally qualified members. These decisions have gone a long way to ensure that the judiciary in general, and minority judicial members of the board in particular, do not, as Legg and others feared, exercise undue influence over the remainder of the board. However, there are three small qualifications to this conclusion. First, the justice minister, in setting up the board, indicated that before nominating any particular candidate the legally qualified members of the board would have to be satisfied as to the legal experience and expertise of that candidate. Second, the board is happy for the executive to ask the relevant sheriff principal or even the lord president, in appointments relating to their courts, whether the vacancy is one that calls for any particular skills or talents, given the existing balance of the bench in their courts. Finally, the board also acts in the knowledge that by statute[38] the first minister must consult with the lord president[39] at the end of the process, since they effectively have a long-stop role in relation to any judicial nominees and can override the board in exceptional circumstances, where they possess knowledge of a candidate that is not available to the board.

The board's decisions on soundings and personal knowledge not only narrowed the sources from which information could be obtained about the candidates but focused the board's attention on the fundamental challenge of 'how to obtain adequate, reliable and verifiable information on every candidate.'[40] The need for such objective evidence led the board to develop the application form into a formidable document in which candidates are required to demonstrate (with examples from their own experience) how they meet the published criteria for judicial appointment. The referee's forms are structured and focused on the same competencies, as is the questioning in the interviews with the short-listed candidates. Nevertheless, a concern remains that by excluding soundings and personal knowledge a candidate with personality flaws might unwittingly be nominated by the board. Soundings and personal knowledge, however, do not necessarily produce objective, reliable information, and in any event any appointment system is capable of making errors. From this perspective the new process can be judged a success if it produces no more mistakes than the old procedure, but gets there through reliance on transparency, fairness, and objectivity. However, influenced by a residual concern about the dangers of excluding soundings and personal knowledge, and by an awareness of the limitations of interviews and references, the Board has some interest in exploring other ways of enhancing their appointment procedures, such as assessment days (including role playing and examinations).[41] The board has also been concerned by the fact that where candidates have served for a period as a temporary or part-time judge[42] no reliable information is available as to their success or otherwise when acting in a judicial capacity. The failure of either the Scots or English jurisdictions to develop effective and reliable monitoring processes for part-time judges is surprising, given the value attached in some circles to such experience in would-be candidates for full-time judicial posts. The board is thus keen to foster debate in appropriate quarters as to the introduction of a formal appraisal program for part-time judges.[43]

Diversity

If trying to establish the best possible procedures for eliciting adequate, reliable, and verifiable information on every candidate is the major current concern of the board, it is equally clear that their biggest challenge for the future will be to tackle that part of their remit that relates to recruiting a judiciary which is as reflective as possible of society.[44] Although the overwhelming majority of commentators and policy makers in the field are supportive of greater diversity among the judiciary, the issue is fraught with judicial sensitivities. The tensions arise partly from a lack of clarity or precision in the terms used in the debate. Thus, critics of the current appointment systems have called for the judiciary to be more 'representative' of the society they are appointed to serve, without specifying what that means. Except in the case of jurisdictions with elected appointees, it presumably cannot mean that the judges are expected to represent different geographic or other segments of the community as members of Parliament do. As the 1996 Home Affairs Select Committee report on the judicial appointment process observed: 'It is not the function of the judiciary to reflect particular sections of the community, as it is of the democratically elected legislature.'[45] It appears that representativeness is being used in a statistical rather than a political sense. The commentators, in short, are asking that the judiciary more accurately constitute a representative sample or cross-section of society. This, too, is problematic. No one is calling for a random selection of individuals or even lawyers as an ideal method of judicial selection. The inescapable minimum requirements of competence and capability militate against statistical representativity in the judiciary, just as the need for impartiality militates against political representativity.[46] Perhaps because of the difficulties with the concept of representiveness, many commentators have suggested that the judiciary should be 'reflective' of society, rather than representing it. This more flexible approach still begs the question of which aspects of society they are supposed to be reflecting, and why. Is it confined to crude discriminators such as age, gender, race, and class, or does it extend to attitudes, values, and cultures? It is not clear that the latter is necessarily always a desirable goal. Suppose that the British National Party or some other party of the extreme right or left was to gain 7 per cent of the popular vote in a general election. Would the commentators expect 7 per cent of the judiciary to reflect such views in their decisions?[47] Moreover, it is a little unrealistic to expect the judiciary to reflect fairly the multiplicity of opinions, values and cultural ideas in a pluralist, postmodern era, where the maxim *tot homines quot sententiae* seems more apt than a chimeral search for consensus. Thus Justice Michael Kirby of the Australian High Court has remarked: 'I know of no serious observer who contends that the judiciary should be representative of all the many minorities in society. But many informed judges now consider that it is desirable that different voices should be heard in the market place of judicial ideas.'[48] Certainly, critics have often argued that judges should between them[49] manifest a somewhat broader range of views as to the political, economic, and social content of concepts such as the 'public interest' than does the current judiciary. What is never clear is how far the concept of 'fair reflection' should go in relation to social, political, or economic values. Rejecting the extremes of left and right sounds sensible, but who is to determine the limits of the acceptable middle ground? More difficult still, how are the values of potential appointees to be elicited, if all are agreed that confirmation hearings of candidates such as occur in the U.S. Senate are to be avoided?

Leaving aside questions of diversity of opinion, almost all of the commentators appear to be agreed that the composition of the judiciary should be reflective of society in the sense of broadly corresponding with the wider community in terms of gender and ethnic make-up.[50] In some jurisdictions this notion has received official endorsement. Thus the Ontario Judicial Appointments Advisory Committee is required by statute to recognize the desirability of 'reflecting the diversity of Ontario society' in their nominations of provincial judicial appointees.[51] In South Africa the Constitution requires that 'the need for the judiciary to reflect broadly the racial and gender composition of South Africa must be considered when judicial officers are appointed.'[52] Indeed, the Commonwealth as a whole has endorsed the principle that 'appointments to all levels of the judiciary should have, as an objective, the achievement of equality between women and men.'[53] Despite this, it was a long time before the Lord Chancellor's Department could bring itself to overtly endorse diversity. In its evidence to the Home Affairs Select Committee in 1996 the department stated that 'the Lord Chancellor has no plans to reconstitute the professional judiciary to reflect the composition of society as a whole.'[54] However, by 2001 the department, in its report on Equality of Opportunity and Promoting Diversity,[55] was commenting: 'The Lord Chancellor is keen to see a judiciary which reflects the diversity of the legal profession, which in turn should mirror our society ... It is not the purpose of the judiciary to be representative of society, but there remains much to be done before the judiciary reflects the diversity of the population it serves in terms of racial and gender balance.' Lest this was seen as a commitment to affirmative action the department quickly added: 'Appointments will always be made on merit from among those who are the most suitably qualified ...'[56] A remarkably similar formulation of words came from Jim Wallace, the then justice minister, in announcing the Scottish executive's intention to establish an independent Judicial Appointments Board in March 2001: 'The Judicial Appointments Board will be expected to have regard to how representative the Bench is of Scottish society and how to encourage applications from under-represented groups ... it will be expected to seek out more qualified women and members of ethnic minorities to serve on the Bench. However, having stressed the importance of diversity let me be quite clear that the over-riding consideration is that all appointments to the Bench must be made on merit.' True to his word, the remit he gave to the Judicial Appointment Board when it was set up in June 2002 included considering 'ways of recruiting a Judiciary which is as reflective as possible of the communities which they serve.'[57]

The arguments put forward for a reflective judiciary appear to be fivefold.

First, the judicial appointment process should be free from direct or indirect discrimination on illegal or unacceptable grounds such as gender, ethnicity, creed, disability, or sexual orientation.[58] Thus there appears to be a reasonable consensus that all properly qualified candidates should have the same chance of judicial preferment. The rub, of course, comes in the words 'properly qualified'; it is here that the unarticulated assumptions that bedevil any discussion of merit selection in the judiciary are to be found. Lady Justice Hale, in an illuminating address to the Society of Public Teachers of Law in 2000, draws on the available research to show the extent to which the then English appointments procedure, both in its process and in the criteria used, worked against women and minorities.[59] Principal among these are the use of soundings, the importance of networks of contacts, and the assumptions associated with merit selection. As we have seen, the Judicial Appointment Board in Scotland has endeavoured to address the first two concerns by declining to allow soundings or to permit its members to impart their knowledge of candidates to other members of the board. However, the last is the hardest to deal with.[60] Nowhere do the statutory qualifications for judicial appointment or the additional appointment criteria used by the board[61] require the candidate to have expertise or widespread experience in oral advocacy.[62] Nor, in the case of candidates for the higher courts, are they required to have had a successful practice as a Queen's Counsel (QC). But in Scotland, at least, these have been unwritten criteria constituting a tacit gloss on the concept of 'merit' which has rarely been departed from. The former militates against the appointment of academics or some employed lawyers; the latter has worked against the appointment of women and ethnic minorities. The standard answer to these criticisms, and to the fact that there are still very few ethnic minority judges, and relatively few female judges at any level above the level of magistrate in Scotland is that the problem will be resolved by the passage of time. As more women and ethnic minorities graduate from law school and work their way through the profession, the diversity imbalance in the make-up of the bench will be resolved. This 'trickle-up' theory consoles the many judges[63] and lawyers who would otherwise feel uncomfortable with the lack of social, gender, educational, and racial diversity in the Scottish bench of today. The added attraction of the theory is that it suggests that little more than tinkering is required to improve the status quo, thus avoiding the major problems associated with such thorny issues as quotas, affirmative action, or positive discrimination. Increasingly, however, an opposing school of thought has been gaining support. These critics allege that the 'trickle' is just that, and that the rate of progress for women and ethnic minorities is not only too slow but likely to peak well before societal proportionality[64] is achieved, because of hidden structural and cultural barriers. As Malleson shows,[65] the growth in number of female QCs and judges of all ranks in England and Wales has been very slow in the last decade, while the perceptions of structural and other barriers has increased more rapidly. The difficulties facing women who take career breaks, the slowness of female solicitor advocates in particular to reach the bench, the retention of judicial soundings, and the greater networking opportunities for men remain for JUSTICE, the Association of Women Barristers and others, barriers which are refusing to go away.[66] Baroness Hale has indicated that most senior judges she meets genuinely believe in the 'trickle-up' theory, but that she finds herself in the opposite camp.[67] In her eyes the hidden assumptions within the notion of merit selection systematically disadvantage women and minorities. The bare statistics of the growing numbers of female solicitors and partners, female advocates, QCs, sheriffs, and Senators of the College of Justice will not solve the debate in the near future, since both schools of thought can gain support from them (see tables 1.1 and 1.2).

However, the evidence from comparable professions is not encouraging. In teaching, academia, and medicine women have been present in the lower ranks for many years without approaching proportionality at the higher levels even now, because of the structural and cultural barriers

Table 1.1
1998 Statistics

Post	All	%	Men	%	Women	%
Senator	27		26	96	1	4
Sheriffs Principal	6		6	100	0	0
Sheriffs	104		93	83	11	11
Part-time/Temp Sheriffs	130		116	89	14	11
Advocates	389		307	79	82	21
Silk	81		75	93	7	9
Partners		100		83		17
Solicitors		100		65		35

that continue to frustrate their efforts to breach the 'glass ceiling' in significant numbers.[68] Nor does the relative dearth of women or ethnic minority equity partners in City firms of solicitors in London[69] (or even Edinburgh and Glasgow) suggest that indirect discrimination is being overcome in that closely related field. Should it ultimately become clear that the 'trickle-up' theory is not working for judges, some other solution will be required. Positive discrimination has few supporters, although some are prepared to say that where two candidates of equal merit present themselves, the one from the minority grouping should be preferred.[70] The other approach is to face up to the protean nature of 'merit' and engage in a serious debate (as the Canadians did fifteen years ago) focusing on the legal and competency-based requirements for appointment and the potential of the candidate to do the job rather than to apply traditional, unwritten concepts of 'merit' such as the view that the only acceptable candidates for appointment to the higher courts are successful silks with at least ten years standing.[71]

The second argument for diversity in the judiciary is that it will enhance democratic legitimacy. As Dame Brenda Hale has observed, 'In a democratic society, in which we are all equal citizens, it is wrong in principle for [judicial] authority to be wielded by such a very unrepresentative section of the population: ... not only mainly male, overwhelmingly white, but also largely the product of a limited range of educational institutions and social backgrounds.'[72] Sir Iain Glidewell's Working Party on Judicial Appointments and Silk adopted Dame Hale's subsequent argument that the judiciary is the link between Parliament and the people,

Table 1.2
2003 Statistics

Post	All	%	Men	%	Women	%
Senator	32		29	91	3	9
Sheriffs Principal	6		6	100	0	0
Sheriffs	136		114	83	23	17
Part Time/Temp Sheriffs	58		48	83	10	17
Advocates	462		356	77	106	23
Silk	97		88	91	9	9
Partners		100		81		19
Solicitors		100		61		39

commenting that the judiciary 'must be seen to reflect the diversity of our society if it is to have the confidence of society as a whole and in particular those who use the courts.'[73] Glidewell continues, 'If the judiciary is seen and continues to be seen as the preserve of the white middle class male, the public's confidence in the judiciary is likely to be undermined.'[74] Malleson supports both lines of thought, arguing that 'in all liberal democracies it is regarded as an inherent good that different social groups should have the opportunity to participate in public life ...'[75] adding that the judiciary, being an institution that exercises official power over individuals' lives, is inevitably a political body. Malleson, like Glidewell, argues that greater diversity in the make-up of the bench will increase accountability and thus public confidence: 'Since the judiciary cannot comply with the democratic requirements of electoral accountability, this method of social accountability amounts to an essential form of legitimacy.'[76] Moreover, Glidewell considers that in areas of particular judicial power and discretion, such as in the field of human rights, greater diversity adds to the quality of justice.[77]

The third and probably the most contentious argument is that greater diversity in the judiciary will change, and hopefully improve, the quality of decision making by the judiciary. The recent emphasis in the United Kingdom on judicial training in racial and gender awareness has been sufficiently sustained to suggest that greater diversity may improve the running of the courts. But would more women or ethnic minority judges enhance the quality of judicial decision making as a whole? On this issue the commentators and critics are of different minds. Feminist scholars are particularly divided, just as they are over the issue of whether the influx of women lawyers to the profession over the last twenty years is altering the style and ethical base of lawyering or merely adding more lawyers to the profession.[78] Regina Graycar points to what she considers to be the entrenched 'male-centredness of law and legal reasoning' and is sceptical that simply appointing more women as judges will change anything. As she notes, 'We may just be adding more women to the bench – nothing more, nothing less.'[79] Malleson[80] is equally sceptical, pointing to the body of American work endeavouring to link social background to judicial philosophy and praxis, and argues that the advent of a more diverse judiciary will not automatically translate into better judicial decision making. The problem is partly the need for impartiality in the individual case. But the difficulty also stems from the dubiety associated with the pursuit of social consensus in a pluralist society, and from the subjectivity of different judges' notions of common sense. On the other hand, Hamilton argues that 'any judge will see the world as a mirror reflecting his/her experiences' and that this influences both their interpretation of their role and their decision making.[81] Bertha Wilson, the first female member of the Canadian Supreme Court, is equivocal on the issue, despite accepting in principle the Gilligan thesis that female judges will speak 'in a different voice' from their male counterparts.[82] Dame Brenda Hale examines the issues of style and substance in relation to gender and judicial decision making, but is even more cautious than Bertha Wilson with respect to whether individual female judges will make any difference. However, she concludes that: 'On the other hand, a generally more diverse bench, with a wider range of backgrounds, experience and perspectives on life, might well be expected to bring about some collective change in empathy and understanding for the diverse backgrounds, experience and perspectives of those whose cases come before them.'[83] Chief Justice Beverly McLachlin of the Canadian Supreme Court is less cautious: 'the presence of women on the Bench can and does make a substantive difference. In so far as women are possessed of special experiences, concerns, and interests, these inevitably affect the way they address the problems that confront them.'[84] Lady Cosgrove, the first female High Court judge in Scotland and the only woman to be elevated to the Scots equivalent of the Court of Appeal,[85] is equally upbeat. 'I believe that women tend to view the world, and what goes on in it, from a different perspective than men, and by bringing the uniquely feminine perspective to bear, women can play a major role in improving the quality of the whole system.'[86] Nor is the effect necessarily confined to gender. Thus Sir

Sydney Kentridge QC, commenting on his time as an acting justice of the newly formed South African Constitutional Court in the late 1990s, noted the considerable diversity on that court in terms of gender, ethnicity, and legal background which led, he felt, not just to diversity of thought but to a maturity of judgment in the court as a whole which it would not otherwise have had.[87]

The fourth argument for diversity is utilitarian. 'Simply put, it represents a sound use of human resources ... modern societies cannot afford to lose the intellectual power and energy of ... [so much of their] ... population.'[88]

The fifth and final argument for diversity is that it enables minority and women judges to act as role models for new entrants to the profession. Thus judges in the United States have pointed to the benefits of the growing numbers of Asian-American as well African-American and Hispanics judges. As one Texan woman judge noted: 'It changes the talk in the hallway, provides minority communities with "a place at the table" ... and provides new minority role models.'[89] Similarly, Beverly McLachlin has observed: 'Symbolically, women on the bench signal to other women and to groups that have been historically marginalized and confined, that they too can excel, and upon excelling, will be recognized and rewarded for their accomplishments.'[90]

Conclusion

Barely twenty months after the establishment of the Judicial Appointments Board for Scotland it is premature to assess the success or otherwise of the enterprise. Nonetheless, even at this early stage it is possible to make some tentative and interim observations. The board appears to be generally perceived by the media and the executive as doing a reasonable job. Moreover, there are indications from a number of quarters, including some of the appointees themselves, that some candidates are being appointed who might not have come to the attention of the lord advocate under the old system. In terms of transparency the Board has broadcast its processes widely in its advertisements, on its website, and in its first Annual Report, as well as through meetings with a range of external organizations. In terms of encouraging diversity, the picture is more mixed. Although it has taken the courageous step of outlawing soundings and personal knowledge in the interests of fairness and equal opportunities, it has not yet been able to tackle the even harder diversity issues associated with the tacit understandings as to the concept of merit selection. Nevertheless, the very existence of the board seems to be having a positive impact on the proportion of female candidates applying for judicial positions. Applications from women rose from 11 per cent in 2001 to 23 per cent in 2003.[91] Although still non-statutory the board also appears to have enhanced the legitimacy of the process by its commitment to objectivity and transparency. The creation of the board and the self-denying ordinance of the executive in restricting its continuing role in the appointment process to that of an exceptional 'long-stop' can be said to have enhanced judicial independence. Similarly, the transparency and objectivity of the board's procedures (and its website and Annual Report) can be said to have enhanced judicial accountability. It is perhaps unfortunate that neither of the Justice Committees have yet invited the board to defend its Annual Report to the Parliament. On the other hand, the board, led by its impressive lay chair,[92] has managed to avoid coming too much under the influence of external agencies and interest groups, including the executive and the judiciary. Yet if the board has so far avoided one of the known dangers associated with judicial appointment boards – co-option – it is too early to say whether it will avoid another, namely, the perceived tendency for boards to make appointments based on extensive experience and competencies rather than on potential. Moreover, the board has suffered rebuffs in relation to its remit which may in the long run undermine its credibility. On balance, therefore, the verdict on the Scottish board might be – a good start, but there are bigger challenges ahead.

NOTES

1 Curiously both the critics and the establishment, or at least lord chancellors as diverse as Lord Hailsham and Lord Mackay of Clashfern, were agreed on the importance of independence and accountability. It was only over the implications of these that opinions differed.

2 All four bodies representing the Scottish judiciary were in favour of the reform, although it was noticeable that they all also favoured a board that would be numerically dominated by judges.

3 Jim Wallace, also the deputy first minister.

4 The executive were strongly advised by the senior judiciary in their response to the Consultation Paper to keep lay participation in the board to a minimum, since their only role could be to keep the lawyers and judges making up the bulk of the board honest.

5 This decline in authority is, of course, not confined to the judiciary but holds true for many professions.

6 The lord advocate. Under the prevailing legislation it was the secretary of state for Scotland who made the decision; however, almost always the real decision was left to the lord advocate.

7 It is clear from judicial biographies and memoirs that successive lord presidents (the highest judge in Scotland) were consulted by lord advocates and considered that there was a constitutional convention whereby their opinion would be sought in relation to all significant judicial appointments. It is equally clear that in some cases lord advocates paid only lip service to this unwritten 'convention.' It was not until the *Scotland Act 1998*, s. 95(4), that the law was changed to require the first minister (who succeeded the secretary of state) to consult the lord president. Ironically, the first minister is not now required to consult the lord advocate, but in practice, it is believed that all first ministers to date have continued to do so.

8 S. 35(1), *Law Reform (Miscellaneous Provisions) (Scotland) Act 1990.*

9 Provided the lord advocate sat in one or other of the Houses of Parliament.

10 Lord Stott appointed himself to the Court of Session bench, quipping later, 'I appointed myself, and a jolly good judge I turned out to be.'

11 See Kate Malleson's chapter in this volume.

12 Scotland is divided into six areas, or sheriffdoms, each with its own sheriff principal who is responsible for the deployment of judicial resources (sheriffs) in that area, as well as for hearing appeals in civil cases from these sheriffs.

13 Thirteen of the last sixteen lord advocates have been elevated to the higher judiciary.

14 Only four of the twenty-eight deans since 1900 did not go on to higher judicial appointment, and two of them are thought to have effectively disqualified themselves by their handling of their business or private lives. The dean is the elected head of the Scottish bar.

15 Deputies to the lord advocate who are experienced advocates and devote three years of their careers to prosecution in the High Court.

16 See Paterson, Bates, and Poustie, *The Legal System of Scotland*, 225–7.

17 [2000] 1 A.C. 119.

18 See, e.g., *Porter v. Magill*, [2002] 1 All ER 465 at para. 103 of Lord Hope's judgment.

19 For a useful discussion of judicial accountability in the United Kingdom see Le Sueur, 'Developing Mechanisms for Judicial Accountability in the UK.'

20 See, e.g., Stevens, 'A Loss of Innocence?', at 399.

21 See Lord Reid of Drem, 'The Judge as Law Maker.' Cited with approval by

Justice Michael Kirby of the Australian High Court in his Hamlyn Lectures on *Judicial Activism* (delivered on 19 and 20 November 2003, Exeter University Law School); by Lord Hoffmann in 'The Role of the Appellate Judge in England,' Address to the Franco-British Lawyers' Society, Glasgow, 20 September 2003; and by Lord Browne-Wilkinson in *Kleinwort Benson Ltd v. Lincoln CC*, [1998] 3 WLR 1095, 1100, who added, 'In truth judges make and change the law.'

22 See Department of Constitutional Affairs, *Constitutional Reform: A New Way of Appointing Judges*, CP 10/03, paras. 34–52.

23 Technically the last word lies with the monarch; however, in terms of U.K. constitutional convention when it comes to judicial appointment the monarch today appoints those whose names have been put forward by the relevant government minister. In some recommending commissions, such as those of Ontario or some of the U.S. merit commissions, the politicians are provided with extensive lists of possible candidates, with or without rankings. Other commissions leave the politicians less room for manoeuvre.

24 Moreover, the longer the self-denying ordinance lasts the harder it will be for the executive to change their stance, and the more the board will grow used to having their recommendations accepted without question.

25 Constitutional Reform Bill 2004.

26 See, e.g, *Politics Now* (Glasgow: Scottish Television, 2004), broadcast on 15 January 2004.

27 The interviews were conducted by a retired senior judge, a layperson, and a senior civil servant. The ultimate appointment was made by the first minister.

28 See Thomas and Malleson, *Judicial Appointment Commissions.*

29 Kennedy, *Eve was Framed*, 267.

30 Hale, 'Equality in the Judiciary,' Fathers' Lecture, 17.

31 Legg, 'Judges for the New Century,' 73. Similarly, Sir Geoffrey Palmer (formerly attorney general, justice minister, and prime minister of New Zealand) has remarked, 'If judges are on the Commission they will exert great weight on the opinion of the lay members. The tendency to turn the judiciary into a self-perpetuating oligarchy ought to be restricted.' See Palmer, 'Judicial Selection and Accountability,' 81–2. See also Professor Robert Stevens's evidence to the Constitutional Affairs Committee on 11 November 2003 at Q.87: 'It is government by the judiciary and most societies think that is not necessarily a good thing, so you need some checks and balances ...'

32 Which they have rarely done since the establishment of the board.

33 The committee drew heavily from criteria in use in the Lord Chancellor's Department as set out in the Peach Report. See the Scotland Judicial Appointments Board, *First Annual Report*, 8–9.

34 Such a stipulation was felt by some to be unfair to QCs who might not consider seeking an appointment as a part-time sheriff and who might not be nominated by the lord president as a temporary judge.
35 Where A means definitely interview, B means possibly interview, and C means do not interview.
36 Which appears to be about to be enshrined in the new English legislation on judicial appointments following negotiations between the lord chief justice and the lord chancellor at the end of 2003, despite the publicly stated criticisms of soundings by the Judicial Appointments Commission in its first two Annual Reports. See Lord Falconer, Speech to the House of Lords, 26 January 2004, *Hansard Parliamentary Debates*, House of Lords, vol. 657, col. 15.
37 Nevertheless, extreme instances may occur where a member of the board has private information concerning a severe conduct allegation against a candidate, such that if the latter was appointed and the allegation proved to be true, it would be significantly detrimental to the public interest and the reputation of the board. In such instances the board has resolved either that the chairman will put the matter to the candidate prior to interview, or where it is as yet unsubstantiated, to withhold disclosure from the board deliberations but request that the executive conduct its own investigations into the allegation before proceeding further.
38 *Scotland Act 1998*, s. 95(4).
39 And de facto also with the lord advocate.
40 See the Judicial Appointment Board's *Annual Report 2002–2003*, para. 39.
41 These have been used in relation to District Court judges in England and Wales and to appoint judges in the Netherlands.
42 An attribute that many judges, referees, and others regard as a positive advantage in a candidate applying for a full-time judicial post. The same problem exists for judges applying for promotion or to go part-time.
43 Such schemes currently exist in England and Wales for deputy district court judges and for magistrates and are also being considered for recorders there.
44 See the Board's *Annual Report 2002–2003*, para. 32.
45 Home Affairs Select Committee report (1996) vol. 2, para. 2.3.3. The former permanent secretary of the Lord Chancellor's Department, Tom Legg, put it even more pithily: 'it is not the function of the judicial branch to represent anyone.' Judges for the New Century, 69.
46 On this, see the helpful discussion by Malleson, *The New Judiciary*, 106–9.
47 In similar vein the Sheriffs' Association, in their Response to the Scottish Executive's (2002) consultation paper *Judicial Appointments: An Inclusive*

Approach, noted that 'there are elements within Scottish Society, including racial and religious intolerance and sexual prejudice, which one would not wish the judiciary to reflect.' Sheriffs' Association Response, 6.

48 Kirby, 'Judicial Accountability in Australia,' 50.

49 As Malleson notes in *The New Judiciary* at 111, even if the judiciary was a statistically accurate reflection of society, this could only impact on the totality of cases, not on individual cases decided by individual judges.

50 In the United Kingdom, at least, there is less agreement on the need to be more reflective of society in relation to age, class, or language.

51 See also the Montreal Universal Declaration on the Independence of Justice, Art 2.13. quoted in Malleson, *The New Judiciary,* 123.

52 S. 174(2).

53 Latimer House Guidelines for the Commonwealth on Parliamentary Supremacy and Judicial Independence, 19 June 1998, 3.

54 See Report on Judicial Selection, vol. 2, para. 2.3.3.

55 Lord Chancellors' Department, *Equality and Diversity,* 1 and 8.

56 Ibid. at 8.

57 Judicial Appointments Board, *Annual Report 2002–2003,* 12, para. 32.

58 The legal community has hitherto been spared the unedifying wrangles of recent years in relation to gay bishops in the Anglican Church. However, Mr Justice Kirby of the Australian High Court has expressed scepticism that he would have been elevated to that court had his sexual orientation been generally known at the time of his elevation (Kirby, 'Judicial Accountability in Australia, at 50). As he observed, there are virtually no openly homosexual judges in the United States, and he could have added the United Kingdom. He notes, however, that the Judicial Service Commission in South Africa has promoted a judge who had declared his homosexuality to the Supreme Court of Appeal. Indeed, one of five candidates for a position on the Constitutional Court of South Africa in 2002 was an openly lesbian judge. (See Evert Knoesen, 'Judicial Service Commission to Appoint New Judges,' available at www.equality.org.za/news/2002/08/30judges.php.)

59 See Hale, 'Equality and the Judiciary.'

60 As Hale wryly observes in 'Equality and the Judiciary' at 492, 'Changing the appointments system will be much easier than changing the assumptions about the qualifications necessary to become a judge.'

61 See Judicial Appointments Board, *First Annual Report 2002–2003,* 8. These were derived in part from criteria applied by the Lord Chancellor's Department.

62 The Lord Chancellor's Department in 2000 was advising applicants that the lord chancellor 'does not regard advocacy experience as an essential require-

ment for appointment to judicial office.' Quoted in Hale, 'Equality and the Judiciary,' 496.

63 Malleson, *The New Judiciary*, 115–23, demonstrates that successive lord chancellors, permanent secretaries, and judges in England have supported this view in the last decade. Again, the commissioner for judicial appointments for Northern Ireland in his Audit Report (February 2003) notes at 67, para. 5.5.7. that 'the "trickle up" view tends to be supported by the senior judges.' The Responses of the Sheriffs Principal and of the Sheriffs Association to the Scottish Executive's consultation paper, *Judicial Appointments: An Inclusive Approach*, are both consistent with the 'trickle-up' approach. Each rejects positive discrimination.

64 For these critics, proportionality with the legal profession is not the issue, since they believe that indirect barriers are artificially constraining progress in the profession.

65 See Malleson, *The New Judiciary*, 116 et seq.

66 Ibid.

67 'Most serious outside observers know that this will not happen.' Quoted in Gibb 'Choice of Judges Fails Democratic Legitimacy.' See also Hale, 'Equality and the Judiciary,' 492. Chief Justice McLachlin, of the Canadian Supreme Court, also rejects the 'trickle-up' thesis; see McLachlin 'Promoting Gender Equality in the Judiciary.' The Commission for Racial Equality, in its evidence before the Constitutional Affairs Committee on 18 November 2003, opposed waiting for the trickle-up effect. In a speech at the first Annual Conference of the Association of Women Judges in England and Wales on 20 March 2004 in Birmingham the lord chancellor indicated concerns as to the efficacy of the trickle-up thesis and an interest in the approach taken in relation to the merit selection of Canadian federal judges in the last fifteen years.

68 See, e.g., Raitt, Callaghan, and Siann, 'Is There Still a Glass Ceiling for Women Solicitors?,' 19.

69 Research in *The Lawyer* (18 August 2003, 1) found that in only one of the top ten firms (in size) in the United Kingdom were more than 20 per cent of the equity partners women.

70 See, e.g., Kentridge, 'The Highest Court: Selecting the Judges,' 62. In fact, both of these approaches are probably incompatible with U.K. equal opportunities legislation; European law might allow the second, though not the first.

71 See McLachlin, 'Promoting Gender Equality in the Judiciary,' at 15.

72 See Hale, 'Equality and the Judiciary,' at 502.

73 Bar Council, *Report of the Bar Council's Working Party on Judicial Appointments and Silk*, para. 2.6.

74 Ibid., para. 2.7.
75 Malleson, *The New Judiciary,* 112.
76 Ibid., 114.
77 Bar Council, *Report of the Bar Council's Working Party on Judicial Appointments and Silk,* para. 2.5.
78 See Gilligan, *In a Different Voice*; Menkel Meadow, 'Portia Redux'; Malleson, Gender Equality in the Judiciary.'
79 Graycar, 'The Gender of Judgements,' 267.
80 Malleson, *The New Judiciary,* 106 et seq.
81 Hamilton, 'Criteria for Judicial Appointment and "Merit,"' 15.
82 Wilson, 'Will Women Judges Really Make a Difference?' Her conclusion (at 515) is that in many areas of law there is no uniquely feminine perspective, but that in others, especially criminal law, 'a distinctly male perspective is clearly discernible.'
83 Ibid., 501.
84 McLachlin, 'Promoting Gender Equality in the Judiciary.'
85 The Inner House of the Court of Session.
86 Robertson, 'Female Judge Appointed to the Legal World's Inner Sanctum.' In keeping with her sentiments Lady Cosgrove was perceived by external observers to have played a key role in the decision of the appeal court that overturned a precedent of 150 years standing by concluding that 'force' by a man overcoming consent was no longer to be an essential ingredient in the crime of rape. Lord Advocate's Reference (No. 1 of 2001) 2002 SLT 466.
87 Kentridge, 'The Highest Court,' 61.
88 McLachlin, 'Promoting Gender Equality in the Judiciary,' 6.
89 See Higgason, 'Diversity Strengthens the Texas Judiciary,' para. 30 et seq.
90 McLachlin, 'Promoting Gender Equality in the Judiciary,' 6.
91 Interestingly, the success rate for female applicants in 2003 was also 23 per cent. One unintended success with respect to diversity has been that the success of prosecutors (procurator fiscals) in some of the early appointment rounds of the board appears to have encouraged considerable numbers of prosecutors to apply for shreival appointments.
92 Sir Neil MacIntosh.

2 The New Judicial Appointments Commission in England and Wales: New Wine in New Bottles?

KATE MALLESON

The decision of the U.K. government in June 2003 to set up a new judicial appointments commission took the legal world by surprise. A Thursday afternoon cabinet reshuffle turned into a constitutional revolution that included a complete overhaul of the judicial appointments process and the creation of a new judicial appointments commission. The unexpected timing of the announcement and the lack of prior consultation about the changes attracted considerable criticism, provoking concern that the proposals might be an attempt on the part of the government to take control of the judicial appointments process.[1] Those fears were laid to rest by the publication of the consultation paper on the new system a month later. Far from being a grab for power, the proposals significantly reduced the role of the executive in the selection process.[2] The clumsy manner in which the reforms were introduced should, therefore, be distinguished from their general desirability. And although the announcement was unexpected, the decision to establish a commission did not come out of the blue. The arguments for change had been rehearsed over many years and by the mid-1990s there was widespread support among reform groups, lawyers, and politicians for reform of the judicial appointments process.

Although the long gestation period of the decision to set up a commission has been frustrating for its supporters, the delay has had advantages. The establishment of the Judicial Appointment Board in Scotland in 2002[3] and the formulation of the framework for a judicial appointments commission in Northern Ireland[4] have provided useful comparative models to draw on in determining the role and function of the commission. Their existence also strengthens the case for change, since the creation of a commission in England and Wales will add to the coherence and consistency of the U.K. judicial selection processes as a whole. In addition to these two new models close to home, a wide range of different commissions is in use around the world, some of which have long track records. As many of the other chapters in this volume show, the powers, procedures, and membership of these bodies differ considerably, reflecting the fact that a commission is not an 'off the shelf' product that can be adopted wholesale, but a system that must be constructed to accommodate the particular legal, political, and cultural conditions of the country.[5] The adaptability of a commission is one of its great strengths, as well as being the reason why the particular model of commission must be thought through carefully. Many lessons can be learnt from the ways in which commissions operate in other systems, but it is neither necessary nor desirable to follow slavishly the detailed arrangements found elsewhere.

The Reason for Setting Up a Commission

In order to assess whether the new appointments system will work in England and Wales it is important to understand why a new body is being set up in the first place, and what it is expected to achieve. The consultation paper made clear that the decision to restructure the judicial appointments process was part of a wider program of modernization that includes the abolition of the office of lord chancellor, setting up a new Supreme Court, and the abolition or reform of the Queen's Counsel system.[6] Together, this package of reforms represents the second phase of constitutional change, building on the introduction of devolution and the incorporation of the European Convention on Human Rights into domestic law in the *Human Rights Act 1998*. The government's underlying purpose for these changes generally and the creation of the judicial appointments commission specifically is to modernize the constitution and the legal system. The consultation paper argues that change to the judicial appointments process is needed because 'Many of the most fundamental features of the system, including the role of the Lord Chancellor, remain rooted in the past.'[7] While the claim that the system is backward-looking is empirically justified, it is not sufficient on its own to justify the uncertainty and extra public expense that will be brought about by a root and branch change to the judicial appointments process.[8] The rationale for the establishment of a commission must be that it will guarantee the independence of the system from inappropriate politicization, strengthen the quality of the appointments made, enhance the fairness of the selection process, promote diversity in the composition of the judiciary, and so rebuild public confidence in the system.

Politicization

The selection of judges on the basis of merit rather than political patronage is the defining feature of a good judicial appointments process. The argument that this can be guaranteed while appointments are in the gift of one minister is, as the government recognized, increasingly difficult to sustain.[9] The government has repeatedly stressed, however, that there has been no credible suggestion that recent lord chancellors have abused their position by appointing judges whose outlook is favourable to the government. Indeed, some recent appointments have patently *not* shared the general political vision of the government of the day. It is notable, for example, that the only senior judge who was once a member of the Communist party, Lord Justice Sedley, was appointed by a Conservative Lord Mackay, while the first two appointments to the Lords of his Labour successor, Lords Millett and Hobhouse, were generally regarded as conservative commercial lawyers. In most cases the political views of the appointees even to the highest courts are neither widely known nor scrutinized. As middle-aged successful lawyers, many no doubt broadly conform to John Griffith's thesis of conservatism, but this generalization tells us little about the particular views of the individual judges that may impact on their decision making.[10] Although we now have sound empirical evidence that individual judges in the House of Lords have taken different approaches to policy questions that have arisen in the cases they have decided, there is currently very little interest in dissecting their views on particular policy or social issues in the way that is familiar, for example, in U.S. Supreme Court appointments.[11]

The success of the current judicial appointments process in removing partisan politics from the system could be seen as grounds for arguing 'if it ain't broke don't fix it.' But there are good reasons for anticipating future political manipulation of the process and making sure that proper safeguards are in place to protect against this danger. The expanding role of the judiciary is an incremental change that predates the *Human Rights Act* and which is slowly redefining the relationship between the branches of state. The view that the United Kingdom is in a transitional phase from parliamentary to constitutional democracy is increasingly credible and has long-term implications for the relationship between the judiciary and the executive.[12] One consequence of this development will be that the conventions which underpin the existing constitutional arrangements, and which by their nature are designed to adapt to changing circumstances, will come under increasing pressure. The convention that judicial appointments in England and Wales are non-partisan is neither so long established nor so tightly defined that it could not be discarded relatively easily.

It is not necessary to look back very far into the constitutional history of the United Kingdom to find examples of political influences at work in the judicial appointments process.[13] Nor is it difficult to imagine a future secretary of state for constitutional affairs (the cabinet minister who replaces the lord chancellor) who feels justified in scrutinizing the ideological views of prospective appointees to the senior judiciary with greater intensity than is the case today. Given the lack of transparency in the current process, political patronage could slip back into the system with very little public awareness or scrutiny. Moreover, the fact that the current arrangements are dependent on the self-control of politicians and lack any structural checks on potential abuse serves to undermine confidence in the system, despite the strong record of non-politicization in recent years.[14] The decision to establish a system which is better able to protect the tradition of selection on merit alone is an attempt to anticipate the changing role of the judiciary and its relationship with the executive and to create an appointments system that is robust enough to withstand future pressure.

Diversity

Establishing sound structural protection against improper political control is intended to secure the long-term health of the appointments system. A more immediate and pressing rationale for change is the need to tackle the lack of diversity in the composition of the judiciary.[15] The narrow background from which the judiciary is drawn, particularly at senior levels, has become its Achilles' heel. Almost the only fact that many people know about judges in England and Wales is that they are generally elderly, white, male barristers educated at private schools and at Oxbridge. Irrespective of whether or not the inclusion on the bench of members of under-represented groups such as solicitors, women, minority lawyers, and disabled lawyers will have a significant effect on the decision making of the courts, the corrosive impact of their absence on the legitimacy of the judiciary is now too great to ignore.[16] The failure of the Lord Chancellor's Department to make significant progress in this area over the last decade, despite the implementation of some important practical changes by the former lord chancellors, Lord Mackay and Lord Irvine, has prompted a radical change of approach by the government.[17] To date, the official response to the lack of diversity in the judiciary has been two-pronged. First, the problem will be solved naturally in time as under-represented groups make their way through the profession and 'trickle up' into the judicial ranks. Second, a significant cause of the lack of diversity in the recruitment pool is an unjustified lack of confidence on the part of non-traditional applicants which, in Lord Irvine's words, 'robbed him' of good candidates.[18] Using the rally call 'don't be shy – apply!', his solution to this problem was to encourage such applicants to come forward. In contrast, the 2003 consultation paper acknowledged that tackling the lack of diversity in the judiciary will require 'fresh approaches and a major re-engineering of the process for appointment.'[19]

The ability of the commission to achieve this goal will depend on whether or not increasing diversity is clearly prioritized within its remit. The evidence from other jurisdictions suggests that the creation of a commission can make a significant difference to the make-up of the judiciary, but that such an outcome is not automatic. Early merit commissions in the United States, for example, did not often affect the composition of the judiciary in terms of gender or ethnic background because this was not generally one of their goals. The focus of the merit commissions was the need to insulate the process from party politics and diversity was a very secondary requirement, if it featured at all. Commissions that have a good record in this area have been specifically tasked with this aim and have the political backing to achieve it. As Lord Irvine discovered to his cost, diversity is only likely to be achieved if equal opportunities are placed at the heart of the judicial appointments process and promoted through sustained and proactive initiatives. An example of such an initiative comes from Ontario, where one of the first actions of the newly established Judicial Appointments Advisory Committee (JAAC) in 1990 was to ask the attorney general to write a personal letter to 1,200 senior women lawyers in the province asking them to consider applying for judicial office. This conscious and innovative attempt to expand the number of women in the recruitment pool produced such a marked increased numbers of applicants from well-qualified women that between 1990 and 1992, 41 per cent of judges appointed by the JAAC were women.[20]

Such results are evidence of the importance of proactive recruitment activities; the long-term effectiveness of these efforts on the part of the commission, however, is dependent on changes that lie beyond the appointments process. Unless the career paths of all lawyers are compatible with judicial office, the recruitment pool will always exclude a significant number of potentially well-qualified candidates. Equally, the structure of the judiciary must be sufficiently open and flexible to allow the most talented of those appointed to all ranks to progress through a judicial career. To date this has been hampered by the presence of an artificial barrier between the upper and lower ranks as a result of which it has been very rare for judges to be appointed to the High Court from the circuit bench or district bench.[21] An important part of the commission's role must therefore be to identify ways of increasing the range of routes both into the judiciary and up the judicial ranks. The changes required to bring this about are both cultural and structural and cannot be achieved by the commission alone. Its efforts will need to be matched by a commitment on the part of the Department for Constitutional Affairs (which replaces the Lord Chancellor's Department), the legal profession, and the judiciary to work together with the commission to ensure that all aspects of their working practices promote and encourage the process of diversification.[22]

Quality of Appointments

While there is almost universal support among judges and lawyers, at least publicly, for the principle of greater diversity, a commonly expressed reservation about the implementation of that goal in practice is the fear that selection on merit may be sacrificed in order to transform the composition of the judiciary. This concern is founded on the assumption that diversity and merit are always in tension, and that appointing from a wider pool means diluting the quality of those selected. Such a fear is justified only if the commission is prepared to appoint less qualified candidates from under-represented groups in preference to better-qualified traditional candidates. But provided the merit criterion is paramount, the diversification of the recruitment pool should, in fact, have the reverse effect and bring about an improvement in the quality of appointments. Unless we believe that white, male barristers from elite chambers are inherently better suited to be judges than any other lawyers, the inclusion of other groups of lawyers in the recruitment will increase competition and so raise standards. There is, however, room for debate about whether the traditional definition of merit is sufficiently wide to incorporate all those candidates who would make good judges. One almost inevitable effect of selecting judges from a narrow group is that the characteristics of that group tend to become synonymous with merit. The evidence from countries such as Canada which have achieved more success in diversifying their judiciaries is that both the cause and effect of their diversification has been the widening of the definition of merit beyond the profile of existing members of the judiciary.[23]

A somewhat different concern regarding the potential impact of a commission on the quality of appointments is the fear that transferring the decision from an individual to a group of people may result in the selection of mediocre compromise candidates.[24] Many of the most celebrated senior judges in England and Wales both past and present have been individualistic mavericks rather than team players. Would such characters command the collective approval of a committee? In some U.S. commissions there is evidence that the need to achieve consensus among commission members has led to the rejection of dynamic, higher-risk candidates in favour of bland, safe appointments. However, this outcome must be seen in the context of the far more politicized U.S. system. Although the 'merit' commissions are intended to reduce the impact of ideological factors, the reality is that the view of the different candidates on political issues may be at least as significant as their intellectual, legal, or other judicial skills. Where commission members are divided along political lines the selection of compromise candidates is often the consequence. The underlying culture of the system in England and Wales is so different in this respect that the risk of a similar outcome is remote. The fact that U.S. commissions have almost always replaced an electoral system has produced a very different political context. State judges are expected, to some extent, to represent the broad political interests of those who select them and this expectation has undoubtedly influenced the way in which commissions operate. This difference is compounded by the fact that the political debate in the United States is dominated by a small number of overarching ideological issues, such as abortion and the death penalty, in a way that has no equivalence in England and Wales.

The Form of Commission

Having established that the goals of the new commission are to strengthen judicial independence, diversify the composition of the judiciary, maintain and enhance the quality of appointments, and raise public confidence in the system, it remains to determine whether the particular powers, procedures, and membership of the new body are most likely to achieve these aims.

The first feature to note of the new system is that it encompasses two commissions, one for the Supreme Court and one for all other ranks of judges. The Supreme Court commission will be a small body, convened only when a vacancy arises, consisting of the president of the Supreme Court (who will chair it) the deputy president, and one of each of the three U.K. appointments commissions/boards (England and Wales, Northern Ireland, and Scotland). The main commission for England and Wales, in contrast, will be responsible for appointing nine hundred full and part-time judges, tribunal members, and lay magistrates. It will have a large secretariat, equivalent to the section of the department that now carries out the day-to-day work for the lord chancellor.

Both the Supreme Court and England and Wales commissions will be recommending commissions, leaving the final selection to be made by the secretary of state for constitutional affairs.[25] However, both are required to put forward only one name to the minister, so that the role of the minister will, in almost all cases, be limited to approving the commission's choice, though she or he has the power to reject that name and ask for a new one to be put forward.

A strength of the new system is that if the minister does reject the name put forward by the commission, she or he must give reasons for doing so. This is an important safeguard against the abuse of ministerial power. In Scotland, in contrast, the first minister has discretion to reject the Judicial Appointment Board's first list of candidates and to ask for another one to be drawn up where there is a 'compelling reason' for doing so. However, there are as yet no guidelines, statutory or otherwise, setting out what constitutes a compelling reason. Nor is the first minister under an obligation to publish her or his reasons for rejecting the board's choice. To date, this issue has not caused difficulties because no names put forward by the board have been rejected, but the arrangements in England and Wales are preferable in ensuring clarity about the type of circumstance in which this could happen.

While the minister must give reasons, it is not clear which reasons will be legitimate. At one end of the spectrum, if the minister's choice was made to promote the policies of the government there could be no doubt that such intervention would constitute improper political influence. At the other end of the spectrum, if the commission's selection had been made without regard to its own proper procedures (whether through incompetence or corruption) then there could be no objection to the minister asking the commission to re-advertise the position or put forward another name from a reserve list of candidates. Likewise, if the minister had obtained reliable information about some aspect of a candidate's professional or personal life that undermined their suitability for appointment, the minister's input would clearly be justified. In such cases the merit of the appointment or the validity of the selection process would be in issue and the minister would be fulfilling an important quality-check function.

In between these two extremes arises the more problematic scenario where candidates are rejected on the grounds that their appointment runs counter to a legitimate policy objective such as the need to enhance the diversity of the judiciary. If, for example, the commission recommended a list of names for a number of vacancies among the part-time judiciary that included no solicitors, women, or minority lawyers, would it be legitimate for the minister to ask it to reconsider its choice or to draw up a new list? The rejection would be on the basis of the collective merit of the candidates rather than their individual merit. In Ontario such a situation arose in the 1990s at a time when there was an explicit drive to recruit more French speakers to the bench. The JAAC submitted a list of names to the minister that did not include any francophone candidates and the minister asked the committee to draw up a new list. The committee re-advertised the posts in French-speaking publications and produced a new list that included both well-qualified English and French speakers. The then chair of the JAAC, reflecting on the action of the minister, considered that this was an appropriate and useful intervention. In South Africa, in contrast, the minister has on occasion rejected a white candidate named first on the Judicial Service Commission's recommended list in favour of a black candidate. These decisions have attracted considerable controversy and criticism. One important difference between these two situations is that in Ontario the names on both the rejected and appointed list were kept confidential, whereas in South Africa the public nature of the process meant that the identities of the candidates were known and the debate about the rejection and selection was inevitably personalized.

The experience of other commissions suggests that setting out clear rules about the way the recommending process works and requiring the commission to provide a full annual account of the process (within the constraints needed to guarantee individual confidentiality) can act as an important safeguard against future manipulation. In Ontario it has been reported that in recent years the government has been requesting longer lists of candidates from the JAAC, arousing suspicion that they are attempting to identify ideologically preferable candidates. Because the length of the list is not fixed by statute and there is no requirement on the part of the committee to publish details of the length of the lists provided, it has proved difficult to scrutinize this change in approach and to determine whether or not it is driven by improper political considerations.

Membership

As the role of the main commission includes the appointment of tribunal members and 30,000 lay magistrates, its workload will be a very heavy one by comparison with most other equivalent bodies. For this reason it will be relatively large by international standards, consisting of fifteen members appointed for relatively short part-time fixed terms.[26] The exact make-up of the body was the subject of intense debate. In particular, there was sharp disagreement about how to strike the right balance between the numbers of legal and lay members. The latter are the conduit through which new approaches and fresh ideas in appointments are brought into the commission. Their experience of other selection systems and recruitment methods, in particular, is vital to the development of an innovative and effective system and provides some safeguard against the danger of self-replication that has plagued the system to date. However, as outsiders to the legal establishment, the lay members may defer inappropriately to the legal insiders, particularly senior judges. One means of guarding against this risk is to ensure an equal number of lay and legal members, as is the case in Scotland, or a majority of lay members, as is the case on the JAAC in Ontario. In the event, the composition of the commission in England and Wales is much more heavily legally dominated than these bodies, consisting of six lay people, five judges, one solicitor, one barrister, one magistrate, and one tribunal member.[27] The one factor mitigating the strong legal presence is that the chair of the commission is a lay member.[28] The very successful chairing of the current Commission for Judicial Appointments established in 2001 to review the appointments process by Sir Colin Campbell had set a good precedent for the appointment of a lay chair. The fact that he is not a lawyer has not hindered his effectiveness in understanding the functioning of the judiciary while his extensive experience of other professional appointments processes has facilitated the ability of the commission to take a fresh and objective look at the judicial appointments system.

One important factor in the success of the commission will be whether its various members are as diverse as possible in terms of background and experience. Diversity will strengthen public confidence in its impartiality and reduce the danger that the commission will be dominated by a single faction or interest group. Commissions that work well in other jurisdictions are generally those which form a strong collective identity and in which the members do not see themselves as representatives of the professional or social groups from which they are drawn. A key to forming this strong sense of identity beyond the narrow interest groups will be the quality and seniority of the lay members. It is vital that the new body attract applications from the most able members of a wide range of public and private institutions.

While there were strong differences in opinion about the best balance between lay and legal members on the commission, there was very little support for including members of Parliament. By statute, no MP can be appointed to the commission. This approach is not universal. The South African Judicial Services Commission and the judicial appointments commission in Israel, for example, both include members of the legislature as a means of enhancing the democratic legitimacy of the system. Nor is it obvious why the inclusion on the commission for England and Wales of one MP from each of the three main parties would give rise to any greater a danger of politicization than the involvement of the secretary of state, who has a clear vested interest in the political outlook of the judges who will scrutinize the government's policies in court. Arguably, the participation of MPs would increase democratic accountability and enhance the legitimacy of the appointments process while posing less of a potential threat to judicial independence than the discretion that will be exercised by the secretary of state for constitutional affairs in the selection of the Supreme Court judges.

The unarticulated assumption that runs through the consultation paper that democratic accountability can only be achieved through the involvement of the executive rather than Parliament requires justification. Just as there was little support for including MPs on the commission, there was an equal lack of enthusiasm for any form of parliamentary confirmation hearing.[29] As the power of the judiciary grows, this unwillingness to address the possibility of including Parliament in the process may become less acceptable. The recent revival of interest in parliamentary involvement in the process in Canada may be a foretaste of future developments in the United Kingdom.[30]

Appointing the Commissioners

Just as important as the make-up of the commission members is the question of how they are appointed and by whom. Many commissions in other jurisdictions, including the Scottish Judicial Appointment Board, leave the selection of the non-judicial members wholly to the executive. In contrast, the secretary of state for constitutional affairs must appoint the commissioners for England and Wales after consultation with an advisory body consisting of the lord chief justice, the chair of the commission (once appointed), and an additional lay member appointed by the minister. In relation to the judicial and legal members the minister must also consult the judicial council and legal governing bodies respectively. What role the advisory body plays in practice and whether it is dominated by the lord chief justice remains to be seen.

The Consultations Process

The question of what degree of influence the judiciary should exercise in the appointments system through their role as members of the commission or in the selection of commission members needs to be considered in tandem with the future role of the consultations process. This system, described by its critics as 'secret soundings,' is a large-scale information-gathering process whereby the views of judges are sought on the suitability of candidates for judicial office. Once a year senior judges are sent a list of candidates for a wide range of judicial office and asked to comment on their suitability. Positive comments from a range of consultees are a prerequisite for appointment. Despite recent changes to the way in which candidates are assessed, the consultations process has remained at the heart of the appointments system.[31] It has also been widely criticized as lacking in transparency and being patronage-based.[32] In 2000 Dame Brenda Hale (as she then was) became the first senior judge to express concern about the weaknesses of the consultations process from the consultees' point of view when she drew attention to the difficulty judges face in making meaningful assessments of large numbers of candidates, most of whom are not well known to them. Her arguments were supported by the findings of the scrutiny commission for judicial appointments, which conducted a full investigation of the consultations process. Its 2003 annual report concluded that the failings of the consultations process were such that it should be abandoned in its current form.

In Scotland, the Judicial Appointments Board has decided not to use consultations in any form on the grounds that they are incompatible with its equal opportunities policy.[33] For the same reason, the personal knowledge of committee members of any of the candidates is not considered. This approach has required the board to consider how to develop new ways of assessing the quality of the candidates. The potential use of performance appraisal reports in the promotion of part-time judges to the full-time bench, for instance, is being examined. If the commission in England and Wales follows the Scottish example it will face similar challenges in the task of identifying merit, though it has something of a head start on the Scottish system since some progress has already been made by the Department for Constitutional Affairs in this area. The development of assessment centres, for example, as an additional method of obtaining information on candidates is proving promising.[34] Interviews are already used for many posts and are likely to be developed further.[35] Abandoning the consultations process will, inevitably, lead to the loss of a source of potentially useful information about some candidates. But the advantages in terms of equity and public confidence are likely to outweigh that cost.

Conclusion

Far from being a grab for power on the part of the government, as some commentators initially feared, the proposal for establishing a judicial appointments commission is a rare and commendable example of the executive giving away a source of political control and potential patronage. The creation of a commission has the potential to secure the long-term independence of the judicial system, to promote the diversification of the bench, and to enhance public confidence in the system. The record of commissions in other jurisdictions in achieving these goals is generally good, although success is not inevitable. The model of commission set up in England and Wales is sufficiently well-constructed to form the basis for a successful new system. Whether or not it does so depends on the quality of the commission members, its ability to form a collective identify beyond that of the interests of the members, and the willingness of ministers to use their powers to appoint the commission and receive recommendations to ensure that the commission functions effectively, rather than seeking to exercise inappropriate political control of the process.

The modernization of the appointments process in England and Wales represents a vital opportunity to rebuild confidence in the way judges are chosen. One of the paradoxes of the recent history of judicial appointments is that public confidence in the process has fallen at the same time as the quality of the appointments made has risen. The current lord chancellor and his recent predecessors, Lord Irvine and Lord Mackay, can take credit for selecting many first-rate candidates, particular to the higher bench. Both the intellectual abilities and the 'people skills' of the judiciary are now higher than at any time in the past. These qualities, combined with the freedom from corruption in the judicial system, are responsible for the international respect which the judiciary in England and Wales currently commands.[36] Yet as complaints about rude, incompetent, or lazy judges have declined, criticisms of the appointments system have grown more intense. Reforms to the system introduced by Lord Mackay and Lord Irvine failed to address these concerns because they were driven by the underlying belief that if the quality of the individuals appointed was high, the system itself was fundamentally sound. The official response to the loss of confidence in the system was therefore to see it as essentially one of perception. The belief that confidence can be separated from the substantive quality of the system fails to appreciate that confidence in the appointments process is a key feature of confidence in the judiciary as a whole. If the way judges are chosen is seen to be lacking in transparency, independence, fairness, or accountability and results in a bench which has a narrow and unreflective composition the legitimacy of the judiciary inevitably suffers. At a time of increasing judicial power and decreasing public deference, the link between confidence in the appointments process and the legitimacy of the judiciary is very clear.

The new commission must therefore work from the premise that while the first and paramount function of the judicial appointments process is the selection of the best possible judges, that is not its only function. The judges it appoints must also be chosen using processes that are independent, open, fair, and inclusive. The challenge the commission will face in guarding against future threats to its independence and reversing existing barriers to equal opportunities should not be underestimated. But the difficulties of this task are mitigated by the fact that the new judicial appointments commission will be inheriting a system in which the job of judging is still highly prized and the quality of applicants is high. If the quality of the appointments process can be made to match that of the judges appointed, the commission in England and Wales will rebuild public confidence in the judicial appointments process and may become a model for other systems looking to reform the way in which they select their judges.

NOTES

1 See, e.g., Lord Alexander, 'Is This a Ruthless Grab for Power?' *The Times* (London), 1 July 2003, Law, 3.
2 Department of Constitutional Affairs, *Constitutional Reform.*
3 Details of the Judicial Appointments Board can be found at: http://www.judicialappointmentsscotland.gov.uk/judicial/JUD_Main. jsp
4 The framework for establishing a commission is set out in the *Justice (Northern Ireland) Act 2002.* The commission, which will be responsible for the process of recommending candidates for appointment up to and including High Court judges will be established by summer 2005.
5 See, e.g., the chapters on the appointments processes in Canada and South Africa. See also Malleson, *The Use of Judicial Appointments Commissions*; Malleson, 'Assessing the Strengths and Weaknesses of a Judicial Appointments Commission.'
6 See Lord Falconer, foreword to Department of Constitutional Affairs, *Constitutional Reform.*
7 Department of Constitutional Affairs, *Constitutional Reform,* para. 18.
8 The government estimates that the additional cost of establishing a commission will be around £3 million a year. Department of Constitutional Affairs, *Constitutional Reform,* para. 85.
9 Lord Falconer states in the foreword to the consultation paper that 'In a modern democratic society it is no longer acceptable for judicial appointments to be entirely in the hands of a Government minister.'
10 Griffith, *The Politics of the Judiciary.*
11 Robertson, *Judicial Discretion in the House of Lords.*
12 See, e.g., Stevens, *The English Judges*; Young, 'Judicial Sovereignty and the Human Rights Act,' 65; Jowell, 'Beyond the Rule of Law,' 671–2.
13 Stevens, *The English Judges.*
14 Department of Constitutional Affairs, *Constitutional Reform,* para. 19.
15 Hale, 'Equality and the Judiciary'; Malleson, 'Promoting Diversity in the Judiciary.'
16 Lord Woolf has noted that the public have a 'right to demand' a judiciary

which is more representative than at present. Lord Woolf, 'The Needs of a 21st Century Judge,' Address to the Judicial Studies Board, London, 22 March 2001, available at http://www.lcd.gov.uk/judicial/speeches/22-03-01.htm.

17 Department of Constitutional Affairs, *Constitutional Reform*, para. 27.

18 In November 1998, Lord Irvine told the Association of Women barristers that 'there will never be more women judges unless more women lawyers put themselves forward for appointment.'

19 Department of Constitutional Affairs, *Constitutional Reform*, para. 28.

20 See Malleson, *The New Judiciary*, 151.

21 The president of the Family Division, Dame Butler Sloss, being a notable exception.

22 Encouragingly, the need for a collective effort is explicitly recognized by Lord Falconer, secretary of state for constitutional affairs, in the foreword to the consultation paper.

23 See F.L. Morton's chapter on judicial appointment in Canada. See also McLachlin, 'Promoting Gender Equality in the Judiciary.'

24 This concern is expressed by Allan in his chapter on New Zealand. See also Stevens, *The English Judges*, 144.

25 Department of Constitutional Affairs, *Constitutional Reform*, para. 42.

26 Members of the Ontario JAAC, for example, are appointed for three-year terms that may be renewed once.

27 It is unfortunate that the European Charter on the Statute for Judges recommends that at least half the members of a commission should be judges. This provision is an understandable attempt at ensuring judicial independence but is a good example of the deficiencies of a 'one size fits all' approach to the very different issues confronting judiciaries in Europe.

28 The JAAC in Ontario and the JAB in Scotland currently both have lay chairs, although the legislation establishing the JAAC allows for either a lay or legally qualified chair.

29 The controversial confirmation hearings of Clarence Thomas and Robert Bork in the United States have cast a long shadow over any proposals for introducing such a process in the United Kingdom. Support for some form of parliamentary scrutiny of this kind, is, however, growing. The former permanent secretary to the Lord Chancellor's Department, Tom Legg, for example, has argued in favour of such a procedure.

30 See F.L. Morton's chapter on Canada in this volume.

32 For example, the piloting of assessment centres, the use of fuller application forms including self-assessment by the candidates, and more extensive use of named referees.

32 Department of Constitutional Affairs, *Constitutional Reform*, para. 24.
33 See Alan Paterson's chapter on judicial appointments in Scotland.
34 The Bar Council Working Party on Judicial Appointments and Silk concluded that the assessments centres provided a 'thorough and professional testing procedure' and strongly recommended that the system should be adopted for all first rung appointments. Bar Council Working Party on Judicial Appointments and Silk, Consultation Paper, 3 March 2003.
35 Candidates are interviewed by a panel made up of a civil servant from the Department for Constitutional Affairs, a judge or retired judge, and a lay person.
36 Department of Constitutional Affairs, *Constitutional Reform*, para. 28.

3 Judicial Appointments in Post-Charter Canada: A System in Transition

F.L. MORTON

[It is an] an iron rule of politics [that] where power rests, there influence will be brought to bear.

V.O. Key, *Politics, Parties and Pressure Groups*

Introduction

An Environics poll released in February 2002 reported that two-thirds of Canadians favour the popular election of Supreme Court judges. While there is virtually no probability of this occurring, this finding is still significant because it clashes with the Canadian practice of executive appointment of the Supreme Court (and the other 1,100 federally appointed judges in Canada) and with no public consultations or parliamentary hearings.

The Environics poll reflects Canadians' growing awareness of judges' increased involvement in political and policy matters since the adoption of the Charter of Rights in 1982. A 2003 Ipsos-Reid poll reported that 71 per cent of Canadians agreed that 'it should be up to Parliament and provincial legislatures, not the courts, to make laws in Canada.' Coming in the midst of a national debate over several judicial rulings ordering provinces to allow homosexual couples to marry, there is a growing perception that judges' personal political and judicial 'philosophies' significantly influence their legal decisions, especially in policy-laden Charter cases. This growing public perception has been confirmed by a number of academic studies.[1]

The appointment of judges in Canada is thus a system in transition. At the risk of simplification, Canada now has an American-style Supreme Court with an unreformed British-style appointments system. Some vigorously defend this new arrangement as combining the best of both traditions – written constitutional rights enforced by strongly independent courts. These defenders include the past and present chief justices of the Supreme Court and recently retired Prime Minister, Jean Chrétien. Critics, however, have challenged this arrangement. They argue that the enhanced policy-making function of the courts require enhanced accountability for the exercise of this new power. Advocates for reform include several retired Supreme Court judges, several prominent academic jurists, and all opposition parties. How these conflicting views will be resolved remains to be seen. The one certainty is that any changes will be shaped by the existing federal character of Canada's judiciary.

Division of Judicial Appointments between the Federal Government and the Provinces

Under the *Constitution Act, 1867,* judicial appointments are made by the two different levels of government to three different levels of courts. Pursuant to section 101 of the constitution, the federal government is responsible for appointing all judges of the Supreme Court of Canada (nine), the Federal Court (twenty-five), and the Tax Court (twenty-five). In addition, the federal government appoints all the judges (just over a thousand) of the 'section 96' provincial superior courts, even though the latter are created and maintained by the provinces. These section 96 courts are the higher trial courts and serve as the first court of appeal for cases originating in section 92 courts. At Canada's founding in 1867, vesting the power to appoint the provincial superior court judges with the new federal government was intended to insure the independence of these courts from local politics or prejudice. It was also a legacy of British imperial rule and (some of) the Canadian founders' desire to subordinate provincial governments to Ottawa. Finally, the provincial governments appoint all the judges (about 1,500) of the provincial courts created pursuant to section 92 of the *Constitution Act, 1867.* Section 92 courts are Canada's lower trial courts in civil, criminal, and family law. In 2002, there were approximately 2,500 judges in Canada. Interestingly, this represents a 50 per cent increase since 1982, the year the Charter was adopted. During the same time period, Canada's population grew by less than 20 per cent.

The Supreme Court of Canada

Appointments to the Supreme Court of Canada are made by the prime minister. There is no requirement for either parliamentary hearings or confirmation of the prime minister's choices.

Canada has a long tradition of ethnic and regional representation in the judicial appointments to the Supreme Court. The *Supreme Court Act* requires that three of the nine justices come from Quebec. This legal guarantee is technically justified by the Court's appellate jurisdiction over Quebec's civil law, but it also symbolizes the 'distinct' status of Quebec as the home of most of Canada's French-speaking citizens. The French-English dualism of the Canadian political tradition also manifests itself in the tradition of alternating the appointment of the chief justiceship between an anglophone and a francophone.[2]

Quebec's guarantee of representation on the Supreme Court sparked a demand by Ontario for equal treatment, which it received. This initial accommodation has evolved into a convention of regional representation on the Supreme Court; thus in addition to the three positions reserved for both Quebec and Ontario, the remaining vacancies are filled by one judge from the Atlantic provinces and two from the western provinces. The expectation of regional balance on the Supreme Court reflects the deep regional cleavages that still shape Canadian politics. There was a similar convention of regional balance governing appointments to the U.S. Supreme Court in the nineteenth century. This practice was a symptom of the relative weakness of the central government and constituted an attempt to reassure the provinces/states that their 'special circumstances' could receive a 'fair hearing' in the national court of appeal. A similar convention exists in contemporary international courts and for the same reasons.[3]

More recently a convention of the representation of women on the Court has developed. In 1982 Prime Minister Trudeau set a precedent by appointing Bertha Wilson, the first woman ever to serve on the Supreme Court of Canada. Prime Minister Mulroney subsequently appointed two more women to the highest Court: Claire l'Heureux-Dubé (1987) and Beverley McLachlin (1989). When Justice Wilson retired in 1991, feminists lobbied unsuccessfully to have her replaced by another woman. However, the number of female justices on the Supreme Court returned to three when Prime Minister Chrétien appointed Louise Arbour to replace retiring Justice Peter Cory in 1999. When l'Heureux-Dubé retired in 2002, Prime Minister Chrétien replaced her with another woman, Quebec jurist Marie Deschamps. Given the high profile of the sexual equality issue in contemporary Canadian politics, it seems that the convention of having at least three women justices is here to stay. Indeed, with the Martin government's appointment of Rosalie Abella and Louise Charron to fill the vacancies created by the departures of Louise Arbour and Frank Iacobucci, four of the court's nine judges are now women. Mulroney also appointed the first Ukrainian-Canadian, John Sopinka (1988), and the first Italian-Canadian, Frank Iacobucci (1991). While it seems unlikely that these appointments will lead to a convention of a Ukrainian- or Italian-Canadian seat, they symbolically reinforced Canada's policy of multiculturalism.

Federalism versus the Charter

In addition to the rules and conventions described above, contemporary Supreme Court appointments are shaped by the often contrary forces of regionalism and rights. Beginning with the Victoria Charter of 1971, a majority of the provinces have lobbied for increased provincial participation in the appointment process and constitutional entrenchment of the convention of regional representation.[4] While their advocates argued that these changes would guarantee a more 'representative' court, critics protested that a provincial veto over Supreme Court appointments would amount to the rejection of 'the basic principle of the judicial process: that judges are judges of the issue, not partisans of the parties to the issue.'[5]

In 1987 the Mulroney government embraced these reforms in the hope that they would increase the legitimacy and authority of the Supreme Court, thus making it a more effective vehicle of 'intrastate federalism' – the representation of regional interests within the institutions of the national government. The 1987 Meech Lake Accord proposed that the federal government be required to appoint Supreme Court judges from lists submitted by the provinces. Since the Meech Lake Accord would have also required three judges from Quebec, this provision would have forced Ottawa and Quebec to reach an agreement on appointments. It was generally understood that provincial nominees, especially those proposed by the Quebec government, would be more de-centralist in their federalism rulings and more reluctant to use the Charter of Rights to impose uniform national standards on provincial policies.

Predictably, this proposal for the provincial nomination of Supreme Court appointments was strongly opposed by the various rights advocacy groups that were benefiting from the Supreme Court's new, more expansive approach to interpreting and enforcing the Charter. Critics alleged that the proposed change would allow provincial governments to mould the political orientation of the Court in a way that would undermine the impact and promise of the Charter. Defenders argued that it was consistent with the spirit of equality of the two levels of government in Canadian federalism, and that provincially nominated judges were likely to be as ideologically diverse on Charter-related issues as federal nominees.[6]

In the end, the Meech Lake Accord was defeated by an odd alliance of small-c conservatives and small l-liberals. The former objected to the absence of Senate reform and the conferring of special status for Quebec. The latter consisted mostly of human rights, native rights, feminist, civil libertarian, and environmental groups, interests that have been beneficiaries of the Charter and the new politics of rights that it has generated. The defeat of the Meech Lake Accord was interpreted by some as the defeat of the politics of federalism by the politics of rights.[7]

A new Canadian version of the politics of rights has blossomed under the 1982 Charter of Rights. The Charter enhanced the potential for Supreme Court judges to influence public policy. With the example of the U.S. Warren Court fresh in their minds, Canadian feminists and civil libertarians were alert to the opportunities offered by influencing the appointment of sympathetic judges. As early as 1981, in anticipation of the enactment of the Charter, the National Action Committee on the Status of Women (NAC) began to lobby for the appointment of a woman 'acceptable to our purposes' to the Supreme Court of Canada.[8] This campaign bore fruit in March 1982 when Prime Minister Trudeau appointed Bertha Wilson to the Supreme Court. Justice Wilson went on to become the Supreme Court's leading practitioner of judicial activism during the first decade of the Charter. Justice Wilson's activism was best exemplified by her outspoken defence of a right of a woman to choose an abortion in her concurring opinion in the Court's 1988 *Morgentaler* decision, which struck down the Criminal Code restrictions on abortion.

In 1985, NAC published a report that observed that with the adoption of the Charter, 'we find ourselves at the opportune moment to stress litigation as a vehicle for social change.'[9] The report went on to recommend the establishment of a legal defence fund to pursue 'systematic litigation strategies' such as those employed by U.S. rights advocacy groups and a complementary campaign of 'influencing the influencers.'[10] The latter identified judges as the key variable in Charter implementation, claiming that rights on paper are meaningless unless the courts correctly interpret their scope and application. The 'influencing the influencers' campaign included influencing the judicial appointment process and the ongoing professional education of judges already appointed to the bench. In Canada, the absence of an open and transparent judicial appointment process makes the latter option a more important access point for influencing 'the judicial mind' than it might be in other systems.

The Supreme Court's 1988 *Morgentaler* decision, which struck down Canada's abortion law, caught Canadians by surprise and alerted them to the new power exercised by judges under the Charter. As Peter Russell observed at the time, 'Filling Supreme Court vacancies ... has always been a little bit political in a subterranean way, and now it will be right at the surface [with] the political interest groups lobbying and pressing the appointing authorities to put people on the court of their persuasion.'[11] Russell's prediction was fulfilled almost before he finished making it. The *Morgentaler* decision was criticized by Angela Costigan, counsel for Choose Life Canada, a national pro-life lobby group, as 'the expression of personal opinion by the judges.' Costigan allowed that in the future her group would try to influence the appointment of judges who shared its position. Norma Scarborough, president of the Canadian Abortion Rights League (CARAL), responded by declaring that while her group had never tried to influence judicial appointments in the past, it would if necessary in the future. 'We are going to protect our position as much as possible,' she declared.[12] When Justice Estey announced his intention to retire several months later, member of Parliament James Jepson, an outspoken pro-life Tory backbencher, declared, 'We now have a chance to put men and women on the bench with a more conservative point of view.' While emphasizing that he had never lobbied for a judicial appointment before, Jepson continued: 'But this one seems to have caught the people's attention. Unfortunately, with the Charter that Trudeau left us, we legislators do not have final power. It rests with the courts ... You have seen the battling in the United States for the [most recent] Supreme Court nominee. Well, it doesn't take a rocket scientist to see we have the same situation here now.'[13] At the time, Jepson's comments represented a sharp break with Canadian practice. In retrospect, they marked the beginning of a growing demand for greater transparency and public participation in Supreme Court appointments.

On the tenth anniversary of the Charter, Chief Justice Antonio Lamer waded into this debate by observing, 'I don't think the America process is a good one.' While he did not rule out the possibility of change, he stressed that 'What we must be very careful not to do is to politicize the process. That's what the Americans have done. We've worked very hard to depoliticize the process. We started 25 or 30 years ago, and I think we have succeeded.'[14] This argument was hard to square with the chief justice's earlier remark in the same interview that 'the Charter has changed our job descriptions.' Prior to the Charter, Lamer observed, judges were trained and expected just 'to apply' and if necessary, 'to interpret' laws. 'But with the Charter,' he continued, 'We are commanded to sometimes judge the laws themselves. It is [a] very different activity, especially when one has to look at Section 1 of the Charter [the reasonable limitations clause], which is asking us to make what is essentially what used to be a political call.'[15] Lamer seemed to admit that under the Charter the Court has become a policy-making court, similar to the U.S. Supreme Court, yet continued to cling to a British-style appointment process associated with the traditional 'adjudication of disputes' model of courts. Critics pointed out that the danger of this hybrid approach is that, rather than preventing the politicization of the appointment process, it will simply drive the politics underground, beyond public knowledge or scrutiny.

An incident pursuant to Justice LaForest's retirement in 1997 suggests that this is occurring. In an interview shortly after he retired, Justice LaForest became the first Supreme Court justice to support public nomination hearings. In September 1997 it came to light that ÉGALE, Canada's leading gay rights advocacy group, was actively lobbying the upper echelons of the Chrétien government for a replacement who would be more supportive of their litigation campaign. Advocates for reform claimed that this showed that the appointment process was already politicized and that holding public hearings for judicial nominees would simply democratize it.[16] A month later a francophone lawyer from New Brunswick, Michèle Bastarache, was appointed to the Court. Within less than a year (April 1998), he joined a majority of the Court in the *Vriend* decision, a major constitutional victory for gay rights and ÉGALE.

Several months later, the influential editor of the *Globe and Mail*, William Thorsell, condemned the practice of choosing judges 'in secret' and called for broader public input and debate in appointing Supreme Court judges. Thorsell was particularly concerned that the judge chosen to replace LaForest, Michèle Bastarache, was 'heavy with political baggage.' Bastarache was a former partner in the prime minister's old law firm; the former co-chair of the national 'Yes Committee' for the Charlottetown Accord Referendum; and a 1993 election adviser to the federal Liberal Party. Thorsell echoed earlier concerns (made before the Bastarache appointment) that the appointment was unduly influenced by the Chrétien government's interest in the outcome of the then pending *Quebec Secession Reference*, a key strategic element of the Chrétien government's 'national unity' efforts to discredit the separatist Parti Québécois government in Quebec.

Stung by mounting public criticism, in December 1998 Prime Minister Chrétien defended the existing appointment process. 'American-style public confirmation hearings before appointing Supreme Court justices,' Chrétien wrote, 'would limit the choice of excellent candidates as many would not wish to undergo the ordeal of public and partisan-motivated attacks.' And it would be wrong, he added, 'if the underlying objective was to shape the court's decision-making process through partisan questioning.'[17]

The issue resurfaced the following year when Justice Peter Cory retired and speculation (and behind the scenes lobbying) about his replacement began. This time the conservative-leaning *National Post* weighed in and took aim at the prime minister's defence of the status quo: 'If judges cannot withstand the heat of an open selection process, how can they expect to determine highly controversial cases that will certainly invite attacks from their critics?'[18] The *Post* editorial went on specifically to oppose the appointment of either Louise Arbour or Rosalie Abella, two women from the Ontario Court of Appeal, because of their alleged proclivities for judicial activism. It then endorsed Ontario Justice David Doherty, whom it described as a 'criminal law genius' and 'resistant to the creeping expansionism of the Charter.' 'Judge Doherty,' the editorial concluded dryly, 'is not, admittedly a woman; but no one's perfect.'

In 1999 this debate was summarized and extended in an influential report by Professor Jacob Ziegel, law professor at the University of Toronto. According to Ziegel,

> In addressing future appointments to the Supreme Court of Canada, there are two key questions. The first is whether we are satisfied with the existing system of appointments which vests complete and unaccountable discretion in the Executive even though the judges of the Supreme Court are the ultimate arbiters of the Canadian constitution and collectively exercise a power as great as that of the federal Cabinet. If this question is answered

no, the second question is what changes we deem desirable to bring transparency and accountability to the selection procedure and to ensure that only the best qualified candidates are appointed. There may be honest differences of opinion about the answer to the second question, but there should be little doubt about the answer to the first. Over the past 15 years there has been a near unanimous chorus of opinion among scholars reinforced by many publicly-sponsored reports that the existing system of appointments is incompatible with a modern federal democratic constitution governed by the rule of law and incorporating one of the most powerful bills of rights in the Western hemisphere.[19]

While these calls for reform were routinely ignored by the government of former Liberal Prime Minister Jean Chrétien (1993–2003), it now appears that action is imminent. The new Liberal Prime Minister, Paul Martin, has indicated his support for reforming the Supreme Court appointments in the direction advocated by Ziegel and other critics. And reform may not be limited to the Supreme Court. In October 2003, the House of Commons gave unanimous, all-party support for a private member's motion to authorize the Standing Committee on Justice to 'study the process by which judges are appointed to courts of appeal and to the Supreme Court of Canada.'

The task of the committee was subsequently complicated by the announcement by two sitting justices (Arbour and Iacobucci) that they planned to leave the Supreme Court at the end of the current term (June 2004). The chief justice quickly indicated that she wanted a full coram of nine judges to be available to hear the Liberal government's controversial reference on same-sex marriage, scheduled to be heard by the Court in Fall 2004. The committee's mandate was thus expanded to include interim recommendations to deal with these two appointments in addition to long-term proposals for reform.

The committee held public hearings in March and April 2004, and released its report in May. The report (written by the Liberal Party majority) rejected submissions calling for U.S.-style parliamentary hearings for judicial nominees as well as the South African model of public interviews. They also ignored suggestions for reforms along the European model of limiting the terms (e.g., nine to twelve years) of high court judges and governments' sharing the appointment power with opposition parties in proportion to the strength of the latter in Parliament.

Instead, the committee proposed several minor changes. For the two pending appointments, they recommended only that the justice minister appear before their committee *after* the appointments 'to explain the process by which the current vacancies on the Supreme Court were filled and the qualifications of the two appointees.'[20] For the longer term, the committee recommended the creation of a nominating committee that would send a list of three to five candidates to the prime minister, who would still have the final choice. The nominating committee would include representatives from each of the political parties in the House of Commons, the relevant provincial governments, the judiciary and the legal profession, and lay members. Once an appointment is made, the committee then recommended that either the justice minister or the chair of the nominating committee appear before a House of Commons committee to explain publicly the process and reasons for the appointment.

Dissenting reports were filed by all three opposition parties. The Conservatives embraced a process of parliamentary review and ratification of appointments. The Bloc Québécois (whose members are exclusively from Quebec) called for nominations to be made by provincial governments. This is also the position of the Quebec government and the system proposed in the 1987 Meech Lake Accord. The New Democrats accepted the proposal for a nominating committee but demanded that the justice minister appear before the Justice Committee to explain his choice *before* the appointment is made, not after.[21]

Significantly, Prime Minister Martin responded to the committee's report by suggesting that it was too timid and intimated that he favoured greater input from Parliament. However, he did not elaborate on the form that input might take. Suffice it to say that it is doubtful that the Justice Committee's report will be the final word on reforming appointments to the Supreme Court of Canada.

Section 96 Provincial Superior Courts

Federal judicial appointments are made by the cabinet on the advice, of the minister of justice, except for chief justices,[22] who are recommended by the prime minister. Historically, patronage was the dominant factor in making these appointments. Depending on whether 'political' was defined strongly (holding office) or weakly (running for office), studies have found that prior to the Second World War, anywhere from 50 to 80 per cent of federally appointed judges had 'political careers' prior to their appointment, and that appointments followed party lines 80 to 90 per cent of the time. The same studies show that patronage declined significantly after the war but did not disappear.[23]

In 1966, dissatisfaction with the continuing effects of patronage on the quality of federal judicial appointments led the Canadian Bar Association (CBA) to create the Committee on the Judiciary to provide a non-partisan source of advice to the federal government on judicial appointments. The CBA committee would receive the names of potential nominees from the minister of justice, review the candidate's record, and then rate the candidate as 'well qualified, qualified, or not qualified.' Under this program, which operated from 1967 until 1988, no candidates receiving an unqualified rating were appointed. The Committee on the Judiciary was replaced under the 1988 reforms (described below) by provincial screening committees.

A succession of Liberal ministers of justice during the 1970s is generally credited with improving the quality of federal judicial appointments. John Turner initiated the practice of systematically collecting names and background information of potential judicial nominees before openings occurred, and this practice was formalized by his successor, Otto Lang, through the creation of a special advisor on judicial affairs. By consulting widely and constantly updating the list of potential nominees, the office of the special advisor was credited with further improving the quality of federally appointed judges.

Notwithstanding improvements in the quality of appointments, the Trudeau government continued to use its judicial appointments to 'section 96 courts' to reward its members and supporters. In 1982 this practice provoked an angry reaction by the newly elected Progressive Conservative Party of Premier Grant Devine in Saskatchewan.'[24] To protest the Liberals' alleged abuse of patronage in judicial appointments in Saskatchewan the Devine government began reducing the number of section 96 judgeships by eliminating positions as they became vacant through death or retirement, thereby denying Ottawa the opportunity to make appointments. This stalemate was not resolved until the defeat of Liberals in the federal election in 1984. The newly elected Conservative government informally agreed to consult more closely with the provinces before making superior court appointments.

The patronage issue again became the focus of public attention following a series of judicial appointments occasioned by Pierre Trudeau's resignation as leader of the Liberal Party and prime minister in 1984. The Trudeau appointments were widely criticized in the press. Brian Mulroney, the new leader of the Progressive Conservative Party, exploited the judicial patronage issue in the 1984 federal election and promised change if elected. The incident also led to new studies by the Canadian Association of Law Teachers (CALT) and the Canadian Bar Association. In 1985 both the CALT and CBA issued reports recommending reform. While the details varied, both reports recommended a process in which an independent nominating commission would recruit and screen potential candidates and then create lists from which the minister of justice would be expected to make appointments. The Mulroney government took these reports under consideration.

Despite the promises of reform made during the 1984 campaign, it turned out that the Mulroney government did not practice what it preached. A 1989 study by Peter Russell and Jacob Ziegel found that of the 228 federal judges appointed during the first Mulroney government (1984–8), 48 per cent had associations with the Progressive Conservative Party. While 86 per cent received a good or better rating from the CBA Committee on the Judiciary, of the thirteen who did not, ten had Tory political connections. Russell and Ziegel conclude that there was only 'marginal improvement' in the judicial selection process during the Mulroney government's first term and that political patronage remained 'pervasive.'

In 1988, the Mulroney government announced a new judicial appointments process that paid lip service to the CALT and CBA reports but did not adopt their recommendation for a true nominating committee. The new system would be administered by the Federal commissioner of Judicial Affairs, who has the rank and status of a deputy minister, and is thus more independent than a member of the Minister's personal staff. Names of candidates would continue to come from many sources including the minister of justice, other members of cabinet, judges, bar associations, law schools, members of Parliament, and provincial office-holders. A novel feature of the new system was the requirement for all candidates to submit full applications to the commissioner of Federal Judicial Affairs.

The commissioner conducts a preliminary investigation to insure that candidates possess the required technical qualifications[25] and then refers their names to the appropriate provincial or territorial committee for screening. Each province (ten) and territory (three) has at least one committee, and there are sixteen in total. Each committee consists of seven persons (including at least one non-lawyer), and is responsible for assessing whether the candidate possesses the required qualifications for appointment. The committee can give three assessments: 'recommended,' 'highly recommended,' or 'unable to recommend.' The committee's recommendations are confidential to the minister, and the committee must be prepared to give reasons for any negative assessments. However, the minister is not obliged to explain himself if he ignores the committee's recommendation. This procedure applies only to new appointments to the federal bench. The government's decision to elevate a sitting judge to a higher judicial office is not subject to review by a provincial screening committee.

The new provincial and territorial committees are not true nominating commissions. Their function is essentially limited to screening the names of candidates provided to them by the commissioner, who, when all is said and done, remains an employee of the federal government. Writing in 1993, Russell and Ziegel critically observed that the 1988 reforms did 'little to address the basic flaws in the appointing system.'

To date there has been no systematic study of the impact of the 1988 reforms. However, a recent pilot project used the Russell-Ziegel methodology to analyse the federal Liberal government's fifty-eight judicial appointments in Alberta (Court of Appeal and Court of Queen's Bench) between 1993 and 2000. This pilot study found that 46.5 per cent (twenty-seven out of fifty-eight) of these judges had a political connection to the Liberal Party. Recalling that the analogous figure in the Russell-Ziegel study was 48.5 per cent, it would appear that little has changed as a result of either the change in government or the new provincial screening committees.[26]

One notable change with respect to federally appointed judges is the significant increase in the number of women. At the beginning of the 1980s only 3 per cent of the federally appointed judges were women. This figure rose to 10 per cent by 1990 and 25 per cent by 2002. Since 1982 there have been seven women appointed to the Supreme Court of Canada (to fill twenty vacancies). The Russell and Ziegel study found that 17.5 per cent of the Mulroney judicial appointments (1984–8) were women.

Section 92 Provincial Courts

At the 'section 92 court' level, patronage was once the dominant criterion for appointment. As recently as 1971, a study of Ontario found that after twenty-five years of Progressive Conservative rule, most 'section 92' provincial court magistrates were past or present supporters of the Progressive Conservative Party. The institution of provincial judicial councils or committees has reduced the practice of judicial patronage, especially in British Columbia, Ontario, Quebec, Saskatchewan, Nova Scotia, and Alberta, where the councils are true 'nominating commissions.'

Today, the procedures for judicial appointments to section 92 courts vary from province to province. In several there are no judicial councils and the appointment of provincial judges is still left to the discretion of the attorney-general. Others have some form of judicial council based on one of two basic models: a screening committee or a nominating commission. The difference is the stage at which the government uses an independent, non-governmental body to assess potential candidates. In the first, the attorney-general conducts the initial recruitment and refers his or her candidate to an independent body for assessment. If approved, the government then proceeds with the appointment. This is basically the same as the 1988 federal practice, since the provincial committees are limited to a screening function.

The alternative model is the nominating commission, which conducts the initial recruitment as well as screening and then presents the government with a list of approved nominees from which it must choose. This is the practice in Ontario, British Columbia, and Alberta, where each province's Judicial Council receives applications for provincial court judgeships. (In Ontario, this body is called the Ontario Judicial Appointments Advisory Committee.) After reviewing the credentials of the applicants, the Judicial Council recommends individuals to the provincial attorney-general. If the attorney-general disagrees with the council's recommendation, he or she is free to request another.

The difference between the two approaches lies in the extent to which they allow political influence. The Ontario, Alberta, and B.C. governments can only make appointments from a pool of candidates who have already been selected by an independent body, while under the screening model, the government is initially unrestricted and uses the independent committees only to confirm choices that the attorney-general has already made. The latter procedure gives the party that forms the government more discretion to favour party members and supporters when making appointments to the bench.

In theory, the potential for undue political influence is significantly reduced by merit selection nominating committees. In practice, it turns out to be more difficult to reduce political influence. While the nominating model clearly restricts the discretion of the appointing government, political influence can come from organized advocacy groups as well as governments. In Ontario, for example, the Conservative government of Premier Mike Harris (1995–2001) became unhappy with the perceived (liberal) bias of the recommendations of the Ontario Judicial Appointments Advisory Committee. The Harris government requested the committee to send longer lists of recommended candidates than had been submitted in the past so that the government would have a wider choice in making a final appointment.

The Ontario Judicial Appointments Advisory Committee was given an explicit 'employment equity' mandate at its creation in 1989. During its first six years of operation, 39 per cent of Ontario's 111 judicial appointments were women – increasing the percentage of women provincial judges in Ontario from 3 to 22 per cent. In addition, three of these new judges were aboriginal, ten were members of racial minorities, and eight were francophones – they included Canada's first aboriginal woman judge, Ontario's first black woman judge, and Canada's first East Asian woman judge.[27] Critics of the committee argued that its appointments were driven more by politics than merit, and this perception contributed to the committee's troubled relationship with the newly elected Conservative Harris government after the 1995 Ontario elections.

Conclusion

It is a paradox that while the Supreme Court of Canada is the court that has experienced the greatest change in its function, it has experienced the least change in how its members are appointed. It is increasingly difficult to reconcile its enhanced political influence under the Charter of Rights with the unfettered discretion of a single politician to choose its members. Until the year 2013 – ten years after former Prime Minister Jean Chrétien left politics – his hand-picked appointees will still constitute a majority on the Supreme Court of Canada. Two of Mr Chrétien's appointees – Justices Bastarache and Deschamps – are not scheduled to retire until 2022 and 2028. With the June 2004 election leading to a minority Liberal government under Paul Martin, a Liberal government will fill the three vacancies created by the voluntary departures of Justices Arbour and Iacobucci in June, and by Justice Major's mandatory retirement in 2006. This means that a party that has averaged about 40 per cent of the votes in the last four elections will have appointed 100 per cent of the judges.

This kind of 'rule-from-the-grave,' one-party domination of a country's highest constitutional court is one more indicator of Canada's democratic deficit and will be the source of ongoing pressure to reform the appointments process. The House of Commons Justice Committee report marks the beginning not the end of the reform process. Four quite distinct constituencies will compete with one another to shape this process.

The first and most powerful voice comes from the defenders of the status quo: the majority of current judges, the Canadian Bar Association, the Canadian Judicial Council, the many Charter-enthusiasts in university law faculties, and of course the Liberal Party of Canada. At the level of principle, the defenders of the status quo successfully invoke the symbols of the Supreme Court as 'the guardian of the Constitution,' separation of powers, and warn against the dangers inherent in any reforms that would 'politicize' the courts. This defence of the status quo has been bluntly stated by the president of the Canadian Bar Association, F. William Johnson: 'Questioning of nominees for judicial appointment in a public setting will do nothing to ensure that the appointment process is depoliticized. In fact, such an approach could prove to do just the opposite. We live by the rule of law and are glad we do. Canadians count on the independence of the judges in their courts to uphold the rule of law. A change to make the appointment process subject to the vagaries of popular politics would wreak havoc on Canadian justice.'[28]

University of Toronto law professor Lorne Sossin has criticized Prime Minister Martin for even allowing parliamentary hearings on judicial appointments because they have facilitated 'the infiltration of politics into the appointment process.'[29]

In practice, the opponents of reform prefer the status quo because it is good for the Liberal Party and coalition of organized interests that have helped it to govern Canada for three-quarters of the twentieth century. What Robert Dahl has said of the U.S. Supreme Court is equally true of its Canadian counterpart: it is a partner in the national governing coalition rather than a check on it.[30] In its first twenty years as 'Guardian of the Charter,' the Canadian Court has been a reliable supporter of feminist, gay, aboriginal, immigrant, and refugee claimant interests, and a vanguard of criminal law reform.[31] It has played a key role in Ottawa's national unity strategy by regularly upholding minority language rights – those of anglophones within Quebec and francophones outside of Quebec – and by its willingness to hear and decide the Liberals' controversial *Quebec Secession Reference* in 1998.[32] The Court has not struck down a single piece of major federal government policy, while upholding government policies against Charter challenges brought by conservative interests.[33]

Why would the Liberal Party want to abandon its monopoly on Supreme Court appointments? As a consequence of the federal government's control of superior court appointments in the provinces, the Liberal Party's defence of the status quo enjoys wide support in the official organizations of the bench and bar as well.

The second force that vies to shape the judicial appointments process in Canada are the identity politics advocates, who argue that the composition of the bench should mirror the diversity of society. This new, post-liberal definition of equality as group parity and representation in public institutions and the workforce is a pre-eminent demand of feminists and multiculturalists. In Canada, as noted earlier, advocates for minority-group representation on the courts have already been successful in influencing judicial selection. The number of women on the Supreme Court has grown from zero to four in just over two decades, and 'diversity' is now one of the official norms used by the justice minister in making appointments.[34] Not only is this norm already entrenched in Canada's judicial selection process, but it enjoys widespread international support as an ethical pillar of the new transnational progressivism found among political elites in other Western democracies.[35]

Despite its political support, the diversity/representation claim suffers several liabilities that may weaken its appeal over time. Appointments based on diversity beg the question why appointments should not simply be based on merit? What does a person's race or sex have to do with being a good judge? Supporters of diversity correctly point out that it is not an either/or choice, but a matter of appointing well-qualified judges from all relevant groups. Also, in the past, merit has sometimes been used as filter, intentionally or not, for screening out prospective appointees from less established groups.[36] Critics respond that whatever may be true in theory, in practice merit is too often sacrificed in diversity-driven appointments.

A second criticism is that diversity is often a cloak for ideology. Just as the NAACP opposed the Republicans' appointment of African-American Clarence Thomas to the U.S. Supreme Court, Canadian feminists would be furious if women like Angela Costigan or Gwendolyn Landolt, lawyers active in pro-life politics, were appointed to Canada's highest court. As Michael Tolley points out in his contribution to this book, half (four of eight) of the Bush nominations being filibustered by Senate Democrats are either women or ethnic minorities.[37] Are Senate Democrats anti-diversity? Hardly. These are simply not the right kind of women and minority members, politically speaking.

Even if the merit versus diversity issue is put aside, other problems remain. Which groups are to be represented? Lawyers, as a class, are arguably one of the least 'representative' groups in any society. And why privilege sex, race, and colour rather than income, geography, or occupation? Does a white woman lawyer from a secular, upper-class family bring more diversity to the bench than a son of recent Eastern European immigrants with strong religious beliefs? A second inconsistency is how to reconcile the claim for group 'representation' with the foundational judicial principle of impartiality. It can be done in theory, but in practice the two often appear to conflict: the judge, qua group member, is expected to 'represent' the 'experience' of the group he or she represents. Where does representation end and advocacy begin? Whether these theoretical inconsistencies will diminish the practical impact of the diversity/representation forces is difficult to predict.[38]

The third strongest force that will shape the future development of Canada's judicial appointments process is federalism, or more specifically, provincial governments' demands for direct input into both Supreme Court and superior court appointments. As noted earlier, strong provincial premiers demanded and won the power to nominate Supreme Court appointees in the ill-fated 1987 Meech Lake Accord. While the nominating power remains a priority of the government of Quebec (and the Bloc Quebecois Party in the House of Commons), this reform appears to have lost much of its support base outside of Quebec. In the recent public hearings of the Commons Justice Committee, it did not figure prominently in the submissions made by scholars and groups from other provinces. It seems improbable that the general public could be rallied into supporting this reform, while its opponents are still present and even stronger than they were in the period 1987–90. Still, when it comes to constitutional amendments, provincial premiers remain the most privileged players apart from the prime minister, and their potential influence should not be underestimated.

A more probable scenario, in my opinion, is that provincial governments – led by Quebec and Alberta – will lobby for returning the power to appoint provincial superior court judges to the provinces. Canada is one of only four federations in the world in which the judges in the member states/provinces are appointed by the central authority.[39] Such central control is an irritant to autonomy-minded provinces, and runs counter to the decentralist trends associated with Canada's dominant north-south trade flows resulting from the North American Free Trade Agreement (NAFTA). Over time this reform would affect the composition of the Supreme Court, since most appointments to the high court are made from appeals court judges in the provinces.

The fourth and weakest force shaping appointments to the Supreme Court is the demand for democratic accountability. Reform in this direction includes parliamentary hearings for nominees, term limits for judges, and sharing of the appointment power with opposition parties. The relative weakness of democratic reform is ironic: the unprecedented political influence of the Supreme Court should logically entail increased accountability.

While the arguments for increased accountability – either of the judges or for the appointing party – are logically coherent, they lack a strong constituency. Other than academics and newspaper editorialists, the only proponents of enhanced accountability for the exercise of judicial power have been the populist, Western-based Reform Party (1988–2000) and its successor, the Alliance Party (2000–3). With the merger of the Alliance and Progressive Conservative Parties in 2004, it is not yet clear what the new Conservative Party of Canada's position will be on judicial appointments. More importantly, reforms in this direction will be opposed vigorously by most of the other constituencies – judges' associations, the legal profession, the Liberal Party, and the identity politics/representation lobby. The Justice Committee's timid refusal to embrace any democratic reforms in its recent report is testimony to the combined influence of these opposing forces.

To conclude, the prospects for significant change seem slight. While the defenders of the status quo will invoke the hoary symbols of judicial independence and separation of powers, the fact is that the Supreme Court of Canada has become a powerful and valued institutional ally of the national governing coalition. The various political interests, governmental and non-governmental, that have benefited from the Court's enhanced policy-making role under the 1982 Charter of Rights will not voluntarily give up the power that ensures the Court as an ally – the power to appoint its members.

V.O. Key's assessment of regulatory bodies applies with enhanced force to powerful national courts of appeal: '[It is an] iron rule of politics [that] where power rests, there influence will be brought to bear.'[40] Indeed, I would take Key's analysis a step further, and propose that the more powerful a national court of appeal becomes, the less independent it becomes. Recall in this regard that the American founders intended not just the U.S. Supreme Court to be 'above politics' but also the Senate and the office of the Presidency.[41] Once the power of an institution is recognized, interested parties will manoeuvre to capture it. The Canadian experience simply demonstrates that this is not an American idiosyncrasy.

In this context, the most likely scenario for reform of appointments to the Supreme Court of Canada will be some form of nominating committee similar to the model proposed by the House of Commons Justice Committee's May 2004 report. While there will be the appearance of input from opposition parties and provincial governments, I would predict that the balance of power will rest with government MPs and strategically selected allies from the Canadian bench and bar. While there will be a great deal of self-congratulation about insulating the 'Guardians of the Constitution' from political influence, all this reform will really do is drive such influence underground. For these reasons, I agree whole heartedly with Professor James Allan's rejection of nominating or screening committees for final courts of appeal as an improvement over the status quo. Such committees will not eliminate 'small p-political considerations'; rather, they would get 'swept under the carpet and out of view.'[42] Under these arrangements, accountability for the judicial exercise of political power will remain blurred.

Canada seems fated to learn yet again that power cannot be depoliticized. The best one can do is to make the exercise of power as transparent as possible, and then create effective checks and balances – 'ambition must be made to counteract ambition ... the interest of the man must be connected with the constitutional rights of the place.'[43] In the case of the power of judicial review, an effective check on its abuse by the courts rests not just with the government but also with the opposition parties and a vigilant media.

One way to achieve this check would be to adopt the European model of giving opposition parties an agency in appointment in proportion to their numbers. Since Canada (or any other common law nation) is unlikely to go down this road, the next best alternative is that proposed by Professor Allan: a system in which the judges of the highest courts are appointed 'openly and directly by the elected government of the day.' Opposition parties – through parliamentary committee hearings – should have the opportunity to quiz the appointees on their approach to interpreting constitutional rules, on the proper balance of power between courts and legislatures, and major issues likely to come before the court. The government will still get the judge it wants, but it can be held accountable for – or get credit for – its appointments at the next election.

Postscript: 4 September 2004

As anticipated, Canada's new Prime Minister, Paul Martin, called a federal election in May 2004. The ensuing campaign featured a partisan debate over judicial appointments to a degree unprecedented in Canadian history. As the Liberals slipped behind the Conservative Party in the early weeks of the campaign, Martin went on the offensive, charging that a Conservative government would use the Notwithstanding Power to undermine the Charter of Rights.[44] This debate played out against the background of the Liberals' reference of the same-sex marriage issue to the Supreme Court of Canada.[45] Martin adamantly declared that a Liberal government would abide by a Supreme Court ruling declaring the traditional definition of marriage an unconstitutional denial of equality rights. Conservative leader Stephen Harper countered that the issue should be decided by Parliament not the courts.

This debate spilled over into the corollary issue of judicial appointments. Liberal columnists wrote about 'the Tories' plans for the Supreme Court.'[46] Conservative columnists responded that 'courts, not legislatures, limit freedoms under the Charter.'[47] Law professors declared that the Tory platform was a 'legal minefield,'[48] and that a Harper government would use the appointment power to engage in American-style 'court-packing.'[49] Conservative commentators retorted that parliamentary confirmation hearings for Supreme Court nominees would merely mean 'democratizing the judiciary.'[50]

In the end, the Liberals prevailed in the election, but managed to elect only a minority government. The consensus of the pundits was that the Charter/notwithstanding clause/judicial appointments issue had helped the Liberals come back in the final week of the campaign, but this has yet to be confirmed by more scientific election studies.

Just over a month later, the judicial appointments issue exploded onto the front pages again, when Prime Minister Martin announced the nominations of Rosalie Abella and Louise Charron to fill the two Supreme Court vacancies from Ontario.[51] As judges on the Ontario Court of Appeal, both nominees had written controversial judgments extending spousal rights to same-sex couples. Liberal Justice Minister Irwin Cotler denied that the nominees' views on gay rights were a factor in their selection, but conservative opinion leaders immediately denounced the Liberals for doing precisely what they had accused the Tories of planning to do during the election – stacking the court with ideologically driven judges.[52]

In a departure from past practice, Cotler agreed to appear before a House of Commons committee to answer questions about the government's choice of Charron and Abella. The committee also included a member of the judiciary and a member of the Canadian Bar Association. This innovation was intended to honour Prime Minister Martin's campaign pledge to give Parliament a role in reviewing Supreme Court appointments. This did not satisfy the Conservative members of the committee. In a dissenting opinion, they criticized the process as a superficial, cursory 'rubber-stamp' exercise. They complained that they were given only one day's notice to prepare for the hearing, which lasted only three hours. Most importantly, they protested that the committee was not allowed to question the nominees directly. In the end, however, the committee's report endorsed the two women nominees as 'eminently qualified.'[53]

There is a consensus among informed observers that the committee process used for screening the Charron-Abella nominations was a temporary measure intended to ensure that there would be a full coram of nine justices to hear the government's marriage reference in October 2004. It is expected that Parliament will continue to press for a more transparent and formal role in the nomination screening process.

NOTES

1 Morton, Russell, and Riddell, 'The Canadian Charter of Rights and Freedoms,' 1–60; McCormick, 'The Most Dangerous Justice'; McCormick, 'Birds of a Feather.'

2 Prime Minister Trudeau's appointment of Brian Dickson as chief justice in 1984 violated this tradition, and appeared to mark its end. But Prime Minister Mulroney followed the tradition in his 1990 appointment of Antonio Lamer, a Quebec francophone, to succeed Dickson as chief justice, and it was confirmed again in 2000, when Prime Minister Chrétien chose Beverley McLachlin, the senior anglophone justice on the Court, to replace Lamer as the new chief justice.

3 See the contribution to this collection by Ruth Mackenzie and Phillipe Sands.

4 See Russell, 'Constitutional Reform of the Judicial Branch,' 227–52.

5 E.D. Fulton, as reported in Stirling, 'A Symposium of the Appointment of Judges,' 137–42.

6 See Russell, 'The Supreme Court Proposals in the Meech Lake Accords,' 99.

7 See Cairns, *Charter versus Federalism.*
8 Justice Committee NAC Memo September 1981, 5; Justice Committee NAC Memo March 1981, 4.
9 Atcheson, Eberts, and Symes (with Stoddart), *Women and Legal Action*, 163.
10 Razack, *Canadian Feminism and the Law*, 36.
11 'Public to Demand Say in Court Appointments,' *Lawyers Weekly*, 12 February 1988, 1.
12 Ibid.
13 'Reduced Role for Politicians Urged in Naming of Judges,' *Globe and Mail*, 16 May 1988, A1.
14 *Globe and Mail*, 17 April 1992, A17.
15 Ibid.
16 F.L. Morton, 'To Bring Judicial Appointments Out of the Closet,' *Globe and Mail*, 22 September 1997, A15. Reprinted in Morton, *Law, Politics and the Judicial Process in Canada*, 154–6.
17 Chétien, 'A Question of Merit,' 15.
18 'Judging the Judges,' *National Post*, 5 June 1999, A15.
19 Ziegel, 'Merit Selection and Democratization of Appointments to the Supreme Court of Canada.' This issue was part of a special series on 'Courts and Legislatures' published by the Institute for Research on Public Policy's (IRPP) in Montreal. The full-text version can be accessed through the IRPP's website: www.irpp.org.
20 Report of the Standing Committee on Justice, etc. *Improving the Supreme Court of Canada Appointments Process*, 4–5.
21 The dissenting opinions of all three opposition parties are included in the committee's published report.
22 In addition to the chief justice of the Supreme Court of Canada and the Federal Court, the prime minister appoints a separate chief justice for the Court of Appeal and the superior trial court of each province except Prince Edward Island, which has only one chief justice.
23 These studies are discussed in greater detail in Russell, *The Judiciary in Canada*, 114–15.
24 *Calgary Herald*, 11 April 1984, A5.
25 That the person is a member of a provincial or territorial bar association and has a minimum of ten years' experience as a practising lawyer and/or judge.
26 Morton, 'Federal Judicial Appointments in Alberta, 1993–2000.'
27 Omatsu, 'On Judicial Appointments: Does Gender Make a Difference?' 177.
28 'Judging our Supreme Court,' Letter to the Editor, *National Post*, 9 June 2004, A17.

29 Lorne Sossin, 'Don't Treat Judges like Politicians,' *National Post,* 6 June 2004, A18.
30 Dahl, 'Decision-making in a Democracy,' 279–95.
31 See Morton and Knopff, *The Charter Revolution and the Court Party.*
32 See Schneiderman, *The Quebec Decision.*
33 See Clarke, 'Social Conservatives in Court.'
34 Report of the Standing Committee on Justice, *Improving the Supreme Court of Canada Appointments Process,* 3.
35 See Fonte, 'Liberal Democracy vs. Transnational Progressivism.'
36 For a defence of the diversity principle, see Kate Malleson's chapter in this volume; see also Alan Paterson's contribution, 'The Scottish Judicial Appointments Board: New Wine in Old Bottles.'
37 Tolley, 'Legal Controversies over Federal Judicial Selection in the United States, n12.
38 See Malleson, 'Gender Equality in the Judiciary,' 1–24.
39 The other three are India, Austria, and Venezuela.
40 Key, *Politics, Parties and Pressure Groups,* 154.
41 See Ceaser, *Presidential Selection.*
42 Allan, 'If it were done when 'tis done, then twere well it were done openly and directly.'
43 James Madison, *Federalist No. 51.*
44 'Martin Puts Focus on Charter But Can't Slow Harper's Surge,' *Globe and Mail,* 16 June 2004, A1.
45 For details, see McKay, 'Confusion on the Hill,' 29–40.
46 Kirk Makin, *Globe and Mail,* 16 June 2004, A6; 'The Conservatives and the Judges,' *Globe and Mail,* 21 June 2004, A12 (unsigned editorial).
47 Lorne Gunter, *Edmonton Journal,* 20 June 2004, A12.
48 'Tory Platform a "Legal Minefield"' *Edmonton Journal,* 21 June 2004, A1.
49 Lorne Sossin, 'Don't Treat Judges like Politicians,' *National Post,* 11 June 2004, A18.
50 Clair Hoy, 'Democratizing the Judiciary,' *National Post,* 7 June 2004, A16.
51 'New Judges Favour Same-Sex Rights,' *National Post,* 25 August 2004, A1.
52 Andrew Coyne, 'A Purely Political Choice,' *National Post,* 25 August 2004, A1; Lorne Gunter, 'Stacking the Court with Activists,' *National Post,* 25 August 2004, A14.
53 'Supreme Court Nominees Win Support,' *Calgary Herald,* 28 August 2004, A9.

4 Legal Controversies over Federal Judicial Selection in the United States: Breaking the Cycle of Obstruction and Retribution over Judicial Appointments

MICHAEL C. TOLLEY

Article II, section 2 of the U.S. Constitution sets forth the broad outlines of the procedures for the appointment of federal judges.[1] The provision is notably short on details of how presidents are to select nominees for vacancies in the federal judiciary, the qualifications of nominees, and how the Senate is to render 'advice and consent.' Despite the text's vagueness on these details, the records of the Constitutional Convention (1787) indicate that the framers debated at length the appropriate role and responsibility of the President and the Senate in judicial selection,[2] and eventually settled on the idea that the power to appoint judges would be shared. In the words of Jack Rakove, 'the framers reached near-consensus on the virtues of combining the "responsibility" of executive nomination with the "security" of senatorial advice and consent.'[3]

Recognizing that the Senate would not always be in session to give advice and consent, the framers, in a provision adopted without dissenting vote and with little discussion,[4] granted to the President alone the power to make recess appointments, which shall expire at the end of the Senate's next session. The text of the recess appointment clause makes no distinction between its application to judges and other presidential nominations (that is, cabinet-level officers or ambassadors). It also leaves in doubt the constitutional meaning of precisely when presidents may bypass the normal advice and consent function of the Senate. Given the vagueness of these provisions and the silences in the historical record dealing with advice and consent and recess appointment, many of the procedures used in the appointment of federal judges have had to be worked out in practice. Forged in the cauldron of real politics, the procedures employed by presidents in finding and selecting judicial nominees and by the Senate in rendering advice and consent have, for the most part, been determined by long-standing institutional norms and traditions.[5]

During President Bill Clinton's two terms in office (1993–2000), Senate Republicans thwarted his attempt to fill vacancies in the lower federal courts by placing 'holds' on over a hundred of his nominations. Sometimes referred to as 'silent filibusters,' holds are extra-parliamentary practices used by senators to prevent a nomination from coming before the Senate Judiciary Committee.[6] Senate Democrats employed the same obstructive tactics throughout President George W. Bush's first term in office (2001–4). When senators of both parties resort to the norm-departing strategy of delay and obstruction, their actions raise several unsettled questions of constitutional law. What does 'consent,' as in 'by and with the Advice and Consent of the Senate,' mean? Is it a simple majority vote or may the Senate establish a rule requiring a supermajority of sixty votes to obtain cloture and end a filibuster on a judicial nomination?[7] Similarly, when presidents of both parties respond to the Senate's obstruction with a norm-departing strategy of their own, their actions raise several questions about the meaning of the recess appointment clause. May presidents circumvent the normal advice and consent role of the Senate and recess appoint judges whose nominations are stalled in the Senate? May presidents recess appoint judges to fill vacancies that did not occur when the Senate was in recess?

Judicial confirmation battles are not unusual. A historical view of the judicial appointments process suggests that intense, partisan struggles between the nominating President and rivals in the Senate have been fairly common. What has been unusual in recent years is the use of new, norm-departing strategies in the struggle over judicial nominations at all levels of the federal court system. Two such strategies are the subject of this chapter: 1) recess appointments by presidents to advance nominations stalled in the Senate, and 2) the Senate's use of holds and filibuster to delay action on judicial nominations.

The use of filibusters and recess appointments raises important constitutional questions. My aim in examining these questions is to determine if the judicial appointments process in the United States is going to be governed by informal norms and traditions worked out between the two political branches and the two rival parties, or by new constitutional limits imposed by formal constitutional amendment or judicial decision. In examining the problems with federal judicial selection in the United States, I hope to shed light on some more general questions. What role should courts play in giving meaning to the ambiguous provisions governing judicial appointments? When the constitution is silent, should courts defer to the norms and traditions that have emerged through the years? How should courts handle disputes over judicial appointments that result from the breakdown of unwritten, institutional norms and traditions that have become attached to this process?

Current Crisis over Federal Judicial Selection

Judicial selection has been the subject of considerable political controversy at all levels of the federal judiciary from the very beginning. In fact, the history of federal judicial selection is replete with epic partisan struggles between the President and the Senate. The struggles over control of the Supreme Court and the lower federal courts in the past decade or so have not been any more intense than some of the bitter contests of earlier times. What has been different is the breakdown of institutional norms formerly used to manage interbranch and interparty conflict on this issue.

As indicated above, during President Clinton's years in office the Republicans, who gained control of the Senate in the 1994 mid-term elections and remained the majority party for all but two of the next ten years, delayed and refused to act on over a hundred of his nominations to the lower federal courts. By not acting on so many of President Clinton's judicial nominees, Senate Republicans managed to preserve the ideological advantage they achieved in the lower federal courts by virtue of the judicial appointments made by Republican Presidents Ronald Reagan and George H.W. Bush from 1981. In departing from its normal practice of bringing judicial nominations to a vote in a timely fashion, the Senate disregarded its long-standing concern for the needs of the judiciary to be fully staffed and subjected lower federal court nominees to a level of scrutiny that had previously been applied only to Supreme Court nominees.

In December 2000, with only a few days remaining in his second term, President Clinton responded to the Senate's delaying strategy with a norm-departing strategy of his own. Clinton recess appointed Roger Gregory, one of four judges he had nominated to the Fourth Circuit Court of Appeals, none of whom received a Judiciary Committee hearing. Though the need to fill the vacancy of the Fourth Circuit was urgent,[8] Clinton's use of the recess appointment power broke two norms: 1) that presidents consult with and ultimately obtain the approval of the home-state senators in all the states in the circuit, not just the state where the court sits (while Gregory had the approval of the two senators from the state of Virginia where the court sits, Senator Helms from North Carolina, a state within the Fourth Circuit, had a 'blue slip hold' on the nomination),[9] and 2) that presidents not make recess appointments to the nation's appellate courts. Both norms had only recently emerged in the federal judicial selection process. Before the 1990s, judicial nominees to the federal courts of appeals, who had the approval of both senators from the judge's home state, were virtually assured confirmation. Since the 1960s, the general understanding between the President and the Senate was that recess appointments were not to be used to fill vacancies in the nation's most important court, that is, the U.S. Supreme Court. But in the 1990s, Senate Republicans broadened the prohibition to include the federal courts of appeals.

Soon after the Gregory appointment, President Bush took the oath of office and the 107th Session of Congress began with the Senate evenly divided between fifty Republicans and fifty Democrats. Since the Vice-President has voting rights in the Senate, the Republicans were technically in charge. In May 2001, when Republican Senator Jim Jeffords switched to Independent, the Republicans lost their majority party status. This arrangement lasted until the mid-term congressional elections of 2002, when the Republicans regained control of the Senate (fifty-one Republicans, forty-eight Democrats, one Independent). Since January 2003, Senate Democrats have been in the minority and have had to resort to filibuster to prevent several judicial nominations from coming to a vote. Failing to muster the sixty votes needed to end the filibuster, the narrow Republican majority had been unable to move seven of President Bush's judicial nominations to a vote.

In January 2004, President Bush used the congressional recess to appoint Charles Pickering to the Fifth Circuit Court of Appeals,[10] in February 2004, he used the power again to recess appoint William Pryor to the Eleventh Circuit Court of Appeals.[11] Bush's two recess appointments were more extraordinary than Clinton's recess appointment of Gregory. When President Bush recess appointed Pickering, he used the power to appoint a judge twice defeated by the Senate: Pickering's nomination was defeated first in 2001 by a party-line vote in the Judiciary Committee, and again in 2003 when the Republicans failed to muster the votes required to end the Democrats' filibuster. When he recess appointed Pryor, Bush used the power during a temporary recess of the Senate (the national holiday recognizing American Presidents; not a *sine die* adjournment) to appoint a judge who had been blocked by the Democrats' filibuster.

President Bush's two recess appointments reveal much about the cycle of obstruction and retribution in federal judicial appointments today. As of March 2004 five of Bush's judicial nominations remain stalled in the Senate,[12] and more filibusters are expected. His recess appointments have increased partisan acrimony, emboldened Senate Democrats to place holds on more nominations, and undermined the goodwill between the parties necessary to achieve compromise on judicial nominations.

Norms and Traditions Governing Federal Judicial Selection

In dividing the appointment power between the President and the Senate, the framers clearly envisioned competition over judicial nominations. The finely crafted compromise became part of the constitution's elaborate system of checks and balances. The fundamental concern, as revealed in the records of the Convention, was how best to balance the needs of filling the judiciary with competent judges against the need to check abuses of the President's discretion.[13] Without a check, the fear was that presidents would allow the corrupting effects of nepotism and patronage to influence the selection process.

Advice and Consent

If the constitutional system the framers created was to work, the competition which was purposefully built into the appointments process would have to be managed. Through the years, many norms and traditions have been adopted to keep the interbranch struggle over judicial appointments from reaching deadlock and disrupting the proper functioning of the judiciary. When vacancies occur, presidents are expected to send their nominations to the Senate, which is in turn expected to act on the nominations in a timely fashion. Normal practice has been for the Senate to work expeditiously to get the nominee a hearing and vote from the Judiciary Committee. If the committee's vote is favourable, party leaders will work to schedule a confirmation vote by the full Senate. Both branches understood that departing from these normal practices would risk undermining the proper functioning of the judiciary.

Though the constitution is silent on the requirement for consent, the practice from the very beginning has been for the Senate to confirm judicial nominees by a simple majority vote. Failing to obtain a majority vote means that the Senate does not consent to the President's nomination. When a Senate minority, intent upon stopping the majority from rendering consent, resorts to the Senate's procedural rule on precedence of motions (Rule XXII), which imposes a supermajority requirement to end a filibuster on any measure, including judicial nominations, it, in effect, raises the standard for confirming judges. The Senate's rule on cloture may be useful in requiring the majority to work with the minority on other Senate business, but when it is applied to judicial nominations, it upsets the delicate balance of power the framers envisioned over judicial appointments.

The phrase 'advice and consent' seems to imply that presidents consult with the Senate before making a nomination. Though the exact constitutional meaning of 'advice' has never been determined judicially, a tradition of consultation developed over judicial nominations to the lower federal courts. 'Senatorial courtesy,' as it is known, is the institutional norm which through the years has compelled presidents to consult with home-state senators before making a nomination to a judicial vacancy in their state.[14] If this courtesy is ignored, the aggrieved senators may prevent the nomination from going forward by not returning the 'blue slip' sent by the Senate Judiciary Committee chair to each of the senators from the state with the judicial vacancy. Though 'blue slip holds' are mainly used to block nominations to vacancies in the district courts, in recent years, they have been used to block nominations to the courts of appeals if a senator whose home state is within the circuit has objections.

By tradition, judicial nominations are sent to the Senate Judiciary Committee for a hearing and a vote on whether the nomination may be sent to the floor. The rules of the Senate Judiciary Committee governing the judicial nominations process have been in flux over the last few years. In October 2003, Senator Patrick Leahy (Democrat) complained that several long-standing rules of the committee had been changed by Republicans, the party then in control of the Senate. According to Senator Leahy, the 'blue slip policy' was changed 'so that even a negative blue slip from both home-state Senators is not sufficient to prevent action on a nominee.' He also complained that the committee's Rule 4 had been changed. This rule once allowed any member of the Judiciary Committee to object to a matter coming to a vote. To override that objection, at least one member of the minority had to vote with the majority in favour of ending debate and bringing the matter to a vote. According to Senator Leahy, the Senate Judiciary Committee Chairman (Orrin Hatch) departed from this rule by allowing votes on nominations that had been cleared by a simple majority vote without the support of at least one member of the minority party.[15]

Recess Appointments

Several norms governing the President's power to make recess appointments have also come under assault. Because recess-appointed judges will be exercising judicial power without the important protection of judicial independence that comes with lifetime tenure, the tradition has been to avoid making such appointments at all. But if the power must be exercised, as it has been in over three hundred cases since 1789, including eleven Supreme Court appointments, then the norm has been for the President to use it narrowly. In short, presidents were expected to fill only vacancies that occurred when the Senate was in formal, *sine die* adjournment (not a temporary recess), and never in a deliberate attempt to circumvent the Senate's responsibility to confirm judicial nominees.

Presidents have long maintained that they have the power to recess appoint federal judges. After President Eisenhower filled three vacancies on the Supreme Court by recess appointments during the 1950s (Chief Justice Earl Warren was recess appointed on 2 October 1953; William Brennan on 15 October 1956; and Potter Stewart on 14 October 1958), the Senate and the Executive Branch eventually agreed that appointments to the nation's highest court were too important to bypass the normal constitutional process of senatorial advice and consent.[16] More recently, the Senate's concern about recess appointments to the Supreme Court has been extended to appointments to the federal appeals courts.

Both old and new norms governing recess appointment of lower federal court judges were transgressed when President Clinton appointed Roger Gregory, and when President Bush appointed Charles Pickering and William Pryor. Broken were the old norms that prohibited the use of recess appointments during short, temporary adjournments of the Senate, or attempts to bypass the Senate's constitutional duty to render advice and consent. Also broken was the new norm that discouraged the use of recess appointments to the nation's appellate courts, including the U.S. Supreme Court and the courts of appeals.

Breakdown of Institutional Norms

Commentators and scholars have attributed the recent departure from institutional norms to increased rancorousness between the parties since the controversial nomination of Judge Robert Bork in 1987. The difficulties President Clinton had with his lower court nominations have been attributed to Republican Party retribution for the Democrats' rejection of Judge Bork. Interbranch and interparty tensions continued into the next administration. Senate Democrats, some believe, have been motivated by the controversial presidential election of 2000 to prevent an illegitimate president from tilting the ideological balance of the federal judiciary.[17] Under normal circumstances, presidents can expect to have their judicial nominations confirmed, even if the party in control of the Senate is not the President's party and despite any objections about the nominee's judicial philosophy. The necessity for the judiciary to be fully staffed with competent judges was understood to outweigh ideological differences. Thus, when the President's party is the party in control of the Senate and he is thwarted in his attempts to place judges of his choosing on the bench by a minority in the Senate, something extraordinary is going on. By using filibuster to prevent President Bush and a Republican majority in the Senate from appointing judges, Democrats are controverting a basic norm governing federal judicial selection.

The Constitutionality of Recess Appointments

Recess appointments of federal judges are not exceptional per se. Presidents have made more than three hundred such appointments since 1789. What was unique in 2000, when President Clinton appointed Gregory, and in 2004, when President Bush appointed Pickering and Pryor, was the fact that each nomination had been opposed by the Senate. In his recent study of the history of recess appointments, Louis Fisher revealed that they are generally not used to bypass the Senate.[18] When the Senate sees the President using the recess appointment power narrowly, making appointments only to prevent disruption of the courts' business and only after consulting with Senate leaders, it rarely objects. This explains in large part the tradition of the Senate subsequently confirming nearly every recess appointed judge.[19] When presidents are perceived to be flaunting senatorial prerogatives and using the recess appointment power to bypass normal advice and consent functions, the Senate is likely to respond differently. The recess appointments of Gregory, Pickering, and Pryor were new, norm-departing strategies in the old battle over judicial appointments, they increased interbranch tensions. They also raise some constitutional questions.

Are recess appointments of federal judges constitutional? Does it make a difference whether the power is exercised broadly, to bypass advice and consent functions and advance nominations stalled in the Senate, or narrowly, to fill urgent vacancies in the judiciary after consultation with Senate leaders? Given the unique circumstances of the Gregory, Pickering, and Pryor appointments, did Presidents Clinton and Bush violate the recess appointment clause of Article II, section 2, clause 3? As I shall explain, the text, history, and the limited case law precedents dealing with the recess appointment clause all indicate that the President's power is constitutional. While recess appointment of federal judges is not unconstitutional, it is certainly bad policy and ought to be exercised narrowly.

Text

The constitution gives the President the power 'to fill up all Vacancies that may happen during the Recess of the Senate, by granting Commissions which shall expire at the end of their next Session' (Article II, section 2, clause 3). The meaning of 'recess' and 'may happen during' will have a bearing on the extent to which presidents may exercise power under the recess appointment clause. History and tradition, rather than judicial decision, have determined that 'recess' means that presidents may fill vacancies any time the Senate is not in session, including brief, temporary adjournments. Presidents have made recess appointments without controversy during temporary adjournments, as well as between formal sessions of the Senate. 'May happen during' has also been given a fairly broad interpretation by historical practice. Presidents have used the recess appointment power to fill vacancies that technically occurred when the Senate was in session, but had remained unfilled after the Senate recessed. Despite the plain meaning of the phrase 'vacancies that may happen during the Recess of the Senate,' history and tradition have recognized the President's power to fill vacancies whenever they occur and whenever the Senate is not in session.

The question whether recess-appointed judges may exercise judicial power without all the protections of judicial independence cannot be answered by analysis of the text alone. The plain meaning of the text does not support the proposition that judges recess appointed to seats on Article III courts (that is, the U.S. Supreme Court, the thirteen courts of Appeals, and the ninety-four district courts) may not exercise judicial power by commission granted by the President. If the framers of Article II, section 2 had wanted to limit the President's recess appointment power, the specific offices to be excluded would have been enumerated. Also, the placement of the recess appointment clause right after the general appointment clause suggests that it applies to the same offices. In other words, the structure of the text does not support the proposition that the recess appointment clause excludes Article III judges. When presidents use the recess appointment power to fill vacancies within the federal judiciary, they may be violating the constitution's principle of judicial independence. Despite the apparent tension between judges with limited commissions, serving on a temporary basis, and the principle of judicial independence, assured by judges holding 'their Offices during good Behavior' (Article III, section 1), the Second and Ninth Circuit Courts of Appeals have ruled that recess-appointed judges possess full powers and authority (see Case Law Developments, below).

History

The records of the Constitutional Convention are largely silent on the framing of the recess appointment clause. All that is known is that the provision was adopted unanimously. There is no indication whether the framers debated how and under what circumstances the power may be used. Alexander Hamilton, writing in *The Federalist Papers, No. 67,* offers only a few scant clues. Though most of his discussion is devoted to rejecting the claim that presidents could use the recess appointment power to fill vacancies in the Senate, he does make the important point that the power was to be an 'auxiliary method of appointment' and not what he called the 'general mode' of appointing officers. That may seem self-evident, but it is worth noting that Hamilton clearly understood the recess appointment power to be 'nothing more than a supplement' to the normal process.

In trying to determine if the recess appointment of federal judges is constitutional or not, the relevant history is not what the framers intended, but how the relevant constitutional actors exercised and reacted to the power in practice.[20] All three branches have recognized, in one form or another, the legitimacy of the President's power to make recess appointments. After President Eisenhower's three recess appointments to the U.S. Supreme Court, the Senate complained about the wisdom of such a policy and worked to forge a new political consensus on the issue. The new norm was the understanding that appointments to the Supreme Court were too important to bypass the normal process of senatorial advice and consent and that any such bypass ought to be avoided. In a decision by the Ninth Circuit Court of Appeals upholding the constitutionality of the power exercised by a recess appointed judge, the court cited the historical consensus in favour of the practice to support its decision.[21]

Case Law Developments

Both the Second and the Ninth Circuit Courts of Appeals have upheld the constitutionality of recess appointments to the federal bench.[22] When these cases reached the Supreme Court, the Court denied certiorari (i.e., denied leave to appeal). While the Supreme Court has not ruled on this question, the two federal appeals court decisions indicate that presidents have the power to recess appoint federal judges and recess-appointed judges have the authority to exercise judicial power.

Prudential Considerations

The obvious problem with recess appointments is that they circumvent the constitutional responsibility of the Senate to advise and consent. But there are other problems, including the rights of litigants in federal court to have their cases handled by judges with all the protections of judicial independence and the rights of the judge, sitting on an Article III court, to all the protections of judicial independence. The judiciary needs to be fully staffed, and recess appointments certainly allow presidents to keep vacancies from affecting the efficient operation of the judiciary. But efficiency must not come at the expense of other important values, such as the quality of justice delivered.

Recess appointment of federal judges is probably not unconstitutional. Two federal appeals courts have upheld the President's power against constitutional challenge. Nevertheless, it is an unwise policy and the norm ought to be that presidents use the power narrowly and not as a strategy to bypass the normal advice and consent functions of the Senate. It is not as if departure from the norm lacks a check or an adequate political remedy. Presidents are certainly aware that recess appointments opposed by the Senate are likely to come at a considerable cost, namely the risk of Senate rejection of the recess-appointed judge and perhaps even future nominations.

Because the political checks are more than adequate, there is no need for judicial intervention on this matter. In addition to threatening future nominations, presidents are likely to have a difficult time finding candidates willing to accept recess appointments. In 1940, Congress passed a law preventing payment of a recessed-appointed judge until the appointee had been confirmed by the Senate.[23] While there are some statutory exceptions,[24] recess-appointed judges generally serve without pay until their nominations are confirmed. The economic reality, together with the realization that a controversial recess appointment is likely to jeopardize their nomination once the Senate returns, might ultimately discourage judicial candidates from accepting recess appointments.

The Constitutionality of Senate Filibusters of Judicial Nominations

As indicated above, under the Senate's rules (Rule XXII), the only way to end a filibuster used to block a judicial nomination is if sixteen members petition, and three-fifths of the entire Senate (sixty members) vote for cloture. Because the use of this rule effectively prevents the President and a majority of senators from fulfilling their constitutional responsibility to appoint judges to fill vacancies in the judiciary, courts need to address the constitutional questions it raises.[25] Several constitutional attacks can be mounted against the Senate rule. First, it arguably violates the advice and consent clause of Article II, section 2, clause 2. By imposing a supermajority requirement on the confirmation of judicial nominees, the rule is contrary to the clear language and history of the advice and consent clause. Second, the Senate rule as applied to judicial nominations arguably violates the separation of powers principle. By setting the bar for consent higher than the simple majority seemingly implied by the text of the constitution, the finely crafted compromise over this shared power has been upset. By allowing a Senate minority the power to delay and ultimately defeat a judicial nomination, the Senate's rule to end a filibuster shifts too much power over the shared process to the Senate.

Arguments based on text, history, and precedent all cast considerable doubt about the constitutionality of the Senate rule of cloture when applied to judicial nominations. In the sections that follow, I shall sketch the broad outlines of these arguments.

Text

The Senate's rule of cloture, requiring a supermajority vote to end a filibuster and bring a judicial nomination to a confirmation vote, violates the language of the constitution. When the framers wanted a supermajority voting requirement, such as the requirement for ratifying treaties (Article II, section 2), approving constitutional amendment proposals (Article V), convicting impeached officers (Article I, section 3), and overriding a presidential veto of legislation (Article I, section 7), they said so explicitly. Unless the framers made explicit provision for a supermajority voting requirement, the general understanding has been that they intended a simple majority vote. To place a supermajority requirement on 'consent' when the constitution is silent on this matter is to read a requirement into the text for which the framers made no provision.

Compare the 'treaty ratification clause' with the 'judicial appointments clause.' Both appear side-by-side in Article II, section 2, clause 2: 'He shall have Power, by and with the Advice and Consent of the Senate, to make Treaties, provided two thirds of the Senators present concur; and he shall nominate, and by and with the Advice and Consent of the Senate, shall appoint Ambassadors, other public Ministers, and Consuls, Judges of the supreme Court, and all other Officers of the United States ...' In rendering advice and consent for the ratification of treaties, the framers were clear that a supermajority vote was required ('two thirds of the Senators present'). If the framers had intended to create a supermajority voting requirement for advice and consent of a wide variety of presidential nominations, they would have said so. When the constitution is silent, as it is here, the general rule of parliamentary procedure, that is, the act of the majority is the act of the body, is assumed to apply.

History

The Senate's rule of cloture when applied to judicial nominations sets the bar for consent higher than the framers of the constitution intended. As explained above, on the occasions the framers wanted a supermajority voting requirement, they provided for it in the text. There is also historical evidence suggesting that a supermajority voting requirement for the confirmation of judicial nominations was considered and rejected by the framers. Early in the convention debate over judicial appointments, there was a proposal to give the power exclusively to the Senate. Since the nominees would be taken from the states, the idea was that the Senate, because it is composed of two senators from each state, would be in the best position to evaluate the judicial candidates. Once this proposal was shown to be wanting, James Madison proposed that the power of appointment be given to the President, subject to a Senate veto by a two-thirds vote. This proposal was also rejected, in part because it placed too much responsibility over appointments in the Executive Branch. In the end, a compromise was reached that delicately balanced the appointment power between the President, who shall nominate, and the Senate, which shall confirm or reject.

In their attempt to divide the appointment power more evenly between the Senate and the Executive Branch, the framers rejected Madison's proposal that only a two-thirds vote by the Senate could defeat a President's nomination. In order for the compromise to make sense, the Senate would have to have more power to stop a nominee. It follows that the framers meant for the Senate to have the power to reject judicial nominees with a simple majority vote. It is difficult to square this understanding of the framers' intent with the Senate's rule of cloture. By allowing a minority in the Senate to defeat judicial nominations, the Senate rule, in effect, upsets the delicate balance by shifting too much power to the Senate.

Unfortunately, *The Federalist Papers* do not address directly the question whether a vote more than a simple majority may be required for judicial nominations. Nevertheless, in passages written on other matters, both James Madison and Alexander Hamilton expressed their general reservations about supermajority voting requirements.[26]

Case Law Developments

The question whether the Senate's rule of cloture is constitutional when applied to judicial nominations has not yet been addressed by the courts. The best analogy may be the cases that raised questions about Congress's power over the rules of quorum and the voting requirements that determine the will of the body. In *United States v. Ballin, et al.* (1892), the U.S. Supreme Court announced the following principle: 'the general rule of all parliamentary bodies is that ... the act of a majority of the quorum is the act of the body.'[27] The question before the high court in this case was whether a vote of 183 members of the House of Representatives, who at the time constituted a majority of the quorum present but less than a majority of the full House, was sufficient to pass a bill. The Supreme Court ruled unanimously that it was.[28]

The *Ballin* principle is still good law, having been relied on by the Supreme Court in *Federal Trade Commission v. Flotill Products, Inc.* (1967).[29] The question in this case was whether a simple majority of the

Federal Trade Commission's quorum was sufficient to exercise the commission's regulatory power. In his opinion for the court, Justice William Brennan explained that a simple majority of a quorum represents the act of the body.[30]

Since the constitution is silent on the Senate's voting requirement on judicial nominations, it follows from these decisions that the general rule ought to be that an act of the majority is the act of the body. Therefore, the Senate's rule of cloture, requiring sixty votes to end a filibuster and move a judicial nomination to a vote, is probably unconstitutional.

Prudential Considerations

The obvious problem with the Senate rule requiring sixty votes to break a filibuster on a judicial nomination is that it allows a minority to block a nominee supported by the majority. But there are other problems as well. By causing breakdowns in the judicial appointments process, the Senate rule ultimately impairs the proper functioning of the judiciary. Unless vacancies are filled in a timely fashion, there will be greater backlogs of cases, an increase in the use of unpublished opinions, and longer delays placed on litigants trying to get into court. Also, an increasing number of meritorious judicial candidates might be reluctant to allow their names to be put forward because of the difficulties many recent nominees have experienced.[31] If recruiting strong candidates becomes more difficult, the quality of the judiciary will suffer.

Judicial Review of Judicial Selection Controversies

When President Bush responded to the filibuster Democrats had placed on seven of his nominations by recess appointing Pickering and Pryor, he raised the stakes in the partisan struggle over control of the courts. The only law that seems to apply today in the area of federal judicial appointments is the *lex talionis*, or the law of an eye for an eye, tooth for a tooth. If the cycle of obstruction and retribution is ever going to end, the rules allowing a minority in the Senate to block nominations indefinitely and the President to bypass with recess appointments may have to change.

In October 2003 Representative Thaddeus McCotter, Republican from Michigan, and the other members of the Michigan congressional delegation proposed an amendment to the U.S. constitution that would require the Senate to affirmatively reject a presidential nomination within 120 days. Otherwise the nomination would be deemed approved.[32] The proposed amendment, modelled on a provision in the Michigan state constitution, was referred to the House Subcommittee on the Constitution. To become part of the constitution, the proposed amendment needs the approval of two-thirds of each House of Congress and three-quarters of the state legislatures within seven years.

The idea that constitutional amendment is the solution to the problem of Senate delay and obstruction is flawed in several respects. If there happened to be enough bipartisan support in Congress to send the proposed amendment to the states for ratification (two-thirds of both Houses), there certainly would be enough support in the Senate to get the cloture rule changed: Senate Rule V requires a two-thirds vote to amend the Senate's rules. A new Senate rule prohibiting the use of filibuster on judicial nominations would make the proposed amendment, in its present form, redundant. Also, in order for the proposed constitutional amendment to work properly, the Senate's rule allowing filibuster of judicial nominations would have to be abolished. Otherwise, forty senators who happened to favour a nomination could get the nomination confirmed against the will of the majority by simply filibustering and preventing a vote for 120 days. If the Senate rule would need to be abolished in order for the new constitutional amendment to work properly, the constitutional amendment would not be necessary to prevent Senate delay on judicial nominations.

Needless to say, today's Senate is hardly poised to abolish the cloture rule or to establish a new norm against delay on considering judicial nominations. The mutual respect and willingness to compromise needed to change the Senate's rules or norms have been lacking for some time. If there is to be any reform, it may very well come through judicial action.

Some, but not all, controversies over federal judicial selection are non-justiciable political questions. There is no 'case or controversy,' for instance, in disputes over the qualifications of nominees or the criteria used by senators to evaluate nominees. On the other hand, some 'cases and controversies' over federal judicial selection may justify judicial intervention.[33] Courts certainly ought not to be barred from remedying an unlawful exercise of power simply because the problem is 'political' in nature. Courts have the power to give meaning to the vague provisions in the text when it is clear that the political stalemate is the result of disputes over the precise constitutional meaning of the text. After all, it was Chief Justice John Marshall who wrote in *Marbury v. Madison*

(1803) that '[i]t is emphatically the province and duty of the judicial department to say what the law is.'[34] Courts should be deferential to the norms and traditions that the political branches have developed to govern an inherently political process only vaguely defined by the constitution. But as the recent controversies over judicial appointments reveal, the problem has not been the use of long-standing traditions and norms; the problem has been the departure from institutional norms and practices for partisan advantage. When there is no realistic hope for an adequate political remedy and the problem seems amendable to a judicial remedy, courts ought to be willing to step into the fray.

Breaking the current political deadlock over judicial appointments may require the same action needed to break the political deadlock over reapportionment in the 1960s. The reapportionment controversy presented a similar cycle of obstruction, delay, and inaction in many state legislatures. The legislative party with the power to reapportion lacked the will to do so because it owed its position to the malapportioned districts which elected them. As the Supreme Court demonstrated in the landmark case *Baker v. Carr* (1962), 'the mere fact that the suit seeks protection of a political right does not mean it presents a political question. Such an objection "is little more than a play upon words."'[35]

Unless the cycle of obstruction and retribution over judicial appointments is broken, the crisis will continue to impair the proper functioning of the judiciary. In his last three 'State of the Judiciary' addresses, Chief Justice William Rehnquist identified the high number of judicial vacancies as a problem which has reached a crisis point.[36] The Senate's norm-departing strategy of delay and obstruction which has caused the judicial appointments' crisis thus presents a justiciable cause of action.

Courts should intervene and declare the cloture rule unconstitutional. Judicial action is needed because the political system is unable to break out of the destructive cycle of obstruction and retribution. To prevent further damage to the proper functioning of the judiciary, courts ought to strike down the Senate's rule of cloture as applied to judicial nominations.

When disputes arise over various aspects of the judicial selection process, such as the disputes over the meaning of senatorial consent and the scope of a president's power to make recess appointments, it will ultimately be the role of the courts to decide what the constitution requires. A judicial ruling declaring unconstitutional the Senate's rule of cloture when applied to judicial nominations would keep a minority from postponing indefinitely a nomination supported by a majority of the Senate. Since filibuster was the threat that made holds possible, such a ruling would also end the extra-parliamentary policy which, on some occasions, had allowed a single aggrieved senator to defeat a nomination. A decision declaring unconstitutional the Senate rule of cloture when applied to judicial nominations may ultimately end the cycle of obstruction and retribution over judicial appointments in the United States.

Epilogue

In May 2005 fourteen U.S. senators (seven Republican and seven Democrat) reached an agreement that defused the latest controversy over federal judicial nominations. The agreement averted a constitutional crisis that threatened to shut down the Senate and preserved the Senate tradition of unlimited debate on judicial nominations in 'extraordinary circumstances.'

Emboldened by the outcome of the November 2004 elections and anxious to confirm several federal appeals court judges whose nominations had been stopped by filibuster, the Republican leaders announced their plans to change the Senate's rule of unlimited debate on matters of judicial nominations. Realizing that the two-thirds vote (sixty-seven senators) needed to change the rules was unlikely to be attained, the Senate majority leader announced his intention of employing what became known as the 'nuclear option' to accomplish a rules change by a simple majority vote. The plan was for the majority leader to ask for a ruling from the presiding officer of the Senate (who happens to be the vice-president of the United States) on whether the minority party's attempt to prevent a judicial nomination from coming to a vote was constitutional. After ruling it unconstitutional, debate on the nomination would be ended by a simple majority vote, and the question of whether to confirm or reject brought to vote.

If the majority's parliamentary manoeuvre had been used, the minority would certainly have carried out their threat to use the Senate's rules requiring unanimous consent to bring the business of the Senate to a halt. The May 2005 compromise, which backed the Senate away from the precipice, included the following agreements. First, the Republican and Democratic signatories agreed to up-or-down votes on three of President Bush's appeals court nominees who had been filibustered (Judges Janice Rogers Brown, William Pryor, and Priscilla Owen). Second, the senators agreed to exercise their advise and consent responsibilities in good faith and would only filibuster nominees in 'extraordinary circumstances.' The meaning of 'extraordinary circumstances' was left undefined in the agreement. Third, the signatories agreed to oppose the use of the so-called 'nuclear option' so long as the agreement is honoured. And lastly, the senators urged the President to consult with members of both parties before submitting judicial nominees for Senate consideration.

The May 2005 compromise may have averted the latest crisis over federal judicial nominations in the United States, but the real test of whether this new understaning as to how the partisan rivals are to handle these matters is expected to come when President Bush attempts to fill the vacancies on the U.S. Supreme Court.

NOTES

1 '... and he [i.e., the President] shall nominate, and by and with the Advice and Consent of the Senate, shall appoint ... Judges of the Supreme Court, and all other Officers of the United States ... which shall be established by Law ...' U.S. Constitution, Article II, section 2, clause 2. 'The President shall have Power to fill up all Vacancies that may happen during the Recess of the Senate, by granting Commissions which shall expire at the End of their next Session.' U.S. Constitution, Article II, section 2, clause 3.

2 Farrand, ed., *The Records of the Federal Convention of 1787*, 2:539–40.

3 Rakove, *Original Meanings*, 260.

4 Farrand, ed., *The Records of the Federal Convention of 1787*, 2: 540, 574, 600, 660.

5 On the relevance of 'norm theory' and its application to the federal appointments process, see generally, Gerhardt, 'Norm Theory and the Future of the Federal Appointments Process'; Gerhardt, *The Federal Appointments Process.* In these works, the author argues that the patterns and practices of presidents and the Senate have produced some distinct and identifiable institutional norms.

6 The Senate's rule on filibuster and cloture makes holds possible. Party leaders may choose to disregard a hold, especially a hold requested by a senator in the minority, but they understand that if they do they may have to face a filibuster. The Senate rule to end a filibuster (Senate Rule XXII 'cloture'; see note 7 below) requires the consent of three-fifths, or sixty members of the Senate. Since 1999 the Senate has tried to end the practice of 'secret holds,' that is, the practice of placing anonymous holds on judicial nominations.

Despite considerable bipartisan support for an amendment to the Senate's standing orders that would require senators to publicly announce their holds on nominations, there has yet to be any change. See 'Senate Resolution 216 – Establishing as a Standing Order of the Senate a Requirement that a Senator Publicly Discloses a Notice of Intent to Object to Proceeding to Any Measure or Matter,' Congressional Record – Senate (108th Congress), 149 Cong Rec S 10923.

7 U.S. Senate, Rule XXII: 'at any time a motion signed by sixteen Senators, to bring to a close the debate upon any measure, motion, other matter pending before the Senate ... is presented to the Senate, the Presiding Officer ... shall at once state the motion to the Senate, and ... he shall lay the motion before the Senate and ... shall, without debate, submit to the Senate by a yea-and-nay vote the question: "Is it the sense of the Senate that the debate shall be brought to a close?" And if that question shall be decided in the affirmative by three-fifths of the Senators ... then said measure, motion, or other matter pending before the Senate ... shall be the unfinished business to the exclusion of all other business until disposed of.'

8 The Administrative Office of the United States Courts had declared Gregory's seat on the Fourth Circuit Court of Appeals a 'judicial emergency.' It had been vacant for nearly a decade, longer than any other seat in the nation. The Administrative Office uses this term to describe long-running vacancies that are affecting the proper functioning of the courts. At the end of 2003, twelve vacancies in the Circuit Courts and ten in the District Courts were deemed 'judicial emergencies.'

9 The blue slip policy, in the words of Senator Patrick Leahy, 'is the enforcement tool to ensure consultation by the Executive Branch with home-state senators about judicial appointments to their states.' It is a long-standing rule developed by the Senate Judiciary Committee that prevented action on a nominee if at least one home-state senator opposed it. 'Statement of Senator Patrick Leahy,' Hearing before the Judiciary Committee on the Nomination of Claude Allen, 28 October 2003.

10 Neil Lewis, 'Bush Seats Judge After Long Fight, Bypassing Senate,' *New York Times*, 17 January 2004, A1.

11 Neil Lewis, 'Bypassing Senate for Second Time, Bush Seats Judge,' *New York Times*, 21 February 2004, A1.

12 As of March 2004, the following appeals court nominees had been either subject to filibuster or threatened with filibuster if they reach the Senate floor: Priscilla Owen, nominated to the Fifth Circuit; Carolyn Kuhl, nominated to the Ninth Circuit; Janice Rogers Brown, nominated to the D.C. Circuit; Brett Kavanaugh, nominated to the D.C. Circuit; and Claude Allen,

nominated to the Fourth Circuit. Only a few months before, this list included Charles Pickering, who had been recessed appointed to the Fifth Circuit, William Pryor, who had been recess appointed to the Eleventh Circuit, and Miguel Estrada, who had withdrawn his nomination to the D.C. circuit, which had been delayed by filibuster for twenty-eight months (see note 31 below).

13 Farrand, ed., *Records of the Federal Convention of 1787*, 2:539–40.

14 According to Henry Abraham, the norm of senatorial courtesy dates back to the First Session of Congress. President George Washington was forced to withdraw his nominee for Naval Officer in the Port of Savannah when it became clear that the full Senate was going to vote to reject the nomination because the two senators from Georgia had not been consulted and were against it. The norm emerged after Washington then named a nominee favoured by the two senators and the full Senate confirmed. *Justices and Presidents*, 27.

15 'Statement of Senator Patrick Leahy,' Hearing before the Judiciary Committee on the Nomination of Claude Allen, 28 October, 2003 (http://leahy.senate.gov/press/200310/102803b.html).

16 See 'The Constitutionality of Recess Appointments.' With recess appointments, there is no nomination, no committee hearing, and no Senate vote. The President simply announces the appointment and signs the judge's commission, which is valid until the end of the next session of the Senate. In most cases, the President also nominates them for the seat, thereby beginning the formal confirmation process once the Senate reconvenes.

17 The controversies over the flawed ballot and the outcome of the presidential vote in Florida were ultimately decided in favour of George Bush. See *Bush v. Gore*, 531 U.S. 98 (2000).

18 Fisher, 'Recess Appointments of Federal Judges.'

19 'Presidents had made approximately 300 judicial recess appointments and ... Congress "has consistently confirmed judicial recess appointees without dissent."' Fisher, 'Recess Appointments of Federal Judges,' 21.

20 According to Professor Whittington, constitutional meaning may lie beyond text and original intent: 'It requires a more integrative approach that connects the Constitution to the actual operation of government institutions and to continuing political conflicts.' See Whittington, *Constitutional Construction*, 228.

21 *United States v. Woodley*, 751 F.2d 1008 (9th Cir. 1985).

22 See *United States v. Allocco*, 305 F. 2d 704 (2d Cir. 1962) and *United States v. Woodley*, 751 F. 2d 1008 (9th Cir. 1985).

23 5 U.S.C. Sect. 5503 (revising the law first passed in 1863).

24 'Section 5503. Recess Appointments. (a) Payment for services may not be made from the Treasury of the United States to an individual appointed during a recess of the Senate to fill a vacancy in an existing office, if the vacancy existed while the Senate was in session and was by law required to be filled by and with the advice and consent of the Senate, until the appointee has been confirmed by the Senate. This subsection does not apply – (1) if the vacancy arose within 30 days before the end of the session of the Senate; (2) if, at the end of the session, a nomination for the office, other than the nomination of an individual appointed during the preceding recess of the Senate was pending before the Senate for its advice and consent; or (3) if a nomination for the office was rejected by the Senate within 30 days before the end of the session and an individual other than the one whose nomination was rejected thereafter receives a recess appointment.'

25 *Judicial Watch, Inc. v. The United States Senate, et al.* was filed in the United States District Court for the District of Columbia in May 2003. Plaintiff is seeking declaratory relief from the harm that the Senate's rule allowing filibuster of judicial nominations is causing. As of March 2004, no decision has been announced.

26 See *The Federalist Papers, Numbers 22 and 58.*

27 144 U.S. 1 (1892).

28 144 U.S. 1 (1892).

29 389 U.S. 179 (1967).

30 'The almost universally accepted common-law rule is ... that ... in the absence of a contrary statutory provision, a majority of a quorum constituted of a simple majority of a collective body is empowered to act for the body. Where the enabling statute is silent on the question, the body is justified in adhering to that common-law rule.' 329 U.S. 179 at 183–4 (1967).

31 Take, for example, the experience of Miguel Estrada. He was nominated by President Bush to a vacancy on the D.C. Circuit Court of Appeals. After a twenty-eight-month delay, he requested that his nomination be withdrawn so that he could return to his legal practice.

32 108th Congress, House Joint Resolution 71.

33 The two principal forms of relief in such cases are declaratory judgment and mandamus. If the Senate is found to have violated its advice and consent duties with Rule XXII, declaratory judgment would be the proper remedy. There are numerous instances of courts using declaratory judgment against a co-equal branch of government.

34 5 U.S. (1 Cranch) 137, 177 (1803).

35 369 U.S. 186 (1962).

36 The Administrative Office of the U.S. Courts reported forty-two vacancies

(eighteen appeals court and twenty-four district court) out of 877 seats in the federal judiciary. Twenty-two of the forty-two vacancies have been declared 'judicial emergencies,' defined as 'any vacancy in a district court where weighted filings are in excess of 600 per judgeship, or any vacancy in existence more than 18 months where weighted filings are between 430 and 600 per judgeship ... and any vacancy in a court of appeals where adjusted filings per panel are in excess of 700 or any vacancy in existence more than 18 months where adjusted filings are between 500 to 700 per panel.' Press release dated 9 October 2003.

5 Judicial Appointments in New Zealand: If it were done when 'tis done, then 'twere well it were done openly and directly*

JAMES ALLAN

In this chapter I want to argue *against* the desirability of any sort of Judicial Appointments Boards that have more than the mildest of advisory powers. In my view, Judicial Appointments Boards that have the power of appointment, the power to nominate a short list from which appointment must be made, or even the power to rate submitted names as 'approved' or 'not approved,' should be avoided. High-level judges should not be chosen by means of any such indirect structure, but rather openly and directly by the elected government of the day (in most instances through the attorney-general).

I also want to set this argument in the context of New Zealand, where only very recently[1] appeals to the Privy Council (as New Zealand's highest court) have been abolished and a new highest court created to take its place. The dangers of political appointments to the bench appear greatest when a brand new highest court is being created from scratch and when all the initial appointments to that new court are being made at the same time, by the same attorney-general. Accordingly, the argument for a vigorous, non-emasculated Judicial Appointments Board – whether it be a nominating or screening committee[2] – should be strongest in precisely the recent New Zealand situation. If such Judicial Appointments Boards are undesirable even in such unusual situations, then *a fortiori* they are undesirable in the far more usual circumstances of filling individual vacancies on the highest courts as they arise.

My contention will be that such boards *are* undesirable even in the recent New Zealand situation in which a highest court was being newly created and the incumbent attorney-general was (legally) unconstrained in whom she could appoint.[3] In attempting to make this argument I shall start by briefly running through the existing appointment process in New Zealand and the court structure in which such appointments are made. Then I will outline how abolition of appeals to the Privy Council came about, the alternative put in its place, the various claims made by the attorney-general and others for how (and from where) the vacancies to this new highest court would be filled, and what eventually happened. That done, I will set out my reasons for believing vigorous Judicial Appointments Boards to be a bad idea.

The New Zealand Court System and the Existing Process of Judicial Appointments

New Zealand was the first country in the world to grant women the franchise (1893); the first to experiment with the welfare state (1890s on); and one of the first to experiment with neo-liberal economic reforms (1980s). Its treatment of the indigenous population – certainly by the standards of the time – can only be described as enlightened. Maori men were granted the vote in 1867 and four of Parliament's then seventy-six seats were reserved for Maori.

All this took place in a country about the same geographical size as Britain or Japan, which is a unitary state rather than a federal one. It happened in a country with a unicameral legislature and no written constitution. Only in 1990 was a Bill of Rights added to that mix, and a strictly statutory one at that – in fact, on its face, one of the most enervated Bills of Rights imaginable.[4]

Within that unitary, unicameral structure, New Zealand had until 2004 a court system with the Privy Council in London at its apex (hearing about a dozen cases a year), beneath which was a Court of Appeal (the highest domestic appeal court and the last stop for all but those dozen appeals a year), below that the first instance High Court (with original jurisdiction), and under that the District Court and other courts such as the Family Court, Environment Court, and Maori Land Court. At the start of 2004 this court structure was altered at its pinnacle, as noted above, when appeals to the Privy Council were abolished and a new domestic highest court, named the Supreme Court, was created to start hearing appeals in June of 2004. All courts below this new Supreme Court were left intact while appeals to it were made by leave only (which was not the case with all Privy Council appeals).

The current process for appointing judges of the High Court and Court of Appeal (and, when it arises in future, of the new Supreme Court) will be familiar to all readers from common law jurisdictions over a certain age. The attorney-general recommends the appointments to the governor-general, who then formally appoints them (see sections 4(2) and 57(2) of the *Judicature Act 1908* and section 17 of the *Supreme Court Act 2003*).[5]

The process adopted by any particular attorney-general is prescribed neither by statute nor by regulation. A past solicitor-general[6] (and currently a justice of the New Zealand Court of Appeal) has outlined the then two-stage process in some detail.[7] There is no reason to think this process has changed in any significant detail, and it basically involves identifying a pool of possible candidates by consulting with a broad range of judges and representatives of various lawyers' organizations. Names of lawyers are brought forward, including those whose careers who have followed less orthodox paths. The long list produced is shortened at a second stage in a meeting between the attorney-general, the chief justice, the president of the Court of Appeal, and the solicitor-general, but it is the attorney-general who decides on the short list and on who will head it. Checks are then undertaken and, when openings occur, potential appointees are contacted to see if they are interested.

Notice that the status quo forces the attorney-general to consult, that the senior judges have a strong say – and possibly what may even approach an informal veto if they are dead set against someone – but that ultimately the attorney-general can appoint the sort of judge (male or female, activist or deferential, from one part of the country or another) she wants. In some situations the attorney-general and her government might be held responsible politically for the choices made. One can imagine electoral pressure coming to bear on a government that had appointed a series of top judges from the same city or with the same interpretive views or whatever. But I will come back to this below.

Abolishing the Privy Council and Creating a Brand New Highest Court

Abolition of the Privy Council as New Zealand's highest court placed this existing appointments process under extreme pressure. Here's why.

Despite much talk and a number of initiatives to abolish appeal to the Privy Council over several decades, as of 2002 it remained New Zealand's highest court. Various explanations for this situation have been offered. The left-wing Labour Party, the political party one would normally have expected to push for abolition, receives the vast preponderance of Maori votes[8] at general elections and Maori have traditionally favoured retaining links to the Crown (and hence to the Privy Council). There has also been a fairly widespread sense that New Zealand's small population, only reaching four million in 2004, is too tiny to produce enough top quality judges. Relatedly, their lordships on the Privy Council have been seen by a significant portion of the population as less likely to veer into the sort of activism that leads to uncertainty in contract cases and to second-guessing Parliament in constitutional cases (though in the last few years, with the advent of the *Human Rights Act 1998* and the ever-increasing influence of European law, that view has been collapsing). Consequently, there has never been any cross-party support in New Zealand for abolition and business groups – not to mention at least half of lawyers – have been adamantly opposed to the idea.

Against that backdrop the Helen Clark Labour government (first elected in 1999 when it defeated the Jenny Shipley National government, and then re-elected in 2002) decided to push for abolition of appeals to the Privy Council. The attorney-general, Margaret Wilson, set up a Ministerial Advisory Group[9] to consider how best, and with what, to replace the Privy Council.[10] That Advisory Group reported in April 2002 and recommended establishing a wholly new highest court to be called the Supreme Court.[11]

What matters for our purposes is this. First, there was no cross-party support for this move to abolish appeals to Privy Council and to create a new Supreme Court[12] (nor was any referendum held). In fact, the Bill doing so was passed on a party political basis by the narrowest of margins, 63 votes out of 120.[13] Second, with the exception of the existing chief justice, the other four new judges to this Supreme Court were to be chosen by the attorney-general.

The second point requires elaboration in two ways. It needs first to be realized that although the chief justice has always sat at the top of the judicial hierarchy, he has done so in a formal sense only. The chief justice is the head of the High Court, but final domestic appeals in New Zealand (before abolition) were heard by the Court of Appeal headed by a president. Certainly in Sir Robin Cooke's[14] time as president of the Court of Appeal in the 1980s and 1990s there was no question that the president was the more important and (save in a formal sense) the more senior judge. Specifying in the Supreme Court Bill (and Act) that the existing chief justice would automatically have a place on the new Court, but the president would not, was thus not as politically neutral as it might have seemed on its face. In fact, the president of the Court of Appeal at the time of abolition, President Gault, was probably the most small 'c' conservative and positivist of the senior judges, while Chief

Justice Elias was undoubtedly the most small 'l' liberal and activist judge. The attorney-general's preference for the latter type of judge was well known.

As for the four new judges to be appointed, the attorney-general did indicate in time that she would consult not just in the standard way, but also with a former governor-general, Sir Paul Reeves.[15] Nevertheless, the final decision on these four appointees would still be hers – a point she emphasized repeatedly.

The proposed abolition in New Zealand of appeals to the Privy Council did not follow the pattern set in Canada and Australia. In both those countries the Privy Council had been replaced by the then existing highest domestic court. In other words, abolition in those countries had *not* been accompanied by the need to appoint a wholly new set of judges to a new highest court. In not simply abolishing a country's highest court without cross-party support but also claiming to be able to appoint in one go all the judges to that new highest court, New Zealand was quite unique (at least in the democratic world).

Attorney-General Margaret Wilson refused to promise that she would simply elevate the four most senior existing Court of Appeal judges to the new Supreme Court, a course of action that many considered to be the only constitutionally proper one. In a nutshell, what ended up happening from the time of the Bill first being proposed until the eventual appointment of the four new judges[16] was this: the attorney-general and the government backtracked and backtracked until eventually the four most senior Court of Appeal judges were indeed appointed to the new Supreme Court. From an initial claim to complete discretion the attorney-general moved to indicating that she would in all likelihood take the advice of a special panel (comprised of the chief justice, the solicitor-general, and the former governor-general), then to saying that she would almost certainly make all appointments from the existing seven-person Court of Appeal, then to saying she would definitely make them from there, and finally to appointing the four most senior Court of Appeal judges.

Political and grassroots opposition, which had grown gradually over time, were clearly successful in forcing the attorney-general (more or less) to follow the Australian and Canadian precedents according to which the most senior existing domestic judges will comprise the court that replaces the Privy Council. To put this climbdown in perspective, recall that the government pushed ahead with abolition itself without holding a referendum on the matter and in the face of (somewhat lesser but still similar) political and grassroots opposition.

In the next and main section of this chapter I want to turn to the question of the desirability of any sort of vigorous Judicial Appointments Board,[17] relating my aversion to such boards to what happened in New Zealand. Among other things, I will argue that had there been some such sort of Judicial Appointments Board in place in New Zealand, then paradoxically it would have been easier (not harder) for the attorney-general to avoid elevating the most senior judges. In other words, her government may well have been successful in its attempt to choose all the new judges to the new highest court it was itself creating.

This argument will form part of a wider attack on indirect structures for appointing top judges.

The Problem of Memes and Self-Selection

In assessing the desirability of creating (or retaining) some sort of indirect structure for the appointment of top judges – of handing such power over to a non-emasculated Judicial Appointments Board with the power to appoint, or to nominate a short list from which selection must be made, or even to rate (unchallengably) submitted names as 'approved' or 'not approved' – context surely matters. One cannot sensibly be for or against such indirect structures in the abstract. At a minimum one needs a general sense of the relative power balance between the judiciary and the other branches of government as well as a grasp of the dominant approach to statutory and constitutional interpretation. Furthermore, one needs to know whether the system in question is a Westminster system or an American-style presidential system, and whether the jurisdiction (as in, say, Australia) has a second legislative chamber which is a genuine House of Review or whether (as in, say, Canada for sure and the United Kingdom almost as assuredly) it does not.

Let me therefore begin this final section by providing a silhouette of that context, for that is all that space allows.

The Role of Judges in the Common Law World

In the last few decades, certainly since the end of the Second World War, there has been a marked increase in the power of the judiciary vis-à-vis the legislature and executive throughout the common law world. I take this claim to be virtually self-evident but if support for it is thought necessary merely consider what Canada's entrenched Charter of Rights has done for the relative power of judges there,[18] and, likewise, what the effects of New Zealand's statutory Bill of Rights have been.[19] Then look at the Australian judiciary's successful attempt to create implied rights (in the absence of a Bill of Rights)[20] and what the American Supreme Court has done since, say, *Brown v. Board of Education.*[21] Even the judges in the United Kingdom have demonstrated less willingness to defer to the elected Parliament.[22] (And all this is without even mentioning the huge power gains of the judiciary in the development of administrative law post the Second World War.)

Personally, I do not think it likely that any legal academic could, with a straight face, argue that the power of the judiciary has not increased – and increased markedly – across the common law world.[23] Of course that increase has not been uniform. Canadian judges seem to me to be at the forefront of activism today[24] – of seeing the role of judges as one of dispensing justice and fairness without too great scruple regarding established precedents, or the actual wording in statutes, or the original intentions and understandings of those who adopted a constitutional provision – while Australian judges are the laggards.[25] But no jurisdiction has been immune.

This trend towards ever greater judicial prominence in social policy making, most notably in the area of contested rights claims,[26] in my view clearly bears on the issue of how best to appoint judges. In the pre–Second World War common law world, where judges deferred to the elected Parliament, governments and attorneys-general had little incentive to appoint on the basis of a candidate's political, social, and moral views. On major social policy issues it was clear to all that the elected legislature would have its way and that judicial candidates' social, economic, and political views could therefore generally be ignored with impunity.

At first glance, today's increasing power (and arguably small 'p' politicization) of the judiciary might seem to tell in favour of taking appointments out of the hands of politicians and giving them to some sort of non–party political Judicial Appointments Board, on grounds more or less analogous to those used to justify taking the power to draw electoral boundaries away from politicians to prevent gerrymandering.[27] But that analogy is flawed and the first glance reaction too hasty.

Where judges are much less likely to defer to the elected politicians on major social policy issues, politicians are in turn more likely to consider a candidate's views on these issues and to opt for seemingly like-minded judges, at least to some extent.[28] If this be granted, then the danger of a direct (what I will call 'status quo') appointments process is of over-politicization of the process. Candidates have to be vetted for their political views on controversial issues. Taken to the extreme, as arguably is becoming the case in the United States, special interest groups soon line up on both sides to examine nominees' views on, say, euthanasia, homosexual rights, abortion, sentencing, what have you. Such screening may even lower the calibre of those prepared to consider judicial appointment. Who knows?

Yet if the direct, status quo appointment process may turn too political, it must be remembered that danger also lurks in opting for the indirect process. The danger on this side of the balance sheet is not simply one of the potential mediocrity of indirectly appointed nominees.[29] The danger is greater than that; it is of a lack of heterogeneity among those ultimately chosen as judges, that we might end up with an insulated, self-selecting lawyerly caste – mediocre or otherwise – whose views on abortion, euthanasia, and other contentious issues are noticeably at odds with the general voting public's. Nor is this a far-fetched worry, as a moment's comparison of the general views of most – not all, but most – New Zealand lawyers (and legal academics) as opposed to the public at large on, say, homosexual rights and sentencing, reveals.

Relatedly, an indirect appointments process can make it difficult, perhaps very difficult, for a political party that has been out of power for some time, but has now won an election, to appoint a judge from among those lawyers who hold minority views (for lawyers that is, they may quite possibly be majority views among the public at large). Those on any Appointments Board may fall victim to the temptation to feel most comfortable with lawyers who share broadly similar world-views. Indeed, the notion of merit itself may come to be viewed through this prism of a candidate's general, small 'p' political views – on the proper role and influence of the jurisdiction's Bill of Rights, for example.

Concomitantly, there is the danger that a political party that has been in power for some time, and that has already made a large number of judicial appointments, may see the advantages of moving to an indirect appointments process before losing power. Having already chosen so many judges, the goalposts constituting what is and is not beyond the pale will have shifted. One more judge in the same mould will appear to many to be the apolitical choice.

My own view is that the danger of over-politicization is the lesser danger. Those who favour as vigorous a democracy as possible in these days of powerful judges have strong grounds for preferring a highest court where homogeneity[30] of background moral sentiments does *not* prevail. And this is where the analogy to non–party political constituency drawing commissions breaks down. When it comes to the task of drawing electoral boundaries, the danger of over-politicization lacks any obvious obverse and corresponding danger (were we to opt instead for the indirect structure). Set out in statute that boundaries are to be regularly shaped, to enclose roughly the same number of voters, to pay heed to topography and communities of interest, and what sort of danger is there that rivals the threat of gerrymandering?

For now, however, let us just say that the judiciary's increasing prominence in settling rights-based disputes (and so in having the last word on a variety of social policy issues) makes *any* appointments process more visible, contestable, and fraught with potential dangers. In the end it will be a matter of choosing the process with the lesser potential downside, and of course reasonable, sincere, even nice people will disagree with each other on which that is. In the meantime more context will help.

Interpretive Approaches

It is not simply that judges have become more powerful vis-à-vis the elected branches of government that bears on the question of how best to appoint them. Relevant, too, is how this happened. The adoption in all liberal democracies, save Australia, of some sort of Bill of Rights has evidently driven much of this shift in power. However, that is not the only cause. The gradual drift away from plain meaning approaches to statutory interpretation towards purposive approaches has undoubtedly given the point-of-application judiciary more room to reach the outcomes they desire in any particular case.[31] As for constitutional interpretation, beyond pockets in the United States and Australia, originalism – the view that constitutional documents should be interpreted in light of either their adopters' original intentions or the original meaning – is these days cursorily dismissed in favour of 'living tree' or 'living organism' type metaphors.[32] The upshot of that is that few baulk at the prospect of judges regularly updating the constitution under the guise of 'keep[ing] pace with civilisation,'[33] keeping abreast of changing social values, and throwing off the dead hand of the past. This is despite the fact that the very purpose of a constitution is to lock things in and make change difficult.[34]

An indirect, Judicial Appointments Board type process not only poses the risk of self-selection and perpetuation of an insulated lawyerly caste, it makes it more difficult to appoint top judges who reject today's interpretive orthodoxy. (In fact, and for similar reasons, it makes more difficult the appointment of all apostate nominees.) The reason is simple, if paradoxical. Lawyers with noticeably divergent views about interpretation will appear too political to appoint. A politician could make such an appointment and be prepared to live with the political fallout; an unelected Judicial Appointments Board would probably prefer to opt for a safer candidate. Over the long term, however, a jurisdiction benefits from dissentient views – judicial as well as generally. It is better off having to listen to the Scalias, Heydons, Dennings, Holmeses, and Brandeises.

The Scope for Political Scrutiny

I have argued that context matters in deciding whether to appoint judges directly via a status quo process or indirectly via a vigorous Judicial Appointments Board. Part of that background context surely involves acquiring a general sense of the relative power of the judiciary as well as a grasp of the dominant approach to statutory and constitutional interpretation. However, one also needs to know what scope there is for political scrutiny of judicial nominees.

The short answer is that Westminster systems offer less scope for scrutiny than an American-style presidential system. In the latter there is a good chance the Senate itself (and the Senate Judicial Committee) will *not* be controlled by the President's party. Nominees can be, and sometimes will be, rejected, and appointments can be delayed even by the minority party. In a Westminster system like New Zealand's, which is unicameral, any vetting committee of the legislature will be controlled by the government. It is difficult to see how judicial appointments could be vetted by legislators in anything remotely similar to the American process.

The same goes for bicameral Westminster systems where the upper House is not a genuine House of Review, elected and capable of blocking lower House Bills. In my view that includes Canada (with its wholly appointed upper House Senate) and the United Kingdom (with its – for now – partly hereditary and partly appointed House of Lords). In those countries, too, any legislative vetting process would be less than full-blooded (if drawn from the lower House) or thoroughly illegitimate (if drawn from the upper House).

However, this is not to assert that giving a role to Parliament – any role – is without value. Even a less than full-blooded legislative vetting committee, one the governing political party would ensure never vetoed nominees, would nevertheless afford opposition politicians an opportunity to question candidates on a wide gamut of issues, including the candidates' views on major social policy issues, on the proper balance between legislature and judiciary, or on which interpretive approaches they think most defensible.

Such a parliamentary vetting committee is clearly of some value, whatever its deficiencies where there is no genuine upper House of Review. Those attendant deficiencies are absent in Australia. There the upper House, the Senate, is a genuine House of Review and moreover one that (due to the STV voting system used and the number of senators per state) is rarely controlled by the government. Presumably Australia could, if it were desired, set up some sort of American-style vetting system. For our purposes, though, the point is that a legislative vetting committee, whether a potentially full-blooded one in Australia or a more circumscribed version as exists in Canada, the United Kingdom, or New Zealand, is distinct from a Judicial Appointments Board. At any rate, the distinction is necessary where the latter is understood as being comprised of independent experts and lay people.[35]

It is these indirect appointing boards that are the focus of this chapter and hence our discussion relates to the choice between the direct status quo appointment process and an indirect process making use of non-politicians. In the former we can expect that merit, talent, and legal ability will often be the decisive criteria of appointment, but that appointees' views on major social policy issues, on interpretive approaches, and on the amount of deference properly shown to Parliament may from time to time enter into a decision. Call these small 'p' political considerations. The first question is whether an indirect process making use of a Judicial Appointments Board can eliminate those small 'p' political considerations or whether they just get swept under the carpet and out of view. The second, concomitant question is whether, assuming they can be eliminated or at least reduced, the benefits outweigh the costs.

Back to New Zealand

My position is that in the New Zealand context the answer to the first of those questions is 'No, a Judicial Appointments Board cannot eliminate small 'p' political considerations but merely masks them.' Assuming, though, that I am wrong in that answer and such considerations can at least be reduced, I would go on to argue that the benefits in achieving that reduction are outweighed by the costs. In particular, I would say that the dangers of over-politicization are easier to combat than the dangers of self-selection, insularity, and too great homogeneity.

Let me try now to make that argument in the New Zealand context (leaving it to the reader to decide whether, in the particular situation of his or her jurisdiction, it applies there too). To begin, though, recall from above that New Zealand still follows the direct, status quo approach to filling top judicial posts. Recall too that New Zealand has a unicameral legislature whose judges have of late adopted an approach to judging that would fall well on the activist[36] side of the ledger (though not yet up to Canadian standards).[37] And finally recall the circumstances surrounding the very recent abolition of the Privy Council as New Zealand's highest court.

Earlier in this chapter I suggested that there are competing dangers involved in choosing between a direct and an indirect appointments process. The former raises the spectre of choices made on overly political grounds. The emphasis, however, must be on the 'overly' in 'overly political.' Too much politicization of the process of appointing judges has bad consequences, seen most obviously in the calibre of those willing to be nominated, in the relationship between the branches of government, and in the public's perception of judicial independence. However, it simply does not follow from this that *some* politicization of the process is also bad.

The status quo, direct system of judicial appointments evidently does have an element of the political to it. A government, having won an election, is entitled to fill vacancies as they occur. As I noted above, there will be good solid grounds – long-term *and* short-term political grounds – for appointees to be chosen largely on the basis of talent, merit, and legal ability. But there will also on occasion be grounds for the government and its appointing attorney-general to consider a nominee's sex, race, geographical origins and place of legal practice, background and, yes, his or her views on interpretive approaches, on the deference (or otherwise) due to the legislature, and on headline social issues.

To think otherwise is to assume that such ancillary considerations never enter into the calculations of Judicial Appointments Boards, that indirect appointments processes are magically apolitical (in the small 'p' sense I have been discussing). Frankly, I do not believe that Appointments Boards always disregard all of the above.[38] Even if it may be true – and I would need convincing on the point – that the indirect process would consider them less frequently than the direct, there is nevertheless the countervailing benefit in direct processes that someone and some political party can be held politically accountable for the selection. There is simply more openness and accountability (for choosing, say, another male or a former politician). Plus, a decision to opt for a less activist type of judge or for someone with unorthodox views on the proper way to interpret constitutional provisions can be deliberately and consciously taken. The government and its attorney-general will have to live with the political ramifications of such a decision, true, but I see no reason why such options should be foreclosed (or made extremely difficult, as surely they would be with an indirect process) in these days of highly powerful judiciaries.

Moreover, in the normal course of events we are talking about a situation in which vacancies arise one at a time and not all that frequently. Where governments of any particular political stripe are voted in and out fairly regularly – in other words, where there is some sort of alternating of which side is in power every five, ten, or fifteen years – then the dangers of over-politicization, if not exactly reduced, are at least counter-balanced.[39] Certainly that has been the case in New Zealand.

Accordingly, in that usual situation of one-off vacancies being filled by governments whose political outlooks change and alternate somewhat regularly, the direct, status quo appointments process has more to recommend it (to my mind) than any sort of non-emasculated Judicial Appointments Board. Undoubtedly that has remained the preponderant view in New Zealand.

However, New Zealand's abolition of appeals to the Privy Council and creation (*ab initio*) of a Supreme Court fell far outside that usual situation. Here was a possibility for one government, and one attorney-general, to appoint *all* the judges of a new highest court. Surely in that situation an indirect process of appointment would be preferable?

Actually not. Even in such a highly anomalous situation the open, direct status quo appointments process was preferable. It was preferable because everyone could see it for what it was; hence political and grassroots opposition could be mobilized against an attorney-general prepared to say (and one supposes to think) that she was entitled to choose all the new judges to a new highest court. The open, direct appointments process made open, direct opposition more feasible and palatable. And that same political and grassroots opposition to the attorney-general doing anything other than appointing the most senior existing judges ultimately succeeded. It is too easy to forget that over-politicization is vulnerable to political counter-attack; an attorney-general and government that is *legally* unconstrained in whom it appoints is *not* thereby politically (and even morally) unconstrained. At any rate, in this most unusual of appointments circumstances political pressure achieved the best results on offer, albeit only slowly and after much backtracking.

Would the same result have been reached had a non-emasculated Judicial Appointments Board been put in place to choose who would fill the vacancies on the newly created Supreme Court? I think the likelihood is against it. The attorney-general's comments at the time gave one every reason to believe that she did not wish to appoint only the most senior judges to the new court. Had such an Appointments Board been set up with the power to nominate a short list from which appointments must be made (a nominating committee in the sense described above), the attorney-general could have stayed within the constraints of such a list and still achieved her goal. More to the point, political opposition would have been blunted;[40] it would have been easier (not harder) for the attorney-general to avoid elevating the most senior judges.

Suppose, instead, that the Appointments Board had been a screening committee and been given the power to rate submitted names as 'approved' or 'not approved.' Unless the board were prepared to reject all names save those of the four most senior existing judges – and coming from an Appointments Board such an action, paradoxically, would have appeared party political – then, again, it is likely that not all the most senior judges would have been elevated. Meanwhile the attorney-general would be in a position to offload some of the responsibility for the choices onto the board. She would have political cover. Quite simply, it is easier to attack the constitutional improprieties of an attorney-general than it is to mount a case against a Judicial Appointments Board, all of whose members appear thoroughly apolitical, legally qualified, and nice.

Even the appointing commission option under which an Appointments Board had, itself, the final power of appointment of all the new judges to the new Supreme Court would have been unsatisfactory. Why, in a democracy, should we be forced to rely on the judgment of such a board? What better outcome, in the event, could it have achieved? Moreover, such Appointments Boards are just as apt to become captured by one political outlook or perspective as any other institution or group.[41]

Accordingly, I repeat my assertion from above. In New Zealand, even in the extremely unusual circumstances of seeking to appoint all the judges to a brand new highest court, indirect appointments processes are best avoided. Any sort of vigorous Judicial Appointments Board would have increased – not decreased – the chances of the attorney-general, Margaret Wilson, getting her way.

Conclusion

New Zealand's recent experience with abolishing appeals to the Privy Council and creating a new highest court requiring five judicial vacancies to be filled has not strengthened the case for indirect appointments processes. In the normal situation of one-off appointments Judicial Appointments Boards pose the risk of a 'great and the good exercise,' of producing an insulated, self-selecting lawyerly caste with too little heterogeneity of outlook, especially as regards the sort of major social policy issues at the heart of rights adjudication.

The direct, status quo appointments process, by contrast, poses the risk of over-politicization. But this chapter has argued that that risk is easier to combat than the too great homogeneity of outlook risk, and anyway is usually counter-balanced where governments are periodically removed by the voters. In addition, some politicization of the appointments process can be a good thing, not a bad thing, particularly in the context of a government deliberately setting out to appoint a judge with unorthodox views.

The perils of over-politicization appear greatest when the situation shifts from the ongoing one-off appointments scenario to the choosing of all the judges to a brand new highest court. Reaching a conclusion that may seem (at least at first glance) counter-intuitive to some, this chapter has also argued that even there the direct status quo appointments process is preferable. Whether these conclusions can be generalized beyond the New Zealand context is best left to the reader.

NOTES

* With apologies to William Shakespeare, *Macbeth,* Act I, Scene VII, lines 1–2. Thanks to Andrew Geddis, Grant Huscroft, and the editors of this book for helpful comments on, and criticisms of, an earlier version of this chapter.

1 See the *Supreme Court Act 2003,* which ended appeals to the Privy Council from 1 January 2004.

2 See F.L. Morton's chapter in this book. On this terminology a nominating committee is the more vigorous option. It recruits, selects favoured candidates, and recommends a short list or single candidate. A screening commit-

tee gets to work at a later stage and assesses the names presented to it. Kate Malleson, in her chapter of this book, uses the terminology of appointing commissions (more virile) and recommending commissions (less virile), which has slightly distinct connotations.

3 Save for the minimal requirement that the appointee have held a practising certificate as a barrister or solicitor for at least seven years. See s. 6 of the *Judicature Act 1908*. More detail on the standard appointment process will be given below.

4 See Allan, 'Turning Clark Kent into Superman.'

5 In New Zealand there is an exception for the office of chief justice. Appointments to this, the highest judicial office, are recommended to the governor-general by the prime minister.

6 In New Zealand, the office of solicitor-general is not an elected office.

7 See McGrath, 'Appointing the Judiciary,' 314–18.

8 Depending on how you determine who is and who is not a Maori, they make up somewhere between 10 and 15 per cent of the New Zealand population.

9 This Advisory Group was chaired by the solicitor-general and appointed by the attorney-general. It was comprised of the usual suspects – presidents of the Law Society and Bar Association, other lawyers' representatives, the president of the Law Commission, Maori representatives, civil servants – but no business representatives and no one obviously opposed to abolition.

10 The terms of reference did *not* include the gateway question of deciding whether it was even a good idea to abolish appeals to the Privy Council.

11 See 'Replacing the Privy Council: A Report of the Advisory Group to the Honourable Margaret Wilson, Government Printer, Wellington.

12 In addition, a sizeable majority of submissions to the Justice and Electoral Select Committee, including the Auckland District Law Society's submission, was opposed to the government's plan and in favour of retention of the Privy Council as the ultimate appellate court.

13 Voting in New Zealand since 1996 has been on the basis of a proportional voting system (MMP) requiring a party to win at least 5 per cent of the party vote or a constituency seat to be represented in Parliament. The three political parties supporting the Bill in the House of Representatives, the Labour Party, the Progressive Party, and the Greens, had received 41.3, 1.7, and 7 per cent respectively of the popular vote at the preceding election – exactly half of the votes cast.

14 Now Lord Cooke of Thorndon.

15 It needs to be said that former Governor-General Reeves was never a lawyer. He was an ex-Anglican archbishop. Whatever expertise he was thought to bring to the table it was not legal expertise.

16 Recall that the statute itself made the existing chief justice a member of the new Supreme Court.
17 Though as will become obvious, screening committees are less undesirable than nominating committees. See note 2 above for the distinction and references to other chapters in this book.
18 See, for instance, Huscroft's (forthcoming) 'The Charter, the Court, and the Limits of Progressive Interpretation'; and Allan, 'The Author Doth Protest Too Much, Methinks.'
19 I set these out in Allan, 'Turning Clark Kent into Superman'; 'Oh That I Were Made Judge in the Land'; 'Paying for the Comfort of Dogma'; and 'The Effect of a Statutory Bill of Rights Where Parliament is Sovereign,' 375.
20 See Campbell, Judicial Activism: Justice or Treason?; Craven, 'The High Court of Australia; and Allan, 'Paying for the Comfort of Dogma.'
21 347 U.S. 483 (1954).
22 See, e.g., Ekins, 'Judicial Supremacy and the Rule of Law'; and Campbell and Young, 'The Metric Martyrs and the Entrenchment Jurisprudence of Lord Justice Laws.'
23 For more on the growth of judicial power see Russell and O'Brien, eds., *Judicial Independence in the Age of Democracy*.
24 So former Canadian Chief Justice Lamer was prepared to say, 'Thank God we're here. It's not for me to criticize legislators but if they choose not to legislate, that's their doing ... People say we're activist, but we're doing our job,' *National Post*, 12 July 1999, p. 1. And current Chief Justice McLachlin has said, 'The *Charter* is still a work in progress, an unfinished project. Perhaps, it will always be.' In 'Coming of Age: Canadian Nationhood and the Charter of Rights,' speech delivered 17 April 2002 at the Association of Canadian Studies Conference, Ottawa.
25 See the articles of two current justices of the Australian High Court, Chief Justice Gleeson, 'The Future of Civil Justice: Adjudication or Dispute Resolution?'; and Justice Dyson Heydon, 'Judicial Activism and the Death of the Rule of Law.'
26 An area that can seem to be without bounds quite often.
27 In New Zealand this boundary drawing is done by a Representation Commission. See the *Electoral Act 1993*, ss. 28–45.
28 A possible or partial exception to this would be where the jurisdiction's highest court is offshore – as was the case in New Zealand before abolition of appeals to the Privy Council.
29 See Kate Malleson's chapter in this book.
30 The point about homogeneity can be buttressed by citing the natural ten-

dency for most humans to identify themselves with the institution where they work; judges working in traditional places like courts are no exception.

31 Lon Fuller's brief and enjoyable 1949 account of why this is so remains the best one available, despite the fact that he himself favoured the purposive approach. See *The Case of the Speluncean Explorers*, in particular the fictitious judgment of Keen J.

32 A prominent exception is U.S. Supreme Court Justice Antonin Scalia. See Scalia, *A Matter of Interpretation* and 'The Bill of Rights: Confirmation of Extant Freedoms or Invitation to Judicial Creation?'; see also Allan, 'Constitutional Interpretation v. Statutory Interpretation.'

33 *Ministry of Transport v. Noort*, [1992] 3 NZLR 260 at 271, per Cooke P. See also *Gosselin v. Quebec*, [2002] 4 SCR 429 at para. 79, per McLachlin C.J.

34 See the introduction by Larry Alexander and the chapter on American constitutionalism by Richard Kay in Alexander, *Constitutionalism*. Antonin Scalia of the U.S. Supreme Court attacks the notion of regular judicial updating of the constitution because it allows judges to frustrate the democratic will. He says: 'It seems to me that a sensible way of approaching this question is to ask oneself whether the framers and ratifiers of the Constitution ... would conceivably have approved a provision that read somewhat as follows: "In addition to the restrictions upon governmental power imposed by the Bill of Rights, the States and federal government shall be subject to such additional restrictions as are deemed appropriate, from time to time, by a majority of the judges of the Supreme Court." To pose that question is to answer it. And if it is absurd as an express provision, why is it not doubly absurd as a supposed implication ...?' Scalia, 'Romancing the Constitution' in *Constitutionalism in the Charter Era*, edited by G. Huscroft and I. Brodie.

35 Of course, there is also the possibility that a Judicial Appointments Board, or appointing commission, might include parliamentarians along with its other members. This is an intriguing suggestion, one floated by Peter Russell. (See Peter Russell, 'A Parliamentary Approach to Reforming the Process of Filling Vacancies on the Supreme Court of Canada,' Submission to the Canadian Standing Committee on Justice, Human Rights, Public Safety and Emergency Preparedness, 23 March 2004). The greater the weighting of legislators on such an Appointments Board, the closer it comes to a legislative vetting committee (and the more I would probably be inclined to support it).

36 In the sense given above. See the main text from note 24 above.

37 See note 19 above. See, too, by way of a brief sample, *R. v. Pora*, [2001] 2 NZLR 37 (where three of seven Court of Appeal Judges thought the doctrine of implied repeal no longer applied – and this in a country without a written constitution and with no entrenched Bill of Rights); *Moonen v. Film and Liter-*

ature Board of Review, [2002] 2 NZLR 750 (where the judges gave themselves – without statutory warrant – the power to issue declarations of inconsistency with the Bill of Rights Act); and *Buchanan v. Jennings*, [2002] 3 NZLR 145 (where the Court of Appeal rewrote, and severely restricted, the long-established parameters of parliamentary privilege).

38 It is not clear to me how one would go about testing the point in a rigorous way.

39 Canada seems to me to stand out as a jurisdiction in which that alternating of governments is a poor description of reality. Since 1963 the Liberal Party has been in power federally for all but eight or nine of the last forty-one years. Add to that the fact that in Canada – unlike the situation in Australia and in the United States – the federal government also appoints the senior judges in the provinces, and one can well understand why it might be possible to claim that Canada's present top judges are far more homogeneous in outlook than in other democracies. Kate Malleson, in her chapter, claims that there is evidence that countries 'such as Canada ... have achieved more success in diversifying their judiciaries.' In my opinion, Professor Malleson's view of what constitutes diversity is too narrow. She appears to focus on candidates' race, sex, background, and socio-economic status. On factors such as these Canada may well have a diverse judiciary. But I think it at least as important to focus on candidates' views of the proper scope, role, and ambit of the Charter, their interpretive views, and their views of the amount of deference properly shown to Parliament. On these criteria Canada's judiciary seems to me to be anything but diverse in its outlook. And my view about the sort of homogeneity and diversity that matters gets some further support from Malleson's concession that at least the sex of judges has little effect on their decision making (see Malleson, 'Gender Equality in the Judiciary').

40 At least to the extent that members of such a Judicial Appointments Board were unable to be painted as party political placemen.

41 In fact, the American Bar Association once ranked Richard Posner as no better than qualified, and possibly lower than that. See Charles Brassley, 'Judging the Judges: A Memo to the ABA,' *Christian Science Monitor*, 11 February 1988, 15, column 1: 'Senator Charles Brassley has alleged that the [ABA's] Standing Committee's political biases explain why the Committee accorded no better than a "Qualified" ranking to the eminent conservative legal scholars Frank Easterbrook, Richard Posner, and Ralph K. Winter, all of whom were confirmed nevertheless.' (Thanks to Michael Tolley for this reference and to Grant Huscroft for the recollection that it was out there somewhere). My point is that the second-order problem of 'who appoints the appointers' cannot be ignored.

6 'The judicial whisper goes around': Appointment of Judicial Officers in Australia

ELIZABETH HANDSLEY

Interest in reform of judicial appointment processes peaked in Australia in the first half of the 1990s. Debate was fuelled by a combination of circumstances and events which had visited unprecedented controversy on the judiciary. A flurry of inquiries and discussion papers did not result in any earth-shifting reforms to appointment processes or criteria, yet there has been a perceptible shift in the sociological make-up of the judiciary. Appointments of women and of people with a professional background elsewhere than at the bar have increased markedly in the last ten years. It is difficult to say whether this development has been the result of a change in perceptions as to the proper criteria for judicial selection or a natural result of the 'trickling up' of non-traditional candidates. I venture to suggest it is a combination of the two. The other major criticism of the process, its opacity and secretiveness, remains largely unaddressed.

The Australian Court System

As a federal system, Australian courts require some explanation. At the apex of the system is the High Court of Australia, constitutionally mandated as not just the arbiter of disputes under the federal constitution but the final court of appeal in all matters arising under state law. The High Court consists of seven judges who hold tenure until age seventy, barring removal by the governor-general, on an address of both Houses of Parliament, praying for such removal on grounds of proved misbehaviour or incapacity. No judge has ever been thus removed, but in the mid-1980s proceedings were commenced against one judge, who died before they could be brought to a close (see below). The constitution further provides that the judges' salaries may not be reduced while they are in office.

In the 1970s the Commonwealth Parliament established two other courts: the Federal Court of Australia and the Family Court of Australia. Both, unlike the High Court, are theoretically liable to be disestablished. However, like the High Court, their members benefit from fixed tenure and salary protection.[1]

All of the states, and both of the self-governing territories (Northern Territory and Australian Capital Territory), have supreme courts. Most states also have intermediate courts of record known as district courts (or, in Victoria, the county court). Judges of state and territory courts do not necessarily enjoy the same level of security as their federal counterparts.

The vast majority of litigation in Australia goes on in the magistrates' courts of the states and territories, formerly known as courts of petty sessions, and in New South Wales known as local courts. The magistracy will not be dealt with in detail here because this book is concerned about public perceptions of the legal system at least as much as more practical matters like the actual quality of justice, and those perceptions are focused on the superior courts. Nor do I propose to consider the vast array of specialist quasi-judicial tribunals that exist in all jurisdictions.

Appointment Processes and Criteria

Appointment processes and criteria can be dealt with briefly as very little is known about them. Judges are formally appointed by the governor or governor-general, typically acting on the advice of the attorney-general. Some prime ministers and premiers have sought a greater role than others in the decision-making process, and the decision would usually come before cabinet for approval, but generally speaking judicial appointments are in the gift of the attorney-general. He or she might or might not consult others outside the government, at one or more stages of the process (for example, in identifying potential candidates or in establishing the relative suitability of those on a short list) but these matters are completely in the discretion of the attorney-general, with one minor and one major exception.

The minor exception is that all jurisdictions have basic eligibility requirements, limiting access to the bench to judges of other courts and legal practitioners of a certain number of years standing. These provisions do little to guide the selection of candidates.

The major exception relates only to the High Court of Australia.[2] Section 6 of the *High Court of Australia Act 1979* (Cth) requires the Commonwealth attorney-general to consult the state attorneys-general before making an appointment to the High Court. It needs to be noted, however, that this is a requirement only of consultation, and nothing the state attorneys say need influence the Commonwealth attorney. Following the introduction of section 6 there was a period of broader state representation on the High Court, with two Western Australians sitting at one time for a brief period (Justice Wilson and Justice Toohey, 1987–9). However, Justice Wilson was replaced by a New South Welshman and Justice Toohey by a Queenslander, with the result that the current composition of the Court is five New South Welshmen (Chief Justice Gleeson, Justice McHugh, Justice Gummow, Justice Kirby, and Justice Heydon), one Victorian (Justice Hayne), and one Queenslander (Justice Callinan).

High Court appointments are always a matter of considerable interest to the media, and the approach of a vacancy invariably brings about a flurry of feature articles speculating on potential candidates and assessing their relative merits. No other court excites the same kind of interest. The reasons for this might include the more overtly political nature of the Court's work and its small size, which makes the numbers manageable for the kind of head-counting in which I myself have just indulged. Moreover, there is an expectation that the number will remain constant, or at least, it should stay an odd number. The political will for an increase is unlikely to be found and a decrease would embroil the government in a political controversy that would not be worth the candle.[3] It thus makes sense to speak of an 'approaching vacancy' on the High Court in a way that does not apply for other courts.

Background to the Intensification of the Debate over Appointments

General Developments in the Legal System

A key factor in the growing interest in judicial appointments in recent years has been the general increasing awareness of issues surrounding legal processes, be they the cost of litigation, delays in court lists, miscarriages of justice, or perceived inadequacies in sentencing. In common with comparable jurisdictions we have also seen a growing 'judicialization' of public policy, as parties have taken to the judiciary issues that political decision makers either would not or could not deal with. There have also been a number of high-profile private law cases of a nature to find their way into public consciousness that one would not have expected to see a generation ago. Further on the private law front, in very recent years a crisis in public liability insurance has caused, among other things, community events to be cancelled or scaled back because of the unavailability, or prohibitive cost, of insurance. This crisis has been (unjustly) blamed on greedy lawyers and spineless judges allowing damages payments to skyrocket, although the real cause is mismanagement within the insurance industry.

Meanwhile, there have been a number of official inquiries into courts and legal processes: examples include the Australian Law Reform Commission's reports on Equality Before the Law (1994)[4] and on the Civil Justice System (2000);[5] the report of the Advisory Committee to the Constitutional Commission on the Australian Judicial System (1987); the Sackville Report on Access to Justice (1994);[6] and the Attorney General's Department's Justice Statement (1995).

All of these developments inevitably feed public debate about how judges are selected and increase pressure on governments to adopt procedures and criteria that they can explain, or at least to select in such a way as to provide a bench with the kind of make-up that people are likely to consider acceptable. As we shall see, while changes in the make-up of the courts have been pursued, little has been done to explain the procedures and criteria for judicial selection.

Alleged Corruption in the 1980s

A second factor in the intensification of the debate over judicial appointments was the controversies affecting the Australian judiciary which emerged in the mid-1980s, with the prosecution of a number of judicial officers for crimes relating to the administration of justice. None raised more legal or community interest than the case of Justice Lionel Murphy of the High Court of Australia, convicted and then acquitted following a retrial of attempting to pervert the course of justice. When a solicitor friend of his honour's was being tried for fraud, Justice Murphy was alleged to have telephoned the presiding magistrate, seeking to influence the outcome of that trial. Even after the acquittal, interested parties continued to pursue Justice Murphy with a view to having him removed from the bench. There were two commissions of inquiry to determine the proper procedure for testing whether the removal provision had been satisfied, that is, whether he could be considered guilty of 'proved misbehaviour' notwithstanding his acquittal.[7] Justicy Murphy died of cancer before the second inquiry could be completed. This remains one of the most interesting chapters of Australian constitutional history, partly because such difficult questions were raised, only to be left unanswered.[8]

The Murphy affair, more than any other, led to much soul-searching about judicial appointment processes. This was partly because Murphy was a judge of the highest court in the land, thereby automatically generating national interest – as we have seen, interest in High Court appointments is high in any event. More significant, however, is the fact that Justice Murphy's appointment itself had been controversial. Immediately prior to his appointment he had been attorney-general in the Whitlam Labor government and, as a long-time senator, he had not spent enough time at the bar to develop the kind of practice that most would have expected for a High Court judge. He had not, for example, taken silk prior to entering politics. It was very easy to brand his appointment 'political' – here was a reformist government appointing one of its key ministers to a post on the court which would judge the constitutionality of so many of its plans.[9] Matters were not helped by the boldly individualistic (and generally pro–human rights) stand Justice Murphy often took in his judgments during his twelve-year tenure on the Court.[10] He sounded so different from any other High Court judge that it was difficult to forget the controversy surrounding his appointment, and when he ran into troubles in the 1980s, it did not take much prompting for his detractors to question whether he should have been appointed in the first place. Murphy's supporters countered that his appointment was no less political than that in 1964 of former Liberal (conservative) Attorney-General Sir Garfield Barwick as chief justice of the High Court. Did it make any difference that Sir Garfield had been a distinguished silk practising at the constitutional bar prior to his appointment? Was advocacy experience really all that important? Were his politics any less apparent in his judgments than Justice Murphy's were in his?

The debate quickly grew into one about what exactly we mean by 'political' and what we mean by 'merit,' providing fodder for the suggestion that it is too easy to be politically biased in what we label as 'political' and that, once we take a realistic view of judicial role – including the fact that judges make choices affected by values – we need to think about more than technical excellence in advocacy skills as the criterion of merit for judicial selection.[11] The themes of this book are presaged in an uncanny way by the events surrounding the Murphy affair: a judge from a non-traditional background and with non-traditional politics, including a commitment to legal realism, finds himself at the centre of a storm over the judicial appointment process and selection criteria, thereby advancing debate on these same matters. Too bad if Australia was not ready to ask the questions this book asks: we had no choice.

The Early 1990s: Legal Realism Entrenched, Judicial Power Expanded

A further factor in the growth of interest in judicial appointments is the awareness of the expanding role of the judiciary. Two key High Court decisions in 1992 sparked widespread debate over judicial power and, consequently, judicial appointment processes. For reasons of space, only one will be considered in detail here.[12]

The case in question, *Mabo v. Queensland (No 2)*,[13] allowed the High Court finally to put to rest the fiction of *terra nullius* that had haunted Australian legal history up until that time. Australia had always been perceived to be a 'settled' colony, meaning that there were no previous inhabitants, or at least, none with anything you could call a legal system. In international law, this meant that the law of the colonists applied automatically, rather than needing to be introduced expressly piece by piece. Thus we speak of the 'reception' of British law on the Australian continent. In *Mabo*, the High Court had to determine whether the law thus received recognized any rights of the original inhabitants over the land they occupied. The answer was yes, British law as properly understood does recognize a kind of native title. This title is very weak, and liable to be extinguished by any acts of the colonizing power that are inconsistent with its survival – for example, the grant of a freehold title to a grazier. However, four years later, even worse controversy broke out when the High Court ruled that a grant of a grazing *lease* did not necessarily extinguish native title.[14] This was the time when calls for review of the selection of High Court judges were heard most loudly.

Those calls were based not only on perceptions (not always inaccurate) about what the Court did, but also on observations about how they did it. There was some irony to this, as it is clearly arguable in a technical legal sense that the High Court did not change the law: there was no binding precedent on the question of *terra nullius*, so the 'Aladdin's cave' explanation of how the result was arrived at would have stood up as well here as it could anywhere. However, there would have been no use in trying to point this out at the time. Critics of the decision could see only the fact that we had always proceeded on the assumption that the country was *terra nullius* prior to the arrival of the British in 1788, and the High Court had moved the goalposts. The High Court had *made law* and if they were going to do that, we had to be much more careful about whom we put on the bench.

It must be hastily added that this debate was not really being fuelled by soul-searching about proper common law method. It only reached such ferocity because of systemic racism against indigenous people and fear at what the future might hold for those who had benefitted from their dispossession. We can be very sure that a High Court that suddenly discovered a hidden treasure trove of property rights for company directors would have hardly registered a murmur on the appointment reform scale. In other words, *what* the Court did was probably far more significant than *how* it did it in driving the debate.

For the calls for reform to the appointment process which emerged in the course of this debate to be coherent, they should have been aiming not to be more vigilant in appointing judges with the 'right' values, but rather trying to find judges with the 'right' judicial method, or those who will not 'make' law. However, for the reasons given above, I believe that the real aim was to find judges who will reach the *conclusions* 'we' like. All in all, it was a shallow, unsophisticated debate which did little to advance understanding of the issues surrounding judicial selection in a legally realistic world. At the same time, it put judicial appointments on the agenda in Australia.

Diversity Issues

The period 1993–4 saw the judiciary coming under intense scrutiny from an entirely different angle, though some of the themes established in debate over *Mabo* were continued. Judges in sex crime cases in a number of state courts made a rash of comments that suggested they subscribed to traditional myths about women and sexual violence. In the reporting of these comments, a picture emerged of a judiciary that was seriously out of touch with the woman-centred perspective on rape that had been gradually seeping into public (and legal) consciousness over the previous decades. In my view these events did more than anything else to put judicial selection on the agenda in Australia, making it practically impossible for governments to avoid taking a hard look at who was eligible for selection and what the criteria should be.

The myths in question are of two types: one is based on the notion that women do not know their own minds when it comes to sex, and are willing to fabricate sexual assault charges if they change their mind; the other is the victim-blaming type, based on the notion that women are not raped if they dress and behave appropriately.

The first case to hit the press (and it really was the media that led the charge here) was *R. v. Johns*, a marital rape case in the Supreme Court of South Australia.[15] In instructing the jury, Justice Bollen made two comments that seemed to be infected by the first kind of myth. He said first that it was acceptable for a husband to use a degree of 'rougher than usual handling' to persuade his wife to have intercourse with him.[16] As one might expect this provoked a storm of protest, as the comment appeared to suggest that violence within marriage is acceptable. Justice Bollen has since explained his comments in a way that avoids this meaning,[17] but the damage was done. Even more unfortunately, the controversy over 'rougher than usual handling' overshadowed the second, far more significant flaw in the instructions, namely, the telling of an inflammatory anecdote about a woman ruining a man's life, and ultimately leading him to suicide, by fabricating a sexual misconduct charge against him.[18] Justice Bollen claimed the anecdote was true but, even if this could be substantiated, its place in jury instructions is highly questionable. It not only brings into the picture traditional (and offensive) views about the propensity of women to lie about sex, but does so in a way that seems calculated to heighten prejudice against women. It is difficult to imagine any jury convicting an accused rapist when they have just heard a story about a man committing suicide over an allegation.

A subsequent case involved a return to the lying-about-sex perspective, as the Victorian judge – again in the course of sentencing – stated that women often say no to sex when they really mean yes.[19]

These events led first to a perception that the judiciary were 'out of touch with community values,' and then to observations about the male-dominated nature of the bench, as well as the fact that the vast majority of judges are from northern European backgrounds (that is, the substantial Italian and Greek communities in Australia, as well as Indigenous people, are underrepresented) and the product of exclusive private schools. There was nothing new about these observations, nor about the taking of the small step from them to questioning who should be allowed to become a judge. The notion of a 'representative' judiciary has a certain appeal, and it was inevitable that governments would come under pressure to appoint more women judges.

None of this is to say that the problems demonstrated in the 'gender bias' cases could necessarily have been avoided with a more careful selection process. Indeed, substantial debate in academic journals ensued over the potential usefulness of enhanced representation of women on the bench for addressing the issues raised in the three cases.[20] Granted, it is difficult to imagine a woman judge – *any* woman judge, from any kind of background – telling a jury that women cause men to commit suicide by telling lies about sex, or that they habitually say no to sex when they really mean yes. But this does not mean that women are immune to the victim-blaming myths. Appointing more women is not automatically a way of removing any risk that rape myths will find their way into judicial thought processes.

The 'more women' argument also overlooks the fact that some rape trials will still be presided over by male judges, and unless having female colleagues is going to disabuse them of the myths – as if by osmosis – the myths will remain as part of the overall judicial armoury unless other steps are taken. Moreover, the cases illustrate the serious need to look at whether rape law reforms have gone far enough and whether they are being fully accepted by judges. It might be that such comments, for example, are incorrect in law, as indeed Justice Bollen's were found to be, on appeal.[21] If they are correct, clearly the law needs to be reconsidered.

In other words, the solutions to the problems exposed by *R. v. Johns* and similar cases lie with judicial education and proper judicial method rather than with judicial selection.

Critical observers of the judiciary could rightly feel ambivalent about the 'gender bias' cases and the debate they prompted. As outlined above, and further developed below, the debate tapped very simplistically into motherhood concepts like representation and accountability without applying or developing any sophisticated understanding of the kind of institution the judiciary is and the place it occupies in the governmental structure. While there is something seductive about the prospect of a 'representative' judiciary that is 'in touch with modern values,' one has to wonder whether the dangers inherent in viewing the judiciary as if its functions were really no different from those of the 'political' branches are too great.

These theoretical reservations notwithstanding, one practical effect of the gender bias controversies was enormous pressure on Australian governments to redress the gender imbalance on the bench. Between 1993 and 2003 there were significant increases in the number of women on the bench of superior courts. Overall the percentage of women rose from about 7 per cent to about 18 per cent. In common with many other jurisdictions, however, the majority of the increases have been clustered at the lower ranks. For example, of forty-three appointments to the Victorian County Court since 1993, eighteen (42 per cent) have been of women; since 2000 the number is twelve out of twenty (60 per cent). There have been some senior appointments: the chief justice of Victoria is a woman, as are the chief judges of the District Courts of Queensland and Western Australia and the president of the Queensland Court of Appeal. Two out of eleven judges of appeal in New South Wales are women. However, following the 2003 retirement of Justice Gaudron, the only woman to have sat on the High Court, that court has joined the Supreme Court of Tasmania as one of only two all-male superior courts in the country.[22]

There is no one simple explanation for the increase. At the bar, various factors have allowed more women to reach the point where they can be considered on traditional grounds. More women entering law schools in the 1960s and 1970s led to more senior women barristers in the 1990s, even if the numbers are still nowhere near representative of the numbers of legally qualified women. Various developments have also made it easier for women (including barristers) to balance work and family life so that the sacrifice of family life required to succeed at the bar does not seem as great as it once was. This is not to say that it is now easy for women to succeed at the bar, but there can be no doubt that it is less difficult than it used to be. The existence of even a handful of successful women barristers removes any excuse a government might have had for not appointing women, and it has been helpful in a climate where governments have been under pressure to appoint more women.

There is anecdotal evidence of a third factor improving women's chances of gaining a judicial appointment in spite of having relatively less success at the bar: senior male lawyers, including judges, have had their consciousness raised by the spectacle of their brilliant daughters struggling to overcome the traditional barriers in the legal profession. The impact of this phenomenon on an informal system could be very great indeed. If, for example, the chief justice is traditionally consulted on prospective appointments, and he happens to have witnessed the difficulties experienced by his daughter as a woman in the profession, he is far more likely to be sympathetic to female candidates. If he is asked to put forward names, he is far more likely to notice women, and far more likely to see 'merit' in any woman's name that might cross his desk. The same holds true for lawyers, generally especially senior barristers, whose views are likely to carry weight in the process.

Attorney-General's Discussion Paper

In September 1993, the Commonwealth Attorney-General's Department published a discussion paper entitled *Judicial Appointments: Procedures and Criteria.* The introduction to the paper does not explain its precise genesis, but it appears to have been commissioned, if not authored, by the then Labour Attorney-General, Michael Lavarch. Comments were invited, to be addressed to the attorney-general's senior adviser. There was no follow-up report. The discussion paper did much, however, to advance debate on judicial appointments, especially on the criteria for appointment. The list of possible criteria has been widely quoted:

- legal skills
- personal qualities (e.g., integrity, high moral character, sympathy, patience, even temper, gender and cultural sensitivity, good manners)
- advocacy skills (noting that this term 'encompasses a variety of skills, some of which are highly relevant to judicial work and some of which might be counter-productive to judicial performance')[23]
- fair reflection of society by the judiciary
- practicality and common sense
- vision
- oral and written communication skills
- capability to uphold the rule of law and act in an independent manner
- administrative skills
- efficiency.[24]

The radical nature of this list cannot be overestimated. Up until the publication of the discussion paper, official accounts of the criteria for judicial selection tended to focus exclusively on advocacy skills, with an occasional nod in the direction of moral character. The list above is distinguished by its implicit reference to what judges actually do, and how we might judge whether it will be done well. The discussion paper is particularly useful in challenging traditional assumptions about the connection between success at the bar and the capacity to be a good judge. For one thing, it states: 'it is doubtful, based on anecdotal evidence of the inquiries that have in fact been made, that Attorneys-General have necessarily confined themselves to considering advocacy as the the only or predominant criteria.'[25] It goes on to point out the specialized nature of some judging and of many barristers' practices: 'One would expect a solicitor ... who appears on the Family Court daily to have a better understanding of the practice and procedure of that court than a barrister who does not practice in that jurisdiction. Equally one might expect a professor of constitutional law to be far more qualified to argue issues of constitutional law than a barrister who has a commercial law practice.[26] It then notes that academic lawyers might well have the same qualities of independence of mind and objectivity that have been lauded as qualifications for judicial service possessed by barristers, and that the managing partner of a large firm of solicitors would have greater managerial expertise than a barrister.[27] Finally, it advances the insightful (yet obvious) proposition that 'some skills necessary for success at the bar may be counter-productive to judicial work.'[28]

Yet the discussion paper, true to its name, makes no recommendations on criteria, on the pool of candidates, or on the process. On this last set of issues, it canvasses in some detail the possible constitution and powers of a judicial appointments commission. While there is no indication in the body of the discussion paper of a preference for one model or another – or indeed for the existence or non-existence of a body of the general kind discussed – the Introduction makes reference to the assumption that there is a need to review the current system. The aims of the reformed process are stated to include making 'the selection process visible and comprehensive and thereby increas[ing] public confidence in the judiciary.'[29] It is therefore possible to conclude that the discussion paper is, broadly speaking, in favour of introducing some kind of body to play a role, if only in advising the attorney-general. (At the Commonwealth level at least, it is arguable that it would be unconstitutional for the executive to allow itself to be dictated to by another body.)

Senate Standing Committee on Legal and Constitutional Affairs Inquiry

In the months following the gender bias cases described above, the Senate referred to its Standing Committee on Legal and Constitutional Affairs for inquiry and report the issue of Gender Bias and the Judiciary. The report from the inquiry was published in May 1994.

The committee took written submissions from the public and held public hearings in Melbourne, Adelaide, and Perth. The views expressed in submissions and evidence fell roughly into two camps: those which defended the courts and the judges,[30] and those which expressed concern that the cases were evidence of a deeper problem within the legal system. The committee clearly sided with the second camp.

Among the committee's recommendations were four relating to the selection of judges:

- that criteria should be established and made publicly available to assist in evaluating the suitability of candidates for judicial appointment;
- that the attorney-general for the Commonwealth should establish a committee to advise him or her on prospective appointees to the Commonwealth judiciary. That committee should include representatives of the judiciary, the legal profession, and the non-legal community;
- that the attorney-general for the Commonwealth should urge the attorney-generals [*sic*] of the states and territories to establish a similar advisory committee in their respective jurisdictions;[31]
- that all jurisdictions, while continuing to select judges on the basis of merit, should strive to increase the diversity of appointees to judicial office.[32]

In other words, the committee saw a need for reform of practice relating to both the criteria and the procedure for selection. The vague wording of the fourth recommendation is explicable given the real controversy over the matter of affirmative action. Even contributors who were generally sympathetic to the need to address gender bias were very wary of any suggestion of tokenism.[33] The recommendation should be understood against its backdrop of a lengthy discussion of the 'pool' of candidates; it is submitted that the committee really meant that the pool should be widened. For example, in the penultimate paragraph previous to the recommendation, the committee said: 'It is also proper that candidates for judicial appointment should be drawn from as wide a pool as practicable. Knowledge of the law, knowledge of the rules of evidence, and a familiarity with all aspects of the conduct of litigation are clearly relevant to judicial appointment. An advocacy practice is but one means by which these attributes can be gained. Many other relevant skills are not necessarily related to practise [*sic*] as an advocate at all.'[34] It is worth noting the way in which the committee, in the last sentence quoted, linked the question of widening the pool with that of revising the criteria, if only by implication.

Objections to the Process: Secretiveness and Opacity

A woman magistrate (now judge) giving evidence before the Senate Standing Committee on Legal and Constitutional Affairs Inquiry into Gender Bias and the Judiciary summarized in evocative terms the effect of the current selection process on perceptions of the judiciary: 'The judicial whisper goes around and someone ends up miraculously on the bench ... Because there is all this mystique, as if it is somehow by magic that it happens, there is a perception – that may or may not be right in certain cases – that it depends on who you know; that it is not based on any objective criteria; and that we do not know what we are trying to achieve when we appoint people.'[35] It is little short of astonishing that the judiciary has survived for so long as an institution whose members are selected behind a veil of secrecy.[36] In recent years, practically every other public institution has been subjected to an unprecedented level of accountability, and in the age of equal opportunity we find firmly entrenched in the public mind belief in the need for clear, fair processes for the bestowal of any kind of benefit – especially one funded by the public purse.

Such processes have a number of functions. First, they ensure a higher level of fairness to candidates. Second, if properly designed they serve the goal of merit, maximizing the likelihood that the best person for the job will be selected. Third, they allow outsiders to feel relatively confident in the integrity and competence of the institution. We might therefore conclude that the opaque and secretive methods of judicial selection still used in Australia are relatively unfair to candidates, relatively ineffective in ensuring merit-based appointments, and relatively uninspiring of public confidence. How have they survived?

First, in an important sense there is no-one to whom to *be* fair because there is as yet no notion of a 'candidate' for judicial office. You do not put yourself forward for it; rather, the quaint tradition remains of thinking of appointment as a 'tap on the shoulder.' At the same time, there is a collegiate sense among senior barristers of entitlement to be considered for appointment – and, in principle, they are so considered. A sense of 'unfairness' towards those people might well emerge if anything were to happen to 'shift the goalposts,' excluding some of them or making them compete in a more open and accountable way.

On the question of quality assurance, it is difficult to trace any dissatisfaction with the judiciary back to the question of judicial selection. To the extent that commentators have done so, it has generally been to argue that the pool of candidates should be widened, and/or that the criteria need to be better adapted to the actual job of a judge in the particular jurisdiction. One rarely sees the suggestion that judicial shortcomings could be remedied by an improvement in selection *processes.* Moreover, as noted above, the job tends to be defined by the kinds of people who have done it. It would thus take quite a leap of the imagination to say that judging could be done better by other kinds of people. There is an even greater leap involved in saying that these other kinds of people could be found by adopting different processes.

The third issue associated with selection process is confidence in the institution. Confidence in Australian courts has undoubtedly been damaged by events that have led people to question selection processes, and possibly by the questioning process itself. But this damage should not be overstated. People are still turning to courts to settle their disputes, and still apparently happy to rely on the courts to protect their liberties and interests.[37] In the absence of proper social science research into public perceptions of the courts and the basis for such confidence as the courts enjoy, it is impossible to say more than that, impressionistically, the courts enjoy greater confidence than is warranted based on the way their personnel are selected.

The primary means mooted in Australia for making the judicial selection process more transparent has been a commission of some sort.[38] Others have been the introduction of advertising for judicial posts, or alternatively of calls for expressions of interest.[39] Issues raised by the notion of a judicial appointments commission include its composition (in particular, whether there should be any lay members and whether these should be in a majority) and its role in the process (whether it should be proactive in seeking out candidates or reactive in commenting on government short list; the degree of bindingness of its findings). As mentioned previously, it would be unconstitutional, at the federal level at least, for the government to delegate the whole selection process to a commission. However, there could be no objection to the establishment of a body to advise the government on its short list or even to create the short list itself.

The establishment of a judicial appointments commission in any Australian jurisdiction is highly unlikely, unless there is another wave of controversies sufficient to convince a government that there is political capital to be made. Even then, the government is much more likely to focus on training, discipline, and removal than on appointments. This is precisely what we saw in New South Wales in the late 1980s, following a wave of judicial corruption cases (including Justice Murphy's): the New South Wales Judicial Commission's remit extends to training and the processing of complaints against judicial officers, but not to any part of the selection process.[40] In those days, even to go that far appeared to be a radical step. Today, there would be little objection in any other jurisdiction to the establishment of an equivalent body, but relinquishing any part of the power over appointments would be too great a blow to the government's own self-interest to be seriously imaginable.

This is not to say that any particular government habitually uses the appointment power for venal or Machiavellian purposes. However little we might know of what goes on, there is no ground on which to argue that judicial appointments are, on the whole, used as an instrument for corrupt purposes. We can also observe that in the last ten years the power has been used in such a way as to respond to community concerns about such matters as gender imbalance. In 1993, for example, when Chief Justice David Malcolm of Western Australia was giving evidence before the Senate Standing Committee on Legal and Constitutional Affairs, he lamented that there was no woman on the fifteen-member Supreme Court of that state, and that only two out of eighteen District Court judges were women.[41] Today, three out of sixteen Supreme Court judges and six out of twenty-two District Court judges are women. In the latter courts, this has been achieved as a result of five out of eleven appointments being of women. Broadly similar patterns can be observed in all other jurisdictions except the High Court and Tasmania. These patterns cannot be the result of a simple 'trickle-up' effect, but must owe at least something to the political will to find suitable women appointments. It must be concluded that the appointments power is used to respond to the demands of public opinion, at least some of the time. In other words, governments act as if they are democratically accountable for the exercise of the power, even if in some strict sense they are not.

However, other, less worthy, ends to which the power can be applied need no introduction. Judicial appointments can repay political favours; they can also remove political enemies. In some jurisdictions they can be used to transplant a political program into the judicial branch and influence the future direction of common and especially constitutional law (a course fraught with risk, but not unknown). No government would voluntarily relinquish even part of so potentially useful a power, as long as the same political capital can be made out of other judicial reforms such as training and complaints processing.

No doubt most if not all governments would also argue that explaining in a publicly acceptable way how one candidate was chosen over others would be no easy matter. Even to divulge the identity of the candidates, it might be argued, would be invidious and discourage qualified people from allowing themselves to be considered. There may be some basis for these objections, but a suitable process can be designed to respond to them.

Objections to the Criteria: Perspectives on 'Fair Reflection'

Whatever justification there might be for governments not divulging their processes of selecting among qualified candidates, there can be no justification for failure to divulge, at an abstract level, the criteria that govern the selection process. Defenders of the status quo reveal a dismaying tendency to attack proponents of change for wanting to dilute 'merit' but rarely show any evidence of having properly reflected on whether the traditionally assumed content of merit really describes what makes a good judge. On one level this is not surprising. Different people have different views even of what the job of a judge is, and there will be correspondingly different views on who is most likely to do that job well. However, it would be no bad thing if participants in the debate were more articulate about these matters, and if debate were conducted at the level of different models of judicial method.[42] Instead, what we have is repeated instances of an assumption that the job of judging is best done by the kinds of people who have always done it.

Following the gender bias controversy described above, debate inevitably came around to the question of the pool of candidates, as it did in both the Senate Standing Committee's report and the attorney-general's discussion paper. In Australia as elsewhere, the bar is not a family-friendly workplace. Very few women have been willing and able to make the sacrifices of family life necessary to succeed at the bar, and it is thus not surprising to find that an appointments process that looks only to the senior bar yields very few women judges. It was only a matter of time before the suggestion was made that there were very good candidates for judicial office in government, in law firms, and in academia – all environments with a higher representation of women. At their most sophisticated, these suggestions make reference to the difference between a barrister's work and that of a judge and to the broadly accepted proposition that judges make value-laden choices, especially in the higher courts. A modern view of what judges do, and should do, brings into question the traditional assumption that forensic skill is the key qualification for a judicial post. In short, these debates lead into a questioning of the content of merit, when it comes to the selection of judges.

It was inevitable that public debate about judicial selection, if it was to emerge at all, would grow out of concrete instances of judging that sections of the public considered unacceptable. The alternative genesis – that debate would be driven by a more abstract questioning of the proper judicial role and the qualities needed to perform that role well – is a pleasant dream, but one unlikely to be realized, especially in a country such as Australia. This state of affairs is unfortunate, because principled arguments about the judicial role and desirable qualities in a judge can easily be confused with purposive arguments from special interests engaging with specific cases. Both types of arguments have the same end-point: the criteria need to be changed and the pool needs to be widened. The difference is that principled arguments tend to place emphasis on the criteria (thus making it acceptable to widen the pool), whereas tendentious ones tend to emphasize the pool (with widening justified in an ex post facto way by the acceptability of the new criteria). In other words, one might think that the criteria should be changed in order to acquire judges better suited to the tasks they will be required to perform, or that they should be changed in order to achieve a more representative bench. The latter argument is easy to dismiss because it looks very much like changing merit for the sake of some goal unrelated to merit. The former is more sound: its starting point is the existing flaws in merit.

These observations may seem of little interest considering that the number of women on the bench has increased considerably in the last ten years. That increase appears to have been influenced in no small way by the events of 1993 and the subsequent calls for a more representative judiciary. However, an understanding of these matters and the different concepts involved is crucial to a critical understanding of what is going on with judicial appointments in Australia. If the changes in government practice have been informed by a desire to create a more representative judiciary – specifically, one with more women – this does not necessarily mean that the criteria have been changed. We could only be confident that the criteria have changed if governments officially said so – as no government has done – and analysis revealed that they were motivated by a desire to improve the criteria – and I maintain it does not. Changes in government practice with respect to judicial appointments appear to be motivated by knee-jerk calls for a 'representative' judiciary which they have been able to create without changing selection criteria, or even broadening the pool in a significant way. Governments have been able to achieve growth in the numbers of women judges (in many cases, from *none* to *some*) simply by picking off the small number of successful women lawyers as they have risen to the top. There have been a few 'creative' or 'courageous' appointments,[43] but in the absence of more information about the process that led to them, there is no reason to believe that they were informed by anything more systematic than a desire to appoint a woman (or *that* woman). None of this is to suggest that these were bad appointments – they simply do nothing to disabuse us of the notion that there has been minimal if any change to the way judges are selected. Decisions are merely responding to a new set of public opinion concerns.

There is much substance to the notion that a representative judiciary is not a worthy policy goal. Some of the more extreme versions of the argument can be dismissed. These are along the lines of 'An ideal legal profession should obviously be composed of 5% convicted criminals, 5% drug addicts, 5% dole bludgers and 30% cretins – just like the rest of the community.'[44] Arguments in favour of a representative judiciary are not so preposterous, they merely overlook the true nature and function of the institution. That is, they overlook the fact that the judiciary is designed to operate independently of any particular viewpoint. Thus a Victorian QC in 1993 criticized 'those who promote causes' for complaining 'that supporters of the cause are not represented on the judiciary, treating it as if it should be a representative body like a legislature.'[45]

Many proponents of a representative judiciary may not mean to refer to representation in this sense; they may mean it in a statistical sense, in the sense we mean when we say, for example, that the number of women judges is not representative of the number of women lawyers, or women citizens. 'Fair reflection' better captures the concern with perceptions of the judiciary as an institution, as distinct from concern with how individual judges carry out their functions. This alternative expression avoids any suggestion that judges do or should represent particular sections of society, reminding us instead of the danger of loss of confidence in the judicial institution if appointments to it appear to be affected by systemic bias *against* particular groups. I suggest that this is really what happened in Australia in the wake of the gender bias cases, and it is this loss of confidence to which governments have sought to respond by appointing more women. It is a pity, however, that the developments in appointments practice will forever be seen as tied to particular debacles in judging, as if the appointment of women could or should change the way that judging is done – particularly if women are seen as likely to judge differently from men because they 'represent' a female point of view. Not only is it problematic to claim that women are inherently likely to have handled such cases differently, it is problematic to suggest – even obliquely – that it would have been right and proper for them to be overtly guided by a sense of representing the interests of their gender.[46]

The attorney-general's discussion paper includes 'fair reflection' as one of many criteria for selection of judges: 'It is a reasonable aim of an appointment process, and consistent with merit principles, that the process can seek to ensure that all sections of society (particularly women, Aboriginal and Torres Strait Islanders, and members of different ethnic groups) are not unfairly under-represented in the judiciary.'[47] It is impossible to find fault with this statement, but worth noting the phrase 'not unfairly under-represented' as a way of emphasizing that the meaning intended is the statistical one, not the democratic one.

Concluding Observations

Judicial appointments in Australia are often said to be 'in the gift of' the executive government. This is an interesting expression, and one rarely heard in any other context. It prompts us to ask whether judicial appointments are essentially employment decisions based on merit, or if they are more like patronage. If we want to believe that they lie at the former end of the spectrum, we have to take it on faith. Not only do we not know what the criteria of 'merit' are, we do not know who is being considered, or by whom.

One telling point about the debate over judicial appointments is that hardly anyone, at any stage, has recognized that it might make sense to have different criteria for appointment to different types of courts, depending on the type of work they do.[48] The common refrain that it is essential to know how a trial works simply makes no sense when it comes to appointment to a court of appeal. Similarly, judges appointed to a court that never uses juries do not need the same skills as those appointed to one that uses them frequently. We would expect to see these distinctions drawn, if debate were being driven by concern about who can do the job best, rather than by some vague notion of who is *entitled* to the very substantial benefit that a position on the bench represents. For this reason, I argue that judicial appointments are conceived in Australia, if only implicitly, more at the patronage end of the spectrum.

In 1996, Livingston Armytage commented that there were 'indications that reform of judicial selection may be imminent in Australia.'[49] Such hopes have proven to be forlorn: there has been no 'reform' as commonly understood, but rather ad hoc and informal developments, prompted more by crisis and controversy than by dispassionate analysis of the demands made on a modern judiciary. In keeping with the age-old tradition of judicial appointments in Westminster-based governmental systems, any changes have taken place in the breast of the individuals involved rather than in public fora. There is no hard evidence that the changes in the make-up of the bench – in particular the increased number of women over the last ten years – are the result of any revision of the criteria or improvements in the process rather than a politically driven urge to cater to public demands for a more 'representative' judiciary. Nor should the trickle-up process be overlooked: 'trickle' is the right expression, but those few women who have managed to make it into the traditional pool for appointments do not appear to have had any difficulty in making it onto the bench.

NOTES

1 For further detail on the structure of the Australian judiciary, see Williams, 'Judicial Independence in Australia,' 174.
2 On High Court appointments generally, see Nicholson, 'Appointing High Court Judges.'
3 The non-appointment of a judge to fill a vacancy in the 1930s 'caused friction.' McQueen, 'The High Court of Australia,' 46.
4 Australian Law Reform Commission, *Equality Before the Law.*
5 Australian Law Reform Commission, *Managing Justice.*
6 Access to Justice Advisory Committee, *Access to Justice.*
7 Commonwealth of Australia, *Report to the Senate, August 1984*; Commonwealth of Australia, *Report to the Senate*; October 1984.
8 See generally Lindell, 'The Murphy Affair in Retrospect.'
9 For a list of cases involving challenges to Whitlam-era legislation, see Blackshield, 'Judges and the Court System,' 121.
10 See, e.g., *SGIC v. Trigwell* (1979), 142 CLR 617, 642; *Dugan v. Mirror Newspapers* (1978), 142 CLR 583, 606.
11 For the more traditional view see Gibbs, 'The Appointment and Removal of Judges,' 144.
12 The second case, *Australian Capital Television Pty Ltd v. Commonwealth* (No 2)

(1992), 177 CLR 106, involved the court in implying a right to freedom of expression into the Commonwealth constitution. It raised debate in legal and academic circles about proper judicial role, and this debate led naturally to a revisiting of views on appointment mechanisms and criteria.

13 *Mabo v. Queensland (No 2)* (1992), 175 CLR 1.

14 *Wik Peoples v. Queensland* (1996), 187 CLR 1.

15 Unreported, 26 August 1992, Bollen J.; discussed and quoted in Senate Standing Committee on Legal and Constitutional Affairs, *Gender Bias and the Judiciary* ('Gender Bias Report'), 1–6. The press picked up the story when the case came up on appeal.

16 See Gender Bias Report, 3.

17 Gender Bias Report, 5 ('I did not have "violence" as properly understood in mind ... I had in mind vigorous hugging or squeezing and pinching. I was directing the jury that if such acts acceptable to, and done in a way acceptable to the wife, did produce a changing of the mind then there was consent').

18 Gender Bias Report, 2.

19 *R. v. Davie* (unreported), Morwell County Court, Bland J., 15 April 1993; discussed in Gender Bias Report, 8–9 ('And often, despite the criticism that has been directed at judges lately about violence and women, men acting violently to women during sexual intercourse, it does happen to the common experience of those who have been in the law as long as I have, anyway, that "No" often subsequently means "Yes"').

20 See, e.g., Cooney, 'Gender and Judicial Selection'; Nicholson, 'Appointing High Court Judges'; Meagher, 'Appointment of Judges'; Harris, 'Appointments to the Bench'; Mason, 'The State of the Judicature,' 131–2; Purvis, 'Judiciary and Accountability'; O'Sullivan, 'Gender and Judicial Appointment.'

21 *Question of Law Reserved on Acquittal Pursuant to Section 351(1A) Criminal Law Consolidation Act (No 1 of 1993)*, Court of Criminal Appeal, 20 April 1993.

22 Only two of the seven Tasmanian Supreme Court judges have been appointed in the last ten years. The issue of gender and High Court appointments has recently been analysed in depth in Davis and Williams, 'Reform of the Judicial Appointments Process.'

23 Commonwealth of Australia Discussion Paper, *Judicial Appointments* [Commonwealth Discussion Paper] 6. For commentary, see Solomon, 'The Courts and Accountability.'

24 Commonwealth Discussion Paper, 5–10. An additional criterion suggested more recently by the chief justice of the High Court is 'the capacity to anal-

yse voluminous information, and to recognise and discard junk.' Gleeson, 'A Changing Judiciary,' 553.

25 Commonwealth Discussion Paper, 17.
26 Ibid., 18.
27 Ibid.
28 Ibid., 19. The current chief justice of the High Court made a similar point as early as 1979. Gleeson, 'Judging the Judges,' 340.
29 Commonwealth Discussion Paper, 4.
30 For example, Mr K. Gee QC submitted that the judges had been the victims of prejudice. Gender Bias Report (1994), 69.
31 Gender Bias Report (1994), 91.
32 Ibid., 105.
33 For example, Chief Justice David Malcolm of Western Australia argued that attempts to increase the representation of women should be limited to the application of a 'tie-breaking' device. Gender Bias Report, 105.
34 Gender Bias Report, 105.
35 Ibid., 77 (quoting Chief Magistrate [now Justice] Sally Brown).
36 See Armytage, *Educating Judges*, 61 ('the lack of accountability ... discloses an extraordinary gap within the framework of civic safeguards').
37 Mason, 'The State of the Judicature,' 131 (citing J.F. Fletcher and B. Galligan, *The Australian Rights Project* (a Presentation to the Law Foundation of New South Wales, 23 July 1993)).
38 See Harris, 'Appointments to the Bench.'
39 Proposals for reform are summarized in Murray and Maher, 'Judging the Judges.'
40 See *Judicial Officers Act 1987* (NSW).
41 Gender Bias Report, 92.
42 See Armytage, *Educating Judges*, 57 ('explicit criteria' should be 'debated and agreed at a level of principle').
43 See Hamilton, 'Criteria for Judicial Appointment and "Merit."'
44 See Armytage, *Educating Judges*, 57 (quoting R.P. Meagher from A. Stevens, 'Roddy Meagher: A Law unto Himself,' *Sydney Morning Herald*, 5 December 1992).
45 Meagher, 'Appointment of Judges,' 198. See also Harris, 'Appointments to the Bench,' 196; Mason, 'The State of the Judicature,' 131; Shaw, 'On the Appointment of Judges,' 462.
46 See Malleson, 'Gender Equality in the Judiciary,' 1–24.
47 Commonwealth Discussion Paper, 6.
48 An exception is Mason, 'Aspects of Judicial Role,' 161.
49 Armytage, *Educating Judges*, 56.

7 Merit Selection and Diversity in the Dutch Judiciary

LENY E. DE GROOT-VAN LEEUWEN

Introduction

The aim of this chapter is twofold. First, I want to explain the evolution of the Dutch judicial appointments system over time, focusing on the resulting composition of the judiciary in terms of gender, political diversity, and class origin. Second, I intend to analyse what may be called the merit/diversity paradox.

The merit/diversity paradox results from the interaction between micro-level selection criteria (in this case, the criteria of individual merit) and macro-level *desiderata*. Of the latter, diversity is most often mentioned, reflecting a belief that the judiciary as a whole should somehow mirror the diversity of society.[1] The dimensions of diversity that are considered important may vary over time and place; in a period of racial tension, for example, ethnic diversity will be considered to be highly relevant. The paradox is that strictly meritocratic selection of individuals may result in an undesired macro-level composition of the bench. For example, if women (as they do) tend to have superior results on the university exams and the psychological selection tests, the composition of the judiciary, if strictly meritocratic, might drift towards an overwhelming female majority.

In order to understand the evolution of the Dutch judicial appointments process it is necessary to appreciate a few fundamental characteristics of Dutch society and its legal system.

Dutch society is a calm society. The Netherlands is one of the oldest and most stable modern nation states.[2] In the nineteenth century the German poet Heinrich Heine remarked that if the end of the world were announced he would go to Holland because everything happens fifty years later there. We may assume that Dutch society has become somewhat more dynamic in more recent years but systemic change is still highly incremental. Sessions of the Second Chamber of Parliament are usually very orderly and unemotional. No single party has ever had an overall majority in Parliament, and thus a coalition parliament is inevitable.[3] For decades the Christian Democrats played a pivotal role in Dutch politics. With the exception of the Occupation years (1940–5) and the years from 1994 to 2002, they were represented in every government after the First World War. Sometimes they formed coalitions with the Social Democrats, sometimes with the Conservative Liberals. This high degree of stability and slow pace of change have a significant impact on the development of the judicial appointments process.

Dutch society is also a consensus society.[4] Many institutions have historically developed through the successful appeasement of tensions between Protestantism and Catholicism. Dutch culture is a culture of bridging contradictions, and there are many mechanisms for diffusing conflict and drawing extremes into the mainstream. In the words of the historian Van der Horst, Dutch society is non-exclusivist; everybody is taken on board, albeit under the silent condition that everybody is supposed to be reasonable, willing to participate in the open discussions that lead to rational consensus.[5] This culture of consensus is unquestioned. In Dutch culture, outspoken criticism and opinions are hidden behind closed doors.

Dutch legal culture is no exception to this model. Dissenting opinions between judges are never published and judges are obliged to maintain secrecy on their deliberations. In order to reach a common decision (or verdict) judges need to negotiate and compromise.[6] Moreover, the judiciary plays a limited political role in society. Although the Dutch legal system is based on a written constitution, according to the Dutch version of the *trias politica* doctrine, no court has the power to strike down legislation as unconstitutional.[7] Judges are not elected and there are no political associations within the judiciary. In the Dutch version of the doctrine of the separation of powers conflict models are abhorred; thus in recent publications on the subject we find titles such as 'Cooperating Powers,' 'Constitutional Partners,' and 'Balancing Powers.'[8] The decision-making process of the private law division of the Supreme Court (studied by Bruinsma)[9] tends to be informal, pragmatic, and consensus-oriented. For every case, for instance, only a few of the justices, selected by a random scheme have official voting power; however, all of the justices participate in the discussions and may propose amendments to drafts, considering themselves as members of the team.

Substantively, judges consider themselves bound by precedents, but when they do reconsider a precedent, they frankly admit that the earlier solution did not work and/or was heavily critiqued in the legal periodicals. The working style is based on getting the job done, without polarization or introduction of extra-judicial motives. Occasionally, judges tend towards activism in the *trias politica*, such as when trying to counterbalance parliamentary decisions. Arguments in such cases are never partisan however, and the court is largely non-activist in politically sensitive cases.

Finally, explicit selection criteria for occupations and professions are fully meritocratic in the Netherlands.

Many of these characteristics described above are visible in the appointment system, the selection and work of the Supreme Court judges. In the next section I will use the Supreme Court as a case study before discussing the general aspects of the Dutch system.

The Supreme Court[10]

The highest court of law, the Supreme Court of the Netherlands (Hoge Raad der Nederlanden), was founded in 1838. It has a general jurisdiction covering private law, criminal law, and tax law. It reviews questions of law only and does not retry cases on the facts. As previously stated, the court does not exercise constitutional review. Cases are heard by three or five justices, depending on the complexity and the importance of the case.

The appointment system of the Supreme Court is different from that of the other courts in the Netherlands. The procedure is based on the 1814 constitution and the 1827 *Act on Judicial Organisation* and has remained almost unchanged from the nineteenth century. When a vacancy arises, the court itself draws up a list of six candidates. These are submitted to the Lower House of Parliament (the Second Chamber, Tweede Kamer der Staten-Generaal), which virtually automatically nominates the first three names on the list to the Crown (the executive in practice).[11] The Crown then chooses from the three names on the list.

After 1948, all justices appointed to the Supreme Court were first on both lists. De facto, therefore, the system is one of co-option; the first candidate of the Supreme Court is always appointed. Numbers two through six on the long list consist of lawyers who will reach the first place on the list at a future vacancy, depending on the expertise required at that time. One interesting ripple in this quiet pond was that in 1975 the Lower House decided to move a female candidate from fifth place on the list to second. This was meant as a signal to put more women on the list; because the female candidate was placed second it did not affect the actual appointment.

Things have not always been this way. During the nineteenth century, the Lower House interfered with many of the appointments. According to van Koppen and Ten Kate this interference should not be interpreted as politically driven.[12] Most members of Parliament during that time were lawyers, and the political High Court judges were drawn from the same very small social stratum; the struggles were in fact for influence between elite (noble and patrician) families.

Considerations of diversity have long been visible in Supreme Court appointments. The constitution of 1814 provided that these justices should as far as possible be chosen from 'all provinces and landscapes.' This diversity criterion was last referred to in 1902, when the court president declared that it had tried to add a Friesian member by putting him first on the list. Considerations of religious diversity have had a longer history. Although not on official selection criterion, the Supreme Court had 'Catholic seats,' the number of which rose to four in 1913. Until 1968, Catholic judges were appointed when a 'Catholic seat' became vacant.

Members of the Supreme Court between 1838 and 1917 were either noble (17 per cent) or patrician (53 per cent). Becoming a lawyer was a traditional occupational choice for men from these families. Since most members of Parliament were lawyers, until 1917 about 80 per cent of the Dutch Parliament, and of course all members of the judiciary, were lawyers and were recruited from a very small social stratum, while many of the judges were recruited from a few upper-class families. As a consequence the political and judicial elite was relatively small.

Courts and Numbers of Judges and Public Prosecutors

The organizational structure of the Dutch judiciary is regulated in the *The Act on the Judicial Organisation* (Wet op de Rechterlijke Organisatie). This Act dates from 1827 and was mainly based on French law. The court system is organized in four layers. Table 7.1 shows the organizational structure and the number of Dutch courts from 1813 onwards.

TABLE 7.1
Number of courts since 1813

Court	1813	1838	1841	1876	1933	2002
Supreme Court	1	1	1	1	1	1
Courts of appeal	7	9	11	5	5	5
District courts	34	34	34	23	19	19
Subdistrict courts	220	150	150	106	62	–

TABLE 7.2
Number of judges and public prosecutors, 1951–2000

	1951	1974	1986	1995	2000
Judges	317	494	694	1223	1546
Public prosecutors	94	152	238	391	450
Total	411	646	932	1614	1996

Only recently has the administrative law system been integrated into the ordinary courts, and it still has its own courts at the top dealing with areas such as spatial planning and environmental law and social security law. These administrative law courts do not appear in table 7.1; the disappearance of the subdistrict courts is due to their integration into the district courts in 2002.

The total judiciary in the Netherlands, members of the Supreme Court, the five courts of appeal, and the nineteen district courts, consists of approximately 1600 judges and about 450 public prosecutors. From 1951 onwards the number of Dutch judges and public prosecutors rose more sharply than did the Dutch population as a whole over the same period. As a fraction of the 16 million population, the Dutch judiciary is still one of the smallest in the Western countries, however.

The Judicial Appointment Process for Judges Other than the Supreme Court

In the Netherlands all cases are tried by professional judges. Juries or lay-assessors are unknown. Apart from the requirements of Dutch citizenship and the absence of certain incompatibilities, the only formal qualification currently required of judicial candidates and candidates for public prosecutors is that they must have a university degree in law.[13]

A mixed recruitment system exists combining the traditional continental career judiciary with the common law, Anglo-American system of appointment from the law profession. In one route young university graduates are selected to undergo six years of judicial training ('raio-opleiding'). Before 1957 this category of so-called insiders was solely trained at a court in the unpaid position of clerk or at the office of the public prosecutor.[14] The other recruitment route is to enter the ranks of the judiciary after at least six years' experience in some other legal post, for example, in a law firm or at the Ministry of Justice. The boundary between insiders and outsiders is not very firm. All insiders have been trainees at some 'outside' place, such as a law firm, as a part of their six-year training period. Many outsiders, on the other hand, have already accumulated some experience as a voluntary judge before entry in the profession.

Judges are appointed for life by the Crown. No minimum age is formally required, and although initially no retirement age was set, today justices of the Supreme Court, as other judges, must retire at the age of seventy. Since judges are not elected in the Netherlands there is no direct role for citizens in the selection of the judiciary.[15] Judicial appointments are prepared by a selection committee which is divided into two parts; one dealing with the young lawyers of the first route and the other with the experienced lawyers who took the second route. The committee commends appointments to the minister of justice, who makes the formal selection decision.

The selection procedure is basically the same for both recruitment routes, comprising a psychological test, a psychological assessment, letters of recommendation, and two or more interviews by a small delegation (different for each interview) from the selection committee. The interviews are largely 'behaviour-oriented,' because non-behavioural aspects such as intellectual capacities are covered by the test and the assessment. Selection criteria for the recruitment of young lawyers are analytical capacity, juridical insight, resoluteness, stress resistance, communicative capacity, and balanced judgment. For the experienced lawyers the criteria are largely the same, but 'orientation towards co-operation' is added.

In 2004 the selection committee as a whole consisted of seventy-one members, dominated by sixty-four lawyers, of whom forty-five (63 per cent) were magistrates (including public prosecutors), all of them of high and middle rank. Of the other occupations, twelve (17 per cent) of the committee members were high-ranking government and university

TABLE 7.3
Number of members of the judiciary with a noble title

Year	Number
1950	40
1966	26
1970	22
1974	21
1979	19
1986	18
2000	13

Sources: Naamlijsten leden rechterlijke macht 1951, 1974, 1979, 1986 en 2000; Schenk, 1970.[17]

personnel, another twelve were solicitors and businessmen, and two were middle-ranking university personnel. Strikingly, the latter two are the only members of the committee from first- or second-generation immigrants. Women comprised 25 per cent of the committee and six members (8 per cent) belonged to the nobility. Members of the committee are recruited by co-option, usually on the initiative of the committee chairman. Proposals for new members are first brought before the committee in order to see if there are any objections.

The Composition of the Judiciary

Class Origin

As said, the recruitment of the judiciary up to the early twentieth century was confined strictly, in practice, to the uppermost layer of society. Limited access to the university and the unpaid position of clerk of the court which used to precede a position on the bench helped to make 'the judiciary ... an almost impregnable fortress to the lower classes.'[16] Some movement towards lowering the recruitment level of the upper classes, however, is discernible in the nineteenth century, when the number of members of the nobility in the Supreme Court began to decline. Table 7.3 shows the process of 'denobilization' of the judiciary as a whole, from 1950 to 2000. Due to the growing number of judges, the figure of 40 in 1950 represents a share of 10 per cent; only 0.7 per cent remained in 2000.

TABLE 7.4
Level of occupation of the fathers of the members of the judiciary in percentages

Level of occupation	1968 (Judges) *n* = 90	1988/89 (Judges, prosecutors [no adm. judges]) *n* = 130	1991 (Judges, prosecutors, trainees [raios]) *n* = 1007	2000 Judges *n* = 669
High	60	51	62	60
Middle	32	42	28	22
Low	8	8	7	8
Unknown	–	–	1	8

Sources: 1968, Van der Land 1970; 1988/9, De Groot-van Leeuwen 1991; 1991, Vrij Nederland-survey; 2000 NJB survey.[18]

Another way of assessing the elite character of the judiciary is to look at the position on the social ladder of the occupation of the father of judges. On this ladder, typically 'high' occupations are mayor, medical doctor, or judge, typically 'middle' occupations are nurse or teacher. Data are available from surveys from 1968, 1988/9, 1991, and 2000. These data are not fully comparable, especially given different definitions of the research population (e.g., judges only or judges plus trainees), as table 7.4 shows. The table indicates fairly consistently, however, that the judiciary has been drawn from the high occupational stratum without significant change over the past thirty years.

The same picture presents itself when looking at the educational background of the fathers of the members of the judiciary. Table 7.5 shows the percentages in 1991 and 2000. Again we notice the overrepresentation of the highest category, and the stability thereof.

The non-representativeness of the social backgrounds of the judiciary is caused primarily by the overrepresentation of the higher strata in the law student population. With respect to social background, law and medicine are the most elitist university studies in the Netherlands.[19] Structuring a representative judiciary would require strong and visible positive discrimination of lower-class candidates, and such a non-meritocratic process does not appear to be desired by actors in the selection system.

As a background for interpreting figures, it may be remarked that overall, the occupational and educational levels of the Dutch population are rising steadily. Relatively, therefore, the predominance of the high stratum among the judiciary is slowly declining.

The Dutch judiciary has an elite character, if 'elite' is defined in terms

TABLE 7.5
Educational background of fathers of the members of the judiciary in percentages

Educational level	1991 (Judges, public prosecutors, trainees [raios]) *n* = 1007	2000 (Judges) *n* = 669
University and polytechnic	51	49
Middle	31	34
Primary education only	18	17

Sources: 1991 Vrij Nederland-survey; 2000 NJB-survey.

of broad social classes; most Dutch citizens are judged by 'higher ups' rather than by their peers. This is not the subject of discussion in Dutch society, however. Public protests are directed against specific behaviour and decisions of judges rather than against the 'class character' of the judiciary in general. This may explain the lack of positive discrimination on class criteria in the selection system.

Gender

One of the most visible changes in the Dutch judiciary during the last half-century is the participation of women.[20] In the Netherlands discussions about the appointability of women started in 1915, with, inter alia, articles on the subject being published in the legal journals. The government requested advice from the Supreme Court on this matter in 1921; this was followed by a discussion in Parliament.[21] The National Women's Council raised the subject again in 1933, but it was only in the post-war spirit of renewal (1946) that the issue was decided. The first female judge was appointed in 1947 (in a juvenile court, naturally).[22]

The participation of women wavered around 5 per cent up to the 1970s, after which it began to rise steadily, reaching 37 per cent in 2000. As table 7.6 shows, women are still strongly underrepresented at the top of the legal pyramid. Except for an indication that female judges may have a somewhat slower career pace than their male counterparts, it is not known if this underrepresentation is due to a simple cohort effect or the result of some form of 'glass ceiling.'[23] In general terms, however, it appears that the higher levels of the judiciary are effectively open to female participation.

TABLE 7.6
Distribution of women throughout the Dutch court hierarchy (%)

	1974	1986	1990	2000
High*	1.3	3.5	5.5	15
Middle**	1.4	9.4	14.5	30
Low***	11.0	25.1	27.8	50

*High: Supreme Court judges, presidents and chief public prosecutors of all courts.
**Middle: crown court judges, middle level of judges and public prosecutors.
***Low: district court judges and public prosecutors.
Sources: 1974, 1986, 1991 de Naamlijsten Leden Rechterlijke macht adapted by de Groot-van Leeuwen 1991; 2000 NJB-survey .

Professional Origin

The professional origin of judges was an issue of debate as early as 1919, when it was said in Parliament that the quality of judicial decisions would improve if the recruitment system allowed for the inflow of more diverse 'life experiences' than those of 'office bureaucrats' alone. In the same vein, in 1975 and 1981 legal scientists expressed fear that the judiciary would become dominated by the career judges from the first ('insiders') inflow route. In reality, however, most of the growth of the Dutch judiciary occurred through the inflow of outsiders. Their percentage rose from 55 per cent of the judiciary in 1986 to 72 per cent in 2000.

Table 7.7 records the occupations of magistrates before their entry into the judiciary.[24] The table shows that in spite of the present-day dominance of the 'outsiders' inflow route, a certain degree of 'bureaucratization' has taken place; many outsiders, obviously, are recruited from government agencies (now at 35 per cent). In a general sense, however, diversity does not seem to have decreased.

Political Preferences

Political preference is a sensitive issue for the judiciary. This recently came to the media forefront, for instance, when it became known that one of the judges sitting on the case of the murder of a right-wing politician was an active member of a left-wing party.

Table 7.8 shows the political preferences of the judiciary over the last thirty years as stated by magistrates in surveys and research interviews.[25]

TABLE 7.7
Occupational background of the members of the judiciary (both inflow routes) in percentages of the judiciary

Occupational background	1951	1974	1986	2000
Bar	45	34	31	32
(Semi-)Government	6	17	13	35
University/polytechnic	1	7	12	13
Business	1	10	13	8
Other	1	6	8	0
None	46	26	22	12

Sources: 1951, 1974, 1986 Naamlijst Leden Rechterlijke macht adapted by de Groot-van Leeuwen 1991; 2000 NJB-survey.

One notable feature is the decline of the Christian Democrats and the rise of the Progressive Liberals, peaking in 1991. The non-politicizing reason-based middle-way style of the latter party had a great appeal for the judges. Several more general conclusions may be drawn from the table. First, the four major parties (Christian Democrats, Conservative Liberals, Labour, and the Progressive Liberals, all four quite moderate and consensus-oriented) have always been present and in equilibrium in the judiciary, as they are in the Dutch society as a whole. Second, diversity has increased of late, with the smaller and more radical parties gaining representation among the judiciary too.

A more subtle phenomenon is a movement from the right to the left (all reasonable, of course, Dutch style), between 1970 and 2000, with the proportion of Christian Democrats and Conservative Liberals falling from 67 to 36 per cent. Interestingly, this change runs counter to that of Dutch society as a whole, which was permissive and community-oriented during the 1970s and is now much more strict and individualistic. Public grumbling about 'class justice' in the 1970s and about judicial 'softies' at present does have some empirical basis, therefore. And although the image of the judiciary compensating for the overall political pendulum of society is tempting, it is hard to imagine what invisible hand would take care of this.

Discussion

In the Netherlands, the judiciary is currently more diverse than before in terms of class origin, gender, occupational background, and political

TABLE 7.8
Political affiliation of the judiciary in percentages

	Judiciary			Dutch population
Party	1970	1991	2000	Elections 1998
Christian Democrats (CDA)	31	17	8	18
Conservative Liberals (VVD)	36	16	22	25
Labour (PvdA)	19	24	29	
Progressive Liberals (D66)	11	39	17	9
Green left (Groen links)	–	4	12	7
Socialist Party (SP)	–	–	2	3
Conservative Christian		–		
(Christen Unie)	–	–	2	3
Others/none	1	8	1	4

Sources: 1970 Van der Land; 1991 VN-survey; 2000 NJB-survey.

affiliation. The selection system, however, formally takes only merit into account and does not pay attention to such characteristics as political affiliation. The Dutch system of selection and appointment of judges is strictly meritocratic in its procedure, criteria, and official descriptions. At the same time, some kind of informal process seems to be at work to solve the merit/diversity paradox and keep the judiciary diversified.

Dutch society, as indicated above, is a consensus society. Consensus-making in the Netherlands is typically a function of the elite, and if the invisible hand responsible for judicial diversity is to be found anywhere, it is within those elite, that is, the judicial selection committee (and the commissions that select the committee). The selection process, containing as it does personal deliberations within the committee as well as objective tests, is thus open to covert collective-level diversity criteria as well as overt ones that focus on individual merit. The diversity criteria are probably never discussed and possibly not even applied consciously by members of the committee. Rather, I surmise that collective-level criteria are acknowledged only, for instance, after a day of interviewing candidate judges when committee members feel satisfied because a nice diversity has been approved. What such diversity involves – gender balance, a balance between quieter and more outspoken candidates, a balance of upper- or working-class backgrounds – may even remain subconscious forever. Every member of the committee shares the satisfaction, however, and everyone contributes to its formation. It is not owned by anyone. It is culture.

NOTES

1 Sloot distinguishes between 'descriptive' and 'substantive' diversity. Descriptive diversity is the diversity that the public can see to exist, such as sex and race. Substantive diversity is the diversity of ideas that exist within the judicial culture. In the present chapter class origin and especially political preferences are relatively substantive dimensions of diversity; Sloot, 'Moeten rechters lijken op de Nederlandse bevolking.'
2 Zahn, *Das unbekannte Holland.*
3 Kranenburg, 'The Political Wing of the "Polder Model",' 35–9.
4 de Groot-van Leeuwen, 'Criticising Judges in the Netherlands,' 153–8.
5 van der Horst, *The Low Sky.*
6 van Duyne, 'Simple Decision Making,' 143–58; van Duyne and Verwoerd, *Gelet op de persoon van de rechter.*
7 Article 120 of the Dutch constitution does not allow for any judicial review of Acts of Parliament. However, it is possible for any judge to declare Acts of Parliament to be at variance with international treaties.
8 Witteveen, *Evenwicht van machten*; de Waard, *Samenwerkende machten;* Heringa, *Constitutionele partners.*
9 Bruinsma, *Cassatierechtspraak in civiele zaken.*
10 This section is largely based on van Koppen and ten Kate, *Tot raadsheer benoemd*; van Koppen, 'The Dutch Supreme Court and Parliament,' 745–80.
11 Between 1841 and 1887 the Lower House of Parliament drew up a list of five nominees instead of three. The change in 1848 was made because the government doubted the quality of the candidates and apparently thought that a longer list might give a higher chance of appointing someone of good quality (Heemskerk, *De Praktijk van de Grondwet*, 63–4). In 1887 a list of three nominees was reintroduced, because the Crown appointed the first candidate on the list.
12 van Koppen and ten Kate, *Tot raadsheer benoemd*; van Koppen, 'The Dutch Supreme Court and Parliament,' 745–80.
13 de Werd, *De benoeming van rechters.*
14 See Pieterman, *De plaats van de rechter in Nederland 1813–1920.*
15 There is body of literature that looks at the impact of the difference between appointed and elected judges in the United States; see, e.g., Bohn and Inman, *Balanced Budget Rules and Public Deficits*; Hanssen, 'The Effect of Judicial Institutions on Uncertainty and the Rate of Litigation,' 205–32; Besley and Payne, *Judicial Accountability and Economic Policy Outcomes.*
16 de Werd, *De benoeming van rechters*, 343; see also Langemeijer, 'De recrutering

van de rechterlijke macht'; Langemeijer, *Taak en opleiding van de rechter*; Pieterman, *De plaats van de rechter in Nederland 1813–1920.*

17 Schenk, 'Telt de rm onevenredig veel adellijke leden?,' 677–8.

18 van der Land, 'Een enquete onder de Nederlandse rechterlijke macht,' 524–32; de Groot-van Leeuwen, *De rechterlijke macht in Nederland*; *Vrij Nederland* 1991, *Nederland Juristen Blad (NJB)* 2000.

19 Koppen, *Een kwestie van discipline.*

20 For the position of women in the judiciary of fifteen countries see Schultz and Shaw, eds., *Women in the World's Legal Professions,* and for the Netherlands the contribution of de Groot van Leeuwen, 'Women in the Dutch Legal Profession (1950–2000),' 341–51 and Ietswaart, 'Choices in Context,' 353–69.

21 On average during this period, the Supreme Court was consulted by the government on legal issues approximately once per year

22 Sloot, 'Officiële uitsluiting van vrouwen in juridische beroepen.'

23 de Groot-van Leeuwen, 'The Equilibrium Elite,' 141–55.

24 Judges who entered through the internal route occupy all of the category of 'no occupation,' but many of those have had some years' experience in another occupation too and are in that category in the table.

25 Asked in the surveys as actual preference.

8 Judicial Selection in Italy: A Civil Service Model with Partisan Results

MARY L. VOLCANSEK

The various schemes devised to name judges in democratic regimes all attempt, in different fashions, to balance the independence of the judges with some form of accountability, while also trying to ensure professional competence. The goal of these judicial recruitment mechanisms is to secure 'quality justice,' which William Prillaman has defined as providing efficiency, independence, and citizen access. Each should fold into the others seamlessly to promote democracy. 'Efficiency coupled with independence lends an air of predictability and bolsters popular faith in the courts.'[1] Popular faith in judicial institutions holds a central place in the reality of courts' legitimacy, even if the perceptions may not be well-grounded.[2] The Italian model of justice has focused on ensuring judicial independence, but many observers suggest that, while it has preserved independence, both efficiency and access have been sacrificed. Though an independent judiciary is typically enshrined as a pillar of democracy, Owen Fiss observed that 'a judiciary that is insulated from the popularly controlled institutions of government – the legislative and the executive branches – has the power to interfere with ... [their] decisions, and thus has the power to frustrate the will of the people.'[3] That may well describe the recruitment and careers of Italian judges, who are totally insulated from outside influences. More directly put, Italian judges may have exercised their independence excessively and given the appearance of being partisan activists. That perception inevitably transforms itself into popular reality.

Recruitment of judges can function to promote or diminish independence. Two forms of judicial independence have been observed: relational and behavioural. The former refers to the autonomy of judges collectively and individually from one another and the judiciary as a whole from interference by other institutions in the political system. The second refers to the ability of judges to behave autonomously as individuals within the judicial corps.[4] The two elements are complementary if a judge is to appear as an impartial third party to whom disputants can bring their claims and expect an unbiased decision based on a priori rules.

Relational models of interactions among institutions of government capture the complexities of governing, in which one institution is usually dependent on others to achieve policy goals. Much recent literature on executive and legislative relations has recognized the interdependence of the two institutions and the strategic decisions that each considers in achieving policy goals.[5] Similarly, courts are now recognized as a factor in the relational equation, as an external veto point,[6] as a threat to political deals achieved by interest groups through the political process,[7] or as a significant but prudent institutional player.[8] The case of the Italian ordinary judiciary presents a novel model, one in which the judiciary has come to have not a competitive or cooperative relationship with the executive and legislative branches, but rather an adversarial one. This situation has evolved for historical, institutional, and political reasons. One's own political ideology and perceptions of events in Italian political life inevitably form the prism through which both process and outcomes of acts by Italian magistrates will be viewed. Though appearances and realities may be at variance, judges in democracies are always well-advised to behave like Caesar's wife, 'above reproach.'

The Italian Magistratura in the First Republic

As in many continental schemes (see, for example, the Provine and Garapon chapter on France), the Italian magistrature has included prosecutors and judges, both of whom carry the title of 'judge.' The magistrature's initial formation at the time of unification in the mid-nineteenth century imitated the Napoleonic system of separation of powers, in which none of the three branches of government could interfere with the internal operations of the others. However, under the Montesquieuian model, the judiciary was not viewed as a co-equal branch of the government, but rather as a weak sister that constituted a mere function rather than a power. More to the point, judges were conceived as no more than the 'mouth of the law,' wielding no independent discretion. As in the Napoleonic system in France, Italian judges prior to the republic were under the executive branch and, from 1907, were governed by the Superior Council of the Magistrature (CSM), an auxillary to the executive for the administration of justice and the guarantor of judicial independence.[9]

Under Fascism Italian magistrates, whether prosecutors or judges, were hardly independent and, in reaction to the abuses of both power and citizen rights under the Mussolini regime, a new, wholly independent judiciary was enshrined in the republican constitution of 1948. The constitution proclaims in Article 101 that 'judges are subject only to the law' and that 'the judiciary is an order that is autonomous and independent of all other powers' (Article 104). To ensure that judges owed no political favours, Article 106 stipulates that 'judges are appointed by means of competitive examinations' and all employment, assignments, promotions, and discipline are governed by the Superior Council of the Magistrature, two-thirds of which is composed of judges elected by their peers, with the other third named by the two houses of Parliament (Article 105). To seal the bubble surrounding the judiciary totally, Article 107 adds that 'judges may not be removed from office.'

Another innovation in the 1948 Republican constitution was the Constitutional Court, a body wholly separate from the magistrature or 'ordinary judiciary.' Responsibility for naming the fifteen judges serving on the Constitutional Court is divided equally among the President of the Republic, Parliament, and the judges on the ordinary and administrative courts. Partisan politics clearly drives the selection process and, though independence should be derived from the judges' nine-year, non-renewable terms, the aspirations of the judges for post-Court careers may lead them to craft decisions with an eye towards their impact on future ambitions.[10]

The complete insularity of the judiciary has coloured its relationships with the political branches of government in varying ways over the last half-century. In the early years of the republic, the judiciary was populated with hold-over Fascist judges. The judicial corps was, according to Paul Ginsborg, 'a closed caste, resentful of its low pay, mainly recruited from the southern law faculties, and alien to the values of the resistance.'[11] The judges were conservative, staunchly anti-Communist, and without sympathy for the working-class struggle.

Tensions between the ordinary judiciary and Parliament have been a constant throughout the republican era. From 1948, when the first parliament was seated, through 1993, the judges notified a total of 4,770 parliamentarians that they were under investigation for some criminal behaviour. Lest those who are familiar with the *Tangentopoli* or *Mani*

Pulite investigations that began in 1991 assume that the investigations resulted from a single incidence of judicial fervour, 72 per cent of those sitting in the first Parliament in 1948 were served with notices of investigation. The proportion never dropped below 24 per cent in a forty-five-year period and reached its pinnacle in 1991–3 when 898, or 94 per cent, of the members of the two houses were under investigation. Antagonism between the legislative and judicial branches has, in other words, been the norm. Parliamentarians reacted actively to the scrutiny of their actions by the judges. Cazzola and Morisi fill fifty-three pages with a mere selection of examples from the parliamentary record of instances in which the legislative representatives retaliated by verbally attacking various judges or the judiciary as a whole from the floor between 1976 and 1994.[12]

The corps of independent judges enjoyed a similar lack of popularity with the public, which exacted a toll on judicial independence in a 1987 referendum in which judges were stripped of their immunity from civil liability in cases in which they had been gravely negligent. The subsequent enabling legislation passed by Parliament appointed, however, the CSM the initial screener of allegations of negligence, making recovery of damages by wronged individuals unlikely. At the same time, a serious reform of the judicial system was passed in 1988, one that converted the previously inquisitorial system into a hybrid adversarial one, designed better to protect the rights of the criminally accused.[13]

The selection of Italian judges, together with the related processes for promotion, assignment, and discipline, must be viewed against this backdrop. Authors of the Italian constitution of 1948 intended to preserve citizen rights from an arbitrary government through establishment of a standard continental civil service model for judges, but they apportioned an extraordinary degree of independence to the judiciary. This bureaucratic model was ultimately transformed into what many see as a partisan apparatus.

The Judicial Career

The recruitment process for judges in post-war Italy was intended as a counterbalance to that of the Fascist scheme under which magistrates were required to be Italian citizens, of the 'Italian race,' registered in the Fascist Party, and with no civil, moral or political disabilities.[14] True to the republican constitutional prescription, selection to the corps of the magistrature has remained based strictly on a competitive examination since the 1960s. This criterion for selection is at variance with the criteria found in Europe and the United States. In Britain, judges are appointed by the executive from among practising lawyers; in France, Spain, and Portugal competitive examinations are followed by completion of a judicial school; and in Germany, aspiring judges are apprenticed to the judiciary and then selected through a competitive examination. Only in Italy is an examination the sole method for selection.[15] The exam, both written and oral, is marked anonymously. No consideration is given to recommendations which in Italy are typically politically inspired and used for political patronage.

The competitive examination as the sole criteria for entering the ranks of the judiciary was predicated upon laudable intentions but has had unintended consequences. Since no one may enter into the magistrature past the age of thirty, the socialization of judges in Italy resides in the hands of law faculties. Law students enter the university directly from the equivalent of an American high school, but study only within a single discipline. At the conclusion of approximately four years of study, a thesis is written and defended. Law faculty curricula are strictly juridical, focusing on law and legal theory without any significant presence of attendant disciplines, such as economics, political science, or sociology, that might inform a judge's decision. There is, moreover, no attention to philosophy or ethics in Italian legal studies.[16]

Thus, a new judge or prosecutor would enter the magistrature around age twenty-three to twenty-five, with no practical experience or training, and receive his or her entire professional socialization from within the established ranks of the judiciary. Until recently, a magistrate could move between the positions of judge and prosecutor, which gave the appearance at least of a prosecutorial bias among judges. Magistrates also regularly seek assignments to other political institutions, even competing for political office at the national, regional, and local levels. They can, moreover, always return to the judiciary without loss of seniority.[17]

In Italy, as in other European countries with civil service models for the judiciary, a high council of the judiciary oversees promotions and retirements. But in Italy, meritorious performance is *not* the criteria for promotion up the ranks. Promotion is based solely on seniority: time and grade. In other words, a new magistrate embarking on a judicial career in his or her mid-twenties can expect to move up the hierarchy steadily, regardless of performance, and eventually reach the highest court, in salary if not in function. A forty to forty-five year career is virtually guaranteed.[18]

Who chooses to take the competitive examinations and why? Women were precluded from all public servant positions until 1963, but their representation in the magistrature has subsequently steadily increased. In 1987, more women than men sat for the magistrature examination, and thereafter the newly entering magistrates have been about evenly divided between men and women. The result is that about one-third of the magistrature was female by 1999, and about 85 per cent of them were under the age of forty-five.[19]

To determine why people entered the Italian judiciary and how they perceived their positions, in 1997 Massimo Morisi sent questionnaires to all of the approximately 8,500 magistrates, of whom 893, or 10.5 per cent, responded. Despite the problem of self-selection in the resulting sample, only the thirty-six to fifty-five age group, those who assumed their positions after 1981, and magistrates educated in the south and the northeast were significantly under-represented. When the respondents were asked if they entered the magistrature because of the prestige, more than half (53.9 per cent) said that they had thought a lot about that; another one-third responded that the prestige of the position had been a consideration. Only 24.4 per cent said that either salaries and/or the prospect of a career, was a primary motivation, though more than half (52 per cent) responded that both entered their decisions 'a little.' Morisi then combined a number of questions and categorized the magistrates as 'committeds' (those who had said that the prestige was not important to them); 'judges' (those who were attracted primarily by the prestige of the position); 'materialists' (those who were attracted by the prospect of the career and salary); and 'ambitious' (those who were motivated strongly by both the prestige and the career of a magistrate). 'Committeds' accounted for 40 per cent of the total, and 'judges' for more than one-third. A mere 5.8 per cent were classified as 'materialists,' while 18.6 per cent were classified as 'ambitious.'[20]

Morisi also asked two questions intended to measure the institutional motivations of the judges: 'When you thought about your decision to enter the magistrature, was it your desire to serve the state?' and 'When you thought about your decision to enter the magistrature, were you desirous of serving the collective?' In responding, 42.7 per cent indicated that a desire to serve the state was a major factor, and only 15.5 per cent said that it was not part of their calculation. A much higher number, 70.2 per cent, said that serving the collective was a major consideration, while 18.5 per cent said that it was a minor one. Only 5.4 per cent said they had not thought about it. Morisi also asked, 'When you thought about the decision to enter the magistrature was the desire to better society a factor?' Fewer than half, 42 per cent, cited this as a major motive, and 20.9 per cent said that it was not a factor at all.[21]

Morisi paints a portrait of a magistrature, albeit based on a limited sample, that is committed to the work and peopled by those who entered the career for altruistic motives. There are a number of reasons to explain the high levels of commitment, among them the guarantee of a lifetime career and steady promotions, with attendant salary increases and official perquisites. The stated commitments to the collective and to work to better society are sentiments most often linked to the left side of the political spectrum.

Superior Council of the Magistrature

The Superior Council of the Magistrature, prescribed by the 1948 constitution though it was not implemented until 1958 (see below),[22] was intended to secure the total independence of the judiciary. It has clearly accomplished that goal. The President of the Republic, the head of state in Italy, is the theoretical presiding officer of the CSM, but in fact the vice-president, who must be a non-judge, usually presides over all deliberations and must preside over disciplinary actions. Two-thirds of the members are judges, elected by their peers; that number is apportioned according to rank within the judicial hierarchy and, since 1990, by geographic region of the country. The remaining one-third, named by Parliament, must be full professors of law or lawyers with a minimum of fifteen years' practice. As in other arenas of political life, the non-judges named to the CSM are apportioned among the parties. From 1976 to 1990, that meant five from the left and five from the centre parties. In 1994, the apportionment shifted to include three from the left, one from the centre, and six from the governing coalition right. In 1998, a more politically representative slate was chosen: four from the left, three from the centre, and three from the right.[23] All members of the council serve four-year, not immediately renewable, terms.[24] The CSM was initially composed of twenty-one members, but that number was raised to thirty, with twenty judges and ten law professors or lawyers, plus three who serve by virtue of their positions, such as the President of the Republic.[25]

An anomaly in the system is the role of the minister of justice, a cabinet-level official in the executive branch responsible for administering the judiciary. An obvious conflict exists between the CSM and the minister of justice, each of whom has a significant interest in judicial personnel decisions, but only the CSM has constitutional authority over those decisions. The minister of justice can initiate disciplinary proceedings against judges, but the CSM maintained that any further involvement by the minister of justice violated the constitution. The Constitutional Court attempted to resolve the conflict by concluding that both the CSM and the minister of justice must concur in promotion and discipline decisions and that the CSM must hear the minister of justice's opinion, but is not bound by it.[26]

Magistrates can be admonished, censured, exempted from office temporarily, dismissed or removed from office permanently, or punished with loss of seniority. These sanctions can be imposed for failure of duties, damaging the prestige of the judiciary, violating the residency requirement, or leaving the precinct without the permission of the official hierarchically superior. Because of the confidentiality of proceedings, precise information on how effective the CSM has been in policing the judicial ranks is spotty. Even so, 'the CSM's own data clearly demonstrate that a single ethical infraction is not sufficient to trigger a serious penalty.'[27]

When the constitution came into force in 1948, there was a strong movement within the judges' union, the National Association of Italian Magistrates, to thwart creation of the CSM. Until the CSM was implemented, the higher ranking judges and prosecutors controlled appointments and promotions and maintained dossiers on magistrates' personal and professional lives.[28] This group of judges came primarily from the higher grades and, thus, were largely hold-overs from the Fascist regime. They succeeded in delaying the CSM for a decade. As the composition of the judiciary changed and younger judges of the lower ranks entered the profession, there was finally a movement to push for implementation of the constitutionally mandated CSM.

Unionization or Politicization?

The existence of a unionized judiciary, indeed a judiciary represented by multiple unions reflecting different political or judicial ideologies, has served as evidence of the politicization of the judiciary for those who criticize the magistrates. The Association General of Magistrates pre-dated the Fascist regime, and a number of its leaders were expelled for attempting to maintain the liberty of unions under the Fascists. It re-emerged after the war as the National Association of Magistrates, but eventually fractured into a variety of currents. By 1961 the National Association of Magistrates had a rival on the right, the Italian Magistrates' Union, and by 1964 had itself dissolved into four different unions: the Democratic Magistrates on the left, the Third Power in the centre, the Independent Magistrates on the right, and the Italian Magistrates' Union continuing on the far right. After realignments between 1969 and 1971, another in 1979, and one in 1989, four unions crossing the ideological spectrum remained: Democratic Magistrates on the left, the Movement for Justice and Proposition 88 on the left-centre, Unity for the Constitution on the centre-right, and Independent Magistrates on the right.[29] Each espouses a judicial position that roughly corresponds to more traditional political notions of right, left, and centre. The Democratic Magistrates champion a conception of the judicial role in which the constitution is viewed as a living document and, therefore, subject to creative jurisprudence. They also value egalitarianism and solidarity in judicial decisions. The Movement for Justice sees itself as a progressive group that wants to preserve the professionalism of the judicial corps, to promote meritocracy in the judiciary and, most importantly, to distance judges from politicians. Unity for the Constitution represents more moderate judges, substantially satisfied with the reforms that have been accomplished recently and anxious to maintain them. They tend to favour amiable, not hostile, relations with active politicians. The Independent Magistrature is the most conservative union and maintains a preference for hierarchy within the judiciary, a prudent connection with the political class, and a moderate, deferential role for the judiciary.[30]

Each union runs a list of candidates for seats on the CSM and receives seats according to a type of proportional representation. From 1976 to 1998, the leftist Democratic Magistrates slowly improved their strength and obtained one-fifth of the judicial seats on the CSM. The Movement for Justice ran its first slate of candidates in 1990 and won three or four seats in each election. Unity for the Constitution, the centre-right grouping, is the largest, holding nine seats from 1976 until 1990, when it dropped to the eight that it still retains. The rightist Independent Magistrature steadily declined, from eight seats in 1981 to four in 1998.[31]

The competing unions of Italian magistrates underscore a fundamental politicization within the corps of judges and prosecutors. By declaring their political preferences so openly the judges have left themselves no mantle of apolitical credibility from which they can derive legitimacy. When politicians, the public, or the media level charges of political motivations at judges, the argument that the judiciary is above politics sounds somewhat specious. The judges have registered at least tentative political persuasions and made public their judicial values. At the same time, since the various magistrates' unions span the political spectrum, the claim of a single driving political ideology for the entire magistrature also has a hollow ring.

Evolution of the Judiciary

The late 1960s witnessed a dramatic shift of the political winds all across Europe, as student and worker groups asserted their rights, often violently. A leftist tilt was also felt within the Italian judiciary, particularly in the Democratic Magistrature. All entrenched interests of the state were challenged, and the Democratic Magistrature was in the forefront of state employees leading the charge. These mainly young, low-ranking judges and prosecutors aimed to reform the antiquated legal system, to reduce delays, and to make the legal system more accessible to all classes of citizens. Some became the so-called assault judges (*pretori d'assalto*), who challenged everything from food additives to pollution, from building code violations to the major economic and political interests of the country. By 1975, most of the attempts to mobilize the state for reform had waned, as Italy entered the 'years of lead,' when radicals on both the left and the right chose to fight the class war through terrorism.[32]

Initially, magistrates and judges were the heroes in the fight against terror, and some were even targets of attacks. At the same time, certain magistrates were overly zealous in their reactions to terrorist attacks, abusing their power to hold people in seemingly indefinite preventive detention. The unreformed judicial machinery continued to creak along at a glacial pace, delaying all justice. Public animus towards the judiciary increased as glaring miscarriages of justice were publicized and several judges were linked to a sinister masonic organization while others were tied to corruption in organized crime. Two referenda were proposed to rein in what appeared to be heavy-handed judges and prosecutors. One called for the popular election of the CSM, and the other for revocation of judicial immunity from civil liability in the case of gross negligence.[33] The former was blocked by the Constitutional Court, but the second referendum reached the electorate in 1987.

The 1987 referendum 'against the judges' was directly motivated by the arrest on drug charges of a popular television personality, Enzo Tortora. Tortora was held in custody or under house arrest from June 1983 until June 1984, when he was elected as a 'symbolic candidate' to the

European Parliament and thereby gained parliamentary immunity. He renounced his immunity, however, and was tried and again returned to house arrest. His conviction was ultimately overturned on appeal more than four years after the initial arrest. When he returned to his television program with more than twenty million viewers, Tortora told his story of judicial abuse and trumped-up charges. He became the public symbol of an off-course judiciary and the 500,000 signatures to petition for a referendum to strip both magistrates and judges of their immunity were easily garnered. The referendum was passed by an overwhelming majority of 80 per cent.[34]

Judges moved from disgrace back to hero stature in 1991 with the advent of the *Mani Pulite* or *Tangentopoli* investigations that altered the Italian landscape for more than a decade. A chief prosecutor in Milan and four of his lieutenants uncovered and pursued a kick-back scheme involving government contracts that ultimately discredited almost an entire generation of politicians. Almost simultaneously with the unravelling of political corruption scandals in Milan, another set of heroic judges/prosecutors were taking on the Mafia in Sicily. The highly publicized investigations by those two sets of prosecutors inspired others across the nation to plunge into corruption and organized crime investigations, and public opinion was firmly behind the crusading judges. By 1993, 898 of the 956 representatives serving in the national Chamber of Deputies and Senate were under investigation.[35]

Political corruption was nothing new in Italy, which raises the question of why *Tangentopoli* happened when it did. A primary explanation is that the existing judicial organization in Italy, one that fostered complete judicial independence, permitted it. There was no means for exerting political control over the judiciary. Secondly, the bonds of those involved in corruption were fragile, unlike those that hold organized crime organizations together, and once one person was caught there was no loyalty to others. An additional explanation has to do with a 1989 legal reform in which a strictly inquisitorial criminal justice system became a modified adversarial one, the so-called *Processo Perry Mason*. Under the new system, the prosecutor, not the judge, was solely responsible for presenting a case and for examining witnesses, with the judge placed as an impartial referee.[36]

The judges were once again cast in the role of villains when Silvio Berlusconi and his Finivest conglomerate of media, retailing, publishing, and public relations came to the attention of the investigators in 1994. Those who were heralded as heroes for their efforts in *Tangentopoli* were seen as persecutors, indeed as Communists intent on gaining power, when they confronted Berlusconi. The Milanese billionaire, the richest man in Italy, had been a close associate of the by then discredited former Socialist Party Prime Minister Bettino Craxi, but when he was under pressure to divest himself of portions of his extensive television holdings, he formed a new political party called *Sforza Italia*, forged a coalition, and was elected prime minister himself in March 1994. Just four months after assuming power Berlusconi attempted to end the *Tangentopoli* investigations by executive decree law. Opposition within his own government prevented the issuance of the decree, and in November of that year Berlusconi was given notice that he, too, was under investigation for bribing the financial police. His government fell one month later, and Berlusconi accused the judges of political conspiracy.[37]

In 2001 Berlusconi and his coalition were elected with large majorities in both houses of Parliament. With his ascension as prime minister, Berlusconi directly controlled three of four private television channels and controlled indirectly the three state television channels. He also controlled large portions of the print media. Berlusconi's critics alleged that he was using his office as a means of protecting his massive business interests from regulation and himself from prosecution. Berlusconi responded that the judges are out to get him and that only he stood between Italy and a Communist takeover. To counter the alleged assault by the judges, his coalition passed a law on 18 June 2003 making the prime minister and four other high-ranking government officials immune from prosecution. The extent of the irregularities in Berlusconi's business dealings were sufficient that the *Economist* magazine featured his picture on its cover and published a five-page open letter to the prime minister in the 2–8 August 2003 issue. The letter raised twenty-eight questions covering Berlusconi's business and political career. The primary one involved the charge of bribing judges, and the magazine documented transfers from Berlusconi's business of almost half a million dollars through various off-shore banks, ultimately to a company owned by one of the judges in a case involving one of Berlusconi's companies. The *Economist* noted the peculiar position of Mr Berlusconi in this case, since he was both a criminal defendant and, as prime minister, the civil co-plaintiff.[38] Notably, in November 2003, one of his co-defendants in the trial, his former lawyer, cabinet minister, and friend, Cesare Previti, was convicted of one count of corruption and sentenced to five years in jail. The other defendants were cleared on all counts, while Previti was cleared on a companion charge.[39] The prime minister was not a party to the case at the time, as a consequence of the immunity law passed at his behest. However, in January 2004, the Constitutional Court invalidated the law.[40]

Like Caesar's Wife

Tensions between the political branches and the judiciary are likely a natural result of separation of powers, but Italy presents an extreme case. As David Nelken observed, there is a profound, reciprocal antagonism between Italian politicians and judges. He argues that this antagonism has been compounded by the transition to an accusatorial system in 1988, because the magistrates continued to act as they had under the old inquisitorial model.[41] It was further aggravated when the head of government came under investigation for criminal acts not only in Italy, where he temporarily granted himself immunity, but also in Spain.

This scenario raises, however, broader systemic issues about the administration of justice. 'Quality justice' is achieved, as you will recall from the introduction to this paper, when the judicial system provides efficiency, independence, and access.[42] Italian justice can score high only on the mark of independence. In Italy, judicial independence is total. Young graduates enter the judicial corps in their mid-twenties, and their entire career is thereafter governed by an incestuous grouping of elected judges and political appointees. In no other major European country are judges recruited to the bench solely on the basis of a competitive examination, promoted solely on the basis of seniority, and have their status and discipline controlled by a group of peer judges, supplemented by law professors or lawyers with political connections.[43] The absence of training or apprenticeship is compounded by a degree of role confusion which, until 1996, allowed judges and prosecutors to serve both functions at the lowest levels and to move from one role to the other.[44] A prosecutorial bias impedes creation of an efficient system of control and leaves ample margins for discretion to the state prosecutor.[45]

As a further complication, the division of the judges into politically connected unions can only heighten the public perception, one that can be exploited by defendants in the press, that the judiciary is politicized. Since approximately 3.5 per cent of the judges are regularly working in non-judicial positions, often overtly political ones, the political tie is even more obvious.

Efficiency and access are the other two elements of Prillaman's equation for achieving quality justice, and without the former, the latter becomes irrelevant. A civil case, first grade, in Italy took on average 1,009 days to complete; a civil case, second grade, required 1,476 days. Justices of the peace were added to handle civil cases involving small amounts of money, and within five years they were overwhelmed with cases. The criminal process is so slow that by 2001 12,000 cases had been filed with the European Court of Human Rights in Strasbourg raising the issue of delays. Even the addition of six hundred new magistrate positions in spring 2003 did not make the wheels of Italian justice turn more rapidly.[46] The process of appeal further extends the time required for resolution. In criminal cases trial between 1989 and 1997, 53 per cent were altered on appeal, most in favour of the defendant. With the courts moving at such a glacial pace, access suffers as well. Furthermore, there are hundreds of appellate judges reaching discordant decisions. The highest appeals court, the *Corte di Cassazione*, has more than four hundred judges, largely because of the seniority system of promotion. Decisions are, perhaps not surprisingly often inconsistent.[47]

One consequence of the absolute independence of the magistrates – both public prosecutors and judges – has been a rise in the number of politically motivated actions by magistrates.[48] The conflict reached, according to Daria Lucca, its maximum point at the end of the twentieth century; the political class in the government branded the judiciary as bad.[49] More importantly, the public agreed. The 1999 *Eurobarometre* found that a mere 36 per cent of Italians had faith in their judicial system.[50] The judges, on the other hand, saw their independence threatened and, in 2002, ninety-five of them petitioned the United Nations Commission on Human Rights to investigate. The commission delegate concluded that there was a threat to judicial independence, but that it was not imminent. Neither the loss of public trust in the judiciary nor the fear of impending encroachments on judicial independence augurs well for achievement of quality justice on the Italian peninsula.

Transitions to democracy are difficult, and though Italy has been a democracy of sorts for more than half a century, it has not yet fully embraced a liberal democratic culture. The first alternation in power occurred in 1996, after fifty years of coalition governments dominated by the now discredited Christian Democratic Party.[51] The 1996 election perhaps signalled that the transition was complete. The genius of democracy lies in its provision of a process for resolving intergroup conflicts,[52] and conflicts are seen as resolved legitimately when the rules are followed and the judges and prosecutors are believed to be legally competent and impartial.

A study of the Russian Constitutional Court over its first decade found that after a few years and one dissolution the court discovered that to develop credibility it must consciously avoid acute political questions, and thus it sidestepped particularly knotty political issues, like those of separation of powers.[53] The Italian Constitutional Court followed a similar path when it was first established, but the Italian ordinary judiciary never recognized a need for prudence or temperance. Their independence protected them. As Italians adjust to a new political scheme in which alternation in power becomes the norm, presumably a stronger liberal democratic culture will take hold. Hopefully consolidation of democracy in Italy will create a climate in which the judicial apparatus can exist in a healthy equilibrium with the other institutions of government. 'Legitimacy resolves itself in legality,' and is compromised when 'judge-legislators ... increasingly take the law in their hand as if there was nothing more to it than having a winning hand.'[54]

NOTES

1 Prillaman, *The Judiciary and Democratic Decay in Latin America*, 15.
2 Connolly, 'Introduction: Legitimacy and Modernity.'
3 Fiss, 'The Right Degree of Independence.'
4 Russell, 'Toward a General Theory of Judicial Independence.'
5 See, e.g., Birchfield and Crepaz, 'The Impact of Constitutional Structures and Collective and Competitive Veto Points on Income Inequality in Industrialized Democracies,' 175–200; Calvert, McCubbins, and Weingast, 'A Theory of Political Control and Agency Discretion,' 588–611; Carey and Soberg Shugart, 'Calling Out the Tanks or Filling Out the Forms?'; Shepsle, 'Institutional Arrangements and Equilibrium in Multidimensional Voting Models,' 27–59; Tsebelis, 'Decision Making in Political Systems'; and Tsebelis, 'Veto Players and Law Production in Parliamentary Democracies.'
6 Volcansek, 'Constitutional Courts as Veto Players.'
7 Landes and Posner, 'The Independent Judiciary in an Interest-Group Perspective.'
8 Epstein, Knight and Shvetsova, 'The Role of Constitutional Courts in the Establishment and Maintenance of Democratic Systems of Government.'
9 Senese, 'Il Governo della Magistratura in Italia Oggi.'
10 Volcansek, *Constitutional Politics in Italy*, 21–3.
11 Ginsborg, *A History of Contemporary Italy*, 149.
12 Cazzola and Morisi, *La Mutua Diffidenza.*

13 Volcansek, 'The Judicial Role in Italy.'
14 Paciotti, *Sui Magistrati.*
15 Guarnieri and Pederzoli, *The Power of Judges.*
16 Guarnieri, *La Giustizia in Italia.*
17 Zanotti, *Le Attivita Extragiudizaria dei Magistrati Ordinari.*
18 Guarnieri, *La Giustizia in Italia.*
19 Paciotti, *Sui Magistrati.*
20 Morisi, *Anatomia della Magistratura Italia.*
21 Ibid.
22 Senese, 'Il Governo della Magistratura in Italia Oggi.'
23 Guarnieri, *La Giustizia in Italia.*
24 De Franciscis, 'Italy.'
25 Salazar, *La Magistratura.*
26 De Franciscis, 'Italy.'
27 Ibid., 59.
28 Volcansek, 'The Judicial Role in Italy.'
29 Guarnieri, *Magistratura e Politica in Italia.*
30 Guarnieri and Pederzoli, *La Magistratura nelle Democrazie Contemporane*; and Paciotti, *Sui Magistrati.*
31 Guarnieri and Pederzoli, *La Magistratura nelle Democrazie.*
32 Ginsborg, *A History of Contemporary Italy.*
33 De Franciscis, 'Italy.'
34 Chimenti, *Storia dei Referendum.*
35 Cazzola and Morisi, *La Mutua Diffidenza.*
36 Bufacci and Burgess, *Italy since 1989.*
37 Ginsborg, *Italy and Its Discontents.*
38 'Dear Mr. Berlusconi ...,' *The Economist,* 2–8 August 2003, 23–8.
39 'One Down,' *The Economist,* 29 November–6 December 2003, 48.
40 'Bocciato il Lodo Salva-Berlusconi,' *La Repubblica,* 14 January 2004, 1.
41 Nelken, 'Berlusconi e i Giudici.'
42 Prillaman, *The Judiciary and Democratic Decay in Latin America.*
43 Guarnieri and Pederzoli, *The Power of Judges.*
44 Volcansek, 'The Judicial Role in Italy.'
45 Di Federico, 'Prosecutorial Independence and the Democratic Requirement of Accountability in Italy.'
46 Lucca, *Giustizia all'Italiana.*
47 Guarnieri, *La Giustizia in Italia.*
48 Guarnieri and Pederzoli, *La Magistratura nelle Democrazie Contemporane.*
49 Lucca, *Giustizia all'Italiana.*
50 Guarnieri, *La Giustizia in Italia.*

51 Bufacci and Burgess, *Italy since 1989.*
52 Przeworski, 'Some Problems in the Study of the Transition to Democracy.'
53 Epstein, Knight, and Shvetsova, 'The Role of Constitutional Courts in the Establishment and Maintenance of Democratic Systems of Government.'
54 Sartori, *The Theory of Democracy Revisited.*

9 The Selection of Judges in France: Searching for a New Legitimacy

DORIS MARIE PROVINE AND ANTOINE GARAPON

A nation's system for selecting judges reveals its presuppositions, not just about judging, but also about effective governance. In France the prevailing view is that the government must be able to act without being second-guessed by courts. The judiciary is independent of the legislative and executive branches in order to ensure that it can resolve disputes fairly, but it is, in a fundamental sense, subordinate to them. Courts interpret the law as it comes to them without undertaking constitutional review. France recognizes the desirability of some independent review of legislation to protect fundamental rights, but not by its courts. The nation's aversion to investing its ordinary judiciary with power of judicial review sets it apart from most modern democracies.

For France the issue is how to organize the judiciary *within* a republican state. Even in a system in which courts are assigned a subordinate role, their effective functioning requires that they be perceived as independent, yet accountable, efficient, but also fair (see Volcansek, this volume). The absence of the power of constitutional review, however, adds a unique dimension to the effort to resolve the tensions among these not-quite-compatible goals. Lacking the power to contradict the elected branches confines French judges to the shadows. Certainly they are much less prominent than judges in Anglo-American nations, and the appointment process is much less openly political. The partisan judicial elections and wrangling over appointments that are so characteristic of the American system are completely absent in France, to everyone's great relief.

In France, judicial selection is almost a bureaucratic affair. Young people are trained for the job in a specialized school and appointed to positions through competitive exams. They rise through the ranks with positive evaluations. Is this approach adequate to the task creating a competent, trustworthy judiciary? Do judges have the intellectual preparation and the flexible procedures needed to resolve the ever-more complex disputes that come before them? Can the system effectively manage burgeoning caseloads? Will judges implement the new rights articulated by the meta-national courts and maintain a sense of justice in the nation's trial courts? How can judges be encouraged to remain aloof from and uninfluenced by powerful interests? How can skilled, talented people be attracted to the judiciary?

Its commitment to judicial passivity puts France somewhat out of step with democratizing tendencies in other parts of the world. The idea that courts should be actively engaged with the problems of modern, globalizing society is gaining ground worldwide, and regional and international courts are springing up to deal with legal issues arising from interdependent economies and internationalising norms (Tate and Vallinder, 1995; Weiler and Haltern, 1998; Sweet, 2000). These courts are making far-reaching decisions, giving life to international economic and human rights treaties and conventions (Volcansek, 1997; Dorr, 1993; Forsythe, 1991). Some of these decisions directly affect France. At the national level, there is a parallel movement throughout the democratic world to accept judicial review; the typical arrangement is to entrust a special constitutional court to exercise this function (Kavass, 1992; Clements, 1994). Although France still rejects the concept of co-equal branches that check and balance each other, the press of experience elsewhere is encouraging it to reconsider its Napoleonic-era devotion to the idea that courts must be under executive domination.

France, the inspiration for much of the civil law world's judicial systems, is in an interesting predicament. In rejecting judicial review, France has rejected the regime-legitimizing function that constitutional courts perform, a valuable asset in a time when politics is becoming increasingly contentious and the nation state is challenged from many directions. The level of French dissatisfaction with government is high. France is under enormous pressure to become more efficient, to integrate its minority populations, and to maintain some semblance of its former importance in the world. The welfare state in France, as everywhere in the world, is running out of steam, and in its place a vision of a more open, individually responsible society is emerging.

In responding to these changes France appears to be handicapped not only by fear of drastic change, but also by its constricted vision of the judicial function. The irony is that French exceptionalism does not rest on a rejection of the idea of the rule of law or a lack of interest in the individual. France is properly viewed as the birthplace of the idea that government should respect individual rights. The French Declaration of the Rights of Man parallels (and predates) the U.S. Bill of Rights in most important respects, guaranteeing equality and liberty, freedom of religion and thought, and the protection of life, liberty, and property (see Morton, 1991: 133–4). The difference lies in their enforceability; the Rights of Man never became operational as a citizen corrective against governmental over-reaching.

The analysis in this chapter therefore begins with the tradition of republican judging, the mindset that explains why judicial work is organized as it is in France. French republicanism constrains courts and empowers the legislature. France constrains courts not just by denying them the power of judicial review, but also by separating and reducing other functions. Ordinary courts are kept quite separate from administrative tribunals. Appellate power is reduced to the bare minimum consistent with providing a right to appeal. Constitutional issues are delegated to a non-judicial body that makes no law and decides no cases. This French finesse of judicial power does avoid certain kinds of confrontations between politicos and judges, but creates institutional problems of its own. The absence in France of a strong sense of judging as an honoured profession makes it hard to recruit top-flight judges. The tendency for prosecutors and judges to be seen in the same light undermines the sense that the criminal courts are fair. Most significantly, the absence of judicial review undermines popular confidence in government, especially among minority populations who are not well represented in any part of public service.

The Tradition of Republican Judging

France can trace its approach to judicial office to Jean Jacques Rousseau, who had little interest in the strategy of dividing powers in order to protect mankind from its baser instincts. Rousseau was not necessarily opposed to executive and judicial authority, but he conceived them as subordinate to the legislature, which he saw as the depository of the general will (Cummins, 1986: 599; Morton, 1991: 135). Nor did Rousseau share John Locke's view that individual rights are prior to government authority and separate from it.

The French revolution sealed the fate of the courts; they never recovered from the enormous loss of prestige suffered when they took the side of the *ancien regime*, which the revolutionaries associated with corruption and support for the royalty. The revolutionary government rejected separation of powers, and ever since, proposals to introduce judicial review to the French appellate courts have been regularly defeated as the first step towards the dreaded *government des juges*. This position has survived various constitutional revisions, including those of 1958, that more precisely outlined individual rights and set stricter limits on government power. Judges are now protected from arbitrary dismissal, but they are not authorized to contradict legislative judgment on matters of constitutional import. The rights of citizens are stated quite precisely, but people cannot litigate to protect them. French legal culture is thus paradoxical in honouring the rights of man, but opposing judicial enforcement of those rights. It could be said that France respects the rights of the citizen, but at a collective, rather than individual, level.

The effort since the revolutionary period has been to avoid courts as nearly as possible in all respects, spelling out the law in codes and regulations as clearly as possible, so as to make law 'judge proof' (Morton, 1991: 134). As Cummins wrote in 1986: 'Despite many changes in the almost two centuries since the French Revolution of 1789, the constitutional system as it relates to the courts has preserved the basic form and inner coherence imprinted on it by the intellectual preferences, historical perspective, and law-making of the revolutionaries and thus has a strong tendency to favour legislative decision and law-making, leaving the role of the courts, however, important it may have been in practice, limited and defined in reference to that central preference' (594). The French have also traditionally been suspicious of executive power. Before the 1958 reforms, the legislature completely dominated the government.

The long-standing conviction that courts must be subordinate began to show signs of change in the 1970s, and especially after the fall of the Berlin wall. French courts became more accustomed to the interventions of the European Court on Human Rights and the European Community Court. Europe's governing bodies, such as the Council of Europe and the European Parliament, were encouraging cross-national comparisons relevant to individual rights with their investigations of policing, welfare, and other institutions (Provine, 1996). This general thawing of attitudes about courts may be challenged as the state moves to deal with new threats to national security in the wake of the September 11, 2001 attack on the World Trade Center. It remains to be seen how France will balance pressures for greater liberty and more attention to individual rights against the need for state-controlled security measures.

One problem is that the basic structure of the French state is not suited to the development of individual rights through judge-made constitutional law. As Howarth and Varouxakis note: 'France became from quite early on a highly centralized and bureaucratised country, where the institutions that constituted "the state" became extremely powerful and influential' (2003: 20). This part of government is largely self-regulating, relying on approximately eight hundred administrative judges to resolve the disputes with citizens that arise in the course of allocating benefits, taxation, and other matters. The corps of administrative judges operates within their own distinctive milieu; the regular judiciary is not involved in overseeing the administrative state, a distinction that is clearly preserved in law. In the words of one revolutionary statute still in effect: 'The judges will not be allowed, under penalty of forfeiture, to disturb in any manner whatsoever, the activities of the administrative corps, nor to summon before them the administrators, concerning their functions' (quoted in Rudden, 1991: 142; Abraham, 1993; 256). This arrangement could not be changed without altering the constitution, which prescribes two 'orders' of courts: ordinary courts (*ordre judiciaire*) and administrative courts (*ordre administratif*) (Dadomo and Farran, 1996: 48–9). When major administrative issues arise, it is politicians and the high administrative elite, the *enarchs*, who are expected to resolve them, not the appellate courts. Their decisions sometimes establish administrative policy, but their point of reference is the laws on the books, not constitutional values.

Constitutional Review in France

The determination to keep constitutional issues out of courts does not leave France entirely without constitutional review. The 1958 constitution created an alternative to judicial review: a constitutional council to review legislation before promulgation for 'compatibility with the constitution.' The council was the outgrowth of a major governmental overhaul that established a stronger presidency and initiated many other important changes. At first the council's jurisdiction was limited to separation of powers issues and voting irregularities. In a 1971 decision, however, the council took it upon itself to apply fundamental norms outlined in the 1958 and earlier constitutions, the so-called *bloc de constitutionnalité*.

This French version of *Marbury v. Madison* created a new, much more expansive, role for the Constitutional Council, and fundamental rights issues soon dominated its agenda. In 1974, Parliament eased the rules for sending legislation to the council, which has helped it grow into a major player in French politics. The checking role of the council is particularly evident in times of stress, as in 1981, when President Mitterand attempted to enact a socialist program over Gaullist opposition. Conflict within government gives the council the last word on the validity of important legislation and has helped it to develop a jurisprudence of sorts. Koopmans concludes that 'it is much more like a true court than in its early days, and its composition as well as its way of proceeding are beginning to show judicial characteristics' (2003: 74; see also 75–6).

Without gainsaying its important role in resolving issues of fundamental rights in proposed legislation, it should be noted that the Constitutional Council lacks many of the powers of a constitutional court. The review process is private, and limited to legislation that has not yet been enacted into law. It does not provide a forum for individuals dissatisfied with a law, or a place for courts to refer constitutional issues. Review is detailed and specific to the proposed law in question. Although Parliament treats its decisions with deference and typically rewrites legislation in light of the council's advice, the decisions have no significance as precedent. The council could never, as American courts frequently do, supervise the administration of a public institution under a consent decree, becoming, in effect, a parallel government in dealing with a social problem (Morton, 1991: 145–6). The council's decisions have no effect on the administrative agencies or courts. There have been attempts to increase the ambit of the council by allowing individuals to petition for constitutional review, but these have so far been defeated (ibid. 148).

The selection of members for the Constitutional Council is a matter of high politics. Nominations are made along party lines, but the turnover is frequent enough that the council is never very far out of step with Parliament and the President. Three of the nine members are appointed by the President of the Republic, who also designates the president of the council; three members are chosen by the President of the National Assembly, and three more by the President of the Senate, all for nine-year, non-renewable terms, with one from each constituency chosen every three years. Those selected include former presidents of France and other prominent people. The chief requirement for selection is acute political sensibility and recognized status as a wise head.

Legal credentials or experience are not required, though so far, those nominated have had them.

The increasing visibility of the Constitutional Council in its role as 'guardian of the constitution' highlights the tension between old and new ways of envisioning law and courts in France. The civil law tradition downplays the role of courts in making law and safeguarding its overall coherence. The major source of law is conceived to be statutes and codes created by legislatures. In the civil law tradition, legal scholars, not judges, are the guardians of the law, studying codes and legislation to understand its inner logic and help to maintain its overall coherence. When there is a dispute about legal meaning, it is their opinion that is sought. Not surprisingly, there is no tradition of parsing cases to search for underlying legal principles. This approach is beginning to show significant signs of strain, however. European judges demonstrate a different model of legal growth, articulating rules of decision and general principles of law that trump provisions in national codes and statutes. These decisions are frequently creative and far-reaching in their implications. They encourage judges in member states to be more wide-ranging in their own decisions. The rise of human rights rhetoric also tends to empower judges at all levels (see Koopmans, 87–91).

Judicial Recruitment

The 'ordinary' magistrates in France, that is, those who are not part of the administrative corps, generally focus on the prosaic work of dispute resolution, hearing auto accident cases, applying the criminal law, and enforcing commercial and private agreements. There are approximately eight thousand of these 'ordinary judges' (in a nation of about 60 million). They are concentrated in the *Tribunaux de grande instance*, which handle the vast majority of both civil and criminal cases, and the *Tribunaux de police*, which occupy themselves with minor police infractions. There are, in addition, regional specialized courts for serious criminal cases and for commercial cases. Atop all of these is the *Cour de cassation.*

The entire culture is oriented to constrain the impact of the personality of the judge. Terms on the top appellate court (*Cour de cassation*) are short. By law and tradition these judges adjudicate upon the narrowest basis possible. The caseload is gargantuan, and it is very difficult to create a coherent jurisprudence within the formulaic system of announcing decisions. Dissents are unheard of. All of this reinforces the civil law mythology that judging is a technical and deductive skill, with no creative or subjective component. At the trial level, the role of the judge is to act as if the civil code already contains the correct answer – the only question is which rule applies. Efficiency is a dominant concern. The system seems unable to face up to what judges have always done in resolving disputes, and it seems unwilling to admit that, in finding solutions to the limitations of codified law, judges have created, in effect, a common law.

The devotion to a technical view of judging is most evident in the way judges in France are prepared for office. Common law countries recruit judges from the ranks of lawyers, while France, following a civil law tradition, trains them for judicial office (see Volcansek and Hamad in this volume for other examples). The schooling is similar for judges and prosecutors – both must graduate from the *École nationale de la magistrature* (ENM) in Bordeaux. Entrance is by competitive exam for those who graduate from their universities with a law certificate, but persons with five years of experience in the civil service or legal practitioners are also eligible. Those who succeed at the exam are appointed *auditeurs de justice* and become part of the judicial corps, receiving a salary as they take courses. The coursework lasts thirty-one months, and includes an introductory cycle of courses followed by a cycle of traineeships in the court system and supporting agencies, such as juvenile facilities. Most of the courses are taught by judges temporarily on leave from their judicial duties. At the end of this period of study a prospective judge takes another exam and is presented with a list of available posts prepared by the Ministry of Justice. Initial appointments are made on the basis of examination scores, those receiving the highest scores getting first pick of the positions. Most of the graduates are appointed to a judgeship in the provinces at the lowest level, where they work as investigating judges or members of the bench that adjudicates minor criminal cases.

This meritocratic system is a complete departure from earlier practice. Until the twentieth century, the selection of judges was based entirely on the power of recommendations that favoured chance and political opinions. This system was much criticized, but it was also difficult to change. After two failed attempts at selection by examination in 1876 and 1906, the decree of 18 February 1908 created a professional exam, which was retained until 1958. At this point the Fifth Republic undertook the most important reforms in the administration of justice since the Revolution. Ordinance 59–77 of 7 January 1959 created the

National Centre of Judicial Studies, which became the ENM in 1970. The new school was modelled on the already well-established *École nationale d'administration*, the elite graduate school that is the source of virtually all of France's governing elite.

The creation of the ENM solved a crisis in recruitment that had arisen in the 1950s. There were at that time too few candidates to ensure quality judges. The establishment of a school with a clear program of study and a capacity to recruit from broad segments of society has made an enormous difference. By the mid-1970s, the number of applicants had increased sharply to more than a thousand per year for about two hundred positions. Women and people of modest economic backgrounds became for the first time a significant part of the student body, and they have steadily moved into the court system. By 1990, women outnumbered men in the lower ranks of the judiciary, though they are still a distinct minority at the top. The rate of pay has also gone up; judges are now paid slightly more than university professors in France.

By 2002, the impact of the ENM on the preparation of the judiciary was evident: 84 per cent of the active judges had graduated from the institution. The remainder have been recruited directly from the civil service or the private sector by special commission. The impact of the ENM on continuing education of judges has also been significant. According to data published in 2000, more than 4,000 magistrates out of 6,847, or about 58 per cent, had taken at least a one-week course at ENM. Many appellate judges had also taken special workshops organized for them.

The judicial branch is governed by the *Conseil supérieur de la magistrature* (CSM), created by the 1958 constitution to assist the President of the Republic as 'guarantor of the independence of the judicial authority.' The President, however, is involved only as a formality; the minister of justice is vice-president of the CSM and its acting head (Dadomo and Farran, 1996: 143–4). The membership – four lay members selected by the other branches, six judges, and six prosecutors – is a careful blend designed to represent relevant constituencies. Members sit for four-year, non-renewable terms. The idea, according to the council's web page, is to 'prevent supporters of corporatism or lobbies from having too much of an influence,' while at the same time ensuring that the judiciary will not 'become an instrument of political power.'

The CSM is in charge of nominating, appointing, and disciplining judges and prosecutors. The most important appointments are those at the highest levels: the *Cour de cassation*, the first president of the Courts of Appeals, and the presidents of the *Tribunaux de grande instance*, a total of four hundred positions. Selections at this level are made not by seniority or written exam, but by oral interviews and recommendations. The process, wholly insulated from political oversight, leaves room for connections, professional repute, and received opinions about the appropriate social and educational background of judges to play a determinative role in judicial careers. The tendency towards insularity is increased by the fact that the CSM divides into two panels in its work, one dominated by judges and the other by prosecutors. The minority of lay members on each panel tend to defer to their professional colleagues.

Disciplinary action is only slightly less insulated from political oversight. Standards are high and broadly stated, including, for example, breaches 'against honour, scrupulousness or dignity' (Lafon, 1996: 34). Conflicts of interest and failure to maintain secrecy and independence from political authority are punishable. Dismissals, however, are very rare. The severity of the rules has encouraged the development of alternatives to full formal proceedings, and every attempt is made to deal with problems administratively. Judges are punished with negative evaluations and poor ratings that influence promotions. Sometimes transfers are negotiated. Or the judge may get a warning, with an amnesty provision after three years that expunges the record. In the most serious cases, the executive, acting through the Ministry of Justice, brings a prosecution before the whole CSM, which convenes as a court. Cases taken to this level include insubordination, failure to respect procedural rules, professional negligence, and scandal in one's private life. The number of prosecutions, however, has always been small. Jacqueline Lafon finds, after an exhaustive survey of misconduct suits, a remarkable consensus about the appropriate rules of judicial conduct over the centuries (1996: 48).

Such independence from political authority, not just in appointment, but also in matters of discipline, is an important accomplishment in a system historically so suspicious of judges. France appears to have been successful in protecting judges from political authorities. This separation from everyday politics, however, comes at a price. Professional values thoroughly dominate the appointment and disciplinary process, and the judiciary's dominate professional union, *l'Union Syndicale des Magistrats*, plays an active role in protecting judges at all costs. Given the low level of regard in which judges are generally held in French society, the system seems quite vulnerable to criticism.

The Debate over Judicial Selection in France

The development of a credible educational program and a governance system that protects the independence of judges have gone far to enhance the status and legitimacy of judicial office in France. The judiciary used to be widely regarded as an occupation for those who lacked the ambition to be practising lawyers or academics. Many people identified judges with the bureaucracy, and polls consistently gave the judicial system poor ratings for efficiency and independence. The state did little to help. For years, working conditions deteriorated as caseloads swelled. These conditions encouraged an organizational movement among judges that began in 1968 and grew to include three unions seeking better pay and working conditions.

Although the establishment of the ENM helped to change attitudes about judges, it did not fully succeed in elevating their calling to the status of an honoured profession. It had been hoped that the ENM, designed on the typically French model of *grandes écoles*, would combine the egalitarian spirit of the Republic with the elitism characteristic of administrative office in France. But it has only partly succeeded in this mission. Elite status depends to a significant extent on the reputation of those who attend. The *École nationale d'administration* has been more successful in creating an elite, high-quality professional corps. Should it attempt to be more selective? What are the appropriate criteria for those who graduate from undergraduate programs with a certificate in legal study? Should the ENM attempt to recruit more practising lawyers, as Anglo-American nations do?

The status and repute of the judiciary are likely to grow as the current generation of young people move into careers. French public opinion is becoming somewhat more favourable towards the idea of litigation to achieve social ends, and human rights discourse is becoming part of everyday vocabulary. People tend to be energized by every show of judicial independence from insider-oriented governance, such as the conviction of President Chirac's protégé, Alain Juppé, for improper use of political funds. Juppé, the mayor of Bordeaux, a former prime minister, a party leader, and a member of Parliament, was widely viewed as Chirac's heir apparent. Chirac responded to this show of independence by trying to short circuit the appointments process with an ad hoc committee of its own made up of the chiefs of the Council of State, Court of Claims, and Court of Cassation. But the judges refused to deal with this new body and the council resumed its function.

Despite this, the fact that Alain Juppé was convicted suggests the potential of the courts in political reform efforts. Some young people are beginning to think that the public interest might be better served by a career in the judiciary rather than in the administrative sector. Preparatory studies in law have now been introduced at prestigious undergraduate institutions. With these developments, ENM is beginning to become a professional destination. Recently, more university graduates took the exams for ENM than for ENA.

Still, it is unlikely that judging will become as highly respected as administrative service in France. Magistrates are respected for their independence from the governing elite, but they do not enjoy equivalent status. They exist, at all levels, a little on the margins, partly because their function is not well understood. The absence of a clear normative base for their actions hurts the reputation of the judiciary. When a judge acts to contain government initiative, the public interpret the decision in various ways. Some see judges as exacting retribution or settling scores against a government that largely ignores them. Others appreciate their independence but are leery of too powerful a role for courts. This cultural predisposition to see the dangers of judicial activism and miss the constraining features of the judicial role tends to dampen enthusiasm for reform-oriented litigation. Class actions and other citizen-initiated efforts to bring court decisions to bear on public policy are virtually unknown in France. Instead, the state is expected to engage in the resolution of social problems without the prompting of lawsuits. Government is widely viewed as more capable of effective action than courts, when government is motivated to act.

With the growing attractiveness of judging as a career and more attention to the role of the judge in deciding important cases, certain weaknesses in the way judges are selected have become more obvious. One criticism is that the first examination that prospective judges take, part of which involves an oral interview, unduly favours middle-class students. The way the oral exam is graded ensures that the successful candidate will be an agreeable person and will have a good grasp of general culture. But does this system select the best judges? Immigrants fare particularly poorly on this part of the exam. In general, the less technical parts of the examination are very difficult for candidates who are not middle class, particularly for those from an immigrant background.

Another criticism is that the current system does not adequately prepare prospective judges for the complex social and economic problems that frequently confront them in their work. The French system, in rejecting the concept of the judge as a neutral, passive, and relatively uninformed umpire, places significant demands on judges. The judge in a complicated criminal case must actively control all aspects of the litigation, particularly its investigative phases. It is lawyers, not judges, who are passive in this system and individual rights are limited. The active role of the investigating magistrate exposes judges to criticism for lack of sufficient technical knowledge and for relentless pursuit of the truth. Particularly critical are the wealthy professionals who are sometimes the object of civil suits – doctors, bankers, businesspersons, and sports figures. Cyclist Lance Armstrong was angry enough with his treatment in a French court that he opted to move his residence to Spain (Armstrong, 2003). It is difficult to know what to make of this criticism because these professionals are self-interested: the judge determined to investigate their activities is a threatening and unwelcome presence in their lives. The youth and lack of expertise of the young judicial recruits may nevertheless be beneficial to society as a whole.

Justice in Many Rooms

In addition to the historic split between administrative and 'ordinary' judges, France has greatly expanded and differentiated quasi-judicial functions in the past fifteen years, multiplying jurisdictional powers, creating extra-judicial and pre-trial authority, and establishing para-judges. Alternative dispute resolution, which was embraced early in France, has become highly institutionalized. Some of these judicial and quasi-judicial roles occur under private auspices. There are professionals who facilitate transactions, and negotiate, arbitrate, and mediate family disputes and disagreements among businesses. Associations of negotiators will soon have the power to sanction their own members. This evolution has been inspired by the proliferation of quasi-judicial powers in the United States and by global economic developments that involve complex transactions (Dezalay, Barth, and Bourdieu, 1998).

Scholars have noted the same centrifugal tendencies in the U.S. system and some, like Judith Resnik, have been critical of this trend (see Resnik, 2002). It is a movement that cries out for limits, but also for sensitivity to the matter of qualifications and expertise. Some changes have been relatively uncontroversial, such as the creation of a new class of judicial assistants. Others are more problematic, especially in a system without a constitutional court. Consider, for example, the fate of a proposal by President Chirac to re-invent the ancient office of the justice of the peace, which he dubbed *juges de proximité.* Chirac's goal was to bring justice closer to citizens with lay judges, and thereby increase the legitimacy of the entire system of justice. The project was short-circuited, however, by the opposition of the Ministry of Justice, which required, as an administrative measure, that a law degree be compulsory for these new positions. The fundamental problem is that France needs to expand its judicial capacity but has committed itself to a single, quite narrow, route to becoming a judge: taking an exam at a relatively young age and moving through the ranks of established judgeships.

France also needs to clarify the relationship between 'ordinary' and administrative judges. The current system separates them completely. There is no general legislation covering the recruitment, retention, and powers of administrative judges. About 25 per cent of the administrative judicial corps is recruited from the *École nationale de l'administration,* where they receive a broad training in civil service norms and practice. The rest come from administrative posts and receive no specifically judicial training before assuming their dispute-resolving responsibilities. Their legal status is a matter of controversy: the Council of State has ruled that administrative judges are not magistrates in the constitutional sense of that term, but the Court of Cassation and the Constitutional Council have applied a broader definition. As Dadomo and Farran conclude: 'Even if they are not *magistrates* within the meaning of the Constitution ... there is no doubt that they carry out the functions of *magistrates* in an administrative court' (1996: 159; see also 155–9). Whatever their precise authority, however, no one would argue that they enjoy the degree of independence the constitution envisions for its regular judges.

The irony is that the regular judges, despite their independence, and despite their specialized judicial training, enjoy less prestige than administrative judges. The association of the administrative judges with the Council of State and with the capital city heightens their image as important persons close to power. The 'ordinary judges' are the provincials in this proudly centralized system. This attitude is reinforced by the fact that France lacks a tradition of judicial lawmaking and tends to downplay the significance of creativity and intelligence in judicial decision making. Merryman's observation is still true: judges in France are thought to be no more than technocratic legal experts, lacking any real power (1985: 56). The fragmentation and minimization of judicial authority that is emblematic of the French judicial system also helps to make judges seem insignificant. It remains to be seen how European pressure to respect procedural niceties in criminal trials will affect this attitude. Over 60 per cent of litigants before the European Court on Human Rights rely on the Convention's procedural provisions in Article 6. Their successful suits are creating an entirely new procedural era in Europe.

Racial, Gender, and Ethnic Diversity on the Bench

France, like other modern nations, is under pressure to diversify governmental offices, including the bench. The traditional republican view of 'one France' without recognized differences has been challenged by a more pluralistic analysis, by feminism, and by the reality of class and ethnic conflict. Women have made relatively rapid gains in this environment. They now dominate the ranks of apprentice judges. Anne Boigeol, writing in 1993, reported a 'homogenation' of careers of men and women at the lower levels (521–2). Top posts, particularly those where political affiliation is a factor, remain less open to women. But even here, feminism has made a difference, at least to the extent that there is a general sense that a bench completely devoid of women would be unacceptable.

The representation of immigrants in the judiciary is much more problematic. The government has not yet dealt effectively with the drastic under-representation of immigrants in government and public life, particularly Muslims from Algeria. There is even a dearth of relevant data with which to study the extent of the phenomenon: France does not keep track of the number of its foreign-born citizens. It is known, however, that the Muslim population in France numbers about 5,000,000, about 8 per cent of the population. Many Algerians immigrated just before and during the war between the two nations; they came to find employment during the economic boom that France experienced in the 1950s and 1960s. This population is overwhelmingly poor. The unemployment rate, about 20–25 per cent, is about twice that of the rest of the population. The Algerian situation remains as it was under French colonial rule in some respects, only now the Algerians are living in the land of the colonizer.

The vast majority of this community have been for a long time practically invisible in French political and social life. They are almost entirely absent, for example, from the Parliament, the courts, and among top civil servants in the administrative sector. They are almost as absent at the local level, even in the areas of large immigrant populations, such as

Lyon. French Algerians are nevertheless the lightning rod for much of the ethnic conflict in France. They are over-represented in street crime and other forms of violence. Some display their fundamentalist faith at every opportunity, in defiance of the French commitment to secularism.

The tendency for French political elites to ignore the obvious may help to account for the rise of Le Pen in French politics. Xenophobia and nationalism are rife in France, with widespread unemployment and underemployment enhancing the influence of the anti-immigrant right. In 2002, one in every four French people said that they agree with most of Le Pen's views in general. There is a perception that the political class is not really aware of the depredations of impoverished immigrants, and that they remain isolated from the crime and delinquency that the less affluent experience. The major parties are reluctant to come to grips with the complexities of this situation, and uncertain how to proceed. It is easier to stay aloof, particularly because this segment of the population is not organized to vote or to express itself in any organized fashion.

This debate is in a period of rapid evolution, as indicated by the nation's tribulations over the appointment of a Muslim prefect and over the issue of headscarves and other religious paraphernalia. Religion is increasingly a flashpoint for ethnic conflict in France. Muslims are believed to be responsible for a rise in anti-Semitic violence. Their demands for sex-segregated swimming pools and gym classes, for prayer breaks, and for other concessions to religion are widely resented in a rigorously secular society. The atmosphere of crisis is surprising only in the sense that the immigrant issue is not new. The issue of accommodating religious practices within the public school system has been a sore point for some time, and past governments have even recognized the need to promote inclusion. *Le Monde* noted recently that two ordinances from 1958, both signed by General De Gaulle, reserved to French Muslims 10 per cent of public employment and offered a special exam for people already in service.

As pressure to acknowledge the rights of minorities grows, particularly with respect to Muslim citizens from Algeria, there will be increasing pressure on the judiciary to become more ethnically diverse. The highly regulated system of judicial recruitment could be reconfigured to create a stronger minority presence through a serious affirmative action policy. France has already demonstrated its willingness to use affirmative action to enhance the representation of women in elected office with *parité*, legislation that requires parties to nominate men and women in equal numbers to all offices. This new law required modification of the French constitution, and yet it was accomplished in reasonably rapid order. While the under-representation of women in elective office has by no means been solved in France, it has been ameliorated, and the issue has become a recognized part of the political agenda.

The Case of the Veil

The controversy over whether Muslim girls may wear a headscarf to school symbolizes the much broader problem of integration of the Muslim population in French society. The issue is not simply overcoming class barriers or cultural difference, but a subtle political resistance to integration on both sides borne of the colonial relationship and differences in beliefs about the proper relationship between state and religion. It is noteworthy, for example, that politicians have cast the conflict in terms of religious paraphernalia, ignoring the more fundamental problems of racism evidenced in ethnic urban ghettoes and the absence of attention to Arab language and culture in the schools and larger society. At this point, France is paying a price for not dealing with two salient facts about the historical situation in Algeria. First France accepted the Jewish residents of Algeria as full French citizens since before the Dreyfus era, but did not extend that same status to Algerian Muslims. The second fact, seldom noted, but nonetheless crucial to understanding the current situation, is that the war of independence failed to build a democratic society in Algeria; Algerian emigrants have no experience with democratic tolerance.

The Council of State at first attempted to resolve the headscarf dispute in a typically administrative way, suggesting that school officials could ask students wearing headscarves to remove them if the student's purpose was to proselytise for their religion, or if the scarf wearing disrupted school activities. The idea was to cool down a volatile issue at the local level if possible. When the controversy refused to go away, the National Assembly voted by an overwhelming majority to ban Muslim headscarves and other religious symbols from the public schools and reinforced the commitment to co-education in sports and other activities. The vote was 494–36 (with 31 abstentions) in the Assembly and equally lopsided in the Senate. Given this overwhelming show of support, the law will bypass the Constitutional Council and take effect without constitutional review. It will almost certainly receive review in the Strasbourg-based European Court of Human Rights, however.

Imagine how differently this debate would have been handled in the United States, where the rights of the girls and the government's historic support for private religious education would surely have figured more prominently into the debate. Where French analysts have tended to focus on the use of public space, those in the United States emphasize individual rights and the state's responsibility to be even-handed (see, e.g., Teitel, 2004). Decades of litigation have encouraged American individualism and sensitivity to the constitutional meaning of religious freedom and state involvement with religion.

Tendencies towards Convergence in Distinctive Systems

There are points of convergence between Anglo-American and civil law nations, even between countries like the United States and France, which are poles apart where the role of the judge in politics and society is concerned. All of these nations must somehow resolve the conflict between pressure for more meritocratic selection of judges and growing demands for political accountability. Diversity in the make-up of the bench is another salient issue everywhere. Even in France, devoted as it is to a modest, technocratic conception of judging, representation of diverse constituencies is considered important. As the power of judicial decrees becomes more widely understood, pressures will grow to develop systems of judicial selection that reward merit, find talent in diverse places, and connect ordinary people to the recruitment process. Canada, for example, has an explicit policy of multiculturalism; judicial appointments are made under an employment equity mandate designed to increase the number of women and ethnic minorities on the bench (see Morton, this volume).

Another point of convergence is the universal need to have enough courts, including a level responsive to the common problems of everyday living. France began with a large, bureaucratically organized and professionally trained judiciary, which it is now trying to open to more citizen-oriented elements. Hence the proposal for *juges de proximité*. Anglo-American nations, where the tradition of local lay judges competent to handle local affairs is well established, are trying to figure out how to professionalize this level without sacrificing informality and access (see Malleson in this volume). In both cases, the issue has so far been conceptualized in terms of professional credentials and localized jurisdiction. The more fundamental issue is whether judging can be rendered more democratically responsive (Olson and Dzar, 2004). With the proper organization and approach, can judges help connect citizens to their government and assist them in understanding the legal rules that affect them?

Both civil and common law nations are also feeling pressure to be more sensitive to international law and universal human rights. The political split within nations and between them is no longer primarily over the appropriate reach of the welfare state, but rather over the desirable degree of international integration. Nations where the internationalists dominate, like France, are thinking about how to train judges to take account of European practice and the decisions of European courts. A white paper prepared by the ENM, for example, proposes that the school undertake an ambitious preparation in European law, including international internships for judges in training. Where important legal posts are concerned, such as the presidency of the Constitutional Council, candidates are assessed according to their attitudes about the influence of Brussels and Strasbourg. These are not trivial questions in France because they resonate with fundamental concerns about which parts of French culture will be preserved and which will be jettisoned in the march towards Europeanization and modernization of the state.

Conclusion

France is fortunate to have the European Court of Human Rights and the European Community court to inject rights-oriented thinking into its policies. The Constitutional Council also helps to highlight the significance of individual rights in the formative stages of lawmaking. But France handicaps itself by not giving its ordinary judges the power to review legislation for constitutional defects. Judicial review would not weaken the French state. On the contrary, it would strengthen state authority by providing a citizen-controlled check on government. Even if French judges gained the power to overturn legislation, there would still be a tendency for social problems to bypass the courts. The French court system, as currently designed, discourages social litigation. To make courts more amenable to change-oriented litigation, the codes of civil and criminal procedure would need to be reformed in a way that would give lawyers more power to present and control their cases. France would have to find better ways to accommodate multiple plaintiffs; she might, for example, consider allowing class-action lawsuits. Such changes would, of course, represent a radical departure from the past.

France, it should be noted, is not under acute pressure to change. In the context of the systems examined in this book, France, at least since the 1958 constitutional revisions, has been a stable democracy. It has no need to revamp its institutions to attract foreign capital or to achieve legitimacy in the world's eyes. It stands in contrast to nations like Russia, which have had 'to purge the judicial corps of old Soviet-era judges, to fight against federal judges "going native" and their impunity, and to improve the accessibility and the reputation of the third branch' (quotation in Trochev, this volume, p. 376).

Still, there is some impetus for change in France. It comes from a fundamental incongruence between current practices and the needs of a globalizing economy that is more rights conscious than in the past, and more prone to use litigation to achieve desired changes. The new emphasis on litigation puts France under pressure to draw together its highly differentiated magistrates into a coherent, self-governing whole. Changing circumstances also make it desirable to bring new expertise to the regular courts, perhaps through more active recruitment from the practising bar and a more wide-ranging education for aspiring judges. Common law nations have an advantage in recruiting judicial personnel from the private sector. The jury system also offers the advantage of a symbolically significant lay check on judicial authority. The connection between courts and citizenry is further reinforced in the United States by the election of some judges and an appointment process that is openly political. These traditions help to legitimate courts by linking them to the public.

This book can be read as an extended essay on ways to give judges more democratic legitimacy, without necessarily resorting to selection as practised in the United States. In France, such a strengthening of democratic foundations will be necessary to attract the best candidates for judgeships. The dilemma is that without changes, the judiciary is destined to remain somewhat on the periphery and it will continue to be difficult to find creative, highly motivated judges. This hurts the judicial branch, but more importantly, it hurts France, which forfeits the contribution that courts could make to the process of orderly social and economic change.

10 The Selection Process of Constitutional Court Judges in Germany

CHRISTINE LANDFRIED

The expansion of judicial power can be observed in a growing number of political systems. In Tate and Vallinder's 1995 volume on judicial power, we find chapters on the United States, the United Kingdom, Australia, Canada, Italy, France, Germany, Sweden, the Netherlands, Malta, Israel, Russia, Southeast Asia, and Namibia.[1] Similarly, Alec Stone Sweet has shown how the judicialization of law-making changes public governance: 'The development of the constitution, as organized by constitutional rule-making, tends to draw actors into specific kinds of legal discourses, thus reinforcing the centrality – and legitimacy – of constitutional justice within the polity.'[2] A considerable amount of research has been conducted on the growth of judicial review or constitutional review[3] and the mechanisms by which the 'judicialization of politics' is shaped. But much less attention has been paid to the selection and election processes of Constitutional Court judges.

In Germany a lack of empirical evidence is one reason for the limited amount of research to date on this subject. While the formal appointments mechanisms are known, the reality of the process by which judges are chosen is not. One of the few journalists who regularly write about the Constitutional Court comments: 'Even the election of the pope is more democratic.' In the opinion of this journalist the judges are chosen in secret circles of political parties.[4]

Why is it important to analyse the politics of the selection of Constitutional Court judges? According to the research literature, while political parties determine the selection process, once elected the party affiliation of judges does not play a decisive role in their decision making.[5] Why should we care about selection if it does not affect the output of constitutional review?

Even if the importance of the selection process in terms of decision-making outcomes is difficult to measure, I want to argue that that process affects the legitimacy of a Constitutional Court. To do this, I will first outline a theoretical approach with which we can analyse the selection process of Constitutional Court judges in a representative democracy. I will then test this approach against the empirical findings of an analysis of the selection process of Constitutional Court judges in Germany. I will describe the formal procedures for selecting Constitutional Court judges and the composition of the court. Third, I want to show that the theory-based empirical findings have normative consequences for the selection process of Constitutional Court judges in a representative democracy. It is the hypothesis of this chapter that there is a correlation between the legitimacy of constitutional review and the selection process of judges. Constitutional review will only be regarded as legitimate in the long run if the principles of transparency, difference, and indirect democratic accountability govern the selection process of judges.

Theoretical Assumptions: The Conditions for Legitimate Constitutional Review

The recruitment of local and state judges in Germany is based on merit. Political considerations, however, do play a role in relation to leading positions in the judiciary. 'Competence remains the standard in selecting presidents, vice presidents, and presiding judges of panels in the various courts, but nearly all commentators agree that judges promoted to these positions of leadership are likely to mirror, to some extent, the political orientation of the ministry or government choosing them.'[6]

Merit is as important at the federal level as it is at the state level, but politics play a greater role in selecting federal judges.[7] Given their enormous political impact one would expect that democratic and transparent rules in selecting Constitutional Court judges are taken seriously – but the opposite is true in Germany. On the ideological premise that the Constitutional Court has no political power it is assumed that the selection process of judges should be governed by impartiality and that the influence of political parties should be reduced. As is often the case, if one denies the political character of an institution or an issue, the pretence of being apolitical is eventually exposed. Notwithstanding the rhetoric, in reality Constitutional Court judges in Germany are selected by a very small group of leading members of political parties both of the Bundestag and of the second chamber of the Bundesrat.[8]

Mary L. Volcansek has shown that a similar process exists for the Italian Constitutional Court. Five of the fifteen judges are named by the two chambers of Parliament, five by the President of the Republic, and five by the judges on the ordinary and administrative courts. The judges named by Parliament and by the President are allocated among the political parties: 'At least two thirds of the membership of the Court, therefore, is part of the lottizzazione or division whereby virtually all sectors of Italian civil life are allocated on the basis of political party affiliation. Despite the lottizzazione, the absolute independence of the judges is claimed. All decisions are unsigned and without dissents, making partisanship difficult to measure.'[9]

Taking into account the undeniable political impact of Constitutional Courts, I want to develop a theoretical approach in which preconditions that must be fulfilled in order to secure legitimate constitutional review are formulated. Here one can utilize the distinction drawn by Fritz W. Scharpf between input-oriented and output-oriented legitimacy.[10] In policy analysis input-legitimacy is concerned with the democratic rules that establish collectively binding decisions. Output-legitimacy relates to the effectiveness of political programs and their capacity to shape society in the interest of the common good. One can similarly speak of input-legitimacy when it comes to the selection process of Constitutional Court judges, and of output-legitimacy when the decisions of the Constitutional Court are at issue. The relation between the two types of legitimacy is instrumental in the sense that for output-legitimacy democratic rules are welcome as long as they serve effective policies,[11] but I also want to make the argument that input and output-legitimacy are more closely connected than they appear in W. Scharpf's analysis.

Democratic rules and input-legitimacy are in my view preconditions for the effectiveness of policies in the area of legislation as well as for the effectiveness of decisions in the area of constitutional review. Constitutional review thus needs both input-oriented and output-oriented legitimacy. The degree to which both types of legitimacy are realized depends on six conditions described below.

Constitutional Court judges have only limited democratic legitimacy because they are not directly elected by the people. The extent of their indirect democratic legitimacy will depend on the procedures for selecting and electing those judges. Transparency in the selection process is the first condition for securing an acceptable degree of legitimacy in a Constitutional Court. Such transparency can only be achieved if the selection of judges does not involve secret bargaining among political parties or a few members of those parties.

According to the German constitution, public governance must be exercised with reference to the will of the people (Article 20 II). The Constitutional Court participating in governance must be indirectly anchored in the sovereignty of the people. A second condition for a legitimate Constitutional Court therefore is that judges are elected by the representatives of the people in Parliament.[12]

A third condition is a selection and election process in which the need for a broad spectrum of professional experience among the judges is taken into consideration. As the court has to decide authoritatively on a broad range of subjects, its members should have at their disposal different educational, professional, political, and societal experiences.

The fourth condition is an ongoing recognition by political and judicial actors that in spite of the fact that a Constitutional Court takes decisions that have political consequences some difference between political and judicial decision making should be maintained. Politicians and judges have to be independent in so far as they have to decide according to specific criteria. In modern political systems in which the problem-solving capacity depends on looking at complex problems from different points of view, the existence of constitutional review can be beneficial in adding a point of view that is different from politics. Of course, judges who enjoy a great deal of independence may still 'decide cases in a manner that is deferential to powerful "others."'[13] But it is a plausible assumption that some institutional arrangements can protect judicial independence better than others.[14]

The other side of the coin is the independence of politicians. They should not carry obedience towards the Constitutional Court too far. The tendency for policy makers in parliaments increasingly to argue as if they were constitutional lawyers[15] is detrimental to democracy. When politicians anticipate constitutional review solely to avoid conflict with the Constitutional Court, and not because they want to ensure conformity with the constitution, they reduce the range of possible solutions to political and social problems. That 'legislators and constitutional judges, within certain legislative processes, are in nearly constant and intimate contact'[16] is not a desirable state of affairs for either the legislators or the judges. If the legislative impact of constitutional courts is a reflection of the growing ineffectiveness of parliamentary law-making, we should address the weaknesses of legislatures rather than give more and more political power to Constitutional Courts.

The fifth condition for legitimate constitutional review is that Constitutional Courts do not transcend their competences. Criteria for an appropriate division of labour between courts and parliaments are difficult to determine. A theory of constitutional review that contains standards for a separation of powers between the two cannot be derived from a subjective point of view or from an existing social consensus, but must be construed from the text and the genesis of the constitution.[17] On the basis of the constitution, criteria for a division of labour between parliaments and courts must be correlated with the functions of both institutions.

According to John Hart Ely, judges of Constitutional Courts are responsible for ensuring that the political process is 'open to those of all viewpoints on something approaching an equal basis.'[18] As long as judges control 'legitimate processes' and not 'legitimate outcomes,' judicial review would be compatible with democracy. I want to maintain Ely's distinction but use it to produce a more flexible interpretation of the appropriate division of labour. In relation to decisions on legitimate processes the courts have broad competences, and the boundaries between courts and parliaments shift in favour of Constitutional Courts. In relation to decisions on legitimate outcomes the courts have only restricted competences and the boundaries shift in favour of parliaments.

The final condition for legitimate constitutional review is the trust of citizens in the Constitutional Court. This trust has, to date, been high in Germany, but once lost it would be difficult to restore. It is all the more important therefore that the crisis of party democracy does not adversely affect the legitimacy of the Constitutional Court as a result of the lack of transparency in the selection of judges. I will now concentrate on the first three conditions, which have to do with the selection and election processes of Constitutional Court judges (table 10.1).

Empirical Findings: The Selection Process of Constitutional Court Judges

The formal procedure for selecting and electing Constitutional Court judges in Germany is prescribed in Article 94 of the constitution and in sections 3, 4, 5, 6, 7, 8, 9, and 10 of the Constitutional Court Law. The constitution stipulates that one-half of the sixteen members of the court are elected by the Bundestag and the other half by the Bundesrat for one term of twelve years (Article 94 II of the Constitution and § 4 of the Constitutional Court Law). Candidates must be lawyers and be at least forty years old. There are two Senates within the court, and three members of each Senate must have worked for at least three years as judges of a Federal High Court. Those judges who are to be elected by parlia-

TABLE 10.1
Conditions for the legitimacy of constitutional review

Independent variables	Dependent variable
1. Transparency of the selection of judges 2. Indirect democratic legitimacy of the election of judges 3. Differences in educational, professional, social, and political experience of judges 4. Taking into account the difference between political and judicial decision making 5. Making a difference between decisions on processes and decisions on outcomes with regard to the competencies of the Constitutional Court 6. Trust of citizens in the Constitutional Court	Input-legitimacy and output-legitimacy of constitutional review in a democracy

ment – the Bundestag – are not elected by the plenary of parliament, however, but by a committee of parliament. The committee for the election of judges of the Constitutional Court consists of twelve MEPs. Thus, the constitutional provision in article 94 which states that Parliament as a whole should elect the judges has been changed into the rule that twelve MEPs should decide who is going to the court in Karlsruhe. This reduced democratic legitimacy has been criticized in literature without any impact on the process.[19]

The members of the parliamentary committee for the election of Constitutional Court judges decide by a two-third majority. A two-third majority is also necessary for the election of a Constitutional Court judge in the Bundesrat. As a consequence of this majority the selection process has become a 'collaborative exercise between the ruling coalition and main opposition parties in both houses.'[20] It is an exercise behind closed doors. The secrecy of decision making inside the parliamentary committee is even written into the Constitutional Court Law, paragraph 6 of which states that members of the committee are obliged to keep secret what has become known about the personal circumstances of candidates. The debates about candidates are also confidential.

To prepare the work in the parliamentary committee and in the Bundesrat the Ministry of Justice keeps one list of all judges who qualify for appointment to the Constitutional Court and another of all judges who have been proposed by a parliamentary party (*Fraktion*), by the federal government, or by a state government (§ 8 II Constitutional Court Law). How the 'short listing' is done and which criteria are relevant in this process is not public knowledge.

It is well known that the preparation of the election is determined by a small number of people within the political parties.[21] In the 1990s, for instance, the 'judge makers' in the Bundestag were Herta Däubler-Gmelin from the Social Democrats and Rupert Scholz from the Christian Democrats; in the Bundesrat they were Bernhard Vogel from the Christian Democrats and Arno Walter from the Social Democrats.[22]

A review of the politics of the selection of judges for the Constitutional Court shows that once a party is in possession of a seat, it holds on to it. This pattern is discernible from the beginning of constitutional review in Germany in 1951 up to 2003 (tables 10.2–10.5).

Analysis of the composition of the court reveals an astonishing continuity in the ability of political parties to retain 'their' chair in the court. It is more difficult, however, to evaluate the impact of the party affiliation of judges on decision making inside the court. Similarly it is difficult to assess the impact of the former professional careers of judges on the quality of constitutional review. If one compares, for instance, the careers of the first generation of judges in 1951 with the careers of judges in office in 1983, there is a trend towards a reduction in the number of judges with professional experience in politics and economics and an increase in the number of judges with careers exclusively in the administration and in the judiciary. In 1951 seven of the twenty-four judges had political experience as ministers, and especially in constitutional assemblies. One was a former member of a trade union, another was a former secretary general of a chamber of trade, three were lawyers having worked in trade and industry, and one was a lawyer having worked in an insurance company. In 1983 only two out of sixteen Constitutional Court judges had experience in politics, and none professional experience in the economy.[23] Thus, we can speak of a 'judicialization' or 'bureaucratization' of the recruitment of Constitutional Court judges. Although in 2004 there were four judges with political experience, it is notable that they all gained if from their experience as Ministers of justice.[24] 'Judicialization' of the recruitment of Constitutional Court judges thus continues.

A more desirable development would be to find judges appointed representing a broad spectrum of professional experience, given the

Table 10.2
Constitutional Court judges and political party affiliation, 1951–1983
First Senate

1951 1954 1955 1956 1959 1962 1963 1964 1965 1967 1968 1970 1971 1972 1975 1977 1979 1983

Höpker-Aschoff (FDP) — Wintrich (CDU) — Müller (CDU) — Benda (CDU) — Benda (CDU) — Herzog (CDU)

Kurt Zweigert (CDU) — Heck (CDU) — Böhmer (nominated by CDU/CSU) — Böhmer — Niedermaier (both nominated by CDU/CSU)

Heiland (SPD) — Haager (SPD) — Heußner (SPD) Heußner (SPD)

Scholtissek (CDU) — Brox (CDU) — Katzenstein (CDU) — Katzenstein (CDU)

Wessel (SPD) — Berger (SPD) — Zeidler (SPD) — Simon (SPD) — Simon (SPD)

Scheffler — Rupp von Brünneck (SPD) — Niemeyer (SPD) — Niemeyer (SPD)

Stein (CDU) — Faller (CDU) — Faller (CDU) — Henschel (CDU)

Ritterspach (CDU) — Hesse (nominated by SPD/FDP) — Hesse (nominated by SPD/FDP)

Drath (SPD) ┐
Lehmann (SPD) ┘

Konrad Zweigert (SPD) ┐
Ellinghaus (SPD) — Kutscher (SPD) ┘

Table 10.3
Constitutional Court judges and political party affiliation, 1983–2003
First Senate

1983	1986	1987	1989	1991	1994	1995	1998	1999	2001	2002	2003
Benda_Herzog (CDU) (CDU)					Haas (CDU)						Haas (CDU)
Böhmer Niedermaier (both nominated by CDU/CSU)	Seidl (nominated by CSU)						Papier (CSU)				Papier (CSU)
Heußner (SPD)			Kühling (SPD)						Bryde (nominated by Greens)		Bryde (nominated by Greens)
Katzenstein (CDU)		Söllner (CDU)				Steiner (CDU)					Steiner (CDU)
Simon (SPD)		Dieterich (SPD)			Jäger (SPD)						Jäger (SPD)
Niemeyer (SPD)			Seibert (SPD)					Hohmann-Dennhardt (SPD)			Hohmann-Dennhardt (SPD)
Faller_Henschel (CDU) (FDP)						Hömig (nominated by FDP)					Hömig (nominated by FDP)
Hesse (nominated by SPD/FDP)		Grimm (nominated by SPD)						Hoffmann-Riem (nominated by SPD)			Hoffmann-Riem (nominated by SPD)

Table 10.4
Constitutional Court judges and political party affiliation, 1951–1983
Second Senate

1951 1952 1956 1961 1963 1965 1967 1968 1970 1971 1975 1977 1981 1983

Katz (SPD) —— Wagner (SPD) —— Seuffert (SPD) —— Zeidler (SPD) —— Zeidler (SPD)

Hennecka —— Rinck (nominated by CDU/CSU) —— Rinck (nominated by CDU/CSU)

Wolff —— Kutscher (SPD) —— Wand (CDU) —— Wand (CDU) —— Klein (CDU)

Klaas (SPD) —— Geller (CDU) —— Rottmann (FDP) —— Rottman (FDP) —— Böckenförde (SPD)

Leibholz —— Hirsch (SPD) —— Mahrenholz (SPD, since 1981)

Federer —— v. Schlabrendorff (CDU) —— Niebler (CSU) —— Niebler (CSU)

Rupp (SPD) —— Steinberger (nominated by CDU/CSU) —— Steinberger (nominated by CDU/CSU)

Geiger (CDU) —— Träger (CDU) —— Träger (CDU)

Leusser (CDU) Schlunck (CDU) ——┐
Friesenhahn ——┘

Fröhlich ┐
Roediger (DP) ┘

Table 10.5
Constitutional Court judges and political party affiliation, 1983–2003
Second Senate

1983	1986	1987	1989	1991	1994	1996	1998	1999	2001	2002	2003
Zeidler (SPD)		Franßen (SPD)		Sommer (SPD)						Gerhardt (nominated by SPD)	Gerhardt (nominated by SPD)
Rinck (nominated by CDU/CSU)	Graßhof (nominated by SPD, but conservative)						Osterloh (SPD)				Osterloh (SPD)
Wand (CDU) — Klein (CDU)						Jentsch (CDU)					Jentsch (CDU)
Rottmann (FDP) — Böckenförde (SPD)						Hassemer (SPD)					Hassemer (SPD)
Mahrenholz (SPD)					Limbach (SPD)					Lübbe-Wolff (SPD)	Lübbe-Wolff (SPD)
Niebler (CSU)		Kruis (CSU)					Broß (CDU)				Broß (CDU)
Steinberger (nominated by CDU/CSU)		Kirchhof (nominated by CDU)						Di Fabio (nominated by CDU)			Di Fabio (nominated by CDU)
Träger (CDU)			Winter (CDU)						Mellinghoff (CDU)		Mellinghoff (CDU)

many political and social issues that are brought before the court. A more diverse judiciary 'may include a wider range of skills and experience which will enhance the quality of its decision-making in a general sense.'[25] An additional rationale, and one which is increasingly important in other jurisdictions such as England and Wales, is 'to strengthen the legitimacy of the judiciary.'[26] In the German Constitutional Court, which has only sixteen judges, there is less opportunity to include members of under-represented groups, but the representativeness of the court is enhanced, at least, by the fact that in 2004 five of the sixteen members were women.

To sum up, we have very little information about the reality of selection politics of Constitutional Court judges. The formal procedure is marred by deficiencies in the democratic structure and in the transparency of the selection arrangements. The election of one-half of these judges is left to a committee of Parliament rather than Parliament in full, further reducing the limited democratic legitimacy of the Constitutional Court. The required two-thirds majority in the committee of Parliament results in bargaining processes between political parties in which candidates who are 'middle-of-the roaders'[27] have the best chance of being elected. The selection process must be characterized as highly lacking in transparency. Only a small group of people within the political parties participate in selecting and electing the judges. There is no hearing of candidates and no debate in the public sphere. Secrecy of decision making in the parliamentary committee is even prescribed in the law. What is presented as a process remote from politics turns out to be a highly party-politicized informal procedure.

Normative Conclusions: Transparency, Difference, and Indirect Democratic Accountability as Principles of the Selection Process of Constitutional Court Judges

Taking the political impact of constitutional review seriously would mean implementing democratic and transparent structures for selecting and electing Constitutional Court judges. Political parties should retain their due rights, but they should not dominate the selection process. If, according to the German constitution, half of the Constitutional Court judges are to be elected by the Bundestag this election must take place in the plenary of Parliament. Parliament as a whole represents the sovereignty of the people, and the indirect democratic legitimacy of Constitutional Court judges must be expressed in an election of one-half of the judges by the Bundestag and one-half by the Bundesrat. A parliamentary committee might prepare the election in the plenary of Parliament, but it cannot replace the representatives of the people. Election of Constitutional Court judges by the plenary of the Bundestag would have the additional advantage of ensuring that such important elections did not take place outside the public sphere.[28]

Since constant communication between the represented and the representatives is a basic requirement of democracy, it would make sense to hold public hearings of the candidates for the Constitutional Court. During these hearings all participants would have the chance to debate the scope and nature of constitutional review in a democracy. Politicians and judges could discuss the function of a Constitutional Court that has a political impact on governance, and abandoning the myth of an unpolitical Constitutional Court, they could deliberate on where the boundaries between political and judicial decision making should lie. Politicians and judges could also learn about the ways in which they have both contributed to an excessive judicialization of politics which is detrimental to democracy. Media coverage of the hearings would allow the public to be better informed about these issues and citizens could make up their own minds.

Hearings would also give all participants the opportunity to learn about the educational, professional, societal, and political experiences of candidates for the Constitutional Court. The recruitment of judges exclusively from the bureaucracy and the judiciary does not deliver the requisite diversity in experience. If one looks at the subjects about which the judges have to decide, ranging among others from social policy to environmental policy to security and foreign policy, it is obvious that members of the Constitutional Court must have a wide range of educational and professional experience at their disposal. The quality of constitutional review grows the greater the range of experiences amongst the members of the Constitutional Court. Opening the selection and election process of Constitutional Court judges to greater democracy, greater transparency, and greater diversity would be in the interest of both the input-legitimacy and the output-legitimacy of constitutional review.

NOTES

1 Tate and Vallinder, *The Global Expansion of Judicial Power.*

2 Sweet, *Governing with Judges,* 152.

3 'Constitutional review' with specialized Constitutional Courts is the European model of testing the constitutionality of laws. In the American model of review, where any judge of any court has the power to declare a law unconstitutional, we speak of 'judicial review.' See Shapiro and Stone, 'The New Constitutional Politics of Europe,' 400. In this contribution on Germany I will use the term 'constitutional review.'

4 Kerscher, 'Selbst die Papstwahl ist demokratischer,' 23.

5 For Germany see Kommers, *The Constitutional Jurisprudence of the Federal Republic of Germany*; and Landfried, 'The Impact of the German Federal Constitutional Court on Politics and Policy Output,' 527. I would be more sceptical. Probably the selection process has more impact on constitutional review than we have assumed so far.

6 Kommers, 'Autonomy versus Accountability,' 145.

7 Ibid., 147.

8 Preuß, 'Die Wahl der Mitglieder des BVerfG als verfassungsrechtliches und-politisches Problem,' 392.

9 Volcansek, 'Political Power and Judicial Review in Italy,' 494.

10 Scharpf, *Interaktionsformen: Akteurzentrierter Institutionalismus in der Politikforschung*, 255.

11 Ibid., 256.

12 Preuß, 'Die Wahl der Mitglieder des BVerfG als verfassungsrechtliches und-politisches Problem,' 389.

13 Russell, 'Toward a General Theory of Judicial Independence,' 7.

14 Ibid., 8.

15 Shapiro and Stone, 'The New Constitutional Politics of Europe,' 403, speak of a 'judicialized legislative deliberation.'

16 Ibid., 404.

17 Böckenförde, 'Die Methoden der Verfassungsinterpretation,' 2089–99.

18 Ely, *Democracy and Distrust*, 74.

19 Preuß, 'Die Wahl der Mitglieder des BVerfG als verfassungsrechtliches und-politisches Problem,' 390.

20 Kommers, 'Autonomy versus Accountability,' 149.

21 Kröger, 'Richterwahl,' 86. Compare Lamprecht, *Vom Mythos der Unabhängigkeit*, 70–88.

22 Kerscher, 'Selbst die Papstwahl ist demokratischer.'

23 Landfried, *Bundesverfassungsgericht und Gesetzgeber*, 40.

24 Christine Hohmann-Dennhardt from the First Senate has been minister of justice in Hessen; Wolfgang Hoffmann-Riem from the First Senate has been minister of justice in Hamburg; Winfried Hassemer from the Second Senate has been data protection officer; and Hans-Joachim Jentsch from the Second

Senate has been minister of justice in Thuringia and member of the Parliament in Hessen.

25 See Kate Malleson's chapter in this volume.

26 Ibid.

27 Kommers, *The Constitutional Jurisprudence of the Federal Republic of Germany*, 155.

28 It is the same argument that Jürgen Habermas applies to the indirect election of the President of the Federal Republic of Germany (Bundespräsident). In spite of being an indirect election by the Bundesversammlung such an election has to be embedded into the context of a public debate. Jürgen Habermas, 'Die Wahl ist frei bis zum Schluss,' *Die Zeit*, 13 May 2004.

PART TWO

Appointing the Judges of International Courts

11 Judicial Selection for International Courts: Towards Common Principles and Practices[1]

RUTH MACKENZIE AND PHILIPPE SANDS, QC

Introduction

In February 1960, the U.K. Foreign Office received an informal enquiry as to its views on a potential Belgian candidate for the forthcoming election of judges to the International Court of Justice (ICJ). The enquiry made its way to the legal adviser, who, in an internal memorandum, provided the following response:

> M. Nisot has a very difficult personality and I should imagine he is somewhat of a problem child from the point of view of the Belgian Government, as he must be almost unplaceable in any normal Foreign Service post, and this probably accounts for the fact that he has been with the Belgian Permanent Mission in New York pretty well since the foundation of the United Nations in one capacity or another.
>
> Nevertheless, despite his cantankerous nature and the jaundiced view that he takes of most things, there are a number of points in his favour. He is completely honest; he is also a man of considerable intellectual ability and a very sound lawyer. Furthermore, although he has strong prejudices, these would mostly operate in our favour and he would bring to the Court a conservative element which, in view of its present general bias, it could well do with.[2]

The legal adviser's memorandum throws some light on the internal workings of what has traditionally been a shrouded process: the manner in which individual candidates emerge for election to international courts. It suggests the way in which informal soundings could make or break a possible candidature. It reveals the role of the senior civil service, and it indicates some of the factors that might be taken into consideration in weighing up the pros and cons of a particular candidate for international judicial office, including personality and political disposition.

In 1960 the selection of international judges was not a subject of wide concern: the ICJ was, in effect, the only functioning international court in existence.[3] However, over the past two decades states have created more than thirty international courts and tribunals, and there are now some 250 international judges. The courts and the judiciary have emerged as important international actors, with the potential to place significant constraints on traditional state freedoms. The existence of these bodies signals a desire to strengthen the rule of law in international relations, and the extent to which that desire will be achieved turns, in part, on the process by which the judges are appointed.

Some international courts and tribunals have a potentially global reach, others operate within regions, while still others operate among only a small group of countries. They address a wide range of subject matters, and can deal with cases of great practical and political significance. While some, such as the European Court of Justice (ECJ), are now well known, with their effects being felt in EU member states almost on a daily basis, there are many others which may be less well known:

- In The Hague, the ICJ has rendered a judgment on a serving foreign minister's immunity from national courts, apparently ruling that the English House of Lords in Pinochet[4] was wrong and also precluding the Belgian courts from exercising jurisdiction over serving heads of government, at least while in office;[5]
- In Geneva, the World Trade Organization (WTO) Appellate Body is a final appeal tribunal for international trade disputes; it may soon be called upon to decide, for example, whether the European Community was entitled to maintain its ban on imports of genetically modified organisms;[6]
- In Hamburg, the International Tribunal for the Law of the Sea (ITLOS) has been asked to bring a halt to Japanese fishing activities for southern blue-fin tuna;[7]
- In Washington, the Inter-American Commission of Human Rights has ordered the United States to protect the basic human rights of foreign detainees at Camp X-Ray, Guantanamo;[8] and
- In The Hague, the International Criminal Tribunal for the former Yugoslavia (ICTY) will decide whether or not former President

Milosevic is individually responsible for genocide in Bosnia and crimes against humanity in Vukovar.[9]

The subjects addressed by these bodies are not minor matters. The fact that they are addressed by courts, rather than political bodies, reflects the extent to which states have been willing to hand over decision-making authority to the new international adjudicators, and to subject themselves to an international rule of law. It is interesting then that, despite the increase in the number and scope of international courts and tribunals, we know remarkably little about our international judges: who they are; their backgrounds; how they were selected to become candidates for election; and how they were actually elected. That information, and the decision-making processes that underpin it, have traditionally been left in the hands of governing elites: politicians, senior civil servants and, very occasionally, members of the bench and bar and academe. Decision-making processes for the nomination and selection of international judges are rarely open to public attention or scrutiny. This is regrettable in so far as it may tend to undermine the legitimacy of those processes and could, over the longer term, diminish the possibility that international judicial bodies can operate effectively.

A comparative examination of judicial selection rules and practices of international courts reveals a range of approaches reflective of the diversity among the courts,[10] although certain common features and common concerns can be discerned. While rules and criteria for the nomination and election of international judges do exist, it is difficult to assess how they are applied in practice. However, as international courts and tribunals are no longer seen as the exclusive domain of states, methods of judicial selection and standards of judicial conduct are coming under increasing scrutiny.[11] Particular attention has been focused on developing nomination and selection procedures that ensure that international judges meet the highest standards of competence and integrity, and that promote the independence of the international judiciary.[12] This chapter outlines approaches to the nomination and election of judges for international courts and tribunals and considers recent debates concerning the improvement of international judicial selection mechanisms.

The Growth of the International Judiciary

The number of international judges has risen significantly in the last fifteen years, although it remains low as compared to most domestic legal systems. The first international court, the Central American Court of Justice, was established in 1907, but it was short-lived. The next international court was the Permanent Court of International Justice established in 1922 and based in The Hague; it was succeeded by the International Court of Justice in 1946, with the creation of the United Nations. The International Court of Justice was and remains the 'principal judicial organ of the United Nations.'

Until the late 1950s, the ICJ and its fifteen judges had a virtual monopoly on the judicial resolution of international disputes. The situation today is much changed. Beyond the ICJ, there is now a wide range of international and regional courts dealing with a variety of subject matters, including free trade, international criminal law, human rights, and law of the sea.[13] Among significant recent developments, in 2002 the International Criminal Court (ICC) was established in the Hague (its eighteen judges were elected in 2003), while, at the time of writing, new regional courts are being established in the Caribbean[14] and in Africa.[15] The judges of these various courts and tribunals are supplemented by the appointment of ad hoc judges whereby, in a number of international courts, a state involved in a case may appoint a judge if it has no national on the bench,[16] as well as by arbitrators sitting on arbitral tribunals established to deal with a particular case. More recently, the Security Council has mandated the establishment of pools of *ad litem* judges for the ad hoc criminal tribunals for the former Yugoslavia and for Rwanda, in order to assist those tribunals in dealing with their caseload within a reasonable period of time.[17] Such appointments can add complexity to the issues of judicial selection and judicial independence.

No rules of general application have been promulgated on the functioning of international courts. To a certain extent each is an island, with its own system of governance and rules, including for the appointment of the judges. However, these courts do have one point in common: states have always been greatly concerned about the manner in which international judges are appointed. This is understandable. If states set up a court and entrust it with functions they inevitably lose a degree of control over what that body does. If it is a court, it is independent, and independence extends to relations with the states which created it, and which may then become parties to cases before it. There are at least two ways in which governments can seek to influence international courts: by controlling the budget, and by deciding who will sit on the court as a judge. The appointment process and the independence of the court are therefore closely connected.

States' concerns about the judicial selection process have been evident from the very beginning of the short history of international courts. The first efforts to move beyond ad hoc arbitration to a permanent international court, during the Hague Peace Conference of 1899, failed because states were unable to agree on how to choose a representative group of judges (out of some fifty states). The issue did not arise for the Central American Court of Justice, in 1907; there were only three state parties, so each could have a judge. In 1922, the Permanent Court of International Justice (PCIJ) became the first international court in which the number of judges was to be smaller than the number of state parties, requiring a process of election; the same situation prevails in the International Court of Justice, with fifteen judges sitting on a court that is now open to more than 180 states. In the early period of the establishment of international courts and tribunals, it was recognized that the 'proper manning' of the courts, and their successful functioning, could only be assured if careful scrutiny was exercised when the actual selection of judges was made. But states were very clear that they wished to exercise control and that their freedom should not be limited. In 1944 Manley Hudson, judge and president of the PCIJ, reviewed the existing rules. His conclusion was: 'No absolute disqualifications can be said to exist in general international law to restrict the freedom of States, though the literature of the nineteenth century evidenced some disposition to list such qualities as infancy and insanity as barring a person's selection.'[18]

Rules Establishing Qualifications and Other Criteria for International Judicial Appointments

The constitutive instruments of the various international and regional courts establish certain criteria to be fulfilled by individual judges, while additional considerations or requirements are imposed as regards the bench as whole. In relation to the qualifications of *individual* judges, typical criteria include:

- high moral character/integrity;[19]
- possession of qualifications required in their respective countries for appointment to highest judicial office, or status of jurisconsults of recognized competence in international law;[20] and
- demonstrated expertise in area of law relevant to the court in question (e.g., human rights; trade; law of the sea).[21]

Thus, for example, Article 2 of the statute of the ICJ provides that: 'The Court shall be composed of a body of independent judges, elected regardless of their nationality from among persons of high moral character, who possess the qualifications required in their respective countries for appointment to the highest judicial office, or are jurisconsults of recognized competence in international law.'

In relation to the formal criteria for appointment to the European Court of Human Rights (ECHR), which are similar to those cited above for the ICJ, a group of European jurists examining the question of appointments to the court recently noted that while these criteria are commonly used, they remain vague and undefined, and aspects of their scope remain unclear.[22] For example, the level of qualification and experience required for appointment to judicial office varies greatly among countries, and the term 'jurisconsults of recognised competence' leaves plenty of room for interpretation.[23]

The Rome Statute of the ICC contains more detailed, multilayered provisions on the qualifications of judges, providing that:

> (a) The judges shall be chosen from among persons of high moral character, impartiality and integrity who possess the qualifications required in their respective States for appointment to the highest judicial offices.
> (b) Every candidate for election to the Court shall:
> i) Have established competence in criminal law and procedure, and the necessary relevant experience, whether as judge, prosecutor, advocate or in other similar capacity, in criminal proceedings; or
> ii) Have established competence in relevant areas of international law such as international humanitarian law and the law of human rights, and extensive experience in a professional legal capacity which is of relevance to the judicial work of the Court;
> (c) Every candidate for election to the Court shall have an excellent knowledge of and be fluent in at least one of the working languages of the Court.[24]

The Caribbean Court of Justice (CCJ) also contains more detailed requirements on qualifications of judges. The agreement establishing the court requires that in making appointments to the office of judge, regard shall be had to 'high moral character, intellectual and analytical ability, sound judgment, integrity, and understanding of people and society.'[25] It further stipulates that:

> A person shall not be qualified to be appointed to hold or act in the office of Judge of the Court, unless that person ...

(a) is or has been for a period or periods amounting in the aggregate to not less than five years, a Judge of a court of unlimited jurisdiction in civil and criminal matters in the territory of a Contracting Party or in some part of the Commonwealth, or in a State exercising civil law jurisprudence common to Contracting Parties, or a court having jurisdiction in appeals from any such court and who, in the opinion of the Commission,[26] has distinguished himself or herself in that office; or
(b) is or has been engaged in the practice or teaching of law for a period or periods amounting in aggregate to not less than fifteen years in a Member State of the Caribbean Community or in a Contracting Party or in some part of the Commonwealth, or in a State exercising civil law jurisprudence common to Contracting Parties, and has distinguished himself or herself in the legal profession.[27]

As regards considerations to be taken into account in the composition of an international court *as a whole*, Article 9 of the ICJ statute provides that: 'At every election, the electors shall bear in mind not only that the persons to be elected should individually possess the qualifications required, but also that in the body as a whole the representation of the main forms of civilization and of the principal legal systems of the world should be assured.'

In some courts, such as the European Court of Human Rights or the European Court of Justice, geographic representation requirements are unnecessary as the bench is composed of one judge nominated or appointed by each participating state. However, where the number of judges does not correspond to the number of state parties to the relevant court, provisions on representation of different geographic areas and legal systems are almost universally found. Provisions requiring some consideration of adequate gender representation on the court are less common.[28] Thus, the protocol establishing the African Court of Human and People's Rights requires that, in selecting judges, the Assembly of the African Union must ensure that the bench as a whole is representative of the main different regions and legal traditions of Africa, and that adequate gender representation is achieved.[29]

Article 36(8) of the Rome Statute of the ICC provides that:

(a) The States Parties shall, in the selection of judges, take into account the need, within the membership of the Court, for:
(i) The representation of the principal legal systems of the world;
(ii) Equitable geographical representation; and
(iii) A fair representation of female and male judges.

(b) States Parties shall also take into account the need to include judges with legal expertise on specific issues, including, but not limited to, violence against women or children.

The Caribbean Court of Justice is designed to exercise original jurisdiction in respect of disputes arising under the revised Caribbean Community treaty,[30] as well as appellate jurisdiction in respect of appeals against certain decisions of the Court of Appeal of a Contracting Party.[31] Given the scope of its jurisdiction, the agreement establishing the court provides that there shall be up to ten judges 'of whom at least three shall possess expertise in international law including international trade law.'[32]

Rules Governing Nomination and Election Processes

Although the selection processes for international judges vary, the general approach is similar in many international courts and tribunals. The states involved in the selection process are entitled to nominate one or more candidates, who are then put up for election by secret ballot, most often by an intergovernmental body representing all the states participating in the court in question. States are often explicitly or implicitly entitled to nominate non-nationals as their candidates.[33]

In the case of the International Court of Justice, candidates are nominated by national groups in the Permanent Court of Arbitration, or national groups appointed specifically for the purpose of making nominations.[34] Each group may nominate up to four persons, no more than two of whom may be of their own nationality. The court's statute is relatively unusual in offering some guidance in relation to the nomination process. It recommends that before making these nominations, each national group consult its highest court of justice, its legal faculties and schools of law, and its national academies and national sections of international academies devoted to the study of law.[35] The fifteen judges are elected by the UN General Assembly and Security Council. In the case of ITLOS, each state party to the UN Convention on the Law of the Sea may nominate up to two candidates; the judges of ITLOS are then elected by secret ballot by the meeting of the state parties.[36] Those elected must obtain the largest number of votes and a two-thirds majority of the state parties present and voting, provided that such majority includes a majority of the state parties.

The judges of the African Court of Human and People's Rights are to be elected by the Assembly of Heads of State and Government of the

African Union. State parties to the protocol establishing the court may nominate up to three candidates, of whom at least two must be their nationals. The African Court protocol offers some guidance as to national nominations, indicating that states should give due regard to adequate gender representation in the nomination process.[37] A different process applies for the European Court of Human Rights, where each of the states parties to the European Convention on Human Rights puts forward three candidates; the candidates are then assessed and voted upon by the Parliamentary Assembly of the Council of Europe and one is elected for each state party.[38] In the European Court of Justice, which is composed of one judge per member state,[39] each member state is responsible de facto for the appointment of its national judge on the court, who is appointed by 'common accord' of the member states.[40] As discussed further below, the Caribbean Court of Justice adopts a novel approach, providing for judges to be selected by a Regional Judicial and Legal Services Commission.

Much attention has been focused on the nomination phase as a key entry point to improving international judicial selection processes. In general, little is known about how candidates for international judicial office emerge at the national level. Notwithstanding the very limited guidance contained in certain court statutes as to issues to be considered or recommended practices in relation to nominations,[41] states retain almost unfettered discretion in this area.[42] There is little or no guidance as to how national nomination processes might be organized or who should be consulted, and no move towards harmonizing approaches to nominations. This leaves open the possibility that informal networks, or other non-transparent mechanisms, will be utilized to identify 'suitable' candidates at the national level.[43] Even states which have introduced more transparent selection mechanisms for some courts have not necessarily similarly transformed nomination procedures for other international courts.[44]

It is also notable that although requirements relating to the bench as a whole are commonly included in the constitutive instruments of international courts, it has not always been the practice that specific rules have been drawn up for elections to clarify how these requirements are met. Indeed there is often no formal common understanding of what the requirements mean in practical terms. In relation to the ITLOS, for example, which requires representation of the principal legal systems of the world, and equitable geographic distribution of judges, Judge Yankov has noted that:

> The concept of 'principal legal systems of the world' has not been sufficiently elucidated and supported by scientific data or legal arguments. There is no such generally accepted definition, since it is a complex notion encompassing many elements, i.e., legal systems in terms of positive law, and legal traditions; national, religious, historical, civilisational and other components; 'common law,' 'continental law,' 'muslim traditional law,' ethnic law and law based on aboriginal tradition, etc. Nevertheless the existing composition of the Tribunal corresponds broadly to the notion of the 'principal legal systems of the world,' whatever that notion would carry within its scope and content.[45]

In effect, this criterion is deemed fulfilled by virtue of the fulfilment of the geographic representation requirement, the latter being a reflection of the UN regional groupings.[46] Thus, Ingadottir notes that: 'Because of the difficulties in defining the principal legal systems of the world, and of categorising states along these lines, the requirement has not been implemented per se at the international courts and tribunals. Rather the requirement has been considered fulfilled through geographical and political arrangements.'[47]

Hence, Article 3(2) of the ITLOS statute provides that there shall be no fewer than three members from each geographical group established by the UN General Assembly. In the ICJ, where no two judges can have the nationality of the same state and the entire bench is to represent the main forms of 'civilization' (as Article 9 of the court's statute puts it) and the principal legal systems, in practice, the five permanent members of the UN Security Council always have a judge. This unwritten custom, still maintained today, may raise issues about independence and seems increasingly anomalous and difficult to justify. The other ten judges comprise two from each of the five regional groupings in the UN system (Latin America and the Caribbean; Western European and others; Eastern Europe; Africa; Asia). In practice, these arrangements meant that in 2004, five of the fifteen ICJ judges would be nationals of member states. This raises the question whether it is really in the interest of the long-term well-being of the ICJ, or the emerging system of global governance, for geographic representation on the ICJ to be skewed towards any particular region, or any particular group of countries.

Where the requirements for the composition of the court go beyond general geographic requirements, more detailed guidance for states or other entities involved in the appointment or election of judges seems appropriate. For example, appointments to the Caribbean Court of Justice must reflect both the specific criteria for individual judges mentioned above and the need for the court potentially to address appeals involving civil, criminal, or constitutional matters, as well as regional trade issues. The first judges have yet to be appointed. The most instructive example to date seems to be that of the International Criminal Court. In addition to the specific criteria for individual judges set out in Article 36(3) of the ICC statute, the elections to the court had to provide not only for the representation of legal systems and for equitable geographic representation, in common with other courts of potentially global reach, but also fair representation of female and male judges and the inclusion of judges with specific expertise in areas of relevance for the court, including violence against women or children. An electoral process was devised[48] to seek to ensure that states addressed each of these criteria in selecting the courts' eighteen judges. Each state entitled to vote was required to vote for at least three candidates from each region, and nine candidates from List A (competence in criminal law and procedure) and five candidates from List B (competence in relevant areas of international law), as well as at least six candidates of each gender. Statements accompanying nominations indicated specific areas of expertise and experience of the candidates.

Tenure and the Re-election of International Judges

The statutes and rules of the various courts and tribunals generally provide that once elected international judges can only be removed by the court itself. In this respect, tenure is not subject to political interference. However, it is noteworthy that international judges generally hold office for relatively short periods in comparison to national judges, although their terms are often renewable by re-election. For example, the term of office on both the International Court of Justice and the International Tribunal on the Law of the Sea is nine years; on the European Court of Justice it is six years. The length of tenure, coupled with the prospect of re-election and the political nature of the election process, raises the question whether individual judges are influenced by the need to secure re-election, particularly towards the end of their term. This has led to calls for consideration of longer but non-renewable terms of office for international judges.[49] The suggestion was taken up in the ECHR in 2004, with the adoption of a nine-year non-renewable term of office.[50]

One objection to longer terms of office may be raised in relation to international courts concerning representativeness: rotation and re-election requirements may serve the interest of all states which are keen to have 'their' nationals or nominees appointed to the bench. This issue does not presently arise in respect of the ECHR, on which each state party has a judge.

Gender and the International Judiciary

A review of various international courts and tribunals reveals that few female judges have been appointed. By way of example, of the fifteen ICJ judges, only one is female; no women have been elected to the twenty-one-judge ITLOS; and a woman was appointed to the seven-member World Trade Organization Appellate Body for the first time in December 2003. The gender balance in some international criminal and human rights tribunals is a little better. In the European Court of Human Rights, of forty-two judges in office in January 2004, ten were women; in the ICTR, four of sixteen judges were women.[51] While some argue that this gender imbalance is merely a result of historical factors and that fairer representation of female and male judges on international courts will be achieved over time, Linehan argues that it is not credible to suggest that the problem at the international level is solely attributable to the lack of a 'pool' of suitably qualified female candidates:

> More likely causes of the low nomination rates are the lack of priority states attach to the issue, persistent ideas about candidates that may work against women and systemic barriers or disincentives for women. It is apparent that many states persist in promoting a particular type of candidate – one with a background in academia, diplomacy and the [International Law Commission] – to which women are less likely to conform. It seems likely also that some states persist in seeing women as 'naturally suitable' candidates only for women's rights and human rights bodies.[52]

Linehan's study, conducted for Project on International Courts and Tribunals in 2000, suggests that the lack of gender balance in the composition of the international judiciary was to a large degree attributable to national nomination processes, rather than solely to election processes.[53] In some tribunals, specific provision is being made to try to ensure a more appropriate gender balance on the bench. Thus, as noted above, the International Criminal Court statute[54] and the protocol on the African Court of Human and People's Rights[55] both contain provisions designed to secure a reasonable gender balance. The election procedure for the ICC, devised in the light of the 'fair representation' provision of the ICC statute, resulted in the election of seven female judges out of a total of eighteen. With regard to nominations, the protocol on the African Court of Human and People's Rights[56] requires states to take gender balance into account in the nomination of candidates, in addition to during the election process proper; and the Parliamentary Assembly of the Council of Europe has sought to encourage states to nominate both male and female candidates for election to the European Court of Human Rights.[57] In 2004, the Parliamentary Assembly requested two governments to present new lists of candidates on the grounds, inter alia, that their original lists did not include candidates of both sexes.[58]

Nomination and Election Processes in Practice

While the precise nature of the criteria to be fulfilled by individual judges and by the bench as a whole vary according to the court concerned, what is of real concern is how any applicable criteria and rules for nomination and election of international judges are applied in practice, and, more significantly, to what extent other informal criteria and considerations are at play.

It is, however, on the whole, extremely difficult to obtain information on any formal basis about national nomination processes and about the considerations that influence countries' votes in international judicial elections. Few, if any, indepth studies on these issues have been conducted.

Given the limited steps taken to date to open up election processes to public scrutiny, elections to international courts such as the ICJ remain highly politicized affairs, often characterized by lobbying and vote-trading.[59] Without the support of some of the more powerful states the electoral prospects for any candidate will be slim. The electoral process for the ICJ involves formal and informal meetings between the candidates and diplomatic representatives of UN members. The state proposing a candidate will use its influence to promote its own candidate (if it does not, the candidate will be perceived not to have the support of the state and the candidacy will be in difficulty). Votes may be promised in return for support in election to other offices in the UN or other intergovernmental organizations.

As previously noted, the nominations of candidates for the ICJ are not, in theory at least, made by governments. According to a UN document prepared before the 1946 ICJ election, the decision to adopt this approach reflected a 'fear that, if governments were entrusted with the function of nominating candidates, they might be influenced by political considerations.'[60] Before making its nominations, the ICJ statute 'recommends' that the national group should consult its highest court of justice, its legal faculties and schools of law, and its national academies and national sections of international academies devoted to the study of law.[61] The extent to which this consultation takes place is not clear. Anecdotal evidence appears to suggest that practice varies widely. In some countries consultation plainly does not happen at all; in others there is informal consultation, and it is apparent that the national group often nominates persons they are told to nominate by the government, while in other cases there is extensive external consultation.

Materials released in the Public Records Office in the United Kingdom throw some light on the kind of considerations that have been at play in judicial nomination processes, at least in some of the early ICJ elections.[62] These materials, relating to nomination and elections for the ICJ in 1946, 1954, and 1960, reveal the role of government officials in the nomination, as well as the influence of a range of criteria and considerations not mentioned in the court's statute. Some general features emerge. First, it is clear that although the nomination is a matter for the national groups at the Permanent Court of Arbitration, in practice the government and the relevant civil servants were not far removed from the process. In nominations for the 1946 elections to the ICJ, for example, the legal adviser at the time was under no illusions as to what his task was, stating that 'we have ... got to persuade tactfully our national group to accept guidance.'[63]

He had earlier noted that '[i]n the past [the views of the Foreign Office and the Lord Chancellor] have been accepted by national groups as having so much weight that they have always followed them.' He recognized, however, that the matter had to be handled carefully: 'We must ... be very careful not to appear to be overriding the prerogative which belongs to them, otherwise we may find that one of them begins to raise objections.'[64]

It is also apparent from the historical materials that the factors which are taken into account are not necessarily the same as those to which the ICJ statute directs attention, and that the criteria set forth in the ICJ statute are not necessarily treated as exhaustive. Thus, for example, the material available from the U.K. Public Records Office reveals that specific concerns raised in relation to nominations and elections to the ICJ in the period from 1946 to 1960 included the political, national, and religious backgrounds of potential candidates; subjective views about the personal qualities of potential candidates; and speculation about the views that candidates were considered likely to espouse if elected to the court. The comments of the U.K. legal adviser with respect to the potential Belgian candidate of the ICJ, M. Nisot, cited at the beginning of this chapter, bear this out, and there are numerous similar instances.[65] In addition, the U.K. records in relation to early ICJ elections reveal efforts to maintain what was considered an appropriate balance in composition of the court that favoured the United Kingdom, including in particular maintaining judges from each of the permanent members of the Security Council, and as membership of the UN broadened, of Commonwealth members.

It is difficult to assess the relevance of these historical materials to modern nomination and election processes. They may simply reflect the specifics of the ICJ (and UN) system and the values that prevailed at the time. But at the very least, the historical material confirms the steps to which governments will go to safeguard their interests and ensure that the 'right' candidates emerge. The formal ICJ election process has not changed, although the composition of the court has. It is readily apparent that far more former foreign office legal advisers, ambassadors, or foreign ministers are represented on the court than previously. Of course, since records are not yet publicly available, it is not possible to verify whether or how far similar considerations have influenced subsequent nominations and elections. Further similar research needs to be done in the United Kingdom and elsewhere in order to get a fuller picture of how international judges are really nominated and elected.

Mechanisms to Enhance Transparency and Effectiveness

In some international courts, efforts have been made to improve the transparency of judicial nomination and election processes, and to avoid or minimize the role of political or other extraneous considerations in nominations and appointments.

The lack of transparency in national nomination processes is frequently compounded by a lack of scrutiny of nominations at the international level prior to the election of judges. In most cases, relatively little information about candidates is formally circulated to states or others involved in the election process, so that there is little information available on which to base an informed decision as to how to vote. In this regard, a notable exception was the first election to the International Criminal Court, where nominations had to be accompanied by a statement specifying how the candidate fulfilled the requirements for office set out in Article 36(3) of the ICC statute.[66] The first elections of judges to the ICC were characterized by a significantly higher level of transparency and public interest than is usual for elections to international courts. This was generated in part by the decision to place details of candidates on the website of the UN, but also owed much to the actions of non-governmental organizations (NGOs), which disseminated information about candidates,[67] gleaned from official sources[68] and from candidates' responses to a questionnaire circulated by NGOs (to which many candidates appear to have responded). Some candidates also met with NGO representatives in New York.[69] It seems likely that the high profile of the ICC elections will sensitize more NGOs and others to the need to engage proactively in similar processes elsewhere.

An additional step envisaged by the ICC statute to enhance the electoral process was the possible establishment of an advisory committee on nominations.[70] Such a body could have played a role in reviewing nominations in order to ascertain whether each candidate fulfilled the requirements set out in the statute and whether the overall requirements of the statute with regard to the composition of the bench were likely to be fulfilled by the candidates available. Despite pressure from NGOs for the establishment of such a body, and support from at least some state parties to the ICC statute, the advisory committee was not established for the first elections. Nonetheless, the possibility remains that such a committee might be established ahead of elections to the court in the future.

Elections to the European Court of Human Rights do incorporate some review of nominations in advance of the election of judges by the Parliamentary Assembly of the Council of Europe. The process of nomination and election of judges to that court has been the subject of rather detailed examination and recommendations in a recent report published by Interights in 2003. As noted above, state parties to the European Convention on Human Rights may nominate up to three candidates for election to the court. The names of the candidates are submitted together with a model curriculum vitae, in the form determined by a resolution of the Parliamentary Assembly.[71] Although the Parliamentary Assembly has recommended that names of candidates be submitted in alphabetical order, states frequently present their nominations ranked in order of preference.[72] Since 1998, a subcommittee of the Parliamentary Assembly's Committee on Legal Affairs and Human Rights has reviewed nominations and ranked candidates in order of preference, without giving reasons.[73] In practice, the subcommittee review is relatively limited, comprising a review of the model curricula vitae and brief interviews with candidates. However, the Interights report found that while the subcommittee represented an improvement on the previous system, its operations 'may mean that not only is it an ineffective filter of candidates, but that it risks adding an additional level of arbitrariness to the appointments' procedure.'[74] Weaknesses in the subcommittee procedure identified in the report included the relative lack of legal and human rights expertise in the sub-committee, and inadequacies in the interview process. The report makes a number of recommendations to improve the judicial selection process, including, for example, the establishment of independent bodies at the national level to nominate candidates; the submission of information by governments of national nomination procedures; and the confirmation of data provided about candidates. The Parliamentary Assembly of the Council of Europe has recommended that the Council of Ministers invite governments to meet additional criteria before submitting lists of candidates for election to the ECHR, including that a call for candidatures has been issued through the specialized press; that candidates have experience in the field of human rights; and that the candidates have sufficient knowledge of at least one of the two official languages of the court.[75] Consideration of similar types of requirements for appointments to other international courts may also be worthwhile.

In an unusual innovation for an international court, the agreement establishing the Caribbean Court of Justice provides for judges to be appointed by a newly established Regional Judicial and Legal Services Commission. Formally then, rather than seeking to improve national nomination processes, the agreement establishing the court seeks to remove states parties from direct involvement in the nomination and election process. This mechanism is designed to insulate the court from political interference both at the judicial selection stage and during the court's operation.[76] In this regard, the role of the president, who is at once the chair of the commission and the senior judge on the court, is critical.[77] The functioning of the commission will be of great interest to those seeking new mechanisms to enhance the independence and accountability of the international judiciary as a whole. At the very least it offers another, apparently 'multistakeholder,' model for the screening of candidates for office: the commission will be able to consult with associations representative of the legal profession and with other bodies and individuals that it considers appropriate in selecting a judge for the court (Article IV(12)). The commission is composed of members drawn from, inter alia, national bar associations, civil society, serving and former chief justices, and academics.[78]

After consultations, the first members of the commission were identified and took office from 20 August 2003.[79] Given its role in the appointment and removal of judges, attention is likely to focus upon the independence of the commission itself and upon the dual role of the president.

Prospects and Conclusions: Towards Common Principles and Practices?

The specific criteria and processes according to which candidates for international judicial office are nominated and international judges are selected are likely to continue to vary according to the court or tribunal concerned. Nonetheless, certain common considerations are relevant and may suggest some move towards some common principles and practices for the future. Foremost among these are the needs of international courts and tribunals to operate effectively and to maintain the trust and confidence of those that use them (including, but not necessarily only, states), as well as those that are affected by their decisions: they need appropriately qualified judges competent in the subject matter addressed by the court, capable of operating in the working languages of the court, and meeting the highest standards of integrity and independence. If the process of international judicial selection is legitimate, then the outcomes of the deliberations of international judges are likely to command respect from the audiences to which judgments are directed. This is principally the parties to the case, but there is a much broader audience at stake, including the national courts that are increasingly called upon to have regard to, take account of, and even apply international judgments.

Existing procedures and practices suggest that there are various avenues through which the nomination and selection of international judges might be made more transparent and more effective. Some of these go to seeking to ensure that states nominate and elect the most appropriate candidates. Such mechanisms include giving additional guidance to states on national nomination processes, for example, by requiring public advertisements and consultation at the national level; introducing procedures for the review of nominations to ensure that candidates fulfil all the required criteria for judicial office – examples here include the review procedure for ECHR candidates, and the proposed advisory committee in the ICC statute; and promoting 'internal' transparency by ensuring that information on candidates is made available to states prior to elections, preferably in a common format. Other mechanisms go to enhancing 'external' transparency – by making information about candidates available to NGOs and the public in general, for example, or providing for wider consultations on candidatures.

More far-reaching options may involve removing judicial selection from the direct authority of states – for example, through the establishment of judicial selection commissions such as that established for the Caribbean Court of Justice (although, of course, it remains to be seen how that commission will work in practice, and in particular whether it results in a bench that meets all the needs and requirements of the court's statute).

This chapter has emphasized that one of the main challenges in making judicial appointments to international courts at present is the lack of available information about existing national nomination procedures and international judicial elections. How do states identify candidates for international judicial office and what influences their vote in practice? Further research on these questions needs to be undertaken at the national level. Efforts to improve procedures for the nomination and selection of international judges may profit from the experience of domestic legal systems surveyed elsewhere in this book on the shortcomings and advantages of different approaches to judicial selection.

NOTES

1 Parts of this chapter are drawn from Sands, 'Global Governance and the International Judiciary; and Mackenzie and Sands, 'International Courts and Tribunals and the Independence of the International Judge,' 271–85.

2 Minutes of Sir Gerald Fitzmaurice on the Possible Candidacy of M. Nisot for the International Court of Justice, 1 February 1960, FO 371/153556/1645/6, cited in Sands, 'Global Governance and the International Community,' 481–2.

3 The European Court of Human Rights was conceived in 1950 and estab-

lished in 1959, but did not render its first judgment until November 1960; the European Court of Justice was created in 1957 and became fully operational in the 1960s.

4 *R. v. Bow Street Metropolitan Stipendiary Magistrate and Others, Ex Parte Pinochet Ugarte (No. 3)* (2000).

5 *Democratic Republic of Congo v. Belgium, Case Concerning the Arrest Warrant of 11 April 2000* (2002).

6 *European Communities – Measures Affecting the Approval and Marketing of Biotech Products – Request for Consultations,* WT/DS 291/1 (United States), 292/1 (Canada), and 293/1 (Argentina).

7 ITLOS, *Southern Bluefin Tuna Cases (Australia and New Zealand v. Japan)* (2000).

8 Inter-American Commission on Human Rights, *Decision on Request for Precautionary Measures (Detainees at Guantanamo Bay, Cuba) 12 March 2002.*

9 See generally http://www.un.org/icty/indictment/english/mil-ii011122e .htm (last accessed 25 April 2004).

10 Information on, and links to, all the international courts and tribunals referred to in this paper can be found on the website of the Project on International Courts and Tribunals at http://www.pict-pcti.org.

11 Keohane et al. suggest that independent selection and tenure is the most important criterion of the independence of an international tribunal. Keohane, Moravcsik, and Slaughter, 'Legalized Dispute Resolution,' 76–7.

12 See, e.g., the ongoing work of the PICT/International Law Association Study Group on the Practice and Procedure of International Tribunals, at http://www.pict-pcti.org; Brandeis Institute for International Judges, *The New International Jurisprudence*; Brandeis Institute for International Judges, *Authority and Autonomy*; Interights, *Judicial Independence*; Ingadottir, *The International Criminal Court*; Shelton, 'Legal Norms to Promote the Independence and Accountability of International Tribunals,' 27–62.

13 See generally Sands, Mackenzie, and Shany, eds., *Manual of International Courts and Tribunals*; and Romano, 'The Proliferation of International Judicial Bodies,' 709.

14 Agreement establishing the Caribbean Court of Justice, 14 February 2001, in force 23 July 2002. Available at www.caribbeancourtofjustice.org.

15 Protocol to the African Charter on Human and People's Rights on the Establishment of the African Court on Human and People's Rights, 9 June 1998, in force 25 January 2004.

16 On ad hoc judges, see, e.g., ICJ Statute, Article 31; ITLOS Statute, Article 17.

17 Security Council Resolution 1329(2000), S/Res/1329(2000), 4240th meet-

ing, 5 December 2000; Security Council Resolution 1431 (2002), S/Res/1431(2002), 4601st meeting, 14 August 2002; Security Council Resolution 1512 (2003), S/Res/1512 (2003), 4849th Meeting, 27 October 2003.

18 Hudson, *International Tribunals*, 34.

19 For example, ICJ Statute, Article 2; Protocol establishing the African Court on Human and People's Rights (ACHPR), Article 11; ICC Statute, Article 36(3); European Convention on Human Rights and Fundamental Freedoms (European Convention on Human Rights), Article 21(1); ITLOS Statute, Article 2(1); Agreement establishing the Caribbean Court of Justice (CCJ) Art IV(11); Treaty Creating the Court of Justice of the Cartagena Agreement (CJAC) Article 6.

20 For example, ICJ Statute, Article 2; European Convention on Human Rights, Article 21(1); EC Treaty, Article 223 (ex Article 167); Statute of the Inter-American Court of Human Rights (IACHR), Article 4; CJAC Treaty, Article 6.

21 For example, ACHPR Protocol, Article 11; ICC Statute, Article 36(3); ITLOS Statute, Article 2(1); WTO Dispute Settlement Understanding (WTO DSU), Article 17; IACHR Statute, Article 4. Some courts, however, do not explicitly incorporate such a criterion. For example, the European Convention on Human Rights does not expressly require judges to possess expertise in international human rights law. A Recommendation of the Council of Europe Parliamentary Assembly adopted in January 2004 recommended that the Committee of Ministers invite governments of member states to ensure that the list of candidates for the office of judge at the ECHR have experience in the field of human rights. Parliamentary Assembly, *Candidates for the European Court of Human Rights, Recommendation 1649,* adopted 30 January 2004 (8th sitting).

22 Interights, *Judicial Independence*, 16.

23 Ibid.

24 ICC Statute, Article 36(3).

25 Agreement establishing the CCJ, Article IV(11).

26 On the commission, see below.

27 Agreement establishing the CCJ, Article IV(10), footnote added by authors.

28 See further below.

29 ACHPR Protocol, Articles 12(2) and 14(3).

30 Agreement establishing the CCJ, Article XII.

31 Ibid., Article XXV. In effect to replace appeals to the Privy Council.

32 Ibid., Article IV(1).

33 For example, European Convention on Human Rights, Article 22; ACHPR Protocol, Article 12; ICJ Statute, Article 5.

34 Each contracting party to the 1899 and 1907 Hague Convention selects up to

four persons to serve as a potential arbitrators as members of the Permanent Court of Arbitration. Those persons constitute the National Group. Each National Group is entitled to make nominations of candidates for elections to the ICJ. They may nominate up to four persons, not more than two of whom may be of their own nationality. Where a UN member is not a party to the PCA Conventions, its nominations may be made by a national group appointed by its government under the same conditions as those prescribed by the 1907 Hague Convention. ICJ Statute, Article 4.

35 ICJ Statute, Article 6; see further below.

36 ITLOS Statute, Article 4.

37 ACHPR Protocol, Article 12.

38 European Convention on Human Rights, Article 22.

39 EC Treaty, Article 221 (ex Article 165).

40 The Draft Treaty establishing a Constitution for Europe contains a provision for the establishment of a panel to give an opinion on candidates' suitability to perform the duties of judge before the governments of the member states make appointments. Under the Draft Treaty, the panel would comprise seven persons chosen from among former judges, members of national supreme courts, and lawyers of recognized competence, one of whom would be proposed by the European Parliament. Draft Treaty establishing a Constitution for Europe, Article III-262, CIG 50/03, 25 November 2003.

41 ACHR Protocol, Article 12; ICJ Statute, Article 6. The Parliamentary Assembly of the Council of Europe has recommended that states nominating candidates for election to the European Court of Human Rights issue a call for candidatures in the specialist press. Resolution 1429 (1999), reproduced in Interights, *Judicial Independence*, 44–5; and Recommendation 1649 (2004). See note 21 above.

42 Interights, *Judicial Independence*, 17.

43 This is considered in more detail below.

44 For example, the United Kingdom advertizes for the candidates for the U.K. judge at the European Court of Human Rights, and for a candidate to be put forward for election to the International Criminal Court. Prior to the ICC process, Schermers described the U.K. nomination process for the ECHR as the only one which was independent and transparent. Schermers, 'Election of Judges to the European Court of Human Rights,' 574.

45 Yankov, 'The International Tribunal for the Law of the Sea and the Comprehensive Dispute Settlement System of the Law of the Sea,' 42.

46 Ingadottir, *The International Criminal Court*, 12.

47 Ibid.

48 Resolution ICC-ASP/1/Res.3, Procedure for the election of the judges for the International Criminal Court, 9 September 2002.

49 See, e.g., Brandeis Institute for International Judges, *The New International Jurisprudence*, 9.

50 Protocol No. 14 to the European Convention on Human Rights and Fundamental Freedoms, adopted by the Committee of Ministers of the Council of Europe on 13 May 2004, Article 2, amending Article 23 of the Convention.

51 Not including the *ad litem* judges.

52 See Linehan, *Women and Public International Litigation.*

53 Ibid., 5.

54 ICC Statute, Article 36(8)(a)(iii).

55 ACHPR Protocol, Article 12(2).

56 ACHPR Protocol, Article 12.

57 Council of Europe Parliamentary Assembly Recommendation 1429 (1999). See now also *Parliamentary Resolution 1366 (2004)*, para. 3 and *Parliamentary Recommendation 1649 (2004)*, paras. 18, 19. Protocol No. 14, adopted by the Committee of Ministers on 13 May 2004, did not take up the Parliamentary Assembly's proposal that Article 22 of the Convention should be amended to require gender balance in the lists of candidates submitted by governments. The Explanatory Report to the Protocol indicates that it was decided not to amend the first paragraph of Article 22 to prescribe that the lists of three candidates nominated by High Contracting parties should contain candidates of both sexes since that might have interfered with the primary consideration to be given to the merits of potential candidates. However, it is stated that parties should do everything possible to ensure that their lists contain both male and female candidates. Council of Europe, *Explanatory Report to the CETS No. 194*, para. 49.

58 Council of Europe, *Assembly to elect 18 judges to the Court, but defers election of three others*, Parliamentary Assembly session, 26-30 April 2004, 27 April 2004, available at http://www.coe.int/T/E/Com/Files/PA-Sessions/april-2004/20040427_news_juges.asp (last accessed 27 April 2004).

59 Brandeis, Institute for International Judges, *Authority and Autonomy*, 9; Interights, *Judicial Independence*, 23-4.

60 United Nations Information Organization Memorandum on the International Court of Justice, 25 September 1945, FO 371/50947/U7369.

61 ICJ Statute, Article 6.

62 Materials relating to the 1946, 1954, and 1960 elections to the ICJ have been more thoroughly reviewed and analysed in Sands, 'Global Governance and the International Judiciary,' from which this section is drawn.

63 Minutes of Eric Beckett on the Nomination of a British Judge to the International Court of Justice, 19 October 1945, FO 371/50947/U8170, cited in Sands, 'Global Governance and the International Judiciary,' 488.
64 Minutes of Eric Beckett on the Appointment of a British Judge on the International Court of Justice, 26 October 1945, FO 371/50947/U8300, cited in Sands, 'Global Governance and the International Judiciary,' 489.
65 See generally Sands (2003) Global Governance and the International Judiciary.'
66 ICC Statute, Article 36(4)(a).
67 See Lawyers Committee for Human Rights, *Election of Judges of the International Criminal Court, 3–7 February 2003, Chart Summarizing the Qualifications of the Candidates.*
68 Such as resumés made available on the UN website.
69 See Lawyers Committee for Human Rights, *Election of Judges of the International Criminal Court, 3–7 February 2003.*
70 ICC Statute, Article 36(4)(c).
71 Council of Europe Parliamentary Assembly, Resolution 1200 (1999); see also Resolution 1366 (2004) and Recommendation 1649 (2004).
72 Interights, *Judicial Independence,* 8.
73 Ibid., 8–9.
74 Ibid., 21.
75 Council of Europe Parliamentary Assembly, Recommendation 1649 (2004), para. 19.
76 See Preparatory Committee on the Caribbean Court of Justice, *The Caribbean Court of Justice,* 32–3; Pollard, *The Caribbean Court of Justice,* 2–3.
77 By April 2004, the post of president had been advertised and was under recruitment, and an advertisement was issued for six judges of the court.
78 The agreement establishing the court (Article V(1)) provided for the constituting of the commission as follows:
(a) The President who shall be the Chairman of the Commission;
(b) Two persons nominated jointly by the Organization of the Commonwealth Caribbean Bar Association (OCCBA) and the Organization of Eastern Caribbean States (OECS) Bar Association;
(c) One chairman of the Judicial Services Commission of a Contracting Party selected in rotation in the English alphabetical order for a period of three years;
(d) The Chairman of a Public Service Commission of a Contracting Party selected in rotation in the reverse English alphabetical order for a period of three years;
(e) Two persons from civil society nominated jointly by the Secretary-

General of the Community and the Director General of the OECS for a period of three years following consultations with regional non-governmental organizations;
(f) Two distinguished jurists nominated jointly by the Dean of the Faculty of Law of the University of the West Indies, the Deans of the Faculties of Law of any of the Contracting Parties and the Chairman of the Council of Legal Education; and
(g) Two persons nominated jointly by the Bar or Law Associations of the Contracting Parties.

79 http://www.caribbeancourtofjustice.org. Biographies of the members of the commission are available on the court's website.

PART THREE

Appointing Judges in New Democracies and Transitional States

12 Judicial Appointments and Promotions in Israel: Constitution, Law, and Politics

ELI M. SALZBERGER

Introduction: Judicial Selection as a Source for Israel's Democracy

It is said that out of the many new states established after the Second World War, few have managed to establish and maintain a real democracy, a liberal democracy.[1] Israel is one of them. Many scholars view this achievement almost as a miracle. Israel inherited the legal system of a colonial regime – the British Mandate. Most of its founders lacked democratic traditions in their countries of origin. It has been in a constant state of war since its establishment. Israel is also one of the few countries in the world in which there is no written constitution limiting the powers of government and guaranteeing individual rights. Separation of powers, both horizontal (between central and regional or local government) and vertical (between the executive and the legislature), does not exist in Israel either. The powers of the executive evolve from a unicameral legislature. Given these circumstances, it seems indeed miraculous that Israelis can be proud of some (though certainly not all) of the unique components of Israeli democracy.

What is the possible explanation for Israel's democratic success? I believe that a key to this enigma lies in the country's legal institutions, and especially its judiciary. The Supreme Court of Israel, together with other legal institutions, including the office of the attorney general and the prosecution agencies, managed to construct important features of Israel's democracy and to protect others. The Israeli case proves that an independent judiciary is perhaps the most crucial condition for a successful democratic state;[2] it is not surprising, therefore, that some scholars prescribing the desirable procedure for the democratization of Iraq hold that the first institution that ought to be established there is an independent judiciary, long before democratic elections are to take place.[3]

The story of the Israeli judiciary, and especially of its Supreme Court, is a fascinating one. In the absence of a constitution to guarantee its independence, the judiciary gradually gained public trust and admiration through the actual conduct of the judges. This began with decisions in the midst of the 1948 Independence War invalidating various ministerial orders (including various orders by David Ben Gurion), continued with the construction of a judicial-made bill of rights from the early 1950s, and culminated with the tough hand the judges have been demonstrating in recent years against irrational and corrupt politicians. In repeated studies from the 1980s onwards, the judicial branch in Israel was ranked second to the army in terms of public appreciation and confidence, whereas the politicians – legislators and government ministers - were ranked in the bottom of the tables.[4]

Public esteem enabled the judges to become crucial partners in public decision making in Israel, and to engage in checking and balancing the decisions of other branches of government. In the 1950s and up to the 1970s, this was done within the legal formalist jurisprudence and discourse. In the 1980s, and especially since the appointment of Aharon Barak to the Supreme Court, and his leadership as the chief justice, the Court shifted from a formalist approach to a non-positivist, value-based discourse. In the 1990s Israel went through an era of enhanced legalization, which was apparent in stronger emphases on constitutional norms and discourse, in the increasing strength of legal institutions, and in a greater public sense of the power of litigation.

The law and the courts have become one of the country's most significant political establishments. The Supreme Court of Israel emerged as the dominant branch of government. It moved centre-stage in the collective decision-making process, affording an unprecedented degree of intervention in the conduct of the other branches of government, and thus attracting both ever-greater attention and growing criticism from the Israeli media and public. The quality of the Israeli judiciary and its Supreme Court in particular was acknowledged recently by Lord Woolf, the lord chief justice of England and Wales, who declared that the Israeli Supreme Court is one of the best courts he is aware of worldwide.[5]

How did this situation come about? How did the Supreme Court of Israel manage to establish its powers in the first place, without any guarantees of structural constitutional independence?[6] I believe that three main sources for the power of the Israeli Supreme Court, which are connected to each other by mutual causal influences, are the Court's jurisdiction and structure as inherited from the Mandatory regime, the Court's composition during Israel's formative years, and the judicial selection procedure established in the early 1950s.

The Supreme Court is the single institution heading the judiciary in Israel. It is the court for appeals in criminal and civil matters, as well as the high court of justice. In the latter capacity the Court hears petitions against all governmental bodies, including various tribunals and courts that are outside the general courts system. Currently, the Court hears more than 10,000 cases a year, sitting in panels of three judges or more. The number of seats in the Court increased from five in 1948 to fourteen today.

From 1948 for nearly three decades, more than half of the Supreme Court seats, together with the occupancy of other key legal positions, such as senior officials in the Ministry of Justice and the State Comptroller office, were held by Jewish German jurists. These jurists formed a pact with those educated in the Anglo-American legal system, establishing a unique Israeli liberal tradition. This tradition was very different from the East European political style that dominated the other branches of government, a style of governance with distinct anti-liberal elements.[7]

The public trust that the Supreme Court judges gained in the first few years of statehood paved the way to the *Judges Act 1953*, which established the procedure for appointment of judges to all courts in Israel. This system, in which the professionals on a judicial appointments commission have the majority vote in the selection of judges, enabled Israel to maintain a Supreme Court with a high degree of professionalism, free of party politics, corruption, and the like. Public trust in the judiciary brought about further strengthening of the structural independence of judges in *Basic Law: Judicature*, enacted in 1984. The semi-accidental composition of the Court, together with the judicial selection procedure, created an independent and liberal Court that managed to construct and protect democracy in Israel. However, the growing role of the Court in public decision making has in the last few years led to increasing attacks from various circles in Israel, and to specific calls to change the procedure for the appointment and promotion of judges.

In the remainder of this paper I will elaborate on the history of judicial selection in Israel, the results of this procedure, and the main contemporary issues under debate.

Historical Survey

The prime objective of the British Mandatory regime (established in 1917 after the occupation of Palestine from the hands of the Ottomans) was not to construct a liberal democracy in Palestine, but rather to create a centralized and effective government that would grant limited autonomy to the local Jewish and Arab populations. These objectives resulted in a compact judicial structure: a three-tiered general courts system comprising peace courts, district courts, and a Supreme Court, from which a discretionary right of appeal to the Privy Council in London was granted.[9]

Appointment of all judges was entrusted to the high commissioner, while the Supreme Court appointees had to be approved in London.[9] Judges were to hold office during His Majesty's pleasure.[10] From the 1930s, however, the high commissioner formed an informal advisory committee, consisting of representatives of the bar and presiding judges, to assist him in judicial selection, and from 1943 the members of this committee were appointed by the chief justice. Jewish and Arab professionals, non-political figures, were appointed to the peace and district courts (by 1948 nine out of twenty district court judges and thirteen out of forty-one peace court judges were Jewish), but the nine-member Supreme Court was manned mainly by British judges, with a representation of one Jew and one Arab. For this reason the Supreme Court also gained the powers of a high court of justice. All petitions against the government or applications for judicial review were under the exclusive jurisdiction of the Supreme Court.[11]

The purpose of this centralized public law enforcement system was to keep the judicial review of government within the hands of the Mandatory regime, or out of the hands of the local judges. When the State of Israel was established in 1948 and the structure of the courts was maintained,[12] however, this feature became one of the sources of the unprecedented emerging power of the Supreme Court. In principle this is still the situation today: every person with a grievance against the government can petition directly to the Supreme Court and does not even have to be represented.[13] For similar reasons the Mandatory regime did not introduce the jury system to the Palestine judicial system. All trials, criminal and civil, were heard and decided by professional judges alone. This feature was also inherited by the Israeli legal system, and it is another source for the contemporary powers of the Israeli judiciary, as compared to equivalent institutions around the world.

Preparations for an independent state had begun a couple of years before the end of the British Mandate and were accelerated after the UN Partition resolution of November 1947. A special body called the People's Assembly was formed, comprising thirty-seven representatives of various organizations and political parties. This body appointed a committee to deal with the legal structure and institutions of the future state. It was decided to maintain the general structure of the three-tiered general courts system, and to leave the conduct and composition of the peace and district courts intact. The Supreme Court was a slightly different story. First, there was a controversy as to its place of seat. Jerusalem was under siege and there were proposals to establish the new Supreme Court in Tel Aviv. More importantly, since most of the Mandatory Supreme Court judges were British, the composition of the Court was an issue to be deliberated. A solution according to which the British judges would be invited to sit in the Court, as they did, for example, in independent Kenya or India, was rejected.[14]

Formally, the first law to be enacted after the *Declaration of the Establishment of the State of Israel* by the Provisional Council (the same People's Assembly that declared itself as a provisional legislature) was the *Law and Administration Ordinance*, which proclaimed the continuity of law and institutions and transferred all powers of the high commissioner to the Provisional Government.[15] This included the power to appoint judges. However, the government declared that because of the great importance of the composition of the Supreme Court, its judges should be appointed by the Provisional Council upon nomination by the minister of justice. In other words, the government delegated to Parliament the competence to appoint judges, maintaining its powers to nominate the candidates. This was the appointment procedure until the enactment of the *Judges Law* in 1953.

The initial composition of the Supreme Court, which, as I argued earlier, is largely responsible for Israel's success as a democratic state, was almost a historical accident. On the establishment of the state of Israel, the first minister of justice was Felix Rosenblüth (Hebraicized to Pinhas Rosen), born and educated in Germany before and during the Weimar era, a rather untypical background for the political map of those days. Rosen formed an inner circle in the spring and summer of 1948 to establish the Israeli Ministry of Justice, which included several 'Yekkes' (the nickname for this small population of German-speaking Jews who emigrated to Palestine in the 1930s with the rise of Nazism).

Rosen's most important impact lay in his proposals to appoint Moshe

Smoira as the first president of the Israeli Supreme Court. In an interview after his retirement, Rosen openly admitted that he preferred Yekkes in the legal establishment because they were honest and law-abiding.[16] This statement can be understood not only as a praise for the German Jewish immigrants, but also as an indication of Rosen's view of the morality of the leaders of Israel's other branches of government, most of whom were born east of the river Oder.

The persistent German presence in the Supreme Court, which amounted to nearly 50 per cent of its judges in the first three decades of the state of Israel, was largely due to Smoira's appointment by Rosen. Of the first five judges of the Court, two were graduates of Anglo-American universities (Olshan and Heshin); two were graduates of Austrian or German universities (Smoira and Donkenblum), and the fifth judge (Assaf) was not a jurist but a rabbi. This initial composition also reflects a political balance of powers. The five judges were not politicians but each represented a connection with the main political forces comprising the government: Smoira and Olshan to Mappai (the Labour movement), Donkenblum to the Liberals, and Assaf – an Ultra Orthodox Jew – to the religious parties, while Heshin had been a district court judge during the Mandate and represented continuity. Gad Froomkin, the only Jewish representative in the Mandatory Supreme Court, was not appointed because he was seen to be too closely identified with the British rule.

The original court did not include any representatives of the left (the Communists and Mapam) or the right (the Revisionist movement), but this fact did not prevent an overwhelming majority of the Provisional Council from approving the composition (by a secret ballot). Some argued that to enable a real selection process a greater number of candidates should be brought for the legislature to choose from, and the suggested composition was also criticized for failing sufficiently to reflect the 'workers' culture' of the emerging state, but no objections were made to any of the individual names.[17]

The balance between the Anglo-American and the Continental-German schools was maintained in the first two additions to the Court – Agranat, who was born in Louisville, Kentucky, and graduated from the University of Chicago, and Silberg, Lithuanian by birth and a graduate of the universities of Marburg and Frankfurt – and continued in the appointment of further judges after the enactment of the *Judges Act* in 1953. It is difficult to see such equilibrium as merely accidental. Of the first twenty-five judges appointed to the Supreme Court between 1948 and 1979 36 per cent were German natives. The legal education of 36 per cent of the twenty-five first judges was obtained in German universities (this figure overlaps with, but does not parallel, the 36 per cent German natives), while 28 per cent obtained their education in English or American universities, 12 per cent in East European institutions and 20 per cent in Palestine-Israel.

Israel is said to have a mixed legal system. Although it inherited British law, many statutes in important areas of law, mainly private law, enacted since the establishment of the state adopted civil law doctrines. This was a direct consequence of the Yekkes' presence in the Ministry of Justice and in the Supreme Court. American influence, mainly in the area of constitutional law, can also characterize Israeli substantive legal arrangements. The Western legal world is usually divided between the Anglo-American legal systems and the European-Continental ones, but it seems that the more important distinction in Israel is not the common law versus Continental law, but the distinction between the liberal tradition, both Central European and Anglo-American, and a very different, East European political style evident in other governmental institutions, a style which, as argued above, has distinct anti-liberal elements. The pact between the Yekkes and the Anglo-Americans is one of the major contributions to the development of an independent judicial branch of government, with a style of government that differs substantially from those of the other branches of government in Israel. The dramatic success of this style of government, which in the last decade has begun to exercise significant power over the other branches, is yet to be explained.

The *Judges Act 1953* increased the structural independence of the judiciary by holding that judges would have tenure until the mandatory retirement age of seventy, and that their salaries could not be decreased separately.[18] But the most significant component of this law was a new procedure for the appointment and promotion of judges. In an interesting move the government and the Knesset gave up their powers to appoint judges and the statute established a committee to perform this task, while giving the formal appointing power to the President of the state. Originally, the composition of the committee was supposed to include two Supreme Court judges, the attorney general, the dean of the Hebrew University Law Faculty (which was then the only law school in Israel), two government ministers, two members of Parliament, and a representative of the bar (then the Legal Council). The composition that was approved in the final version included three Supreme Court judges, two representatives of the bar, two cabinet ministers, and two Knesset members, but not the academic representative or the attorney general. This change was significant as it guaranteed a majority of five to four for non-politicians (the judges and the bar members) and it gave the three Supreme Court judges an advantage, as they constituted the largest group in the committee. As a balancing measure the minister of justice (one of the two ministers in the committee) was to preside over this committee.

Opposition to the motion was voiced by the left – the Communists and Mapam – who argued that the power to appoint judges should be left with the Knesset, so that the politics of judicial appointments will be clear and transparent to the public. However, the law was eventually passed by a large majority.[19]

The system of appointing and promoting judges adopted in 1953 remains in force today. In 1984 the Knesset replaced the *Judges Act* with *Basic Law: Judicature*, which retained the procedure for the selection of judges but upgraded its normative status to make it part of Israel's constitution. In addition, small changes in the wording of the article strengthened the status of the selection committee as the final decision-making body regarding the appointment and promotion of judges and reinforced the fact that the role of the President of the state is purely a formal one.

In 1984, therefore, the Knesset reaffirmed the system and increased the structural independence of the judiciary, at the same time reaffirming the jurisdiction of the Court and its substantive powers.[20] Although currently the process for changing basic laws (by a majority vote in the Knesset) is formally as easy as changes to regular legislation, informally the Knesset is more cautious in amending basic laws, and in the future the amalgamation of the basic laws into a coherent constitution will remove the possibility of changing the selection procedure by simple majority. The 1984 law can thus be seen as increasing the structural independence of the judiciary.

Analysis of the Judicial Selection Process in Israel

The basic framework of judicial selection for the general courts system in Israel has been in place for more than fifty years now. Its most important component is the judicial appointments and promotions statutory committee. The nine-member committee represents the three branches of government plus the legal profession. Politicians – two members of

Parliament elected by the Knesset, traditionally one from the opposition, and two government ministers, one of whom is the minister of justice and chair of the committee – have an important input, but the majority of members are professionals – two bar members, elected by the Council of the Bar for three years, and three Supreme Court justices, the President of the Court and two judges elected by all the Court's members for a period of three years. The Supreme Court judges are the largest block.[21] The general success of this system led to the adoption of its principles in relation to other specialized courts, such as labour courts, military courts, and even religious courts, each with the necessary variations.[22]

Candidates for judicial positions can be practising lawyers or legal academics with a minimum period of experience (five years for the peace court, seven years for the district court, and ten years for the Supreme Court) prior to the nomination.[23] The law also allows a 'significant jurist' to be a nominee to the Supreme Court, provided that he or she gains the support of three-quarters of the selection committee members. In practice, most peace court judges are selected from among private and public practitioners (mainly prosecutors). Most district court judges are either peace court judges who gain promotion or senior prosecutors or other state legal office holders nominated directly to the district court. The Supreme Court judges are either district court judges who gain promotion, or very senior state legal officers, such as the attorney general or state attorney, or, more rarely, senior academics.[24]

Nominations for the committee's consideration can be made by the minister of justice, the president of the Supreme Court, and any three members of the committee.[25] In practice, this requirement means that in most cases the nominees are agreed upon by the minister and the president of the Court. The committee also elects the president of the Supreme Court when this position becomes vacant (with the retirement of the incumbent at the age of seventy). Traditionally the most senior judge in the Court is automatically elected to be the president.

The balance between professionals and politicians in the selection committee brought about several interesting features in the composition of the Israeli courts, and especially that of the Supreme Court. From the early days of the committee's work, it was the politicians who pushed for a more representative Court. The religious parties in the Knesset demanded a seat be reserved for an Orthodox judge. David Ben Gurion wanted a judge from a Spharadic background. He initially expressed this wish in the early 1950s, and repeated it more vocally following the 1959 riots in Wadi Salib, Haifa. Menachem Begin, shortly after he was elected to the prime minister's office in 1977, expressed a desire to see an Arab judge on the Supreme Court bench. The judges in the committee, who almost always voted en bloc after consultation with their fellow Supreme Court judges, were generous in appointing Spharadic, Orthodox, and Arab judges to the lower courts, but insisted that appointment to the Supreme Court should be based solely on merit.

Eventually, a seat for a religious judge was reserved on the Supreme Court bench. The first composition of the Court even included a rabbi who was not a jurist; after Rabbi Assaf passed away an Orthodox jurist was appointed to the bench (Moshe Silberg) and unofficially at least one seat has always been reserved for an Orthodox Jew since that time. The first Spharadic was appointed to the Supreme Court in 1962 (Eliyahu Mani) and since then at least one seat has been unofficially reserved for a Spharadic judge.[26] The first woman judge was appointed to the Supreme Court in 1977 (Miriam Ben Porat), and the number of women judges has increased steadily to about a third of the Court. Its next President is going to be a woman (Dorit Beinish)[27] and in the Israeli judiciary as a whole there is now a majority of women judges.

Although Arab judges are well represented in the peace and district courts, the first Arab was appointed as a temporary Supreme Court justice only in 2000 (Zuebi); after his one-year term another Israeli Arab was appointed on a temporary basis (Gubran),[28] and in May 2004 he gained a permanent seat. The bottom line, therefore, is that, mainly due to the politicians' input in the selection process, in comparison to other countries, the composition of the courts in Israel, including the highest court, has always been more heterogeneous from the perspective of ethnic origins, gender, and religious beliefs.[29]

Having said this, the three-judges bloc in the committee managed to maintain the ideological tone of the Court, which has always been more liberal and dovish than that of the government and the Knesset. To be more precise, on a left-right axis with regard to the most important issues of public controversy in Israel – peace, security, and human rights – the Court has always been left of the other branches of government. The same applies to the Court's position with regard to the second important area of public debate – the relation between religion and the state. The Court has always been more liberal than the other branches. With regard to economic and social policies, in the era of Israeli socialism, or under the rule of the Labour movement (which lost its hegemony in 1977 after thirty years in power), the Court can be seen as having held more liberal views than that of the government, but in recent years, with the dominance of libertarian government policies, the Court is slowly shifting left to represent a more social justice–orientated stance.

In terms of ideological position, the politics of the Israeli Supreme Court are very different from the rather traditional Conservative tenor (and composition) of the English judiciary, and the law is not perceived as an upper class and Tory territory.[30] The Israeli Court is also different from the American Supreme Court, which, depending on vacancies, and because of the political nature of judicial selection, swings towards the political colours of the current administration, with lasting effects on future administrations. In other words, while in the United States one can point to periods in which the Supreme Court has been more liberal than the administration and other times in which it has been more conservative than the administration, in Israel the Supreme Court has always maintained a more progressive stance than other branches of government.

The former dean of Tel Aviv University Law Faculty recently defended the ideology of the Court, basing his argument on System analysis.[31] The law, argued Menachem Mauntner, in response to calls to bring about a more diverse Supreme Court not only in terms of ethnicity, gender, and religion, but also in terms of values and ideologies, is a separate cultural system and thus membership in the Court is exclusive to those who subscribe to liberal values. The commitment to this value system, according to Mautner, ought to be a pre-condition for appointment.

Another vantage point in the ideological position of the Court on levels of both normative and positive analyses relates to the separation of powers. The Israeli structure of government lacks important components of separation of powers, which can limit the raw power of the majority and shift the collective decision-making outcome from a simple majority towards a more qualified or super majority. Lack of vertical separation between central and local government, lack of vertical separation between the legislature and the executive, and a unicameral legislature with strict proportional representation system leave the judiciary, and especially the Supreme Court, as the only balancing power against the raw majority. This structural explanation can explain not only the stances that the Supreme Court taken but also the intensity of its voice and role in collective decision making in Israel.[32]

On the level of positive analysis one can argue that the unprecedented judicial activism in Israel in the last decade is the result of the lack of proper separation of powers combined with the decreasing ability of the political branches of government to reach coherent and far-sighted or long-term public decisions. In these circumstances decision-making powers are delegated to the courts. This was not the case in the era of the Labour hegemony, and indeed, the increasing activism of the judiciary, and especially that of the Supreme Court, can be traced to the early 1980s, when that hegemony ended.

On a normative level of analysis one can justify the Court's activism as the only counter-majoritarian mechanism and as a device for considering long-term issues beyond the election cycles.[33] Whatever the case may be, the independence of the judiciary provided by the political branches in their legislation, among which is the procedure for judicial selection, enabled the Supreme Court to fulfil this task.

The Contemporary Debate about Judicial Selection in Israel

It is this last development – the growing intervention of the Court in the decision making of the other branches – which brought about a wave of criticism and calls for reforms. The attack on the Court was launched about seven years ago by Ultra Orthodox circles, especially the Shas party, and by the extreme right wing in Israel. It is fascinating to observe how these circles adopted insights from the American Critical Legal Studies movement, portraying the law as part of politics, and the Supreme Court justices as an old elite that tries to maintain its domination through the tool of law.

More recently some mainstream Likud Knesset members, headed by the speaker of the Knesset, have joined these attacks. A motion in the Knesset to establish a constitutional court, bypassing the Supreme Court, was defeated several months ago by a very close vote (ironically, those who put forward this motion, the right wing and Ultra Orthodox, do not believe in a constitution and constitutional values.[34] In January 2004, however, the Knesset passed a decision expressing concerns about the Supreme Court trespassing into the legislature's territory.[35] This can be seen as the lowest point in the history of the relations between the judiciary and the other branches of government since the 1952 clash between the minister of justice and the president of the Supreme Court over sentencing policies, which culminated in an unprecedented letter sent by the president of the Court, Itzhak Ulshan, to the members of the Knesset.[36]

In 2000 mounting criticism of the Court led to the appointment of a committee to re-examine the selection procedure of judges.[37] The committee, headed by the former attorney general and Supreme Court justice Itzhak Zamir, praised the existing system.[38] It highlighted all of the features added to this system since 1953, which were meant to make the selection process more transparent and procedurally just,[39] and it recommended secondary changes which are currently being implemented. They focus on making the selection procedure more professional and transparent.

Thus, for example, although it recommended that the selection committee's deliberations should not be open to the public, it did propose to publish more widely the names of the candidates on the committee's agenda twenty-one days before its deliberations. This added to the existing rule, which enables the general public to submit objections to a specific candidate chosen by the committee during a period of twenty-one days following the committee's decisions.[40] It also proposed to invite all the candidates for a first judicial position for a one-week assessment course in which a more extensive and multi-disciplinarian impression can be obtained of them.[41] Similarly, a sub-committee (three members from the selection committee) is to hold interviews with the candidates. The investigating committee rejected calls to make the judiciary more representative, but it did recommend a more reflective composition of the courts, asserting that they ought to reflect the composition of the Israeli public.

The differences between 'representative' and 'reflective' appear marginal at first glance, but in fact they are substantial. Various politicians called for a more representative court in order to overcome its anti-majoritarian nature. In other words, they want the Supreme Court to represent the various views in society in a similar way to the Knesset. The committee rejected this view, emphasizing that the essence of the Supreme Court is to balance the majority. The committee agreed, however, that a greater effort should be made to include judges from different ethnic and religious backgrounds. Implicitly, the committee embraced Mautner's view that judges should be loyal to the spirit of law, that is, to basic liberal and democratic values, but within these parameters an attempt should be made to grant a voice to different groups in society.[42]

These recommendations, which are now being implemented, have not prevented various politicians from declaring their intention to try and change the law, especially the composition of the selection committee (increasing the number of politicians and other representatives outside the profession, or decreasing the number of judges from three to two, thus breaking their dominance). Recently, the Knesset has considered new legislation that will force the judges on the committee to provide an independent assessment of each of the nominees, rather than a collective decision of all the Supreme Court judges (who are currently being consulted on the candidates before each meeting of the selection committee). The Constitution and Law Committee of the Knesset is reviewing all Basic Laws to prepare for their amalgamation into a unified constitutional document, and in the course of this process changes to the selection committee's composition are likely to be put on the table.

Conclusion

Like Israeli substantive law, the institutional structure of the Israeli judiciary can be portrayed as a mixed system. Like most common law countries it has a general courts system with a Supreme Court that functions as a court for criminal and civil appeal and as a court for public law cases, as well as a constitutional court (in most civil law countries constitutional courts are totally separated from the general system and this is also the case for administrative courts). Likewise, the judges in Israel are senior jurists whose judicial position is a second or third career. There is no career-based judiciary as found in most Continental countries. The judiciary in Israel is rather compact, comprising about five hundred judges in a three-instances hierarchy. These judges enjoy the highest salaries in the public sector and a high social status.

The main institutional features which more closely resemble the Continental system are the lack of jury, the role of the minister of justice as the top administrator of the system, and the selection process of judges. Selection committees dominated by professionals were more common until recent years in civil law countries (e.g., Spain, Italy, Portugal, and France), although some common law countries are currently considering a shift towards this mode of judicial selection.

Since the Israeli judicial selection process was established in 1953, and especially since the enactment of the *Courts Act 1984* and accompanying regulations, the process has been marked by increasing formalization. Vacancies for judicial positions are formally publicized; candidates must complete an application form, accompanied by recommendations; they have to go through a preliminary interview by a sub-committee of the selection committee and attend a one-week evaluation course, and their names are published twenty-one days before the committee considers their applications. Judges who seek promotion have to go through a parallel formal process and present ten judgments and recommendations of the president of their courts.[43] The Zamir committee proposed to establish an advisory committee for judicial promotions, appointed by the judicial selection committee and comprised of senior district court judges, who currently have no formal voice in the selection process.[44] This recommendation has not been yet implemented.

Israeli scholars are unanimous in the view that over the last fifty years the judicial selection committee has broadly been a great success. The judiciary established its reputation for independence, integrity, and intellectual ability in the early years of its existence and improvements to the process of judicial selection have built on these foundations. The appointments process has been an important factor in the successful establishment of the state of liberal democracy in Israel. Nonetheless, the current Israeli political sphere can be characterized by the increasing ineffectiveness of the decision making of the political branches of the state and increasing delegation to the courts, which manifests itself in increased judicial activism.[45] Correspondingly, we witness a delegitimating campaign against the legal establishment, one symptom of which is the mounting calls to change the selection process of judges. The combination of the two developments – the delegation and the delegitimizing – poses a danger to Israeli democracy.

The story of the Israeli Supreme Court can serve as an interesting case study in the development of a theory of the state. On the one hand, it supports the Madisonian argument that the right structure of government, and more specifically the right division of powers, can be sufficient to nourish a liberal democracy. On the other hand, it proves that such division ought to be entrenched in a formal constitution. Otherwise, changing and difficult circumstances, combined with irrational political forces, can undermine a vital foundation on which the future success of the democratic process rests. While reform of the judicial selection process in Israel towards more transparency and procedural justice might be desirable, I hope that the baby will not be thrown out with the bath water.

NOTES

1 A real democracy is not merely a system in which representatives are periodically voted into duty by a majority of the citizens. A real democracy, a liberal democracy, is a political system in which the rule of law is enshrined to pro-

tect individuals and minorities, founded on the principles of individual liberty, civic equality, popular sovereignty, and government by the consent of the governed.

2 On a similar claim regarding the connections between an independent judiciary and economic success see North, *Institutions, Institutional Change and Economic Performance.*

3 See, e.g., Spears, 'Sitting on the Dock of the Day,' 171.

4 A recent survey of the confidence of Israelis in state institutions in comparative perspective is Arian, Nahmias, Navot, and Shany, *The Israeli Democracy Index.*

5 Lord Woolf's Address at the Hebrew University, as reported in *Haaretz,* 5 December 2003.

6 On structural judicial independence see Salzberger, 'A Positive Analysis of the Doctrine of Separation of Powers,' 350–2.

7 On the 'German' presence in the Israeli Supreme Court and its heritage see Oz-Salzberger and Salzberger, 'The Hidden German Sources of the Israeli Supreme Court.'

8 The Mandatory structure of government was regulated by the *Palestine Order in Council 1922,* which can be regarded as the constitutional norm during the rule of the British from 1917 to 1948.

9 This was regulated first by s. 14 of the *Palestine Order in Council 1922,* which referred to all appointments in the civil service and later, specifically to judicial selection in the *Courts Ordinance 1940.*

10 S. 15 of the *Palestine Order in Council 1922.*

11 Ibid., s. 43.

12 The first statute enacted by the new Israeli legislature was the *Law and Administration Ordinance 1948.* The law provides for the principle of continuity of the Mandatory law and institutions. S. 17 deals specifically with the judicial system.

13 To this institutional feature one should also add the substantive component. The Supreme Court, sitting as a High Court of Justice, has the competence to 'deal with matters in which it deems necessary to grant relief in the interests of justice and which are not within the jurisdiction of any other court or tribunal' (s. 15 of *Basic Law: Judicature,* previously s. 7 of the *Courts Act 1957*). The intention of the Israeli legislature was to keep the Mandatory jurisdiction of the High Court of Justice, regulated in s. 43 of the *Palestine Order in Council* and s. 7 of the *Courts Ordinance 1940,* which read 'The Supreme Court, sitting as a High Court of Justice, shall have jurisdiction to hear and determine such matters as are not causes or trials, but petitions or applica-

tions not within the jurisdiction of any other court and necessary to be decided for the administration of justice.' However, in the course of translation the 'administration of justice' turned into the broader concept of 'interests of justice'; this is the formal foundation for the Court's very broad perception of its jurisdiction and for judicial activism in Israel.

14 Gadbois, 'The Selection of Indian Supreme Court Judges.'

15 *Law and Administration Ordinance 1948*, s. 14. The continuity of law is regulated in s. 11.

16 Erel, *The Yekkim*, 187.

17 On the parliamentary debate see Rubinstein, *Shoftei Ertertz*, 66–8.

18 SS. 15–21 of the *Judges Act 1953*.

19 The debate is transcribed in *Divrei Haknesstet* (the official Gazette) 9: 423–43, 2431–50.

20 See note 13 above. Despite the fact that by 1980 the Supreme Court already had a record as an activist court, especially as a High Court of Justice (allowing applications from Palestinians in the territories occupied by Israel in 1967, and invalidating a law of the Knesset on the grounds that it violates an entrenched article in a basic law), the Knesset has not changed its jurisdiction, and by encoding the jurisdiction in a basic law it, in fact, increased the power of the Court.

21 One can argue that the members of the bar are also politicians of a sort. Indeed, the candidates for elected positions in the bar sometimes ran on political tickets, or with some association with political parties. However, as lawyers are the direct clients of courts and judges, professional considerations in this committee usually outweigh political ones.

22 For example, for selection of judges for the labour courts one of the ministers on the committee is the minister for Labour and Welfare (*Labor Courts Act 1969*, s. 4). Composition of the selection committees for the military courts and the various religious courts is regulated by the respective acts dealing with these courts' competence and institutional set-up.

23 S. 2 of the *Courts Act [Consolidated Version] 1984*.

24 The current president of the Court, Aharon Barak, for example, was a law professor who was appointed attorney general in 1975 and to the Supreme Court in 1979. Itzhak Zamir went the same route. Two other law professors were appointed directly to the Supreme Court: Menachem Elon and Itzhak Engelrad.

25 S. 7 of the *Courts Act [Consolidated Version] 1984*.

26 On the politics of special seats on the Supreme Court see Birnhack and Gusarski, 'Designated Chairs, Dissenting Opinions and Judicial Pluralism.'

27 The unbroken tradition is that the committee selects the president of the Court according to seniority. In other words, the most veteran Supreme Court judge is automatically elected to this position.

28 On temporary appointments to the Israeli Supreme Court see Salzberger, 'Temporary Appointments and Judicial Independence.'

29 In a dramatic meeting of the selection committee on May 2004 four new judges were selected for the Supreme Court: two women, one of whom is the state attorney, despite vocal opposition from some politicians who portrayed her as politicians persecutor; the first Arab to gain a permanent seat in the Court; and the former attorney general, who is an Orthodox Jew.

30 See Shapiro, *Courts*; Salzberger, 'The English Court of Appeal,' 223–51; and, on the personal backgrounds of the English judiciary, Atkins, 'Judicial Selection in Context.'

31 Mautner, 'The Selection of Judges to a Supreme Court in a Multi-Cultural Society.'

32 For a more elaborate and analytical explanation see Salzberger, 'A Positive Analysis of the Doctrine of Separation of Powers'; Voigt and Salzberger, (2002) 'Choosing Not to Choose'; Salzberger and Voigt, 'On Constitutional Processes and the Delegation of Power.'

33 On a complete normative argument regarding the role of the courts in a liberal democracy see Salzberger and Koren, 'The Effects of Cyberspace on the Normative Economic Analysis of the State.'

34 The Knesset official Gazette no. 678 19.5.03.

35 See http://www.knesset.gov.il/Tql//mark01/h0000969.html#TQL. This decision was voted after the Court, in a case challenging budgetary cuts in social benefits for the poor, asked the state to provide a policy statement with regard to standards of minimal existence, based on the *Basic Law: Human Dignity and Freedom.*

36 On this affair see Rubinstein, *Shoftei Ertertz,* 97–101.

37 Formally, this committee was appointed by the Judicial Selection Committee; in practice, it was the government who initiated appointments.

38 *The Report of the Committee for the Examination of Judicial Selection.*

39 These procedural requirements are mostly regulated by the *Courts Act [Consolidated Version] 1984* and accompanying regulations.

40 The duty to publish the names of the candidates and the twenty-one-day-objections phase are regulated by *The Adjudication Regulations (The Working Practices of the Judicial Selection Committee) 1984,* as they were amended in 1997.

41 Chapter 8 to the Committee Recommendations.

42 In a sense this is what exactly happened in the early years of the state, when

the Yekkes interacted with the Anglo-Americans on the bench, creating a unique Israeli liberal tradition.

43 For more details on the formal procedure preceding judicial appointments and promotions in Israel see Shetret, *Justice in Israel.*

44 S. 71 of *The Report of the Committee for the Examination of Judicial Selection.*

45 For more on the growing judicial activism in Israel see Shetreet, 'The Critical Challenge of Judicial Independence in Israel.'

13 The Politics of Judicial Selection in Egypt

MAHMOUD M. HAMAD

Introduction

The rule of law is a prerequisite as well as a defining characteristic of a modern state. But the law, in its procedural as well as substantive aspects, is administered by justices and judges 'so that it has become a truism that the quality of justice depends more on the quality of the [persons] who administer the law than on the content of the law they administer.'[1] Hence, judicial selection and its political implications have great significance for political scientists, politicians, and citizens alike, particularly in developing countries where democracy is not yet the only game in town.

The politics of judicial selection in Egypt is the theme of this chapter, which argues for the existence of a linkage between the type of regime's legitimacy, the degree of judicial independence, and the politicization of judicial selection. Max Weber, long ago, argued that any regime based solely on force is inherently unstable. In order to endure, the ruler has to base his claim to obedience on some legitimate grounds. Weber stated, 'Like the political institutions historically preceding it, the state is a relation of men dominating men, a relation supported by means of legitimate (i.e., considered to be legitimate) violence. If the state is to exist, the dominated must obey the authority claimed by the powers that be. When and why do men obey? Upon what inner justifications and upon what external means does this domination rest?'[2]

According to Weber, in principle, there are three inner justifications, hence basic legitimations of domination: tradition, charisma, and legality.[3] These three 'pure' types of legitimation – 'traditional,' 'charismatic,' and 'legal' – are but one of Weber's lasting marks on social and political science.[4] Weber also advocated the notion that charismatic authority might suppress legality. He recognized that 'charisma can undermine the working of legal-bureaucratic institutions.'[5] Nassar's revolutionary-charismatic regime established its legitimacy on direct personal appeal to the populous. Rational-legal legitimacy receded to the shadows. In order to achieve control over the society and the polity, the revolutionary regime opted for a politically accountable judiciary rather than an independent one. This led to substantial executive intervention in judicial selection. Charismatic-based legitimacy thus hindered judicial independence.

Sadat, who did not enjoy the charisma of Nasser, wanted to replace the charismatic legitimacy of the regime, at least in part, with elements of institutionalism and legality. Sadat's regime was of a transitional nature. While preaching legality, in practice, executive-judicial relations retained the stamp of the previous era. Mubarak, on the other hand, lacks both the charisma and the revolutionary credentials of his predecessors. Consequently, he has moved to invigorate the legal base of legitimacy for his regime. This has led to less executive intervention in judicial selection and judicial politics in general. However, Mubarak used his authority over the most senior judicial appointment to influence judicial behaviour, especially in the Supreme Constitutional Court (SCC).

This chapter begins by outlining the structure of the Egyptian judiciary and judicial selection procedures. It then examines practice in three particular regimes: executive intervention in judicial selection in the Nasserite Era (1954–70); the politics of judicial selection under Sadat (1970–81); and judicial selection under Mubarak (1981–present).

The Current Judicial Selection Procedures

Since their establishment over a century ago, Egyptian courts have not only become important components of the social and political landscape but have been imitated throughout the Arab world.[6] The Egyptian legal system established in the 1880s was modelled on the French legal system. However, the 'French' institutions in Egypt have sometimes developed in a way slightly different than they did in France. Furthermore, the Egyptian legal system has developed some institutions that are not found in France, although they do have counterparts in other civil law legal systems.[7] The most important of these is the Supreme Constitutional Court. The Egyptian legal system is thus *sui generis*, comprised of both regular court and exceptional court systems. The regular court system consists of civil and criminal courts, the State Council (a separate administrative court structure), and the Supreme Constitutional Court.[8]

Judicial selection in Egypt is based on the typical civil law model of continental Europe.[9] Magistrates enter the judicial service without any significant prior legal experience,[10] by taking an entrance exam shortly after completing their university education.[11] Judicial appointment is highly prestigious and extremely competitive. 'Judges, especially those in senior positions, and their counterparts in the *niyaba* (public prosecution office) are definitely of high status in Egyptian society, and are accorded considerable respect. They are paid, even at the lower levels, relatively well as government salaries go.'[12]

The official prerequisites for admission to the office of magistrate are: (1) the candidate must be an Egyptian citizen who enjoys his civil rights, all the required guarantees of morality, and good reputation, (2) the candidate must have an LLB from an accredited university or an equivalent degree from Al-Azhar, and (3) the candidate must be at least twenty-one years old for the office of public prosecutor, and thirty years old for the court of first instance.

The judicial appointment process is formally merit-based. Applicants' files are tightly screened to confirm their appropriateness in character and intellect for the bench. Applicants must demonstrate their legal competence and suitability of character before a committee composed of the attorney-general and top sitting judges. Those judges function as gatekeepers to the bench.

In addition to these formal eligibility requirements, a number of other factors determine the make-up of those appointed to the judiciary. First, until relatively recently women were barred from holding senior positions and from sitting as judges, despite the fact that Egyptian women have long worked in the country's judiciary. It was only in 1998 that Counsellor Hind Tantawi was appointed head of the Administrative Prosecution Body, whose current head, Counsellor Nagwa Sadeq, is also a woman. Though the Egyptian constitution guarantees the equality of men and women, generations of women law graduates have been denied appointment as deputies to the prosecutor-general, the traditional starting point in the career of any judge. Nonetheless, the first woman justice, Tahani El-Gebali, was recently appointed to the Supreme Constitutional Court and two female judges were appointed to the SCC's Commissioners' Body. The debate over allowing women to serve as judges is at least half a century old. Traditional segments of Egyptian society are firmly opposed to any changes to the current system. On the other hand, many liberals and feminists, especially within the National Council for Women, have advocated equal access to the bench regardless of gender. This struggle is still unfolding but there is no indication of drastic changes in the foreseeable future.[13]

The second important characteristic of successful judicial candidates is a suitable family background. In practice this usually means that they should be from the upper-middle or upper stratum of society.[14] Thirdly, none of a candidate's immediate relatives should have been accused of anti-regime sentiments or activities. When the appointment process is finalized, the President of the Republic issues a presidential decree to appoint the new group of magistrates.

Newly recruited magistrates are trained in the field as well as at the National Center of Judicial Studies located in Cairo.[15] There are now proposals to change the training program at the Center to something similar to the thirty-one month program of the French L'École Nationale de la Magistrature.[16]

The State Council has a similar recruitment process. Senior members of the council, such as the president and vice-presidents, serve as gatekeepers to the administrative judiciary. However, the Administrative Prosecution Body is a separate entity with a different selection process.

The two main streams of the Egyptian court system, the ordinary judiciary and the State Council, resemble the French system.[17] The first position in the ordinary judicial structure is assistant district attorney, where the fresh appointee stays for one year. The appointee then expects to be promoted to the rank of associate district attorney, which he stays at for about two years. The third rank is district attorney. Based on seniority and competence, the appointee moves to the rank of first class district attorney. This rank is divided into two sub-ranks, A and B. Upon reaching the age of thirty, district attorneys may move to the court structure. Judge rank B is the gateway to the court system. Afterwards the judges are advanced within the judicial structure based on seniority and merit.

The State Council has a similar hierarchal structure. The first position is that of an assistant agent. After acquiring two law school graduate diplomas, one of which must be in public law or administrative sciences, the assistant agent will be promoted to the rank of an agent. He then moves, depending on seniority and academic and practical performance to the subsequent higher ranks.

In regard to the selection process of the highest court of the land, the SCC, Article 3 of the Supreme Constitutional Court Law of 1979 stipulates that the Court is to be headed by the chief justice and staffed by a number of other justices. The law does not specify the exact number of justices. In order to be appointed, justices must meet certain eligibility requirements as stipulated by the Supreme Constitutional Court Law of 1979. A justice must be of Egyptian nationality, have at least an LLB in law, be of good behaviour, be free of any criminal conviction, and be at least forty-five years old. An appointee must be selected from among the following categories:

a. Current or former members of the judicial bodies holding the rank of a counsellor or equivalent for at least five consecutive years.
b. Current or former law professors who have held the position of a professor at an Egyptian university for at least eight consecutive years.
c. Attorneys-at-law who have practised before the Court of Cassation or the high administrative court for at least ten consecutive years.[18]

The President of the Republic appoints the chief justice. The President, based on the advisory opinion of the Supreme Council of Judicial Bodies, also appoints associate justices. Each justice is selected from a choice of two candidates: the chief justice nominates one candidate and the General Assembly of the SCC nominates the other.[19]

The constitution guarantees the independence of the judiciary[20] in Article 166, which proclaims that 'judges shall be independent, subject to no authority other than the law, and that no authority may intervene in judiciary cases or in the affairs of justice.' Judges are appointed for life and may not be dismissed without serious cause. In practice, however, the executive authority enjoys considerable influence over the judiciary, in so far as the appointments of judges are a presidential prerogative.

Theoretically, the President of the Republic *formally* appoints all judges at different ranks. In actuality, new appointees are chosen either by the High Judiciary Council in the case of the ordinary courts, or by the State Council leadership in the case of new council appointees.[21] However, it is notable that the chief executive enjoys absolutely free discretionary power in appointing the most senior members in the judicial structure. The president of the Court of Cassation, who is also the president of the High Judiciary Council, is chosen from among the vice-presidents without any input from the Court's General Assembly or the

High Judiciary Council. It became a norm in the 1980s and 1990s that the most senior vice-president receives the appointment, but there is no guarantee that this practice will continue if the President of the Republic wishes to abandon it.

The president of the State Council is similarly appointed on presidential discretion from among the vice-presidents. The only procedural requirement is the advisory opinion of a special general assembly composed of the president, vice-presidents, deputy-presidents, and counsellors who have served in this capacity for at least two years.[22]

Furthermore, the attorney-general, who supervises the work of all public prosecutors and who has the final authority to initiate criminal proceeding, is also appointed on presidential discretion without any input from the judicial body or the legal profession. The only requirement is that the appointee be of the rank of president of the Court of Appeal or counsellor in the Courts of Cassation, or First Public Attorney. The High Judiciary Council has no say in this process.

In addition, the chief executive has unqualified authority to appoint the chief justice of the SCC. The President can select any person who satisfies the professional requirements mandated by the SCC law. This discretionary power is enormously important because of the chief justice's influence over the SCC's composition and direction.

The Revolutionary Era (1954–1970)

Following the 1952 Revolution, which led to the overthrow of the monarchy and the rule of Mohammed Ali's dynasty, leaders of the military regime were keen to hold absolute power in order to secure a commanding position within the polity and society. Nasser, like other revolutionary leaders, was not deeply impressed with idea of the rule of law. As Rosberg argues, 'Nasser himself was not ideologically committed to the idea of an independent judiciary or the rule of law.'[23] Nasser wanted to radically change society from above, and he did not appreciate judicial claim to due process. He not only feared that the courts could be slow in grasping the message of the revolution, he also suspected that counter-revolutionary elements had infiltrated its ranks. Many of Nasser's public statements affirmed how concerned he was with the law's power to obstruct implementation of government policy.[24] This might explain why the Egyptian legal institutions were significantly weakened during the Nasserite Era.

Radical elements within Nasser's regime thought to use certain 'revolutionary' methods to domesticate the regime's opponents in the judicial structure. The regime was first concerned with a number of rulings by the State Council (*Maglis al-Dawla*) that overturned government laws and regulations. On 29 March 1954, regime thugs physically beat Dr al-Sanhuri, the president of the State Council and Egypt's greatest legal scholar. In the following month, the Council of Ministers issued a new law prohibiting those who assumed ministerial posts under the monarchy from sitting on the bench. Many believe that the law was mainly drafted to purge al-Sanhuri, who was a minister under the overthrown regime.

In 1955, and after a number of highly publicized anti-regime rulings, the revolutionary regime drafted Law 165, which stipulated that all members of the State Council should be reappointed by a decree of the Council of Ministers within fifteen days. This law gave the regime a free hand to restructure the council, and purge some of its leading members. Twenty prominent members of the State Council, including its vice-president, were forcibly retired or transferred to non-judicial positions. 'These moves were particularly damaging to judicial independence since *Maglis al-Dawla* was the only institution through which citizens could challenge administrative acts. By 1955 the *Maglis al-Dawla* was formally stripped of its power to cancel administrative acts.'[25] Tarek Al-Beshri, a former State Council judge, documented the impact of this 'reform' process on the nature of rulings and opinions from the council in the post-1955 era.[26]

Nasser's preference for an expansion of executive powers at the expense of autonomous rule-of-law institutions continued into the late 1960s. The final and most significant blow to Egyptian judicial institutions came in the late 1969 'massacre of judiciary.' In the wake of the 1967 defeat and with increasing calls from both the Judges Association[27] and the Lawyer's Syndicate[28] for political and judicial reform, the regime responded with a massive array of legislation. Judge Sherif summarizes this attack all too briefly, stating:

> After the unfortunate result of the Six-Day War of 1967 an increasing judicial tendency to move towards democratization was shown. The political leadership at the time aimed to continue its domination over the judiciary and began to express a wish to have judges enrolled in the sole political party like any other group of people. Judges claimed that this step would detract from their independence, and they therefore condemned the proposal. The reaction of the executive to this resistance was the issuance of a chain of decree laws to reorganize all judicial bodies.[29]

On 31 August 1969, Nasser surprised the judiciary and virtually the whole country by issuing four presidential decrees:

- Presidential decree No. 81, which established the Supreme Court.
- Presidential decree No. 82, regarding the restructuring of the judicial bodies.
- Presidential decree No. 83, which instituted the Supreme Council of Judicial Bodies.
- Presidential decree No. 84, concerning the formation of the Judges Association.[30]

Nasser decided that judicial autonomy was too great a threat to the regime. Utilizing his legislative powers he dismissed 189 judges, including the president of the Court of Cassation, fifteen counsellors at the same court, all members of the board of the Judges Association, and other key judges and prosecutors in various parts of the judicial system. To ensure that resistance to executive power would not easily re-emerge, Nasser created the Supreme Council of Judicial Bodies,[31] which gave the regime greater control over judicial appointments promotions and disciplinary action.

Presidential decree No. 81 consolidated executive control over the process of judicial review through the creation of a new, executive-dominated Supreme Court. This newly established court was given the exclusive power of judicial review and replaced the system of 'abstention control' in which each individual court practised constitutional interpretation and periodically abstained from enforcing laws that they deemed to violate articles of the constitution.[32] In an explanatory memorandum to decree 81/1969, the regime made no attempt to hide the purpose of the new court when it openly declared: 'It has been clear in many cases that the judgments of the judiciary are not able to join the march of development which has occurred in social and economic relations.'[33]

Essentially, the new Supreme Court centralized the process of judicial review and placed it under tight control of the regime. Court justices were appointed directly by the President for three-year terms and the court was regularly stacked with pro-regime justices.[34] In the unlikely event that judicial resistance to executive policy emerged, the President could easily appoint new justices to replace the old. 'From 1969–1979, when the Supreme Court was in operation, it made over 300 rulings, not one of which significantly constrained the regime.'[35]

It seems that Nasser was able, at last, to domesticate his opponents within the judiciary and hence dramatically increase the accountability of the court to the executive branch. These measures had severe political costs, as the regime lost all claims to legality and due process. The charismatic leadership of Nasser was able to stabilize the political system even under these conditions, but this situation depended heavily on Nasser's persona and consequently could not be sustained after his death in 1970.

The Transitional Era (1970–1981)

The constitutional proclamation of 1971, issued shortly after Sadat came to power in late 1970, affirmed the crucial significance of the rule of law, stating 'The sovereignty of law is not only a guarantee for the freedom of the individual alone, but is also at the same time the sole basis for the legality of authority.' The 1971 constitution, also known as the permanent constitution, included a new chapter entitled 'Sovereignty of the Law.' Article 64 stipulated that 'Sovereignty of the law shall be the basis of rule in the State.' Article 65 went further to proclaim, 'The State shall be subject to law.' The same article linked this new conception of the role and mission of the state to the judiciary: 'The independence and immunity of the judiciary are two basic guarantees to safeguard rights and liberties.'

President Sadat wanted to create an image of liberalism, openness, and respect for the rule of law in order to accomplish a number of tasks. First, although a member of the Free Officers,[36] Sadat lacked Nasser's charisma and he wanted to build a rational-legal base of authority that might compensate for this lack. Second, Sadat embarked on a process of de-Nasserization. Sadat's assertion that he wanted to create a 'state of institutions' was a direct assault on the individualistic leadership of his predecessor. Third, Sadat wanted to please his new constituency in the United States and the West. This was closely related to his program of changing Egypt's foreign policy westward. All that said, Sadat did not want to relinquish his firm grip on power.

While the President repeatedly affirmed his commitment to institutionalism and the rule of law, his promises in this regard did not materialize. The judiciary remained mostly under the repressive legal framework of Nasser. The executive-dominated Supreme Council of Judicial Bodies continued to be the ultimate authority for all courts. Article 173 of the 1971 constitution states, 'A Supreme Council, presided over by the President of the Republic shall supervise the affairs of the judicial organizations.' Sadat did not dismiss judges or purge the judiciary, but he added many layers of judicial bodies outside the regular court system. The more notable among them are discussed below.

First, he established the Socialist Public Prosecutor. Article 179 of the constitution stipulates that 'The Socialist Public Prosecutor shall be responsible for taking the measures which secure the people's rights, the safety of the society and its political regime, the preservation of the socialist achievements and commitment to socialist behavior.' The President of the Republic appoints the socialist prosecutor and he must be confirmed by the People's Assembly.

Second, Sadat established the Political Parties Court (Law 40/1977). When Egypt's constitution was amended to allow a multi-party system, a new body was created to determine the legality of new parties and their eligibility to contest elections. While generally referred to as the 'Parties Court,' this body is as much a political body as it is a judicial one.

Third, the Court of Ethics was created to try cases of corruption and illicit economic gain. The Socialist Public Prosecutor is the only body authorized to bring cases to this court. While most of its members are professional judges, respected public dignitaries are added to the bench as well, as half of its members are political appointees.

Fourth, the State Security Court–Emergency Section was established with much more direct executive involvement in its composition and jurisdiction. These courts allow no judicial appeal, but the military governor (under a state of emergency) is allowed to affirm the verdict or order a retrial.

To summarize, Sadat continued to base his legitimacy on the 1952 Revolution (and later on 1973 War); however, he included elements of legality to substitute for the lack of charisma. By refraining from purging judges, Sadat was able to preserve an image of legality. Nonetheless, the many layers of special courts, usually staffed by judges with weaker guarantees of independence, led to a fragmented judicial body. 'The fragmentation of the judicial system can therefore be seen as a means of politically neutralizing ordinary courts while preserving their institutional independence.'[37]

The Post-Revolutionary Era (1981–present)

Mubarak's regime marked a new era in the judicial selection process. Upon ascending to office in 1981, Mubarak inherited a severe legitimacy crisis from his predecessor; the economy was in turmoil, all leading leaders of the legal opposition were in detention, and corruption scandals implicated many leading politicians and businessmen, including members of Sadat family. The 'young' President was not part of the revolutionary officers, and could not found his legitimacy on the 1952 Revolution. Also, Mubarak looked like a pale figure in the shadows of Nasser and Sadat. He had to look to a more rational-legal source if he wanted to appear as a legitimate leader, and Mubarak thought to highlight the rule of law in his quest for legitimacy.

The role of the judiciary thus took centre-stage in Mubarak's speeches. While the President rarely meets justices and judges, whenever he speaks about the Egyptian judiciary he expresses his gratitude and appreciation for their noble mission. 'The judiciary is the high bench that everyone looks to for its fairness.'[38] Also, Mubarak repeatedly affirms his adherence to court orders by insisting that 'the respect for the high bench is the basic duty and obligation of the ruler.'[39]

On a practical level, Mubarak worked to strengthen the judiciary. The regime issued a law that gave members of the public prosecution office full judicial immunity. He also signed Law 35 of 1984, which restructured the High Judiciary Council under the chairmanship of the president of the Court of Cassation. Hence, control of judicial affairs was reserved to senior members of the judiciary who serve in the council.[40]

Additionally, the regime issued Law 136 of 1984, which gives full immunity to the State Council and grants its senior members functional authority over its members. These moves were practically welcomed by the court. The president of the Judges Association praised Mubarak, stating 'the President's actions have repeatedly shown his deep commitment to the rule of law and the protection of justice.'[41]

As a result of these reforms, 'in the 1980s, the courts, acting as a coordinate and coequal branch of government, began to issue opinions that severely imposed on the powers of the executive and legislative branches. National and security courts quashed convictions; administrative courts held that executive actions banning political activity or publications were inconsistent with applicable laws; and the SCC exercised judicial review in an aggressive fashion.'[42] But Mubarak's tolerance of judicial power proved to be limited. Faced with an intense violent threat from Islamists in the 1990s, Mubarak decided to transfer terrorism cases outside the ordinary court system, and even the state security court, to the military courts. These military courts are mostly staffed with officers and are not subject to the appeal process of the civilian courts.

Mubarak did not use extra-legal measures to interfere in the judicial appointment process. The regime preferred to enlist the judicial cooperation of certain key judges by providing some material incentive. For example, a number of judges loyal to regime policy were appointed as governors or heads of other important governmental agencies.[43] Recognizing the political significance of the SCC,[44] however, Mubarak decided to interfere vigorously to domesticate the Court, and he used his authority over the appointment of the chief justice to influence its agenda and rulings. As stated above, the law does not set the exact number of justices.[45] Although he is theoretically *primus inter pares* – and has but one vote among the justices of the court – the chief's potential influence may outweigh that of any ordinary presiding officer. The SCC system gives the chief justice extraordinary power to shape the Court's jurisprudence. The chief justice has the right to 'assign the date of the session on which proceedings on the case or application will commence.'[46] More to the point, whether or not he is in the majority, the chief justice will either write the opinion or assign it to a judge of his choosing.[47] He can also assign the opinion to a judge who is not in the majority.[48] When the opinion is issued, it will not disclose how justices cast their votes. Indeed, the law classifies such information, and justices or court officials who reveal it are subject to discipline.[49]

Nonetheless, the most important power of the chief justice is his ability to nominate justices to the Court, and his sole authority to nominate the president of the Commissioners' Body and its members.[50] The Commissioners' Body represents the Egyptian institutionalized version of the law clerks in the U.S. Supreme Court.[51] Its principal duty is to prepare all cases, disputes, claims, and petitions to be heard by the Court. The head of the Commissioners' Body must meet the same eligibility requirements as the justices of the Court. Other members must meet the same requirements applicable for their peers, as provided for in the Judiciary Law. Receiving an appointment as commissioner at the SCC is considered a privilege for mid-career judges in the State Council or other judicial branches.[52] For an extended period of time, Commissioners' Body appointment did not raise a flag because the internal requirement process – a type of internal promotion largely based on merit – ensured that the chief justice would represent the consensus of the court.

If the chief justice has the same ideological commitment as the majority of justices, the SCC's General Assembly and the chief justice will nominate the same candidate. This procedure effectively gives the Court full control over the appointment of justices. Indeed, in the 1980s and 1990s the SCC had greater influence over its composition and ideological development than any other constitutional court in the world.[53]

The processes of internal requirement dominated SCC selection between 1979 and 2001. This meant that, in most cases, judges received an appointment at the Commissioners Body. A commissioner who proved his competence would be promoted to a senior rank within that body. The next step was to be selected by the chief justice or the General Assembly of the Court for an SCC position. He could then move onward with seniority and aptitude to the rank of chief justice.

Former Chief Justice al-Morr is a perfect example of the internal requirement process. He was appointed to the Commissioners' Body when the Court was founded in 1979. In 1983, after serving for four years, he was promoted to the rank of senior member; in 1984 he was selected to be an SCC justice. After seven years of serving as a justice, al-Morr was finally promoted to chief justice in 1991. He served in this capacity for seven more years until, by the virtue of age, retired in 1998. 'In the period from 1990 to 1997 the SCC became ever more assertive under the leadership of Chief Justice Awad al-Morr.'[54]

Upon al-Morr's retirement, a presidential decree was issued to promote the most senior justice to the rank of chief justice. On this occasion it was Justice M. Wali al-Din Galal who received the appointment. Mubarak and other members of the regime probably thought that the retirement of al-Morr would end the activist and liberal-oriented era of SCC. Chief Justice Galal proved them wrong, however, as the SCC, under his leadership, maintained an identical ideological commitment. The Court issued a number of rulings to expand the political and civil rights of the citizenry. For example, the SCC deemed unconstitutional a provision of the Press Law requiring the approval of the Council of Ministers before publishing a newspaper.[55]

The most daring SCC decision was related to Article 24 of the Law of Political Participation (73/1956), which governs the monitoring of parliamentary elections. According to the SCC, the constitution gives the judiciary the exclusive right to supervise all stages of legislative elections. The relevant article of the Political Participation Law was ruled unconstitutional because it stipulates that state and public sector employees can head local election committees.[56] Since the parliamentary elections of both 1990 and 1995 were carried out according to the Political Participation Law – that is, without the complete and effective supervision of the judiciary – the assemblies themselves are, in turn, illegitimate. This ruling struck at the heart of the regime-managed liberalization. In the following parliamentary election, the first under full judicial supervision, many leading members of the ruling NDP ware handsomely defeated.

With the departure of Chief Justice Galal in late 2001, Mubarak would have ample opportunity to interfere in the SCC selection process. The President stunned everybody, including SCC justices, with his choice of M. Fathi Naguib for the post. Naguib, who was recently appointed president of the Court of Cassation and president of the High Judiciary Council, was a well-known regime supporter. Mustafa nicely summarizes the public reaction to this move:

> Opposition parties, the human rights community, and legal scholars were stunned by the announcement. Not only had Fathi Naguib proved his loyalty to the regime over the years, but he was the very same person who had drafted the vast majority of the regime's illiberal legislation over the previous decade, including the oppressive law 153/1999 that the SCC had struck down only months earlier. Moreover, by selecting a Chief Justice from outside the justices setting on the Supreme Constitutional Court, Mubarak also broke a strong norm that had developed over the previous two decades.[57]

Chief Justice Naguib announced that he would increase the number of justices in the court. Established practice since 1979 had set the number of justices at nine,[58] but Naguib increased that number dramatically. Currently, there are fifteen SCC judges.[59]

Naguib's new recruits came predominantly from the ordinary courts and mainly from the Court of Cassation and Cairo Court of Appeal. This recruitment also broke an established norm of recruiting the SCC justices from the State Council. While there are no detailed studies of the different ideological commitments of the administrative and regular court justices, State Council judges are typically more inclined to restrict government authority in comparison to regular court judges. In an effort to preserve the regime's legitimacy, Naguib also nominated the first-ever female SCC justice, the nationalist lawyer Tahani El-Gibali.

The SCC under Chief Justice Naguib took a conservative and less active role. Contrary to all other SCC justices, he accepted the idea of prior constitutional review. This proposal, which was widely condemned under al-Morr, would strip the SCC of its judicial review power in favour of a more advisory role before the drafting of legislation.[60] He also affirmed his belief in the absence of any political role for the SCC.[61] The chief justice even criticized prior SCC rulings. Mustafa quotes him as saying: 'They [SCC justices] were issuing rulings that were bombs in order to win the support of the opposition parties. They were very pleased with the rulings, but the rulings were not in the interest of the country. This needed to be corrected. Now the president [Mubarak] can be assured that the court will make rulings that are in the interest of the country and yet still maintain its independence.'[62]

The chief justice delivered on his promise. Naguib's Court did not trouble the regime with any major ruling. The most important SCC ruling under his chairmanship was to exempt the People's Assembly decision on presidential nomination from any judicial revision. The Court stated that this very important decision is a procedural matter. It is neither legislation nor a legislative act and hence does not fall within the jurisdiction of the Court.[63]

The untimely death of Naguib in August 2003 caught the regime off guard. The government had been debating a law that aimed to extend the mandatory retirement age of all justices to sixty-eight. This would have enabled Naguib to serve until 2006 (he was born in 1938). Mubarak again opted to choose a chief justice from outside the SCC. His appointee was Mamdouh Marra,' the president of the Cairo Court of Appeal.

Marra', like Naguib, had for years proved to be a loyal soldier of the regime. Like his predecessor, he rose within the ranks of the Ministry of Justice to the rank of deputy-minister for judicial supervision.[64] This is the position that Naguib had held before being nominated to the presidency of the Court of Cassation. While it is too early to investigate the political implications of this selection, many believe that the new chief justice will follow the line of his predecessor. This argument finds support in some SCC recent rulings, which in general do not contradict the political line of the regime.[65]

Conclusion

Since the 1952 Revolution, judicial selection in Egypt has remained a political matter. However, the politicization of judicial selection has varied in intensity and form. This chapter argues that the degree of politicization is a function of the regime's strategy to achieve political legitimacy. Charismatic or revolutionary leaders, like Nasser, could easily base their political legitimacy on a direct appeal to the people. Legality and the rule of law could be sacrificed in order to hold the judiciary accountable to the political authority and hence executive intrusion became the norm in this era.

Sadat, while a member of the Free Officers, did not enjoy the charisma of Nasser and wanted to base his political legitimacy, at least in part, on institutionalism and legality. Consequently, he moderately strengthened the independence of the court while at the same time preserving its accountability to the regime.

Mubarak enjoys neither the charisma nor the revolutionary credentials of his predecessors. It is no wonder, therefore, that he moved to revitalize the legal base of legitimacy for his regime. The balance between independence and accountability has moved further in the direction of establishing a semi-equal judicial branch.

While Egypt still has a long way to go to be considered a full-fledged democracy, there is no doubt that, since the death of Nasser in 1970 and especially after Sadat's assassination in 1981, the rule of law as a base of the regime's legitimacy has been augmented. This trend led to less executive intervention in judicial selection and judicial politics. This was reflected in the more subtle and legal forms of intervention in judicial selection. For instance, Mubarak has not opted for extra-legal measures to influence the judiciary. The President, nonetheless, has utilized his constitutional powers to appoint like-minded justices to top posts within the judicial structure. Those justices, especially the chief justice, used promotion from the regular court system to check the activist orientations of the State Council's justices who historically dominated the Supreme Constitutional Court. To conclude, it is safe to say that because of the magnified impact of judicial decisions, judicial selection will remain a sensitive political matter in twenty-first-century Egypt.

NOTES

The author wishes to thank Professor Susan Olson for her useful comments and suggestions. The editorial assistance of Melissa Goldsmith is appreciated.

1 Abraham, *The Judicial Process*, 1.

2 Weber, *Politics as a Vocation.*

3 Ibid.

4 Weber recognized that 'the pure types are rarely found in reality. But today we cannot deal with the highly complex variants, transitions, and combinations of these pure types, which problems belong to "political science."' *Politics as a Vocation*, 79, n4.

5 Christian Boulanger, 'The Charisma of, Rationality in, and Legitimacy through Law: A Neo-Weberian Analysis of Post-Communist Constitutionalism,' paper presented at the 2001 Law and Society Association and ISA RCSL Joint Meeting, Budapest, 4–7 June 2001, 12.
6 Brown, *The Rule of Law in the Arab World*, 1.
7 Hill, *Mahkama! Studies in the Egyptian Legal System, Courts and Crimes, Law and Society*, 1.
8 An elaborate exceptional court system exists parallel to the ordinary court system. This study focuses exclusively on the regular courts. Special courts like State Security Courts, Emergency courts, or Military Courts have special appointment procedures, which are not discussed here.
9 For more details about this model please see the excellent chapters on France and Italy in this volume.
10 The term 'magistrate' refers to junior members of the prosecution body as well as the junior judges.
11 Law education in Egypt is conducted through national universities, Al-Azhar, and the Police Academy. The curriculum includes all of the normal courses in any modern law college. In addition, certain other groups of courses are related to the Islamic legal system. Thus the construction of the syllabus for the LLB in Egypt is a reflection of the history of the legal development in the country. See Serag, 'Legal Education in Egypt,' 616.
12 Hill, *Mahkama*, 41.
13 For more details about the different opinions on this issue please see Ebid, *The Independence of the Judiciary*, 250–6; Hassnin, 'An Interview with Ahmed Medhat Al-Maraghi,' *Al-Ahram* (Cairo), 15 May 2002; Elbendary, 'Women on the Bench.'
14 While there are no official figures to investigate the socio-economic status of the new judicial appointees, based on my fieldwork and personal contacts with justices and public persecutors, I assume that over one-half of the new appointees are relatives of sitting or former judges. Siblings of government ministers, MPs, governors, university professors, and top officials of the military-bureaucratic establishment are privileged to receive a judicial appointment.
15 Bernard-Maugiron and Dupret, eds., *Egypt and Its Laws.*
16 *Al-Akhbar* (Cairo), 11 December 2003.
17 See chapter 9, 'The Selection of Judges in France,' in this volume.
18 However, in practice, all but one of the SCC's justices came directly from other judicial bodies, mainly the State Council and the ordinary courts.
19 The SCC's General Assembly includes all justices and senior members of the Commissioners' Body.

20 Russell points out that the term 'judicial independence' is often used to refer either to the institutional guarantees judges enjoy or to the degree of autonomy they display in relation to litigants and political branches. See Guarnieri and Pederzoli, *The Power of Judges*, 5.

21 These procedures are very similar to the French system. See Abraham, *The Judicial Process*, 35.

22 Article 83 of Law 47 of 1972.

23 Rosberg, 'Roads to the Rule of Law,' 124.

24 Ibid., 125–6.

25 Mustafa, 'Law versus the State,' 49.

26 Al-Beshri, *Studies about Egyptian Democracy*, 200.

27 The Judges Association was established on 11 February 1939. It accepts all members of the courts and the public prosecution. The second article of its charter states that its purposes are to 'strengthen the cohesiveness and collaboration among all justices, guard their interests, facilitate social collaborations among them, [establish a] credit union for the members, and help the families of passed away judges.' A fifteen-member board of directors, elected by the members, runs the association. See Nassar, *The Battle for Justice in Egypt*, 36.

28 Established in 1912, the Lawyers' Syndicate is one of Egypt's most liberal professional associations. The bar is renowned for fighting for political and civil rights.

29 Sherif, 'Attacks on the Judiciary,' 15.

30 For more details see Imam, *The Massacre of the Judiciary*.

31 The executive branch dominated this council. The President of the Republic assumes its chairmanship and the minister of justice acted as a vice-president. In addition to the heads of the judicial bodies, the president had the right to appoint two members. This council replaced the Higher Judiciary Council as the ultimate source of authority within the judiciary.

32 Judges had resisted the implementation of laws that restricted freedoms by enforcing only the letter and not the spirit of these laws. Furthermore, in the absence of an authoritative force of constitutional interpretations, lower courts would make constitutional interpretations themselves and refuse to implement laws they found unconstitutional. See Rosberg, 'Roads to the Rule of Law,' 156.

33 Mustafa, 'Law versus the State,' 58–9.

34 According to Article 7 of the Court Law, the President of the Republic has the sole authority to appoint the chief justice. The president can even disregard the age limit for his retirement. The president also appoints the deputy-chief justice and justices after gathering the opinion of the Supreme Council

of Judicial Bodies. The law did not specify the number of the Court's justices, giving the president the further right to appoint additional justices when he deems necessary. Fouzi, *Constitutional Review of Legislations*, 54–61.

35 Mustafa, 'Law versus the State,' 59–60.

36 The Free Officers are the young group of army officers, led by Nasser, who carried the 1952 Revolution against the king. They played an important role in Egyptian politics in the 1950s and 1960s.

37 Guarnieri and Pederzoli, *The Power of Judges*, 79.

38 Mubarak's speech at the opening of the fourth legislative session of the People's Assembly, 24 June 1984; Farhod, 'The Place of the Judiciary in the Egyptian Political System,' 293.

39 Mubarak's speech at the opening of the First Conference of Justice, Cairo, 20 April 1986, in Farhod, 'The Place of the Judiciary,' 293.

40 The council is headed by the president of the Court of Cassation, and it includes the President of the Cairo Court of Appeal, the attorney-general, the two most senior deputy-presidents of the Court of Cassation, and the two most senior presidents of the Courts of Appeal. See Article 77* of Law 35 of 1984.

41 The Speech of Judge Yahi Al-Rafai at the opening session of the First Conference of Justice, Cairo, 20 April 1986, in Farhod, 'The Place of the Judiciary,' 296.

42 Lombardi, 'State Law as Islamic Law in Modern Egypt, 170–1.

43 The list currently includes the former president of the State Council, Dr Godat Al-Malt, who after reaching the age of retirement was appointed as the chairman of the crucial Central Authority of Accounting. The current governor of Giza, Mahmoud Abu El-Lial, is also a former judge.

44 Nabil Abdel-Fattah highlights the political significance of the SCC stating, 'The Supreme Court's rulings reveals that it functions to entrench and foster the sovereignty of law, democracy, and human rights, as these concepts have come to be understood across the civilized world.' *Al-Ahram* (Cairo), 10–16 August 2000.

45 Law 48 of 1979 – regarding the proclamation of the law on the Supreme Constitutional Court.

46 Article 41 of Law 48 of 1979.

47 Sherif, 'The Freedom of Judicial Expression, The Right to Concur and Dissent,' 145.

48 'In the Egyptian system, the decision of any court is a unified opinion of all its members, none of the judges being able to present his or her own views separately. Therefore, the public never knows what an individual judge has decided in a particular case, and consequently it is nearly impossible for

them to be certain of the judge's own personal beliefs.' Sherif, 'The Freedom of Judicial Expression,' 139.

49 The Court simply issues one opinion and no dissents are published. If there are three or more conflicting opinions, the chief justice counts the number of votes for each position, identifies the two positions that have the most support, and drops all the others. The justices are then required to cast their votes again, and are only permitted to vote for one of the two remaining opinions. El-Morr, Nosseir, and Sherif, 'The Supreme Constitutional Court and Its Role in the Egyptian Judicial System,' 42–3.

50 Article 23 of the Court Law dictates that 'The President of the Commissioners Body and its members are appointed by a presidential decree after a nomination by the Chief Justice and consulting with the Court General Assembly.'

51 For more information on the role of law clerks in the Supreme Court see Abraham, *The Judicial Process*, 263–9.

52 For more details see El-Morr, Nosseir, and Sherif, 'The Supreme Constitutional Court.' 43–4.

53 Rutherford, 'The Struggle for Constitutionalism in Egypt,' 298.

54 Mustafa, 'Law versus the State,' 134.

55 *Al-Ahram* (Cairo), 7 May 2001.

56 The regime used to appoint public sector's employees to staff polling locations in order to manipulate election results.

57 Mustafa, 'Law versus the State' 250–1.

58 El-Morr, Nosseir, and Sherif, 'The Supreme Constitutional Court,' 42–3.

59 *Al-Ahram* (Cairo), 9 November 2002.

60 Naguib comments at his meeting with the editors-in-chief of some major Egyptian newspapers. *Al-Ahram* (Cairo), 14 January 2003.

61 Naguib interview, *Al-Ahram* (Cairo), 9 November 2002.

62 Mustafa, 'Law versus the State,' 254.

63 *Al-Ahram* (Cairo), 12 May 2003.

64 *Al-Ahram* (Cairo), 27 August 2003.

65 See, e.g., the SCC legal opinion on the supplementary elections of the People's Assembly and the other legal opinion on which judicial bodies may supervise elections. *Al-Ahram* (Cairo), 8 March 2004.

14 Judicial Selection in Post-Apartheid South Africa

FRANÇOIS DU BOIS

If judicial power is an essential component of democracy,[1] then its expansion in South Africa during the past decade was inevitable. Along with universal franchise, the constitutional changes inaugurated by the 1994 elections introduced a package of reforms to the courts and the judiciary.[2] Foremost among these was the enactment of a Bill of Rights authorizing the courts, for the first time, to invalidate legislation and to enforce positive duties imposed on the state. Equally important was the creation of a Constitutional Court (CC) exercising final decision-making power over constitutional matters, as well as the establishment of a Judicial Service Commission (JSC) and constitutional provision for a Magistrates' Commission (MC) to govern the higher and lower judiciary respectively.[3] The creation of the JSC in particular was directly linked to the expansion of judicial power. A new process of judicial appointment was considered necessary to ensure that this power would be exercised by independent yet accountable judges whose demographic profile and jurisprudential orientation would be in keeping with the transformed constitutional order.

The JSC commenced work in October 1994 with the appointment of the first members of the CC, and it has since then played a role in the appointment of all judges. It has won well-deserved praise for its transformation of the judicial appointment procedure,[4] although an examination of its operation reveals the complexities of the purposes for which it was established.

Background

Like everything else in South Africa, these new commissions and courts operate against a background of stark racial division. Despite the abolition of legally codified racial separation and discrimination, racial division is a contemporary reality and continues to affect the administration of justice. Nelson Mandela's famous objection in 1962 to being tried by a white magistrate[5] has been echoed more than once since 1994.[6] Perhaps predictably, the courts remain dismissive of applications for recusal based on the racial identity of judicial officers.

These cases highlight two central aspects of the South African legal system. First, the racial identity of judicial officers is deeply contentious, and this fact is central to the social legitimacy of the judiciary. Already in 1986 the Human Sciences Research Council, an official, state-funded body, reported that the various population groups differed greatly in their estimation of the quality of justice meted out in the courts, and that the solution lay partly in the appointment of black judges and magistrates.[7] Second, it highlights the continuity of South African law in this regard: there is still no entitlement to be judged by 'your own,' not even when the facts and context of a case are suffused with racial division and conflict. The CC, the pride of the post-1994 legal order and the major force in the transformation of the law, has put it this way:

> While litigants have the right to apply for the recusal of judicial officers where there is a reasonable apprehension that they will not decide a case impartially, this does not give them the right to object to their cases being heard by particular judicial officers simply because they believe that such persons will be less likely to decide the case in their favour, than would other judicial officers drawn from a different segment of society ... Judicial officers are ... required to 'administer justice to all persons alike without fear, favour or prejudice, in accordance with the Constitution and the law.' To this end they must resist all manner of pressure, regardless of where it comes from. This is the constitutional duty common to all judicial officers. If they deviate, the independence of the Judiciary would be undermined, and in turn, the Constitution itself.[8]

Several other chapters in this volume attest to the universality of the tension between a society (or at least a large part thereof) that measures the judiciary by its representativity, and a legal establishment for which the touchstone is professional impartiality born of mastery of the law and the acquisition of lawyerly virtues. They also show that the attitude expressed in this quotation is far from idiosyncratic. However, one of the notable features of the South African constitution is that it addresses and seeks to mediate this tension. When judicial officers (a term covering magistrates as well as judges) are appointed, they must not only be 'appropriately qualified' and 'fit and proper,' '[t]he need for the judiciary to reflect broadly the racial and gender composition of South Africa must [also] be considered.'[9] Primary responsibility for this task is vested in the JSC and MC; this chapter explores the functioning of these bodies in light of the tension between representativity and technical accomplishment as means for the pursuit of judicial legitimacy.

The specific duty placed on these bodies to 'reflect broadly' the racial and gender segmentation of South African society – that is, to make the judiciary more representative of major social divisions – can be contrasted with the subtly different goal of diversity, which values variety as such. The chapters on Australia, Canada, and the United Kingdom in particular advocate a more diverse judicial corps, not only exposing how false conceptions of 'merit' can, and do, mask prejudice and vested interests, but also indicating how greater diversity on the bench may improve the administration of justice. Yet they are also critical of representativity as an aim in judicial appointments, fearing that it might result in a dilution of the quality of the judiciary through the implementation of a quota system. As the South African experience described in the rest of this chapter shows, however, 'diversity' and 'representativity' cannot be sealed off from each other in this way. Enhancing the legitimacy of judicial power – which is the aim of promoting a diverse bench – may require more than the pursuit of diversity. When the judiciary suffers from a significant legitimacy crisis as a result of its identification in the eyes of the public with specific sectors of society, gaining public support for it necessitates shifting the perceived balance of power. As success in this endeavour requires not only greater variety, but sufficient variety, and variety of the right sort, it demands moving beyond diversity and pursuing representativity instead. The South African experience recounted below demonstrates this truth, revealing at the same time how conflicts between the goals of diversity and representativity can result. As the reference in the provision quoted in the preceding paragraph to gender and race alone suggests, and some judicial appointments discussed herein confirm, the attention that the pursuit of representativity fixes on 'variety of the right sort' all too easily allows dimensions of diversity that may be less central to social conflict (e.g., sexual orientation and physical handicaps) to fall by the wayside. Moreover, as the controversies discussed below reveal, the friction accompanying transformation of the judiciary cannot be finessed through pointing to the poverty of traditional notions of judicial merit and to the contribution that a more diverse judiciary would make to improving the quality of justice meted out in the courts. Sometimes, as the JSC's record shows, hard choices have to be made between diversity and representativity, and between lawyerly excellence and social legitimacy.

The Commissions

Prior to 1994, neither judges nor magistrates in South Africa were appointed through mechanisms specifically designed to foster independence. The procedures resembled those found in the United Kingdom and its other ex-colonies.[10] Magistrates were appointed by the minister of justice, and were civil servants subject to the *Public Service Act* of 1984 and to direction and control by senior civil servants who exercised disciplinary powers, determined salaries and conditions of service, and controlled promotions as well as transfers between courts. Not surprisingly, in 1983 a Commission of Enquiry stated, 'This state of affairs is quite incompatible with the doctrine of the separation of powers and represents a glaring anomaly in the exercise of the judicial function in South Africa. The identification of the lower courts with the Executive sullies the administration of justice in South Africa.'[11] Judges, on the other hand, were appointed by the President on the advice of the minister of justice. Although the minister seems as a rule to have tendered such advice after consultation with, or at the initiative of, the head of the relevant court, the same commission found that '[I]ndividual merit has not always been the decisive factor ... [A]ppointments to the Bench ... have in the past sometimes been made without prior consultation with the Chief Justice or the Judge President concerned.'[12] Indeed, there are clear examples at different periods of South African history of Jewish lawyers being passed over in favour of 'WASPS,'[13] of a deliberate policy of appointing Afrikaners, and of appointments made in the face of opposition from bar and bench.[14]

Both the Interim and the Final Constitution distinguish the appointment and regulation of judges from that of magistrates. The latter fall under the purview of the MC, the composition and powers of which are laid down in ordinary legislation rather than in the constitution. Judges only are appointed with the participation of the JSC; it is specifically provided that their salaries, allowances, and benefits may not be reduced; and the circumstances in which they may be removed from office are prescribed in the constitution itself. The composition of the JSC is constitutionally prescribed.[15] It has twenty-three permanent members, three of whom are judges – the chief justice (who heads the CC) as chairperson, the president of the Supreme Court of Appeal (SCA), and a judge president (head of a High Court) 'designated by' all judges president. Five members of the legal profession are appointed by the president upon nomination by their constituencies: two advocates, two attorneys, and one legal academic. In addition to these eight members of the legal profession, there are eleven politicians – the minister of justice, six members designated by the National Assembly (three of whom must be members of opposition parties) and four designated by the other house of Parliament, the National Council of Provinces. A further four members are chosen by a political process: they are designated by the President as head of the national executive (i.e., the national cabinet), after consulting the leaders of all the parties in the National Assembly. When a High Court vacancy is considered, the judge president of that court and the premier of the province in which it is situated are added to the JSC ad hoc. In addition to its role in respect of judicial appointments, the JSC has any further powers and functions assigned to it in the constitution and national legislation, and may advise the national government on any matter relating to the judiciary or the administration of justice. The constitution also grants the JSC vital decision-making power regarding the dismissal of judges by Parliament.[16] When it considers anything other than the appointment of a judge, the JSC must sit without the members designated by the two houses of Parliament.[17]

The JSC's specific powers depend on the extent of a judge's powers and their political sensitivity. In order to enhance accountability, and to foster a harmonious relationship with the other branches of the state, political input increases along with a judge's power to countermand political choices and the symbolic importance of a particular office. In respect of appointments to the High Court and the Supreme Court of Appeal and of judges president (and their deputies), its power is determinative, since the President must make such appointments 'on the advice of' the JSC.[18] It is important to note that this includes most of such 'promotions' (apart from elevation to the CC) as are open to judges, namely appointment to the SCA and as a (deputy) judge president, as well as lateral transfers. Appointments to the CC and the offices of chief justice, president of the SCA, and their Deputies, however, involve greater freedom of action on the part of the President and broader political participation. Appointment to these four offices are the prerogative of the President as head of the national executive, but he must consult the JSC and in the case of the chief justice and deputy chief justice, the leaders of all parties represented in the National Assembly as well.[19] In the case of CC judges, the JSC must provide the President with a list of nominees with three names more than the number of vacancies; the President may, if he finds an insufficient number of acceptable nominees on the list, require of the JSC to amend the list once.[20] The President appoints from the list, exercising this power as head of the national executive, after consultation with the chief justice (as head of the CC) and the leaders of the parties represented in the National Assembly.[21] The President's powers, and those of the JSC, are circumscribed by a constitutional requirement that at all times at least four members of the CC must already have been judges at the time they were appointed to the CC.[22] Constitutional Court judges must be South African citizens; otherwise, any appropriately qualified woman or man who is a fit and proper person may be appointed, subject to the duty to consider the need for the judiciary to reflect broadly the racial and gender composition of South Africa.[23]

From this it is clear that the JSC is, as Kate Malleson points out in her chapter, a 'hybrid' institution, one that has both decision-making and recommending powers. It also exhibits a duality of another kind: its membership combines politicians with legal professionals, thus precluding its decision-making powers from being the exclusive domain of either political or professional interests. The JSC therefore embodies a specific conception of how to balance independence and accountability in the appointment process. The South African approach steers clear of the dangers inherent in a self-selecting judiciary, described in the chapter on the Netherlands, yet also limits the discretionary power of the executive to a greater extent than is the case in comparable institutions in Canada and Namibia, and in the proposals mooted for England and Wales and Australia.[24] South Africa's inclusion of a sizeable block of politicians in the JSC, and restriction of the number of appointments in respect of which the executive truly makes the final decision, means that accountability is primarily pursued through the composition of the institution charged with judicial selection. Such an indirect form of accountability has obvious potential drawbacks, which have led some to call for a return to appointments by an executive accountable to Parliament,[25] and others to criticize the composition of the JSC.[26] However, ensuring that appointments are the product of collective decision making involving all major interested parties fosters debate among them on the murky concept of judicial merit, and may limit potentially destructive public disagreements between politicians and the legal establishment. It also eliminates the necessity of searching for what is likely to be an elusive mechanism for holding the executive to account in respect of the exercise of a discretion to make appointments from a list of recommendations.[27] Moreover, as the chapter in this volume on Zimbabwe makes plain, an appointment commission that lacks decision-making power and a representative membership is especially vulnerable to subversion by the executive.

The South African approach invites attention to the composition of the selection body, and this has recently led to an important judicial evaluation of the success with which independence and accountability have been balanced in the case of the MC. In *Van Rooyen v. The State*, the CC set aside a High Court decision that magistrates lacked the independence demanded by the constitution. This was plainly of great significance, as magistrates constitute the great bulk of judicial officers and adjudicate the overwhelming majority of cases.[28] Although the manner in which the MC functions means that there would be little point in examining it here in the same detail as the JSC – its proceedings lack the public profile of those of the JSC and hence any meaningful scrutiny by the press and legal profession – this challenge to the independence of a selection commission sheds light on a central difficulty that must be faced when such bodies are entrusted with judicial transformation.

Unlike the JSC, the composition of which has remained stable during the approximately ten years of its existence (although the individual incumbents of its various positions have of course changed), the composition of the MC was significantly altered through amendment of the *Magistrates Act* in 1996. This gave greater power to the executive in the appointment of MC members than it had enjoyed when the MC was first created in 1993, and added eight members of Parliament to the commissioners. The High Court decided that the restructured MC lacked independence, as its composition was now considered to be ultimately dominated by the parliamentary majority.[29] The CC, however, held that the High Court had failed to pay due attention 'to our history of racial and gender discrimination which had to be addressed after the adoption of the interim Constitution.' It stressed 'the transformative purpose of the interim Constitution and the 1996 Constitution,' which involved not only changes in the legal order, but also changes in the composition of the institutions of society. Prior to 1994 these, including the MC as it was constituted in 1993, were largely under the control of white men.[30] In the CC's view, 'There was a pressing need for the racial and gender disparities within the Commission to be changed, and for the Commission to be re-composed so as to become more representative of South African society. The changes made facilitated this, and that would have been understood by an objective observer taking a balanced view of all the relevant circumstances.'[31] This episode shows that it would be misguided to think of such institutions as standing outside conflicts over transformation, as uninvolved, neutral arbiters between the pursuit of diversity and other priorities. Their own accountability and legitimacy are subject to the same forces and demands for representativity as affect the judiciary.[32] As products of the pursuit of transformation, reflecting this goal in their very constitution, they can be expected to take representativity as a lodestar. Instead of balancing merit against diversity, they may transform its meaning, and sometimes prefer the latter to the former. As the next section shows, something of this is evident in the workings of the JSC. Equally important, however, is the prominent place this controversy gives to the manner in which the members of such a body are chosen. Precisely because their role is so central, it is essential that the process itself be seen to be simultaneously independent and transformative. The English proposal of an appointments commission seems promising,[33] although this may simply shift the controversy to *its* selection and at any rate seems ill-suited to a system such as the South African one, where accountability is pursued primarily through the composition of the commission.

The JSC in Practice

Transformation

The JSC has contributed to a remarkable transformation of the judiciary's demographic profile. Whereas there were only three black (male) and two (white) female judges in the higher courts among 166 in early 1994, by September 2003 34 per cent were black and 12 per cent female.[34] In other words, between 1994 and late 2003 the percentage of white judges in the higher courts was reduced from 98 per cent to 64 per cent. Although white men (128 out of 214, or 60 per cent) still predominate in the 2003 figures, the composition of the judiciary is much closer to the constitutional ideal of broadly reflecting the racial and gender composition of the country's population: there are fourteen white women, forty-two African men, eight African women, eight coloured men, two coloured women, eleven Asiatic men, and two Asiatic women.[35] Women and black judges are present at all levels of the judiciary, and seven of the eleven courts are now headed by black judges (but none by women, although there is one female deputy judge president). The significance of these figures is enhanced by the fact that a large proportion of current judges, about 40 per cent, was inherited from the previous dispensation.

The openness of the selection process has been crucial in bringing this about. Twice a year, the JSC conducts well-publicized open interviews, following widely distributed calls for applications for judicial vacancies and published lists of candidates inviting comments. It consults with, and elicits views from, the judiciary and legal profession, and its proceedings and decisions are reported and commented on in the media.[36] Although its pre-interview screening and its post-interview deliberations take place in closed session, it has made available a transcript of its discussions concerning the general approach and priorities to be pursued in making selections.[37] This transparency promotes public accountability on the part of the JSC as well as the judges, and has contributed to making the transformation of the judiciary much less controversial than it is likely to have been if judicial appointments had remained in the hands of the executive.

Perhaps most significantly, the advertising of judicial vacancies and the nomination of candidates by diverse sources means that the identification of potential judges is no longer confined to sitting judges and the minister of justice.[38] A considerably broader range of interested and knowledgeable persons is now involved in finding suitable candidates. They are not limited to official representatives of the legal profession in the (advocates') General Council of the Bar and the (attorneys') Law Society of South Africa, but include groups dedicated to the transformation of South African law and the judiciary, such as the Black Lawyers Association, the National Democratic Lawyers Association, and Advocates for Transformation. These organizations have been very active indeed in identifying and supporting candidates whose presence on the bench would serve the cause of transformation, and in commenting on short-listed candidates. In a situation in which the overwhelming majority of legal practitioners, especially advocates, and particularly those in the experienced and senior reaches of the profession, are white males, the existence of this entry-point for views from outside the professional establishment has been vital.

A second way in which the JSC's procedures have lessened the constraints on transformation flowing from the demographics of the legal profession concerns the expansion of the range of professional backgrounds from which judges are now drawn. Prior to 1994, the bench was the exclusive preserve of advocates, which was, and remains, a more white and male corner of the profession than either attorneys' practices or legal academia.[39] The JSC's appointments have changed that. Judges appointed from the ranks of attorneys and academics now sit on all levels of the superior courts, and this has been an important route for the entry of black and female judges into the judiciary: both women (one black, one white) sitting on the CC were academics at the time of their appointment, and of the three (white) women holding permanent appointments to the SCA, two were academics and the other an attorney when they were first appointed as judges. A significant number of black judges of both genders appointed to the bench since 1994 were practising attorneys at the time of their appointment.[40]

The JSC's procedures have helped to make this possible.[41] They enable those whose interaction with the judiciary has been indirect and infrequent to make their ambitions known. As importantly, advertisements, nominations, public comments, a candidates' questionnaire eliciting information about experience, accomplishments, and publications, and interviews all serve to provide the kind of information to the JSC that in the past was, and could then perhaps only have been, obtained by way of the knowledge senior practitioners and judges gleaned through observing advocates in court. The augmentation of available information through a more open process has enabled expansion of the pool of candidates. Nevertheless, women are still rare among the candidates appearing before the JSC – much more so than black men.[42]

A related, perhaps paradoxical, aspect of the JSC's appointment procedures must also be noted. This is the dependence of the JSC on what amounts to a preliminary sifting by the minister in conjunction with the heads of the courts. The JSC is very reluctant to consider anyone who has not served as an acting judge. This helps to level the field on which 'non-traditional' candidates compete with established advocates, since it allows them to gain the courtroom experience and demonstrate the qualities essential for appointment. It is therefore an important element in the JSC's efforts to transform the judiciary.[43] However, the JSC plays no role in acting appointments, as the constitution stipulates that these are to be made by the minister (president in the case of the CC) with the concurrence of the head of the court to which the appointment is made.[44] This enables the executive and senior judiciary to act as gatekeepers to judicial appointments, the significance of which is enhanced in the case of 'non-traditional' would-be judges, for whom such appointments may be the only way to prove their mettle and gain the necessary experience. At this crucial juncture in the appointment process things have therefore remained much as they were, with a combination of political and judicial decision makers determining the outcome through a closed process.

This is perhaps inevitable in a system where, in the absence of a continental-style formally trained career judiciary, described in the chapters on France, Italy, and Japan, qualification for judicial office depends on the qualities gained and demonstrated in courtroom settings. First, there is no better way to assess suitability than on the basis of performance.[45] Second, acting appointments serve other purposes as well, not least to clear up backlogs, and are made with such frequency and at such unpredictable intervals that it is not readily conceivable that they could be accommodated within the logistical constraints that result from the combination of the JSC's size and procedures. Perhaps no more can be expected of a body like the JSC than that it functions as an ultimate safeguard, controlling permanent appointments.[46] It is nevertheless worrying that the minister's control over acting appointments has, on at least two occasions, led to public controversy,[47] and may have been used to delay the consideration of candidates for permanent appointment.[48]

There are also other grounds for concern over the extent to which the South African model of balancing independence and accountability leaves significant pockets of power in the hands of politicians. A 2002 appointment to the Constitutional Court, for example, was delayed and marred by controversy after the leader of the main opposition party in Parliament claimed that the President had merely informed him of the choice he had made, and thus failed to consult him as required by the constitution.[49] The JSC has also been said, by its most steady journalistic observer, to be 'overloaded with politicians and subject to lobbying influences that candidates and the public know nothing about.'[50]

Balancing Diversity, Merit, and Representativity

JSC selections made in the pursuit of judicial transformation have met with some criticism, and not only from opposition politicians or those with one foot in the past. So, for example, the doyen of pre-1994 anti-apartheid lawyers, Sir Sidney Kentridge QC, has said that while the JSC represented a 'huge advance on the old system,' and had succeeded in eliminating some poorly qualified candidates who might otherwise have hoped for political favour, it had not been rigorous enough 'in ensuring that legal knowledge and experience accompany the other qualities needed for the transformation of the judiciary.'[51] Concern about the quality of appointees has also been expressed in the pages of newspapers.[52] Others have decried the slow pace of transformation.[53] And a chairman of the General Council of the Bar, who was an early advocate of a judicial appointments commission,[54] has objected that the 'Constitution is, in fact, undermined when demographics – and these with broad, selective and inexact brushstrokes – are used to overpaint the core values of the Constitution,' of which one 'is explicitly "non-racialism" ... and which together are the very antithesis of a mere numbers game.'[55]

The last-quoted remarks are particularly interesting, as they were written in response to a controversial appointment made to fill the first vacancy that arose on the CC. As required by the constitution, the JSC put four names before the President. One was black: Judge Sandile Ngcobo, active in public interest legal practice before 1994, appointed to the Cape High Court in 1996, and subsequently also acting president of the Labour Appeal Court.[56] Three were white: Judge Edwin Cameron, another post-1994 appointee to judicial office, who, after glittering academic success at Oxford, had practised anti-apartheid public interest law and published forceful scholarly critiques of the previous judiciary; Judge Kees van Dijkhorst, who had served prior to 1994, presiding over politically contentious trials, and subsequently emerged as a strong proponent of limiting the constitutional right to silence;[57] and the more conventional Judge André Erasmus. Press comment drew attention to the contribution to diversity that Judge Cameron could make as an HIV-positive, openly gay man.[58] After the JSC interviews, an influential national newspaper said in its main editorial that 'it would be a travesty of justice if Judge Cameron were not appointed to the post.'[59] Yet this is what happened. Judge Ngcobo was selected by the President, eliciting the following response from the bar chairman in the article quoted above: 'When a brilliant South African, known for his commitment to constitutionalism, his scholarship and his dedication, is passed over by the President for appointment to the CC in the circumstances which recently applied, legitimacy is not advanced. The institution is not enhanced; only a racial quota is.'[60] Yet the opposite was argued with equal force. An op-ed page column headed 'Black Eye' insisted that 'there is no way the government can continue to replicate white domination of levers of power as if there have not been two elections in which black people said resoundingly they wanted change and control over their lives and country,' and accused Cameron's supporters of hankering for the past while masquerading as champions of fairness and democracy.[61]

This episode highlights at least three things that are of particular importance to understanding such a commission's specifically recommending functions. First, electoral accountability via the involvement of political office holders in the appointment process makes a difference. If the bar chairman's views, and the similar ones of 'senior jurists' referred to in newspapers, are taken to represent those of the legal fraternity, then it is clear that the meaning, pace, and direction of judicial transformation are strongly influenced by the balance of power between the legal and the political establishments. When the demographic transformation of public institutions enjoys strong political priority and public support, as it does in South Africa, a process that places the ultimate decisions in the hands of politicians, as is the case with CC judges, favours and accelerates representativity. This seems to be borne out by the contrast between the composition of the CC and SCA: after four 'new appointments' to the CC, the majority of its judges are now black, while the SCA, in respect of which the JSC enjoys final decision-making power, remains largely white even though most of its current members were appointed after 1994.

Second, it shows that the involvement of a judicial selection commission, even one which, like the JSC, has a membership carefully designed to represent the interests of different groups, and follows a transparent procedure, does not eliminate controversy and suspicions that professional accomplishment plays second fiddle to political objectives. All four nominees had been vetted, assessed, and judged suitable for appointment by the JSC. Its filtering process should, in principle, have reassured everyone that each nominee was qualified for appointment to the CC, thus making it a matter of indifference, from the point of view of merit, who was ultimately selected by the President. That debate nevertheless flared up shows that such a commission provides only limited insulation against political controversy. This is confirmed by other events. Individual judges, particular courts, and the judiciary as a whole have continued to be the targets of criticism, often at least implicitly tied to their race, arising from suspicions born of the role and selection of judges before the advent of democracy and the JSC.[62] These have been sufficiently severe to provoke public expressions of concern, and calls for restraint, by senior judges[63] as well as the minister of justice.[64]

Third, the Cameron controversy focuses attention on the essentially contested character of terms such as 'transformation,' 'diversity,' and 'merit.' Especially in a context, like the South African one, where these ideals are subscribed to by all concerned,[65] they define the problem rather than resolve it. The debate shifts from their relevance to their meaning, enhancing the scope for political contestation. This is further underlined by the filling in 2001 of another CC vacancy with a black male judge. The appointee, Moseneke J., had served on the High Court bench for a few months after relinquishing a high-flying business career he had taken up upon leaving practice at the bar, which he had joined after studying for a law degree during a ten-year spell as a political prisoner.[66] This time, a journalist who attended the interview pointed out, two white JSC nominees might also have qualified as 'transformation' candidates: one was a prominently gay woman and the other a blind man; she had no doubt however, that the latter would not be selected by the President, despite having performed best during the interviews.[67] The third unsuccessful nominee, another black male judge, was eventually appointed to the CC in 2003, along with a white male judge, when two further vacancies arose.[68]

The appointment of three black male judges to replace three white male judges who had sat on the eleven-member CC since its creation has dramatically changed the racial balance on this court, but it has also left its gender composition intact and maintained its heterosexual orientation. Viewed from one perspective, the CC bench has certainly become more representative than it was at the start; from other perspectives, however, neither representativity nor diversity have been advanced after the first round of appointments. Political priorities determined which understanding of representativity won out, and accorded less weight to diversity than to representativity.[69] At this point it is helpful to turn to the JSC's own record.

Giving Substance to 'Diversity' and 'Merit'

The JSC from the start grappled with the meaning of concepts such as 'merit,' diversity,' and 'transformation.' When it had to nominate the first members of the CC, the JSC resolved to look beyond the narrow requirements of legal skills and expertise, and also to consider positive attributes such as independence, open-mindedness, intellectual ability, fairness, judgment, perceptiveness, stamina, industry, courage, and integrity, as well as negative characteristics such as a personal history of hypocrisy, dishonesty, opportunism, and expediency.[70] Moreover, it decided to treat diversity as 'a component of competence,' rather than an independent requirement vying with competence, by focusing – as does the constitution – on representativeness at an institutional level. This led the JSC to reject a quota system that would directly reflect the demographic composition of the population.

Some five years later, by which time it had made a considerable number of selections, and had been the target of criticisms concerning the pace of transformation as well as the quality of new appointees, the JSC again publicized its views. It released the transcript of a discussion by its members on selection criteria. This again stressed a broad understanding of 'competence,' the then chief justice adding the 'capacity and the ability to give expression to the values of the Constitution' and experience of 'the values and needs of the community in which he serves' to technical skill.[71] The discussions supported the notion that transformation, too, was a broad concept; not merely a matter of 'replacing a white face with a black face,' it also encompassed the 'intellectual transformation' of the judiciary. There was nevertheless some divergence of views about the weight to be accorded to the symbolic importance of appointments and to technical ability when these clash with other priorities, and the trade-off between potential and demonstrated technical skill also received different emphases. A general concern was evident with the continuing impact of the legacy of apartheid on the availability of suitable black candidates, particularly in light of the many other spheres of activity – not least the practising profession itself – that needed the participation of black lawyers. Indeed, the present chief justice and chair of the JSC said at this meeting that, 'each time the pool gets diminished by an appointment ... the quality of the people coming through the pool gets weaker and weaker.'

Although they bring some substance to the meaning of merit and diversity, these general interpretations do not resolve the issue of the potential conflict between different criteria when it comes to the selection of individuals,[72] as the Cameron controversy demonstrates. How the JSC does this cannot be determined with precision, as its deliberations on individual candidates take place behind closed doors. This is particularly problematic in view of the pursuit of accountability, in part, through the inclusion of a significant contingent of political appointees in the JSC – nothing is known about the extent to which political affiliation tallies with decision-making patterns within the JSC, or about the extent to which the politicians and the lawyers on the commission agree, disagree, and compromise with each other. Fortunately the open interviewing process makes it possible to shed at least some light on how the JSC approaches these criteria.

A random examination of press reports and available transcripts reveals several points. Most generally it shows, as one newspaper report put it, that candidates are 'made to justify their political leanings, their judgments, their failure to do community work and their attitude to transformation.'[73] Of these, the most frequently asked type of question concerns a candidate's attitude towards, and understanding of, judicial transformation. This type of question was asked of all candidates bar one in the April 2001 interviews,[74] and press reports suggest that it has often been raised during the life of the JSC.[75] Personal questions with a more specifically political thrust are asked more selectively and somewhat less frequently, but are the second-most common type of question. They have ranged from questions about membership of organizations closely associated with the apartheid establishment[76] or the current government,[77] or perceived as secret,[78] through some concerning allegiance to political parties of all stripes,[79] to more general questions concerning candidates' resistance to apartheid within the ambit of their professional activities.[80] This aspect of the interviews has at times been controversial, and resulted in complaints to the JSC that 'certain commissioners had indulged in hostile or politically-motivated questioning of candidates.'[81] Although present in most rounds of interviews, questions about community involvement have been asked rather less frequently.[82] Personal problems, particularly alcohol abuse, have also received attention.[83] All of these questions feature in the questionnaire that candidates are required to complete and submit prior to the interview.

Several types of questions have a more direct bearing on the adjudicatory tasks of judges. The most common question here, asked of all the candidates interviewed in April 2001, was also the most general one: how the candidate had experienced his or her acting appointment. Candidates have on several occasions been confronted with detailed questioning on shortcomings in their performance, in their handling of the law and in their discharge of the administrative duties of a judge.[84] The quality and significance of their judgments, especially as evinced by their presence or absence from the law reports, has also been the subject of questions, particularly to candidates seeking elevation to higher judicial offices.[85] Questions focusing on administrative and managerial issues, notably as pertaining to promoting the transformation of the bench, have been prominent in the case of candidates for appointment as judge president or deputy judge president.[86] Some candidates have also been asked about their relevant legal experience[87] and areas of expertise.[88] In addition, candidates have been asked about aspects of their professional behaviour that might reflect adversely on their professional integrity,[89] as well as their ability to interact harmoniously with colleagues.[90] Some have also been asked about their language proficiency,[91] and, after the well-publicized resignation of a recently appointed judge for financial reasons, about the adequacy of judicial remuneration for their needs.[92]

Although not entirely absent, direct and substantive legal questions that would shed light on a candidate's approach to specific current legal issues have been comparatively rare. A study of the first interviews for the CC in October 1994 classifies about 25 per cent of the questions asked of all candidates as legally substantial, with curriculum vitae and skills-related questions coming a very close second.[93] In this and subsequent rounds of CC interviews, general legal questions were also asked, concerning matters such as the role of the CC, its relationship to democracy and to the political process, and the interpretation of the Bill of Rights.[94] However, there have been few examples of direct questioning on more specific matters. The most prominent instance occurred where the candidate had previously published widely discussed and controversial views on the impact of the constitutional right to silence on the criminal justice system.[95] Apart from this, the closest the JSC has come to probing such views seems to have been to ask candidates for the SCA to discuss their attitude to the role of that court in promoting the impact of the constitution on all fields of law, at a time when this issue was very prominent in criticisms of the SCA.[96]

Despite some candidates' experience of the interviews as humiliating, particularly in the early days of the JSC's existence,[97] there are clear indications that the process serves to cultivate a sense of public accountability among the judiciary. For example, a candidate who had on several occasions unsuccessfully sought appointment to the SCA, each time being quizzed about his long-standing membership of the Freemasons, eventually resigned from this organization, citing as his reason the 'strong public perception that membership thereof was incompatible with judicial office.'[98] Further evidence is provided by candidates disclosing alcohol problems and reporting their progress since previous (unsuccessful) interviews in dealing with it.[99] To this must be added the very fact of willingness to undergo public questioning, sometimes prominently reported in the press, in which candidates' allegiance to the new constitutional order, their general legal views, and their past performance are probed.

The interviewing process provides some glimpses into JSC members' views on candidates' suitability. Thus in the April 2001 interviews members on several occasions declared their 'allegiance to' a particular candidate, and in several instances made comments or asked questions that revealed support for a particular candidate.[100] However, it is remarkable how few JSC members take an active part in questioning candidates.[101] The only member in the April 2001 interviews to question all of them was the chairperson, Mr Justice Chaskelson, who initiated questioning, although the heads of court each questioned all the candidates for appointment to their respective courts quite closely. Next came the two most senior politicians, the minister of justice and the chairman of the Parliamentary Portfolio Committee on Justice. Considerably fewer candidates were questioned by the two representatives of advocates, a mere two by the attorneys' representatives, and only one by the representative of legal academics.[102] The rest of the members, all political appointees, asked questions of one or two candidates only. This hampers any effort to infer from the interviews how the JSC interprets, balances, and prioritizes its selection criteria. The similarity of the questions asked by JSC members of diverse origin is nevertheless striking. No single group monopolizes a particular type of question: judges, representatives of the profession, and political appointees all, on occasion, ask questions about transformation, political allegiances, and professional conduct and experience. This suggests that the commissioners heed the call by a previous minister of justice that 'it is extremely important that people who join the JSC do not see themselves as representing any particular constituency.'[103]

The private nature of the JSC's deliberations after interviews makes it very difficult to assess the weight that is given to different questions and candidates' answers, the more so as some selections have appeared surprising in view of what transpired at the interviews.[104] The thrust of the JSC's questioning suggests that it pays great attention to candidates' general allegiance to the new constitutional order, with its commitment to moving away from the apartheid past and to the demographic and ethical transformation of the legal order. As one JSC member (representing advocates) recently put it,

> It lays great store by the mindset of the candidates. In JSC parlance such a person is referred to as a 'transformed/transformation' candidate and has to possess certain attributes. These traits apply without distinction to black

> and white candidates. They have to demonstrate a commitment to the values that underpin the Constitution, such as respect for the human dignity of each and every person, the achievement of equality, the advancement of human rights and freedoms, non-racism and non-sexism, the supremacy of the Constitution and the rule of law.[105]

Professional accomplishment, technical expertise, and views about trends and questions in the law seem, except in the case of CC and SCA candidates, to come second to candidates' impartiality, integrity, and industry, although it must be said that much of the former could be gleaned from their answers to the written questionnaire. From this it appears that, as far as competence for judicial office is concerned, the interviews are generally aimed at establishing whether a candidate meets a certain threshold of technical ability and experience rather than at identifying high flyers. The approach followed seems to be, as Judge Chaskelson put it during the JSC's discussion on the qualities to be looked for, that there is 'a certain level of technical ability which is required of a judge and a person who does not meet that technical level ought not to be appointed,'[106] but that beyond this threshold it is the search for demographic diversity that counts. The JSC member already quoted explained this rather well: 'Where the candidate otherwise qualifies for appointment, the fact that a particular appointment will have a symbolic value that gives a positive message to the community at large, may tip the scales ... especially where there is competition for a vacancy. A hypothetical example would be the appointment of an Indian female judge to a Division where there were no female judges at all and wherein Indians were by law previously denied the right of residence.'[107]

The JSC's exercise of its determinative powers bears this out. A telling example is the appointment towards the end of 2003 of a suburban attorney as judge of the Cape High Court in preference to one of the country's most renowned and active human rights lawyers, pre- and post-1994.[108] The unsuccessful candidate was a white man; the appointee, a black woman, became the first to hold a permanent position on that court. Moreover, the JSC in several instances went against the views expressed by practitioners as well as serving judges, where this served the cause of racial transformation.[109] However, the JSC has on the whole avoided automatically appointing candidates from under-represented groups and has on several occasions chosen to appoint white men. This is most noticeable in the case of appointments to the SCA, the majority of which have been of white men. In light of the continuing impact of the social and educational legacy of apartheid and gender discrimination on the make-up of the legal profession, the limited demographic transformation of this court suggests that the JSC has interpreted 'competence' according to the specific role that this court plays in the legal system. As the SCA, which has final authority over all non-constitutional questions, is entrusted with the intricate doctrinal development of civil and criminal law, exceptional experience, technical flair, and reputation in professional circles – going well beyond ordinary judicial competence – are needed of those who sit in it. Placed alongside the fact that CC and SCA candidates seem to be subjected to more searching questions on legal and jurisprudential matters than High Court candidates, this indicates that the JSC seeks to balance diversity and merit in part by moving the competence threshold to fit the character of the court in question.

Conclusion

'The ultimate goal of legal reform,' the chief justice and chair of the JSC recently said, 'must be a normative system that is accepted by the community, internalised in their day to day attitudes, and where necessary, enforced by a judiciary which is an institution respected by the public, and whose independence, integrity and competence is beyond question.' To this he added that: 'The impartiality of the judiciary is more likely to be respected by the public if it is seen to be drawn from all sectors of the community than will be the case if it is drawn from one race and one gender as, for all practical purposes, was the case prior to 1994. It is not only the Constitution and our commitment to establishing a non racial society, but equity and common sense as well, that demands that this be done.'[110]

In implementing their mandates, the JSC and MC have succeeded in changing the racial and gender profile of the bench, diversifying the range of life-experiences[111] and professional backgrounds represented among the judiciary, and in crafting a judicial corps whose attitude to public accountability differs markedly from their predecessors.' This has meant following the same course as the post-apartheid government, whose overriding aim has, naturally, been to eradicate the vestiges of a racial and patriarchal oligarchy. The JSC has clearly not functioned as a disinterested arbiter of the conflict between candidates' lawyerly excellence and their racial and gender profiles. It has adopted a definition of competence that blends 'lawyerliness' with socio-political awareness, and has tried to resolve the tension between representativity and expertise partly by tailoring that definition to fit the specific functions of particular courts. Moreover, the role of politicians and political appointees within the MC and JSC, and their final decision-making power over the selection of CC judges and those who hold the highest judicial offices, have served as an entry point for political priorities. 'Transformation' has remained a fuzzy concept and it is difficult to discern coherence in the JSC's overall balance of its various components.

It would nevertheless be a mistake to conclude that this selection process has compromised the independence of the judiciary. Social development, as the chief justice also indicated, 'involves an interrelationship between the legislature, the executive and the judiciary.'[112] They are interdependent institutions, and their shared commitment to the constitution is one that 'both keeps us separate and binds us together. Separate because we each have a different role under the Constitution; and yet binds us together because we make the same commitment in respect of our functions, and depend each upon the other for the fulfilment of these commitments.'[113] It follows that judicial independence should be assessed in a way that does not assume an adversarial relationship between the judicial and the other branches of the state, but is consonant with the sharing of fundamental values between them, and their harmonious co-existence. What matters is whether the courts can play their different role within this context of interdependence and shared commitment, and whether the overall result reflects societal aspirations and values. Looked at in this light, the decisions of post-apartheid judges at all levels, and indeed of those whose appointment pre-dates 1994, engender confidence rather than concern. There is no evidence of subservience to government – in fact, the opposite is true.[114]

This is not to say that the new method of selecting judicial officers has miraculously overcome all hurdles. The effects of the legacy left by apartheid, and of gender discrimination, are frequently and rightly cited as impediments to the pace of judicial transformation more generally.[115] The dearth of women on the bench, and among candidates appearing before the JSC, remains a matter of serious concern. The JSC has gone some way to overcome this by diversifying the pool of potential candidates, expanding the sources of information on candidates, and having regard to potential as well as accomplishment. It has also embarked on a judicial education program, including the nurturing of potential candidates.[116] But the creation of appointable candidates requires more resources and wider initiatives than are possessed by a body focused on judicial appointments, especially in a jurisdiction that draws its higher judiciary from the ranks of private practitioners.[117] Even so, the discrepancy between the racial and gender transformation of the bench points to the influence of broad political priorities on the understanding of diversity and representativity: the need to overcome the legacy of apartheid and to render all public institutions more legitimate in the eyes of the public puts racial representativity at the forefront of concern, and may, for example, in the case of sexual orientation, sometimes displace other dimensions of diversity. This is particularly evident in the case of the CC, the very existence of which symbolizes the establishment of a new legal order, and which has an appointment process directly linked to political accountability. But, as the controversy over the Budlender candidacy shows, it is also present in the JSC's own nominations, and can be hard to square with that court's professed 'broad concept' of transformation.

Nor has the selection of judicial officers by bodies that weld together different interest groups and political tendencies stilled controversy over perceived hidden motives behind judicial decisions and appointments,[118] or ensured that court decisions are obeyed without fail.[119] This is important, as the JSC's open and public proceedings means that interviews serve not only to inform commissioners, but also, via the media, to influence public opinion about the judiciary. The tension between the ends of 'non-racialism' and 'non-sexism' and the means of selecting black and female judges whenever possible remains a source of contention. Although there has certainly been much less criticism than would have attended judicial transformation through the old-style executive appointment process, the JSC and MC have not insulated the legitimacy of the judiciary from the faultlines and conflicts in South African society. Strikingly, the only empirical research so far conducted on the legitimacy of post-apartheid legal institutions reportedly indicates that the CC enjoys comparatively low levels of public support, that its legitimacy varies along racial lines, and that it has failed to develop a distinctive public profile.[120]

All of this suggests that South Africa's approach to reconciling independence and accountability in the judicial appointments process may not have fulfilled the hopes held out for it, and might indeed have been less successful in promoting public confidence than some of the other models discussed in this volume. However, institutional design can never eliminate the impact of history and social structure: the sting of controversy over appointments could perhaps be blunted by the adoption of more precise selection criteria, described elsewhere in this volume,[121] but it is doubtful that it could ever be drawn altogether in such a deeply divided society. However, should that be the goal? Don't vigorous and persistent debates over the judiciary show, in a democracy, that the critical social engagement with public affairs on which both independence and accountability depend is alive and well despite the expansion of judicial power?

NOTES

1 See, e.g., Dworkin, 'Equality, Democracy and Constitution.'

2 Constitutional reform took place in two phases. The first involved the enactment of the 'Interim Constitution' (Act 200 of 1993) by the last apartheid legislature after a multi-party negotiating process, while the second phase saw the enactment of a 'Final Constitution' (Act 108 of 1996) by the legislature elected in 1994. The latter is referred to when mention is made of the constitution in this chapter. The institutions discussed in this chapter are, in the main, found in both documents.

3 The MC was created by the 1993 *Magistrates Act* and its existence given constitutional force by section 109 of the Interim Constitution, a provision not reiterated in the Final Constitution. Both the Interim and the Final Constitution contain detailed provisions regarding the JSC. The division between superior and lower (i.e., magistrates') courts and their personnel dates back to British colonial rule in what was then the Cape Colony. It is similar to that found in Australia, as described by Elizabeth Handsley in this volume. Although a very few magistrates have since 1994 enjoyed temporary appointments as acting judges (largely to deal with backlogs in criminal cases), and one (Kondile J.) has been appointed permanently to the Natal High Court (see Bench Press, 'JSC Announces Permanent Appointments'), these remain distinct classes of judicial officers, with no career progression from the lower to the higher courts. See further du Bois, 'History, System and Sources.'

4 See, e.g., Corder, 'Judicial Authority in a Changing South Africa.'

5 See Mandela, *Argument for the defence in S v Mandela*, 125–8.

6 See *S. v. Collier* 1995 (2) SACR 648 (C) at 649–52. For the converse situation, see *S. v. Shackell* 2001 (4) SA 1 (SCA), which rejected an appeal on the grounds of perceived judicial bias against the conviction by a black judge, whose son had been murdered by a white policeman while in custody, of a white policeman for the murder of a black prisoner.

7 Human Sciences Research Council, *Law and Justice in South Africa*. This was endorsed by editorials in the journal of the General Council of the Bar,

Consultus – see the October 1988 and April 1991 issues. See also Koen and Budlender, 'The Law is Fraught with Racism.'

8 *President of the Republic of South Africa and others v. South African Rugby Football Union and others* 1999 (4) SA 147 (CC). The case involved an application for recusal brought against members of the CC on the ground of their perceived ideological and personal ties with the President, whose decision to appoint a Commission of Enquiry was being challenged. Emphasizing the seriousness of the case and the court's determination, the judgment was – highly exceptionally – published as that of 'The Court,' leaving the author(s) unidentified.

9 S. 174 of the constitution. Note that South Africa does not have a lay magistracy – legislation stipulates the minimum legal qualifications required of magistrates.

10 See the chapters in this volume on Australia, Canada, and the United Kingdom.

11 *Fifth and Final Report of the Commission of Enquiry into the Structure and Functioning of the Courts,* 1:24.

12 Ibid., paras. 1.3.2 and 1.3.3 at 59.

13 White Anglo-Saxon Protestants.

14 See Forsyth, *In Danger for their Talents,* 38–46; van Blerk, *Judge and Be Judged,* 112–45.

15 S. 178 of the constitution.

16 See s. 177 of the constitution.

17 S. 178(5) of the constitution.

18 The JSC is also involved in the appointment of judges to some specialized courts, e.g., the Labour Courts and Competition Appeal Court.

19 S. 174(3) of the constitution.

20 S. 174(4) of the constitution.

21 Ibid.

22 S. 174(5) of the constitution.

23 S. 174(1) and (2) of the constitution.

24 See the relevant chapters in this volume.

25 See *First Interim Report of the Commission of Enquiry into the Rationalisation of the Provincial and Local Divisions of the Supreme Court,* vol. 4, extracts from the evidence of Mr Justice Flemming.

26 Gauntlett, 'Dear President Mbeki ... An Open Letter to the President,' describes the JSC as failing 'embarrassingly, to comply with the Latimer House Commonwealth guidelines for the appointment of judges.'

27 For acknowledgment of this need in the case of purely recommending commissions, see especially the chapter in this volume by Malleson.

28 There are approximately 1,700 magistrates as against about 200 judges.

There are more than 250 magistrates' courts but only 13 High Courts. See du Bois, 'History, System and Sources,' and Olivier, 'Is the South African Magistracy Legitimate?'

29 *Van Rooyen and others v. The State and others* 2001 (4) SA 396 (T).

30 *Van Rooyen v. The State (General Council of the Bar of South Africa Intervening)* 2002 (5) SA 246 (CC), para. 47.

31 Ibid., para. 61. A former chairman of the MC has described this reconstitution of the MC as a 'retrograde step' creating 'a body dominated by politicians and so bloated as to be unmanageable.' See van Dijkhorst, 'The Future of the Magistracy.'

32 It is noteworthy that as currently constituted the JSC has a rough parity of white and black members, but a significant majority of men.

33 See the chapter in this volume by Malleson.

34 For these figures, see Maduna, 'Address at the Banquet of the Judicial Officers' Symposium'; and Moerane, 'The Meaning of Transformation of the Judiciary in the New South African Context,' at 665 and 713 respectively. Maduna, 'Address,' at 666, also states that out of a total of 1,784 magistrates, whites now comprise 918 (51.46 per cent) and blacks 866 (48.54 per cent). Here, and in the main text, the term 'blacks,' in accordance with standard South African usage, includes 'Coloureds' (mostly persons of mixed racial descent), 'Asiatics' (persons of Indian descent), and 'Africans' (perhaps best described as 'the most indigenous' of the population groups). For the complexity of racial labels in South Africa, see Ford, 'Challenges and Dilemmas of Racial and Ethnic Identity in American and Post-apartheid South African Affirmative Action,' at 1985–6. According to the 2001 population census, Africans constitute 79 per cent of the population, Whites 9.6 per cent, Coloureds 8.9 per cent, and Asiatics 2.5 per cent. See http://www.statssa.gov.za.

35 Maduna, 'Address.'

36 See Corder, 'Judicial Authority in a Changing South Africa'; Malleson, 'Assessing the Performance of the Judicial Service Commission.'

37 See 'How to Judge a Judge.'

38 See Flemming J., evidence in First Interim Report of the Commission of the Enquiry into the Rationalisation of the Provincial and Local Divisons of the Supreme Court.

39 South Africa has a split legal profession similar to that in England, advocates (barristers) specializing in court appearances and associated specialist work, and attorneys (solicitors) in general legal practice. However, the latter can now also obtain the right of appearing in the superior courts, previously closed to them. See generally du Bois, 'History, System and Sources,' 32–6.

40 See, e.g., Bench Press, 'Five Attorneys Appointed to the Bench.' The presence of former academics and attorneys in their midst has not been received favourably by all judges, however. See, e.g., Ngoepe, 'White Paper on the Judicial System: Memorandum by Pretoria Judges,' 30.

41 This conforms with the experience, and hopes expressed, in other jurisdictions. See especially the chapters on Australia, Canada, and the United Kingdom in this volume.

42 See 'Women are Still not Contenders,' *Sunday Times* (Johannesburg), 18 April 1999, reporting that just three out of twenty-two nominees at a JSC session were women while the nineteen male candidates were 'split almost exactly down the middle in terms of colour.' The JSC's interview schedules show that in April 2000 there was one woman among the fourteen candidates interviewed for High Court positions, in October 2000 there were four women among thirty-four candidates, in April 2001 no women were among the seventeen candidates, in April 2002 there were five women (of whom two were seeking transfers) among twenty-three interviewees, and in April 2003 the thirty-two interviewees included only five women. Sometimes the picture is less gloomy: in October 2003, four women and five men were interviewed for a seat on the CC – see Bench Press, 'Constitutional Court.'

43 This was emphasized by a spokesperson for the minister of justice, quoted in Carmel Rickard, 'Acting Judges won't Be Scrapped from SA Legal System – Despite UN Criticism,' *Sunday Times Online* (Johannesburg), 18 March 2001, available at www.sundaytimes.co.za/business/legal/2001/03/18/carmel01.asp.

44 S. 175 of the constitution.

45 See note 84 and accompanying text for evidence of this in JSC interviews.

46 The use of acting judges was nevertheless criticized by the UN Special Rapporteur Dato' Param Cumaraswamy, who commented that this practice 'could adversely affect the independent character of tribunals, especially when these appointments are used as a form of "short probation."' See UN Commission on Human Rights, *Report of the Special Rapporteur on the Independence of Judges and Lawyers, Addendum: Mission to South Africa*, 4.

47 In 1999, the judge president of the Natal High Court resigned after the minister refused to make two acting appointments he had requested on the ground that expertise was needed to counterbalance the inexperience of recent appointees in the pursuit of transformation, and the Cape judge president was asked to stay on in an acting capacity beyond the normal retirement age although his deputy, Judge Hlophe, seemed a shoe-in as his successor. See Carmel Rickard, 'Who Exactly is Running the Judicial show?'

Sunday Times (Johannesburg), 12 December 1999; 'Backing for Hlophe,' *Cape Times* (Cape Town), 6 December 1999.

48 See note 47 above regarding Judge Hlophe (who was appointed as JP when the JSC eventually advertised the position) and the long hiatus in filling vacancies in the SCA. See 'High Court Bench "Still Too Pale and Male,"' *Cape Argus* (Cape Town), 19 April 1999; 'The Custodian of Our Constitutional Democracy,' *Mail and Guardian* (Johannesburg), 17–22 December 1999; Gauntlett, 'Dear President Mbeki ... An open letter to the President.'

49 Mathatha Tsedu, 'Moseneke is the Perfect Candidate to Transform Our Justice System,' *Sunday Times* (Johannesburg), 17 November 2002.

50 Carmel Rickard, 'Is the Price of Transformation Too High?' *Sunday Times* (Johannesburg), 21 April 2002.

51 Kentridge, 'The Highest Court,' 69.

52 Rickard, 'Is the Price of Transformation Too High?' wrote that 'the general quality of candidates and appointments has become so poor it's time the public was concerned.'

53 See, e.g., 'Justice Minister Calls for Transformation of Judiciary in Budget Vote Speech' and 'Transforming the Judiciary: How Far, How Fast?' *Business Day* (Johannesburg), 16 January 2003, reporting President Mbeki's statement at a party conference that the judiciary is not transforming fast enough and that this may threaten the credibility of the courts.' Tsedu, 'Moseneke is the Perfect Candidate,' above n48, concluded that not enough was being done to bring about racial transformation on the bench.

54 Gauntlett, 'Appointing and Promoting Judges.'

55 Gauntlett, 'A Matter of Race?,' 4.

56 For a biographical sketch, see 'Respect for Constitutionalism Shaped by Life and the Law,' *Sunday Independent* (Johannesburg), 6 June 1999.

57 See 'Grueling Questions have Aspirant Judges Grappling on their Benches,' *Sunday Independent* (Johannesburg), 25 April 1999 and 'Delmas Judge Comes Out with Guns Blazing,' *Cape Argus* (Cape Town), 20 April 1999.

58 'Cameron Favoured for Post,' *Mail and Guardian* (Johannesburg), 23 April 1999.

59 'Commission Needs to Do Some Soul-searching,' *Sunday Times* (Johannesburg), 25 April 1999.

60 Gauntlett, 'A Matter of Race?'

61 Mathatha Tsedu, 'So-called Liberals Still Question Every Black Appointment,' *Sunday Independent* (Johannesburg), 6 June 1999.

62 See, e.g., Gauntlett, '"Racial Bias" in the Judiciary; Chairman's Contribution,' 'Judge Bashing.'

63 See press statement by the judges of the Witwatersrand High Court (1999); Davis, Marcus, and Klaaren, 'The Administration of Justice,' 884.

64 See 'Stop Hammering Judges, Pleads Maduna,' *Cape Argus* (Cape Town), 6 June 2000.

65 See, e.g., the sources cited in notes 53–5.

66 See the biographical sketch in 'The High Court Judge Who "Does the Dishes,"' *Sunday Times* (Johannesburg), 3 November 2002.

67 Carmel Rickard, 'Presidential Eye Set to Fall on Moseneke for the Constitutional Court,' *Sunday Times Online* (Johannesburg), 22 July 2001, available at http://www.sundaytimes.co.za/business/legal/2001/07/22/index.asp.

68 See 'Two New Constitutional Court Judges Appointed.' In the other CC appointment to date, a male judge of Indian descent was replaced by another.

69 It is again interesting to contrast this with the results of the exercise of the JSC's decision-making powers: although the SCA is racially less representative than the CC, it is more diverse, not least because both gay judges referred to above now grace its bench.

70 Judicial Service Commission, *Guidelines for Questioning Candidates for Nomination to the Constitutional Court*, 3–7.

71 See 'How to Judge a Judge,' which is the source of the information and quotations in this paragraph.

72 Malleson, 'Assessing the Performance of the Judicial Service Commission,' 47.

73 'Grueling Questions have Aspirant Judges Grappling on their Benches.'

74 Transcripts of interviews for judgeships held in Cape Town, April 2001 (on file with the author). I am grateful to Siri Gloppen for kindly making this available to me.

75 'Basil Wunsh Appointed to TPD Bench' (candidate Wunsh); 'Experience "Must Not Be Sacrificed on the Altar of Change,"' *Cape Argus* (Cape Town), 20 April 1999 (candidate Van Dykhorst); 'High Court Bench "Still Too Pale and Male"' (candidate Hlophe). 'JSC Grasping the Transformation Nettle,' *Mail and Guardian* (Johannesburg), 29 January 2001 (candidate Horn was asked: 'Where do you see yourself fitting in as a white man?').

76 See 'Grueling Questions have Aspirant Judges Grappling on their Benches' (candidates Donen and Claasen); 'Johannesburg Attorney to Preside over Land Claims Court' (candidate Gildenhuys); 'Law Society Welcomes Durban Attorney Thumba Pillay to High Court Bench' (candidate Booysen).

77 See the Judicial Service Commission, Selection Interviews for Constitutional Court Judges, *passim*, 3–6 October 1994, available at http://www.concourt.gov.za/interviews/index.html; Transcripts of interviews for judgeships held in Cape Town (candidate Cachalia).

78 For example, the Freemasons. See Carmel Rickard 'Court Hopeful Quits the Masons – Preview of the Judicial Service Commission Hearings,' *Sunday Times Online* (Johannasburg), 7 April 2002, available at www.sundaytimes.co.za/business/legal/2002/04/07/carmel04.asp.

79 See Transcripts of interviews for judgeships held in Cape Town (candidates Wessels, Rampai, and Cachalia).

80 News, 'Roger Cleaver Appointed to CPD Bench' (candidate Cleaver); 'Johannesburg Attorney to Preside over Land Claims Court' (candidate Sithole).

81 Seligson, 'The Judicial Service Commission,' 13.

82 Only candidates Cachalia and Galgut seem to have been asked about this in the April 2001 interviews – see Transcripts of interviews for judgeships held in Cape Town.

83 See 'Legal Titans Set for Showdown,' *Sunday Times* (Johannesburg), 29 October 2000, reporting one JSC member as saying rather hyperbolically that the JSC is 'continually confronted by alcohol problems among judges and candidates.'

84 See 'Grueling Questions have Aspirant Judges Grappling on their Benches' (candidates Donen, Peko, and Sithole); Transcripts of interviews for judgeships held in Cape Town (candidate Majoli); and the works cited in note 58. This can be controversial: see Shadrack Gutto, 'A Moment of National Disgrace,' *This Day* (Johannesburg), 3 August 2004 condemned such questioning of candidate Motata.

85 See Carmel Rickard, 'What's Secret? You Be the Judge,' *Sunday Times* (Johannesburg), 23 March 2003 (candidate Mailula quizzed over listing only one judgment given since her appointment in 1995 as having been reported; whereas the official questionnaire asks that no more than ten of a candidate's most significant judgments be noted, she listed only six).

86 See, e.g., Carmel Rickard, 'Bringing a Woman's Touch to the Bench: New Deputy Judge President Takes Sensitivity to Heart,' *Sunday Times* (Johannesburg), 28 October 2001; Carmel Rickard, 'Things They Said at This Week's Hearings of the Judicial Service Commission,' *Sunday Times Online* (Johannesburg), 4 February 2002, available at www.sundaytimes.co.za/business/legal/2001/02/04/carmel03.asp.

87 See 'Johannesburg Attorney to Preside over Land Claims Court' (candidate Moshidi) and Transcripts of interviews for judgeships held in Cape Town (candidate Nugent).

88 See Transcripts, of interviews for judgeships held in Cape Town (candidates Wessels, Cachalia, Mthiyane, and Galgut).

89 See 'Basil Wunsh Appointed to TPD Bench' (candidate Satchwell); Tran-

scripts of interviews for judgeships held in Cape Town (candidate Rampai); 'The Law's Brightest and Best Do Battle for Top Post,' *Business Day* (Johannesburg), 21 October 2002 (candidate Skweyiya); 'Commission Needs to Do Some Soul-searching'; and 'Oops! Unfortunate Omission By Would-be Judge,' *Sunday Times* (Johannesburg), 14 April 2002.

90 See 'Basil Wunsh Appointed to TPD Bench' and 'First Two Women on the Bench' (candidate Satchwell); Transcripts of interviews for judgeships held in Cape Town (candidates Galgut and Hugo).

91 See Transcripts of interviews for judgeships held in Cape Town (candidates Rampai, Wessels, and Majoli).

92 See Transcripts of interviews for judgeships held in Cape Town (candidates Galgut and Cachalia).

93 Calland, *A Step in the Right Direction*, 13. An additional 10 per cent of questions concerned candidates' special, mostly legal, interests, however.

94 Ibid., Appendix One; sources cited in nn65–6.

95 See 'Grueling Questions have Aspirant Judges Grappling on their Benches' (candidate Van Dykhorst).

96 See Transcripts of interviews for judgeships held in Cape Town (candidates Melunsky, Mthiyane, and Nugent).

97 See Rickard, 'Is the Price of Transformation Too High?'; Kentridge, 'The Highest Court,' 70; and Flemming J.'s evidence, First Interim Report of the Commission of Enquiry into the Rationalisation of the Provincial and Local Divisions of the Supreme Court.

98 Rickard, 'Court Hopeful Quits Masons.' See also Kentridge, 'The Highest Court,' 70; and the strongly expressed view of some judges that this has led some of those who should be appointed to refuse to be nominated. See Fleming J.'s evidence, First Interim Report of the Commission of Enquiry into the Rationalisation of the Provincial and Local Divisions of the Supreme Court, and Ngoepe, White Paper on the Judicial System.

99 'Legal Titans Set for Showdown.'

100 See Transcripts of interviews for judgeships held in Cape Town (candidates Cachalia, Melunsky, Nugent, and Galgut); 'Johannesburg Attorney to Preside over Land Claims Court' (candidate Bam). Helpful leading questions were also asked in the 1994 Constitutional Court interviews. See Calland, *A Step in the Right Direction.*

101 This is also true of the 1994 interviews, where 67 per cent of the questions were asked by only 25 per cent of the commissioners, while almost 68 per cent of legally substantive questions were asked by only two commisioners. See Calland, *A Step in the Right Direction*, 13–14.

102 This is in marked contrast with the 1994 CC interviews, which, according to

Calland, *A Step in the Right Direction*, 22, were dominated by the legal academics' representative.

103 See 'How to Judge a Judge,' 19.

104 'Commission Needs to Do Some Soul-searching' reports that two successful candidates had been questioned extensively over basic mistakes made during their acting appointments, while a third was facing allegations of professional impropriety. A year later, however, a candidate who was questioned extensively about her failure to disclose that she had been dismissed from a company's board, and about her conviction by the bar for a professional misdemeanour, failed in her bid. 'Oops! Unfortunate Omission by Would-be Judge.'

105 Moerane, 'The Meaning of Transformation of the Judiciary in the New South African Context,' 713–14.

106 'How to Judge a Judge.'

107 Moerane, 'The Meaning of Transformation of the Judiciary in the New South African context,' 714.

108 See *De Rebus* (October 2003): 10; (December 2003): 12. The two candidates were Roseni Ally (successful) and Geoff Budlender (unsuccessful). The latter has long been a leading light in the Legal Resources Centre, which conducted much anti-apartheid litigation, and most recently spearheaded the centre's efforts to ensure the implementation of socio-economic rights through cases such as *Government of the Republic of South Africa v. Grootboom* 2001 (1) SA 46 (CC); *Minister of Health v. TAC (No. 2)* 2002 (5) SA 721 (CC). When, in April 2004, Budlender was again passed over by the JSC, this time in favour of a black male candidate (Daniel Dlodlo), a storm erupted in the press about the role and relevance of race as a criterion, and commentators' views were split along racial lines: see Carmel Rickard, 'The Bench is Closed to Pale Males, Struggle Credentials or Not,' *Sunday Times* (Johannesburg), 18 July 2004; Dumisa Buhle Ntsebeza, 'Why Majority Black Bench is Inevitable,' *Sunday Times* (Johannesburg), 25 July 2004; Gutto, 'A Moment of National Disgrace.'

109 On treatment of the views of the General Council of the Bar, see 'Law Society Welcomes Durban Attorney Thumba Pillay to High Court Bench' and 'Grueling questions have Aspirant Judges Grappling on their Benches' (candidates Donen and Peko); regarding the views of judges, note the eventual appointment of Judge President Tshabalala of the Natal High Court despite initial public opposition from a large portion of that court's judges (see 'Law Society Welcomes Durban Attorney Thumba Pillay to High Court Bench,' and the failure to appoint Judge Van Dykhorst, first as deputy judge president and later as judge president of the Transvaal High Court, despite

widespread support for him from judges and practitioners, including Advocates for Transformation (see 'Commission Needs to Do Some Soul-searching'; 'Approaching the Bench,' *Sunday Times* (Johannesburg), 1 April 2001; and Transcripts of interviews for judgeships held in Cape Town.

110 Chaskalson, 'Address at the Opening of the Judges' Conference,' 662.

111 E.g., the SCA now contains someone who started his working life as a manual labourer, messenger, and driver (Mthiyane J.A. – see Carmel Rickard, 'Controversial Judicial Seat could Finally Be Filled This Week,' *Sunday Times Online* (Johannesburg), 25 October 2002, available at www.sundaytimes.co.za/business/legal/2000/10/25/carmel02.asp) alongside Rhodes Scholars, and the CC has a former long-term political prisoner in its ranks (Moseneke J; see 'The High Court Judge Who "Does the Dishes"').

112 Chaskalson, 'Address at the Opening of the Judges' Conference,' 659.

113 Ibid., 659–60.

114 The CC's rejection of the government's health care policy on Aids (*Minister of Health v. TAC (No. 2)* 2002 (5) SA 721 (CC)) is a spectacular example, but equally important are a series of recent SCA decisions holding public officials liable for failure to prevent third parties from harming individuals (e.g., *Minister of Safety and Security v. Van Duivenboden* 2002 (6) SA 431), several High Court decisions calling officials (including provincial ministers) personally to account for failing to fulfil statutory duties to provide welfare benefits (surveyed in Plasket, Administrative Justice and Social Assistance), and decisions of High Court judges to call the President before the Court (*SARFU and Others v. President of the RSA and Others* 1998 (10) BCLR 1256 (T), reversed on this point by the CC in *President of the Republic of South Africa and others v. South African Rugby Football Union and others* 2000 (1) SA 1 (CC)) and to reject the reform of the Magistrates' Commission (*Van Rooyen and Others v. The State and Others* 2001 (4) SA 396 (T)).

115 See the sources cited in notes 34, 53, and 55.

116 Moerane, 'The Meaning of Transformation of the Judiciary in the New South African Context,' 718.

117 This may even require structural change superseding the division between lower courts and superior courts and those who serve in them, by expanding the pool of candidates to include magistrates – this has been endorsed by judges, the minister of justice, and a leading JSC member: see Maduna, 'Address at the Banquet of the Judicial Officers' Symposium,' 666 and Moerane, 'The Meaning of Transformation of the Judiciary in the New South African context,' 718. Other matters that have been mentioned are inadequate remuneration, poor conditions of service compared to the facilities of private practitioners, the need to enhance the numbers and experi-

ence of black and female practitioners, and identifying potential candidates with a view to training for judicial office and 'career pathing.' See Maduna, 'Address' 666–7; Moerane, 'The Meaning of Transformation,' 717–18; and 'How to Judge a Judge.' Much of this suggests that part of the problem lies in the structure of legal practice and courts South Africa inherited from British colonial rule.

118 See 'Racial Divisions Among Judges Affect Us All,' *Mail and Guardian* (Johannesburg), 28 May–3 June 1999; 'The Custodian of Our Constitutional Democracy,' *Mail and Guardian* (Johannesburg), 17–22 December 1999; and the sources cited in notes 1–4. The leader of the largest opposition party has accused the government of 'using the rhetoric of transformation to push through judicial appointees that are loyal to its views': 'ANC Stacking Courts with Loyal Judges – Leon,' *Mail and Guardian Online,* 10 March 2003, available at www.mg.co.za/Content/13.asp?ao=11950&t=1 (last accessed 11 February 2005).

119 See Plasket, 'Administrative Justice and Social Assistance'; 'Judges' Orders Being Ignored,' *Sunday Times* (Johannesburg), 1 April 2000; and *S v. Mamabolo (E TV and Others Intervening)* 2001 (3) SA 409 (CC), where an official was convicted of contempt of court for criticizing a judge's order. The judiciary recently felt it necessary to call collectively on the government to ensure that all court orders are observed diligently by officials. See 'Symposium Statement,' 650.

120 Gibson, *Overcoming Apartheid,* 300–27.

121 See especially the chapters on Australia and England and Wales.

15 A Judiciary in Transition: Reflections on the Selection of Judges in Namibia

SUFIAN HEMED BUKURURA

Namibia (previously known as South West Africa) achieved its political independence in 1990. At the time, the world in general, and Africa in particular, had witnessed various forms of dictatorship regimes, including military rules, one-party states, and life presidencies. It was around the same time that the World Bank reported on the causes of Africa's decline and made important recommendations for the revival of the continent's fortunes.[1] Just before the World Bank report there were international developments regarding the judiciary.[2] Although the extent to which these international developments influenced the form and substance of the 1990 constitution of Namibia may not be very clear, one is tempted to infer that the content and conclusions of these reports significantly informed those involved in the negotiation and drafting processes. The constitution of Namibia, therefore, became well known for the way in which it skilfully married conventional constitutional arrangements with imaginative ideas. It appeared to go beyond independence constitutions drafted in the 1960s. Provisions for the separation of powers, protection of the rule of law, and safeguarding of the independence of the judiciary were, for example, complemented by executive accountability through consultation and approval requirements,[3] as well as provisions regarding national reconciliation and affirmative action.

It is partly in this context that a clear understanding of the process of selecting judges in post-independence Namibia has to be located. Put differently, an attempt to unravel the dynamics and complexities of selecting judges in post-independence Namibia has to take into account the historical background of the country as well as legal developments around the world. This will both create a holistic picture of the processes and complexities at play and locate them in a broader perspective.

The discussion that follows begins with a brief account of the history of Namibia, in which the judicial branch and judges are but component parts. I then turn to the constitutional and legal mechanisms established for the selection of judges after independence, and an analysis of some of the controversies that have arisen. A cautious conclusion is drawn that, although a workable compromise appears to have been found, it has not completely closed the debate on the need for further reforms.

Historical Context: The Judiciary in the Tortuous Past

Namibia, like other African countries, was subjected to many years of colonial domination. Colonialism, therefore, influenced the manner in which governance institutions were created and operated. Most importantly, courts and judges were introduced as part of colonial mechanisms, and were unknown in pre-colonial arrangements.[4] Namibia's history has a further dimension: colonialism was accompanied by racial segregation, otherwise known as apartheid.[5] German colonialism took its toll, but it is South Africa's apartheid system that seems to have left the most visible scars on the administration of justice in general, and the selection of judges in particular.

Colonialism and Apartheid

Namibia was subjected to German occupation from 1884 to 1915.[6] It also became part and parcel of the South African administration, with its attendant apartheid system, in the period 1915–1990. German colonisation ended when South African troops occupied the territory during the First World War. In 1920, under the Treaty of Versailles, that occupation was transformed into a League of Nations mandate, in terms of which South Africa was mandated to administer Namibia 'to promote the utmost material and moral well-being and the social progress of the indigenous inhabitants of the territory' on behalf of the British Crown. This was the starting point of South Africa's entrenchment of apartheid.

South Africa 'exported' its administrative machinery, including its legal system and the judiciary, to Namibia. Appeals from the Namibian High Court were from 1920 heard by the Appellate Division of the Supreme Court of South Africa,[7] and appointments to these courts were, in many ways, related to political and legal developments in South Africa.[8]

The Judiciary in the Era of Domination

One of the characteristics of apartheid was the treatment of the majority, described as non-white, as an underclass, and the conscious and deliberate exclusion of that majority from meaningful involvement in political, social, and economic spheres. Consequently, non-whites did not occupy positions of influence in any government institution, including the judiciary. Judges of the apartheid era were selected from minority white males only. It has been noted in regard to appointments and promotion to the South African Supreme Court, which has resonance for Namibia as well, that even among qualified and experienced whites, judges were mostly selected from a preferred category of Afrikaner nationalist sympathizers.[9] In other words, selection of judges, even from among white males, was not based entirely on merit, but on a patronage system.[10] The majority black men and women were excluded from judicial office.[11]

This situation, which is a recurring theme in several post-independence government reports, is aptly described in one of the Ministry of Justice reports as follows: 'It was inconceivable during the apartheid era for a black magistrate or judge to preside over a case where the defendant or the accused person was white. It was inconceivable for a black magistrate or judge to sentence a white criminal to a term of imprisonment ... [I]t is clear from this state of affairs that before independence, blacks were at the receiving end of the administration of justice in Namibia.'[12] As one would expect, marginalization and exclusion of the majority led to deep resentment.[13] At the political level, a lack of trust and confidence was partly expressed in the war of liberation that lasted many years.

Any analysis of the pre-independence judiciary in Namibia (and undoubtedly South Africa itself) is incomplete without mention of another significant factor: during the apartheid era, most judges became part and parcel, and an important pillar, of the oppressive machinery. Instead of putting the brakes on or mitigating the rigours of oppression, courts and judicial officers consciously or unconsciously supported the regime.[14]

In sum, three historical underpinnings have to be considered in reflecting on the selection of judges in Namibia: the judicial branch and judicial officers had no indigenous roots in the African soil; colonialism was oppressive in character; and apartheid ensured the deliberate exclusion of the majority. This tragic history had both short- and long-term consequences.[15] In the short term, the 'non-white' majority of Namibians were subjected to laws made by and for them by the minority. It is also correct to say that disputes involving the majority of Namibians were adjudicated upon by judges who were not appointed from among their number, and with whom they shared little, if at all. In other words, the majority of Namibians were deliberately excluded from both law-making processes and consideration for selection as judges.

The exclusion of the majority of Namibians from the legal processes had more far-reaching consequences as well. Blacks and women neither obtained the necessary qualifications nor acquired the requisite experiences to become part of the pool from which future judges could be appointed. The exclusion also invariably affected public perceptions about the administration of justice in general, and the institution of the judiciary and court processes in particular. The implications of these horrific circumstances were bound to linger on many years after the apartheid system had ended. As will be shown below, some of the intricate questions raised by the selection of judges in post-independence Namibia are linked partly to, and informed by, almost seventy years of the country's colonial connection to South Africa. Both the institution of the judiciary and the selection of judges were bound to be haunted by the ghosts of their past.

Change in Continuity: Daunting Challenges

Against the background of its torturous past, an independent Namibia faced the daunting challenge of becoming a constitutional democracy. As will soon be made clear, the transition has not been easy. As much as seeds of building the future were planted, some components of the past had to be retained to avoid chaos and confusion.[16] Discrimination and past imbalances, for example, informed post-independence policies and legislation, and continue to be points of reference when issues of change are raised. In this section post-independence initiatives are examined in the context of pre-independence barriers and constraints.

From the Past into the Future

The end of South Africa's rule of Namibia followed a combination of factors, including many years of liberation struggle and the involvement of the international community through the United Nations. The Namibian constitution was hailed around the world for its approach and vision. It signified a break from the country's apartheid brutality and was a significant development in the creation of a constitutional democracy. Several rhetorical statements are made in the preamble, including the following. The constitution shall be the supreme and fundamental law of the land;[17] the government is responsible to freely elected representatives of the people, operating under a sovereign constitution and a free and independent judiciary. Some of these statements are a re-affirmation of globally recognized principles and can be traced back to the South West African Peoples Organisation (SWAPO), the national liberation movement, and documents prepared several years before independence. Two important policy statements prepared by the Lusaka-based United Nations Institute for Namibia (UNIN) need to be mentioned.[18] Both documents stated that in the new Namibia fundamental rights would be protected, principles of the rule of law and independence of the judiciary would be respected, and courts would be independent. Both documents demonstrated awareness of, and made observations about, options available for the selection of judges.[19]

More significant, however, is the way in which the new constitution translated those pre-independence aspirations into constitutional reality, creating a hierarchy of courts and protecting them from external interference by specifying the mechanism in which judges of the High Court and Supreme Court would be selected: through the Judicial Service Commission and presidential appointment. Before examining those provisions, it is important to mention Article 23, which attempts to link the events and processes of the past to aspirations of the future. It provides:

> (1) The practice of racial discrimination and the practice and ideology of apartheid from which the majority of the people of Namibia have suffered for so long shall be prohibited and by Act of Parliament such practices, and the propagation of such practices, may be rendered criminally punishable by the ordinary Courts by means of such punishment as Parliament deems necessary for the purposes of expressing the revulsion of the Namibian people at such practices.
> (2) Nothing contained in Article 10 hereof shall prevent Parliament from enacting legislation providing directly or indirectly for the advancement of persons within Namibia who have been socially, economically or educationally disadvantaged by past discriminatory laws or practices, or the implementation of policies and programmes aimed at redressing social, economic or educational imbalances in the Namibian society arising out of past discriminatory laws or practices or for achieving a balanced structur-

ing of public service, the police force, the defence force, and the prison service.
(3) In the enactment of legislation and the application of any policies and practices contemplated by Sub-Article (2) hereof, it shall be permissible to have regard to the fact that women in Namibia have traditionally suffered special discrimination and that they need to be encouraged and enabled to play a full, equal and effective role in the political, social, economic and cultural life of the nation.

As will be explained below, this provision became an important foundation upon which most post-independence attempts to redress the injustices and imbalances of the past have been based.[20] This is heavily emphasized in one of the earliest government documents in which government ministries outlined their priorities. Among the five priority areas for the Ministry of Justice, for example, three were, in one way or the other, related to dealing with the past. These include promotion of the policy of affirmative action, intensive training programs to improve standards and ensure better performance, and the training of staff in the fields of law and law-related disciplines.[21]

Before looking at the selection of judges we need to highlight the organization of the judiciary. Article 78 of the constitution provides for the establishment of a Supreme Court, High Court, and lower courts[22] in Namibia. This provision outlines the hierarchy of courts in the country and the constitutional and legal requirement for their independence, and prohibits interference by members of other branches of government. Also provided for, in clear and certain terms, is a positive duty upon other organs of government to assist the courts to protect their independence, integrity, and effectiveness. A positive duty is imposed on the other organs to exercise their muscle and assist the least dangerous and weakest branch of government, the judiciary.

Selecting Judges: The Judicial Service Commission (JSC)

The constitution entrusted the function of selecting judges in Namibia to the Judicial Service Commission (JSC).[23] For a clear picture of the process, Articles 85 and 82 of the constitution must be read together with reference to the *Judicial Service Commission Act.* According to Article 85(1), the JSC is comprised of the chief justice, a judge appointed by the President, the attorney-general, and two persons nominated by the professional organizations of the legal profession.[24] In view of the history and past composition of the judiciary and legal profession, it was not surprising that at independence the JSC was not only all white, it was also male dominated. Flowing from these dynamics, Steytler has noted, was the recommendation, and subsequent appointment of, the first post-independence chief justice and judge president.[25] It is not an understatement to suggest that there was much unease among politicians and members of the general populace about that state of affairs.[26]

The Judicial Service Commission in Namibia, as anywhere else where such a body exists, was expected to play an important part in ensuring that a positive image and reputation of the judiciary was maintained, because that image and reputation was bound to be in the spotlight.

Whereas members of the legal fraternity in other countries in southern Africa consistently express grave doubts about the competency and impartiality of judges, Namibia's higher courts have been spared such experiences. In other words, despite the initial unease, the administration of justice in the Supreme Court and High Court appears to have been relatively smooth and uncontroversial. However, that does not mean that perceptions of some influential people and opinion makers have changed. From time to time, and depending on the legal issues at stake, the issue of imbalance in the composition of the judiciary and the legal profession, from whom judges are appointed, emerges.

Article 85(1) of the constitution provides that an Act of Parliament will be passed to complement and give detail to the functions of Judicial Service Commission. That law was enacted in 1995,[27] and of interest here is section 5(1), which states: 'Whenever the Judicial Service Commission is required by the provisions of the Constitution or any other law to make a recommendation to the President for the appointment of a person to a judicial office, the Commission shall, as far as is practicable, have due regard to affirmative action and the need for a balanced structuring of judicial offices.'

Although government documents do not explicitly justify affirmative action and balancing of the judicial structure to reflect the demographics of the Namibian society on the basis of any international principle, support for it is found in the Montreal Declaration, Article 2.13 of which states as follows: 'The process and standard of judicial selection shall give due consideration to insuring a fair reflection by the judiciary of the society in all its aspects.'

The policy of discrimination practised by South Africa (in South Africa itself and in Namibia), was not in anyway geared towards achieving social inclusion. On the contrary, it was antithetical to it. Supporters of apartheid may be pleased to hear and take comfort from suggestions that, by its very nature, the function of adjudication does not necessarily require reflection of social diversity in the composition of the judiciary. Sir Antony Mason (chief justice of Australia, 1987–95)[28] notes:

> The composition of the judiciary is another current topic of debate. The Judiciary, like other Australian institutions, is not representative of various elements which make up Australian society. No doubt some elements in society, particularly minority groups, believe that they would have greater confidence in the Judiciary if it were more representative, just as they would have more confidence in our political institutions if they were more representative of the diverse elements of society. But, unlike the politician, the judge is not appointed to represent anyone. The judge's paramount responsibility is to be impartial and to decide the contest between the parties by applying the relevant principles of law as the judge understands or enunciates them to the facts as found.

As Elizabeth Handley's chapter makes clear, this approach was contested in Australia. It is a recurring theme in the debate on judicial appointments in many different jurisdictions, but is highly problematic. In particular, it undervalues one important characteristic of contemporary governance: the success of institutions of governance in general, including the judiciary, is heavily dependent on public trust and confidence. When the majority of society are excluded from an institution, public confidence in that institution is likely to be fundamentally undermined. As discussed above, most Namibians were marginalized and deliberately excluded by the apartheid policy, and did not trust, or have confidence in, political institutions in general and the courts in particular. The significance of social representation in such circumstances cannot be underestimated.

Recognizing that public confidence in courts and the judicial officers who preside over them is essential, the Montreal Principles included representation of the whole society as an important consideration in the selection of judicial officers.[29] The drafters of Namibia's independence constitution and the *Judicial Service Commission Act* of 1995, consciously or unconsciously, expressed those sentiments through the language of 'affirmative action' and 'balanced structure of the judicial office.'

According to Articles 85 and 82 and the *Judicial Service Commission Act*, the JSC selects candidates for judicial office and sends its recommendations to the President who, under the terms of Article 85(1), makes the appointment. In situations where the President does not accept the JSC's recommendations, section 5 stipulates the procedure to be followed: the President is to refer the matter back to the JSC, giving written reasons for the rejection and requesting the commission to make fresh recommendations.[30] It is not known whether the JSC in Namibia has ever made a recommendation that was rejected by the President.

Namibia's Judicial Service Commission has been well aware of the delicate situation it faces and has, consequently, chosen to act very cautiously. In the past thirteen years, only nine judges have been selected and subsequently appointed to permanent positions.[31] There are several plausible explanations for this, two of which need to be emphasized, as they both have historical undertones. First, there has been a very narrow pool from which to select judges. Second, senior legal practitioners, who are mostly white males, have been reluctant to put themselves forward for selection.

In these circumstances, an inference can be drawn that the JSC's caution, has, in some way, led to the adoption of tentative and short-term solutions. The notable ones are the sporadic recommendation of judges from beyond the borders of Namibia,[32] and the use of ad hoc and acting judges in both the High Court and Supreme Court. As will be shown below, both approaches appear to have some partial benefits.

The appointment of expatriate judges has been a common feature of post-colonial countries with few appropriately qualified nationals. In most cases, these judges were either retired in their own countries or in the twilight of their careers. They not only brought experience to the bench, but also served as transitional appointments in the absence of qualified locals. Naturally, with the passage of time, they reached retirement age and their positions fell vacant.

Ad hoc and acting appointments, as the titles suggest, are only short-term appointments. According to Articles 82(3) and (4), such appointments are made by the President at the request of the chief justice (in case of Supreme Court),[33] or the judge president (in the case of appointments to the High Court). In effect, the appointment of acting judges is an easy process, as observed by the High Court in *Zemburuka v. S*, where it was stated as that:

> The threshold requirements for the appointment of an ad hoc Judge for the Supreme Court are that, (a) in cases involving the determination of constitutional issues or the guarantee of fundamental rights and freedoms, (b) the Chief Justice is of the opinion (c) that it is desirable that such per-

> sons should be appointed to hear such cases by reason of their special knowledge of or expertise in such matters and (d) requests the President to so appoint them. Those requirements for the appointment of Acting judges of the Supreme Court are that (a) a casual vacancy exists on its Bench and (b) the Chief Justice requests the president to appoint an acting Judge to fill it (at 21–22).[34]

In Namibia, unlike England, acting and ad hoc appointments have not necessarily been used as a training ground for potential candidates. So far not more than one of those subsequently appointed to permanent positions went through that route. Acting and ad hoc appointments in Namibia have been used merely as short-term and stop-gap measures, so that wherever a qualified Namibian acquires sufficient experience, there is a very great likelihood that there will be a post available to which such person can be appointed. The appointments of Justices Mainga,[35] Hoff,[36] and Shivute[37] from among the ranks of magistrates are illustrative.

One serious concern that the JSC might not have an immediate solution for, and may have to grapple with for a longer time, is gender inequality.[38] Women, who together with non-whites were discriminated against under the old regime, have not made meaningful inroads into the higher judiciary. Whereas some women have been appointed to positions of influence including ombudsman (appointed in December 1996), attorney-general (appointed in March 2001), and more recently, prosecutor general (appointed in December 2003),[39] only one woman, an expatriate, has so far been appointed as a judge of the High Court. Other qualified women, however, have been appointed on an ad hoc basis.

The picture in Namibia therefore mirrors that of many other jurisdictions in Africa and elsewhere, where women do not appear to be 'trickling up' into the higher ranks of the judiciary.

The explanation for the slow pace of transformation in the judiciary since the establishment of the JSC is complex. Although there is a general consensus as to the desirability of change, deep-seated institutional problems have limited the extent of change in practice. One important factor has been the composition of the legal profession.

Transformation of the Legal Profession

In Namibia, like other countries in the common law system, practising lawyers have invariably been the main pool from which judges were selected.[40] In view of Namibia's history, the profession was predominantly composed of white males. Any meaningful balancing of the judiciary, therefore, required that access to the legal profession be changed. The government embarked on transformation of the legal profession with the introduction of the 1995 Legal Practitioners Bill. That became an arena of acrimonious debate between the profession and the government. Among the aspects chosen for reform, two are discussed here. First, the government attempted to recognize foreign legal qualifications and, consequently, to permit Namibians who studied law outside South Africa to be admitted into the profession. Second, the government moved to bring the two branches of the profession, attorneys and advocates, together into one. Seven advantages were outlined for the fusion of the profession, one of which was the broadening of the pool from which judges may be appointed.[41] Practitioners argued that although they supported the transformation in principle, they objected strongly to any intrusion into professional independence (which erodes the rule of law) and to any lowering of established professional standards. The ensuing conflict is expressed in a government report as follows: 'This provoked considerable resistance to the extent that petitions were sent to the International Bar Association and to the UN Human Rights Commission with a view to stopping the fusion.'[42] When the Bill ultimately became law, with the government proclaiming victory, damage had already been done. The government, for its part, viewed the objections partly as an unnecessary detraction from its program of transformation and partly as an undue protection of entrenched interests. On the other hand, lawyers admitted into the profession through the reformed system mistrusted their mainstream colleagues. These feelings are partly manifested in the creation of an exclusively non-white grouping – the Namibian Law Association (NLA) – within the statutory Law Society of Namibia (LSN).[43] Some members of the NLA suggest that it is just a forum in which interests of non-white lawyers, most of who were admitted after 1995, are aired and discussed. That assertion conveys an incomplete picture of the association and, mostly importantly, the background of its membership. In a wider perspective, the existence of the NLA within the LSN creates an impression that serious differences may still exist along racial lines within the profession, fourteen years after independence.

Public Utterances and Demonstrations

Since independence some members of Namibian society have demonstrated to express their concerns regarding particular court decisions.[44] For the purposes of this paper, however, only recent demonstrations following the *Sikunda* case will be alluded to.[45] The case involved an individual whose liberty was infringed, with the imminent threat of further violations. The sixty-two-year-old Sikunda Snr had been arrested and imprisoned pending deportation. The matter arose at a time when certain parts of the country were experiencing what the government referred to as a 'high level of insecurity.'

Concerned about Sikunda Snr's liberty, his son brought an urgent application before a High Court judge. The first judge issued an interim order for Sikunda Snr's release. It was first alleged, and later confirmed by the High Court, that the minister of home affairs, and/or his officials, disregarded that interim order. The case was then taken before another High Court judge for hearing. After several court appearances and hearings of the matter, the judge withdrew (recused himself), and another bench had to be constituted.

On the face of it the issues in the case appeared very simple: the exercise of powers of arrest; and the detention and removal of a person considered to be a security risk by the minister of home affairs acting on the advice of, and in consultation with, the Security Commission. Both the minister and the Security Commission seem to have understood that these powers needed to be exercised as a matter of urgency because national security was at stake. But in acting urgently and speedily prescribed national and international minimum safeguards and protections were breached.

Following the decision of the High Court, demonstrators, organized by the ruling SWAPO party in Windhoek, took to the streets and read a petition to the President. Among the demands made, two are of particular relevance: that judges should be elected and that trial by jury should be introduced. Whereas politicians made remarks of a general nature, demonstrators made specific demands with direct relevance to the judiciary and in particular to the selection of judges. Both demands appear to be linked to the overall issue of the accountability of judges.

Although members of the general public might not have obvious avenues through which to express their views on the nature of the judiciary or the selection of judges, a high-profile case and judicial pronouncements as in the *Sikunda* case provided an opportunity, however limited, for public views to be aired.

Conclusion

Namibia was under colonial domination for many years. That domination ended only thirteen years ago. This paper set out to explore the selection of judges in the peculiar circumstances of colonialism and apartheid, and especially, the long-term damage done by racial discrimination. Attempting to transform procedures and processes that are well entrenched was not going to be easy, as the government of Namibia has discovered since coming to power. Nonetheless, attempted initiatives could only find justification in the context of the historical realities of the country, on the one hand, and the significance of the institution of the judiciary and the work that it does in the new dispensation, on the other.

If the judiciary is to command respect and trust in the new Namibia, its composition must reflect to some degree the diversity of the society in which it operates. Although diversity of the judiciary might not have been an imperative in the past, its significance cannot be underestimated in contemporary circumstances. Achieving diversity, however, has to be approached carefully without compromising the essential qualities expected of the institution and its members. The selection process, through the Judicial Services Commission, seems to have constituted a workable compromise. It does not in any way mean that the process has been uncontested. Public demonstrations, at least, suggest that a different approach might have been preferred. Although it is unlikely that the process of selecting judges may be revisited in the near future, concerns have been voiced in the context of a politically sensitive issue of 'perceived' national security.

NOTES

In the preparation of this chapter assistance and comments were received from numerous friends and colleagues. Norman Tjombe and Evelyn Zimba, of the Namibian Legal Assistance Centre, kept me informed of developments in Namibia and drew my attention to relevant documents. John C. Mubangizi, David H. Hulme, and Sandy Singh of the Faculty of Law, University of KwaZulu-Natal, read and commented on various aspects of the chapter in its draft form. To all I am deeply indebted.

1 World Bank, *Sub-Saharan Africa*.

2 Several international declarations were made in the 1980s; see, e.g., the United Nations Basic Principles on the Independence of the Judiciary (1985), which was preceded by the Syracuse Principles (1981), the Tokyo Principles (1982), the New Delhi Standards (1982), and the Montreal Declaration (1983), outlined in Shetreet and Deschenes, eds., *Judicial Inde-*

pendence, chapters 32, 33, and 35–9. See also Special Issue: Centre for the Independence of Judges and Lawyers (CILJ) Bulletin: A Compilation of International Standards (1993).

3 See Cottrell, 'Constitution of Namibia: An Overview,' 56–78; Hatchard and Slinn, 'Namibia: The Constitutional Path to Freedom,' 650.

4 On conflicting views regarding adoption of English law in East Africa, for example, see Morris and Read, *Indirect Rule and the Search for Justice*, esp. chapter 3.

5 For an understanding of the connection between apartheid and colonialism, see Mamdani, *Citizen and Subject*.

6 On the racial segregation program during German rule, see, e.g., Melber, 'Namibia: The German Roots of Apartheid,' 74–5.

7 See, e.g., Administration of Justice Proclamation 21 of 1919 and Appellate Division Act 12 of 1920.

8 See, e.g., Account of the Proceedings on the Day the High Court of South-West Africa was Opened (6 January 1920), 170–3 on the installation of judges in Namibia, and The Appellate Division, 293.

9 See, e.g., Cameron, 'Legal Chauvinism, Executive-mindedness and Justice,' 42; Gauntlett, 'Appointing and Promoting Judges,' 23; Kentridge, 'Telling Truth about Law,' 652. See also Millner, 'Eclipse of a Judiciary,' 887.

10 At some point, the selection of judges on the basis of patronage in the Transvaal Division of the High Court of South Africa manifested itself in the allocation of cases. Certain judges, for example, presided over 'politically oriented' cases. See Dugard, 'The Judiciary and National Security.'

11 Dlamini, 'The Appointment of Black Judicial Officers'; Gauntlett, 'Appointing and Promoting Judges.'

12 Republic of Namibia, *Ministry of Justice Annual Report 1990–1998*, 2. It has been suggested, for example, that in 1988, two years before Namibia achieved its political independence, whites constituted only 5 per cent of the country's population. See Republic of Namibia, *White Paper on National Policies and Sectoral Ministries*, 7.

13 See, e.g., Corder, 'Establishing Legitimacy for the Administration of Justice in South Africa.'

14 The ways and dimensions in which courts sustained the apartheid system have been extensively documented. In addition to numerous journal articles there are several full-length studies. These include Abel, *Politics by Other Means*; Corder, *Judges at Work*; Dugard, *Human Rights and the South African Legal Order*; Forsyth, *In Danger for their Talents*; Dyzenhaus, *Hard Cases and Wicked Legal Systems*; Ellman, *In Time of Trouble*; and Mathews, *Freedom, State Security and the Rule of Law*.

15 One cannot help noting the significance of and extent to which Namibia's past history shapes post-independence policies. It is referred to at length and many times in public speeches as well as in government documents. See, among others, Republic of Namibia, *White Paper on National Policies and Sectoral Ministries*; Republic of Namibia, *Ministry of Justice Annual Report 1990–1998*; Republic of Namibia, *Namibia: A Decade of Peace, Democracy and Prosperity, 1990–2000.*

16 Provisions of the constitution meant to ensure continuity include Articles 138(2), 140, and 141. Article 140 authorized all laws in force at the date of independence to remain in force until repealed or amended by Act of Parliament, or until declared unconstitutional by a competent court. Article 141, on the other hand, provides that any person holding office under any law shall continue to hold such office unless and until he or she resigns or is retired, transferred, or removed from office in accordance to law.

17 In addition to the Preamble and Article 1(6), the supremacy of the constitution of Namibia is also dealt with in Articles 32(1), 63(1), and 78(2).

18 United Nations Institute for Namibia (UNIN), *Constitutional Options for Namibia,* and United Nations Institute for Namibia, *Towards a New Legal System for Independent Namibia.*

19 See UNIN, Constitutional Options for Namibia, 45, and UNIN, Towards a New Legal System, 56.

20 S. 174(2) of the constitution of South Africa 1996, on its part, categorically provides that 'the need for the judiciary to reflect broadly the racial and gender composition of South Africa must be considered when judicial officers are appointed.' See François du Bois's chapter in this book.

21 Republic of Namibia, White Paper on National Policies and Sectoral Ministries, 38. See also Speeches made at the inauguration of the Faculty of Law, University of Namibia, 18 February 1994, in Faculty of Law, *Speeches: Inauguration of Law Faculty.*

22 Namibian lower courts, unlike the High Court and Supreme Court, are presided over by magistrates. The procedure for selection of magistrates is substantially different from that of judges. It is partly for that reason and partly for want of space that selection of magistrates is omitted in the present discussion.

23 The functions of the Judicial Service Commission extend beyond selection of judges to include recommendations for the appointment of the prosecutor general as well as the ombudsman (Article 88(1) and 90(1), and the investigation into the conduct of judges (Article 84(3)).

24 The independence of the JSC was alluded to by the Supreme Court in *Ex parte Attorney General, Namibia: In re the Constitutional Relationship between the Attorney General and the Prosecutor General* (1995).

25 Steytler, 'The Judicialisation of Namibian Politics.'

26 In Namibia, like South Africa, public unease with the judiciary arose from the role played by the judiciary during apartheid. South Africa decided to have a broad-based JSC composed of a wide selection of people. See s. 105(1) of the *Constitution of South Africa Act 200* of 1993 and s. 178(1) of *Constitution 1996, Act 108.* See also Corder, 'The Appointment of Judges.'

27 Act 18 of 1995 came into effect on 20 November 1995, Government Notice 220/95.

28 See Mason, 'The State of the Judicature,' 131. Kirby, 'Modes of Appointment and Training of Judges,' 545, and Williams, 'Judicial Independence in Australia,' 186–7, recognize, without necessarily approving, the idea of a judiciary that is representative of society. On the other hand, however, Shetreet writes approvingly, adding that a representative judiciary is a necessary imperative of social diversity. See Shetreet, 'Who will Judge,' 775–8.

29 It has been suggested that the requirement of social representation as one of the qualities of a judge can also be found in the Code of Jewish Law. See, e.g., Goldstein, 'The Appointment of Judges,' 806. On the value of public confidence in the judiciary, see, e.g., Kenny, 'Maintaining Public Confidence in the Judiciary.'

30 This is in sharp contrast to what used to happen in Kenya during the presidency of Daniel Arap Moi. Because JSC recommendations were not legally binding upon the President, it was not uncommon for the President to disregard recommendations without giving reasons and appointing anybody he wanted to be a judge. See Days et al., *Justice Enjoined*, 17.

31 Article 33(8) requires appointments of judges and other constitutional positions to be published in the Government Gazette. The information on appointments referred to here has been obtained from various government gazettes and supplemented by Government Proclamation 1 August 2003.

32 Of the nine judges on permanent appointments, four were appointed from outside Namibia: Mr Justice N.R. Hannah (served as chief justice in Swaziland); Mrs Justice M. Gibson (from Britain); Mr Justice A.M. Silungwe (chief justice in Zambia); and Mr Justice S.V. Mtambanengwe (served on the High Court in Zimbabwe). Other appointments to the High Court include Mr Justice G.J.C. Strydom, a white Namibian, first appointed judge president in 1991; Mr Justice P.M. Teek, a black Namibian appointed in April 1992; and Mr Justice J.D.G. Maritz, a white Namibian appointed in August 1999.

33 Until 2003, for example, the chief justice was the only permanent member of the Supreme Court. Other justices of the court were appointed from time to time either as ad hoc or acting judges. On 1 March 2003, Mr Justice Teek was appointed to the Supreme Court. See Proclamation 22 of 2003, Government

Gazette 3034. It is believed that this appointment was made in anticipation of the retirement of Chief Justice Strydom, who had been in that post since 1 March 1999.

34 *Zemburuka v. S* (Unreported) HC Case No. CA 119/2002, 30 September 2003.

35 Appointed to the High Court on 27 September 1999. See Proclamation 22 of 2003, Government Gazette 3034.

36 Appointed to the High Court on 1 March 2001. See Proclamation 22 of 2003, Government Gazette 3034. Justice Hoff was first appointed in acting capacity on 14 April 1999. See Proclamation 1 of 1999 Government Gazette 2022.

37 Appointed to the High Court on 1 March 2001. See Proclamation 22 of 2003, Government Gazette 3034. Justice Shivute was later appointed judge president on 6 June 2003 (see Proclamation 22 of 2003, Government Gazette 3034), ahead of other judges of the High Court.

38 Problems of gender inequality and achievements made since independence are examined in detail in Republic of Namibia, *Namibia National Progress Report on the Implementation of the Beijing Platform for Action*, 53. The report shows that between July 1995 and March 1998 there has been an increase of women in senior positions in the Ministry of Justice. The increase, for example, is noted among magistrates (20 per cent to 29 per cent); state prosecutors, (40 per cent to 44 per cent); legal advisers (40 per cent to 60 per cent); legislative drafters (21 per cent to 27 per cent); and government attorneys (40 per cent to 50 per cent). See also Republic of Namibia, *Namibia: A Decade of Peace, Democracy and Prosperity*, 267.

39 See Menges Werner, 'Imalwa gets PG (Prosecutor-General) post – as expected,' *The Namibian*, 1 December 2003, 1, where it is stated that the newly appointed prosecutor general will assume her office on 1 January 2004.

40 See, e.g., Kahn, 'The Judges,'

41 See Republic of Namibia, *A Decade of Peace, Democracy and Prosperity*, 268. So far no judge has been appointed from the pool created by the fusion of the profession. However, three black Namibian judges (Justices Mainga, Hoff, and Shivute, referred to in notes 35, 36, and 37 above) have been appointed from among magistrates.

42 Republic of Namibia, *Ministry of Justice Annual Report 1990–1998*, 13. See also Attorney-General Vekuii Rukoro and response by Advocate Dave Smuts, interviews by Cupido, *Namibia Review* 4:4–7.

43 It is not entirely clear how diverse interests of the Law Society of Namibia generally and those of the Namibian Law Association in particular have con-

verged lately. The two bodies separately launched court challenges against the *Legal Practitioners Amendment Act 10* of 2002. See *Olyvia Martha Ekanjo-Imalwa v. The Law Society of Namibia and Another* (2003) (unreported) HC(P) A11/03, 11 August 2003.

44 See *S v. Heita and another*, [1992] 3 SA 780 (NmHC) and review of it in Steytler, 'The Judicialisation of Namibian Politics,' 493. The National Society for Human Rights, a non-government organization with observer status at the African Commission for Human Rights, has a full account of negative statements by politicians about judges and courts. See specifically National Society for Human Rights, *Namibia: The Judiciary under Siege*. See also various NSHR Human Rights Annual Reports for subsequent years.

45 *Sikunda v. The Government of the Republic of Namibia & Others* (unreported) HC case no. A327/2000, 9 February 2001.

16 Creating a Compliant Judiciary in Zimbabwe, 2000–2003

DEREK MATYSZAK

Background

When the peace deal at the end of Zimbabwe's war of independence was brokered at Lancaster House under the auspices of Britain, the legal teams of the former adversaries played no part in drafting the new constitution for the country.[1] The British Foreign Office took care of that, simply handing the parties a document that was supposed to give effect to the compromises reached. Numerous clauses thus entered the constitution by default, including those provisions relating to judicial selection. Given the similarity between the process of judicial selection provided for the new Zimbabwe and other post-colonial Commonwealth countries in Africa,[2] it is reasonable to suppose that the British Foreign Office used a pro forma for constitution-making during the decolonization process. It is thus of some interest that these constitutions are all noteworthy for their inadequate checks on executive power and a system of judicial appointments that contains insufficient protection from executive interference.

The manner in which judicial appointments are made in Zimbabwe is provided for in sections 84 and 85 of the 'Lancaster House' constitution. Selection is made by a Judicial Services Commission[3] (JSC) and the system has remained unchanged since the country's independence. This chapter outlines some of the techniques used to subvert the process of judicial appointments by an executive determined to remove all constraints on its power while retaining the possibility of asserting a fidelity to the rule of law, no matter how cynical such an assertion might be.

Zimbabwe in Crisis

Since independence in 1980 Zimbabwe has been ruled by governments formed by President Robert Mugabe's ZANU PF party, with no real challenge from a viable opposition. This situation changed, with profound consequences, in February 2000, when the government's proposed new constitution for the country was rejected in a nationwide referendum. The referendum had been viewed widely as a test of the government's popularity and its outcome was thus regarded as the government's first defeat at the polls. Furthermore, it was regarded as a litmus test for the impending parliamentary and presidential elections due in June 2000 and March 2002 respectively. For the first time since independence there was a possibility of ZANU (PF) being dislodged at the polls.

The response of ZANU (PF) to this situation was swift and dramatic. The compromises reached at Lancaster House had left the key issue of land distribution unresolved, and the bulk of prime farmland remained in the hands of about 4,500 white farmers.[4] At successive elections agrarian reform had been raised by ZANU PF as a campaign strategy, but little had been done thereafter. Following its defeat in the referendum, under the guise of agrarian reform, the government launched a campaign to establish total control over all sections of society. Farm invasions by a government-sponsored militia began two weeks after the referendum. The government claimed that the invasions were due to the demand for land, which until then had only been contained by the promise of a new constitution that would have addressed the issue.[5]

In response to the widespread local and international denunciation of the human rights abuses that accompanied this campaign,[6] the discourse of Mugabe and his government became informed by anti-white, anti-imperialist,[7] pseudo-Pan-Africanist propaganda. The media, controlled by the government,[8] provided ample broadcasting opportunities for this and it is difficult to exaggerate the pervasiveness and intensity of the propaganda. The three select quotations below are indicative of its essence:

> The human rights NGOs supporting the MDC[9] under the guise of the NCA,[10] ... are well known for using equal political and civil rights to justify unequal economic rights. And that is what the British want to see in Zimbabwe: a spectacle of getting the Black majority to use political rights to defend unequal rights between Blacks and Whites under the guise of democracy.[11]

> In our situation in Zimbabwe this fundamental issue of land reforms has pitted the Black majority who are the right holders and, therefore, the primary stakeholders to our land against the obdurate and internationally well-connected racial minority, largely of British descent and brought in and sustained by British colonialism, now being supported and manipulated by the Blair Government.[12]

> These (Whites) do not deserve to be in Zimbabwe and we shall take steps to ensure that they are not entitled to our land in Zimbabwe. These, like Bennet and Coltart,[13] are not part of our society. They belong to Britain and let them go there. If they want to stay here, we will say 'stay' but your place is in prison and nowhere else. Those who are compliant, let them come out and let them show they want to be part of us, otherwise time is not on their side.[14]

The judiciary was not to be left out of the campaign. A compliant judiciary was seen by the government not only as a desirable end in itself, it was also necessary to contain legal actions arising from land invasions; to avoid judicial review of Draconian legislation enacted as part of the campaign;[15] to avoid review of legislation introduced to enhance Mugabe's electoral chances; and to avoid due scrutiny of the extra-legal methods (including endemic intimidation and violence) deployed in the elections.

A compliant judiciary required the removal of those judges seen as hostile and the appointment of new judges who were perceived to be sympathetic to the government's aims. A different modus operandi was adopted in each case. Given that the High Court consisted of only twenty-three judges and the Supreme Court then of five, the reconstitution the government required did not demand extensive changes. The appointment of compliant judges was relatively easy, and underscores the evident weakness of the system of appointments provided by Britain at Lancaster House.

Appointing 'Compliant' Judges

Zimbabwe's Present System of Judicial Appointments

There are three tiers of courts in Zimbabwe: the Magistrates Courts, the High Court and, at the top of the pyramid, the Supreme Court. The Supreme Court hears appeals from lower courts. It also hears most constitutional matters, either as a court of first instance or on referral of such matters to it by the Magistrates Court and the High Court. This chapter will examine only the position of judges, and not that of the magistrates. Suffice it to say that the magistrates form part of the public service and are not appointed by the JSC. As such, they are an easy prey to governmental pressure and manipulation.[16]

The President appoints judges 'after consultation with the Judicial Services Commission.'[17] The process of consultation is ostensibly more than merely perfunctory. Section 84(2) of the constitution provides that if the appointment of a chief justice or a judge of the Supreme Court or the High Court is not consistent with any recommendation by the JSC in terms of subsection (1), the President must cause Parliament to be informed as soon as possible. This implies that the President will act upon such recommendation in the normal course of events. But if he does not, there is no consequence other than that Parliament must be informed. There is no indication of the action that Parliament may take if it is unhappy with the President's actions in this regard. Even when this process faced its severest test during the 2000–3 period, there was not a single instance where the President ignored the recommendation of the JSC. The reasons for this are twofold. First, there is no provision in the constitution laying down how candidates for possible appointment as judges are selected for consideration by the JSC. The process is legally opaque,[18] but it is commonly known that persons within the Ministry of Justice are tasked to find 'suitable persons.' Hence only candidates who are acceptable to the government are proposed to the JSC. Second, the composition of the JSC itself is of obvious importance. This is provided for in section 90(1) of the constitution and comprises:

a) the Chief Justice, or if there is no Chief Justice ... the most senior available judge of the Supreme Court;[19]
b) the Chairman of the Public Services Commission;
c) the Attorney-General; and
d) no less than two or more than three other members, with prescribed qualifications, appointed by the President.

The President appoints the chairman of the Public Services Commission under the terms of section 74 of the constitution and the President appoints the attorney-general after consultation with the JSC in accordance with section 76. The attorney-general is an ex officio member of cabinet.[20] Hence of the possible six members of the JSC, at least three and possibly four are directly appointed by the President. The remaining two are members by virtue of their office, and are themselves appointed to such office by the President after consultation with the JSC. There is no indication as to how long the members who are appointed as specific presidential appointees in terms of paragraph (d) – as opposed to being members ex officio – remain as such. It is thus not clear if such persons only sit on an ad hoc basis to consider particular appointments or whether they remain in the post indefinitely.[21] In any event, the obvious power of the President over this process is as clear as it is extensive. After the year 2000, when the President found it necessary to ensure the appointment of those sympathetic to his government, it was obvious to all that the JSC would cooperate in this regard.[22] It is also important to note that there is no limitation on the number of judges, and more particularly Supreme Court Judges, that can be appointed.

Removing 'Undesirable' Judges

Term of Office and Salaries

A judge holds office until the retirement age of sixty-five, unless, before reaching such age, the judge has elected to retire at the age of seventy. However, such election for later retirement is subject to acceptance by the President, after consultation with the JSC, of a medical report confirming the judge's mental and physical fitness to continue in office. The office of a judge may not be abolished (without his or her consent) during his or her tenure of office.[23] Further security is provided by the fact that the judges' salaries are secure and cannot be reduced[24] while they are in office and are chargeable to and payable from the Consolidated Revenue Fund. The salaries are determined under an Act of Parliament.[25]

Removal from Office

A judge may be removed from office only on the basis of an inability to discharge the functions of office, whether this inability arises from 'infirmity of body or mind or any other cause, or misbehaviour.'[26]

A tribunal appointed by the President considers the removal of a judge on the following grounds.[27] In the case of the chief justice, it is the President who considers whether the fitness of the chief justice ought to be investigated[28] and who appoints the tribunal. In the case of all other judges, the chief justice advises the President of the need for such an investigation.[29] The tribunal selected by the President consists of no less than three people. These people must hold specified qualifications. They must be either a former judge of the Supreme Court or High Court, a judge of an equivalent court from a country with a Roman-Dutch or English common law heritage and where English is an official language, or a lawyer with at least seven years standing in the profession.[30] The lawyer of at least seven years standing must be chosen by the President from a list of at least three people submitted by the profession's governing body, the Law Society of Zimbabwe.[31] However, this qualification upon the President's power may be bypassed as there is no requirement that the three are selected so that each category is represented. All three members may simply be former judges if the President so chooses. The tribunal considers the question before it, reports on its findings, and recommends to the President as to whether the question of removal should be referred to the JSC. The tribunal's procedures are governed by the *Commissions of Inquiry Act*.[32] This Act does not require public hearings, or even a publication of findings.[33] The President is obliged to act in accordance with the recommendation of the tribunal.[34] If the JSC recommends the removal of the judge, the President is also obliged to act in accordance with this recommendation. A judge is suspended from duty until the process is finalized.[35]

Once again, the President's power is extensive. He has full power to appoint persons to the tribunal whom he considers might give the sort of recommendation he would favour. Even then, the final recommendation for removal is not made by the tribunal but by the JSC. A JSC with half the members selected ad hoc and especially for the outcome the President deems desirable is both possible and legal.

Government's Actual Modus Operandi after 2000

Obviously, in the crucial 2000–3 period, the referral for investigation of all those judges the government deemed undesirable to a tribunal that had never previously been convened would have been highly suspicious – the more so if the tribunal had found each and every judge guilty of misconduct. Thus certain tentative moves were made which clearly sought to lay the groundwork for other ways to remove judges. The government's first step in this regard was to bring the judges within the ambit of its anti-white and anti-West propaganda campaign. In a manoeuvre to disenfranchise whites in the June 2000 elections, the government had introduced new laws prohibiting dual nationality.[36] The state-owned printed media then ran xenophobic articles alleging that the white judges on the bench were British and had no right to be there. Minister of Information Jonathan Moyo was reported as saying: 'No sane Zimbabwean should expect the judiciary to be headed by a foreigner – especially a British – 20 years after our independence, just like it would be insane to have a foreign or British president or speaker of parliament.'[37]

A pro-state weekly newspaper reported that at least six white judges had lost their Zimbabwean citizenship as a result of the new legislation and were British. This was followed up by a report claiming: 'A source in the President's Office had earlier told *The Zimbabwe Mirror* that Mugabe had hinted at forcing the judges to retire from the bench if it is proved that they hold dual citizenship. "President Mugabe told a South African journalist yesterday (Wednesday) that he will look into the matter of the judges and he thinks the judiciary is too British," said the source.'[38]

Although there is no constitutional requirement that judges be Zimbabwean citizens, the paper sought to get around this by claiming that a 'reliable source' had indicated: 'All currently serving judges were appointed on the understanding that they are Zimbabweans. If they are not Zimbabwean, they are guilty of deception.'[39] This attempt to lay a basis for dismissal was not pursued. The government shifted its approach to one of portraying white judges as racist relics of the former Smith regime.[40] The Minister of Justice, Legal and Parliamentary Affairs, Patrick Chinamasa, played a leading role in this vilification of white judges. In a speech delivered to the Law Society on 11 November 2000 Chinamasa set out his agenda:

> In 1965, Ian Smith tore up the Constitution in order to take the country back in history, to avoid freedom for Africans and the restoration of their sovereignty as a people ... What was the judiciary's response to this illegality. Only one judge resigned in protest, maybe two ... The rest of the judges who undoubtedly shared the racist paradise epitomized by the Smith Government expended their energies legitimizing the illegal regime ... Happily for Ian Smith, the judiciary and the executive and legislative arms shared the same racist vision. I have taken some time to dwell on this point because most of the public criticisms today centre on the perceived conflict between the judiciary and the executive. Do they have shared values and vision? I am asked to explain how judges who served the racist Smith regime so faithfully can serve this government. How can personnel so high up in the pecking order of a regime grounded in a racist grundnorm faithfully serve a democratic state? Reference is made to Mr. Justice Blackie who

> was a member of parliament for the Rhodesian Front from 1975, Mr. Justice George Smith who served as cabinet secretary for the Smith Government, the present Chief Justice Gubbay who was appointed to the bench by the Smith Government in 1977, Mr. Justice Adam who, whilst unsoiled by the UDI years,[41] somehow turned up at Lancaster House Constitutional Conference as a member of the Smith Legal team and delegation and Mr. Justice Ebrahim who was State Counsel in the Director of Public Prosecutions under the Smith regime at a time when coloured people were not accepted into the public service.

Chinamasa's anxiety to portray the judiciary as an inheritance of the Smith regime was contradicted by the facts. At the time that Chinamasa made these observations, the only judge who had not been appointed after independence was the chief justice, and even he had been elevated to the Supreme Court after independence.[42] All the other judges had formally been appointed by Mugabe. Although Chinamasa later proclaimed that the government wished to 'indigenize' the judiciary,[43] this had not been an issue until the 2000 referendum. As late as 1996 one white person and one person of mixed race were appointed to the bench.[44] As judgments on the land issue began to be handed down in favour of white farmers, the government sought to portray them as evidence of racism and 'bias in favour of the Judge's kith and kin.' This is notwithstanding the fact the some of the judgments were passed by recent pro-government appointees or by non-whites. Furthermore, given the clear lawlessness involved in the land invasions, there was little that counsel for the government could say in argument in these cases, and several key judgments on the land issue were in fact given by consent between the plaintiffs' and state counsel.[45]

Despite this vilification, the government remained anxious to be able to assert an adherence to the rule of law. Thus while comments by government ministers were often contemptuous of the judges, Chinamasa on several occasions acknowledged that his government had no power to fire judges and there was no overt and general unlawful attempt to remove them from office. It was left for the militia to take the hint. On several occasions, that which the government could not achieve lawfully, it left to the militia to do unlawfully.[46] The militia was repeatedly portrayed as being beyond the government's or anyone's control. The government announced that the concerns of the militia were political, not legal, and thus could not be solved via the police or the courts.[47] Two weeks after Chinamasa's speech to the Law Society, the militia invaded the Supreme Court demanding the removal of 'racist' judges, forcing the Court to adjourn the proceedings. There was no condemnation of this action by the government. At the end of 2000 and the start of 2001 the militia intensified its campaign against the judiciary, issuing threats to invade judges' homes and drive them from the country.[48] The most prominent militia leader, Dr Chenjerai 'Hitler' Hunzvi (then a member of Parliament),[49] vowed to oust the entire Supreme Court bench and four non-black High Court judges. He is reported to have said in Parliament: 'We are not afraid of the High Court ... this country belongs to us and we will take it whether they like it or not. The judges must resign. Their days are now numbered as I am talking to you ... I am telling you what the comrades want, not what the law says.'[50]

The deputy chairman of ZNLWVA's[51] Harare branch, Mike Moyo, warned, 'The judiciary must go home or else we will chase them and close the courts indefinitely until President Mugabe appoints replacements.'[52] This particular threat was followed by one to remove judges by force if they did not resign within a fortnight. Moyo was also quoted as saying, 'The judiciary of Ian Smith is still with us now, joined by some black puppet judges who are making their own laws instead of following laws made by Parliament.'[53]

No condemnation of this intimidation was forthcoming from the government. In view of the statements from government ministers themselves that had preceded the intimidation, even if there was no direct evidence that the militia were acting on the government's instructions, they could at least be said to be acting with its tacit approval. It seems likely that the token increase in security for judges during this period was intended to create an argument to counter this perception, rather than being prompted by any concern for the judges' well-being.[54]

While the judges found these threats intimidatory,[55] they do not appear to have caused the resignation of the High Court judges who left the bench prematurely during this period, and others stayed on. Having failed to purge the High Court of judges it found undesirable, the government deployed other strategies to undermine judicial independence.[56] Of crucial significance was the change in the method of allocating cases to the judges. Previously cases had been assigned by the registrar of the court[57] on a roster basis. Justice Chidyausiku, then judge president, halted the roster system and took direct charge of the allocation of cases – a system that was continued by the new judge president when Justice Chidyausiku was later appointed chief justice.[58] The result was that cases with important political implications were allocated to judges who were believed to be government sympathizers. Those judges seen as unwilling to do the government's bidding were sidelined. The resignation of three judges from the bench between 2001 and 2002 had more to do with the fact that they could play no role as a checking mechanism on the executive, and felt that they were merely lending credibility to an illegitimate system, than with the threats made against them by the militia.[59]

Reconstituting the Supreme Court

The key to controlling the judiciary lay in having influence over the final court of appeal, and that required replacing the incumbent chief justice, Justice Gubbay. Justice Gubbay was accordingly singled out as a special target for the hostility directed towards the bench. The judge president of the High Court, Justice Chidyausiku, whose sympathy for the ruling party had been made clear through the controversial Constitutional Commission,[60] began to position himself for the post of chief justice. In 2000 he had given a remarkable judgment that purported to suspend the effect of a Supreme Court ruling to allow the peasant occupiers of commercial farms time to bring a class action. Not surprisingly, the Supreme Court overruled his decision.[61] Chidyausiku JP then used his opening of the 2001 Bulawayo High Court session (at the very time when the campaign against the chief justice was at its most intense) to defend publicly his own judgment and criticize the Supreme Court for nullifying his decision. He further indicated that the incumbent chief justice, Justice Gubbay, should recuse himself in all cases concerning the land issue on account of a speech the chief justice had given ten years earlier. In that speech the chief justice had suggested that an attempt to amend the constitution to allow for the expropriation of land without compensation might be in conflict with the 'essential features' doctrine in relation to the constitution.[62] The chief justice, with the full support of the Supreme Court bench, publicly reprimanded Justice Chidyausiku and required him to 'avoid making inflammatory statements' on the land issue.[63] By being seen to be at loggerheads with the sitting chief justice on the land issue, Justice Chidyausiku was perfectly poised to step into Gubbay's position, anticipating correctly that the post would shortly be vacant.

OUSTING OF THE CHIEF JUSTICE

The events surrounding the ousting of the chief justice will be related in some detail, as they serve as an archetype of the methods used by the government to achieve its objectives through the exertion of behind the scenes pressure, while at the same time asserting adherence to the rule of law. Although the chief justice was to reach mandatory retirement age in fourteen months' time, the government was not prepared to wait that long. It was clear that in order to achieve its objectives the chief justice would have to be replaced before the presidential election. Furthermore, the election victories of several ZANU PF members of Parliament had been successfully challenged in the High Court. The government wanted a new chief justice in place by the time these cases came on appeal.[64] In its determination to expedite the departure of the chief justice, the government came closer to overt lawlessness than in relation to its behaviour towards any other judge.

Concerned by the verbal attacks and the physical invasion of the Supreme Court without any action or condemnation on the part of government, the chief justice and a fellow judge of appeal[65] arranged a meeting with the vice-president at the end of January 2001. Rather than receiving a sympathetic ear, the judges were lambasted in the very manner that they had come to complain about and were accused of attempts to frustrate the government's land reform 'program.'[66] It was suggested that in the heated emotions of this meeting the chief justice had said he would resign if the situation continued. Taking advantage of this the minister of justice visited the chief justice in his chambers on 2 February 2001. It is not known what happened at this meeting. However, the state-owned press indicated that the minister had determined to treat the chief justice's comments as an offer of resignation. The minister told the chief justice that his offer had been accepted. The retirement was then reported as a fait accompli. The suggestion was made in the media that a deal had been struck whereby the chief justice would go on leave from 1 March 2001 as a way of serving out the last few months before an early retirement in June of that year, some fourteen months before reaching the age of compulsory retirement.[67] While details of the agreement and what had passed between the minister and the chief justice were not made public, drawing on the events and statements from the government that had preceded the chief justice's departure, the opposition press suggested that the chief justice had effectively been forced from office.[68] Whatever arrangement was made, it swiftly unravelled. Such was the urgency with which the government wished to instal Justice Chidyausiku as chief justice that the minister of justice wrote to the chief justice on 22 February 2001 requesting that he convene a meeting of the

JSC for the purpose of appointing an acting chief justice. Through his lawyers, Gubbay indicated that he had never agreed to the appointment of an acting chief justice during his leave and that to do so would conflict with past practice and be premature.[69] The government, however, was determined that Gubbay should be gone by 1 March 2001 and Chidyausiku installed in his place. Accordingly, the minister of justice responded by publicly stating that the chief justice had reneged on the 2 February 2001 agreement.[70] This, and the refusal to convene the Judicial Services Commission,[71] the minister alleged, constituted misconduct. In the circumstances the minister said, the government had two options. One was to invoke section 87(2) of the constitution to convene a tribunal for the dismissal of the chief justice on the grounds of misconduct. The minister indicated it had chosen the other option, reportedly addressed to Gubbay CJ as follows: 'you will be paid four month's salary in lieu of leave. This means that your term of office as Chief Justice terminates on 28 February 2001, by which time you should have cleared your belongings from your chambers.'[72]

The government stated that it would regard any court over which Gubbay presided after that date as improperly constituted. The chief justice was also given ten days to vacate his official residence. This 'option' was obviously unconstitutional. The chief justice refused to leave on this basis and indicated that he would reconsider his retirement.[73] In response to a question on this issue in Parliament relating to the stand-off with the chief justice, the minister of justice stated: 'As far as government is concerned there will be no Chief Justice tomorrow. We now refer to him as former Chief Justice.'[74]

While Gubbay reported for work at his chambers on 1 March 2001, the government did not immediately put into effect its threat to convene a tribunal to investigate him for misconduct. However, various members of government responded to Gubbay's actions by insisting that he vacate his office. One minister stated, 'I don't know what he thinks he is doing in there, but this country has no chief justice. If he thinks he is going to stay he has another think coming.' Once again the comment was followed by action by the militia. The following day, Joseph Chinotimba, a prominent member of the militia and leader of the November 2000 invasion of the Supreme Court, forced his way past security into the Supreme Court building. Although unable to get to the office of the chief justice, by way of a commandeered security official's cell phone, he ordered the chief justice to leave. The order was accompanied by a threat that if the chief justice did not leave the militia would declare war on him.

Later that day Gubbay concluded an agreement drawn by his lawyers and those of the government. He agreed to the appointment of an acting chief justice and it was agreed that Gubbay would be entitled to all rights and privileges of chief justice during his leave. The government then put out an agreed statement. The government's cynicism in this regard can be readily gauged by the preceding events. In the statement Justice Gubbay was probably, though rather futilely, attempting to protect the remaining members of the bench. The statement read as follows:

> The Minister and Chief Justice acknowledged the importance of the independence of the judiciary. They affirmed that any action by any party to undermine or interfere with that independence was contrary to the interests of the people of Zimbabwe. The Minister has assured the Chief Justice, on behalf of the Government, that no steps will be taken to unlawfully cause the suspension, removal or resignation of any of the judges of Zimbabwe. The agreement recognizes the immense contribution and loyalty to Zimbabwe of the Chief Justice ...[75]

Only two months previously Mugabe had stated that Gubbay was the guardian of 'white rascist farmers.'[76] As had been widely predicted by the media[77] (in view of his prior manoeuvrings), Justice Chidyausiku was appointed acting chief justice a week later.[78] He is the first chief justice to be appointed to the post directly from the High Court and took the position ahead of numerous other judges considered senior in terms of experience and standing by the legal profession.[79] Once again the process of judicial selection can be seen to be inadequate. The media had correctly predicted Justice Chidyausiku's appointment on the basis of his clear political allegiance – rather than judicial experience, competence, or suitability. While Justice McNally was the obvious candidate for the post in terms of experience and seniority, it is arguable that a black Zimbabwean would have been more suitable. Such a candidate was available from the Supreme Court bench in the form of Justice Sandura, of greater experience and seniority than Chidyausiku and a former judge president of the High Court. Justice Sandura had not, however, shown any particular partiality to the government's policies.

Shortly after his appointment Justice Chidyausiku assured a visiting delegation of the International Bar Association (IBA) that he would protect judges from attack and uphold the rule of law and the independence of the judiciary.[80] Given that his appointment was due to the resignation of Gubbay under such pressure that the IBA regarded it as forced, and that Justice Chidyausiku had himself added to that pressure, the value to be placed on his assurances was questionable.[81]

PRESSURE ON THE REMAINING SUPREME COURT JUDGES

A week after the 2 February meeting between the chief justice and vice-president, the minister of justice began meetings with the other Supreme Court judges. They were informed that the government had lost confidence in the Bench and that a vote of no confidence in it had been passed by a ZANU (PF) parliamentary caucus. The minister claimed that the purpose of his meeting was to convey this message to the judges.[82] However, one judge revealed that they were asked to advance their retirement and resign.[83] The minister allegedly indicated that the judges' safety could not be guaranteed, though this was denied by him.[84] Justice McNally is reported to have said, 'We were told very nicely and politely we should take our leave and go, otherwise anything could happen. They didn't want me to come to any harm.'[85] Such a statement, it should be recalled, was made in a situation where anti-white propaganda was being broadcast daily by the state media and where the threat to remove white farmers from their farms had resulted in the murder of six white farmers[86] without the prosecution of any of the perpetrators – despite the fact that one group had abducted their victim from a police station.

In light of these threats the opposition[87] introduced a motion in Parliament a few days later condemning the pressure being placed on the judiciary. The government's contradictory pronouncements in this regard were highlighted on 23 February 2001, when Chinamasa in the course of the debate stated: 'we have said that time has come to indicate our displeasure and that we have withdrawn confidence in the judges. But we are not firing anybody. The judges who have decided to remain on the Bench can stay and no harm will come to them.' Later that same day, at a seminar concerning a proposed establishment of an anti-corruption commission,[88] he stated: 'I have no power to fire any judge, in as much as I do not want to see most of them remaining on the Bench. The problem is that there was foolish magnanimity on our part. We did not reform the judiciary after obtaining independence. We have a situation where litigants, especially on the land issue, bring their cases before judges, some of whom served in the same Rhodesian government that took away land from the blacks.' He then was reported to have said that the government: 'would continue to pile up the pressure on the judiciary because that seem[s] to be the only way to push them out.'[89]

Before the parliamentary debate on the issue closed, ZANU (PF) used the state-owned television station to request that all of its MPs be in Parliament on 28 February 2001. They defeated and inverted the Movement for Democratic Change motion to support the judiciary,[90] replacing it with a vote of no confidence in the judiciary. One ZANU (PF) parliamentarian stated, 'when we are at this stage of pursuing our revolution, they [judges] need also to play the tune ... they also need to bend down and do like what the revolution requires us to do.'[91] Another ZANU (PF) legislator proposed that a parliamentary commission of enquiry into the judiciary be established. Expressing his pleasure at the supposed removal of the chief justice, the MP went on to say that he did not regard 'his mandate' as complete without the removal of the entire Supreme Court bench.[92] Five days later, the militia leader, Chenjerai 'Hitler' Hunzvi, announced that he did not recognize the deal with Justice Gubbay and that he would continue his campaign, through violence if necessary, until all white judges had been removed.[93]

To their credit, notwithstanding these threats, the targeted appeal court judges remained on the bench. Chidyausiku CJ thus found himself a lone voice on a bench of five. In two key cases, one relating to the land issue and one to the elections, he gave the single minority judgment in favour of the government.[94] Chidyausiku CJ had anticipated the rather uncomfortable position of being the lone voice supportive of government on the Supreme Court bench, reportedly stating that he would not take up the appointment unless the Supreme Court was completely reconstituted. Having failed to secure the resignation of the remaining judges and thus gain control over the Supreme Court indirectly, the government decided to solve the problem by resorting to the more time-honoured method of stacking the court. Despite assurances to the International Bar Association to the contrary,[95] in July 2001 three new judges were appointed to the Supreme Court, bringing the complement of the Court to eight for the first time.[96] As one opposition newspaper noted: 'Two of those appointees were reported last weekend to have benefited from the Government's opaque land lease scheme. In other words, they will be asked to deliver judgments on the legality of a land redistribution process of which they are recipients.'[97]

All were regarded as supportive of the government and all were appointed ahead of more senior judges. Their appointments meant that the new chief justice could convene a bench composed entirely of judges known to be sympathetic to the government in ordinary cases, and a bench of five in constitutional cases with only one judge from the former Supreme Court included. The new Court immediately reversed a key judgment on the land issue given by the Gubbay Court, with a strong dissenting opinion from the single judge from the former court.[98] Since this time the newly appointed Supreme Court justices have consistently ruled in favour of the government at every possible opportunity, often on tenuous grounds.[99] The fifth judge from the former bench has almost always given a dissenting opinion.[100] Several of these judgments were crucial pillars in securing President Mugabe's controversial election victory in 2002.[101]

Gaining Further Control over the High Court

Having secured control of the Supreme Court the government continued to try to increase its influence in the High Court through both intimidation and inducement. Two judges who had given crucial judgments against the government were very shortly thereafter arrested on suspicion of criminal offences on very dubious grounds.[102] Even if the suspicion had been reasonable (and it seems that it was not in either case), it is clear that there was no need to arrest either of the two, and that summons would have been a more appropriate procedure. In one of these cases the Supreme Court determined that the arrest had been unreasonable when the matter came before it as a constitutional matter. Chidyausiku CJ did not preside over this case.[103] The arrests were clearly vindictive and intended to be intimidatory. That was the stick part of a carrot and stick approach. Compliant judges have been the beneficiaries of land handed out to government supporters. Three black women judges who had failed to secure farms for themselves are alleged to have approached the chief justice to ask him to use his influence to ensure an allocation of land to them.[104] Given that a significant proportion of cases coming before the High Court concerned land occupations, it is difficult to see how the judges' impartiality could remain intact after they had been given expropriated farms.[105] The peculiar situation was highlighted when one judge, who had moved a caravan onto a farm to secure his occupation of it, was alleged to have breached a High Court order by threatening the white farm owner.[106]

Conclusion

While the government's influence in the courts is not entirely unfettered, it is reasonably secure through partiality in the allocation of cases, intimidatory tactics, and inducements. Where these fail to produce a satisfactory outcome, the government may be reasonably confident that the reconstituted Supreme Court will deliver a more favourable judgment on appeal wherever possible. And while the government has certainly not adhered to the spirit of the law and notions of judicial independence, it is difficult to point to any area where it has breached the letter of the law in regard to judicial appointments. It has thus achieved its objective of obtaining a compliant judiciary while maintaining a façade of fidelity to the rule of law.

NOTES

1 Walter Kamba, a delegate at the Constitutional Conference, interview by author, University of Zimbabwe (17 October 2003).

2 See Madhuku, *The Constitution and the Independence of the Judiciary*, and the chapter by S.H. Bukurura in this volume.

3 Appointment by way of a Judicial Services Commission was first introduced in the 1979 constitution of Zimbabwe-Rhodesia. Until then appointments had been by the head of the executive in consultation with the chief justice. See the Federation of Rhodesia and Nyasaland Order-In-Council, 1953, s. 47, and the *Constitution of Rhodesia Act 54*, 1969, s. 63.

4 International Bar Association, *Report of Zimbabwe Mission, 2001,* 7.4 (IBA Report).

5 While the government has denied directing the militia, the facts are otherwise. See Zimbabwe Human Rights Non-Governmental Organisations Forum, *Politically Motivated Violence in Zimbabwe, 2000–2001*, and IBA Report, 38.

6 See generally *Politically Motivated Violence in Zimbabwe 2000–2001.*

7 Government adopted an *ignorantia elenchi,* using as a campaign strategy the slogan 'Zimbabwe will never be a colony again.' Britain was the prime target of this aspect of the campaign.

8 The government is the sole radio and television broadcaster in Zimbabwe, having introduced legislation that effectively makes it impossible for privately owned stations to operate. In 2003 the government used similar legislation to close the only privately owned daily newspaper, thus effectively silencing the opposition media in all but two weekly papers.

9 The Opposition Movement for Democratic Change.

10 The National Constitutional Assembly comprising various NGOs.

11 'Observers Impartiality in Doubt,' *Sunday Mail* (Harare), 11 June 2000.

12 Putsch Commey, 'African Leaders Etch Lasting Impact on Earth Summit,' *The Herald* (Harare), 25 October 2002.

13 Two white parliamentarians and members of the opposition MDC.

14 President Mugabe quoted in *The Daily News*, 30 October 2002.

15 The two most obvious examples are the *Public Order and Security Act*, chapter 11:17, and the *Access to Information and Privacy Act*, chapter 10:27. For a brief critique of these pieces of legislation, see Legal Resources Foundation, *Justice In Zimbabwe*, 9–54.

16 The head of the Public Services Commission is appointed by Mugabe under s. 74 of the constitution. The prosecution service is likewise susceptible to outside influence, and has been party to over- and under-prosecution on behalf of the government. Anecdotal evidence has indicated that all promotions in both sectors is approved by the President's Office before being rubber stamped by the Public Service Commission.

17 S. 84(1) of the constitution.

18 As an indication of the government's deliberate opaqueness in this regard it is worth noting that when two different ministries were approached for a list of judges' profiles known to be held by them for the purpose of researching this chapter, the request was refused by both on the grounds that judges are 'too important' for this information to be made public.

19 There is no indication as to who determines seniority or how it is determined.

20 S. 76(3b)(a).

21 From personal discussions with members of the legal profession and a judge, there does seem to have been some continuity in the composition of the JSC, at least until 2000.

22 New appointees to the High Court bench after 2000 were widely perceived to have personal ties to the government and ruling party. They included former non-constituency (appointed) MP and member of the government's Constitutional Commission, Rita Makarau; her law firm partner Annie Gowora; former UZ law lecturer and member of the government's Constitutional Commission, Ben Hlatswayo; ex-combatant Charles Hungwe; Godfrey Chidyausiku's brother's daughter, Antonia Guvava, formerly director of the Legal Advice Division in the Attorney-General's Office; and ex-combatant George Chiweshe (previously judge advocate in the Zimbabwe Defence Forces). See Zimbabwe Human Rights NGO Forum, *Enforcing the Rule of Law in Zimbabwe*, 43.

23 S. 86(3).

24 One way of indirectly forcing judges from office is to reduce their salaries to an unsustainable level. While Zimbabwe's constitution expressly prohibits

this, at the time of writing inflation is running at 400 per cent and rising. This means that the same effect could be achieved through the expedient of simply not increasing the salary. That power, however, vests in Parliament and not with the President.

25 S. 88.

26 S. 87(1).

27 S. 87.

28 S. 87(2).

29 S. 87(3).

30 S. 87(4).

31 S. 87(5).

32 Chapter 10:07.

33 According to the newly constituted Supreme Court, publication is at the President's discretion: *Zimbabwe Lawyers for Human Rights & Anor v. The President of the Republic of Zimbabwe* S.C. 12/03.

34 S. 87(7).

35 S. 87(8).

36 Government then (unlawfully) used the fact that some whites chose to retain a foreign nationality as a ploy to remove them from the voter's roll.

37 Farai Dzirutwe, 'Opposition Forces Triggered Political Violence,' *Sunday Mail* (Harare), 4 June 2000.

38 'Mugabe Threatens to Fire Judges,' *The Mirror* (Harare), 16 June 2000.

39 Ibid.

40 Ian Smith's Rhodesian Front party had unilaterally declared independence from Britain in 1965 in order to prevent the adoption of universal suffrage in the country.

41 A reference to the 1965 Unilateral Declaration of Independence.

42 At independence, the judiciary was exclusively white and male. See Biti, 'Judiciary Bashing, a Predatory State, and the Rule of Law in Zimbabwe,' 97–108.

43 'Indigenization' in the Zimbabwean context is understood to mean the appointment of black Zimbabweans to particular positions.

44 Justice James Devitte, an advocate well known for his human rights work while in practice, and senior advocate Michael Gillespie.

45 See IBA Report, 7.24 et seq.

46 A day after the minister of information announced that the opposition newspaper *The Daily News* would be silenced, its printing presses were destroyed by a bomb. See 'Liberators Say Bombing was Barbaric,' *Daily News* (Harare), 29 January 2001. The perpetrators were widely believed to be members of the militia. No one was arrested for the offence.

47 Mugabe was reported as saying, 'The land issue is not for the courts. It seems the judges did not hear me clearly on this one ... We will take the land in a political struggle. If the courts want compensation then they should go to Britain ... If the technicalities continue to hamper the process, I together with Vice-Presidents ... will do it on our own. The courts can do whatever they want, but no judicial decision will stand in our way. My own position is that we should not even be defending our position in the courts. We cannot ... brook interference or court impediment to the land acquisition programme.' Quoted in Zimbabwe Human Rights NGO Forum, *Enforcing the Rule of Law in Zimbabwe.* See also 'President Attacks Judiciary,' *Financial Gazette* (Harare), 14 December 2000; 'Mugabe Steps Up Anti-White Campaign,' *Zimbabwe Independent* (Harare), 15 December 2000; and Legal Resources Foundation, *Justice In Zimbabwe,* 27.

48 War veteran leader Mike Moyo stated, 'We are now moving to our next strategy and we will occupy [the judges] properties. We will only vacate their properties after they have boarded planes back to Britain.' 'Retired Chief Justice Gubbay Living in Fear,' *Daily News* (Harare), 23 February 2001.

49 Although Dr Hunzvi's war creditials have been questioned, the 'Hitler' part of his name was purportedly his nomme de guerre during the war of liberation.

50 *Parliamentary Debates* 27, 26:2686; 'Chengetai Zvaunya Chinamasa Defends Judges from War Vet Attacks,' *The Standard* (Harare), 10 December 2000.

51 Zimbabwe National Liberation War Veteran's Association.

52 To the speaker 'home' is a reference to Britain.

53 'The Judiciary Crisis in Zimbabwe: Who Is Overstepping Their Boundary,' *The Herald* (Harare), 24 January 2001.

54 Court reporter, 'War Vets Plan to Attack Judges,' *Daily News* (Harare), 14 December 2000.

55 See the IBA Report, 9.10.

56 Justices Smith and Blackie reached the age of retirement in April and July 2002 respectively. There are now no white judges on the High Court bench, as opposed to four at the commencement of the 2000 crisis.

57 The registrar is a public servant appointed by the Public Services Commission controlled by the President. He would certainly feel bound to take instructions from the judge president.

58 Justice Garwe, who had been allocated land under the government's controversial program and was generally seen as sympathetic to the government. He was appointed judge president ahead of more experienced and senior judges.

59 Interview by the author with one of the resigning judges, Harare, 27 December 2003.

60 Indicative of this is the fact that when various commissioners objected to some of the proposed clauses of the draft as being at variance with public opinion, rather than putting the issue to the vote, Chidyausiku JP announced that the draft had been accepted 'by acclamation.' The Constitutional Commission had been established by the government to draw a draft constitution for the country. Participation in its proceedings was seen as controversial as it was believed to have been established to pre-empt a similar exercise initiated by civil society which had preceded that of the government.

61 See *Commercial Farmers' Union v. Mhuriro & Others* (2000) (2) ZLR 405 (S).

62 See IBA Report, para. 10, for an analysis of this. Both Mugabe and the government's minister of information had declared Gubbay 'unfit' to hear cases involving the land issue. See the *Telegraph* report on this issue in November 2000 (available at http://www.telegraph.co.uk/news/main.jhtml?xml=/news/2000/11/06/w zim06.xml).

63 'Chief Justice Publicly Warns Chidyausikyu,' *Financial Gazette* (Harare), 18 January 2001.

64 The government had used its control over the process of allocating cases to have many of these cases heard by sympathetic judges. It then proceeded to use the same mechanism to delay the appeal process in cases where it had been unsuccessful. Although election petitions are required to be heard as a matter of urgency, nearly three years after the elections some of these petitions are still awaiting a hearing, and none have been finalized. It is clear that not all of the petitions will have been heard by the time the next elections are due. The significance of this is underlined when it is considered that, notwithstanding the manner in which ZANU PF undermined the democratic process, they only secured three more elected seats than the opposition.

65 Justice Wilson Sandura.

66 'Program' has been put in inverted commas here, as it is precisely because there was no program as such that the Supreme Court found against the government in several rulings. See Legal Resources Foundation, *Justice in Zimbabwe,* 55.

67 'Chief Justice Gubbay Retires from the Bench,' *The Herald* (Harare), 3 February 2001.

68 See, e.g., Collin Chiwanza, 'Gubbay Dismissal Unlawful,' *Daily News* (Harare), 9 February 2001.

69 Gubbay's letter to the minister was reported in *The Herald* of 27 February 2001 as follows: 'The Chief Justice is to proceed on leave on 1 March, pending his retirement on the 30th June 2001. Accordingly, in terms of section 85(1) of the Constitution, the office of the Chief Justice will neither be

vacant nor will the present incumbent be unable, for any reason, to perform the functions of his office.'

70 'Gubbay to Leave Office Tomorrow,' *The Herald* (Harare), 27 February 2001.

71 There is no indication in the constitution as to who is responsible for convening the JSC, though it seems as a matter of practice this was done by the chief justice.

72 'Gubbay to Leave Office Tomorrow,' *The Herald* (Harare), 27 February 2001.

73 'I am Not Going Says Defiant Gubbay,' *The Herald* (Harare), 28 February 2001.

74 'Gubbay Rescinds Retirement Decision,' *The Herald* (Harare), 1 March 2001.

75 Itai Musengeyi, 'Standoff Broken as Gubbay Agrees to Go,' *The Herald* (Harare), 3 March 2001.

76 'War Vets Plan to Attack Judges,' *Daily News* (Harare), 14 December 2000.

77 See, e.g., Basildon Peta, 'Chidyausiku to Replace Gubbay,' *Financial Gazette* (Harare), 23–31 January 2001.

78 He was appointed to the substantive post in August 2001.

79 In April, participants in a closed seminar organized by Zimbabwe Lawyers for Human Rights reportedly called for judicial appointments to be free of political influence. Some two hundred black lawyers petitioned the JSC against Chidyausiku's appointment as chief justice. The lawyers who protested were reportedly described by Information Minister Jonathan Moyo as 'so-called black lawyers ... speaking for Rhodesians,' 'the usual black Uncle Toms' fronting for 'the usual white liberal gang in the judiciary.' He urged them 'to desist from compromising the judiciary by making unfounded, irresponsible and malicious political attacks on targeted individual judges,' a cynical exhortation in view of the minister's own attacks. See 'Appointment of Chief Justice is President's Constitutional Prerogative,' *The Herald* (Harare), 24 May 2001, 27 June 2001.

80 IBA Report, 10.24.

81 The more so in view of the fact that Chidyausiku had suggested that he might not take up appointment as chief justice unless the Supreme Court bench was 'reconstituted.'

82 Pedzisai Ruhunya and Collin Chiwanza, 'Judge Refuses to Go,' *Daily News* (Harare), 10 February 2001.

83 'Two More Judges Targeted in Attack against Zim Judiciary,' *The Namibian* (Windhoek), 12 February 2001, available at http://www.namibian.com.na/2001/February/africa/01D281AE37.html (last accessed 11 February 2005).

84 Ruhunya and Chiwanza, 'Judge Refuses to Go.'

85 'Two More Judges Targeted in Attack Against Zim Judiciary'; see also *IBA Report*, 10.18.

86 Information supplied by the Commercial Farmers Union.

87 The Movement for Democratic Change.

88 Hosted by Transparency International Zimbabwe.

89 Luke Tamborinyoka, 'Judges to Stay,' *Daily News* (Harare), 23 March 2001.

90 The Zanu (PF) majority voted for its 'amendment' – ruled by the Speaker as 'proper, procedural and admissible' – to delete the motion in its entirety and to substitute a proposal that the President set up an (unconstitutional) enquiry into what they alleged to be unspecified 'misconduct' among the judiciary. *Parliamentary Debates* 27,24; 27,44; 27,46.

91 *Parliamentary Debates* 27,44:4383–4.

92 'Judges Angry,' *The Standard* (Harare), 4–10 February 2001. The judges were Justices Sandura, Muchetere, McNally, and Ebrahim. That two of the judges were black Zimbabweans emphasizes the fact that issue was not about 'indigenizing' the judiciary.

93 *IBA Report*, 10.20.

94 *Minister of Lands, Resettlement and Rural Development v. Paliouras & Anor* S-55-2001; *Stevenson v. Minister of Local Government & Ors* 2001 (1) ZLR 321 (H).

95 IBA Report, 12.34.

96 On a more positive note, also unprecedented was the appointment of a woman.

97 'Chidyausiku Needs to Win Public Respect,' *Zimbabwe Independent*, 24 August 2001.

98 *Minister of Lands Agriculture and Rural Resettlement & Others v. The Commercial Farmers Union* S-111-2001.

99 See Legal Resources Foundation, *Justice in Zimbabwe*, 54–78.

100 At present there is only one member of the Gubbay Court remaining on the Supreme Court bench, Justice Wilson Sandura. Of the others, Muchetere J.A. died in December 2001, McNally J.A. retired in 2001, and Ebrahim J.A. retired in March 2002.

101 *Registrar-General of Elections v. Combined Harare Residents Association & Another* S-7-2002; and see the judgments critiqued in Legal Resources Foundation, *Justice in Zimbabwe*, 79–83.

102 Justice Blackie had issued a warrant of arrest against the Minister of Justice, Legal and Parliamentary Affairs, P. Chinamasa for failing to appear in court to answer a charge of contempt and had issued a further contempt of court order against him. This resulted in the minister threatening to organize a tribunal to have the judge investigated for misconduct and a (contemptuous) diatribe against the judge by the minister of information. Shortly

thereafter, Justice Blackie was arrested on allegations of corruptly setting aside on review a woman's conviction for theft. Such reviews are presided over by two judges and Blackie J. had allegedly failed to obtain the consent of the second judge who had sat in with him in the matter. See Legal Resources Foundation, *Justice in Zimbabwe,* 34–40 for an account of this. A second judge, Justice Paradza, was arrested after finding against the government in its attempt to unlawfully dislodge the opposition party mayor of Harare.

103 The judgment is not yet available, but will presumably be reported as *Paradza v. Minister of Home Affairs & Others.*

104 Interview with a prominent human rights lawyer who did not wish to be named, 6 June 2003.

105 At the Law Society Summer School in October 2003 Justice Gwaunza, who had been allocated a farm by the government, was asked how she could preside over cases involving issues raised by land seizures. She replied that she felt she could be impartial. She was then pressed as to how she could rule on the legitimacy of a process from which she had benefited. She told the questioner to move to another question.

106 See Africa Roundup, 13 January 2003, available at http://headheeb.blogmosis.com/archives/015076.html (last accessed 11 February 2005).

17 The Politics of Judicial Selection and Appointments in Japan and Ten South and Southeast Asian Countries

DAVID M. O'BRIEN

In contrast with the increasingly contentious process of appointing federal judges and the costly and competitive state judicial elections in the United States, judicial appointments in Japan and South and Southeast Asia are generally noncontroversial, though there have been exceptions. The appointment of Japanese judges, in some respects, stands apart from other judicial appointment systems in South and Southeast Asia, namely, those in Bangladesh, Nepal, Pakistan, Thailand, Singapore, Indonesia, the Philippines, Cambodia, the Lao People's Democratic Republic, and Vietnam.[1] These latter countries, however, share family resemblances in having judicial appointments based on either (1) a separate judicial career system somewhat like Japan's; (2) a judicial career system that is part of a larger civil service system; or (3) a system that is dominated by political parties and in which judges are subject to considerable executive, legislative and party influence, oversight, and control.

Japan's Career Judiciary

Although judges are formally appointed by the prime minister and the cabinet, the Japanese judiciary enjoys a high degree of institutional independence, while individual judges exercise little judicial independence on the bench, as a result of the judicial appointment process.[2] That appears largely due to the recruitment and appointment of judges from within a career judiciary, controlled by the Legal Training and Research Institute (LTRI) and under the supervision its General Secretariat and the chief justice of the Supreme Court of Japan.

The Japanese judiciary is unitary, unlike the system of judicial federalism in Australia, the United States, and elsewhere, with both a national judicial system and separate state judiciaries. At its apex is the Supreme Court of Japan, which is composed of fifteen justices who generally decide cases as petty benches composed of five justices each; major cases and administrative matters are decided by the entire Court, which sits *en banc* as the Grand Bench.[3] Below the Supreme Court are eight high courts, located in the major cities, as well as six branches in other cities. There are approximately 331 high court judges, appointed by the cabinet on the recommendation of the Supreme Court and subject to periodic reassignments and mandatory retirement at age sixty-five. Appeals to these courts come from district courts and family courts. District courts are the principal trial courts of the system. There are 50 of them, located in all major cities and another 203 branches in smaller towns. There are also 50 family courts and 203 branches located alongside the district courts. They have specialized jurisdiction over family and domestic matters and utilize conciliation procedures. Unlike other courts in Japan, they are staffed primarily by lay conciliators, appointed by the Supreme Court. Below these courts are 438 summary courts with 806 judges, who have jurisdiction over minor civil and criminal cases.

The Japanese judicial system now employs more than 21,000 judges, clerks, secretaries, marshals, and other personnel. The LTRI turns out virtually all the country's attorneys, prosecutors, and judges. The entire system is supervised by the Supreme Court, with primary responsibility under the direction of the chief justice and the General Secretariat. The latter consists in one secretary general, seven bureau chiefs, and about 800 judges and other officials. Consequently, Japanese judges and courts are highly professional and tightly controlled, in contrast to the decentralized, relatively non-bureaucratic, and far more independent federal courts in the United States.

With the exception of Supreme Court justices, the lower courts are staffed by career judges who must survive a series of professional hurdles, beginning with admission into a university. Unlike legal education in the United States, but like that in Great Britain, Germany, and France, students study law as undergraduates and earn a BA in law. After graduation, most take bar exam cram courses in preparation for the National Law Examination. That test, which may be taken numerous times, is rigorous. Out of the more than 20,000 students who annually take the test, only about 1,000 pass; prior to changes in the 1990s only about 500 were permitted to pass. Graduates of the leading law schools tend to be favoured. However, in 2004 several public and private universities opened new law schools. After two to three years of study, students in these programs nevertheless still need to be admitted into the LTRI.

Only after passing the national examination, submitting a thesis, and passing a personal interview are students admitted into the LTRI. There, at government expense, they pursue a two-year course of study. After graduating they may then apply to become assistant judges, although there are only as many positions as there are vacancies due to retirements, which amount to approximately a hundred a year. Some students are deemed unsuited and denied appointments, though the number has steadily declined from thirty-four in the 1970s to fifteen in the 1980s and a single rejection in the 1990s.[4] Still others are discouraged by faculty at the LTRI from applying for judgeships.

Judicial careers begin with a ten-year appointment as an assistant judge, another apprenticeship. But assistant judges function like full judges after five years. They may become associate judges on a three-judge district court or preside over a single-judge court. After a decade, they become full judges, though subject to reappointment every ten years. During the course of their careers, they are reassigned many times and to several different courts, or to other positions within the judiciary, such as to the LTRI or as law clerks at the Supreme Court. A judge may move from a district court to being an acting high court judge, sitting as a so-called left-hand associate. After five more years, the judge may then become a regular high court judge, sitting on the right side of a more senior presiding judge; the designation of left- and right-hand judges denotes their seniority. Eventually, the judge may be elevated to the position of a presiding judge on a three-judge court. A very few are then given an opportunity to become chief judges (presidents) on Japan's most prestigious high courts. From that select group, who will by now have reached their mid-sixties, a few will be rewarded with an appointment to the Supreme Court or to the most coveted position of chief justice. The chief justice ranks in status with the prime minister, the only other government official ceremoniously appointed by the emperor. The chief justice recommends to the Judicial Conference of the Supreme Court and to the cabinet all lower court appointees and reappointments, consults on appointments to the Supreme Court, and otherwise oversees the entire operation of the judiciary.

Already selective, the Japanese judiciary becomes increasingly competitive the higher up a judge moves within the judicial hierarchy. Over the years and along the way, a few are denied reappointments; however, the number of rejections has declined from seven in the 1950s to three in the 1960s, one in 1970, none in the 1980s and 1990s, and one in 2003. Many more, though, are encouraged to abandon their judicial careers and to move into private practice. Reassignment to less desirable courts, salary rankings, and the remote but real possibility of being denied reappointment are powerful incentives for achieving conformity.

Unlike lower court judges, not all members of the Supreme Court are career judges. The appointment process and tenure for Supreme Court justices is also somewhat different from that for lower court judges. The drafters of the constitution and the Court Organization Law of 1947 modelled the appointment process for justices along the lines of the so-called Missouri Plan.[5] The basic elements of the plan are as follows: (1) a nonpartisan commission nominates three candidates for every vacancy; (2) from those three, the governor appoints one judge; and (3) the judge must then be approved by the voters at the next general election. If approved, the judge receives a twelve-year appointment.

Although modelled after the Missouri Plan, the constitutional and statutory provisions for the appointment of Supreme Court justices have been modified or circumvented. When a vacancy occurs in the Supreme Court, cabinet officials consult with the chief justice and the General Secretariat, who oversee the appointment and assignments of lower court judges, as well as bar associations and administrative heads if a practitioner, administrator, or a diplomat is to be appointed. As with the selection and promotion of lower court judges, the chief justice largely determines the appointments of members of the Supreme Court, including his own successor. In other words, appointments are formally made by the prime minister and the cabinet, but only on the recommendation of the chief justice. There is no 'advice and consent' process comparable to the U.S. Senate's confirmation of the President's nominees to federal courts. As a result, little media attention is paid to judicial appointments in Japan, and the appointment of Supreme Court justices, like lower court judges, becomes known only after the fact.

The selection and appointment of justices is also conditioned by the stipulation in Article 31(1) of the Court Organization Law that they 'shall be among persons of broad vision and extensive knowledge of law, who are not less than 40 years of age.' That article further specifies:

> At least 10 of them shall be persons who have held one of the positions mentioned in item (1) or (2) for not less than 10 years, or one or more of the positions mentioned in the following items for the total of 20 years or more: (1) President of the High Court; (2) Judges; (3) Judges of the Sum-

> mary Court; (4) Public Prosecutors; (5) Lawyers; (6) Professors or assistant professors in legal science in universities which shall be determined elsewhere by law.

In practice, only those who have reached the pinnacles of their careers are considered, and a convention was established, in the words of Chief Justice Yakaahi Hattori, that 'Supreme Court justices are appointed in roughly equal numbers from among three broad groups: (1) inferior court judges; (2) practising lawyers; and (3) public prosecutors, law professors, or other persons of broad knowledge and experience.'[6] Even that ratio in representation has evolved over the years. The rule became for there to be six career judges, four lawyers, two former bureaucrats, two prosecutors, and one law professor on the Supreme Court. As the ratio of career judges, lawyers, bureaucrats, and law professors changed, the balance tipped farther towards reinforcing the influence of the chief justice and General Secretariat over the composition of the Court.

No less significantly, somewhat like the Missouri Plan, the constitution of Japan provides for a system of judicial retention elections, or 'popular review' as it is known. After their appointment, according to Article 79(2), members of the Court 'shall be reviewed by the people at the first general election of the members of the House of Representatives following their appointment.' Thereafter, justices face retention elections after each ten years of service. Under the system, voters place an 'X' in a box next to the name of a justice they think should be dismissed; otherwise, the ballot is counted as a vote for retention. Popular review has been rendered virtually meaningless, however, since voters know very little about the justices and there is little media coverage. Moreover, an end-run around the system has been made by the practice of appointing older and older justices. Justices are simply not on the bench long enough to stand for election after ten years. Article 50 of the Court Organization Law mandates retirement at age seventy, and because justices are typically appointed in their sixties, few face retention elections, and none have been rejected. Furthermore, the average age of appointees has inched up incrementally from 61.2 in the 1950s to 62.9 in the 1960s, 63.7 in the 1970s, and 64 in the 1980s and 1990s.[7] Appointing older justices results in higher levels of turnover, and the chief justice and the General Secretariat in turn have more opportunities to reward a greater number of those who have reached the peak of their careers and proven loyal and reliable.

In sum, the appointment of judges in Japan is largely determined by the recruitment, training, and promotion of career judges admitted into the LTRI and overseen by the chief justice and the General Secretariat. Most judges begin their careers in their mid-twenties and serve until sixty-five, though some may extend their careers until age seventy by serving on the Supreme Court or a summary court. Throughout their careers they have periodically spiralling assignments in various courts within the overarching judicial hierarchy. Their careers are governed by senior judges and the central personnel bureaucracy of LTRI. These two features – spiralling career paths within a judicial hierarchy that is closely overseen and controlled by a judicial bureaucracy – set the Japanese judiciary apart not only from other judicial selection systems within Asia (with the possible exception of South Korea), but also from those in Western Europe and North America. Not even Germany's judicial system,[8] which Japan's judicial system most closely resembles, shares both of these features. From beginning to end, Japanese judicial careers are determined by senior judges and judicial peers, not political branches or agencies outside the courts. As a result, the Japanese judiciary maintains its institutional independence and integrity, though at the price of conformity and the sacrifice of the independence of individual judges on the bench.

Judicial Appointments in South and Southeast Asia

Like Japan, the ten countries in South and Southeast Asia examined here all have unitary judicial systems, though Pakistan is a federal state and it and some other countries also have separate religious courts. However, unlike Japan, and with the exception of Singapore, all are economically developing countries and in the continuing process of making transitions to democracy and establishing the rule of law. As a result, judicial systems in these countries confront serious economic problems in judicial administration that also affect the recruitment and appointment of judges. Unlike Japan, each of these countries is also ethnically and culturally diverse and bears some legacy of colonialism.

In spite of the diversity and variations, the processes of judicial appointment in South and Southeast Asia revolve around basically three systems. First, somewhat as in Japan, judicial appointments are made from national judicial career systems in Pakistan, Thailand, and the Philippines. Second, judges are appointed from a career judiciary that is part of the country's general civil service system in Bangladesh, Nepal,

Singapore, and Indonesia. Third, Cambodia, the Lao People's Democratic Republic, and Vietnam have mixed or non-career judicial appointment systems in which the executive, legislature, and ultimately political parties exercise the principal influence over, if not completely control, judgeships.

Separate Independent Judicial Career Systems

Pakistan, Thailand, and the Philippines have separate judicial career systems, modelled along the lines of the Japanese system and those in Western Europe. Yet, each is different.

Pakistan has a system of superior and subordinate courts combined with a third tier of special courts and administrative tribunals.[9] The superior judiciary includes the Supreme Court, composed of the chief justice and sixteen justices; four high courts for different provinces that have between six and fifty judges; and a federal Shariat Court for Islamic disputes. The subordinate courts are civil and criminal district (trial) courts. Special sessions courts, along with high courts, deal with banking controversies, and quasi-judicial tribunals handle other specialized matters such as tax disputes.

Judicial appointments are made after a combination of civil service examinations, conducted by the Public Service Commission in each province, and interviews by panels of senior high court judges for the appointments of regular subordinate judges. District and sessions judges may be promoted from positions as civil judges or magistrates; members of the practising bar may also apply after ten years of experience and taking the public service exam. For superior courts – the regional high (appeals) courts and the Supreme Court – appointments are made from senior judges and lawyers by the President based on consultations with the chief justice and the regional government in which a high court vacancy is filled. These judges may be drawn either from district or sessions courts, or from the practising bar if they are at least forty-five years old.

In appointing the chief justice the President and the government have considerable discretion, but for all other superior court appointments, the recommendation of the chief justice is deemed binding.[10] As with high court judges, however, Supreme Court justices may be appointed on a permanent or a temporary ad hoc basis. In practice, the selection and appointment of justices is also governed by an unwritten rule for maintaining representation of provinces on the Supreme Court, similar to the practice in the nineteenth century of maintaining geographical representation on the Supreme Court of the United States.

Historically, there have been recurring power struggles between the executive, regardless of the political party in power, and the chief justice and the Supreme Court over judicial appointments. In 1996, the Supreme Court of Pakistan issued an extraordinary and historic decision in what is known as the 'Judges' Case,'[11] asserting its power and laying down new rules for executive-judicial relations in the appointment of justices. The ruling held, among other matters, that ad hoc judges could not be named to the Court in lieu of filling permanent positions; acting chief justices could be appointed for a maximum of ninety days and could not consult with the executive branch on the appointment of judges; and the senior-most judge of a high court should be appointed as chief justice, unless there were persuasive reasons for not doing so. Most importantly, the constitutional provision authorizing executive appointment of judges 'after consultation' with the chief justice was interpreted to mean that the chief justice's recommendations on judicial appointments are binding on the executive.

Tensions between the judiciary and the government again erupted over the appointment of Chief Justice Sajjad Ali Shah in 1997. Ten justices of the Supreme Court ruled that his appointment was illegal; he was forced to go on leave and retired in 1998. The following year, the government of Nawaz Sharif was overthrown in a military coup led by General Parvez Musharraf. He in turn required judges to swear an oath of loyalty to him and the coup. Several justices refused to do so, but in 2000 the Supreme Court upheld the imposition of military rule,[12] drawing criticism that judicial independence and the rule of law were thereby sacrificed.

Thailand has one of the most complex unitary judicial systems in the region. There is a separate constitutional court, a Supreme Court, a court of appeals, and over a hundred trial courts in cities and provinces, along with nine provincial juvenile courts. There are also special courts with limited jurisdiction for labour, child and family, bankruptcy, and international trade disputes. With the exception of its constitutional court, Thailand has a career judicial system. All judges are career civil servants. Notably, Thailand's fifteen-member constitutional court is the only judicial body empowered to exercise judicial review, but that review is restricted to laws passed by the legislature and does not extend to regulations or rules issued by the executive branch.

Five justices on the constitutional court are appointed based on their election by the Supreme Court, two others based on their nomination and election by the administrative court. All other judges are appointed by the Judicial Service Commission (JSC), which monitors written and oral examination. The JSC is chaired by the chief justice of the Supreme Court and includes twelve other members elected (four each) by law school deans, political scientists, and representatives of major political parties.

Judicial candidates must be at least twenty-five years old and hold a BA in law. If they pass the examination, they are admitted to a year-long traineeship or internship, working for four different judges – two of whom handle criminal matters and two involved with civil litigation. As civil servants, judges (except on the constitutional court, where terms are limited to nine years) serve on the bench until they reach the mandatory retirement age of sixty. They may, however, be reappointed to two five-year terms and serve on the bench until age seventy. In spite of having a civil service judiciary and codes of conduct, the code is infrequently enforced and the bar association remains weak. As a result, the Thai judiciary faces serious problems in recruiting qualified people and is considered (along with the judiciaries in Bangladesh, the Philippines, and Indonesia) to be one of the most corrupt in South and Southeast Asia.

The Philippines has a unitary judicial system that includes the Supreme Court, composed of fifteen justices; and a court of appeals, which sits in separate regional divisions and consists of a presiding justice and fifty-two associate judges. Below the high courts are thirteen metropolitan and municipal trial courts; there is also a separate court for tax appeals and tribunals for family, commercial, and Sharia (Islamic) law.[13]

The Philippines's 1993 constitution vests the power in the President to appoint judges; the appointments are not subject to confirmation by the Senate and the House of Representatives. But in practice, since 1986 the Judicial and Bar Council has recommended a list of potential appointees to vacancies in the judiciary, from which the President makes the appointments. The Judicial and Bar Council includes the chief justice of the Supreme Court, the secretary of justice, a representative of Congress, a member of the Philippines Bar Association, a law professor, a retired Supreme Court justice, and a representative of the private sector. The President and the legislature nonetheless exercise considerable influence over judicial appointments, since the President retains final authority over appointing judges and the legislature approves the composition of the Judicial and Bar Council.

Besides constitutional requirements, such as age, judicial candidates must pass (as of 2001) a course given by the Philippines Judicial Academy. While this process and the central role accorded to the Judicial and Bar Council aim at promoting meritorious judicial nominees, in practice the President and the Judicial and Bar Council confront lobbying and considerable pressure from political parties, bar associations, other interest groups, and the legal academy. These external political pressures on the judicial recruitment process may serve to strengthen judicial accountability, but they also extract a cost and appear to promote the dependency of judges and courts on external political bodies and interest groups.

Judicial Career Systems That Are Part of the Civil Service System

Bangladesh, Nepal, Singapore, and Indonesia include judgeships, at some or all levels, within their larger national civil service systems. Despite that commonality, there are crucial differences in recruiting and selecting judges among these countries.

Since becoming an independent state in 1971, Bangladesh has preserved its common law traditions.[14] Bangladesh has no separate constitutional court but instead maintains a two-tier judicial system, along with special criminal and civil courts. The Supreme Court is at the apex of the judiciary yet works by high court appellate divisions that include approximately fifty judges. Below are district and magistrates courts. Other courts include those for trials of public servants; a tribunal for crimes against women and children; courts under the *Special Powers Act* of 1974; courts with jurisdiction over administrative, bankruptcy, environmental, labour, and family disputes; juvenile courts; and other courts for civil matters.

Traditionally, Bangladesh employed a slightly different appointment system for each of three levels of courts: Supreme Court justices, judges on subordinate courts, and magistrates. The first are appointed by the President, whereas the latter two are named by the President upon the recommendation of the chief justice and the prime minister. In practice, when the chief justice retires, the next senior justice is elevated.

The career path for the 746 subordinate lower court judges in 61 district courts, and for magistrates, begins with passing an examination given by the Public Service Commission, after completing an undergraduate BA in law. Approximately 100,000 graduates compete for the 600 to 1,000 annual vacancies. Assistant judges are recruited through this process by the Ministry of Justice; the ministry in turn makes recommendations for the appointment and promotion of judges to the Supreme Court, which generally acts accordingly.

However, in a historic decision with sweeping implications for the appointment of judges and the operations of courts, the Bangladesh Supreme Court Appellate Division held in the 1999 *Masdar Houssain* case that a constitutional amendment was not necessary for ensuring the independence of the judiciary. The case was brought by two hundred lower court judges, who argued that they should be independent of the national civil service system.[15] The Supreme Court agreed, and on the basis of its interpretation of the constitution and the importance of judicial independence, issued twelve directives that, when fully implemented, may strengthen the independence and separation of the judiciary, including its control over the process for judicial appointments. Among the directives, the government was directed to provide a separate budget for the Supreme Court, which it has done. The government was also directed to separate the recruitment of judges from the Bangladesh civil service and to establish a Judicial Service Commission (JSC) for the recruitment, appointment, and promotion of judges, which continues to be conducted by the Ministry of Law, Justice and Parliamentary Affairs in consultation with the Supreme Court. In addition, the government was directed to reorganize the judiciary and specifically barred from ad hoc recruitment and reassignments of judges to work as legal officers for governmental ministries. Although four years after the ruling in *Masdar Hossain* the government has yet to fully implement all of the directives and has repeatedly sought delays in their implementation, the media and bar association have given them extensive attention and promoted public awareness and debate over the importance of a separate, independent judiciary with its own appointment system removed from the national civil service system.

Whereas the common law tradition remains firmly rooted in Pakistan, it made inroads in Nepal only in the last half-century.[16] Nepal's 1990 constitution established a legal system that remains modelled on the continental system and the Napoleon Code. Nepal has one Supreme Court, which has jurisdiction over matters referred to it by the King's council, constitutional amendments, and civil and criminal appeals from appellate and other special courts. There are 16 courts of appeal, with jurisdiction over civil and criminal appeals of decisions rendered by 75 district courts, and a total of 237 judges.

Nepal combines a judicial career/civil service system in ways that minimize the external influences of the executive and legislative branches over judicial recruitment. Moreover, in the high courts, Nepal has a mechanism – the so-called Coordination Committee – for recruiting both career and non-career judges, thereby providing opportunities for divergent views on the bench.

In general, judicial appointments to regular courts in Nepal are made by the King based on recommendations of the Judicial Council. The Judicial Council is composed of the chief justice, the minister of justice, two senior Supreme Court justices, and a jurist named by the King. The chief justice is appointed on the recommendation of the Constitutional Council. The Constitutional Council's composition is basically that of the Judicial Council, except that it includes the opposition leader in the House of Representatives. Since 1990 the practice has been to elevate the senior associate justice to the chief justiceship, thereby minimizing political conflicts over that pivotal position, which heads the Judicial Council and oversees the appointment of all regular judges. By contrast, judges on the military court are appointed by the army from a pool of commissioned officers. Appointments to administrative, labour, tax, and special courts are made by the government from regular appellate court judges, senior lawyers, experienced administrators, and tax experts.

Regular lower court judges are appointed by the Judicial Council and judges recruited for the district courts must have passed a judicial service test administered by the Civil Service Commission (CSC). The CSC recommends judicial nominees to His Magistry's Government (HMG), which prepares a list of candidates for judicial service, subject to their approval by the chief justice, who has the formal power of making appointments. The Judicial Council also makes recommendations for the appellate bench and typically solicits recommendations from the Nepal bar association, which actively monitors judicial appointments and charges of judicial corruption. For appointments to appellate courts and the Supreme Court, the Judicial Council works with a Coordination Committee in order to achieve a mix of career and non-career judges on the high courts. The Nepal bar association, including practising attorneys and academics, provides lists of eligible lawyers for appointment to appellate courts and the Supreme Court, and assesses the qualifications of proposed judicial nominees for the Judicial Council. In practice, career judges generally outnumber non-career judges on the appellate courts and in the Supreme Court.

Singapore's judges are among the highest paid not only in Asia but in the world, and its judiciary is considered one of the most reliable. Nonetheless, lower court judgeships in Singapore are not considered highly prestigious, largely because they are temporary assignments for those serving in the country's civil service system. Singapore has a constitutional tribunal that sits apart from the Supreme Court, a high court, and a court of appeals. Below these courts are subordinate courts with specialized jurisdiction.[17] They include civil and criminal courts, juvenile and family courts, coroner's courts, and small claims courts. Singapore has a mixed career judicial selection, appointment, and promotion system. The President, on the recommendation of the prime minister, appoints the chief justice and other members of the Supreme Court, court of appeals judges, and 'Judicial Commissioners' – members of the Supreme Court who have only limited terms, but who may receive a full-term appointment and who nevertheless otherwise exercise full judicial powers. These high court judges and justices tend to be recruited from the attorney-general's office. Very few come directly from private legal practice; for more than a decade no member of the Supreme Court was appointed from private legal practice until the appointment of Chief Justice Yong Pung How in 1999.

Recruitment for the subordinate courts is done by the Singapore Legal Service, composed of the chief justice, the attorney-general, the chair of the Civil Service Commission, another member of the Singapore Supreme Court, and two additional members of the Civil Service Commission. Notably, subordinate judges tend not to make their careers serving on the bench but are periodically transferred to other positions within the public legal service. In addition, they face periodic performance reviews and no security of judicial tenure.

By and large, judicial appointments are politically non-controversial, and none have been challenged constitutionally. The judicial appointment process, even at the high court levels, has little transparency and the public shows little concern over the lack of publicity. Since subordinate judges serve limited terms and are frequently transferred to other positions within Singapore's legal services, judges enjoy little prestige, apart from being civil servants, and there is little appreciation for judicial independence apart from general standards for the civil service.

Indonesia, like the Philippines, has developed a unitary and consolidated judicial system. Under its Supreme Court, which includes 51 justices and works by divisions, there are four sets of courts with different jurisdictions: first, regular courts – 26 appeals courts and 326 trial courts – with general civil and criminal jurisdiction; second, 305 courts with jurisdiction over religious matters; third, military courts; and fourth, courts with limited jurisdiction over disputes with the government and administrative agencies.[18]

In Indonesia, judges are civil servants subject to selection, appointment, transfers, and promotion by the Ministry of Justice, a part of the executive branch. However, in 2004 responsibility for judicial recruitment from the ranks of the civil service transferred to the Supreme Court, thereby, perhaps, diminishing some of the external political influences on the judiciary and increasing the control of the Supreme Court over lower court judges. Still, the approximately two hundred annual new judicial recruits will continue to be selected by the Ministry of Justice, after they have earned high grades and a BA from a law school. They must then pass written and oral examinations before admission into a one-year program at the Ministry of Justice Education and Training Center. Upon graduation, they are assigned to a district court for more training before becoming government employees as judges and beginning their judicial careers. Unlike the training program for judges in Japan, however, until their appointments as full-time government employees, judicial recruits in Indonesia do not receive full or adequate state funding. Thus, the judicial recruitment process works to disadvantage poor and middle-class candidates interested in pursuing a judicial career. Moreover, judicial recruitment in Indonesia is burdened by low prestige and salaries and inadequate court facilities, especially in rural areas. Furthermore, like other Indonesian civil servants, judges face civil service performance reviews and work under its direction for promotions and transfers. They must retire at age fifty-five unless they are promoted to a high court or the Supreme Court, in which case they may retire at age sixty and sixty-five, respectively.

Party-Dominated Judicial Systems

Cambodia, Lao, and Vietnam all have party-dominated judiciaries. While they share much in common, there are important differences. Cambodia, Lao, and Vietnam bear the imprint of the continental civil law tradition, but each in its own way reflects an unique accommodation of traditional legal cultures with more recently imported socialist legal influences.[19]

Notably, judges in these three countries are appointed for very short (usually five-year) terms, with no employment security. They are paid very low salaries, suffer from inadequate court facilities, and remain subject to extensive oversight by local and national party officials. In Vietnam, for instance, lower court judges are paid about US$20 per month, barely enough for a judge to live on and not enough to support a family. In Lao judges on the Supreme People's Court receive about US$26 per month, and lower court judges are paid between US$22 and $23 per month.

Judicial recruitment is also difficult: inadequate legal education and training facilities have led in turn to a shortage of lawyers, particularly in Cambodia and Lao, and until very recently in Vietnam. Cambodia has only 249 registered members in its national bar association – the only persons authorized to practice law – in a country of 11 million people. Those who have law degrees earned them in Vietnam or Russia. Judges in Lao may have degrees from Vietnam's only law school, in the capital Vientiane, which only recently was transformed from a post-secondary school and still has inadequate facilities, personnel, and instructional materials. After graduating, judicial candidates must complete a one-year on-the-job training program, but are not required to take and pass a bar examination.

Unlike Lao and Vietnam, Cambodia has a separate constitutional court, below which is the Supreme Court (as of 1997), an appellate court, eighteen provincial courts, two municipal courts, and a military court. There are only 139 judges, of which less than half have law degrees, a result of Pol Pot and the Khmer Rouge's purging and extermination of the educated classes between 1975 and 1979.

Under the 1993 constitution, Cambodian judges are formally appointed and promoted by the King in accordance with recommendations of the Supreme Council of Magistracy and the Ministry of Justice. Prior to 1993 they were appointed and promoted by the Ministry of Justice in the executive branch and under the control of the Communist Party, after the overthrow of the Khmer Rouge by the Vietnamese military. But in practice, recent judicial appointments have been made on the basis of brokered deals among the leading three political parties. There were no clear, established rules for judicial selection and promotion, although demonstrated party loyalty and connections are necessary.

In 2002, however, the prime minister issued a decree establishing a Magistrates School and laying down minimal qualifications for judicial applicants. Under the new guidelines, individuals may apply for judicial positions if they have an undergraduate law degree and are at least twenty-one years old and not older than thirty, or if they have a post-graduate degree and are less than thirty-eight years old. Applicants from within the government must have the same qualifications and at least five years of governmental experience; candidates nominated by the government need have only a BA and five years' government experience.

Although individuals' applications for judgeships are considered, the judiciary has very low prestige. Low salaries, inadequate facilities, and a reputation of being ineffective, corrupt, and subject to reversal and reprisals from party officials mean that the recruitment of judges in Cambodia remains extremely problematic.

Lao has a three-tier system with the Supreme Court at the apex, three regional appellate courts, and trial courts in provinces and municipalities. There are also special military courts. In Lao, judges are civil servants and do not undergo special legal training apart from a one-year internship. There are 194 judges in the country, with 9 on the Supreme Court, 95 provincial courts, and 90 district court judges.

Since 1993, the Ministry of Justice has appointed either practitioners or new law school graduates from the one law school in Vientiane for a one-year period of on-the-job-training in local district courts. The president of the constitutional court then evaluates them and, with the consent of the provincial authority and counterparts in the Lao Revolutionary Party at the provincial and district levels, recommends to the Ministry of Justice their appointment as 'provisional judges,' before their actual appointment by the Standing Committee of the National Assembly. Judges are also promoted and disciplined on the recommendation of the Ministry of Justice by the Standing Committee of the National Assembly. But as in Cambodia, there is a dearth of skilled and trained lawyers and judges, as well as poor legal education facilities from which to recruit judges.

In Lao as in Vietnam, although judges are civil servants, a single political party governs all branches of government, including the judiciary. The Lao People's Revolutionary Party not only controls the legislature, executive, and judicial branches, its party organization parallels all levels of the governmental structure, from the top down to the local grassroots level. Party committees monitor, and ultimately control, judges and other governmental officials and civil servants. In other words, judicial appointments, promotions, assignments, and tenures are subject not only to hierarchical controls and oversight within the government, but also to external party pressures at regional and local levels of governance, as are judges in Cambodia and Vietnam.

Vietnamese courts are under the supervision of the National Assembly and the Communist Party. There is a three-tiered system of courts: the Supreme People's Court, 61 People's Courts at the provincial level, and 620 People's Courts at the district level. Since 1994, there has also been a court with limited jurisdiction over economic disputes, and two other specialized courts for administrative and labour disputes, as well as a military court. The Supreme People's Court and provincial people's courts work by divisions for criminal, civil, economic, labour, and administrative matters.

In 2002 Vietnam undertook judicial reforms that provide detailed guidelines for the selection, appointment, promotion, and discharge of judges. But, as of late 2003, the Standing Committee of the National Assembly had failed to release them. Under guidelines laid down in the Court Organization Law of 1993, judges must be 'loyal to the motherland,' and 'firmly defend the socialist legal system.' They must at least have a law degree and demonstrate a 'judicial capacity of resolving cases,' as well as four years of legal experience for appointment as a district judge, six years for appointment as a provincial judge, and at least eight years of legal experience to qualify for an appointment to the Supreme Court. Previously, because of the lack of legally trained people, most of the district court judges were selected from the military and local leaders in the Communist Party, but in the last five years the practice has been to appoint experienced law clerks to district courts and to elevate district court judges to positions on higher courts.

As in the Lao People's Democratic Republic, the selection and promotion of Vietnamese judges is subject to close internal and external supervision, though somewhat greater influence by the chief justice is exercised over the selection and appointment of lower court judges. The President appoints the chief justice of the Supreme People's Court. The President also appoints the other justices of the high court, but only with the agreement of the chief justice and the Central Committee on Judicial Selection (CJS) of the National Assembly.

Lower court judges are appointed by the chief justice on the CJS's recommendation, and in practice after consulting the Party Committee are responsible for monitoring the court on which a vacancy is to be filled. Indeed, judicial applicants must have the approval of the local party committee and submit its vote on the candidate's application. Likewise, promotions, transfers, and salaries are determined by the chief justice and the chief judge of a local court in consultation with the head of the local party committee. Moreover, Vietnamese judges serve only five-year terms – terms timed to elections for the National Assembly – and they are not guaranteed reappointments or promotions; indeed, when their terms expire, judges must reapply for a new position and complete a new application form. As noted earlier, Vietnamese judges are among the most poorly paid judges in the region, and judgeships are considered only part-time employment. Hence, there is a strong internally dependent relationship between lower court judges and chief judges and the chief justice, as well external supervision by the national, regional, and local Communist Party committee.

Conclusion

The sources of influence and control over judicial appointments vary considerably from Japan to and throughout South and Southeast Asia. In Japan, although judges are formally appointed by the prime minister and the cabinet, under the control of the Liberal Democratic Party for most of the last half-century, judges are part of a highly professional career judiciary supervised by the Legal Training and Research Institute and its General Secretariat and the chief justice of the Supreme Court. There have been no major public controversies over judicial appointments; indeed, they lack public visibility.

By contrast, in the single-party dominated countries of Lao and Vietnam, judges are recruited, appointed, and promoted under the close supervision of the Lao People's Revolutionary Party and the Communist Party, respectively. Cambodia has few qualified lawyers and relatively few judges, who are appointed by the King but on the basis of brokered deals among the three leading and competing political parties in the legislature.

In Thailand, judges are career civil servants appointed and under the direction of the Judicial Service Commission; in Singapore and Indonesia, they are part of the national civil service system. In the Philippines, the Judicial and Bar Council recommends judicial nominees to the President, who formally appoints judges, though both the Judicial and Bar Council and the executive branch face considerable pressure and lobbying from competing political parties, bar associations, and interest groups.

In South Asia, the Pakistan judiciary has often been under enormous pressure and engaged in power struggles with the government – regardless of which political party was in power or whether under military rule. Still, the chief justice, the Supreme Court, and higher court regional judges largely determine the appointment and promotion of lower court judges. Likewise, the chief justice and the Bangladesh Supreme Court exercise considerable influence over judicial appointments and have directed the government to create a separate Judicial Service Commission for the training and recruiting of judges. In Nepal, the King formally appoints judges, but in practice only on the recommendation of the Judicial Council, which is headed by the chief justice of the Supreme Court.

In spite of the range of differences in the principal sources of influence and control over the recruitment and appointment of judges in South and Southeast Asia, several commonalities stand out. First, with the exception of a few controversial appointments in Bangladesh and Pakistan, judicial recruitment and appointments are generally noncontroversial, largely because the selection processes lack transparency and command little public attention. Second, except for Japan and national supreme courts in the other countries, lower court judges in South and Southeast Asia enjoy low or even little prestige. Third, in most countries in South and Southeast Asia, even those that base judicial recruitment on open civil service examinations, there are *no well-established criteria or guidelines* for judicial appointments. The absence of transparency is particularly acute in countries like Cambodia, Lao, and Vietnam. But even in countries like the Philippines, Thailand, and Bangladesh, which employ civil service examinations, the criteria for judicial appointments remains opaque. Finally, the problem of the lack of transparency also relates to the *process of selection, appointment, and promotion*. Whether the process is controlled by bodies external to the judiciary or centralized and internalized within the judiciary itself, the actual process in most countries appears hidden from the public and little understood.

NOTES

This paper was prepared for the meeting of the International Political Science Association's Research Committee on Comparative Courts, in London, England, in January 2004. The author appreciates the assistance of Professor Yasuo Ohkoshi. This paper benefited from a grant from Tokyo International University and the author's research as an international consultant for The Asian Foundation's project on judicial independence conducted for the Asia Development Bank.

1 With the exception of Japan, the countries discussed were selected as a result of a study done by the author for The Asia Foundation and the Asia Development Bank; the overview report and country-level summaries of that study are available on the website of the Asia Development Bank at http://www.adb.org/documents/events/2003/reta5987/default.sop. Although not all

countries in South and Southeast Asia are covered here, the selection provides a reasonable cross-representation of judicial selection processes in the region. It would have been impossible to cover all countries in the region, given limitations on the length of the chapter. Apart from the sources cited in the notes below and the country-level summaries of the judiciaries in the region on the Asia Development Bank's website, useful overviews of these and other legal systems may be found in Kritzer, ed., *Legal Systems of the World.*

2 This point is further developed in O'Brien and Ohkoshi, 'Stifling Judicial Independence from Within,' 37.

3 For further discussion see Itoh, *The Japanese Supreme Court*; and Okudaira, 'The Japanese Supreme Court,' 67.

4 Further discussed in O'Brien and Ohkoshi, *To Dream of Dreams.*

5 The Missouri Plan was first adopted by that state in 1940; subsequently, almost half of the other American states enacted some version of it. The plan embodies a merit system that the American Bar Association and the American Judicature Society championed as an alternative to partisan judicial elections in state courts in the United States. See, generally, Sheldon and Maule, *Choosing Justice.*

6 Hattori, 'The Role of the Supreme Court of Japan in the Field of Judicial Administration,' 69, 72.

7 Based on and further discussed in O'Brien and Ohkoshi, 'Stifling Judicial Independence from Within.'

8 See Kommers, 'Autonomy versus Accountability,' 131–4.

9 For further discussion see Newberg, *Judging the State*; and Khan, *Constitutional and Political History of Pakistan.*

10 See *Al-Jehad Trust v. Federation of Pakistan*, PLD 1996 SC 324.

11 Ibid.

12 *Syed Zafar Ali Shah v. General Pervaiz Musharraf*, PLD 2000 SC 869.

13 See Bakker, *The Philippines Justice System*; and Narvasa, *Judicial Power in the Philippines.*

14 See Ahmed, 'The Problem of the Independence of the Judiciary in Bangladesh'; and Patwari, 'Independence of Judiciary in the Third World.'

15 *Secretary, Ministry of Finance v. Masdar Hossain* 20 (2000) BLD (AD) 104; 52 (2000) BLD 82.

16 See Bond, 'Nepal.'

17 See Tan, ed., *The Singapore Legal System.*

18 See, CYBERconsult, *Law Reform in Indonesia.*

19 See Woodside, *Vietnam and the Chinese Model*; and Nicholson, 'Vietnamese Legal Institutions in Comparative Perspective.'

18 Judicial Selection in Russia: Towards Accountability and Centralization

ALEXEI TROCHEV

At the beginning of the new millennium, Russia is continuing to experiment with ways of selecting its judges for both higher and lower courts. While in the early 1990s Russia quickly adopted 'life tenure' for judges of higher and lower courts in order to champion judicial independence from the political branches of government and to raise the prestige of the judiciary, the current (2001–3) phase of judicial reform enhances the accountability of the judiciary by imposing a mandatory retirement age of sixty-five for *sitting* judges and term limits on important judicial posts, and by strengthening the role of the federal President in the process of staffing the courts.[1]

How can we explain these zigzag-like changes in judicial selection in Russia? To critics of President Putin's 'managed democracy,' they are not surprising at all: more control of the executive over judicial recruitment helps to entrench his authoritarian rule.[2] Indeed, many argue that popular politicians, who do not fear losing elections, prefer dependent and accountable courts.[3] However, a move towards greater judicial accountability to the elected branches of government could also occur if politicians view courts as too powerful and too independent, as Peter Russell and Kate Malleson suggest in the introduction to this volume. Moreover, even in liberal democracies 'activist' constitutional courts 'may provide an efficient institutional way for hegemonic sociopolitical forces to preserve their hegemony and to secure their policy preferences,'[4] because dominant political elites can influence judicial decision making via judicial recruitment and ideological propensities.[5] Indeed, in addition to recruiting loyal judges, between 1967 and 2003, precisely during the era of 'global diffusion of judicial power,' political majorities in more than a dozen countries in Europe, Asia, and Africa attempted to modify the terms of judicial tenure de jure or de facto in order to enhance judicial accountability.[6]

While the dynamics of judicial reform are unique for each country, Russia's current move towards greater judicial accountability represents a complex effort to purge judicial corps of old, Soviet-era judges, to prevent corrupt judges and federal judges from 'going native,' and to improve the accessibility and the reputation of the third branch of government. The introduction of new mechanisms of judicial selection were a product of compromise between various domestic interests – federal and regional elites, and the judicial community. No less important was the personal commitment of highly popular federal President Vladimir Putin, who, unlike his predecessor, pledged to nearly double the size of the Russian judiciary by hiring an additional 10,000 judges, to raise the judicial salaries, and to expand the power of judges. President Putin told his staff that, once out of power, he did not want to suffer from corrupt judges, and ordered his staff to screen out any suspicious judicial candidates.[7] Hiring the best candidates for judgeships to boost public respect for Russia's courts was one way of achieving larger objectives, such as the attraction of significant investment for the Russian economy and land reform.[8] However, concentrating the judicial appointment power in the hands of the federal President may bring back the Soviet-era practice of issuing guidelines to judges on how to resolve certain politically sensitive cases, and political pressures on the thousands of newly hired judges may kill the seeds of judicial independence sown during the 1990s.

This paper opens with a brief review of the functioning of the Russian judicial system. It then discusses the struggles over courts in the context of Russian federalism of the 1990s and explores the patterns of staffing federal courts during the first term of President Putin (2000–3). It concludes by assessing the impact of Putin's reforms on the future of the Russian judiciary.

The Structure and Activism of Russian Courts

Russia's federal judiciary has three branches: the courts of general jurisdiction, the Constitutional Court, and *arbitrazh* courts. The courts of general jurisdiction, or regular courts, which hear all cases outside the jurisdiction of other courts, consist of a traditional hierarchy of about 2,500 district courts, 89 regional courts, and the Russian Supreme Court (to which were added, in 2000, a new lower rung, the justices of the peace), and a separate hierarchy of 151 military courts. In 2003, regular courts handled almost a million criminal cases, five million civil cases, and three million cases involving administrative offences. More importantly, these courts actively exercised judicial review powers: in 2002, they heard 5,500 challenges to regional laws and gubernatorial decrees and struck down 4,700 (85 per cent) of them.[9] Similarly, military courts handle hundreds of thousands of complaints against administrative decisions of military officials and find in favour of complainants in 90 per cent of these cases.[10] In 2002, the Russian Supreme Court heard 213 cases against the federal government and ruled in favour of the complainants in 23 per cent of them.[11] This trend increased in 2003, but in February 2004, the Russian Constitutional Court, acting on the petition of the federal cabinet, declared this power of the Supreme Court unconstitutional.[12]

The nineteen-member Russian Constitutional Court (RCC) (founded in 1991), with narrowly defined jurisdictions, stands alone and does not form a hierarchy with regional constitutional courts. Between 1992 and 2003, this court received 120,000 petitions from individuals, corporations, regions, other courts, and politicians, and issued over 800 decisions, a significant share of which reversed federal and regional policies. Between 1995 and 2003, the RCC struck down 118 laws, upheld 59 pieces of federal and regional legislation, and offered its own binding statutory interpretation in over 100 cases.

The *arbitrazh* courts, established in 1991 to hear disputes among firms and between firms and the government, exist at the trial level in eighty-one regions and include twenty appellate circuits of three to five regions (introduced in 2003), ten cassation circuits of eight to ten regions (added in 1995), and the Higher *Arbitrazh* Court. Their caseload is growing by 15–20 per cent each year and reached one million cases in 2003; roughly half the cases involved disputes between businesses and the government.[13] Similar to their colleagues in regular courts, *arbitrazh* judges appear to adjudicate in an impartial manner. For example, they did not hesitate to rule against the federal government in economic disputes between the Federation and the regions, and in disputes over taxes they sided with taxpayers in 65–70 per cent of the cases and tended to award larger sums to private firms as compared to tax authorities.[14]

Russia's regions do not have separate judicial systems, although federal law empowers regions to establish constitutional courts and Justice of the Peace courts. As of February 2004, only fifteen out of eighty-nine regions staffed their own constitutional courts, emulating German

Lander. Contrary to theories that link democratization and vibrant 'electoral markets' with judicial empowerment,[15] these courts were created and persisted in the regions with authoritarian political regimes, and failed or were not created in the regions with high electoral uncertainty.[16] The constitutional courts determine whether regional and local laws and decrees comply with the regional constitutions through a posteriori abstract and concrete constitutional review procedures. Between 1992 and November 2003, these courts issued over 330 decisions on the merits of the case, having struck down about equal proportions of executive and legislative acts in 60 per cent of the cases, which included numerous politically charged disputes between regional legislatures and governors over fiscal policies, electoral procedures, and socio-economic rights.[17]

At the same time, most Russian regions had Justice of the Peace (JP) courts up and running by 2003, although not all regions could afford or wanted them. Between 2000 and November 2003, they hired (sometimes enthusiastically, sometimes under pressure from the federal centre) about 5,500 JPs, although the federal budget allocated salaries for 6,470 of them. In 2002, JPs handled 22.4 per cent of all criminal cases (up from 11.2 per cent in 2001), 45 per cent of all civil cases (up from 24 per cent in 2001), and half of all administrative offences.[18] In short, these new local judges substantially relieve overloaded regular courts, quickly become overworked themselves, and compose a significant portion (30 per cent) of Russia's judiciary.

Entering the second decade of post-Communist transformation, the Russian judiciary is diverse compared to many other judiciaries around the world: women account for almost 60 per cent of 18,000 regular court judges, for about two-thirds of 3,000 *arbitrazh* judges and 5,500 JPs, and for one-third of 72 regional constitutional court judges. Women also dominate court clerkships, an important reservoir of judicial applicants. However, in common with many of the jurisdictions covered in this volume, the number of women in senior ranks of the judiciary is much lower. The 115-member Russian Supreme Court has 16 women justices, and only 4 of 26 Russian Constitutional Court justices appointed have been women. Also, similar to many civil law jurisdictions, Russia's judicial hierarchy exhibits strong patterns of internal dependency in which chairs of courts and senior judges exert enormous influence over the appointments to the bench and the workload and careers of rank-and-file judges.[19]

To sum up, the Russian judiciary appears to be both active and activist in its willingness to address numerous important issues of public policy. This judicial activism, together with the statutory expansion of judicial authority, has attracted both federal and regional political elites who have tried their best to recruit loyal judges.

Whose Judges: Regional or Federal?

Russia began to experiment with reform to the process of judicial recruitment shortly before the collapse of the USSR, when the Russian Parliament established a Constitutional Court in the fall of 1991. A key issue of contention during the lengthy passage of the RCC statute concerned the design of recruitment rules to the bench of the court.[20] As Canadian provinces did in the 1980s (see F.L. Morton's chapter in this volume), Russia's regions proposed to formalize regional representation on the bench of the new RCC. However, Parliament defeated these proposals amidst fears of the disintegration of Russia, and, in late October 1991, elected thirteen justices (three of them from the regions) out of twenty-three candidates to serve 'an unlimited term' subject to mandatory retirement at the age of sixty-five. Although the last four RCC justices appointed between 2000 and 2003 came from various Russian regions, regional governments did not seem to play any significant role in their nomination. Thus, while it is too early to say whether geographical or gender representation in the RCC will be crystallized as a constitutional convention, similar to the Pakistani or Canadian models (on Pakistan, see David O'Brien's contribution in this volume), both Russian Presidents seem to agree that at least three out of sitting nineteen RCC justices should be women.

In 1992, Parliament approved the introduction of life tenure for all other federal judges, following an initial probationary five-year appointment to the bench. At the same time, the 1992 Federation Treaty placed the creation of courts and judicial recruitment in both federal jurisdiction and joint jurisdiction between the federal centre and the twenty-one republics. While politicians and jurists in Moscow argued among each other over whether to allow regions to have their own judicial systems, similar to the United States, regional politicians went ahead and set up judiciaries in their regions. Some of these republics chose to establish their own constitutional courts while other regional (and even local!) governments attempted to appoint judges to regular and *arbitrazh* courts.[21]

For example, in 1993, contrary to the federal requirement of life tenure for all judges, the Kabardino-Balkariya legislature tried to re-appoint all judges in the region to five-year terms subject to compulsory retirement at sixty. The Russian Supreme Court challenged these restrictions in the RCC, and the latter quickly invalidated them as unconstitutional encroachments on the principle of judicial independence and on exclusive federal jurisdiction.[22] Already in the second year of its existence, the RCC did not hesitate to address sensitive political questions over rules of judicial selection in the context of constitutional ambiguity and the breakdown of the previous political regime. As I will show below, Russia's top courts followed Michael Tolley's advice (see his chapter in this volume) to defer to the norms and traditions that the political branches have developed to govern judicial appointment process only vaguely defined by the constitution, and to set the rules of the game in this inherently political process.

The new 1993 Russian constitution, however, broke sharply with the trend towards decentralizing the courts by providing for a unitary court system established under federal law, financed exclusively from the federal budget, and staffed by judges subordinate to the constitution and federal law. While judges on the highest courts (Constitutional, Supreme and Higher *Arbitrazh* Courts) were to be appointed by the Federation Council, the upper chamber of the Russian Parliament, upon nomination by the President, judges on 'other federal courts' were to be appointed directly by the President.[23]

The 1993 constitution was nonethelss a product of compromise between the federal centre and the regions. While Article 71 removes regional control over the organization of the courts, under Article 72 the personnel of courts belong to the joint federal-regional jurisdiction.[24] Under the new rules, President Yeltsin immediately began making judicial appointments. In some cases, the leaders of certain regions directly asked him to appoint certain judges,[25] while other regions refused to accept the new system of judicial appointments and continued appointing judges to their highest courts, and even passed laws, including constitutions, that legitimated these practices. With no Constitutional Court operating in Moscow between October 1993 and March 1995, there was no way to challenge these unconstitutional enactments.

In general, President Yeltsin responded to this potential constitutional crisis through diplomacy, seeking the consent of the chiefs of regions to the new appointment procedures and signing bilateral treaties between the federal government and several regions which established the appointment of judges as an area of joint jurisdiction.[26]

Moreover, in 1995, President Yeltsin vetoed a federal bill that empowered the Russian Supreme Court chairman to appoint chairs of lower courts, and signed a federal law requiring the President to appoint federal judges only after hearing the opinion of regional legislatures.[27] In addition, initial appointment to the bench was shortened from a five- to a three-year term.[28] This led to a bizarre situation: when federal elites were deadlocked over a nominee for the chair of a regional court, they sometimes lobbied regional governors to influence President Yeltsin's choice among judicial candidates.[29]

The 1996 Law on Judicial System was yet another product of bargaining among federal political elites, judicial bosses, and the regions. While this law did not transfer any existing courts to the regions, the latter regained a potentially decisive voice in judicial appointments. Before a candidacy for a judicial appointment of any kind reached the President's office, it had to pass the scrutiny of the regional legislature, thus giving the latter an effective veto. This regional veto was strengthened by chronic underfunding of federal courts: while federal budgets repeatedly failed to provide adequate pay raises for judges and funds needed for basic operations of courthouses (utilities, transportation, building repairs, and even stamps), often the municipalities (themselves dependent on regional and republican governments) came to the rescue by providing supplementary off-budget funds for their courts.[30] In the spring of 1998, precisely when soon-to-be-president Vladimir Putin began his meteoric rise in the Kremlin, Yeltsin's staff contemplated a bill empowering regions to set up their own appellate courts in parallel with existing regular courts. Even after the Russian Supreme Court declared illegal the attempts of Ingushetia's governor to hold a March 1998 referendum on the establishment of a regional court system, President Yeltsin appointed a conciliatory commission to allow Ingushetia a greater say in judicial recruitment.[31]

Judicial bosses fiercely opposed regional court systems, fearing they would destroy their dominant position in the judicial community by introducing a competition between regional and federal courts. Thus, between 1998 and 2000, the Russian Supreme Court invalidated all cases appealed to it from courts in Bashkortostan and Tatarstan on the grounds that some of their judges had been appointed illegitimately, that is, these judges had begun their work without waiting for the presidential approval.[32] In the same period, the Russian Constitutional Court repeatedly rejected petitions from sub-national governments who asked to be allowed to establish U.S.-style regional court systems and ruled that all courts belonged to a unitary national judicial system.[33] In addition, the RCC narrowed the role of the regions in selecting federal judges to simple notification of federal authorities about particular judicial nominees. In the Constitutional Court's view, the opinion of the region about a judicial applicant binds neither the Supreme Court chairman in nominating her nor the President in appointing her.[34] In short, Russia's top courts prepared a solid legal footing for President Putin's crackdown on regional violations of federal laws, including illegal encroachments on the part of the regions in the processes of recruiting federal judges and financing federal courts.[35]

Moreover, President Putin agreed that regional consent in selecting federal judges was redundant and time-consuming, and proposed to remove it over vocal opposition from several regions.[36] As a result, in December 2001, changes in the 1992 Law on the Status of Judges and in the 1996 Law on the Judicial System removed the legislatures of the regions from the process of appointing and promoting federal judges. The veto power that had been achieved by the regions in 1996, itself based upon the constitution's placement of judicial appointments in joint jurisdiction, was eliminated.

Under these legislative changes, the federal centre appears to have regained the final say over judicial appointments and has ended the practice of confirming judicial candidates who proved loyal to local authorities during their initial three-year term on the bench.[37] While in the beginning of his term, President Putin agreed with the Moscow mayor's choice for the Moscow City Court chair, in 2003, Putin ignored the opinion of the mayor in appointing the heads of Moscow Appellate *Arbitrazh* Courts. Similarly, in 2003, the Supreme Judicial Qualification Commission, a federal body, picked federal judges for Bashkortostan and Ingushetia, prompting Bashkortostan's legislature to challenge this removal of regional consent in the RCC as an unconstitutional elimination of a regional prerogative in the joint federal-regional jurisdiction.[38] Putin's legal advisers replied that regional legislatures would be in charge of appointing Justices of the Peace and 'representatives of the public' to the regional judicial qualification commissions (JQCs) (see below).

Enthusiastic about Putin's pledge to raise judicial salaries and to hire 10,000 judges, federal judges hoped that this new, simplified procedure would speed up the process of staffing the courts. However, as I will demonstrate, these hopes did not materialize: regional governors remained agile in using informal channels to lobby for their judicial nominees, while the presidential administration became quickly overloaded in trying to accomplish four tasks at the same time: hiring thousands of new judges, lobbying for its own judicial candidates, breaking the cycle of internal judicial dependency, and preventing corrupt candidates or governors' cronies from getting on the federal bench.

Staffing Russian Courts: Against Judicial Hierarchy?

The formal qualification requirements for appointment to the Russian judiciary are very limited, a subject of constant criticism by the judicial community.[39] For example, the candidate for the Russian Supreme Court and Higher *Arbitrazh* Court must have reached thirty-five years of age and have ten years of legal work experience, broadly defined. All judicial applicants must possess a higher legal education and have neither committed any 'compromising acts' nor suffered from certain diseases, the list of which is compiled by the Council of Judges. Federal judges appointed to the bench for the first time serve probationary three-year terms, after which they can be appointed for life until reaching the compulsory retirement age of sixty-five.

All candidates for first-time judgeships (except in Constitutional Courts) have to pass an exam, administered by the JQC of the region with the vacancy. Currently, judges of various specializations, appointed by court chairs, dominate the special ten- to sixteen-member examination commissions in charge of testing candidates' legal knowledge and professional preparation. During what many view as a 'tough,' open-book, two-hour oral exam, the candidate has to solve two cases from judicial practice, write a draft outline of the judgment (if necessary) and answer three questions from various branches of law related to the vacant position (e.g., commercial law, for nominees for *arbitrazh* courts, and labour law for candidates for regular courts). Thus, the Russian system is beginning to address Elizabeth Handsley's concern (see her chapter in this volume) that different judicial positions require different sets of professional knowledge and skills. Yet the actual degree of differentiation in testing the candidates depends on the will and the capacity of judicial chiefs in preparing separate exam questions and keeping them up to date.[40]

Successful candidates must then obtain a 'recommendation' from a regional JQC, which screens candidates for regular, *arbitrazh*, and the Justice of the Peace courts. From 1993 to 2002, this body was composed exclusively of judges.[41] In that period, regular courts in eighty-five regions, seventy-six *arbitrazh* courts, thirteen military courts, the Russian Supreme Court, and the Higher *Arbitrazh* Court each had their own JQCs, which made these commissions particularly vulnerable to pressure by judicial bosses. Eighty-five JQCs of regular courts thus rejected only 276, or 5 per cent, of 5,367 judicial nominees sponsored by the court chairs in 1999, and 8.6 per cent of nominees in 2000. Between 1997 and September 2000, the thirty-two-member Supreme JQC in charge of selecting the chairs of regional courts and judges of the Russian Supreme Court and the Higher *Arbitrazh* Court rejected 86 out of 436 nominees (20 per cent) for these politically important posts.[42] The Russian Constitutional Court repeatedly ruled that candidates who were rejected by the JQC could ask regular courts to annul the JQC decision. This recourse, however, lacked teeth because judges rarely disagreed with their peers and court chairs.[43]

By the fall of 2002, in an effort to break judicial corporatism and to 'depoliticize' the composition of JQCs, all of them, including the Supreme JQC, had to include several 'representatives of the public' and could no longer include chairs and vice-chairs of any court, MPs, or government officials. Inserting one representative of the Russian President in every JQC and having a single commission in every region also makes it easier to monitor the initial stages of judicial recruitment.[44] Thus, the twenty-nine-member Supreme JQC has eighteen judges elected by the All-Russian Congress of Judges based on quotas for the regular, *arbitrazh*, and military courts, ten lay members appointed by the Federation Council, and one presidential representative. Depending on the number of judges in the region, regional JQCs have twenty-one, thirteen, or eleven members with seven, four, and two laypersons respectively, appointed by the regional legislatures. While regional JQCs have to be reappointed every two years, the Supreme JQC has a four-year term.

Clearly, these measures attempt to accommodate the prerogatives of the regions in staffing federal courts, the power of the federal President to monitor the work of the JQCs, and some measure of judicial autonomy by granting 60 per cent of the seats of the JQCs to judges. Moreover, the judicial community succeeded in allowing the newly staffed JQCs to begin their operation after one-half of their members was appointed. Not surprisingly, regional conferences of judges quickly elected their representatives to JQCs, who in turn swiftly elected chairs of these commissions without waiting for the representatives of the 'public.' Moreover, many chairs of regional courts took an active part in pre-screening of laypersons of the JQCs.[45]

Powerful governors also joined the race in staffing JQCs in order to minimize the access of political opposition to them. In the regions with weakly organized civil society, powerful governors secured the exclusive right to nominate the representatives of the 'public' to these commissions without any competition.[46] Regions with visible NGOs and divided political elites took longer to appoint JQC members because of vibrant competition over nominees. Here, regional legislators approached this issue seriously because the vote gave them a real say in hiring judges, and designed elaborate procedures for staffing JQCs to minimize the influence of judicial bosses.[47] Finally, regional legislatures with severe political polarization faced fierce conflict among politicians and judges over appointments to JQCs and continued to staff these commissions throughout 2003.[48]

The judicial bosses of the highest courts tightly controlled appointments to the Supreme JQC, ignoring proposals from the regions and disallowing any competition for eighteen spots reserved for judges.[49] The process of appointing ten lay members to the Supreme JQC was not open to competing political forces, given that Putin's administration tightly controlled the selection. By July 2002 the Federation Council, which appoints the representatives of the public to the Supreme JQC, had received forty-two nominations, quickly appointed eight of them (all men, mostly well-known law professors), and refused to vote on one nominee directly sponsored by ten regions whose candidacy was not approved by the Putin's staff.[50]

How did the JQC reform affect the work of these commissions? Increasingly, the JQCs advertise vacancies on the bench, conduct a merit-based selection of nominees, and inform the public about the time and place of their meetings. In 2002, the rules were changed so that the JQCs can now recommend only one candidate for each judgeship. In addition, the court chair now has the power to ask the JQC to retract its recommendation, strengthening internal judicial dependency because this veto power of judicial chiefs (which could be over-ridden by two-thirds of the JQC members) is the only effective remedy for rejected candidates. While rejected nominees have a right to appeal the rejection in court, and the court can overturn the rejection, this remedy again lacks teeth because the court cannot re-open the competition and order the JQC to retract its recommendation.[51] In addition, court chairs use informal methods to learn about judicial nominees. For example, the chair of Moscow Circuit *Arbitrazh* Court openly admitted that she routinely receives dossiers of candidates from the JQC, invites them for a chat, and 'keeps the process of judicial selection under control.'[52] However, having presidential and 'public' representatives at the JQC may allow judges to disagree with the court chiefs and the governors, and several JQCs have not hesitated to advertise their resistance to judicial chiefs.[53]

Before deciding whether to recommend a judicial candidate, some regional JQCs test the nominee on the following eight criteria: professionalism, susceptibility to conflicts, leadership, physical development, accessibility, self-control, IQ, and moral qualities. Judges like these psychological tests with hundreds of questions because they allow subjective judgments about the 'moral qualities' of the judicial candidate to be hidden behind the veil of 'objective scientific criteria.'[54] Several court chairs require all judicial applicants to take these tests, ignoring their confidential, voluntary, and non-binding nature.[55]

Finally, the JQCs also request background checks on judicial candidates and their relatives from the police, customs, and state security agency to guard against nepotism and to 'prevent organized crime figures inside the judicial system.'[56] Currently, JQCs take these background checks seriously to play along with the Russian President's efforts to root out judicial corruption and to improve public trust in the judiciary at the cost of slowing down judicial recruitment.[57] In 2002, the Supreme JQC considered 191 judicial nominations, approved 151 of them, and rejected 40 nominations (21 per cent), 39 of them in the merit-based competition that tends to centre on prestigious courts in large cities and affluent regions. In the same period, all regional JQCs reviewed 6,736 judicial nominations, recommending 6,060 (90 per cent) of them.[58] In short, it appears that competitive merit-based judicial selection accounts for a slight increase in the rejection rates, as compared with previous years.

To sum up, the role of the JQCs in staffing Russian courts is growing, and no judge in Russia (except the federal and regional constitutional court judges) can be appointed without the recommendation of a JQC. The use of party lists in the forthcoming regional legislative elections is bound to inject more politics into the process of staffing regional JQCs, which, in turn, may politicize the process of judicial recruitment even further.[59] While the type of political regime in the regions accounts for the timing and intensity of struggles over staffing regional JQCs, there appears to be no direct link between the type of regime and the degree of transparency in screening judicial candidates in the regions. In 2003, one could easily find accessible and closed JQCs in both 'democratic' and 'authoritarian' regions in Russia. The best predictor seems to lie in the willingness and capacity of judicial chiefs to open up court statistics, to publish them on the web, and to allow media in the JQC meetings.[60]

The Russian President: Centralizing Judicial Recruitment

As should be clear by now, Russia's judicial bureaucracy dominates the process of staffing courts from top to bottom, inviting collusion between the heads of the judicial corps, governors, and private businesses, who actively lobby for their preferred judicial candidates.[61] Although court chairs no longer sit in the JQCs and no longer head their courts for life, they can be reappointed to head another court and their renewable six-year terms make them dependent on the nominations by the chairs of the Russian Supreme Court and Higher *Arbitrazh* Court.[62] This nomination, together with the recommendation of JQCs that are often under the de facto control of the chairs of regional courts, effectively restricts the choice of the Russian President in appointing federal judges.

Although federal law gives the Russian President two months to decide whether to appoint the judicial candidate, in practice it usually takes a year, as President Putin attempts to centralize judicial selection even at the cost of an overloaded judiciary. All paperwork first goes to the Department of Cadres Policy in the Presidential Administration. The department repeats, among other things, various background checks with the help of law enforcement agencies and presidential envoys in seven federal districts, new, high-ranking federal officials appointed in 2000.[63] Putin's envoys are responsible for screening all nominees for judgeships at the regional level and below, and for reporting to the Presidential Commission on Judicial Nominations, a second body in charge of screening nominees. Rejections of nominations for a judgeship by this commission and by Putin himself reflect badly on the performance of envoys. It should be noted that to date the role played by presidential envoys in most judicial appointments has reportedly been formal, as they rubber stamp the names of candidates who have survived the many earlier stages of vetting.[64]

Judges across Russia repeatedly complain that the Presidential Administration reviews judicial nominations too slowly, and that this results in an overloaded judicial system.[65] The complaints seem plausible, given that the judicial recruitment process has been complicated by the addition of a new stage – review by the presidential envoy – to the five previous stages: the initial nomination, review by the regional JQC, security clearance by the law enforcement agencies, screening by the Presidential Commission on Judicial Nominations, and final confirmation by Putin himself.

While, under both Presidents, the Commission on Judicial Nominations rejected up to 5 per cent of judicial nominations, the focus of its work under President Putin shifted to the candidates for regional and *arbitrazh* courts. Between 2002 and 2003, this commission failed to endorse 7.5 per cent of nominees for *arbitrazh* courts (10 per cent in 2003 alone), suspecting them or their relatives of nepotism, corruption, links with organized crime, or close ties with governors.[66] The expected retirement of ten Higher *Arbitrazh* Court Justices, including the chairman and seventeen heads of regional *arbitrazh* courts (who should reach sixty-five by January 2005) is likely to further politicize and slow down federal judicial recruitment. More importantly, it is widely believed that President Putin himself rather than the governors, oligarchs, or judicial bosses will have the final say in filling these vacancies, with far-reaching consequences for Russian judicial and market reforms.[67] This is a dramatic departure from the practice of the 1990s, when the role of the President in staffing the courts was 'relatively minor.'[68]

The challenge of hiring an additional 2,200 federal judges during 2004, replacing 400 federal judges now forced to retire at age 65, and staffing 20 newly created *arbitrazh* appellate courts and 521 soon-to-be created administrative courts is bound to exacerbate delays in the appointment of judges. While President Putin pledged to increase the size of the federal judiciary by 3,000 in 2002 alone, he managed to appoint only 1,298 regular judges that year, half as many as he did in 2001 (2,456 judges). In the same year he appointed 244 *arbitrazh* judges and promoted 30 of them.[69] By October 2003, out of 23,290 judgeships throughout Russia, there were 2,787 vacancies on the lower courts and 431 in federal courts at the regional level, and it could take up to two years to fill a vacant judgeship, especially in the *arbitrazh* courts.[70] Moreover, President Putin has begun to appoint the chairs of 20 newly created appellate *arbitrazh* courts, and appears to allow these chairs to pick judges loyal to them, thus exacerbating internal judicial dependency within these new courts. Improved funding for the judiciary also means that court clerks, who are now subordinated to court chairs, will form a significant pool of judicial candidates in the next several years. Indeed, one of the latest Putin appointees, the chair of Samara *Arbitrazh* Court, viewed his main role as 'building the vertical of judicial power' in that region.[71]

Finally, the true test of Putin's commitment to judicial independence will come when he will be asked to reappoint for life over 10,000 federal judges, after their initial three-year appointments expire during his second presidential term (2004–8). Which judges will be promoted, which ones will not be re-appointed, and why? Russians may never have the answers and may continue to distrust the authorities unless the presidential office makes its role in the process of staffing the courts transparent to the public.

Conclusion

Putin's judicial reform during his first term (2000–3) was a work-in-progress during which the federal government, regional elites, and the judicial community fought over the limits of judicial empowerment, independence, and accountability. Russian courts are expanding their power of judicial review of executive rule-making, which is still far more common than legislation, at all levels of government. This expansion is in its early stages, and the division of powers among constitutional, regular, and *arbitrazh* courts is still ambiguous.[72] Moreover, similar to the judiciary in Japan and Pakistan, Russian courts attempted to define the rules of judicial recruitment, and federal political elites seemed to accept them. The fact that Russia's top courts simultaneously paved the way for some aspects of judicial appointment reform and posed obstacles for other ones stresses the importance of Michael Tolley's emphasis on the role of the judges in the judicial selection game. Here, the greatest progress has been achieved in opening court statistics, holding competitive judicial selection at the public meetings of the JQCs, hiring press officers for federal courts, and using court websites to address the problem of public distrust in Russian courts, which remains high on Putin's agenda.[73]

These measures, together with hiring thousands of judges, raising their salaries, treating courts as an equal branch of government, and removing regional legislatures from the judicial selection process, have done much to combat the tendency for federal courts in the regions to become captives of local power brokers and to ensure that the federal courts remain federal in more than name. President Putin is strengthening his own role in judicial selection by having his officials recheck all judicial nominations, retaining the power to appoint chairs of all federal courts in the regions, and nominating chairs for the top federal courts (except the RCC). During his second term in 2004–8, Putin will appoint judges on newly created politically important administrative and *arbitrazh* courts and decide on the promotion of thousands of federal judges whose initial three-year terms will have expired.

However, regional governors continue to use informal ways to influence judicial selection by preparing to host these newly created courts, by negotiating deals with judicial bosses, and by controlling laypersons in the regional JQCs.[74] The use of party lists in the forthcoming regional legislative elections and reappointments of several thousands of JPs in Russian regions are bound to generate further controversies over judicial nominations.

Over two-thirds of Russian judges will be scrutinized by the political branches of government in the next several years. Will this close scrutiny overcome internal judicial dependency and improve the reputation of Russian courts at home and abroad? Since we know that 'activist' courts provoke politicians to recruit loyal judges no less actively, there is no doubt that both the regional governments and the federal government will try to co-opt or pressure politically important courts, that is, courts most likely to hear civil complaints against local authorities and federal government agencies. The ease with which Russian politicians experiment with judicial selection rules under vague constitutional provisions suggests that we will see more political struggles not only over particular judicial nominations, but also over the procedures of judicial recruitment. Russia will not enjoy a strong, stable, and independent judiciary until these procedures cease to change every time a new federal president comes to power.

NOTES

1 See Solomon, 'Putin's Judicial Reform,' 118.

2 See, e.g., Reddaway and Orttung, eds., *The Dynamics of Russian Politics*; and McFaul, Petrov, and Ryabov, *Between Dictatorship and Democracy*.

3 See, e.g., Epstein and Knight, 'Constitutional Borrowing and Nonborrowing,' 196; Ginsburg, *Judicial Review in New Democracies*; Magalhães, 'The Politics of Judicial Reform in Eastern Europe,' 43; Ramseyer, 'The Puzzling (In)dependence of Courts,' 721; Russell, 'Adjudication and Enforcement of Laws in a Federal System,' 40–51.

4 Hirschl, 'The Struggle for Hegemony,' 73. See also his *Towards Juristocracy*.

5 Tsebelis, *Veto Players*; Russell, 'Adjudication and Enforcement of Laws in a Federal System.'

6 Trochev, '"Tinkering With Tenure."'

7 Ignateva and Naidenov, 'Pravyi krainii. V chetverg poutru s Dmitriem Kozakom.'
8 Trochev and Solomon, 'Courts and Federalism in Putin's Russia.'
9 'Rabota sudov Rossiiskoi Federatsii v 2002 godu,' 71. On 2003, see Mikhailina, Sudi rasskazali o prestupleniiakh i nakazaniiakh.
10 Postupat' po zakonu i po sovesti, 13. For an excellent analysis of the growth of administrative justice in Russia, see Solomon, 'Judicial Power in Russia,' 549.
11 'Rabota sudov Rossiiskoi Federatsii v 2002 godu,' 69.
12 Sterkin, 'Pravitelstvo zabilo gol v svoi vorota.'
13 'Arbitrazhnye sudy Rossii v 2003 godu rassmotreli okolo odnogo mln del.'
14 See Hendley, 'Suing the State in Russia,' 122; Solomon, 'Judicial Power in Russia;' Trochev and Solomon, 'Courts and Federalism in Putin's Russia.'
15 See note 2 above.
16 Trochev, 'Less Democracy, More Courts,' 513.
17 See Trochev, 'The Constitutional Courts of Russia's Regions,' 7; and Trochev and Solomon, 'Courts and Federalism in Putin's Russia.'
18 See 'Rabota sudov Rossiiskoi Federatsii v 2002 godu,' 70–1; and Solomon, 'The New Justices of the Peace in the Russian Federation,' 381.
19 For an indepth analysis of internal judicial dependency in post-Soviet Russia, see Foglesong, 'The Dynamics of Judicial (In)Dependence in Russia,' 62; and Solomon and Foglesong, *Courts and Transition in Russia.*
20 Henderson, 'The First Russian Constitutional Court,' 105.
21 Naidenov, 'Sudiam daiut srok,' 1; Trochev, 'Less Democracy, More Courts.'
22 The Russian Constitutional Court decision 18-P of 30 September 1993, *Vestnik Konstitutsionnogo Suda RF* [hereinafter *VKS RF*] (1994), No. 6, 26; Fleiner and Khakimov, eds., *Federalism: Russian and Swiss Perspectives.*
23 See Article 128 of the 1993 constitution.
24 For the criticism of this compromise, see Morshchakova, ed., *Kommentarii k zakonodatelstvu o sudebnoi sisteme Rossiiskoi Federatsii,* 43.
25 Zherebtsov, Kak zakalialas Vysshaia kvalifikatsionnaia kollegiia sudei, 6.
26 See Trochev and Solomon, 'Courts and Federalism in Putin's Russia.'
27 Kleandrov, *Status sudi,* 57–8.
28 The Russian Constitutional Court repeatedly affirmed the constitutionality of setting this initial 'probationary' term. See Morshchakova, *Kommentarii k zakonodatelstvu o sudebnoi sisteme Rossiiskoi Federatsii,* 126.
29 Zherebtsov, 'Kak zakalialas Vysshaia kvalifikatsionnaia kollegiia sudei.'
30 See Solomon and Foglesong, *Courts and Transition in Russia,* 13.
31 Shakhrai, 'Vystuplenie na zasedanii Politicheskogo konsultativnogo soveta,' 26.

32 'Nepravilnye sudi Tatarstana'; Kurmanov, 'Judicial System in Russia,' 66–7; Trochev and Solomon, 'Courts and Federalism in Putin's Russia.'
33 Russian Constitutional Court decisions: #3-P of 1 February 1996, *VKS RF* 1 (1996); #32-O of 12 March 1998, *VKS RF* 3 (1998): 66; #10-P of 7 June 2000, *VKS RF* 5 (2000); #91-O of 8 June 2000, *id.*; and #92-O of 27 June 2000, *id.*
34 Russian Constitutional Court decisions: #20-O of 1 April 1996; #32-O of 19 April 1996; and #1-O of 23 January 1997 (all unpublished); #217-O of 27 October 2000, *VKS RF* 2 (2001): 8; #252-O of 21 December 2000, *id.*, 62.
35 Putin, Novoi Rossii nuzhna silnaia nezavisimaia sudebnaia sistema, 1–2.
36 See Kurmanov, 'Judicial System in Russia,' 66; 'Podgotovleny izmeneniia v zakon o statuse sudei RF.'
37 Abrosimova, Sudoustroistvo i status sudi, 94.
38 'V sostav Verkhovnogo suda respubliki voidut deviat novykh sudei'; 'Respublika Ingushetiia. Attestovany federalnye sudi'; The Russian Constitutional Court decision 428-O of 4 December 2003, available at the website of the Russian Constitutional Court, http://ks.rfnet.ru/opred/o041203d.htm.
39 See Foglesong, 'The Dynamics of Judicial (In)Dependence in Russia'; and Solomon and Foglesong, *Courts and Transition in Russia.*
40 'Trudno li stat sudiei?' (Is it Difficult to Become a Judge?) interview with the chairwoman of the examination commission at the Yaroslavl JQC, '16 January 2004, http://cdyar.yaroslavl.ru; Egorov, 'Nas ne obmanuli, potomu chto nam nichego ne obeshchali.'
41 For their work in the 1990s, see Foglesong, 'The Dynamics of Judicial (In)Dependence in Russia'; and Solomon and Foglesong, *Courts and Transition in Russia.*
42 The data are available on the website of the Russian Supreme Court at http://www.supcourt.ru.
43 Portnov, 'Mina dlia Femidy,' 4.
44 Article 11 of the Federal Law of 14 March 2002 on the Bodies of Judicial Community in the Russian Federation, *Sobranie zakonodatelstva RF* 11 (2002), st. 1022; Ukaz Prezidenta RF #196 of 13 February 2004, 'O naznachenii predstavitelei Prezidenta RF v kvalifikatsionnykh kollegiiakh sudei subektov RF,' *Sobranie zakonodatelstva RF* 7 (2004), st. 509.
45 Biriukova, 'Biudzhetnyi defitsit sokratilsia'; OO 'Sutiazhnik,' 'Otkrytoe pismo,' 17 May 2002 (unpublished document); 'Pskovskaia oblast. Deputaty oblastnogo sobraniia ne smogli izbrat predstavitelia obshchestvennosti v kvalifikatsionnuiu kollegiiu sudei.'
46 Maratova, 'Kabardino-Balkaria President Continues to Influence Judicial System.'
47 Glebova, 'Femida zrit v koren'; Ignatenko, 'Deputat sude ne kollega.'

48 'V kvalifikatsionnoi kollegii sudei Sankt-Peterburga ostalis vakantnymi dva mesta dlia predstavitelei obshchestvennosti.' (

49 Ignateva, 'Pomni o Strasburge,' 2.

50 'Komitet SF po pravovym i sudebnym voprosam otklonil popravki v novyi UPK'; 'Komitet Soveta Federatsii po pravovym i sudebnym voprosam vse-taki rekomendoval odobrit zakon 'O vnesenii izmenenii i dopolnenii v UPK RF'; 'Otchet o rabote Komiteta Soveta Federatsii po pravovym i sudebnym voprosam v 2002 godu'; Katanian, 'Kadrovyi vopros bez podteksta,' 3.

51 Morshchakova, *Kommentarii k zakonodatelstvu o sudebnoi sisteme Rossiiskoi Federatsii*, 123.

52 Perekrest, 'Izobretaiutsia izoshchrenneishie sposoby vnedreniia v sudebnuiu sistemu.'

53 'Na zasedaniiakh kvalifikatsionnoi kollegii sudei Amurskoi oblasti v 2003 godu,' 2004; Ponomarev, O Kvalifikatsionnykh kollegiiakh sudei.

54 Kleandrov, *Status sudi*, 79–93; Materov, 'Ob uluchshenii podbora kandidatov na dolzhnosti sudei,' 95; Mikhailina, 'Budushchie sudi budut risovat' nesushchestvuiushchikh zhivotnykh'; Perekrest, 'Izobretaiutsia izoshchrenneishie sposoby vnedreniia v sudebnuiu sistemu.'

55 'Rekomendatsii po eksperimentalnomu ispolzovaniiu metodov psikhodiagnosticheskogo obsledovaniia kandidatov na dolzhnost sudei, utv. Prikazom Generalnogo direktora Sudebnogo Departamenta pri Verkhovnom Sude RF ot 17 dekabria 2002 goda N147'; Shadrunov, 'Stat sudiei neprosto,' 8; 'Sudebnaia reforma: den za dnem. Sudebnyi psiholog.'

56 'Valentin Kuznetsov: My sudim sudei.'

57 For attempts to estimate the nature and extent of corruption in Russian courts see Enyutina, 'Korruptsiya v sudebnykh organakh.' and Satarov, Prorzhavevshee pravosudie, 87.

58 Rossiiskaia iustitsiia 2003. 'Deiatelnost kvalifikatsionnykh kollegii sudei v 2002 godu,' 74.

59 See Kurmanov and Sultanov, 'Vzaimootnosheniia zakonodatelnykh (predstavitelnykh) organov gosudarstvennoi vlasti i kvalifikatsionnykh kollegii sudei subektov RF.'

60 Trochev, 'Russian Courts on the Web,' 7.

61 Abrosimova, 'Sud i ispolnitelnaya vlast,' 129; Foglesong, 'The Dynamics of Judicial (In)Dependence in Russia,' 79; Trochev and Solomon 'Courts and Federalism in Putin's Russia.'

62 Morshchakova, *Kommentarii k zakonodatelstvu o sudebnoi sisteme Rossiiskoi Federatsii*, 115.

63 See Reddaway and Orttung, *The Dynamics of Russian Politics*, vol. 1.

64 See Trochev and Solomon, 'Courts and Federalism in Putin's Russia.'

65 Mikhailina, 'Sudi rasskazali o prestupleniiakh i nakazaniiakh'; Kriuchkova, 'Polpredskaia KADRil.'
66 Overall, the commission rejected on these grounds 35 nominations for all federal judgeships (1.4 per cent) in 2001, 52 (3.4 per cent) in 2002, and 161 (4.6 per cent) in 2003. Perekrest, 'Viktor Ivanov.'
67 'Predsedatel Vysshego arbitrazhnogo suda Veniamin Iakovlev v dekabre etogo goda pokinet svoi post.'
68 Foglesong, 'The Dynamics of Judicial (In)Dependence in Russia,' 79.
69 Lebedev, 'Doklad o rabote sudov za 2002 god'; 'Internet-interviu s V.F. Iakovlevym 'Rabota arbitrazhnykh sudov v 2002 godu.'
70 Postanovlenie Soveta Sudei RF, O nekotorykh voprosakh, sviazannykh s naznacheniem sudei federalnykh sudov obshchei iurisdiktsii i arbitrazhnykh sudov.
71 Naumova, 'Samarskii arbitrazh poluchil predsedatelia.'
72 Trochev, 'Competing for the Judge-Made Law.'
73 'Putin for Increasing Trust in Court System.' See also Solomon, 'Glavnyi vopros dlia rossiiskoi sudebnoi vlasti – kak dobitsia doveriia obshchestva?,' 5–6.
74 In addition, throughout Putin's first term, local authorities across Russia continued to provide questionable bonuses to judicial salaries and de facto controlled the distribution of housing for federal judges. See Trochev and Solomon, 'Courts and Federalism in Putin's Russia'; 'Postanovlenie Mera goroda Irkutska 'O pooshchrenii rabotnikov sudebnykh organov po itogam raboty za 2003 god' #031-06-1678/3,' 23 December 2003 (unpublished document); 'Pravitelstvo Peterburga pomozhet sudiam reshit kvartirnyi vopros.'

19 Improving the Quality of the Judiciary in China: Recent Reforms to the Procedures for Appointing, Promoting, and Discharging Judges

COLIN HAWES

In this paper, I will begin by briefly describing the judicial appointment system in the People's Republic of China (PRC) prior to the mid-1990s. I will then analyse the major reforms that have taken place in the decade since 1995, which have corrected some of the most serious defects of the earlier period. Finally, I will conclude by discussing various problems that still require resolution if China's judiciary is to improve its generally poor reputation. I focus not only on the appointment of judges, but also on their promotion/demotion, evaluation, and discharge, as all of these aspects are intimately related under the current judicial system.

Introduction: Chinese Judges 1949–1995

Soon after establishing the People's Republic of China in 1949, the ruling Chinese Communist Party (the Party) set up a basic system of people's courts at the local/district (basic level), provincial/municipal (intermediate and superior), and central (Supreme People's Court) levels, governed by a rudimentary legal framework.[1] However, during the 1950s and early 1960s, it was the Party, with its committees spread throughout the country and in every work unit, which generally meted out justice and discipline. When cases did come before the courts – for example, when serious criminals were apprehended – it was a foregone conclusion that judges would defer to their local Party committee when deciding guilt or innocence and fixing a sentence.[2]

The Party also controlled the appointment of judges, or 'adjudicators,' through political committees at each level of government.[3] Some older judges, who had been trained in university law schools prior to

1949, were permitted to stay on after the Communist Revolution in order to transmit their legal knowledge to the younger generation. Others were appointed as judges after obtaining degrees at institutions of higher learning, or were simply transferred into the judiciary from non-legal administrative or military leadership positions.[4]

From the early 1950s onwards, judges who had been educated prior to 1949 were increasingly purged from the ranks of the judiciary, due to their suspect class background. Like other intellectuals and professionals, many were forced to become ordinary workers or were sent to reform camps for 're-education through labour.'[5] From the mid-1960s, after leftist radicals gained sway in the Party and launched the Cultural Revolution, Chinese society as a whole descended into a three-year period of anarchy followed by several years of extreme revolutionary fervour. The fledgling Chinese court system was completely dismantled and all remaining judges were removed from their positions. Ad hoc justice was meted out by military tribunals and revolutionary committees, with horrifying results.[6]

It was only in the late 1970s, when a more moderate leadership regained control, that the government began to emphasize the need for a stable and effective legal system to prevent the human tragedy of the previous decade from recurring. Courts were re-established and judges were appointed in great numbers. Countless new laws, both substantive and procedural, were passed during the next two decades, as China attempted to develop a legal system that could maintain social order while at the same time sustain a modern and prosperous economy and attract foreign investment.[7]

Despite the plethora of new legislation, however, during the 1980s and into the 1990s there was widespread and increasing public dissatisfaction with the Chinese judicial system. Many judges, especially those in local level courts, became notorious for their corruption, inefficiency, and lack of knowledge of the law.[8] The problems had become so serious by the mid-1990s that top political and judicial leaders, such as Jiang Zemin, then Communist Party Secretary, and XiaoYang, president of the Supreme People's Court, publicly admitted that much of the court system was dysfunctional and that far-reaching reforms were essential.[9] Improving the quality of the judiciary became a top priority on the government's reform agenda. As Jiang Zemin declared in a speech reported in *People's Daily* in 1996, 'We must move ahead with judicial reform, ensuring that we create a system that guarantees the independent and fair exercise of adjudicative and supervisory review powers by judicial organs. We must put in place a system of accountability for wrongly decided and unjust judgments, and increase the effectiveness of our judiciary and enforcement personnel.'[10]

The government's stated aim for legal reform was to create a 'nation governed by the rule of law,' as opposed to one in which individual leaders, political factions, or criminal elements could set up their own local fiefdoms and govern based on their own personal whims. Yet without an effective legal system staffed by incorruptible and well-trained judges, this laudable objective would remain simply a pipe dream.[11]

There were several root causes of the 'inferior quality' of the judiciary in the 1980s and '90s. In the next section I will describe the defects of the judicial system prior to the latest round of judicial reforms. I will then turn to the ways in which the Chinese government has attempted to address these defects through the *Judges Law of the People's Republic of China* (1995) and accompanying regulations and administrative reforms over the subsequent decade.[12]

Defects of the Judicial Appointments System Prior to 1995

One of the most obvious flaws of the judicial system prior to the implementation of the *Judges Law* in 1995 was that specialized legal knowledge or experience was not a prerequisite for judges to be appointed. Indeed, even a tertiary education was not mandatory, let alone a law degree. A large number of judges were simply transferred into the judiciary from military or Party posts, having received no formal legal training. Others were appointed by Party officials based on personal connections and political orthodoxy rather than professional standards. Still others were given preference for appointments because their parents were judges, a practice that was widespread in civil service and administrative organs during the Communist period.[13] It is no surprise, therefore, that many judges lacked the ability to apply China's increasingly complex body of statutory law to individual fact situations, or to produce convincing and well-reasoned judgments.

Educational qualifications aside, the fact that all judges in courts at the district, intermediate, and superior provincial levels were appointed and could be discharged at any time by the government at the corresponding level (more specifically, by the local Party Committee) meant that the legal merits of cases were often ignored in favour of political expediency. Political corruption at the local level would simply be reflected in local court decisions as judges became tools for local leaders to enforce their power.[14]

The internal personnel structure of courts also militated against a meritocratic system favouring competent and honest judges. Within each court, judges would be appointed at one of twelve administrative ranks, in the same manner as any other local government or civil service functionary. Those who were transferred in from non-legal positions would start at a rank commensurate with their seniority. Promotion up the ranks then occurred based on years worked and correct 'political attitude.'[15] In other words, judges who ingratiated themselves with the leadership within their court – which was controlled by People's Court political committees working in conjunction with the local government – would automatically be promoted. By contrast, judges who attempted to exercise their judicial independence and took a stand against local political interests, including the interests of senior judges within their own court, could expect rapid demotion or discharge. Besides controlling the promotion process, the court political committees also controlled housing, benefits, health care, and other day-to-day matters for all personnel within the court, including judges.[16] A rash moment of judicial independence could have serious repercussions both for the judge's professional career and his or her basic living conditions.

Finally, the process by which cases were adjudicated and judgments produced prior to the late 1990s again allowed incompetent and corrupt judges to escape censure and even rise through the ranks. In general, all first instance cases were heard by panels of at least three judges. Before judgment was given, one of these judges would produce a written summary of the facts and relevant law and the panel's preliminary decision. This report was not made public or disclosed to the parties, but was circulated to a court adjudication committee, at which the court president normally presided. The court president or the committee could approve the decision, suggest changes in the application of the law, or reverse the decision. In the case of a reversal, no new trial would be held. The panel would simply revise its earlier holding based on the committee's recommendations and then read the final judgment to the parties without any indication that its decision had been overturned or revised.[17]

One negative consequence of this group decision-making process was a lack of individual accountability among judges. First, court presidents could not be certain which of the judicial panellists was responsible for erroneous decisions, hence they would find it difficult to single out judges for incompetence or obvious partiality. Second, the frequency of successful appeals from judgments was also an unreliable indicator of a judge's incompetence, as judgments were often influenced, for better or worse, by the court president and members of the adjudication committee. Obviously, under such a system most judges would automatically seek their superiors' 'approval' for all but the most clear-cut cases, as this would absolve them from responsibility when appeal courts overturned their decisions.[18]

When one adds to all these problems the fact that remuneration of judges remained at the meagre level of minor civil service functionaries, and that there was no clear prohibition on judges' ex parte contacts with the parties before them – indeed, it became common practice for each side separately to invite the judge to a restaurant to try to 'resolve' their case – it is no surprise that the public generally viewed the judicial system of the 1980s and '90s as ineffective and totally corrupt.[19] At the same time, the public perceived that the superior provincial courts were staffed by better-qualified judges who were less influenced by local interests. Consequently, appeal rates were extremely high, causing lengthy backlogs of cases at the superior court level and leading inevitably to a decline in the quality of appeal judgments as well.[20]

Judicial Reform since the Mid-1990s

How has the government and the Supreme People's Court attempted to deal with these systemic problems, specifically as they relate to the appointment and evaluation of judges? Large-scale reform of the judicial system has been ongoing since the mid-1990s, and although it has been an uphill struggle to alter the mindset of a whole generation of judges trained under the previous system, there are some obvious signs of progress. Clear, if incremental, improvements have occurred, both in the quality of new judges entering the profession and in the legal persuasiveness of judgments, more and more of which are being made publicly available.

Many of the reforms were originally outlined in the *Judges Law* and then refined and further explained by subsequent regulations and Supreme People's Court interpretations. In this section, I will show how these reforms, which break down into several broad categories, have attempted to address the various flaws identified above.

Stricter Entry Standards for Judges and Greater Emphasis on Legal Knowledge

It was only in 1983 that legal knowledge became one of the official criteria for the selection of judges,[21] and throughout the 1980s and early

1990s the standards for evaluating that knowledge remained extremely vague. In practice, many judges were first transferred from non-legal positions and then obtained their legal knowledge 'on the job,' through night school, correspondence courses, and occasional seminars. Only with the promulgation of the *Judges Law* in 1995 did a law degree or its equivalent become a prerequisite for entry into the judiciary.

Section 9 of the *Judges Law* sets out the following entry requirements, which include not only educational criteria but moral, physical, and political criteria as well:

> To be appointed as a judge one must fulfil the following conditions:
> 1. Be a citizen of the PRC;
> 2. Be at least 23 years old;
> 3. Uphold the PRC Constitution;
> 4. Display good political and professional qualities and moral conduct;
> 5. Be physically healthy; and
> 6. Have graduated from a post-secondary educational institution majoring in law, or have graduated from a post-secondary institution majoring in another field but possessing specialized legal knowledge, [in both cases] with two years' work experience; or have received a bachelor of laws with one year's work experience; or if one has received a master's degree or doctorate in law, the work experience requirement may be waived.

On top of these basic requirements, section 12 of the *Judges Law* states that those who wish to be appointed as judges must also pass a national judicial entrance examination: 'New judges will be appointed based on strict evaluation methods and criteria that include both demonstrated skills and moral conduct; candidates will become qualified for selection after passing a national standard judicial examination and satisfying the basic criteria for becoming a judge.'

Such an examination has been held every two years in China since 1995.[22] Further guidelines for this examination are set out in the 'Interim Measures Regarding the Examination for Appointing Adjudicators and Assistant Adjudicators' (promulgated 1996, revised 1999). Besides reiterating the educational qualifications required to take the examination, which parallel those set out in the *Judges Law*, the measures make it clear that the examination is now mandatory for anyone who wishes to become a judge and that the prior 'work experience' required of candidates must be in the area of law. These two points were not stated clearly in the *Judges Law*.[23]

Having satisfied these basic qualifications, candidates are then appointed as judges based on the recommendation of the court president (or, in the case of higher level courts, the chief justice of the court) to the People's Congress at the level of the court in question. Court presidents and chief justices are themselves appointed directly by the People's Congress at the same level. For example, the SPC grand chief justice is appointed by the National People's Congress, and the chief justice of each province is appointed by the Provincial People's Congress.

With respect to the chief justice, vice chief justice, court president, and vice-president positions, including the so-called grand justices of the Supreme People's Court (SPC), more rigorous criteria were also introduced in amendments to the *Judges Law* in 2001 to reduce the numbers of purely political appointees. Section 12 of the *Judges Law* now includes the following clause: 'Chief justices and vice chief justices of the People's Courts should be selected on the basis of merit from among current judges or from those who meet the required criteria for becoming judges.' In other words, they too must have a law degree or its equivalent. Previously, there were no clear criteria for appointments to such higher level judicial positions.

Though it is too early to see the effect of this amendment, it is clear that legal factors are already beginning to exert stronger influence on the appointment of SPC grand justices. Among the nine current SPC justices, the majority are legal scholars with research degrees who previously held faculty positions in Chinese law schools. For example, Cao Jianming, appointed to the SPC in 1999 and currently ranked as the second-most senior justice in the SPC, holds a master's of law degree, and was for many years a professor of law at the Eastern China Politics and Law University and served as dean of the Faculty of Law from 1997 to 1999. Other grand justices, such as Wan Exiang and Shen Deyong, have similar backgrounds in academia.[24]

Nevertheless, the grand chief justice of the SPC apparently continues to be a political appointee directly chosen by the National People's Congress through an opaque selection process. Xiao Yang, the current incumbent, was previously a career politician and Party official, holding successive positions as Party Secretary in various towns and districts in Guangdong Province before being promoted to the Guangdong Provincial Procuratorate and finally to the Ministry of Justice. He served as minister of justice from 1993 to 1998 prior to his appointment as grand chief justice in 1999. While he did receive some legal education at the university level during the late 1950s, it is not clear whether he completed his law degree, and his focus was obviously on politics for the greater part of his career.

It will be interesting to see whether Xiao Yang's successor is drawn from a primarily legal or political background, and hence whether the grand chief justice will become subject to the rules that govern all other new appointees to leadership positions within the Chinese courts.

In the case of the provincial and municipal superior courts, the effects of the 2001 amendments are less clear. The great majority of current provincial and municipal chief justices do not appear to have any legal background, having instead risen through the ranks of the Party in local and provincial political posts. To give just two examples, Qin Zheng'an, chief justice of the Beijing Municipal Superior Court, received university training in science in the late 1960s, and following the Cultural Revolution, worked his way up through Party posts in the Beijing Municipal Education Ministry, followed by Party Secretary positions in various Beijing district governments. His first legal position came in 1997, when he was appointed as vice chief justice and Party Secretary of the Beijing Superior Court, with his promotion to chief justice coming just one year later. Similarly, Ding Shifa, chief justice of the Liaoning Provincial Superior Court, received a university degree in Chinese language in 1969, then rose through a series of Party posts in the Shenyang Municipal and Liaoning Provincial governments. In 2002, he was appointed provincial chief justice after serving for five years on the Liaoning Provincial Party Committee's Political and Legal Affairs Bureau.[25] Presumably, it will only be after the present incumbents retire or are otherwise removed from their positions that such provincial and municipal chief justices will be drawn from the ranks of judges or legal scholars.

The new set of basic requirements for the appointment of judges to Chinese courts is certainly an improvement on the system that existed prior to 1995. However, many commentators have pointed out that the current system still sets the bar for entry into the judiciary remarkably low in comparison with jurisdictions elsewhere in the world, and still allows far too much political influence on the appointments process. These are points to which I will return in my concluding section.

Training Programs and Other Measures for Existing Judges

Many thousands of judges were appointed under the previous system, and legislators clearly felt reluctant to simply remove those judges who do not meet the stricter educational requirements in force today. Therefore, rather than demanding that sitting judges take the same examination as new appointees, which might result in many losing their positions, the government instead introduced mandatory retraining and skills upgrading courses, taught at various judicial institutes around the country, in an attempt to increase judges' legal knowledge. Section 9 of the *Judges Law* allows for such alternative treatment of existing judges in the following provision, which is appended to the six criteria listed above: 'Those adjudicators who were appointed before the promulgation of this law and who do not meet the [educational] criteria set out in s-s.9(6) should submit to training programs, with the content of such programs to be determined by the Supreme People's Court.'

In addition to such training programs, which judges are supposed to attend once every three years,[26] all judges must also submit to annual performance evaluations organized by their court. Criteria for these evaluations include productivity, intellectual quality, carrying out adjudicative duties properly, demonstrating understanding of legal issues, and a conscientious attitude towards their work.[27] Following evaluation, each judge will be placed in one of three categories: excellent, work acceptable, or work unacceptable. Their ranking will directly affect their remuneration level, retraining requirements, and promotion or demotion prospects.[28] The work of evaluation is supposed to be carried out by judicial evaluation committees set up in each court, although in practice the court president will normally control the process.[29]

Unlike in many jurisdictions elsewhere in the world, in China it is relatively easy to remove judges from their position, or to transfer them to positions where they cannot participate in adjudication work. Section 11 of the *Judges Law* states that the People's Congress at the level equivalent to each court may remove judges of that court on the recommendation of the president of the court. Where political issues are involved, however, it is likely that the local government will take the initiative.

Section 40 of the *Judges Law* lists the wide range of possible causes for discharge, which include:

> 40(1) Receiving an evaluation of 'work unacceptable' for two consecutive years;
> (2) not performing competently in one's current position and refusing to accept an alternative posting [i.e., a demotion];
> (3) refusing a reasonable change in one's duties as a result of reforms to adjudicative bodies or reduction of personnel;
> (4) missing work or taking unauthorized vacations without good reason

for over fifteen consecutive days, or for an aggregate of thirty days within any calendar year; and

(5) not carrying out one's duties as a judge and refusing to correct the problem when requested to by one's superiors.

Clearly, there is as yet no concept of tenure for judges in China. As Hu and Feng observe, the reasons for discharging judges are virtually identical to those for discharging regular Chinese civil servants, a point that I will analyse further below.[30] This situation is obviously a two-edged sword: it allows courts to remove incompetent judges or put pressure on them to improve their legal knowledge, but at the same time it discourages even competent judges from asserting their independence when doing so would ruffle the feathers of their immediate superiors or local political interests.

Even SPC grand justices may be removed from their positions, presumably for the same reasons as regular judges outlined above. However, removal of an SPC justice requires both the recommendation of the SPC grand chief justice and the approval of the standing committee of the National People's Congress. As a result, SPC justices are at least immune from the influence of local or provincial power interests.

On the positive side, the *Judges Law* does establish relatively objective criteria for removing judges, rather than simply leaving decisions entirely to the discretion of court presidents or local Party leaders. And the criteria, though somewhat vague, are solely concerned with professional performance or structural changes within courts leading to new personnel requirements. Moreover, section 8(3) of the *Judges Law* emphasizes that judges may not be discharged, demoted, or disciplined except for legally justifiable reasons, and only by means of a procedure set down in law. Since the implementation of the *Judges Law*, therefore, a discharge of a judge for purely political reasons is more difficult to justify and some evidence of professional incompetence or intransigence on the part of the judge is required.

Improving the Quality and Transparency of the Judgment Writing Process

Apart from changes in the appointment, promotion, and evaluation of judges in China, major reforms are also ongoing in the area of judgment writing and publication. In the case of some progressive local courts, these reforms are not merely a matter of improving judges' formal writing skills, but involve opening up the whole adjudication process to public scrutiny. There are two central aims of the reforms, both relevant for the purposes of our discussion: (i) to discourage judges from engaging in unsavoury or corrupt adjudication practices behind closed doors – since they must now publicly justify every judgment that they make; and (ii) to encourage competent judges to display their legal reasoning powers and judicial wisdom, in order to facilitate a more objective evaluation of their performance, and so ensure that promotion will be based squarely on professional merit rather than personal relationships.

Many courts have now started to post notarized texts of complete judgments on freely accessible and searchable websites.[31] Such publication is significant because previously available published judgments were almost invariably edited and shortened to a greater or lesser degree, possibly distorting their contents in some cases.

The most promising freely accessible collection of posted judgments I have located is on the Chinacourt site, which currently contains a total of 982 original judgments from various levels of Chinese courts, dealing with all major areas of law. If this site continues to expand, it may soon become a relatively comprehensive legal source, useful for both legal practitioners and scholars.[32]

Equally significant, some local court presidents have begun to encourage panels of judges to include dissenting opinions or separate concurring reasons *within* the judgments themselves.[33] The name of each judge is given alongside the opinion that he or she endorses. In previously available published versions of judgments, the disposition section always began with the phrase 'this court holds ...,' with no indication given of any differences of opinion, or even how many judges were involved in the final decision.

The separate identification of judges on the panel, especially with the encouragement of publicly expressed dissenting and separate concurring opinions, is not only a departure for Chinese courts, it goes far beyond what many European civil law jurisdictions currently allow,[34] and seems more similar to the practice of common law appeal courts.

As the president of the Guangzhou Maritime Court, one of the courts that enthusiastically promotes such experiments, points out, the refusal of Chinese courts to publicize the differing opinions of individual judges on judicial panels means that the final decision-making process remains behind closed doors and secret.[35] He argues that requiring all judges to write and publish their own separate opinions in each judgment will allow talented and knowledgeable judges to shine, while showing up in stark relief the failings of unqualified members of the panel. This will help court presidents to make decisions regarding promotion based on merit rather than on personal connections, winnowing out incompetent judges and preventing them from engaging in adjudicative work.[36] Jin also notes that the existing system, by promoting collective and relatively anonymous decision making, has prevented Chinese judges from becoming publicly known and respected in society, unlike the 'Lord Dennings' of common law jurisdictions. The opportunity to become famous rather than remaining obscure, faceless bureaucrats should encourage judges to produce and sign their names to well-reasoned and fair opinions.[37]

Of course, publishing complete judgments, especially those that include dissenting or separate opinions, assumes that a court has a sufficient number of judges qualified to draw their own well-considered conclusions from the evidence and apply laws to complex fact situations. This is not the case in many Chinese courts, as noted earlier.[38] In such an environment, it is not surprising that the Supreme People's Court has preferred to promote incremental improvements on the national scale, such as citing and quoting relevant laws or regulations and dealing with all of the claims of parties in the judgment, rather than encouraging dissent and assertion of individuality among judges.[39]

Reducing the Influence of Court Presidents, Adjudication Committees, and Higher Courts

One further consequence of allowing individual judges to express their own opinions is that court presidents and adjudication committees will be forced to delegate some of their powers. Currently, court presidents in courts of every level can choose to supervise or refer to the adjudication committee any case being heard in their court. As noted above, the president or committee can then require changes to the judgment before it is given.[40] One local court president has argued that delegation of power would give more credit to judges who produce cogently reasoned opinions, while exposing to public scrutiny those not up to the task of adjudication. It would also reduce the workload of the court presidents and committee members, allowing them to focus on truly intractable cases rather than routine decisions, and resolving one of the major bottlenecks in the Chinese court system.[41]

Some moves have been made in this direction by the government. For example, the amended *Criminal Procedure Law* now restricts interference by the adjudication committee to cases that are 'complex or difficult,' and discourages judicial panels from referring problems up the judicial chain before giving judgment.[42] Realistically, however, one wonders how many court presidents and adjudication committee members will be willing to relinquish their power in this way, allowing judges in their courts publicly to disagree with each other and giving the impression that they can no longer influence the outcome of every case.

A similar issue is interference by higher level courts on the decisions of judges of lower level courts *before* the first instance judgment is pronounced. Such interference is still justified by many judges, including some SPC grand justices, as a means of preventing obviously erroneous decisions from having deleterious effects on the parties involved. Lower court judges can seek the opinion of a higher court judge with more experience, and adjust their decisions accordingly.[43] However, many scholars criticize such practice because it further erodes the independence of individual judges and reverses the regular procedure laid down in the *Organizational Law of the People's Courts*, whereby decisions at the first instance may be appealed to a higher court. If the higher court has already given its opinion, any appeal would simply be futile for the parties involved.[44] Scholars also express concern at the casual nature of such external advice, which is frequently given over the telephone after a short summary of the facts by the lower level judge.[45] I discuss this issue of judicial independence in more detail in the final section below.

Remaining Problems with the Judicial Appointment System

The various measures implemented since 1995 to improve the quality of Chinese judges and the integrity of their decision-making process are a step in the right direction. Perhaps even more crucial for the future is the encouraging fact that both the Chinese government and the Supreme People's Court have publicly exposed and attempted to address the serious defects of the Chinese justice system. They have allowed some local courts to experiment with more far-reaching reforms – even including those influenced by common law approaches – in order to test their suitability in the Chinese legal context. They have also organized numerous conferences and seminars and sponsored the publication of a wide range of opinions from among the judiciary and the scholarly community on the best means of deepening reform over the next decade.[46]

In pointing out problems that remain with the current system, we should not forget the broader context that underlies all aspects of social reform in China. Within both government and court hierarchies, diverse and sometimes contradictory interests struggle for supremacy, with progressives arrayed against conservatives, centralizing interests vying with localizing interests, and international-minded cosmopolitans competing with xenophobic nationalists. Likewise, the government and Supreme People's Court must constantly engage in a balancing act between promoting innovation and maintaining social stability in a rapidly changing society. Such competing interests and broader social factors help to explain the frustratingly gradual and seemingly half-hearted nature of reform in certain sensitive areas.[47]

With these qualifications in mind, I will conclude this discussion by identifying the major shortcomings that must still be dealt with to ensure that Chinese judges will be appointed and evaluated under a fair and objective process, and that their decisions will inspire public respect and confidence rather than the present continuing cynicism and derision.

Entry Standards for Judges Still Too Low

Many commentators have criticized the entry criteria set out in the *Judges Law* for being too lax. Those who have reached the age of twenty-three, fulfilled the educational and work criteria set out in section 9, and passed the judicial examination are more or less assured of finding a position.[48] However, this does not mean that they actually have the knowledge and experience to serve as judges. Even those at the high end of the educational spectrum may only possess a law degree plus two years' working experience. And the judicial examination, though similar to North American bar exams in terms of style and degree of difficulty, gives little indication of a candidate's aptitude for writing opinions or applying the law to complex fact situations, since most of the answers are in multiple choice format.[49]

The inevitable result is that court presidents and adjudication committees must supervise newly appointed judges until they have built up sufficient experience on the bench to adjudicate by themselves. To avoid such an undesirable situation, some legal practitioners have argued that the minimum age of judges should be raised to thirty or thirty-five, and that judges should be required to work in a law-related occupation for ten years prior to being eligible for appointment to the bench.[50] These sensible proposals may ultimately be adopted in China. However, one must not forget that, as of 1999, only 28 per cent of Chinese judges possessed a law degree, and that this was a tenfold increase over the number of degree-holding judges in 1979. Of those 28 per cent, moreover, many obtained their degrees by taking correspondence courses or night classes rather than attending a formal university program.[51] For the time being, therefore, educational qualifications will remain a higher priority for the courts than practical legal experience.

Lack of Judicial Independence

Section 8.2 of the *Judges Law* states that judges have the right to adjudicate cases according to the law without interference from 'administrative organs, social groups and individuals.' Though this right appears on the surface to resemble Western concepts of judicial independence, in practice individual judges in China still face two major obstacles that hamper their ability to adjudicate purely according to the law.

First, although theoretically the prohibition on interference by 'administrative organs' includes government bodies, such as ministries, agencies, and the like, it apparently does not include the Party itself.[52] Moreover, as we noted earlier, the position of judges is still little different from other local government and civil service functionaries, in that judges at each level can be readily discharged by the government body at the same level. As a result, when faced with political cases involving either dissidents or allegedly corrupt Party and government officials, judges will invariably defer to the stated or unstated wishes of the local or central government when deciding guilt or innocence.[53] It is true that, in recent years, many hundreds of Party and state officials, including some at the exalted rank of municipal or provincial Party Secretary, have been tried in the courts and convicted of corruption and other offences, with the death penalty meted out to the most serious offenders.[54] Yet there is a widespread public perception in China that the vast majority of Party officials engage in corrupt practices to a certain degree, and those who actually face prosecution are not always the worst offenders; rather, they are simply the losers in factional struggles within the Party hierarchy. In most such cases, courts merely act as a vehicle through which sentences are handed down, with guilt effectively established before the accused even stands trial. Judges would be foolish to question the evidence against such alleged offenders and still hope to keep their positions on the bench.

A similar situation applies to those charged with opposing the Party or the government. Take, for example, the recent spate of trials of supporters of the banned spiritual movement Falungong. A judge who unilaterally decided to acquit such people on the constitutional grounds of freedom of religious belief would almost certainly face immediate discharge, and the decision would inevitably be overturned at a higher level. The government made a policy decision to treat Falungong not as a religious belief but as a harmful and subversive superstition, and no Chinese court, let alone an individual judge, would venture to overturn such a decision on constitutional grounds.[55] This situation is unlikely to change without major political and constitutional reform accompanied by the establishment of a secure tenure system for individual judges.

At the same time, the majority of cases passing through Chinese courts do not directly involve political interests, and in these cases courts are now generally able to adjudicate without the kind of external interference that was common even as recently as the 1980s.

This brings us to the second obstacle to judicial independence: internal interference by court presidents, adjudication committees, and higher level courts. Most Chinese courts still attempt to maintain a public image of unanimity when deciding cases, despite private differences of opinion among individual judges. This is done both by requiring panels of judges to produce a single judgment signed by all of the sitting judges – whether they agree with it or not – and by requiring that any doubtful or difficult cases be referred to the adjudication committee, and sometimes to higher level courts as well, *before* judgment is given.[56] Some legal scholars have justified such an approach by interpreting section 8.2 of the *Judges Law* to mean that judges collectively in each court should be independent from external interference, but that individual judges should not be independent from other judges within the same court. Support for this interpretation comes from section 125 of the *Constitution of the People's Republic of China*, which states: 'The People's Courts will independently carry out adjudication based on the law without interference by administrative organs, social groups, or individuals.'

In other words, it is the courts that are independent, not the judges. Faced with such reasoning, one scholar has remarked sardonically that under the current system judges are not 'adjudicators' at all, but 'communicators': in other words, they merely communicate to the parties the decisions made by their superiors.[57]

Likewise, as noted earlier, there is still occasional interference by higher level courts in the work of lower level courts, which is usually justified by the 'supervisory' role accorded to the superior courts under the *Organizational Law of the People's Courts.* In fact, only the SPC is given this supervisory role over lower courts (in section 30 of the *Organiza-*

tional Law) and rarely exercises it.[58] However, many superior courts have apparently taken it upon themselves to perform this pre-judgment advisory role, even though other sections of the *Organizational Law* clearly state that such courts should wait until the first instance judgment has been pronounced and the decision appealed.[59]

The crux of this problem, like many others, is the overall quality of the judiciary. As we noted above, a handful of local courts have been experimenting with reforms that promote a much higher degree of judicial independence within the court, with individual judges actively encouraged to produce dissenting opinions and take final responsibility for their decisions. Yet such reforms are unlikely to be implemented on the national level until the general educational level of judges improves. Indeed, if judges still lack the basic skills and knowledge to correctly apply and explain the law, a truly independent judiciary with judges' positions protected by a tenure system could prove more of a curse than a blessing! At the very least, a major effort must be made to identify and remove incompetent judges before the concept of judicial independence can be seriously debated in China.

Lack of Clear Standards for Disciplining Judges

Another problem that the recent reforms have not satisfactorily addressed is how to deal with judges whose conduct violates acceptable professional or moral standards. While section 32 of the *Judges Law* does list unacceptable behaviours that are subject to discipline, these are extremely broad in scope and the exact form of discipline for each offence is not clearly specified. Offences include disseminating opinions that harm the national reputation; participating in illegal groups or in gatherings, demonstrations, and other activities aimed at opposing the state; taking part in strikes; accepting bribes and engaging in corrupt behaviour; distorting the law for the sake of one's personal relations; extorting confessions by torture; covering up or fabricating evidence; revealing or misusing state secrets and secrets related to judicial work; neglecting one's duties to the extent of making erroneous decisions or causing serious loss to a party; purposely delaying adjudication so that one's work is adversely affected; using one's position to obtain private benefits for oneself or others; engaging in profit-seeking activities; privately meeting with parties or their representatives and accepting gifts and invitations from parties or their representatives; and finally, engaging in any other conduct that 'violates law and discipline.'

Despite this apparently comprehensive coverage, Chinese commentators have noted that it is not at all clear what kind of disciplinary action will be attached to each violation.[60] Possible punishments range from warnings through demotion and discharge to criminal prosecution for illegal activities,[61] but there is no detailed breakdown of recommended sanctions for non-criminal offences in either the *Judges Law* or any other public regulations. Likewise, there is no code of conduct explaining to judges what each of the offences actually entails – what, for example, is meant by 'harming the national reputation'? As a result, most decisions on discipline that do not directly involve political issues are simply left to the discretion of individual courts.[62]

When compounded by the lack of individual accountability of judges for their decisions, the result of such a vague disciplinary framework is that corrupt or incompetent judges who maintain good relations with their immediate superiors in the court and Party routinely get away with offences such as accepting gifts and invitations from parties to their cases. On the other hand, upright judges may find themselves demoted simply for challenging an erroneous decision of the court president or adjudication committee and thereby 'violating [court] discipline.'[63]

Lack of Political Will to Remove Incompetent Judges and Improve Efficiency

Although statistics regarding the low educational levels of judges are still shocking, they are misleading in one sense. Many of the so-called judges within Chinese courts do not carry out any adjudicative functions, but are responsible only for administrative tasks. This is another indication that until very recently the government viewed the judiciary simply as an arm of the civil service, and adjudication was considered to be a form of administration. Under such a system, there was no anomaly in terming both court administrators and adjudicators as 'judges.' One study has estimated that, of the 142 judges sitting in a district court in Shanghai, some 26, or approximately 17 per cent, do not engage in any adjudicative work. If one also subtracts the number of so-called assistant judges, who generally do not have the right to adjudicate, but may act on the judge's behalf for preliminary or procedural matters, the number of true judges decreases still further to just 64, or approximately 45 per cent of the total.[64]

Moreover, as one study has pointed out, China has a much higher proportion of judges in relation to the total population than many other countries. Citing figures from 1992, the authors note that China had

140,000 'judges' out of a total population of 1.166 billion, or one judge for every 8,328 people. By contrast, Canada currently has approximately 2,500 judges out of a population of 30 million, or one judge per 12,000 people. In other words, even adjusting for the difference in overall population, China still has around 1.5 times as many judges per person as Canada.[65] The difference is even more striking with other countries, such as the United Kingdom,[66] so there is clearly inefficiency built into the current system.

What is even more pressing than recruiting more judges, now that entry standards have been tightened up, is to remove the enormous number of incompetent and superfluous judges, so that better qualified judges can do their jobs without internal court interference from ill-qualified superiors. Indeed, once a basic core of qualified judges is trained and hired, they will be able to adjudicate individually without the need for three-person judicial panels and frequent references to adjudication committees. This will immediately raise the efficiency of courts while still allowing for a large reduction in the number of judges. Some scholars have therefore proposed that all judges in district and provincial level courts who cannot pass the judicial examination or its equivalent should be removed from their positions. Those over fifty should be immediately pensioned off, and younger judges should be transferred to non-judicial positions, losing their title as judges, so that they have no further opportunity to carry out adjudicative work.[67]

Such proposals, while very sensible, are doubtless made with the knowledge that they will not be applied in practice, at least in the near future. Older judges tend to be among the most senior personnel in each court – including many chief justices and court presidents – and they have had time to build up the strongest ties to local power interests. They will strongly resist efforts to reduce their influence on the adjudication process. Their political superiors in the local government will also be loath to lose a useful group of allies within the courts merely in the interests of abstract ideals such as judicial impartiality and legal competence.

Low Remuneration of Judges

Judges in China are often tempted to abuse their positions to gain material benefits. Some Chinese scholars have therefore proposed that judges be paid much higher salaries than their current civil service rates to lessen the financial temptation of corrupt activities. High remuneration should also attract better-qualified applicants to take the judicial examination. However, the government is reluctant to give preferential treatment to judges when other government officials still receive relatively meagre salaries. Moreover, as we have seen, the concept of judicial independence is not yet firmly enough entrenched in China for the government to distinguish judges from other kinds of civil servants. Changes in this area will likely depend on greater national economic prosperity in the future and broader reforms to the Chinese political structure.[68]

Negative Influences of 'Local Protectionism'

A final problem that continues to plague the Chinese court system is the tendency of many courts to favour local economic and political interests when adjudicating disputes. For example, a court may refuse to enforce a 'foreign' (i.e., out of province) judgment that would result in a local state-owned business going bankrupt or cutting jobs. One obvious way of addressing this problem would be to transfer the power of appointing and discharging judges to a higher level of government, and to give judges more secure tenure, thus freeing them from the pressure to conform to the desires of local government and business elites.[69]

Another solution, proposed in a central government policy document but not yet implemented, is for judges to serve a maximum of three years in any one court before being transferred to a court in another jurisdiction.[70] If adopted, such a system would be an interesting throwback to imperial China, when local magistrates faced a similar three-year rotation to prevent them from developing strong local ties and power bases, thereby threatening the authority of the emperor and the central government.[71] The difference today is that judges, unlike imperial magistrates, are no longer members of the executive, and do not control the local political power structure. If their appointment, promotion, and discharge are still influenced by local governments at the same level, they will presumably continue to toe the local Party and government line during their three-year postings, whether or not they come from the region themselves. One wonders whether this proposal is simply an attempt to avoid implementing more painful and far-reaching reforms, such as removing large numbers of older judges and reducing local government influence over the judiciary. Only such radical changes will help to create a competent and truly independent judiciary with the power to stand up against local political interests without fear of reprisals.

Conclusion

Though it will certainly take many years to restructure the Chinese courts and remove a whole generation of incompetent and often corrupt judges, the fact that concerned legal practitioners and scholars are permitted publicly to criticize the current system and to experiment with deeper reforms at the local level is a sign of great progress. As with corresponding political and economic reforms in China, advances in the legal sphere are rarely as sudden or dramatic as Western liberal democrats might wish. It may turn out, however, that in the long term China's incremental attitude towards change will produce a more stable and effective set of legal institutions than found in nations in which democratic legal systems have been imposed before the wider society was ready for them.

NOTES

1 Hu and Feng, *Sifa gongzheng yu sifa gaige yanjiu zongshu,* 164; Peerenboom, *China's Long March towards Rule of Law,* 44; Lubman, *Bird in a Cage: Legal Reform in China after Mao,* 73–4.
2 Peerenboom, *China's Long March towards Rule of Law,* 46; Lubman, *Bird in a Cage,* 76. As Peerenboom notes, at 44–5, there were brief periods during the mid-1950s and early 1960s when the court system achieved a level of relative independence from the executive. However, courts were generally viewed with suspicion by the Communist government until at least the late 1970s.
3 Hu and Feng, *Sifa gongzheng yu sifa gaige yanjiu zongshu,* 164–5. Note that the term that I translate as 'judge' (*faguan,* literally meaning 'legal official') was not favoured by the Communist government, which preferred the term 'adjudicator' (*shenpanyuan*) as having fewer class connotations. 'Officials' were associated with the exploiting classes of the pre-revolutionary Nationalist regime. The term *faguan* only returned to favour with the passing of the *Judges Law* (*Faguan fa*) in 1995.
4 Lubman, *Bird in a Cage,* (1999), 47–8.
5 Ibid., 73.
6 Hu and Feng, *Sifa gongzheng yu sifa gaige yanjiu zongshu,* 165; Lubman, *Bird in a Cage,* 100–1.
7 Alford, 'A Second Great Wall?,' 193ff.; Hu and Feng, *Sifa gongzheng yu sifa gaige yanjiu zongshu,* 165–6.
8 Lubman, *Bird in a Cage,* 278–80.
9 See, e.g., the annual reports of Xiao Yang, SPC Chief Justice, such as *Zuigao*

renmin fayuan gongbao, 1999.1:16 and 1999.2: 51–4. Cf. Hu and Feng, *Sifa gongzheng yu sifa gaige yanjiu zongshu*, 344–52.

10 Cited in Liu and Xiaoyu, 'Guanyu faguan guanli zhidu gaige de ruogan wenti yanjiu,' 136.

11 Lubman, *Bird in a Cage* (1999), 126–30, esp. 128. Lubman notes that the 'nation governed by the rule of law' slogan is usually attributed to Jiang Zemin, in a speech addressing a Party conference in 1996. For a thorough discussion of 'rule of law' in modern China, see Peerenboom, *China's Long March towards Rule of Law.* Peerenboom notes, at 56–63, that there are various, sometimes competing, theories among Chinese scholars and policy makers as to what rule of law exactly entails.

12 I use the Chinese text of the *Judges Law* in *Falu xiaoquanshu* (Laws and Regulations of China) (2002), 1:36, which incorporates some amendments passed in 2001. All references to provisions in the *Judges Law* are to this edition, and all translations are my own unless otherwise indicated below. A slightly quirky English translation of the *Judges Law* is available at the following website: http://en.chinacourt.org/public/detail.php?id=2692

13 Lubman, *Bird in a Cage*, 256; Hu and Feng, *Sifa gongzheng yu sifa gaige yanjiu zongshu*, 170–1.

14 Lubman, *Bird in a Cage*, 263–6.

15 Hu and Feng, *Sifa gongzheng yu sifa gaige yanjiu zongshu*, 171.

16 Peerenboom, *China's Long March towards Rule of Law*, 280–1.

17 Hu and Feng, *Sifa gongzheng yu sifa gaige yanjiu zongshu*, 172–5. For further discussion of the adjudicative process, see Hawes, 'Dissent and Transparency in Recently Published Chinese Court Judgments.'

18 Hawes, *Dissent and Transparency* 13–14.

19 For judges' remuneration, see Hu and Feng, *Sifa gongzheng yu sifa gaige yanjiu zongshu*, 202, 205. For judicial corruption, see Lubman, *Bird in a Cage*, 260, 278–80.

20 Yan and He, 'Lun caipan wenshu gaige de ji ge wenti,' 895–6.

21 Hu and Feng, *Sifa gongzheng yu sifa gaige yanjiu zongshu*, 166. This requirement was set out in the *Renmin fayuan zuzhi fa* (Organizational Law of the People's Courts), s.34.2.

22 Hu and Feng, *Sifa gongzheng yu sifa gaige yanjiu zongshu*, 167. For Chinese readers, past papers and other information on the national judicial examination can be found at the following website: http://www.chinacourt.org/flfw/

23 Hu and Feng, *Sifa gongzheng yu sifa gaige yanjiu zongshu*, 167.

24 Information on the backgrounds of these SPC justices, and those of the chief justice and provincial/municipal judges described below, comes from the Chinacourt website, at http://www.chinacourt.org/dfg/.

25 Ibid. For general surveys of the SPC, now slightly outdated but still useful, see Finder, 'The Supreme People's Court of the People's Republic of China'; and Nanping Liu, *Judicial Interpretation in China.*

26 The three-year requirement was set out in a central government policy document issued in 1998, entitled 'Five Year Reform Plan for the People's Courts.' However, it is likely that the actual frequency of training programs varies from region to region, for economic reasons.

27 *Judges Law,* s. 23.

28 *Judges Law,* s. 24.

29 *Judges Law,* s. 48–9; Hu and Feng, *Sifa gongzheng yu sifa gaige yanjiu zongshu,* 199–200.

30 Hu and Feng, *Sifa gongzheng yu sifa gaige yanjiu zongshu,* 201.

31 One of the best of these is the Guangzhou Maritime Court site, http://www.ccmt.org.cn. The site, which is constantly updated and expanded, as at March 2004) contained 531 GMC judgments, dating from the previous three years. It also included around 412 original maritime and commercial judgments from other Chinese courts. The site is rather misleadingly titled 'China Foreign-Related Commercial and Maritime Trials [Website],' but the judgments from the GMC include many purely domestic cases. The site seems to work best using Internet Explorer (not Netscape). For the GMC judgments click on the tab *haishi* ('maritime') at the top right of screen, then select Guangzhou, and click on *caipan wenshu* ('judgments') to go to the indexed tables of GMC judgments. To obtain the full judgment texts, click on the red highlighted text in each table.

32 See www.chinacourt.org/sfws. The Chinacourt site also contains useful information in Chinese about the recent adjudicative reforms in China.

33 Many examples can be found (in Chinese) on the GMC website: http://www.ccmt.org.cn. See also Jin, 'Gaige caipan wenshu de shuxie fangshi shi shenhua shenpan fangshi gaige de tupokou,' for a justification of this practice.

34 MacCormick and Summers, *Interpreting Precedents,* 110: '[In France], it is generally thought that such [dissenting and separate concurring] opinions would weaken the legitimacy of the courts, because their decisions would be seen, not as the expression of the truth, but as the mere private opinion of a majority of the court.'

35 Jin, 'Gaige caipan wenshu de shuxie fangshi shi shenhua shenpan fangshi gaige de tupokou,' 2 (2001).

36 Idid., 2; Zhengjia Jin, interview by author, Beijing China, 25 June 2002 [hereinafter, Jin interview].

37 Jin, 'Gaige caipan wenshu de shuxie fangshi shi shenhua shenpan fangshi gaige de tupokou,' 2.

38 See Lubman, *Bird in a Cage*, 253–8.

39 See the cautious stance of the *Administrative Measures of the Supreme People's Court on the Publication of Judgment Texts* (*Zuigao renmin fayuan caipan wenshu gongbu guanli banfa*), promulgated 15 June 2000 [hereinafter *Measures*]. Chinese text in *Zuigao renmin fayuan gongbao* (2000) 4:118.

40 The legal basis for these powers is set out in the 2002 SPC Regulations, cited in the preceding note.

41 Jin interview.

42 Peerenboom, *China's Long March towards Rule of Law*, 286.

43 See Hu and Feng, *Sifa gongzheng yu sifa gaige yanjiu zongshu*, 153, citing former SPC justice Liu Jiashen.

44 Ibid., citing the legal scholar He Weifang.

45 Peerenboom, *China's Long March towards Rule of Law*, 314–15.

46 The comprehensive collection of papers by judges and legal scholars from all over China, edited by Cao Jianming and others, on which I have heavily relied in preparing this chapter, is a good example of such recent publications. See Cao Jianming et al., eds., *Zhongguo shenpan fangshi gaige lilun wenti yanjiu.*

47 For these broader institutional and social issues, see Potter, *The Chinese Legal System*, esp. chapters 1–2.

48 Hu and Feng, *Sifa gongzheng yu sifa gaige yanjiu zongshu*, 197.

49 See sample examination papers from the past few sessions in Chinese at http://www.chinacourt.org/flfw/.

50 Liu and Chen, 'Guanyu faguan guanli zhidu gaige de ruogan wenti yanjiu,' 159.

51 Hu and Feng, *Sifa gongzheng yu sifa gaige yanjiu zongshu*, 182–3, 188; Liu and Chen, 132, 139; Lubman, *Bird in a Cage*, 253–4.

52 Hu and Feng, *Sifa gongzheng yu sifa gaige yanjiu zongshu*, 172–3; Lubman, *Bird in a Cage*, (1999), 214.

53 Lubman, *Bird in a Cage*, 263–6.

54 Peerenboom, *China's Long March towards Rule of Law*, 133.

55 For a detailed discussion of Falungong from the perspective of rule of law, see ibid., 91–102.

56 Hu and Feng, *Sifa gongzheng yu sifa gaige yanjiu zongshu*, 173.

57 Ibid., 177, citing the legal scholar Xu Yichu.

58 See Chinese text of *Organisational Law of the People's Courts* in Shu; further references are to this edition.

59 See *Organizational Law of the People's Courts*, s. 14.

60 Wang Liming, *Sifa gaige yanjiu*, 436–7.

61 *Judges Law*, s. 34.

62 Wang, *Sifa gaige yanjiu*, 437.

63 Lubman, *Bird in a Cage*, 260, 278–9.

64 Liu and Chen, 'Guanyu faguan guanli zhidu gaige de ruogan wenti yanjiu,' 132–3. Cf. Wang Guiping, 'Zhongguo faguan zhidu de fansi yu chonggou,' 158.

65 See the chapter by F.L. Morton in this volume figures.

66 Liu and Chen, 'Guanyu faguan guanli zhidu gaige de ruogan wenti yanjiu,' 132. In the United Kingdom, for example, there are five times fewer judges per person than in China. However, there are also large numbers of U.K. magistrates who perform various adjudicative functions in local British courts.

67 Wang, 'Zhongguo faguan zhidu de fansi yu chonggou,' 159–60.

68 Hu and Feng, *Sifa gongzheng yu sifa gaige yanjiu zongshu*, 205–6; Wang, 425–9.

69 Lubman, *Bird in a Cage*, 266–9.

70 Hu and Feng, *Sifa gongzheng yu sifa gaige yanjiu zongshu*, 168, from the 'Five Year Plan for Reform of the People's Courts.'

71 For traditional Chinese magistrates in the Qing dynasty (1644–1911), see Ch`ü, T`ung-tsu, *Law and Society in Traditional China.*

Conclusion

PETER H. RUSSELL

The Inescapable Political Nature of the Process

The one clear conclusion to be taken from the accounts of appointing judges in the nineteen preceding chapters is that no matter how the process is constructed it always has a political dimension. This is bad news for those who want to take the politics out of appointing judges. The desire to insulate the appointment of judges from politics is an understandable human aspiration. The defining function of the judiciary is to adjudicate disputes about citizens' and governments' rights and duties. If the adjudicative function is to be carried out in an even-handed way it would seem essential that those who perform the function somehow be chosen in a way that rises above the contested realm of politics. But alas, we humans are incapable of such apolitical action in operating our institutions of governance. What this book shows is that our choice is between a process in which the politics is open, acknowledged, and possesses some degree of balance or a system in which political power and influence is masked, unacknowledged, and unilateral. The book also shows that while reform in appointing judges is always possible, the options in each national context are highly constrained by the country's political culture and circumstances.

In the United States, as Michael Tolley reminds us, the process of selecting judges has been political from the very beginning. This is what we should expect in a country that has acknowledged the judiciary's political role in its very foundation, and in its constitution provided for an open political process in the appointment of its federal judges. The politics of that process – presidential nomination and appointment with 'the advice and consent' of the Senate – is a raw kind of politics in which conflicting considerations of ideological and policy are ventilated in a public arena. The current crisis in that system described in Tolley's chapter shows how it can break down when partisanship, fuelled by ideological absolutism, is so fierce that there is a lack of respect on both sides of politics for the political conventions that moderate the political contest over the appointment of judges. The Americans are not likely to restructure a process so enshrined in their constitutional history. They will avoid a crisis if their political leadership recovers a capacity for the modicum of moderation essential for the operation of their system. Elsewhere in the democratic world, no matter how much reformers may aspire to a more open and democratic system of appointing judges, they are unlikely to risk the raw politics of the American model.

In chapters on other long-established liberal democracies based, primarily, on the common law legal culture – Australia, Canada, New Zealand, and different components of the United Kingdom – we can see how the politics of appointing judges has 'come out of the closet,' so to speak. In her introduction to this volume, Kate Malleson points to the global increase in judicial power as a crucial factor in increasing political interest in how judges are appointed. Once judges are recognized as having a discretionary kind of power on controversial issues of public policy there is bound to be more concern about who they are and how they are chosen. We can see this tendency clearly at work in F.L. Morton's chapter on Canada, where controversy over the judiciary's interpretation of a constitutional *Charter of Rights and Freedoms* has made the appointment of the judiciary, especially at the highest level, a major political issue. Similarly, Jim Allan's chapter on New Zealand relates political interest in the appointment of judges to that country's adoption of a quasi-constitutional *Human Rights Act*, plus the creation, following the abolition of Privy Council appeals, of a new national Supreme Court.

In the United Kingdom, the incorporation of the European Convention on Human Rights into domestic law has expanded the potential power of domestic judges and contributed to political interest in appointing judges. But Kate Malleson's chapter on England and Wales and Alan Paterson's on Scotland indicate that other factors are at work in building momentum for reforming the traditional system of appointing judges. Judicial reform in the United Kingdom is part of a larger process of modernization. Vesting the highest judicial authority in Law Lords and an officer of state who is both a member of the cabinet and speaker of a parliamentary chamber will not likely survive Britain's transition from a purely parliamentary democracy to a constitutional democracy. Part of the modernization process is an unmasking of the power of a judicial elite to recreate itself and the social exclusiveness of that elite. Alan Paterson speaks of 'the decline in moral authority of the judiciary' and 'a more demanding consumer society' as contributing to public interest in reforming how judges are appointed. In Australia, which stands alone among the Anglo common law democracies in resisting the constitutionalization of rights, the appointment of judges has been less of a political issue. Nonetheless, Elizabeth Handsley's chapter reports that controversial judges and controversial judicial decisions on 'cutting edge' issues such as the rights of women and indigenous peoples are beginning to quicken political interest in a judicial selection system that is more transparent and likely to produce a more socially diverse judiciary.

The supposition that it is the growth or recognition of judicial power that produces political interest in the appointment of judges receives support from chapters on liberal democracies which have civil law legal cultures. The institutionalized role of political parties in selecting the members of Germany's Constitutional Court described by Christine Landfried is a classic example of politicizing the process of selecting the judges of a court which from the beginning was recognized as having a major role in German government. But Landfried's analysis also shows that the control of judicial appointments by party notables may result in a process that is as closed and unaccountable as when judicial elites control appointments. In Italy, as we learn in Mary Volcansek's chapter, a different kind of judicial power has had a very different effect on judicial appointments. The prosecution and trial of corrupt politicians by an aggressive magistracy has attracted much more political attention than the exercise of judicial review by that country's Constitutional Court. The politics of managing the judicial system is played out primarily among rival judicial unions. The magistrates collectively insulate themselves from the power of politicians and the higher judiciary by making success in competitive exams the only point of entry and ensuring that promotions are governed solely by seniority. Leny de Groot-van Leeuwen's chapter on the Netherlands takes us to a politically calmer European democracy with a judicial system and a legal culture that is less rigorously civilian. The Dutch have long recognized the 'pragmatic' role of judges in developing the law and their lawyers have constituted a powerful and respected profession. Though the Netherlands has not yet adopted domestic constitutional judicial review, recognition of judicial power is evident in the formal control the Dutch parliament has maintained over appointments to its Supreme Court and the reflection of the country's balance of political forces in the committee that selects the members of its lower courts. In Europe, France stands out as the country that, as Doris Marie Provine and Antoine Garapon put it, is marked by 'devotion to judicial passivity.' This denial of judicial power extends to the constitutional review of legislation, a function carried out by a wholly political Constitutional Council. In this setting, the politics of judicial selection operates within the judicial hierarchy itself in the selection of judges for the country's highest courts.

The chapters on Japan and Egypt deal with two countries in which the judiciary is based very much on the French model. David O'Brien's chapter shows that control over Japan's career judiciary is even more concentrated in the hands of a judicial elite than is the case in France. While the *Conseil superieur de la magistrature* which manages the French judiciary has some politically appointed lay members, in Japan it is the chief justice and his General Secretariat who control entry to and promotion within the Japanese judiciary. The domination of Japanese politics by a single party has facilitated a hegemonic alliance between judicial and political elites. Rather than removing politics from the appointment and promotion of judges, this alliance has insulated judicial politics from public exposure and debate. Egypt too has emulated the French judicial model, including its separate system of administrative law tribunals. But, as we learn in Mahmoud Hamad's chapter, the rule of law is much stronger in Egypt after major regime changes from Nasser, to Sadat, to Mubarak, although it still depends on an uneasy and politically vulnerable alliance between the President and the senior judiciary. While President Mubarak, much more than his predecessors, tries to derive legitimacy from closer adherence to the rule of law, he did not hesitate to use his control over the appointment of the chief justice, who heads the judicial hierarchy, to tame judicial activism when it threatened to impose unwelcome limits on his regime.

Chapters on three newer democracies, Israel, Namibia, and South Africa, show how an awareness in constitution making of the social and political significance of judicial power can produce carefully crafted constitutional provisions for the appointment of judges. The challenge for both Namibia and South Africa, emerging from decades of white domination rule, has been to design systems that are true to their liberal democratic constitutional foundations, including an independent judiciary, but at the same time can produce, fairly quickly, a judiciary that their black majorities will trust and respect. In both cases, the chosen mechanism is a Judicial Services Commission (JSC), an institution favoured by former British colonies. Though judicial commissions now operate in many parts of the world, and in an interesting historical twist, are now the chosen instrument of judicial reform in the United Kingdom, they come in many shapes and sizes. What they all have in common is an attempt to establish some balance in the political and professional forces that control judicial appointments. It is doubtful if any other country's commission has the same range and depth of membership as the South African Judicial Services Commission described by François du Bois, with three senior judges, eight lawyers, eleven politicians (three of whom must be members of opposition parties), and four persons chosen by the President in consultation with the leaders of all parties in the National Assembly. Sufian Hemed Bukurura's chapter on Namibia describes a JSC that is much smaller and more professionally dominated, but which has nonetheless functioned as an important vehicle of judicial independence. The same cannot be said for Zimbabwe, whose independence constitution also provided for a Judicial Services Commission. Derek Matyszak's chapter shows how the composition of Zimbabwe's JSC is so thoroughly under presidential control that President Mugabe has been able to ensure that it will appoint a 'compliant judiciary' who will reject legal challenges to his authoritarian regime.

The judicial appointments committee which, since 1953, has played the primary role in selecting the Israeli judiciary does not bear the JSC label but nonetheless performs the JSC selection function in a very powerful manner. It does this in a liberal democracy whose judiciary, in Eli Salzberger's view, has emerged as a dominant branch of government. The Israeli committee is more professionally oriented than the South African model, with judges and lawyers occupying five of its nine positions, while two cabinet ministers and two Knesset members provide its political component. The political struggle over its composition that has developed in recent years suggests that its domination by jurists from the secular, liberal side of Israeli politics means that it cannot provide the political balance needed in the selection of the members of a judiciary that has come to play such an important role in the country's most contested political issues.

Judicial power and judicial politics have been prominent features of a newer democracy, post-Communist Russia. In reading Alexei Trochev's chapter one is struck by the size of the contemporary Russian judiciary and its activist inclinations. It is equally clear that this surge of judicial power has occurred on far from settled constitutional foundations. Judicial review by a Constitutional Court has survived, but only by the judges showing a prudent sense of the limits of their mandate. In the Putin era the politics of judicial selection has been part of a larger political struggle to strengthen power at the centre of the Russian federation. The major reform of the judicial selection process has been minimizing the role of regionally based politicians. Although this limits the system's political pluralism, it has left a very powerful role for 'judicial bosses' to operate alongside 'political bosses.' In a political context where the fall from power may be swift and fast, Trochev suggests that rulers like Putin have an interest in maintaining a judicial system that will treat them fairly when they are no longer on top.

In China, a Communist state that has made no pretence of moving to liberal democracy, the situation is obviously very different. The rulers here fear no sudden fall from power and have no interest in an activist judiciary that might apply constitutional limits on their rule. But we can see in Colin Hawes contribution to the volume that the regime has developed an interest in developing a large and technically proficient judiciary as an instrument for maintaining social order. A judiciary that knows some law and appears capable of handling private commercial disputes in a consistent and predictable manner will also assist China in gaining greater access to international trade and investment. 'Progressives' struggle against 'conservatives' to supplant political loyalty and military service as criteria for judicial appointments. While this is a political struggle, it is kept 'in house' – within the Party. This is not a regime that tolerates open debate about the institutions of government.

The glimpse that the second part of David O'Brien's chapter affords of other Asian countries indicates that there is little scope for a politics of appointing judges in this part of the world. This reflects a general underdevelopment of the judicial branch of government in countries whose judiciaries tend to be almost undifferentiated sections of the civil service. There are some interesting exceptions. In Pakistan, we see that a Supreme Court endeavouring to check executive control of appointments was quickly brought under control by a military dictator. In Bangladesh, a high court ruling has led to the introduction of that favourite institution of former British colonies, a Judicial Services Commission, and separation of judicial selection and appointments from the regular civil service. And in Cambodia, O'Brien reports that a system of brokered politics among leaders of the three main political parties has recently come into play in appointing the members of the country's skeletal judiciary. In Lao and Vietnam, however, one-party Communist rule continues with Party control of the membership of emasculated, poorly paid, and inadequately prepared judiciaries similar to those found in China before its recent effort at reform. There will be no politics of judicial appointments, open or behind the scenes, in non-democratic countries with weak judiciaries.

As for International Courts, appointment processes as analysed by Ruth Mackenzie and Philippe Sands most certainly have a political dimension. Courts rendering justice across national borders in an era of globalization form one of the fastest growing arenas of judicial power. The politics in appointing the members of these tribunals has its own distinctive character. Despite formal provisions designed to have judges 'elected' by an intergovernmental body of jurists, states that have agreed to subject themselves to the adjudication of these tribunals find diplomatic ways of protecting their interests in the election process. All countries accepting an international court's jurisdiction may be free to nominate their own nationals, but as Mackenzie and Sands tell us in relation to the new International Criminal Court, without the support of some of the more powerful states, candidates have little chance of success.

Independence and Accountability

The analyses presented in this volume are concerned about two dimensions of judicial appointing systems: their capacity for satisfying procedural norms, and their capacity for producing a good judiciary. Although these dimensions are obviously intertwined – analysts and reformers will argue that a particular appointment process is likely or unlikely to produce the best kind of judiciary – for the sake of analytical clarity let me deal first with what we might learn from the authors' discussion of the normative qualities of a good process for selecting and appointing judges.

As Kate Malleson indicates in the Introduction, the normative concern about process that most frequently comes up is striking the right balance between independence and accountability. Most – perhaps even all – of the authors would agree with Alan Paterson's statement that 'Judicial appointment procedures have to be independent of undue political influence and democratically accountable' (13). Note that Paterson speaks of 'undue political influence,' not the total absence of political influence. The kind of political influence on the appointment of judges that is not only undue, but even 'due' or desirable, is a focal point of much of the discussion about reforming the process. The desire for a process that is 'democratically accountable' pulls in the opposite direction from the independence norm in that it requires that the process for selecting judges be subject to the influence of the democratic citizenry – all the more so when the judiciary appears to be weighing into important issues of public policy. Interestingly, none of the chapters shows any interest in making judges directly accountable to the people by creating an elected judiciary. The Japanese system imported a touch of the elected model from some of the American states by requiring Supreme Court justices to be reviewed by the people in the first general election following their appointment. But David O'Brien reports that public disinterest and the appointment of older justices who retire before the next election have rendered this constitutional requirement virtually a dead letter. The democratic accountability norm for most authors and reformers requires that those who do the selecting and appointing be answerable to the people and their elected representatives for what they do and how they do it.

Striking the right balance between independence and democratic accountability is a concern of liberal democratic regimes. A liberal democratic regime is one in which the government, no matter how popular it is or claims to be, is subject to legal restraints on how it exercises its power, restraints that are applied by a judiciary the government does not direct or control. Certainly, some of the states whose judicial structures and appointment systems are discussed in this volume are not yet and may never become liberal democracies. In these countries the dominant normative concern is the efficiency and effectiveness of the judiciary in providing a creditable and accessible means of settling disputes that do not threaten the political interests of the government. As Hawes puts it, in China it is the courts that are independent, not the judges. The regime is endeavouring to protect the court system from interference by other administrative organs or societal groups while keeping the judges under the tight control of a judicial hierarchy controlled at the top by Party leaders whose interference can never be viewed as 'undue,' and whose accountability is to the regime's ideology rather than to the people.

Within the liberal democracies the common law and civil law judicial systems as they evolved developed somewhat different ways of meeting the independence and accountability norms. Accountability in appointing the judiciary of the common law Anglo democracies was provided by vesting the appointing power and responsibility in senior elected members of the executive – typically a minister of justice and a prime minister or president. With the notable exception of the United States, no institutional checks and balances were built into this system of executive control over the selection and promotion of judicial personnel. Concerns about independence were met by downplaying the political significance of the judiciary's work, by selecting judges from the top echelons of an independent legal profession, and by guaranteeing judges security of tenure after their appointment. In civil law countries the presence of elected members of government and in some cases opposition politicians in the bodies responsible for judicial selection gave a modicum of accountability to the process, even though control over entry to the judicial service and subsequent advancement was largely in the hands of senior judges. Entry to judicial service by a system of competitive examinations along with the security enjoyed by a career judiciary went a long way to satisfying concerns about independence from outside the judiciary.

The advent of the age of judicial power in common law countries has aroused concerns about continuing to vest unfettered power of government control over appointment to and advancement within judiciaries that are supposed to be rendering impartial justice in disputes to which the government itself is very often a party, and which deal with controversial issues of public policy. It is interesting that the reforms attracting most interest do not emulate the American model of balancing a highly political and ideologically directed executive control of nominations with a robust and equally political challenge to nominees in a chamber of the legislature. Instead, the approach most widely favoured is to build checks and balances into the selection process by placing the responsibility for identifying the best candidates for judicial office in the hands of a commission or committee on which the government is represented but which is not controlled by the government. The decisions of such commissions or committees may in effect be determinative, so that they function not as nominating bodies but as appointing bodies. This appears to be the case for Israel's judicial appointments committee and South Africa's Judicial Services Commission, except for appointments to the Constitutional Court and the highest chief justice and deputy chief justice positions. In these systems it is the participation of elected politicians in the selection process that provides political accountability. The committees functioning in Scotland and at the provincial level in Canada, and those proposed for England and Wales, for the new U.K. Supreme Court and for federal judicial appointments in Canada, are designed as nominating committees with final decision left in the hands of accountable politicians. In these models accountability may be reinforced by requiring that, if ministers reject committee recommendations, they give reasons for their rejection and go back to the committee for further nominations.

Judicial appointment or nominating committees are not winning favour everywhere in the common law world. The contributions to this collection on Australia and New Zealand indicate little support for this approach to reform in the antipodes. Critics of nominating or appointing commissions are concerned about internalizing the politics of judicial selection. This is the core of Jim Allan's argument against adopting such a committee process in New Zealand. Allan argues that such a committee would likely be dominated by a 'self-selecting lawyerly caste' and precludes the appointment of those who challenge prevailing views on adjudication. Similarly, F.L. Morton argues that the nominating committee currently under consideration at the federal level in Canada will drive political influence on judicial appointments underground by shielding it from public view. While unfettered government control over judicial appointments may maintain democratic accountability for judicial appointments, it still raises questions about judicial independence. In this age of judicial power, with judges playing such a prominent role in governance, independence from a country's politics is neither possible nor desirable. A more realistic norm for a judiciary that can command respect from the country's main political divisions is one that contains a mixture of political persuasions, including differing views on the proper approach to adjudication. If one political party dominates government for a considerable period of time and exercises its control over appointments in a partisan or ideological way, there is a serious risk of a politically unbalanced judiciary.

In the traditional common law appointing systems, as well as in systems using nominating or appointing commissions, lack of transparency in how candidates for judicial office are assessed and selected has been a key accountability concern. South Africa, with its practice of public interviewing by the JSC, goes further than any other common law country in enabling the public to see and hear the leading candidates under consideration. In his account of this aspect of the South African system, du Bois acknowledges that some candidates have found public interviews to be a humiliating experience but concludes that it has enhanced the accountability of the system. Elsewhere in the common law world, reformers prefer the more discrete practice of private interviews by the appointing or nominating body. In some instances accountability is enhanced by advertising vacancies and disclosing selection criteria. Of the new systems now under consideration in the common law world, the least accountable appears to be the commission proposed for England and Wales, which has no elected politicians in its membership and no devices to enhance transparency.

Among the civil law liberal democracies, the Italian system of appointing judges solely on the basis of competitive examinations and advancing through the ranks solely on the basis of seniority is the most insulated from extra-judicial politics. Mary Volcansek's analysis raises serious issues about the democratic accountability of such a system. In Italy the judiciary has become virtually an independent political force. Among other things, this means that little can be done by accountable politicians to overcome the judiciary's inefficiency or inaccessibility in discharging the ordinary, non-political adjudicative functions of courts. The judicial appointing systems of France and Japan are almost as insulated from extra-judicial politics as Italy's. However, the judiciary's relative political passiveness makes this less of an issue in these countries. Among the civil law countries, the Netherlands has the most complex judicial appointing system, combining a career judiciary with the appointment of experienced lawyers and using a large, professionally dominated appointing committee. The result is a politically diverse judiciary tilting somewhat to the liberal left and serving as a counterweight to a rightward mutation in the country's politics.

Russia, a country on the cusp of liberal democracy, employs its own unique form of judicial nominating committee. The very name of these committees, Judicial Qualification Committees (JQCs), connotes an aspiration to free judicial selection from political manipulation and control. But Trochev's account shows that while JQCs have been an important factor in developing a more independent judiciary in post-Communist Russia, they are not without their own distinctive politics. Under Putin, reform of the JQC system has been in the direction of reducing judicial domination and increasing accountability by adding lay persons and elected politicians to the committees.

In all of the civil law liberal democracies with high courts or tribunals exercising the power of constitutional judicial review, there is an open acknowledgment of the inherent political nature of this function. All of these countries require some political pluralism in making appointments to these powerful arbiters of constitutional disputes. Among the common law liberal democracies, only the United States, with its provision for open critical review of the administration's nominees by the political opposition, provides an institutional check on government in making these appointments. It would seem unlikely that other common law countries that have adopted some form of constitutional judicial review, notably Canada, New Zealand, and the United Kingdom, will for much longer withstand pressure to introduce an element of political pluralism into the system of appointing their highest judges. Even if they do this, Christine Landfried's analysis of the 'election' of the members of Germany's Constitutional Court by party chieftains on parliamentary committees shows that political pluralism alone is no guarantee of an open appointing process that meets the norms of a discursive democracy.

Judicial Merit, Diversity, and Representativeness

A system of judicial selection and appointment must be assessed not only by how well it meets procedural norms, but also by its capacity for producing a high quality judiciary. Indeed, some might argue that the primary test of any process of judicial selection is its ability to appoint persons solely on the basis of their technical or professional merits. But this volume makes it clear that in this age of both democracy and judicial power, what constitutes a high quality judiciary or judge is changing and broadening. It will no longer do to juxtapose technical merit against other considerations of character, experience, and background and assume that a strong and effective judiciary requires only the former.

In Asian countries that are just beginning to build creditable court systems, judicial reform is essentially a matter of recruiting educated young people with a modicum of education and legal knowledge and remunerating them well enough to keep them in judicial service. China seems to be leading the way in this regard. Reforms introduced since the mid-1990s have considerably raised the requirements for entry to the judiciary. The fact that this country, the world's most populous, now has a very large pool of university and law school graduates to draw from has made it possible for China to make post-secondary legal education and success in national examinations requirements for appointment to the judiciary. It is interesting to note that the formal qualifications for the Chinese judiciary include more than professional education and ability – they also require good political qualities, moral conduct, and physical health. In the liberal democracies, including Namibia and

South Africa, formal legal education and professional experience or, in civil law countries, success in entry examinations, have long been qualifications for holding salaried, permanent judicial positions. In the case of Namibia, such a high entry qualification has been a serious obstacle to recruiting judges from the majority population.

Though legal education and ability remain prerequisites for appointment to the judiciaries of the more industrialized liberal democracies, a broadening and deepening of the professional qualities considered desirable for judicial office has been occurring. This is especially evident in the common law world, where an outstanding career as a legal advocate has traditionally been the key qualification for judicial office. Countries in which advocates or barristers form an elite professional cadre separate from the rest of the legal profession are now catching up to countries like Canada and the United States, which have unified legal professions and have long recruited their judges not only from the ranks of courtroom lawyers but from legal professionals who have achieved eminence in many other settings, including government, business, and the universities. There are signs that such a widening of the pool of professionals from which judges are selected is underway in the United Kingdom and even in Australia, the crustiest bastion of common law tradition. In South Africa, the recruitment of judges from a broad spectrum of legal professionals has been an essential condition of transforming the judiciary from a bastion of white domination. An attorney-general's discussion paper in Australia shows a move away from an exclusive focus on advocacy skills as the litmus test of eligibility for judicial office. Administrative and writing skills, evidence of practicality, common sense, and social vision have been added to the list of criteria. It is in assessing these skills and qualities of mind and character that lay members of selection commissions can make a major contribution. Scotland's commission, with 50 per cent lay membership and a lay chair, has eliminated from its assessment process 'judicial soundings' that in the past were virtually the sole basis for assessing 'merit.'

In civil law systems, where all or most of the judiciary are appointed after university graduation without any extended period of professional practice, there has been less scope for expanding considerations of professional merit. In these countries it is the structure and character of legal education that is the major influence on shaping the pool from which the judiciary is recruited. Italian judges, who take their legal education directly after secondary school in programs narrowly focused on the single discipline of law, will have a much more limited intellectual formation than the university graduates who compete in the examinations for entry to France's École national de la magistrature in Bordeaux. In Russia, whose judicial system straddles the common law/civil law divide, specialized knowledge and experience are now being given weight in recruiting for different types of courts. As law in advanced industrial countries becomes ever more complex, the need for expertise in particular areas of law will increasingly be a factor in judicial selection, not only in common law countries, but also in civil law countries like France, Germany, and the Netherlands, in which there is more than one way of qualifying for judicial office.

Much more controversial than widening the scope of professional merit is the growing concern about a judiciary's representative character. In large measure this tendency is an understandable reaction against the social exclusiveness of judiciaries in the past – their domination by male lawyers drawn from the more affluent and conservative sections of society and from the mainstream or most powerful ethnic group. It should be no surprise that in a democratic age demanding social inclusiveness in all phases of public life and loading ever-increasing responsibilities on judiciaries that there should be a movement towards judiciaries that are more representative of the societies they serve. Much of the argument is about whether diversity should be achieved gradually, as members of formerly excluded groups gain access to legal education and professional opportunity and 'trickle up' to the level of professional eminence needed for judicial appointment, or through programs of affirmative action that take proactive measures to redress the legacy of historic, systemic discrimination. In Australia the 'trickle-up' approach seems to be carrying the day, whereas in the United Kingdom, as in the Canadian provinces, bolder 'affirmative action' policies are favoured. A trickle-up strategy would clearly not have served South Africa's transformative objective very well. Du Bois's chapter shows the remarkable progress South Africa has made in recruiting more blacks and more women to its higher courts. In civil law countries, where professional experience is not required for appointment to the bench, educational reform can produce judicial diversity much more quickly. This is evident in the chapters on France and Italy, where males no longer dominate the judiciary – at least at the lower levels. However, little has been done in France to represent its expanding Islamic population. In Egypt, on the other hand, women are still totally excluded from serving in the ordinary courts. The situation in Russia is very much the opposite of this, with women occupying 60 per cent of the positions in the regular courts and two-thirds of the positions in the *arbitrazh* courts dealing with industrial disputes. But in Russia too male justices dominate the highest echelons of the judicial hierarchy: only three of the Constitutional Court's twenty-four members are women.

A court or judiciary's representativeness is a collective quality that can contribute to what political scientists call its legitimacy. Citizens are more likely to respect and trust courts whose judiciaries include people like themselves. A lack of legitimacy could mean a reluctance to look to the courts for justice and a tendency to resolve differences in more disruptive ways. Increasing the diversity of backgrounds of the judiciary may also improve the quality of judicial decision making. Part of the knowledge needed for intelligently deciding the issues that come before courts these days is first-hand experience with these issues and the communities in which they arise. This is as true for first level trial courts, particularly with respect to sentencing, as it is for courts of appeal and constitutional courts. And yet there is a good deal of muttering – some of which can be heard in the pages of this volume – about considerations of diversity being in conflict with and detracting from judicial 'merit.' Du Bois acknowledges that in some instances in South Africa a white lawyer considered in professional circles to be a real 'high flyer' has lost out in a competition for a high judicial office to a black lawyer whose professional reputation was not quite so high. Even so, it may be that if such appointments improve the collective quality and legitimacy of the judiciary they more than compensate for the loss of some technical brilliance.

The fact that so many kinds of difference exist in any society raises the question of which differences should count for judicial representation. The papers in this volume make it clear that there is no common universal answer to this question. The kind of diversity that comes to be recognized as desirable depends very much on political context and the issues seen as salient to judicial decision making. In the liberal West, the emancipation of women has prompted efforts to expand the participation of women in judiciaries not because it is assumed all women hold the same views but, among other reasons, to ensure that the juridical talent in the female half of the population is not lost to judicial service. Longstanding structures of governance and politics in the Netherlands require that the judiciary have a proper balance of Catholic and Protestant judges. The absence from the French judiciary of citizens with an Algerian/Islamic background, and the severe under-representation of Israel's conservative and non-European population on that country's judiciary, raise serious questions about the judiciary's ability to deal sensitively with issues touching matters of vital concern to the under-represented groups. In some federal countries territorial diversity is a requisite quality for membership of the highest court. This is true in the case of the Canadian Supreme Court, even though, except for Quebec with its distinct system of civil law, it is a practice driven primarily by symbolic politics rather than the functional needs of the court. The diversity required for the International Court of Justice and the new International Criminal Court extends beyond the political imperative of national and regional diversity to the functional requirement of including jurists versed in the principal legal systems of the world.

In this age of judicial power, in which constitutional courts and supreme courts in all parts of the world are becoming ever more engaged in deciding cases that deal with highly controversial political issues, diversity of a political nature is likely to become a dominant concern in staffing these courts. The political diversity that comes into play at this level relates not only to ideological differences that animate the country's system of political competition but to ideological or philosophical differences about adjudication and the proper role of the judiciary in constitutional democracy. Important as these latter differences are in both the popular and scholarly discussion of high court decisions, they are very difficult qualities to identify and to balance in an appointing process. Yet, getting this element of diversity right on a country's highest court in the future may become the acid test of an acceptable appointing system.

Table of Cases

Al-Jehad Trust v. Federation of Pakistan, PLD 1996 SC 324.

Australian Capital Television Pty Ltd v. Commonwealth (No 2) (1992), 177 CLR 106.

Brown v. Board of Education, 347 US 483 (1954).

Buchanan v. Jennings, [2002] 3 NZLR 145.

Commercial Farmers' Union v. Mhuriro & Others, 2000(2) ZLR 405 (S).

Democratic Republic of Congo v. Belgium, Case Concerning the Arrest Warrant of 11 April 2000, ICJ, General List No. 121, Judgment of 14 February 2002.

Dugan v. Mirror Newspapers (1978), 142 CLR 583.

Ex parte Attorney General, Namibia: In re the Constitutional Relationship between the Attorney General and the Prosecutor General (1995), 8 BCLR 1071 (SC).

Gosselin v. Quebex, [2002] 4 SCR 429.

Government of the Republic of South Africa v. Grootboom (2001), 1 SA 46 (CC).

Kleinwort Benson Ltd v. Lincoln CC, [1998] 3 WLR 1095.

Mabo v. Queensland (No 2) (1992), 175 CLR 1.

Minister of Health v. TAC (No. 2) (2002), 5 SA 721 (CC).

Minister of Lands Agriculture and Rural Resettlement & Others v. The Commercial Farmers Union, Judgement no. S-111-2001.

Minister of Lands, Resettlement and Rural Development v. Paliouras & Anor, Judgement no. S-55-2001.

Minister of Safety and Security v. Van Duivenboden 2002 (6) SA 431.

Ministry of Transport v. Noort, [1992] 3 NZLR 260.

Moonen v. Film and Literature Board of Review, [2002] 2 NZLR 750.

Olyvia Martha Ekanjo-Imalwa v. The Law Society of Namibia and Another, (unreported) HC case no. (P) A11/03, 11 August 2003.

Porter v. Magill, [2002] 1 All ER 465.

President of the Republic of South Africa and others v. South African Rugby Football Union and others (1999), 4 SA 147 (CC).

President of the Republic of South Africa and others v. South African Rugby Football Union and others, 2000 (1) SA 1 (CC).
Question of Law Reserved on Acquittal Pursuant to Section 351(1A) Criminal Law Consolidation Act (No 1 of 1993), Court of Criminal Appeal, 20 April 1993.
R v. Bow Street Metropolitan Stipendiary Magistrate and Others, Ex parte Pinochet Ugarte (No. 2), [2000] 1 AC 119.
R v. Davie (unreported), Morwell County Court, Bland J., 15 April 1993.
R v. Pora [2001] 2 NZLR 37.
R v. Bow Street Metropolitan Stipendiary Magistrate and Others, Ex Parte Pinochet Ugarte (No. 3), House of Lords, [2000] 1 AC 147.
Registrar-General of Elections v. Combined Harare Residents Association & Another Judgement no. S-7-2002.
Russian Constitutional Court decision #10-P of 7 June 2000, (2000) *VKS RF* 5.
Russian Constitutional Court decision #1-O of 23 January 1997 (unpublished).
Russian Constitutional Court decision #20-O of 1 April 1996 (unpublished).
Russian Constitutional Court decision #217-O of 27 October 2000, (2001) *VKS RF* 2:8.
Russian Constitutional Court decision #252-O of 21 December 2000,(2001) *VKS RF* 2:62.
Russian Constitutional Court decision #32-O of 12 March 1998, (1998) *VKS RF* 3:66.
Russian Constitutional Court decision #32–O of 19 April 1996 (unpublished).
Russian Constitutional Court decision #3-P of 1 February 1996, *VKS RF* 1 (1996)
Russian Constitutional Court decision #91-O of 8 June 2000, (2000) *VKS RF* 5.
Russian Constitutional Court decision #92-O of 27 June 2000, (2000) *VKS RF* 5.
S v. Collier, 1995 (2) SACR 648 (C).
S v. Heita and another. [1992] 3 SA 780 (NmHC).
S v. Mamabolo (E TV and Others Intervening), 2001 (3) SA 409 (CC)
S v. Shackell, 2001 (4) SA 1 (SCA).
SARFU and Others v. President of the RSA and Others (1998), 10 BCLR 1256 (T).
Secretary, Ministry of Finance v. Masdar Hossain 20 (2000) BLD (AD) 104; 52 (2000) BLD 82.
SGIC v. Trigwell (1979), 142 CLR 617.
Sikunda v. The Government of the Republic of Namibia & Others, (unreported) HC case no. A327/2000, 9 February 2001.
Southern Bluefin Tuna Cases (Australia and New Zealand v. Japan) (2000), 39 ILM 1359.
Stevenson v. Minister of Local Government & Ors 2001(1) ZLR 321 (H).
Syed Zafar Ali Shah v. General Pervaiz Musharraf, PLD 2000 SC 869.

Russian Constitutional Court decision 18-P of 30 September 1993 (1994) *Vestnik Konstitutsionnogo Suda RF* 6.

Van Rooyen and Others v. The State and Others, 2001 (4) SA 396 (T).

Van Rooyen v. The State (General Council of the Bar of South Africa Intervening) 2002 (5) SA 246 (CC).

Wik Peoples v. Queensland (1996), 187 CLR 1.

Zemburuka v. S., (unreported) HC, Case No. CA 119/2002, 30 September 2003.

Zimbabwe Lawyers for Human Rights & Anor v. The President of the Republic of Zimbabwe S.C., December 2003.

Bibliography

Abel, R. *Politics By Other Means: Law in the Struggle against Apartheid, 1980–1994.* London: Routledge, 1995.

Abraham, Henry J. *Justices and Presidents: A Political History of Appointments to the Supreme Court.* 3rd ed. New York: Oxford University Press, 1992.

– *The Judicial Process.* 6th ed. New York: Oxford, 1993.

– *The Judicial Process: An Introductory Analysis of the Court of the United States, England, and France.* New York: Oxford University Press, 1998.

Abrosimova, Elena. 'Sudoustroistvo i status sudi.' In Boris Topornin and Igor Petrukhin, eds., *Sudebnaia reforma: problemy i perspektivy*, 94. Moskva: IGPAN RAN, 2001.

– 'Sud i ispolnitelnaya vlast.' In Igor Petrukhin, ed. *Sudebnaya vlast*, 129. Moskva: Prospekt, 2003.

Access to Justice Advisory Committee. *Access to Justice: An Action Plan*, edited by Ronald Sackville. Canberra Australian Government Publishing Service, 1994.

Account of the proceedings on the day the High Court of South-West Africa was opened (6 January 1920), *South African Law Journal* (1920) 37:170–3.

Ahmed, Naimuddin. 'The Problem of the Independence of the Judiciary in Bangladesh.' *Bangladesh Journal of Law* (1998) 2:133.

Al-Beshri, Tarek. *Studies about Egyptian Democracy.* Cairo: Dar Al-Nahadah, 1998 (in Arabic).

Alexander, Larry. 'Introduction.' In Larry Alexander, ed., *Constitutionalism: Philosophical Foundations.* Cambridge: Cambridge University Press, 1998.

Alford, William P. 'A Second Great Wall?: China's Post-Cultural Revolution Project of Legal Construction.' *Cultural Dynamics* (1999) 11, no. 2: 193.

Allan, James. 'Constitutional Interpretation v. Statutory Interpretation: Understanding the Attractions of "Original Intent."' *Legal Theory* (2000) 6:109.

– 'Turning Clark Kent into Superman: The New Zealand Bill of Rights Act 1990.' *Otago Law Review* (2000) 9:613.
– 'The Effect of a Statutory Bill of Rights Where Parliament Is Sovereign: The Lesson from New Zealand.' In Tom Campbell, Keith Ewing, and Adam Tomkins, eds., *Sceptical Essays on the Human Rights Act 1998.* Oxford: Oxford University Press, 2001.
– 'Oh That I Were Made Judge in the Land.' *Federal Law Review* (2002) 30:561.
– 'The Author Doth Protest Too Much, Methinks.' *New Zealand Universities Law Review* (2003) 20:519.
– 'Paying for the Comfort of Dogma.' *Sydney Law Review* (2003) 25:63.
Appellate Division, The. *South African Law Journal* (1920) 37:293.
'Arbitrazhnye sudy Rossii v 2003 godu rassmotreli okolo odnogo mln del.' *RIA Novosti.* 11 February 2004. http://www.rian.ru.
Arian, Asher, David Nahmias, Doron Navot, and Daniel Shany. *The Israeli Democracy Index.* Jerusalem: The Israeli Democracy Institute, 2003.
Armstrong, Lance. *Every Second Counts.* New York: Broadway Books, 2003.
Armytage, Livingston. *Educating Judges.* The Hague: Kluwer, 1996.
Atcheson, M. Elizabeth, Mary Eberts, and Beth Symes (with Jennifer Stoddart). *Women and Legal Action: Precedents, Resources and Strategies for the Future.* Ottawa: Canadian Advisory Council on the Status of Women, 1984.
Atkins, Burton. 'Judicial Selection in Context: The American and English Experience.' *Kentucky Law Journal* (1989) 77:577.
Australian Law Reform Commission. *Equality before the Law: Women's Access to the Legal System*, vols. 1 and 2. Report No. 69. Canberra: Australian Government Publishing Service, 1994.
– *Managing Justice: A Review of the Federal Civil Justice System.* Report No. 89. Canberra: Australian Government Publishing Service, 2000.
Bakker, Jan Willem. *The Philippines Justice System.* Leiden: Leiden Centre for the Independence of Judges and Lawyers, 1997.
Bar Council. *Report of the Bar Council's Working Party on Judicial Appointments and Silk.* London: Bar Council, 2003.
Bar Council Working Party on Judicial Appointments & Silk. Consultation Paper, Chair Sir Ian Glidewell (General Council of the Bar, London, 2003). 3 March 2003. http://www.barcouncil.org.uk/documents/GlidewellConsultation.pdf.
Bench Press. 'JSC announces Permanent Appointments.' *De Rebus* (May 1998): 5.
– 'Constitutional Court.' *De Rebus* (October 2003): 10.
– *De Rebus* (October 2003): 10.
– *De Rebus* (December 2003): 12.

– 'Five Attorneys Appointed to the Bench.' *De Rebus* (December 2003): 12.

Bernard-Maugiron, Nathalie, and Baudouin Dupret, eds. *Egypt and Its Laws.* London: Kluwer Law International, 2002.

Besley, Timothy, and A. Abigail Payne. *Judicial Accountability and Economic Policy Outcomes: Evidence from Employment Discrimination Charges*, Working Paper, Department of Economics. London School of Economics, London, June 2003. http://econ.lse.ac.uk/staff/tbesley/papers/courts.pdf.

Binder, Sarah, and Thomas Mann. 'Slaying the Dinosaur: The Case for Reforming the Senate Filibuster.' *Brookings Review* (1995) 13:42.

Birchfield, Vicki, and Markus M.L. Crepaz. 'The Impact of Constitutional Structures and Collective and Competitive Veto Points on Income Inequality in Industrialized Democracies.' *European Journal of Political Research* (1998) 34:175.

Biriukova, Irma. 'Biudzhetnyi defitsit sokratilsia.' *Kaliningradskaia pravda*, 24 May 2002.

Birnhack, Michael, and David Gusarski. 'Designated Chairs, Dissenting Opinions and Judicial Pluralism.' *Iyunei Mishpat* (1999) 22:499 (in Hebrew).

Biti, T. 'Judiciary Bashing, a Predatory State, and the Rule of Law in Zimbabwe.' *Zimbabwe Human Rights Bulletin* (1999) 1:97.

Black, Charles. 'A Note on Senatorial Confirmation of Supreme Court Nominees.' *Yale Law Journal* (1970) 79:661.

Blackshield, A.R. 'Judges and the Court System.' In Gareth Evans, ed., *Labor and the Constitution 1972–1975*, 121. Melbourne: Heinemann Educational Australia, 1977.

Böckenförde, Ernst-Wolfgang. 'Die Methoden der Verfassungsinterpretation – Bestandsaufnahme und Kritik.' *Neue Juristische Wochenschrift* (1976) 29:2089.

Bohn, Henning, and Robert Inman. Balanced Budget Rules and Public Deficits: Evidence from the U.S., NBER Working Paper 5533, 1996.

Boigeol, Anne. 'La magistrature française au feminine: Entre spécificité et banalisation.' *Droit et société* (1993) 25:521.

Bond, Johanna. 'Nepal.' In Kritzer, ed., *Legal Systems of the World.*

Brandeis Institute for International Judges. *The New International Jurisprudence: Building Legitimacy for International Courts and Tribunals.* Waltham, MA: Brandeis Institute for International Judges, 2002.

– *Authority and Autonomy: Defining the Role of International and Regional Courts.* Waltham, MA: Brandeis Institute for International Judges, 2003.

Brown, Nathan J. *The Rule of Law in the Arab World: Courts in Egypt and the Gulf.* Cambridge: Cambridge University Press, 1997.

Bruinsma, Freek. *Cassatierechtspraak in civiele zaken.* Zwolle: W.E.J. Tjeenk Willink, 1988.

Bufacci, Vittori, and Simon Burgess. *Italy Since 1989: Events and Interpretations.* London: Palgrave, 2001.

Cairns, Alan C. *Charter versus Federalism: The Dilemmas of Constitutional Reform.* Montreal and Kingston: McGill-Queen's University Press, 1992.

Calland, Richard. 'A Step in the Right Direction: An Analysis of the Interviews of the Nominees for Membership of South Africa's First Constitutional Court.' LLM dissertation, University of Cape Town, March 1995.

Calvert, Randall L., Matthew D. McCubbins, and Barry R. Weingast. 'A Theory of Political Control and Agency Discretion.' *American Journal of Political Science* (1989) 33:588.

Cameron, E. 'Legal Chauvinism, Executive-mindedness and Justice: LC Steyn's Impact on South African Law.' *South African Law Journal* (1982) 99:38–75.

Campbell, David, and James Young. 'The Metric Martyrs and the Entrenchment Jurisprudence of Lord Justice Laws.' *Public Law* [2002]:399.

Campbell, Tom. 'Judicial Activism: Justice or Treason?' *Otago Law Review* (2003) 10:307.

Canada Justice Committee. 'NAC Memo' Justice Committee Report. March 1981, 4.

Cao Jianming et al., eds. *Zhongguo shenpan fangshi gaige lilun wenti yanjiu.* Beijing: Zhongguo zhengfa daxue chubanshe, 2001.

Carey, John M., and Matthew Soberg Shugart. 'Calling Out the Tanks or Filling Out the Forms?' In John M. Carey and Matthew Soberg Shugart, eds., *Executive Decree Authority.* Cambridge: Cambridge University Press, 1998.

Cazzola, Franco, and Massimo Morisi. *La Mutua Diffidenza: Il Reciproco Controllo tra Magistrati e Politici nella Prima Repubblica.* Milan: Feltrinelli, 1996.

Ceaser, James. *Presidential Selection: Theory and Development.* Charlottesville: University of Virginia Press, 1979.

Centre for the Independence of Judges and Lawyers Special Issue: Centre for the Independence of Judges and Lawyers (CILJ) Bulletin: A Compilation of International Standards. Geneva: CILJ, 1993.

Chairman's Contribution. 'Judge Bashing.' *Advocate* (August 2003): 3.

Chaskalson, Arthur. 'Address at the Opening of the Judges' Conference.' *South African Law Journal* (2003) 120:657.

Chen, Jianfu. *Chinese Law: Towards an Understanding of Chinese Law, Its Nature and Development.* The Hague: Kluwer Law International, 1999.

Chrétien, Jean. 'A Question of Merit: Ensuring Quality and Commitment in High Court Appointments.' *National* (Canadian Bar Association) (December 1998): 15.

Chimenti, Anna. *Storia dei Referendum.* Bari: Editori Laterza, 1993.

Chu'ü, T'ung-tsu. *Law and Society in Traditional China.* Paris; La Haye: Mouton, 1965.

Clarke, Donald C. 'Power and Politics in the Chinese Court System: The Enforcement of Civil Judgments.' *Columbia Journal of Asian Law* (1996) 10:1.

Clarke, Jeremy Andrew Stuart. 'Social Conservatives in Court: A Reassessment of Canadian and U.S. Experience.' Masters thesis, University of Calgary, 2003.

Clements, Luke. *European Human Rights.* London: Sweet and Maxwell, 1994.

Commissioner for Judicial Appointments for Northern Ireland. *Audit Report.* 2003.

Commonwealth of Australia. *Report to the Senate, August 1984: The Select Committee on the Conduct of a Judge.* Parl Paper No 168/1984.

– *Report to the Senate, October 1984: The Select Committee on Allegations concerning a Judge.* Parl Paper No 271.

– *Judicial Appointments: Procedures and Criteria,* Commonwealth Discussion Paper. Attorney-General's Department, Canberra.

Connolly, William. 'Introduction: Legitimacy and Modernity.' In William Connolly, ed., *Legitimacy and the State.* New York: New York University Press, 1984.

Constitutional Reform: A New Way of Appointing Judges. Department of Constitutional Affairs consultation paper. July 2003.

Cooney, Sean. 'Gender and Judicial Selection: Should There Be More Women on the Courts?' *Melbourne University Law Review* (1993) 19:20.

Corder, Hugh. *Judges at Work: The Role and Attitudes of the South African Judiciary 1910–1950.* Cape Town: Juta, 1984.

– 'The Appointment of Judges: Some Comparative Ideas.' *Stellenbosch Law Review* (1992) 3:207.

– 'Establishing Legitimacy for the Administration of Justice in South Africa.' *Stellenbosch Law Review* (1995) 6:202.

– 'Judicial Authority in a Changing South Africa.' *Legal Studies* (2004) 24:253.

Cottrell, J. 'Constitution of Namibia: An Overview.' *Journal of African Law* (1991) 35:56.

Craven, Gregory. 'The High Court of Australia: A Study in the Abuse of Power.' 31st Alfred Deakin Lecture. Melbourne: Alfred Deakin Lecture Trust, October 1997.

Cummins, Richard J. 'The General Principles of Law, Separation of Powers, and Theories of Judicial Decision in France.' *International and Comparative Law Quarterly* (1986) 35:54.

Curtis, Thomas. 'Recess Appointments to Article III Courts: The Use of Historical Practice in Constitutional Interpretation.' *Columbia Law Review* (1984) 84:1758.

CYBERconsult. *Law Reform in Indonesia: Results of a Research Study Undertaken for the World Bank.* Jakarta, Indonesia: CYBERconsult, 1997.

Dadomo, Christian, and Susan Farran. *The French Legal System.* 2nd ed. London: Sweet and Maxwell, 1996.

Dahl, Robert A. (1958) 'Decision-making in a Democracy: the Supreme Court as a National Policy-Maker' *Journal of Public Law* 6:279.

Davis, D.M., G.J. Marcus, and J. Klaaren. 'The Administration of Justice.' *Annual Survey of South African Law* [2000]:877.

Davis, Rachel, and George Williams. 'Reform of the Judicial Appointments Process: Gender and the Bench of the High Court of Australia.' *Melbourne University Law Review* (2003) 27:819.

Days, D.S. III, et al. *Justice Enjoined: The State of the Judiciary in Kenya.* New York: Robert F. Kennedy Memorial Centre for Human Rights Publication, 1992.

De Franciscis, Maria Elisabetta. 'Italy.' In Mary L. Volcansek, ed., *Judicial Misconduct: A Cross-National Comparison,* 49. Gainesville: University Press of Florida, 1996.

de Groot-van Leeuwen, L.E. *De rechterlijke macht in Nederland, Samenstelling en denkbeelden van de zittende en staande magistratuur.* Arnhem: Gouda Quint, 1991.

– 'The Equilibrium Elite; Composition and Position of The Dutch Judiciary.' *The Netherlands' Journal of the Social Sciences* (1992) 28:141.

– 'Criticising Judges in the Netherlands.' In Michael K. Addo, ed., *Freedom of Expression and the Criticism of Judges.* Aldershot: Ashgate/Dartmouth, 2000.

– 'Women in the Dutch Legal Profession (1950–2000).' In Ulrike Schultz and Giesekla Shaw, eds., *Women in the World's Legal Professions.* Oxford: Oxford University Press, 2003.

de Waard, B.W.N. *Samenwerkende machten: wetgeving en rechtspraak in dienst van het recht.* Zolle: Tjeenk Willink, 1994.

de Werd, Marc. *De benoeming van rechters, Constitutionele aspecten van de toegang tot het rechtersambt in Nederland en in de Amerikaanse deelstaat New York.* Arnhem: Gouda Quint, 1994.

'Deiatelnost kvalifikatsionnykh kollegii sudei v 2002 godu.' *Rossiiskaia iustitsiia* (2003) 6:74.

Dezalay, Yves, Bryant Garth, and Pierre Bourdieu. *Dealing in Virtue: International Commercial Arbitration and the Construction of a Transnational Legal Order.* Chicago: University of Chicago Press, 1998.

Di Federico, Giuseppe. 'Prosecutorial Independence and the Democratic Requirement of Accountability in Italy.' *British Journal of Criminology* (1998) 38:371.

Dlamini, C.R.M. 'The Appointment of Black Judicial Officers.' *Consultus* (1990) 3:31.

Dorr, Neal. 'An Introduction to Human Rights Developments since 1945.' In Liz Heffernan, ed., *Human Rights.* Dublin: Round Hall Press, 1993.

du Bois, François. 'History, System and Sources.' In C.G. van der Merwe and Jacques E. du Plessis, *Introduction to the Law of South Africa*. The Hague: Kluwer Law International, 2004.

Dugard, J. *Human Rights and the South African Legal Order*. Princeton, NJ: Princeton University Press, 1978.

– 'The Judiciary and National Security.' *South African Law Journal* (1982) 99:655.

Dworkin, Ronald. 'Equality, Democracy and Constitution: We the People in Court.' *Alberta Law Review* (1990) 28:324.

Dyzenhaus, D. *Hard Cases and Wicked Legal Systems*. Oxford: Clarendon Press, 1991.

Ebid, Mohamed Kamel. *The Independence of the Judiciary: A Comparative Study*. Cairo: Judges Club Publishing, 1991.

Egorov, Sergei. 'Nas ne obmanuli, potomu chto nam nichego ne obeshchali.' *Pchela* (August–October 2003): 43.

Ekins, Richard. 'Judicial Supremacy and the Rule of Law.' *Law Quarterly Review* (2003) 119:127.

Elbendary, Amina. 'Women on the Bench.' *Al-Ahram Weekly*, 9–15 January 2003.

Ellman, S. *In Time of Trouble: Law and Liberty in South Africa's State of Emergency*. Oxford: Clarendon Press, 1992.

El-Morr, Awad, Abdel Rahman Nosseir, and Adel Omar Sherief. 'The Supreme Constitutional Court and Its Role in the Egyptian Judicial System.' In Kevin Boyle and Adel Omar Sherif, eds., *Human Rights and Democracy: The Role of the Supreme Constitutional Court of Egypt*, 42. London: Kluwer Law International, 1996.

Ely, John H. *Democracy and Distrust. A Theory of Judicial Review*. 4th ed. Cambridge: Harvard University Press, 1982.

Enyutina, Galina. 'Korruptsiya v sudebnykh organakh.' *Working Papers of the St. Petersburg branch of TRACC*. 2003. http://www.mosorgcrimrescenter.ru/Research/Biggr/Enutina/part1.htm.

Epstein, Lee, and Jack Knight. 'Constitutional Borrowing and Nonborrowing.' *I·CON International Journal of Constitutional Law* (2003) 1:196.

Epstein, Lee, Jack Knight, and Olga Shvetsova. 'The Role of Constitutional Courts in the Establishment and Maintenance of Democratic Systems of Government.' *Law and Society Review* (2001) 35:117.

Erel, Shlomo. *The Yekkim: Fifty Years of German-speaking immigration to Israel*. Gerlingen: Bleicher Verlag, 1985 (in Hebrew).

European Communities – Measures Affecting the Approval and Marketing of Biotech Products – Request for Consultations by the United States, WT/DS 291/1.

European Communities – Measures Affecting the Approval and Marketing of Biotech Products – Request for Consultations by Canada, WT/DS/292/1.

European Communities – Measures Affecting the Approval and Marketing of Biotech Products – Request for Consultations by Argentina, WT/DS/293/1.

Faculty of Law. *Speeches: Inauguration of Law Faculty*. Windhoek: Faculty of Law, University of Namibia, 1994.

Falu chubanshe, ed. *Falu xiaoquanshu* (Laws and Regulations of China). Beijing: Falu chubanshe, 2002.

Farhod, Ahlam M.A. 'The Place of the Judiciary in the Egyptian Political System.' PhD dissertation, Cairo University, 1998 (in Arabic).

Farrand, Max, ed. *The Records of the Federal Convention of 1787*. New Haven, CT: Yale University Press, 1937.

Fifth and Final Report of the Commission of Enquiry into the Structure and Functioning of the Courts. Volume 1. Pretoria: Government Printer, 1983.

Finder, Susan. 'The Supreme People's Court of the People's Republic of China.' *Columbia Journal of Asian Law* (1993) 7:2.

First Interim Report of the Commission of Enquiry into the Rationalisation of the Provincial and Local Divisions of the Supreme Court. Volume 4. Pretoria: Government Printer, 1997.

– News (1999) 'First Two Women on the Bench.' *De Rebus* (September 1999): 547.

Fisher, Louis. 'Recess Appointments of Federal Judges.' *CRS Report for Congress* (Congressional Research Service Report for Congress, Library of Congress). 5 September 2001.

Fisk, Catherine, and Erwin Chemerinsky. 'The Filibuster.' *Stanford Law Review* (1997) 49:181.

Fiss, Owen. 'The Right Degree of Independence.' In Irwin P. Stotzky, ed., *Transition to Democracy in Latin America: The Role of the Judiciary*. Boulder, CO: Westview Press, 1994.

Fleiner, T., and R. Khakimov, eds. *Federalism: Russian and Swiss Perspectives*. Kazan: IHAST, 2001.

Foglesong, Todd. 'The Dynamics of Judicial (In)Dependence in Russia.' In Russell and O'Brien, eds., *Judicial Independence in the Age of Democracy*.

Fonte, John. 'Liberal Democracy vs. Transnational Progressivism: The Future of the Ideological Civil War Within the West.' http://www.hudson.org/files/publications/transnational_progressivi sm.pdf (accessed 2002).

Ford, Christopher A. 'Challenges and Dilemmas of Racial and Ethnic Identity in American and Post-apartheid South African Affirmative Action.' *UCLA Law Review* (1996) 43:1953.

Forsyth, C.F. *In Danger for their Talents: A Study of the Appellate Division of the Supreme Court of South Africa 1950–1980.* Cape Town: Juta, 1985.

Forsythe, David P. *The Internationalization of Human Rights.* Lexington, MA: Lexington Books, 1991.

Fouzi, Hisham M. *Constitutional Review of Legislations: A Comparative Study of Egypt and the United States.* Cairo: Cairo Center for Human Rights Studies, 1999.

Fuller, Lon. 'The Case of the Speluncean Explorers.' *Harvard Law Review* (1949) 62:616.

Gadbois, George H., Jr. 'The Selection of Indian Supreme Court Judges.' Paper presented at Conference on Judicial Selection, London School of Economics and Political Science. London, February 2004.

Gauntlett, Jeremy. 'Appointing and Promoting Judges: Which Way Now?' *Consultus* (April 1990): 23.

– 'A Matter of Race?' *Consultus* (December 1999): 3.

– 'Dear President Mbeki ... An Open Letter to the President.' *Advocate* (First Term 2000): 3.

– '"Racial Bias" in the Judiciary.' *Advocate* (Second Term 2000): 4.

Gerhardt, Michael. *The Federal Appointments Process: A Constitutional and Historical Analysis.* Durham, NC: Duke University Press, 2000.

– 'Norm Theory and the Future of the Federal Appointments Process.' *Duke Law Journal* (2001) 50:1687.

Gibbs, Harry. 'The Appointment and Removal of Judges.' *Federal Law Review* (1987) 17:141.

Gibson, James. *Overcoming Apartheid: Can Truth Reconcile a Divided Nation?* Cape Town: HSRC Press, 2004.

Gilligan, Carol. *In a Different Voice.* Cambridge: Harvard University Press, 1982.

Ginsborg, Paul. *A History of Contemporary Italy: Society and Politics 1943–1988.* London: Penguin Books, 1990.

– *Italy and Its Discontents: Family, Civil Society, State, 1980–2001.* London: Palgrave, 2003.

Ginsburg, Thomas B. *Judicial Review in New Democracies: Constitutional Courts in Asian Cases.* New York: Cambridge University Press, 2003.

Glebova, Marina. 'Femida zrit v koren.' *Versty.* 3 October 2002.

Gleeson, Murray. 'Judging the Judges.' *Australian Law Journal* (1979) 53:338.

– 'The Future of Civil Justice: Adjudication or Dispute Resolution?' *Otago Law Review* (1999) 9:449.

– 'A Changing Judiciary.' *Australian Law Journal* (2001) 75:547.

Goldstein, W. 'The Appointment of Judges: Guidelines of Jewish Law and South African Principles.' *South African Law Journal* (2000) 117:797.

Gosudarstvennoe Sobranie-Kurultai-Respubliki Bashkortostan. 'Zapros o proverke sootvetstviia p. 3 st. 6, pp. 6 i 7 st. 6.1 Zakona RF 'O statuse sudei v RF' Konstitutsii RF.' Unpublished, 17 May 2003.

Graycar, Regina. 'The Gender of Judgements.' In Margaret Thornton, ed., *Public and Private: Feminist Legal Debates*, 262. Oxford: Oxford University Press 1995).

Griffith, John. *The Politics of the Judiciary*. 5th ed. London: Fontana Press, 1997.

Guarnieri, Carlo. *Magistratura e Politica in Italia*. Bologna: Il Mulino, 1992.

– *La Giustizia in Italia*. Bologna: Il Mulino, 2001.

Guarnieri, Carlo, and Patrizia Pederzoli. *La Magistratura nelle Democrazie Contemporane*. Rome: Editori Laterza, 2002.

– *The Power of Judges: A Comparative Study of Courts and Democracy*. Oxford: Oxford University Press, 2002.

Hale, Brenda. 'Equality and the Judiciary: Why Should We Want More Women Judges?' *Public Law* (Autumn 2001): 489.

Hamilton, Barbara. 'Criteria for Judicial Appointment and "Merit".' *Queensland University of Technology Law Journal* (1999) 15:10.

Hanssen, Anders F. 'The Effect of Judicial Institutions on Uncertainty and the Rate of Litigation: The Election versus Appointment of State Judges.' *Journal of Legal Studies* (1999) 28:205.

Harris, Bede. 'Appointments to the Bench – The Role of a Judicial Services Commission.' *Adelaide Law Review* (1993) 15:191.

Hassnin, Magdah. 'An Interview with Counsellor Ahmed Medhat Al-Maraghi.' *Al-Ahram* (Cairo), 15 May 2002.

Hatchard, J. and P. Slinn. 'Namibia: The Constitutional Path to Freedom.' *Commonwealth Law Bulletin* (1991) 17:644.

Hattori, Yakaahi. 'The Role of the Supreme Court of Japan in the Field of Judicial Administration.' *Washington Law Review* (1984) 60:69.

Hawes, Colin. 'Dissent and Transparency in Recently Published Chinese Court Judgments.' Paper presented at Association for Asian Studies Annual Meeting, New York, March 2003.

– 'Seeds of Dissent: The Evolution of Published Commercial Law Court judgments in Contemporary China.' *Australian Journal of Asian Law* (2003) 5:1.

Heemskerk, J. *De Praktijk van de Grondwet*. Utrecht: Beijers, 1881.

Henderson, Jane. 'The First Russian Constitutional Court: Hopes and Aspirations.' In Rein Mullerson, Malgosia Fitzmaurice, and Mads Andenas, eds., *Constitutional Reform and International Reform in Central and Eastern Europe*. The Hague: Kluwer Law International, 1998.

Hendley, Kathryn. 'Suing the State in Russia.' *Post-Soviet Affairs* (2002) 18:122.

Heringa, A.W. *Constitutionele partners: rechterlijke beslissingen als instrument van samenwerking tussen rechter en wetgever.* Deventer: Kluwer, 1996.

Heydon, Dyson. 'Judicial Activism and the Death of the Rule of Law.' *Otago Law Review* (2004) 10:493.

Higgason, R. 'Diversity Strengthens the Texas Judiciary.' *Houston Lawyer* 40 (June 2003): para. 30.

Hill, Enid. *Mahkama! Studies in the Egyptian Legal System, Courts and Crimes, Law and Society.* London: Ithaca Press, 1979.

Hirschl, Ran. 'How to Judge a Judge.' *De Rebus* (October 1999): 18.

– 'The Struggle for Hegemony: Understanding Judicial Empowerment Through Constitutionalization in Culturally Divided Polities.' *Stanford Journal of International Law* (2000) 36:73.

– *Towards Juristocracy: The Origins and Consequences of the New Constitutionalism.* Cambridge: Harvard University Press, 2004.

Howarth, David, and George Varouxakis. *Contemporary France: An Introduction to French Politics and Society.* London: Arnold, 2003.

Hu, Xiabing, and Feng, Renqiang. *Sifa gongzheng yu sifa gaige yanjiu zongshu.* Beijing: Qinghua daxue chubanshe, 2001.

Hudson, Manley O. *International Tribunals: Past and Future.* Washington: Carnegie Endowment for Peace and Brookings Institution, 1944.

Human Sciences Research Council. *Law and Justice in South Africa.* Pretoria: HSRC, 1986.

Huscroft, Grant. 'The Charter, the Court, and the Limits of Progressive Interpretation' in Brodie and Huscroft, eds., *Constitutionalism in the Charter Era.* LexisNexis, forthcoming.

– 'Deputat sude ne kollega.' *Vladivostok.* 16 January 2003.

Ignateva, Iuliia. 'Pomni o Strasburge.' *Obshchaia gazeta.* 30 November 2000, 2.

Ignateva, Iuliia, and Igor Naidenov. 'Pravyi krainii. V chetverg poutru s Dmitriem Kozakom.' *Obshchaia Gazeta,* 13 December 2001.

Imam, Abdullah. *The Massacre of the Judiciary.* Cairo: Madboli Bookstore, 1976 (in Arabic).

Ingadottir, T. *The International Criminal Court: Nomination and Selection of Judges, A Discussion Paper.* ICC Discussion Paper 4. (New York and London: Project on International Courts & Tribunals, 2002).

Inter-American Commission on Human Rights *Decision on Request for Precautionary Measures (Detainees at Guantanamo Bay, Cuba) 12 March 2002* (2002) 41 ILM 432.

Interights. *Judicial Independence: Law and Practice of Appointments to the European Court of Human* Rights. London: Interights, 2003.

International Bar Association. *Report of Zimbabwe Mission, 2001.* London: International Bar Association, 2001.

'Internet-interviu s V.F. Iakovlevym 'Rabota arbitrazhnykh sudov v 2002 godu.' *SPS Konsultant Plius.* 20 February 2003. http://www.consultant.ru/news/interview/yakovlev.html

Israel. Report of the Committee for the Examination of Judicial Selection (Chairman: J. Yizhak Zamir). Jerusalem, March 2001 (in Hebrew).

Itoh, Hiroshi. *The Japanese Supreme Court.* New York: Markus Wiener, 1989.

Jin, Zhengjia. *'Gaige caipan wenshu de shuxie fangshi shi shenhua shenpan fangshi gaige de tupokou.'* Unpublished, Spring 2001, Guangzhou Maritime Court, Beijing, China.

Jowell, Jeffrey. 'NAC Memo' Justice Committee Report, September 1981, 5.

– 'Justice Minister Calls for Transformation of Judiciary in Budget Vote Speech.' *De Rebus* (July 1998): 12.

– 'Beyond the Rule of Law: Towards Constitutional Judicial Review.' *Public Law* (Winter 2000): 671.

Kahn, E. 'The Judges: The Claim of the Practicing Advocates to a Monopoly on the Appointment of Judges.' *Businessman's Law* (1989) 18:201,249.

Katanian, Konstantin. 'Kadrovyi vopros bez podteksta.' *Vremia MN.* 27 February 2003, 3.

Kavass, Igor I. *Supranational and Constitutional Courts in Europe: Functions and Sources.* Buffalo and New York: William S. Hein, 1992.

Kay, Richard. 'American Constitutionalism.' In Larry Alexander, ed., *Constitutionalism: Philosophical Foundations.* Cambridge: Cambridge University Press, 1998.

Kennedy, Helena. *Eve was Framed: Women and British Justice.* London: Vintage, 1993.

Kenny, Susan. 'Maintaining Public Confidence in the Judiciary: A Precarious Balance.' *Monash University Law Review* (1999) 25:209.

Kentridge, Sidney. 'Telling Truth About Law.' *South African Law Journal* (1982) 99:648.

– 'The Highest Court: Selecting the Judges.' *Cambridge Law Journal* (2003) 62:55.

Keohane, R.O., A. Moravcsik, and A.-M. Slaughter. 'Legalized Dispute Resolution: Interstate and Transnational.' In J.L. Goldstein, M. Kahler, R.O. Keohane, and A.-M. Slaughter, eds., *Legalization and World Politics,* 73. Cambridge: MIT Press, 2001.

Kerscher, Helmut. 'Selbst die Papstwahl ist demokratischer. Verfassungsrichter werden von einer geheimen Kungelrunde der Parteien ausgesucht.' *Süddeutsche Zeitung.* 5 December 1998.

Key, V.O. *Politics, Parties and Pressure Groups.* New York: Thomas Y. Crowell, 1958.

Khan, Hamid. *Constitutional and Political History of Pakistan.* New York: Oxford University Press, 2001.

Kirby, M. 'Modes of Appointment and Training of Judges: A Common Law Perspective.' *Commonwealth Law Bulletin* (2000) 26:540.

– 'Judicial Accountability in Australia.' *Legal Ethics* (2003) 6:41.

Kleandrov, Mikhail. *Status sudi.* Novosibirsk: Nauka, 2000.

Koen, Raymond, and Debbie Budlender. 'The Law is Fraught with Racism: Report on Interview Research into Perceptions of Bias in the Criminal Justice System.' *Stellenbosch Law Review* (1997) 7:80.

'Komitet SF po pravovym i sudebnym voprosam otklonil popravki v novyi UPK.' *IA Regnum.* 9 July 2002. http://www.volgainform.ru/allnews/41400.

'Komitet Soveta Federatsii po pravovym i sudebnym voprosam vse-taki rekomendoval odobrit zakon 'O vnesenii izmenenii i dopolnenii v UPK RF.' *IA Regnum.* 10 July 2002, Available at http://www.regnum.ru/allnews/41399.html.

Kommers, Donald. *The Constitutional Jurisprudence of the Federal Republic of Germany.* 2nd ed. Durham, NC: Duke University Press, 1997.

– 'Autonomy versus Accountability: The German Judiciary.' In Russell and O'Brien, eds., *Judicial Independence in the Age of Democracy,* 145.

Koopmans, Tim. *Courts and Political Institutions: A Comparative View.* Cambridge: Cambridge University Press, 2003.

Koppen, J.K. *Een kwestie van discipline; over de externe democratisering van het wetenschappelijk onderwijs.* Amsterdam: Thesis, 1991.

Kranenburg, Mark. 'The Political Wing of the "Polder Model".' In Mark Kranenburg, *The Netherlands, a Practical Guide for the Foreigner and a Mirror for the Dutch.* Amsterdam: Prometheus/NRC Handelsblad, 2001.

Kritzer, Herbert, ed. *Legal Systems of the World.* Santa Barbara: ABC-CLIO, 2002.

Kriuchkova, Irina. 'Polpredskaia KADRil.' *UralPolitRu.* 18 June 2002. http://www.uralpolit.ru/sverd/?article_id=563.

Kröger, Klaus. 'Richterwahl.' In Christian Starck, ed., *Bundesverfassungsgericht und Grundgesetz,* 86. Tübingen: J.C.B. Mohr, 1976.

Kurmanov, Midkhat. 'Judicial System in Russia: A Perspective from Tatarstan.' In Thomas Fleiner and Rafael Khakimov, eds., *Federalism: Russian and Swiss Perspectives.* Kazan: Institute of History of the Academy of Sciences in Tatarstan, 2001.

Kurmanov, Midkhat, and Evgenii Sultanov. 'Vzaimootnosheniia zakonodatelnykh (predstavitelnykh) organov gosudarstvennoi vlasti i kvalifikatsionnykh kollegii sudei subektov RF.' *Pravosudie v Tatarstane* 2. http://www.usdrt.ru/2003/2_2003/5_2_2003.html.

Lafon, Jacqueline Lucienne. 'France.' In Mary L. Volcansek, ed., *Judicial Misconduct: A Cross-National Comparison.* Gainesville, FL: University Press of Florida, 1996.

Lamprecht, Rolf. *Vom Mythos der Unabhängigkeit.* 2nd ed. Baden-Baden: Nomos, 1996.

Landes, William M., and Richard A. Posner. 'The Independent Judiciary in an Interest-Group Perspective.' *Journal of Law and Economics* (1975) 18:875.

Landfried, Christine. 'The Impact of the German Federal Constitutional Court on Politics and Policy Output.' *Government and Opposition* (1985) 20:527.

– *Bundesverfassungsgericht und Gesetzgeber.* 2nd ed. Baden-Baden: Nomos, 1996.

Langemeijer, G.E. 'De recrutering van de rechterlijke macht.' *Civis Mundi* (1974) r. 9/10.

– *Taak en opleiding van de rechter.* Gent: np, 1974.

Latimer House Guidelines for the Commonwealth on Parliamentary Supremacy Judicial Independence, 19 June 1998.

– 'Law Society Welcomes Durban Attorney Thumba Pillay to High Court Bench.' *De Rebus* (November 1998): 13.

Lawyers Committee for Human Rights. *Election of Judges of the International Criminal Court, 3–7 February 2003, Chart Summarizing the Qualifications of the Candidates.* http://www.humanrightsfirst.org/international_justice/icc/election/election_chart.pdf (last accessed 11 February 2005).

Leahy, Patrick. 'Statement of Senator Patrick Leahy.' Hearing before the Judiciary Committee on the Nomination of Claude Allen, 28 October 2003. http://leahy.senate.gov/press/200310/102803b.html.

Lebedev, Viacheslav. 'Doklad o rabote sudov za 2002 god' *Bulleten zakonodatelstva i sudebnoi praktiki* 1 (March 2003). http://www.usd.khv.ru/Content/b_nomer_06.html.

Legal Resources Foundation. *Justice In Zimbabwe* Special Report. Harare: Legal Resources Forum, 2002. http://www.lrf.co.zw/.

Le Sueur, Andrew. 'Developing Mechanisms for Judicial Accountability in the UK.' *Legal Studies* (2004) 24:73.

Legg, Thomas. 'Judges for the New Century.' *Public Law* (2001) 61.

Lindell, Geoffrey. 'The Murphy Affair in Retrospect.' In H.P. Lee and George Winterton, eds., *Australian Constitutional Landmarks.* Port Melbourne: Cambridge University Press, 2003.

Linehan, J. *Women and Public International Litigation, Background Paper.* Prepared for a seminar held by the Project on International Courts and Tribunals and Matrix Chambers, London, 13 July 2001. http://www.pict-pcti.org/ (last accessed 11 February 2005).

Liu, Nanping. *Judicial Interpretation in China: Opinions of the Supreme People's Court.* Hong Kong: Sweet & Maxwell Asia, 1997.

Liu, Zhongding, and Chen Xiaoyu. 'Guanyu faguan guanli zhidu gaige de ruogan wenti yanjiu.' In Cao Jianming, et al. *Zhongguo shenpan fangshi gaige lilun wenti yanjiu,* 130. Beijing: Zhongguo zhengfa daxue chubanshe, 2001.

Lombardi, Clark Banner. 'State Law as Islamic Law in Modern Egypt: The Amendment of Article 2 of Egyptian Constitution and the Article 2 Jurisdiction of the Supreme Constitutional Court of Egypt.' PhD dissertation, Columbia University, 2001.

Lord Chancellor's Department. *Equality and Diversity*. London: LCD, October 2001.

Lord Reid of Drem. 'The Judge as Law Maker.' *Journal of the Society of Public Teachers of Law* 12 (1972): 22.

Lubman, Stanley. *Bird in a Cage: Legal Reform in China after Mao*. Stanford: Stanford University Press, 1999.

Lucca, Daria. *Giustizia all'Italiana*. Rome: Carocci Editore, 2003.

MacCormick, Neil, and Robert S. Summers, eds. *Interpreting Precedents: A Comparative Study*. Aldershot: Ashgate/Dartmouth Publishing, 1997.

Mackenzie, R., and P. Sands. 'International Courts and Tribunals and the Independence of the International Judge.' *Harvard International Law Journal* (2003) 44, no. 1:271.

Madhuku, Lovemore. *The Constitution and the Independence of the Judiciary: A Survey of the Position in Southern Africa*. (2001; Unpublished), on file with University of Zimbabwe law library.

Madison, James. *Federalist No. 51*. In Alexander Hamilton, James Madison, and John Jay, *The Federalist Papers*. New York: Bantam Dell, 1982.

Maduna, Penuell. 'Address at the Banquet of the Judicial Officers' Symposium.' *South African Law Journal* (2003) 120:663.

Magalhães, Pedro C. 'The Politics of Judicial Reform in Eastern Europe.' *Comparative Politics* (1999) 32:43.

Malleson, Kate. *The Use of Judicial Appointments Commissions: A Review of the US and Canadian Models*, Lord Chancellor's Department, Research Paper no. 6. Lord Chancellor's Department, 1997.

– 'Assessing the Strengths and Weaknesses of a Judicial Appointments Commission.' *Amicus Curiae*, May:13.

– 'Assessing the Performance of the Judicial Service Commission.' *South African Law Journal* (1999) 116:36.

– *The New Judiciary*. Brookfield, VT: Ashgate, 1999.

– 'Promoting Diversity in the Judiciary: Reforming the Judicial Appointments Process.' In Phil Thomas, ed., *Discriminating Lawyers*. London: Cavendish Press, 2000.

– 'Gender Equality in the Judiciary: Why Difference Won't Do.' *Feminist Legal Studies* (2003) 11:1.

Mamdani, M. *Citizen and Subject: Contemporary Africa and the Legacy of Late Colonialism*. Princeton, NJ: Princeton University Press, 1996.

Managing Justice: A Review of the Federal Civil Justice System ALRC Report 89. Canberra, ACT: Australian Government Publishing Service, 2000.

Mandela, Nelson. *Argument for the defence in S v Mandela*, Pretoria, 22 October 1962. Excerpted in Nelson Mandela *No Easy Walk to Freedom*. London: Heineman, 1973.

Maratova, Lyudmila. 'Kabardino-Balkaria President Continues to Influence Judicial System.' *EWI Russian Regional Report* (2002) 26.

Mason, Anthony. 'Aspects of Judicial Role.' *Journal of Judicial Administration* (1993) 3:156.

– 'The State of the Judicature.' *Australian Law Journal* (1994) 68:125.

Materov, N.V. 'Ob uluchshenii podbora kandidatov na dolzhnosti sudei.' *Vestnik Vysshego arbitrazhnogo suda RF* (2003) 12:95.

Mathews, A. *Freedom, State Security and the Rule of Law: Dilemmas of the Apartheid Society*. Cape Town: Juta, 1986.

Mautner, Menachem. 'The Selection of Judges to A Supreme Court in a Multi-Cultural Society.' *Mechkarei Mishpat* (2003) 19:423 (in Hebrew).

McCormick, Peter J. 'Birds of a Feather: Alliances and Influences on the Lamer Court 1991–1997.' *Osgoode Hall Law Journal* (1998) 36:340.

– 'The Most Dangerous Justice: Penetrating the Voting Patterns of the Lamer Court, 1990–1997.' *Dalhousie Law Journal* (1999) 22:93.

McFaul, Michael, Nikolai Petrov, and Andrei Ryabov. *Between Dictatorship and Democracy: Russian Post-Communist Political Reform*. Washington, DC: Carnegie Endowment for International Peace, 2004.

McGrath, John. 'Appointing the Judiciary.' *New Zealand Law Journal* (1998): 314.

McKay, John. 'Confusion on the Hill.' In Daniel Cere and Douglas Farrow, eds., *Divorcing Marriage: Unveiling the Dangers in Canada's New Social Experiment*. Kingston and Montreal: McGill-Queen's University Press, 2005.

McLachlin, Beverley. 'Promoting Gender Equality in the Judiciary.' Seminar to the Association of Women Barristers, House of Commons, 2 July 2003.

McQueen, Rob. 'The High Court of Australia: Institution or Organisation?' *Australian Quarterly* (1987) 59:43.

Meagher, D.R. 'Appointment of Judges.' *Journal of Judicial Administration* (1993) 2:190.

Melber, H. 'Namibia: The German Roots of Apartheid.' *Race and Class* (1985) 17:63.

Menkel Meadow, Carrie. 'Portia Redux.' *Virginia Journal of Social Policy and Law* (1994) 2:75.

Merriman, John H. *The Civil Law Tradition: An Introduction to the Legal Systems of Western Europe and Latin America*. 2nd ed. Stanford: Stanford University Press, 1985.

Mikhailina, Iuliia. 'Budushchie sudi budut risovat' nesushchestvuiushchikh zhivotnykh.' *Gazeta*. 24 December 2002.

– 'Sudi rasskazali o prestupleniiakh i nakazaniiakh.' *Gazeta.* 28 January 2004. Available at http://www.gzt.ru.

Millner, M.A. 'Eclipse of a Judiciary: The South African Position.' *International & Comparative Law Quarterly* (1962) 11:886.

Moerane, M.T.K. 'The Meaning of Transformation of the Judiciary in the New South African Context.' *South African Law Journal* (2003) 120:708.

Morisi, Massimo. *Anatomia della Magistratura Italia.* Bologna: Il Mulino, 1999.

Morris, H.F., and J.S. Read. *Indirect Rule and the Search for Justice: Essays in East African Legal History.* Oxford: Clarendon Press, 1972.

Morshchakova, Tamara, ed. *Kommentarii k zakonodatelstvu o sudebnoi sisteme Rossiiskoi Federatsii.* Moskva: Iurist, 2003.

Morton, F.L. 'Judicial Activism in France.' In Kenneth Holland, ed., *Judicial Activism in Comparative Perspective.* New York: St Martins Press, 1991.

– *Law, Politics and the Judicial Process in Canada.* 3rd ed. Calgary: University of Calgary Press, 2002.

– 'Federal Judicial Appointments in Alberta, 1993–2000: A Pilot Study.' Unpublished, on file with University of Calgary, 2003.

Morton, F.L., and Rainer Knopff. *The Charter Revolution and the Court Party.* Peterborough: Broadview Press, 2000.

Morton, F.L., Peter H. Russell, and Troy Riddell. 'The Canadian Charter of Rights and Freedoms: A Descriptive Analysis of the First Decade, 1982–1993.' *National Journal of Constitutional Law* (1994) 5:1.

Murray, Andrew, and Felicity Maher. 'Judging the Judges.' *Alternative Law Journal* (1998) 23:185.

Mustafa, Tamir. 'Law versus the State: The Expansion of Constitutional Power in Egypt, 1980–2001.' PhD dissertation, University of Washington, 2002.

'Na zasedaniiakh kvalifikatsionnoi kollegii sudei Amurskoi oblasti v 2003 godu.' http://www.oblsud.tsl.ru (accessed 25 January 2004).

Naidenov, Igor. 'Sudiam daiut srok.' *Obshchaia gazeta.* 30 November 2000, 1.

Namibia, Republic of. *White Paper on National and Sectoral Policies.* Windhoek: Government Printer 1991.

– *Ministry of Justice Annual Report 1990–1998.* Windhoek: Government Printer, 1998.

– *Namibia National Progress Report on the Implementation of the Beijing Platform for Action.* Windhoek: Department of Women Affairs, 1999.

– *Namibia: A Decade of Peace, Democracy and Prosperity,* 1990–2000. Windhoek: Office of the Prime Minister, 2000.

Narvasa, Andres. *Judicial Power in the Philippines.* Manila: Supreme Court of the Philippines, 1997.

Nassar, Momtaz. *The Battle for Justice in Egypt.* Cairo: Dar Al-Shrouq, 1974 (in Arabic).

National Society for Human Rights. *Namibia: The Judiciary under Siege: Special Report for 1995.* Windhoek, National Society for Human Rights, 1995.

Naumova, Elena. 'Samarskii arbitrazh poluchil predsedatelia.' *Kommersant-Samara.* 13 January 2004.

Nelken, David. 'Berlusconi e i Giudici: Legittimi Sospetti?' In Jean Blondel and Paolo Segatti, eds., *Politica in Italia: I Fatti dell'Anno e le Interpretazioni.* Bologna: Il Mulino, 2003.

'Nepravilnye sudi Tatarstana.' *Novosti Instituta Prav Cheloveka.* 22 September–4 October 2000. http://www.hrights.ru/hrights/archnews/archnews22_09_4_10_2000.htm.

Newberg, Paula. *Judging the State: Courts and Constitutional Politics in Pakistan* Cambridge: Cambridge University Press, 1995.

Ngoepe, B.M. 'White Paper on the Judicial System: Memorandum by Pretoria Judges.' *Advocate* (First term 2000): 27.

Nicholson, P. 'Vietnamese Legal Institutions in Comparative Perspective.' In Kanishka Jayasuriya, ed., *Law, Capitalism, and Power in East Asia.* London: Routledge, 1998.

Nicholson, Pip. 'Appointing High Court Judges: Need for Reform?' *Australian Quarterly* (1996) 68:68.

North, Douglas. *Institutions, Institutional Change and Economic Performance.* Cambridge: Cambridge University Press, 1990.

O'Brien, David M., and Yasuo Ohkoshi. 'Stifling Judicial Independence from Within.' In Russell and O'Brien, *Judicial Independence in the Age of Democracy.*

O'Brien, David M., with Yasuo Ohkoshi. *To Dream of Dreams: Religious Freedom and Constitutional Politics in Postwar Japan.* Honolulu: University of Hawaii Press, 1996.

Okudaira, Yasuhiro. 'The Japanese Supreme Court.' *Law Asia* (1972) 3:67.

Olivier, M. 'Is the South African Magistracy Legitimate?' *South African Law Journal* (2001) 118:166.

Olson, Susan M., and Albert W. Dzar. 'Revisiting Informal Justice: Restorative Justice and Democratic Professionalism.' *Law and Society Review* (2004) 38:139.

Omatsu, Maryka. 'On Judicial Appointments: Does Gender Make a Difference?' In Joseph F. Fletcher, ed., *Ideas in Action: Essays on Politics and Law in Honour of Peter Russell,* 177. Toronto: University of Toronto Press, 1999.

O'Sullivan, Dominic. 'Gender and Judicial Appointment.' *University of Queensland Law Journal* (1996) 19:107.

'Otchet o rabote Komiteta Soveta Federatsii po pravovym i sudebnym voprosam v 2002 godu.' *IA Regnum,* 20 January 2003. http://www.regnum.ru/allnews/81744.html.

Oz-Salzberger, Fania, and Eli Salzberger. 'The Hidden German Sources of the Israeli Supreme Court.' *Tel Aviv University Studies in Law* (2000) 15:79.

Paciotti, Elena. *Sui Magistrati: La Questione della Giustizia in Italia.* Rome: Editori Laterza, 1999.

Palmer, Geoffrey. 'Judicial Selection and Accountability.' In B.D. Gray and R.B. McClintock, eds., *Courts and Policy: Checking the Balance.* Wellington: Brookers, 1995.

Paterson, A.A., T. StJ. N. Bates, and M. Poustie. *The Legal System of Scotland.* 4th ed. Edinburgh: W. Green, 1999.

Patwari, A.B.M. Maifizul Islam. 'Independence of Judiciary in the Third World: The Case of Bangladesh,' *Journal of the Asiatic Society of Bangladesh* (1994) 39:131.

Peerenboom, Randal. *China's Long March towards Rule of Law.* Cambridge: Cambridge University Press, 2002.

Perekrest, Vladimir. 'Izobretaiutsia izoshchrenneishie sposoby vnedreniia v sudebnuiu sistemu.' *Izvestiia,* 25 September 2003. Available at http://www.izvestia.ru/community/article38899.

– 'Viktor Ivanov: Glavnoe – iskliuchit vozmozhnost popadaniia v sudebnuiu sistemu sluchainykh liudei.' *Izvestiia.* 28 January 2004. http://www.izvestia.ru/community/article43559.

Pieterman, R. *De plaats van de rechter in Nederland 1813–1920, Politiek-Juridische ideeenstrijd over de scheiding van machten in de staat.* Arnhem: Gouda Quint, 1990.

Plasket, Clive. 'Administrative Justice and Social Assistance,' *South African Law Journal* (2003) 120:494.

'Podgotovleny izmeneniia v zakon o statuse sudei RF.' *IA Finmarket.* 20 December 2000. http://www.infoport.ru/main_popup.php?ID=233075

Pollard, D. *The Caribbean Court of Justice (CCJ): Challenge and Response* (2000). Available at http://www.caricom.org (last accessed 16 September 2004).

Ponomarev, Lev. 'O Kvalifikatsionnykh kollegiiakh sudei.' (2002) Available at http://www.hro.org.

Portnov, Vitalii. 'Mina dlia Femidy.' *Rossiiskaia gazeta.* 25 November 2000, 4.

Postanovlenie Soveta Sudei R.F. (2003) 'O nekotorykh voprosakh, sviazannykh s naznacheniem sudei federalnykh sudov obshchei iurisdiktsii i arbitrazhnykh sudov.' 28 November 2003. Available at http://www.supcourt.ru/ojc/aj/aj_dcs/2003/2003–108.htm.

'Postupat' po zakonu i po sovesti.' *Rodnaia gazeta.* 14 November 2003.

Potter, Pitman B. *The Chinese Legal System: Globalization and Local Legal Culture.* London and New York: Routledge, 2001.

'Pravitelstvo Peterburga pomozhet sudiam reshit kvartirnyi vopros.' *IA Rosbalt.* 16 April 2004. http://www.rosbalt.ru/2004/04/16/156108.html.

'Predsedatel Vysshego arbitrazhnogo suda Veniamin Iakovlev v dekabre etogo goda pokinet svoi post.' *RIA Novosti.* 11 February 2004.

Preparatory Committee on the Caribbean Court of Justice. *The Caribbean Court of Justice: The History and Analysis of the Debate.* Georgetown: CARICOM, 2000.

Press Statement by the judges of the Witwatersrand High Court. *South African Law Journal* (1999) 116:886.

Preuß, Ulrich K. 'Die Wahl der Mitglieder des BVerfG als verfassungsrechtliches und –politisches Problem.' *Zeitschrift für Rechtspolitik* (1998) 10:392.

Prillaman, William C. *The Judiciary and Democratic Decay in Latin America: Declining Confidence in the Rule of Law.* Westport, CT: Praeger, 2000.

Provine, Doris Marie. 'Courts and the Political Process in France.' In Jacob et al., eds., *Courts, Law, and Politics in Comparative Perspective.* New Haven: Yale University Press, 1996.

Przeworski, Adam. 'Some Problems in the Study of the Transition to Democracy.' In Guillermo O'Donnell, Phillippe C. Schmitter, and Laurence Whitehead, eds., *Transitions from Authoritarian Rule: Comparative Perspectives.* Baltimore, MD: Johns Hopkins Press, 1991.

'Pskovskaia oblast. Deputaty oblastnogo sobraniia ne smogli izbrat predstavitelia obshchestvennosti v kvalifikatsionnuiu kollegiiu sudei.' *IA Region-Inform*, 26 November 2002. http://www.regions.ru/newsarticle/news/id/924398.html.

Purvis, Rodney. 'Judiciary and Accountability: The Appointment of Judges.' *Australian Journal of Forensic Sciences* (1994) 26:56.

Putin, Vladimir. 'Novoi Rossii nuzhna silnaia nezavisimaia sudebnaia sistema.' *Rossiiskaia gazeta.* 26 January 2000, 1.

'Putin for Increasing Trust in Court System.' *RIA Novosti*, as translated in *Johnson's Russia List #8168*, 15 April 2004. http://www.cdi.org/russia/johnson/8168–5.cfm.

Qi, Gengsheng, Yang Tailan, and Xu Chunjing. *'Lun woguo sifa jieshi de wanshan yu jianli fuhe guoqing de panli zhidu.'* In Cao Jianming et al., eds., *Zhongguo shenpan fangshi gaige lilun wenti yanjiu*, 325. Beijing: Zhongguo zhengfa daxue chubanshe, 2001.

Raitt, F., M. Callaghan, and G. Siann. 'Is There Still a Glass Ceiling for Women Solicitors?' *Journal of the Law Society of Scotland* (2000) 45:19.

'Rabota sudov Rossiiskoi Federatsii v 2002 godu.' *Rossiiskaia iustitsiia* (2003) 8:69–71.

Rakove, Jack. *Original Meanings: Politics and Ideas in the Making of the Constitution.* New York: Vintage Books, 1997.

Ramseyer, Mark. 'The Puzzling (In)dependence of Courts: A Comparative Approach.' *Journal of Legal Studies* (1994) 23:721.

Razack, Sherene. *Canadian Feminism and the Law: The Women's Legal and Education Action Fund and the Pursuit of Equality.* Toronto: Second Story Press, 1991.

'Rekomendatsii po eksperimentalnomu ispolzovaniiu metodov psikhodiagnosticheskogo obsledovaniia kandidatov na dolzhnost sudei, utv. Prikazom Generalnogo direktora Sudebnogo Departamenta pri Verkhovnom Sude RF ot 17 dekabria 2002 goda N147.' *Pravosudie v Tatarstane* 1. http://www.usdrt.ru/2003/1_2003/7_1_2003.html.

Reddaway, Peter, and Robert W. Orttung, eds. *The Dynamics of Russian Politics. Vol. 1.* Lanham, MD: Rowman & Littlefield, 2003.

Replacing the Privy Council: A New Supreme Court – A Report of the Advisory Group to the Honourable Margaret Wilson, Attorney-General, April 2002. Wellington: Office of the Attorney-General, 2002.

Report of the Standing Committee on Justice, etc. *Improving the Supreme Court of Canada Appointments Process.* Canada, House of Commons, 2004.

Resnik, Judith. 'Uncle Sam Modernizes His Justice: Inventing the Federal District Courts of the Twentieth Century for the District of Columbia and the Nation.' *Georgetown Law Journal* (2002) 90:607.

'Respublika Ingushetiia. Attestovany federalnye sudi.' *ARN Regions.Ru.* 16 May 2003. http://www.regions.ru/article/news/id/1106742.html.

Robertson, David. *Judicial Discretion in the House of Lords.* Oxford: Clarendon Press, 1998.

Romano, C. 'The Proliferation of International Judicial Bodies: The Pieces of the Puzzle.' *NYUJILP* (1999) 31, no. 4:709.

Rosberg, James H. 'Roads to the Rule of Law: The Emergence of an Independent Judiciary in Contemporary Egypt.' PhD dissertation, MIT, 1995.

Rubinstein, Elyakim. *Shoftei Ertertz (The Judges of the Land).* Jerusalem: Shoken Publications, 1980 (in Hebrew).

Rudden, Bernard. *A Sourcebook on French Law.* Oxford: Clarendon Press, 1991.

Rukoro, Vekuii, and Dave Smuts. Interview of Attorney General and Advocate Dave Smuts, interviews by Braam Cupido. *Namibia Review* (1995) 4:4–7.

Russell, Peter H. 'Constitutional Reform of the Judicial Branch.' *Canadian Journal of Political Science* (1984) 17:227.

– *The Judiciary in Canada: The Third Branch of Government.* Scarborough, ON: McGraw-Hill Ryerson, 1987.

– 'The Supreme Court Proposals in the Meech Lake Accords.' *Canadian Public Policy* (1998) 14:93.

– 'Toward a General Theory of Judicial Independence.' In Peter H. Russell and

David M. O'Brien, eds., *Judicial Independence in the Age of Democracy*, 7. Charlottesville: University of Virginia Press, 2001.

– 'Adjudication and Enforcement of Laws in a Federal System.' In Peter H. Solomon, Jr, ed., *Legal and Economic Aspects of Federalism in Russia and Canada*. Toronto: CREES University of Toronto, 2004.

Russell, Peter H., and David M. O'Brien, eds. *Judicial Independence in the Age of Democracy: Critical Perspectives from around the World*. Charlottesville: University of Virginia Press, 2001.

Rutherford, Bruce K. 'The Struggle for Constitutionalism in Egypt: Understanding the Obstacles to Democratic Transition in the Arab World.' PhD dissertation, Yale University, 1999.

Salazar, Carmela. *La Magistratura*. Rome: Editori Laterza, 2002.

Salzberger, Eli. 'A Positive Analysis of the Doctrine of Separation of Powers, or: Why Do We Have an Independent Judiciary.' *International Review of Law and Economics* (1993) 13:349.

– 'The English Court of Appeal: Decision-Making Characteristics and Promotion to the House of Lords.' In Stuart Nagel, ed., *Handbook of Global Legal Policy: Among and Within Nations*, 223. New York: Marcel Dekker, 2000.

– 'Temporary Appointments and Judicial Independence: Theoretical Analysis and Empirical Findings From the Supreme Court of Israel.' *Israel Law Review* (2001) 35:481.

Salzberger, Eli, and Elkin Koren. 'The Effects of Cyberspace on the Normative Economic Analysis of the State.' In Alain Marciano and Jean-Michel Josselin, eds., *Law and the State: A Political Economy Approach*. Edward Elgar, forthcoming.

Sands, P. 'Global Governance and the International Judiciary: Choosing Our Judges.' *Current Legal Problems* (2003) 56:481.

Sands, P., R. Mackenzie, and Y. Shany, eds. *Manual of International Courts and Tribunals*. London: Butterworths, 1999.

Sartori, Giovanni. *The Theory of Democracy Revisited*. Chatham: Chatham House Publishers, 1987.

Satarov, Georgii. 'Prorzhavevshee pravosudie' *Otechestvennye zapiski* (2003) 2:87.

Scalia, Antonin. *A Matter of Interpretation*. Princeton: Princeton University Press, 1997.

– 'The Bill of Rights: Confirmation of Extant Freedoms or Invitation to Judicial Creation?' In Grant Huscroft and Paul Rishworth, eds., *Litigating Rights*. Oxford: Hart Publishing, 2002.

Scharpf, Fritz W. *Interaktionsformen. Akteurzentrierter Institutionalismus in der Politikforschung*. Opladen: Leske & Budrich, 2000.

Schenk, W. 'Telt de rm onevenredig veel adellijke leden?' *Nederlands juristen Blad (NJB)* [1970]: 677.

Schermers, H.G. 'Election of Judges to the European Court of Human Rights.' *European Law Review* (1998) 23:568.

Schneiderman, David P., ed. *The Quebec Decision: The Supreme Court Opinion on Quebec and Related Documents.* Toronto: James Lorimer & Co., 1999.

Schultz, Ulrike, and Gisela Shaw, eds. *Women in the World's Legal Professions.* Oxford: Hart Publications, 2003.

Scotland. Judicial Appointments Board. *Annual Report of the Judicial Appointments Board 2002–2003.*

Scottish Executive. *Judicial Appointments: An Inclusive Approach,* Consultation Paper. Edinburgh: Scottish Executive, 2002.

Seligson, Milton. 'The Judicial Service Commission.' *Advocate* (December 2001): 12.

Senate Standing Committee on Legal and Constitutional Affairs. *Gender Bias and the Judiciary.* Canberra: Commonwealth of Australia, 1994.

Senese, Salvatore. 'Il Governo della Magistratura in Italia Oggi.' In Pier Luigi Zanchetta, ed., *Governo e Autogoverno della Magistrature nell'Europa Occidentale.* Milan: Franco Angeli, 1987.

Serag, Mohamed. 'Legal Education in Egypt' *South Texas Law Review* (2002) 43:616.

Shadrunov, Valerii. 'Stat sudiei neprosto.' *Russkii sever.* 9 April 2003, 8.

Shakhrai, Sergei. 'Vystuplenie na zasedanii Politicheskogo konsultativnogo soveta.' In *Materialy zasedaniia Politicheskogo konsultativnogo soveta 20.02.1998 g.* Moskva: PKS, 1998.

Shapiro, Martin. *Courts: A Comparative and Political Analysis.* Chicago: University of Chicago Press, 1981.

Shapiro, Martin, and Alec Stone. 'The New Constitutional Politics of Europe.' *Comparative Political Studies* (1994) 26:400.

Shaw, J.W. 'On the Appointment of Judges' *Australian Law Journal* (2000) 74:461.

Sheldon, Charles H., and Linda S. Maule. *Choosing Justice: The Recruitment of State and Federal Judges.* Pullman, WA: Washington State University Press, 1997.

Shelton, D. 'Legal Norms to Promote the Independence and Accountability of International Tribunals.' *Law and Practice of International Courts and Tribunals* (2003) 2, no. 1: 27.

Shepsle, Kenneth A. 'Institutional Arrangements and Equilibrium in Multidimensional Voting Models.' *American Journal of Political Science* (1979) 23:27.

Sherif, Adel Omar. 'The Freedom of Judicial Expression, The Right to Concur and Dissent: A Comparative Study.' In Kevin Boyle and Adel Omar Sherif, eds., *Human Rights and Democracy: The Role of the Supreme Constitutional Court of Egypt*, 145. London: Kluwer Law International, 1996.

– 'Attacks on the Judiciary: Judicial Independence – Reality or Fallacy?' In Eugene Cotran, ed., *Yearbook of Islamic and Middle Eastern Law*, Volume 6, 1999–2000, 15. London; Kluwer Law International, 2001.

Sheriffs' Association Response to Scottish Executive's Consultation Paper. *Judicial Appointments: An Inclusive Approach.*

Shetreet, Shimon. 'Who Will Judge: Reflections on the Process and Standards of Judicial Selection.' *Australian Law Journal* (1987) 61:766.

– *Justice in Israel: A Study of the Israeli Judiciary.* Dordrecht: Martinous Nijhoff, 1994.

– 'The Critical Challenge of Judicial Independence in Israel.' In Peter H. Russell and David M. O'Brien, eds., *Judicial Independence in the Age of Democracy.* Virginia: University of Virginia Press, 2001.

Shetreet, Shimon, and Jules Deschenes, eds. *Judicial Independence: The Contemporary Debate.* Dordrecht: Martinus Nijhoff Publishers, 1985.

Sloot, Ben P. 'Officiële uitsluiting van vrouwen in juridische beroepen.' *Nederlands Juristen Blad (NJB)* (1980) 45/46:1186.

– 'Moeten rechters lijken op de Nederlandse bevolking.' *Trema* (2004) 2:49.

Solomon, David. 'The Courts and Accountability: Choosing Judges.' *Legislative Studies* (1995) 9:39.

Solomon, Peter H. Jr. 'Putin's Judicial Reform: Making Judges Accountable as Well as Independent.' *East European Constitutional Review* (2002) 1/2:118.

– 'Glavnyi vopros dlia rossiiskoi sudebnoi vlasti – kak dobitsia doveriia obshchestva?' *Rossiiskaia iustitsiia* (2003) 6:5.

– 'The New Justices of the Peace in the Russian Federation: A Cornerstone of Judicial Reform?' *Demokratizatsiya* (2003) 11:3.

– ed. *Legal and Economic Aspects of Federalism in Russia and Canada.* Toronto: CREES University of Toronto, 2004.

– 'Judicial Power in Russia: Through the Prism of Administrative Justice.' *Law and Society Review* (2004) 38:549.

Solomon, Peter H. Jr, and Todd S. Foglesong. *Courts and Transition in Russia: The Challenge of Judicial Reform.* Boulder, CO: Westview Press, 2000.

South Africa. Judicial Service Commission. *Guidelines for Questioning Candidates for Nomination to the Constitutional Court.* 26 September 1996.

Spears, Jeffry L. 'Sitting on the Dock of the Day: Applying Lessons Learned from the Prosecution of War Criminals and other Bad Actors in Post-Conflict Iraq and Beyond.' *Mil. L. Rev.* (2004) 176:96.

Sterkin, Filipp. 'Pravitelstvo zabilo gol v svoi vorota.' *Strana.Ru*, 27 January 2004. Available at http://www.strana.ru.

Stevens, R. 'A Loss of Innocence?' *OJLS* (1999) 19:365.

Stevens, Robert. *The English Judges: Their Role in the Changing Constitution.* Oxford: Hart, 2002.

Steytler, N. 'The Judicialisation of Namibian Politics.' *South African Journal on Human Rights* (1993) 9:477.

Stirling, G.M. 'A Symposium of the Appointment of Judges.' *Alberta Law Review* (1973) 2:301. Reprinted in F.L. Morton, *Law, Politics and the Judicial Process in Canada,* 3rd ed., 137. Calgary: University of Calgary Press, 2002.

– 'Two New Constitutional Court judges appointed.' *De Rebus* (January/February 2004): 15.

'Sudebnaia reforma: den za dnem. Sudebnyi psiholog.' *Ulianovskii oblastnoi sud,* 28 April 2003. http://www.scourt.vens.ru.

Sweet, Alec Stone. *Governing with Judges. Constitutional Politics in Europe.* Oxford: Oxford University Press, 2000.

Symposium Statement. *South African Law Journal* (2003) 120:648.

Tan, Kevin, ed. *The Singapore Legal System.* 2nd ed. Singapore: Singapore University Press, 1999.

Tate, C. Neal, and Torbjorn Vallinder. 'The Global Expansion of Judicial Power: The Judicialization of Politics.' In Tate and Vallinder, eds., *The Global Expansion of Judicial Power,* 1.

Tate, C. Neal, and Torbjörn Vallinder, eds. *The Global Expansion of Judicial Power.* New York and London: New York University Press, 1995.

Teitel, Ruti. 'Through the Veil, Darkly: Why France's Ban on the Wearing of Religious Symbols Is Even More Pernicious Than It Appears.' In *Findlaw,* 22 February 2004. Available at http://writ.findlaw.com/commentary/w0040216_teitel.html.

Thomas, C., and K. Malleson. *Judicial Appointment Commissions.* LCD Research series No. 6/97. December 1997.

Thornton, Margaret, ed. *Public and Private: Feminist Legal Debates.* Melbourne: Oxford University Press, 1995.

Trochev, Alexei. 'The Constitutional Courts of Russia's Regions: An Overview.' *EWI Russian Regional Report* (12 December 2001) 44:7.

– 'Russian Courts on the Web.' *Bulletin on Current Research in Soviet and East European Law* (2002) 2:7.

– 'Competing for the Judge-Made Law: Politics of Intra-judicial Conflicts in Russia and the Czech Republic.' Paper presented at the 35th National Convention of the American Association for the Advancement of Slavic Studies, Toronto, Canada, 21 November 2003.

– '"Tinkering With Tenure": The Russian Constitutional Court in Comparative Perspective.' Paper presented at the Law & Society Annual Meeting, Pittsburgh, PA, 7 June 2003.

– 'Less Democracy, More Courts: The Puzzle of Judicial Review in Russia.' *Law and Society Review* (2004) 38:513.

Trochev, Alexei, and Peter H. Solomon, Jr. 'Courts and Federalism in Putin's Russia.' In Peter Reddaway and Robert W. Orttung, eds., *The Dynamics of Russian Politics. Vol. 2.* Lanham, MD: Rowman & Littlefield Publishers, forthcoming.

'Trudno li stat sudiei?' Interview with the Chairwoman of the examination commission at the Yaroslavl JQC. 16 January 2004, http://cdyar.yaroslavl.ru.

Tsebelis, George. 'Decision Making in Political Systems: Veto Players in Presidentialism, Parliamentarism, Multicameralism and Multipartyism.' *British Journal of Political Science* (1995) 25:289.

– 'Veto Players and Law Production in Parliamentary Democracies: An Empirical Analysis.' *American Political Science Review* (1999) 93:591.

– *Veto Players: How Political Institutions Work.* Princeton: Princeton University Press, 2002.

United Kingdom. Department of Constitutional Affairs. *Constitutional Reform: A New Way of Appointing Judges.* CP 10/03, 2003.

UN Commission on Human Rights. *Report of the Special Rapporteur on the Independence of Judges and Lawyers, Addendum: Mission to South Africa* UN doc E/CN.4/2001/65/Add.2, 25 January 2001.

United Nations Institute for Namibia. *Constitutional Options for Namibia: A Historical Perspective.* Lusaka: UNIN, 1979.

– *Towards a New Legal System for Independent Namibia.* Lusaka: UNIN, 1981.

'V kvalifikatsionnoi kollegii sudei Sankt-Peterburga ostalis vakantnymi dva mesta dlia predstavitelei obshchestvennosti.' *Agentstvo Biznes Novostei.* 3 July 2003. http://www.abnews.ru.

'V sostav Verkhovnogo suda respubliki voidut deviat novykh sudei.' *IA BASHINFORM.* 17 January 2003. http://www.regnum.ru/allnews/81250.html.

'Valentin Kuznetsov: My sudim sudei.' *Izvestiia.* 18 July 2003.

van Blerk, Adrienne. *Judge and be Judged.* Cape Town: Juta, 1988.

van der Horst, H. *The Low Sky; Understanding the Dutch.* Schiedam: Scriptum Books, 1996.

van der Land, R. 'Een enquete onder de Nederlandse rechterlijke macht.' *Ars Aequi* [1970]:524.

van Dijkhorst, Kees. 'The Future of the Magistracy.' *Advocate* (First Term 2000): 39.

van Duyne, Petrus C., and Jan R.A. Verwoerd. *Gelet op de persoon van de rechter: Een observatie-onderzoek naar het strafrechtelijk beslissen in de raadkamer,* vol. 58. Staatsuitgevrij, 's-Gravenhage, 1985.

van Duyne, Petrus C. 'Simple Decision Making.' In D.C. Pennington and S.

Lloyd-Bostock, eds., *The Psychology of Sentencing: Approaches to Consistency and Disparity*. Oxford: Centre for Socio-Legal Studies, 1987.

van Koppen, Peter J. 'The Dutch Supreme Court and Parliament: Political Decisionmaking versus Nonpolitical Appointments.' *Law & Society Review* (1990) 24:745.

van Koppen, Peter J., and Jan ten Kate. *Tot raadsheer benoemd, Anderhalve eeuw benoemingen in de Hoge Raad der Nederlanden*. Arnhem: Gouda Quint, 1987.

Vivier, San. 'Johannesburg Attorney to Preside Over Land Claims Court.' *De Rebus* (August 1995): 463.

Voigt, Stefan, and Eli Salzberger. 'Choosing not to Choose: When Politicians Choose to Delegate Powers.' *Kyklos* (2002) 55:289.

– 'On Constitutional Processes and the Delegation of Power, with Special Emphasis on Israel and Central and Eastern Europe.' *Theoretical Inquiries in Law* (2002) 3:207.

Volcansek, Mary L. 'The Judicial Role in Italy: Independence, Impartiality and Legitimacy.' *Judicature* (1990) 73:322.

– 'Political Power and Judicial Review in Italy.' *Comparative Political Studies* (1994) 26:494.

– *Law Above Nations: Supranational Courts and the Legalization of Politics*. Gainesville: University Press of Florida, 1997.

– *Constitutional Politics in Italy: The Constitutional Court*. Houndsmills: Macmillan Press Ltd., 2000.

– 'Constitutional Courts as Veto Players: Divorce and Decrees in Italy.' *European Journal of Political Research* (2001) 39:347.

Wang Guiping. 'Zhongguo faguan zhidu de fansi yu chonggou.' In Cao Jianming et al., eds., *Zhongguo shenpan fangshi gaige lilun wenti yanjiu*, 146. Beijing: Zhongguo zhengfa daxue chubanshe, 2001.

Wang Liming. *Sifa gaige yanjiu*. Beijing: Falu chubanshe, 2000.

Weber, Max. *Politics as a Vocation*. Munich: Duncker & Humblodt, 1919. Extracts available at http://www.mdx.ac.uk/www/study/xWeb.htm.

Weiler, J.H.H., and Ulrich R. Haltern. 'Constitutional or International? The Foundations of the Community Legal Order and the Question of Judicial Kompetenz-Kompetenz.' In Anne-Marie Slaughter, Alec Stone Sweet, and J.H.H. Weiler, eds., *The European Court and National Courts – Doctrine and Jurisprudence: Legal Change in its Social Context*, 331. Oxford: Hart Publishing, 1998.

Whittington, Keith E. *Constitutional Construction: Divided Powers and Constitutional Meanings*. Cambridge, MA: Harvard University Press, 1999.

Williams, John M. 'Judicial Independence in Australia.' In Russell and O'Brien, eds., *Judicial Independence in the Age of Democracy*, 174.

Wilson, Bertha. 'Will Women Judges Really Make a Difference?' *Osgoode Hall Law Journal* (1990) 28:507.

Witteveen, W. *Evenwicht van machten.* Zwolle: Tjeenk Willink, 1991.

Wolfe, Christopher. 'The Senate's Power to Give "Advice and Consent" in Judicial Appointments.' *Marquette Law Review* (1999) 82:355.

Woodside, Alexander B. *Vietnam and the Chinese Model.* Cambridge: Harvard University Press, 1971.

World Bank. *Sub-Saharan Africa: From Crisis to Sustainable Development, a Long Term Perspective Study.* Washington, DC: World Bank, 1989.

Xinbian Zhonghua renmin gongheguo changyong falu fagui quanshu. Beijing: Zhongguo fazhi chubanshe, 1999.

Yan, Chengrong, and Nenggao He. 'Lun caipan wenshu gaige de ji ge wenti.' In Cao Jianming et al., eds., *Zhongguo shenpan fangshi gaige lilun wenti yanjiu,* 895. Beijing: Zhongguo zhengfa daxue chubanshe, 2001.

Yankov, A. 'The International Tribunal for the Law of the Sea and the Comprehensive Dispute Settlement System of the Law of the Sea.' In P. Chandrasekhara Rao and R. Khan, eds., *The International Tribunal for the Law of the Sea: Law and Practice,* 33. The Hague, Boston: Kluwer Law International, 2001.

Young, Alison. 'Judicial Sovereignty and the Human Rights Act.' *Cambridge Law Journal* (2002) 61:65.

Zahn, E. *Das unbekannte Holland; Regenten, Rebellen und Reformatoren.* Berlin: Siedler, 1984.

Zanotti, Francesca. *Le Attivita Extragiudizaria dei Magistrati Ordinari.* Padua: CEDAM, 1981.

Zherebtsov, Anatolii. 'Kak zakalialas Vysshaia kvalifikatsionnaia kollegiia sudei.' *Rossiiskaia iustitsiia* (2003) 7:6.

Zhonghua renmin gongheguo falu fagui quanshu. 12 vols. Beijing: Zhongguo minzhu fazhi chubanshe, 1994.

Zhonghua renmin gongheguo zuigao renmin fayuan gongbao. Beijing: People's Court Press, 1985–.

Ziegel, Jacob. 'Merit Selection and Democratization of Appointments to the Supreme Court of Canada.' *Choices* (1999) 5, no. 2: 3.

Zimbabwe Human Rights NGO Forum. *Enforcing the Rule of Law in Zimbabwe.* Special Report. Harare: Zimbabwe Human Rights NGO Forum, 2001.

– *Politically Motivated Violence in Zimbabwe 2000–2001.* Harare: Human Rights Forum, 2001). http://www.hrforumzim.com/evmp/evmpreports/polmotviol0108/polviol0 108.htm.

Contributors

Jim Allan is the Garrick Professor of Law at the University of Queensland and was previously associate professor of law, University of Otago, New Zealand. His primary areas of research interest are legal philosophy, constitutional law, and bills of rights scepticism. He has written two monographs, *Sympathy and Antipathy: Essays Legal and Philosophical* (2002) and *A Sceptical Theory of Morality and Law* (1998). He has also published many articles and book chapters.

Sufian Hemed Bukurura is an associate professor in the School of Law at the University of Durban-Westville, South Africa. He has written on the balance of liberation and constitutionalism, and on constitutionalism and the administration of justice in Namibia.

Leny E. de Groot-van Leeuwen is professor at the Law Faculty of the Radboud University Nijmegen, the Netherlands. She has published several books and articles in the field of the sociology of law, primarily on the legal profession, including *De rechterlijke Macht in Nederland* (1991); 'The Equilibrium Elite: Composition and Position of the Dutch Judiciary,' *The Netherlands Journal of Social Sciences*, 28, no. 2 (1992); and (together with Wouter T. de Groot) 'Dining Out in the Trias Politica: Involvement of the Dutch Judiciary in the Legislative Process,' *International Journal of the Legal Profession*, 10, no. 3 (November 2003).

François du Bois studied law at the Universities of Stellenbosch and Oxford, and is an associate professor at the University of Cape Town. His research and publications focus on the changing South African legal system. He is joint editor of the *South African Law Journal*.

Antoine Garapon qualified as a judge and doctor of law and spent many years as a juvenile magistrate before becoming secretary general of the Institut des Hautes Études sur la Justice. He is a member of the editorial board of *Esprit* and has published extensively. His recent works include *Punir en démocratie* with Frédéric Gros and Thierry Pech; 2001), *Albert Camus: Réflexions sur le terrorisme* (2002), *Des crimes qu'on ne peut ni punir, ni pardonner* (2002); *Les juges: Un pouvoir irresponsable?* (2003); *Juger en Amérique et en France: Culture juridique française et common law* (with Ioannis Papadopoulos; 2003). In addition, he is editor of the series *Bien commun,* published by Éditions Michalon.

Mahmoud M. Hamad is a senior lecturer in political science at Cairo University in the Faculty of Economics and Political Science. He is currently a PhD candidate at the University of Utah in the Department of Political Science. He specializes in comparative judiciary with a particular emphasis in Middle East judicial systems. He has published extensively in many Egyptian and Arab periodicals.

Elizabeth Handsley was educated at the University of New South Wales and Northwestern University, and held academic posts at the University of New South Wales and Murdoch University (Perth, Western Australia) before taking up her current position at Flinders University (Adelaide, South Australia) in 1996. She has a long-standing interest in the constitutional position of judges following from her involvement in the development of a gender awareness training program for Western Australian judges in the early 1990s. She teaches constitutional law, torts, and media law and is currently researching the regulation of food advertising to children.

Colin Hawes received his initial training in Chinese literature, obtaining his BA from the University of Durham and a PhD from the University of British Columbia. His book on Song dynasty poetry is forthcoming from State University of New York Press. More recently, he has focused on Chinese law and legal culture, especially judicial reforms in contemporary PRC society. Having completed his LLB in 2003, he is currently working as an associate lawyer in a Vancouver law firm that deals mainly with East Asian clients.

Christine Landfried holds the Chair of Comparative Government at the University of Hamburg, Germany. She was the president of the German

Political Science Association (DVPW) between 1997 and 2000 and is a former fellow at the Institute for Advanced Studies, Berlin. She has a doctorate and an MA in political science from the University of Heidelberg.

Ruth Mackenzie is principal research fellow and assistant director, Centre for International Courts and Tribunals, Faculty of Law, University College London.

Kate Malleson is a professor in the Department of Law at Queen Mary, University of London. In 2003–4 she was a specialist adviser to the House of Commons Constitutional Affairs Select Committee, assisting it in its review of the provisions of the Constitutional Reform Bill. Her work includes *The Legal System* (2003); *The New Judiciary: The Effects of Expansion and Activism* (1999); 'Creating a Judicial Appointments Commission: Which Model Works Best?' *Public Law* (Spring 2004); and 'Modernising the Constitution: Completing the Unfinished Business,' *Legal Studies* (Spring 2004).

Derek Matyszak is a lecturer in procedural law at the University of Zimbabwe. He holds a BA and an LLB from Capetown University.

F.L. (Ted) Morton is a professor of political science at the University of Calgary. His books include *The Charter Revolution and the Court Party* and *Charter Politics* (both with Rainer Knopff); *Morgentaler v. Borowski: Abortion, the Charter and the Courts*; and *Law, Politics and the Judicial Process in Canada*, 3rd ed.

David M. O'Brien is Leone Reaves and George W. Spicer Professor at the University of Virginia. He has served as a judicial fellow at the Supreme Court of the United States, as visiting fellow at the Russell Sage Foundation, and Fulbright visiting professor in constitutional studies at Nuffield College, Oxford University. He has held the Fulbright chair for senior scholars at the University of Bologna and been a Fulbright researcher in Japan. Among his publications are *Storm Centre: The Supreme Court in American Politics*, 5th ed., which received the American Bar Association's Silver Gavel Award; *To Dream of Dreams: Religious Freedom and Constitutional Politics in Postwar Japan*; a two-volume casebook, *Constitutional Law and Politics*, 4th ed.; and *Supreme Court Watch.* He has co-edited a book with Peter H. Russell, *Judicial Independence in the Age of Democracy: Critical Perspectives from around the World.*

Alan Paterson is currently professor of law at Strathclyde University Law School and director of the Centre for Professional Legal Studies there. He is a member of the Council of the Law Society of Scotland, president of the Society of Legal Scholars, and serves on the Judicial Appointments Board in Scotland. His work on the judiciary includes a D.Phil (Oxon.) on the Appellate Committee of the House of Lords; *The Law Lords* (1982); 'Becoming a Judge,' in R. Dingwall and P. Lewis, eds., *The Sociology of the Professions* (1983); 'Scottish Lords of Appeal' *Juridical Review* [1988]: 235; and (with C. Himsworth) 'A Supreme Court for the United Kingdom: Views from the Northern Kingdom,' *Legal Studies* [2004]: 99.

Doris Marie Provine is the director of the School of Justice & Social Inquiry, Arizona State University. She has written on the issue of non-lawyer judges in local courts (*Judging Credentials: Non-lawyer Judges and the Politics of Professionalism*) and has served on the bench as a town justice in Virgil, New York. Her other work on courts includes a book on case selection in the U.S. Supreme Court, a reference book for judges on strategies to pursue settlement in civil cases, and articles and chapters on judicial self-governance in the federal circuits, the politics of courts in France, and the development of European human rights. Other current projects include participation in a volume on the future of the American judiciary with support from the Annenberg Foundation.

Peter H. Russell is a university professor emeritus at the University of Toronto, where he taught political science from 1958 until retiring in 1996. He has published widely in the fields of constitutional, judicial, and aboriginal politics. He was the founding chair of Ontario's Judicial Appointments Advisory Committee.

Eli M. Salzberger is a professor of law at the University of Haifa, Israel. He holds an LLB from Hebrew University of Jerusalem and a D.Phil (Oxon). He has written articles and books on higher judicial bodies (including the Supreme Court and the House of Lords) and the interaction of law and society. His forthcoming work deals with law and economics in cyberspace.

Philippe Sands, QC, is a professor in the Faculty of Laws, University College London. He is also the director of the Centre for International Courts and Tribunals, University College London.

Michael C. Tolley is an associate professor of political science at Northeastern University in Boston, Massachusetts. His research and teaching interests are in the field of public law and judicial process, specifically American constitutional law, comparative constitutional law, and judicial behaviour. He is now president of the Research Committee for Comparative Judicial Studies, an affiliate of the International Political Science Association.

Alexei Trochev is a PhD student at the University of Toronto, currently completing his dissertation on the first decade of the Russian Constitutional Court. He has taught Russian and comparative constitutional law at Promor State University Law School in Arkhangelsk, Russia. His research focuses on judicial reforms in non-democratic regimes and the impact of state capacity on judicial power. His work on post-Soviet Constitutional Courts has appeared in the *Law and Society Review*, and *I-CON: International Journal of Constitutional Law and the East European Constitutional Review.*

Mary L. Volcansek is dean of the AddRan College of Humanities and Social Sciences and professor of political science at Texas Christian University. Her scholarship focuses on law, courts, and politics in the United States and in Europe, as well as on transnational courts. Her most recent book is a volume edited with John F. Stack, Jr, *Courts Crossing Borders: Blurring the Lines of Sovereignty.*